D1538522

Craig Evans is Professor and Director of the Graduate Program in Biblical Studies, Trinity Western University, Langley, BC, Canada. James Sanders is Professor of Intertestamental and Biblical Studies at the School of Theology, Claremont, California.

JOURNAL FOR THE STUDY OF THE NEW TESTAMENT
SUPPLEMENT SERIES
148

Executive Editor
Stanley E. Porter

STUDIES IN SCRIPTURE IN EARLY JUDAISM
AND CHRISTIANITY
5

Series Editors
Craig A. Evans
James A. Sanders

Sheffield Academic Press

Early Christian Interpretation of the Scriptures of Israel

Investigations and Proposals

edited by
Craig A. Evans
and
James A. Sanders

Journal for the Study of the New Testament
Supplement Series 148

Studies in Scripture in Early Judaism and Christianity 5

Copyright © 1997 Sheffield Academic Press

Published by Sheffield Academic Press Ltd
Mansion House
19 Kingfield Road
Sheffield S11 9AS
England

Printed on acid-free paper in Great Britain
by Bookcraft Ltd
Midsomer Norton, Bath

British Library Cataloguing in Publication Data

A catalogue record for this book is available
from the British Library

ISBN 1-85075-679-1

CONTENTS

Part III

ACTS, EPISTLES AND REVELATION

PREFACE

The present volume is the fifth in the series Studies in Scripture in Early Judaism and Christianity, a series that has grown out of the Society of Biblical Literature program unit Scripture in Early Judaism and Christianity, founded by the editors and currently chaired by Kenneth E. Pomykala. The series produces occasional volumes that are published as Supplements to the *Journal for the Study of the Old Testament*, *Journal for the Study of the New Testament*, and *Journal for the Study of the Pseudepigrapha*. The first two volumes appeared in 1993: *Paul and the Scriptures of Israel*, edited by C.A. Evans and J.A. Sanders (JSNTSup, 83; SSEJC, 1) and *The Pseudepigrapha and Early Biblical Interpretation*, edited by J.H. Charlesworth and C.A. Evans (JSPSup, 14; SSEJC, 2). A third volume appeared in 1994: *The Gospels and the Scriptures of Israel*, edited by C.A. Evans and W.R. Stegner (JSNTSup, 104; SSEJC, 3). A fourth volume appeared earlier this year: *The Things Accomplished among Us: Prophetic Tradition in the Structural Pattern of Luke–Acts*, by R.I. Denova (JSNTSup, 141; SSEJC, 4). As in the case of these previous volumes, *Early Christian Interpretation of the Scriptures of Israel: Investigations and Proposals* represents a collection of studies concerned with the function of Israel's Scriptures in later sacred writings. The studies in this volume, however, are more specifically concerned with questions of method, of probing into how ancient writers understood Israel's scriptural heritage and called upon it in their own exegesis and argumentation.

Almost all of the papers were read at annual meetings of the Society of Biblical Literature and then subsequently were revised for inclusion in the present volume. The editors wish to express their thanks to the many scholars who with industry and enthusiasm took part in the sessions of the Scripture in Early Judaism and Christianity program unit and especially to those scholars whose papers were prepared for inclusion in this volume.

Craig A. Evans, James A. Sanders
Spring 1997

ABBREVIATIONS

AB	Anchor Bible
ABD	Anchor Bible Dictionary
AGJU	Arbeiten zur Geschichte des antiken Judentums und des Urchristentums
AJSL	*American Journal of Semitic Languages and Literatures*
AJT	*American Journal of Theology*
AnBib	Analecta biblica
ANET	J.B. Pritchard (ed.), *Ancient Near Eastern Texts*
ARW	*Archiv für Religionswissenschaft*
ASNU	Acta seminarii neotestamentici upsaliensis
BA	*Biblical Archaeologist*
BAGD	W. Bauer, W.F. Arndt, F.W. Gingrich and F.W. Danker, *Greek–English Lexicon of the New Testament*
BDB	F. Brown, S.R. Driver and C.A. Briggs, *Hebrew and English Lexicon of the Old Testament*
BDF	F. Blass, A. Debrunner and R.W. Funk, *A Greek Grammar of the New Testament*
BETL	Bibliotheca ephemeridum theologicarum lovaniensium
BHS	*Biblia hebraica stuttgartensia*
BHT	Beiträge zur historischen Theologie
BibOr	Biblica et orientalia
BJS	Brown Judaic Studies
BNTC	Black's New Testament Commentaries
BR	*Biblical Research*
BTB	*Biblical Theology Bulletin*
BZ	*Biblische Zeitschrift*
BZNW	Beihefte zur *ZNW*
CBQ	*Catholic Biblical Quarterly*
CBQMS	*Catholic Biblical Quarterly*, Monograph Series
CNT	Commentaire du Nouveau Testament
ConBOT	Coniectanea biblica, Old Testament
CRINT	Compendia rerum iudaicarum ad Novum Testamentum
CSCO	Corpus scriptorum christianorum orientalium
CTA	A. Herdner, *Corpus des tablettes en cunéiformes alphabétiques*
DJD	Discoveries in the Judaean Desert
EBib	Etudes bibliques
EKKNT	Evangelisch-Katholischer Kommentar zum Neuen Testament
ETL	*Ephemerides theologicae lovanienses*

EvQ	*Evangelical Quarterly*
EvT	*Evangelische Theologie*
ExAud	*Ex Audito*
FRLANT	Forschungen zur Religion und Literatur des Alten und Neuen Testaments
GKC	*Gesenius' Hebrew Grammar*, ed. E. Kautzsch, trans. A.E. Cowley
HBT	*Horizons in Biblical Theology*
HeyJ	*Heythrop Journal*
HKNT	Handkommentar zum Neuen Testament
HNT	Handbuch zum Neuen Testament
HR	*History of Religions*
HSS	Harvard Semitic Studies
HTKNT	Herders theologischer Kommentar zum Neuen Testament
HTR	*Harvard Theological Review*
IB	*Interpreter's Bible*
IBS	*Irish Biblical Studies*
ICC	International Critical Commentary
IDB	G.A. Buttrick (ed.), *Interpreter's Dictionary of the Bible*
IDBSup	*IDB*, Supplementary Volume
Int	*Interpretation*
ISBE	G.W. Bromily (ed.), *International Standard Bible Encylopedia*, rev. edn
JAOS	*Journal of the American Oriental Society*
JBC	*Jerusalem Bible* Commentary
JBL	*Journal of Biblical Literature*
JCS	*Journal of Cuneiform Studies*
JEH	*Journal of Ecclesiastical History*
JJS	*Journal of Jewish Studies*
JPS	Jewish Publication Society
JSNT	*Journal for the Study of the New Testament*
JSNTSup	*Journal for the Study of the New Testament*, Supplement Series
JSOT	*Journal for the Study of the Old Testament*
JSOTSup	*Journal for the Study of the Old Testament*, Supplement Series
JSPSup	*Journal for the Study of the Pseudepigrapha*, Supplement Series
JTS	*Journal of Theological Studies*
Judaica	*Judaica: Beiträge zum Verständnis. . .*
LCL	Loeb Classical Library
LSJ	Liddell–Scott–Jones, *Greek–English Lexicon*
MeyerK	H.A.W. Meyer (ed.), Kritisch-exegetischer Kommentar über das Neue Testament
MNTC	Moffatt NT Commentary
NCB	New Century Bible
Neot	*Neotestamentica*
NICNT	New International Commentary on the New Testament
NIGTC	The New International Greek Testament Commentary
NJBC	*New Jerusalem Bible* Commentary

NovT	*Novum Testamentum*
NovTSup	*Novum Testamentum* Supplements
NRSV	New Revised Standard Version
NTAbh	Neutestamentliche Abhandlungen
NTD	Das Neue Testament Deutsch
NTS	*New Testament Studies*
NTTS	New Testament Tools and Studies
OG	Old Greeek
PVTG	Pseudepigrapha Veteris Testamenti graece
RB	*Revue biblique*
RechBib	Recherches bibliques
RevExp	*Review and Expositor*
RevQ	*Revue de Qumran*
RHE	*Revue d'histoire ecclésiastique*
RHR	*Revue de l'histoire des religions*
RSR	*Recherches de science religieuse*
RSV	Revised Standard Version
SB	Sources bibliques
SBLDS	SBL Dissertation Series
SBLMS	SBL Monograph Series
SBLSCS	SBL Septuagint and Cognate Studies
SBLSP	SBL Seminar Papers
SHR	Studies in the History of Religion
SJLA	Studies in Judaism in Late Antiquity
SJOT	*Scandinavian Journal of the Old Testament*
SJT	*Scottish Journal of Theology*
SNT	Studien zum Neuen Testament
SNTSMS	Society for New Testament Studies Monograph Series
SPB	Studia postbiblica
SSEJC	Studies in Scripture in Early Judaism and Christianity
STDJ	Studies on the Texts of the Desert of Judah
StudBib	*Studia biblica*
StudNeot	Studia neotestamentica
SVTP	Studia in Veteris Testamenti pseudepigrapha
TBü	Theologische Bücherei
TBT	*The Bible Today*
TDNT	G. Kittel and G. Friedrich (eds.), *Theological Dictionary of the New Testament*
TNTC	Tyndale New Testament Commentaries
TRE	*Theologische Realenzyklopädie*
TTod	*Theology Today*
TU	Texte und Untersuchungen
TZ	*Theologische Zeitschrift*
UBSGNT	United Bible Societies' *Greek New Testament*
UF	*Ugarit-Forschungen*
USQR	*Union Seminary Quarterly Review*
VT	*Vetus Testamentum*
WBC	Word Biblical Commentary

WMANT	Wissenschaftliche Monographien zum Alten und Neuen Testament
WTJ	*Westminster Theological Journal*
WUNT	Wissenschaftliche Untersuchungen zum Neuen Testament
ZAW	*Zeitschrift für die alttestamentliche Wissenschaft*
ZNW	*Zeitschrift für die neutestamentliche Wissenschaft*
ZRGG	*Zeitschrift für Religions- und Geistesgeschichte*
ZTK	*Zeitschrift für Theologie und Kirche*
ZWT	*Zeitschrift für wissenschaftliche Theologie*

LIST OF CONTRIBUTORS

G.K. Beale
Gordon-Conwell Theological Seminary, South Hamilton, MA

H. Alan Brehm
Southwestern Baptist Theological Seminary, Fort Worth, TX

Mary Katharine Deeley
Seabury–Western Theological Seminary, Evanston, IL

Pamela Eisenbaum
Iliff School of Theology, Denver, CO

Peter E. Enns
Westminster Theological Seminary, Philadelphia, PA

Charlotte Fonrobert
University of Judaism, Bel Air, CA

Charles A. Gieschen
Concordia Theological Seminary, Fort Wayne, IN

Mary R. Huie-Jolly
Pacific Theological College, Suva, Fiji Islands

Sylvia C. Keesmaat
Institute for Christian Studies, Toronto, Canada, ON

Deborah Krause
Eden Theological Seminary, St Louis, MO

William S. Kurz, SJ
Marquette University, Milwaukee, WI

Vasiliki Limberis
Temple University, Philadelphia, PA

Stanley E. Porter
Roehampton Institute London, England

Jeffrey S. Rogers
Furman University Greenville, SC

Wolfgang Roth
Garrett-Evangelical Theological Seminary, Evanston, IL

Christopher D. Stanley
McKendree College, Lebanon, IL

William Richard Stegner
Garrett-Evangelical Theological Seminary, Evanston, IL

Diana M. Swancutt
Duke University, Durham, NC

J. Ross Wagner
Duke University, Durham, NC

John T. Willis
Abilene Christian University, Abilene, TX

Part I

METHODS AND CANONS

THE SOCIAL ENVIRONMENT OF 'FREE' BIBLICAL QUOTATIONS IN THE NEW TESTAMENT

Christopher D. Stanley

The Nature of the Problem[1]

The authors of the documents that we call the New Testament drew most of their argumentative methods from contemporary rhetorical practice. One of the more common techniques they used to seal an argument was to adduce a verse from the Jewish Scriptures that could be read as supporting or at least illustrating their position. What makes this usage remarkable is the way the authors simply assumed that these Jewish texts spoke directly to the needs and circumstances of their Christian audience. For them, the question was not whether, but how the authoritative text was to be understood and applied.

This process of 'Christianizing' the Jewish Scriptures was in fact a highly subjective enterprise. Meanings that no one could have dreamed of associating with a particular passage were 'uncovered' with the aid of a hermeneutic that viewed the entire history of Israel as foreshadowing events in the life of Jesus of Nazareth and his followers. The words of the prophets were said to have been written not for their own day, but for 'the time of the end'; the voice of the preincarnate Jesus was heard echoing throughout the Psalms. The underlying principle was summed up by the apostle Paul in Rom. 15.4: 'For whatever was written in former days was written for our instruction, that by steadfastness and by the encouragement of the Scriptures we might have hope.'

Of course, some passages proved more pliant than others to the rhetorical and practical interests of the nascent Christian community. In many cases the wording of the biblical text had to be altered to indicate the precise sense in which the author meant the verse to be understood

---

1. This article is a slight revision of a paper that was presented in the Scripture in Early Judaism and Christianity Section at the 1992 Annual Meeting of the Society of Biblical Literature.

and/or applied. Barnabas Lindars has identified dozens of places where early Christian apologetic interests reshaped the wording of biblical quotations.[2] Krister Stendahl argued for a school environment as the most likely setting for the extensive reworking of the biblical text that he discovered in Matthew's quotations.[3] My own studies have shown that fully 60% of the apostle Paul's nearly one hundred biblical quotations were adapted in some way to suit their present context.[4]

But the early Christians were not the only ones to employ this technique. Incorporating interpretative elements into the wording of a quotation was a common literary practice throughout the ancient world.[5] Nevertheless, questions remain. Why did the literary standards of antiquity diverge so sharply from our own? What made Graeco-Roman society (including its Jewish component) so tolerant of even the most obvious 'interpretative renderings' of its ancestral texts (Homer, the Jewish Scriptures, etc.)? What literary and/or social factors contributed to the continuance of what we today would view as an intolerably permissive state of affairs? This article is devoted to an examination of these and related questions.

The Social Environment

In the modern world, a writer who quotes selectively from another author's work is expected to reproduce the original text verbatim and to follow a well-defined format for acknowledging the source of the outside materials. Where the author has added or deleted words for the sake of clarity, brackets and ellipse markers are inserted to indicate this fact. Readers, for their part, are trained to expect a verbatim rendering and the appropriate documentation whenever secondary materials are cited. Any deviation from these rules can elicit charges of tampering with the text, or even plagiarism.

Not so in the ancient world. Footnotes are a modern invention, the product of a print-oriented society in which pages are numbered and

---

2. B. Lindars, *New Testament Apologetic* (Philadelphia: Westminster Press, 1961).

3. K. Stendahl, *The School of St. Matthew* (ASNU, 20; Lund: Gleerup; Copenhagen: Munksgaard, 1954).

4. C.D. Stanley, *Paul and the Language of Scripture* (SNTSMS, 74; Cambridge: Cambridge University Press, 1992), pp. 252-64.

5. Stanley, *Paul*, pp. 267-350.

readers can generally check the wording of a quoted text. Looking up quotations in an ancient scroll, on the other hand, was virtually impossible. Not only were books expensive and hard to obtain, but they also contained no system of references (page numbers, chapters, verses, etc.) by which a reader might locate a passage within a broader composition. As a result, ancient readers often kept notebooks into which they copied materials that they felt might prove useful at a later date.[6] Particularly important passages would be committed to memory.

This state of affairs has led many investigators to cite 'quotation from memory' as the most likely explanation for the relatively 'free' citation technique encountered in the literary works of antiquity, including the New Testament. According to these interpreters, Graeco-Roman society around the turn of the era remained a fundamentally oral culture, in which true literacy was uncommon and memory quotation the rule. In this sort of environment (so the argument goes) mistakes and interpretative elements were bound to creep into the wording of any quotation, no matter how familiar the source. The weakness of this explanation should be obvious. The ancients were trained from childhood to quote the basic texts of their culture from memory (Homer for the Greeks, the Bible for the Jews).[7] How can one call it 'memory error' when educated people fail to quote even the most common passages with accuracy? The fact that deviations in wording typically improve the 'fit' between the quotation and its new rhetorical context also tells against this explanation. Paul Achtemeier rightly describes Graeco-Roman society as 'a culture of high residual orality which nevertheless communicated significantly by means of literary creations'.[8] To overemphasize either the oral or the literary aspects of that culture is to court misunderstanding.

6.   On the use of notebooks in antiquity, see Stanley, *Paul*, pp. 74-78.

7.   On the importance of rote memorization in the educational systems of antiquity, see H.I. Marrou, *History of Education in Antiquity* (trans. G. Lamb; New York: Sheed & Ward, 3rd edn, 1956). Numerous examples of ancient memory feats are cited (and critically examined) in W. Harris, *Ancient Literacy* (Cambridge/London: Harvard University Press, 1989), pp. 30-33, 301. B. Gerhardsson (*Memory and Manuscript* [trans. E.J. Sharpe; Lund: Gleerup; Copenhagen: Munksgaard, 1961], chapters 9–11) offers a fine discussion of the role of memorization in the rabbinic educational system, but his retrojection of this system into the Second Temple period remains problematic.

8.   P. Achtemeier, '*Omne verbum sonat*: The New Testament and the Oral Environment of Late Western Antiquity', *JBL* 109 (1990), p. 3. A lengthy discussion of the dynamic interplay between oral and written culture in the ancient Mediterranean world can be found in Harris, *Ancient Literacy*, chapter 2.

More helpful than broad generalizations about the oral nature of ancient society and the importance of 'quotation from memory' are specific observations about the ways in which citizens of the ancient world would have encountered the 'text' of a literary composition. Though the level of literacy in the Graeco-Roman world remains a subject of debate, it seems likely that for the bulk of the population, the most common means of experiencing a 'text' was in the form of an oral recitation or performance. Episodes from the Homeric epics were recited regularly at public festivals and private parties. Performances of classical and contemporary plays drew huge and enthusiastic audiences to the local theaters. Reciting and listening to artfully prepared speeches was a highly popular form of entertainment. For the Jewish community, one could add here the regular public reading and translation of the Scriptures that took place in the synagogue every Sabbath and at festivals. Except where individual listeners might have committed a passage to memory, the audience in these situations had no way to check the oral performance of a text against its written form. In such a context, the wording of the recitation actually supersedes the written text; cloaked in the authority of the original, it retains the power to move its hearers regardless of how closely it adheres to the original composition. For the ancients, moving the audience was the chief aim of any oral performance, involving not only the hearers' emotions, but their beliefs and wills as well. This was true for the meturgeman's translation of the Torah as much as the rhapsode's interpretation of Homer. 'Interpretative renderings' were thus an integral part of every public presentation of a written text, a reality well understood and perhaps even anticipated by ancient audiences.

In the Jewish sphere, moreover, a longstanding tradition allowed for repeated reinterpretation and even rewriting of cerain portions of the biblical record so as to draw out its significance for a later time. Already in the canonical text, the book of Deuteronomy covers much of the same ground as the books of Exodus, Numbers, and Leviticus, and the book of Chronicles offers an even closer rewriting of the book of Kings. In several instances narrative sections in the prophetic corpus overlap the versions given in the historical books. Numerous examples of the reuse of biblical traditions, motifs, and even specific language can be seen throughout the literature.[9] While it is doubtful whether Jewish

---

9. See especially M. Fishbane, *Biblical Interpretation in Ancient Israel* (Oxford: Clarendon Press; New York: Oxford University Press, 1985).

readers around the turn of the era would have understood the notion of
'inner-biblical exegesis', their constant exposure to such 'interpretative
renderings' within the pages of Scripture itself would have shaped the
expectations of the most illiterate listeners at the regular readings in the
Jewish synagogues. The growth of the so-called 'oral Torah', that body
of interpretative traditions and legal rulings that circulated orally alongside the written text, no doubt reinforced this blurring of the lines
between text and interpretation in early Judaism.

Among the more literate members of society, the opportunities for
exposure to written texts were much broader. Alongside copies of the
work itself, an educated reader would have had access to many 'rewritten' or adapted versions of the same basic text. On the Graeco-Roman
side, the most obvious examples are the various expansions of the
Homeric narrative that were included in the so-called 'Homeric cycle'
from classical times onward. Many popular plays were also framed
around familiar episodes from the *Iliad* or *Odyssey*, as a vehicle for
driving a point home to a viewing audience. A similar approach can be
seen in that set of Jewish texts that modern investigators call 'rewritten
Bible'. Included here are such diverse works as the book of *Jubilees*, the
Temple Scroll and Genesis Apocryphon from Qumran, Pseudo-Philo's
Biblical Antiquities, and Josephus's *Jewish Antiquities*.[10] More extensive reworkings of the biblical text to serve a later interest can be seen
in the testamentary literature of early Judaism (*Testament of Abraham,
Testaments of the Twelve Patriarchs*, etc.) and in such documents as the
Life of Adam and Eve and *Joseph and Aseneth*. Although little is known
about the circulation of some of these texts, the sheer number of works
extant makes it unlikely that any educated Jew could have been ignorant
of the entire genre. Since works of this sort were being composed
throughout the period in question, there is ample reason to suppose that
they reflect the same 'free' attitude toward the biblical text that one sees
in the biblical quotations of both Jewish and Christian authors.

Indirect contacts such as these—oral recitation, 'inner-biblical exegesis', and 'rewritten' texts—helped to shape the way even the *literati* of

10. See the discussions by D.J. Harrington, 'The Bible Rewritten (Narratives)', in
R.A. Kraft and G.W.E. Nickelsburg (eds.), *Early Judaism and its Modern Inter-
preters* (Atlanta: Scholars Press, 1986), pp. 239-46, and P.S. Alexander, 'Retelling
the Old Testament', in D.A. Carson and H.G.M. Williamson (eds.), *It is Written:
Scripture Citing Scripture: Essays in Honor of Barnabas Lindars* (Cambridge:
Cambridge University Press, 1988), pp. 99-121.

Graeco-Roman society (including educated Jews) viewed the archetypal texts of their culture. But many of these same people also carried on a regular program of studies in the primary texts as well. From infancy the epics of Homer (and/or the Jewish Scriptures, as the case may be) served as the cornerstone of the ancient educational system, so much that one occasionally sees references to a person who could repeat the entire corpus by heart. The sheer breadth of quotations from these basic texts in the literary product of antiquity, combined with the close integration of the quoted texts into their new argumentative contexts, is sufficient to show that ancient authors did not cease their studies in the Homeric epics (or the Jewish Scriptures) once they completed their formal educations. Surely these direct and repeated encounters with the primary text would have more than offset any broader societal tendencies toward a looser, more 'interpretative' rendering of the ancient classics.

Or would it? In an era when books are published and printed in thousands or even millions of standardized copies, it is easy to forget that for the ancient reader, no two manuscripts of a literary work were exactly alike. In fact, one of the first tasks of every schoolmaster was to collate the readings of his students' manuscripts to insure that everyone in the class was working from the same text.[11] While many of the differences between manuscripts were clearly accidental, recent studies suggest that intentional interpolations and 'interpretative renderings' played a greater role in the scribal practices of antiquity than many have recognized.

Stephanie West has examined the wealth of papyrus fragments from the *Iliad* and *Odyssey* that have turned up in the sands of Egypt.[12] Her studies show that the manuscript tradition for the Homeric epics remained quite fluid until the text was standardized in the mid-second century BCE, with additional lines, transpositions, and other variants appearing throughout the period. In her view, such variations can only be attributed to the activities of rhapsodes and/or scribes who sought to update or 'improve' the traditional texts.[13] Even more revealing is the

11. See Marrou, *History*, p. 165.

12. S. West, *Ptolemaic Papyri of Homer* (Papyrologica Coloniensis, 3; Cologne: Westdeutscher Verlag, 1967).

13. On the influence of rhapsodes on the language of ancient manuscripts, see L.D. Reynolds and N. Wilson, *Scribes and Scholars: A Guide to the Transmission of Greek and Latin Literature* (Oxford: Clarendon Press, 2nd rev. edn, 1974), pp. 23-27, and

evidence from Qumran, where ancient biblical manuscripts have yielded a wealth of clearly interpretative variants. A careful analysis of the evidence leads Shemaryahu Talmon to speak of a 'controlled freedom of textual variation' that arose out of the scribe's dual role as copyist and interpreter of the sacred text. According to Talmon, 'The limited flux of the textual transmission of the Bible appears to be a legitimate and accepted phenomenon of ancient scribal tradition and not a matter which resulted from sheer incompetence or professional laxity'.[14] A similar scribal ethos can be traced in the various tendentious adaptations and 'interpretative renderings' that made their way into both the Samaritan Pentateuch and the Greek version of the Jewish Scriptures.[15]

Thus it appears that even regular scholarly study in the 'original text' would have offered no true counterbalance to the broader societal trend toward 'interpretative renderings' of both the Homeric epics and the Jewish Scriptures. In fact, one could argue that the social realities of the transmission process actually reinforced this more 'liberal' attitude

D.L. Page, *Actors' Interpolations in Greek Tragedy* (Oxford: Clarendon Press, 1934). On the frequency of scribal emendations and interpolations, see G.M. Bolling, *External Evidence of Interpolation in Homer* (Oxford: Clarendon Press, 1925); M. van der Valk, *Textual Criticism of the Odyssey* (Leiden: A.W. Sijthoff, 1949); R. Renehan, *Greek Textual Criticism: A Reader* (Cambridge, MA: Harvard University Press, 1969); and M.J. Apthorp, *The Manuscript Evidence for Interpolation in Homer* (Heidelberg: Carl Winter, 1980).

14. S. Talmon, 'The Textual Study of the Bible: A New Outlook', in F.M. Cross and S. Talmon (eds.), *Qumran and the History of the Biblical Text* (Cambridge, MA: Harvard University Press, 1975), p. 326 (cf. the extended discussion in pp. 338-78). P. Skehan ('Qumran and Old Testament Criticism', in M. Delcor [ed.], *Qumrân, sa piété, sa théologie et son milieu* [BETL, 46; Paris: Duculot, 1978]), discussing the variant readings in 1QIsaᵃ, speaks similarly of 'an exegetical process at work within the transmission of the text itself' (p. 151). See also M.J. Mulder, 'The Transmission of the Biblical Text', in *idem* (ed.), *Mikra: Text, Translation, Reading and Interpretation of the Hebrew Bible in Ancient Judaism and Early Christianity* (CRINT, 2.1; Assen: Van Gorcum; Philadelphia: Fortress, 1989), pp. 90-95; I.L. Seeligmann, 'Indications of Editorial Alteration and Adaptation in the Massoretic Text and the Septuagint', *VT* 11 (1961), pp. 201-21; J. König, 'L'existence et l'influence d'une herméneutique sur la transmission du texte hébreu de la Bible', *RHR* 187 (1975), pp. 122-25.

15. On the Samaritan Pentateuch, see A. Tal, 'The Samaritan Targum of the Pentateuch', in Mulder (ed.), *Mikra*, pp. 200-16. Good recent summaries of LXX translation technique include S.P. Brock, 'Translating the Old Testament', in Carson and Williamson (eds.), *It is Written*, pp. 87-98, and E. Tov, 'The Septuagint', in Mulder (ed.), *Mikra*, pp. 168-78. The latter article includes a list of similar studies on individual books (p. 168 n. 22).

toward the written text. The issue can be approached from two different angles. On the one hand, the very fact that no two manuscripts were exactly alike would have fostered a wholly different view of the 'fixed-ness' of the original text than that which prevails in modern print-oriented societies. While the basic parameters of the text were no doubt regarded as fixed, no single manuscript could ever claim to have pre-served the precise and unalterable wording of the original composition. In fact, the application of a rudimentary form of 'textual criticism' (albeit of a highly subjective nature) was a *sine qua non* for the use of any ancient manuscript, especially where the reader had been exposed to differing copies of the same work over the course of a lifetime. In other words, the physical *realia* of the manuscripts would have encouraged not a reverence for the wording of this or that exemplar, but rather a critical attitude toward the text of any individual manuscript.

More important for the present study are a variety of insights that have emerged in recent years concerning the role and function of the scribe in antiquity. Shemaryahu Talmon's conclusions about scribal practices at Qumran can be applied *mutatis mutandis* to the activities of scribes throughout the ancient world. As an acknowledged expert in both copying and interpreting the written text, the scribe (סופר/ γραμματικός) occupied a prestigious position in ancient society, as 'a comprehensive literate who could be author, editor, transmitter, scribe, or copyist when performing different aspects of his profession'.[16] With such a multifaceted role, says Talmon, 'it surely must be agreed that [the scribe's] literary techniques would not automatically change whenever he turned from one task to another. Quite to the contrary, it may be taken for granted that some basic canon of literary conventions would be followed by him in all the variegated performances of his craft.'[17] The result was a 'controlled freedom of textual variation' that can be seen even now in the manuscript tradition of antiquity.[18] In view of the prominent place of scribes as the authorized guardians and interpreters of the ancestral texts, it can be presumed that their approach to the written word would have exercised a decisive influence on the way doc-uments were viewed and handled in the society at large, especially among the *literati*.

Thus we arrive at a coherent and holistic explanation for the rela-

16. Talmon, 'Textual Study', p. 336.
17. Talmon, 'Textual Study', p. 337.
18. Talmon, 'Textual Study', p. 326.

tively 'free' approach to the written text that can be seen throughout Graeco-Roman antiquity. From oral recitations to 'rewritten' texts to the practices of the dominant scribal culture, written works were handled in a way that valued 'interpretative freedom' over slavish adherence to the original text. Only when a particular text-type was declared 'canonical' and the prevailing authorities wielded sufficient power to procure widespread acceptance was the fluid approach of this earlier period replaced by a concern for reproducing the precise wording of a fixed text. The only place in the ancient world where a single text-type appears to have obtained this kind of authoritative backing is in the sphere of rabbinic Judaism.[19]

Intentional Adaptations?

This leads to a final question. Given the degree to which literary and cultural factors shaped the way in which quotations were handled in the ancient world, how appropriate is it to describe the editorial intrusions of the New Testament authors as 'intentional adaptations' of the biblical text? Two possible answers to this question can be immediately set aside. On the one hand, the evidence of the quotations themselves makes it difficult to argue that the authors were simply unaware that they were not always following the precise wording of their *Vorlagen*. Neither the close and repeated links between the revised wording of a citation and its later context nor the sophisticated literary artistry seen in certain 'combined citations' can be explained by a theory of arbitrary lapses in memory. On the other hand, it would be equally inappropriate to think of the New Testament authors as surreptitiously manipulating the wording of the biblical text to create artificial prooftexts to support their own

---

19. Present evidence suggests that by the early second century CE the rabbis had set their stamp of approval on a single text of the Hebrew Bible, the so-called 'proto-Masoretic' text, which was then preserved according to rigid standards of copying and use. See F.M. Cross, 'The History of the Biblical Text in Light of Discoveries in the Judaean Desert', *HTR* 57 (1964), pp. 281-99; D. Barthélemy, 'Text, Hebrew, History of', *IDBSup*, pp. 878-84; and B.J. Roberts, 'Text: Old Testament', *IDB*, IV, p. 583. Biblical citations in the rabbinic literature seem for the most part to follow the wording of the 'Masoretic' Hebrew text: see J. Bonsirven, *Exégèse rabbinique et exégèse paulinienne* (Paris: Beauchesne, 1939), p. 336. Of course, conclusions about rabbinic citation practices must remain tentative in view of the lack of a critical text for the rabbinic materials and the possibility that later copyists systematically 'corrected' the wording of rabbinic quotations toward the Masoretic text.

tendentious arguments. The bulk of the adaptations that can be identified in the New Testament have little effect on the meaning of the original text, and those that do can normally be explained as the result of a sincere attempt to understand the meaning of a particular passage within the context of the author's own culture and/or community.

A more adequate explanation would view the New Testament authors as working consciously but unreflectively within the bounds of contemporary literary conventions that shaped the way quotations might be handled. In the case of the apostle Paul, such a view of his activities finds support in his often-noted lack of reflection on the broader hermeneutical issues implied in his own use of Scripture. Only in 2 Cor. 3.7-18 and such isolated verses as Rom. 4.23-24, 15.4, and 1 Cor. 9.10, 10.11 does Paul offer any hint as to the principles that guided his 'Christian' reading of the Jewish Scriptures, and even these statements illuminate only a fraction of his explicit appeals to Scripture. In some cases the hermeneutical process leads Paul to reshape the wording of a biblical quotation; in others, the original text is deemed sufficient to express what Paul wants his readers to glean from the passage at hand. In both cases the result could still be called an 'interpretative rendering' of the biblical text, a contextual application in which introductory expressions, interpretative comments, explicit deductions, and (in many cases) changes in wording combine to relate the authoritative words of Scripture to the needs of a later audience.[20]

Like Paul, each of the New Testament authors has a method of reading and applying the language of Scripture that is uniquely his own. But when we see one of these authors incorporating interpretative elements into the wording of an explicit biblical quotation, we should remember that the author is simply following the accepted literary standards of the day.

---

20. For a detailed examination of Paul's usual citation practice, see the study cited in note 4.

SCRIPTURE IS AS SCRIPTURALISTS DO:
SCRIPTURE AS A HUMAN ACTIVITY IN THE QUMRAN SCROLLS[*]

Jeffrey S. Rogers

Introduction: W.C. Smith's Concept of Scripture

Wilfred Cantwell Smith's monumental study, *What Is Scripture? A Comparative Approach*, represents a fundamental challenge to the adequacy of prevailing conceptions of Scripture in both scholarly and confessional communities. Smith lays down the challenge when he claims concerning these conceptions, 'All are beginning to be seen as starkly idiosyncratic, and limited; one might even say, demonstrably inadequate. The time has come to move on to a significantly new orientation.'[1] The significantly new orientation that Smith proposes in his encyclopedic historical and comparative investigation is grounded in his assertion that '*scripture is a human activity*' rather than a text or set of texts.[2] 'Studying Scripture', then, is attending to the attitudes and actions of people ('scripturalists' in this paper) who engage in the activity that Scripture is.

According to Smith, the nearly world-wide propensity of people to 'privilege' certain texts appears at first glance 'to be legitimately described as people's separating out some piece of literature from all others and "elevating" it to a special, yet puzzling, status'.[3] However, the perspective of this initial glance is 'seriously inadequate'.[4] Smith writes,

*   I am indebted to my Furman Advantage Research Fellow Jennifer Allsbrook Bibb and my colleague Dr Claude N. Stulting for their critical reading and valuable suggestions.

1.   *What Is Scripture? A Comparative Approach* (Minneapolis: Fortress Press, 1993), p. 67.

2.   Smith, *What Is Scripture?*, p. 18 (emphasis in the original and consistently so, as the repeated exclamation indicates: 'Scriptures are not texts!' [pp. 19, 223]).

3.   Smith, *What Is Scripture?*, p. 230.

4.   Smith, *What Is Scripture?*, p. 230.

What has been going on here is not that persons and groups have raised a form of language to serve transcendent functions, so much as the other way around. The scriptural phenomena begin with people's awareness of involvement in transcendence; and persist so also. That awareness has then been somehow *reduced* to speech or writing, has been brought down to earth and given accessible form in words. It is impossible, we suggest, to understand the world's scriptures without such a perception.[5]

In fact, that it is *text* (in the sense of 'written material') is secondary or incidental.[6] As Smith points out,

Scripture is not differentiated from other forms of literature. . . so much as distinguishable from—however closely integrated with—other forms of a people's symbolizing of the transcendent within and among and around them.[7]

Scripture, then, is a human activity that has been and is for many people in many religions a distinctive and powerful component in their experience of self, the world, and the transcendent.

Scripture as a Human Activity in the Qumran Scrolls

The scrolls discovered in the vicinity of Khirbet Qumran are a veritable treasure trove for the investigation and elucidation of what Smith calls the 'scripture movement' prior to its consolidation in the second through the seventh centuries CE in Judaism, Christianity, and Islam.[8]

5.   Smith, *What Is Scripture?*, p. 231.

6.   According to Smith, the typically Western emphasis on Scripture as *written material* rather than as *oral/aural event* ('recital', 'proclamation', 'performance', or 'enactment') has given rise to the primacy of a concept of Scripture as 'text' (see Smith, *What Is Scripture?*, pp. 7-10). The result has been that the experiential dimension of Scripture has been almost entirely ignored (on this point see, additionally, n. 27 below).

7.   Smith, *What Is Scripture?*, p. 231. Compare, similarly, T. Jacobsen's consideration of Mesopotamian 'religious literature' (along with 'cult drama', 'fashioning divine images', and 'building temples') as an *action* in relation to 'the presence of numinous power' (*The Treasures of Darkness: A History of Mesopotamian Religion* [New Haven: Yale University Press, 1976], pp. 13-17).

8.   See Smith, *What Is Scripture?*, p. 56. In his third chapter, 'Scripture as Form and Concept: Historical Background', Smith charts the rise of the phenomenon of Scripture, beginning in the ancient Near East in Babylonia and pre-Israelite Canaan at least as early as the second millennium BCE and culminating in the emergence of the Qur'an in the seventh century CE. Although in the West notions of Scripture have been

Dated variously from the late third century BCE to the middle of the first century CE, the scrolls derive from an enormously important nexus in the history of Scriptures and the history of religion.

In the Early Jewish context to which the scrolls testify, a clearly delineated canon has yet to emerge; but a basic element of 'Scripture' is already evident: 'inherited texts treated as highly special, and indeed of cosmic quality'.[9] However, it is essential to recognize that the 'treatment' these inherited texts receive is not a 'use' or an 'interpretation', understood as a literary technique or a conceptual manipulation of texts. As James A. Sanders has put it, 'hermeneutic techniques. . . are not as significant as the hermeneutic axioms which underlie those techniques'.[10] The distinctively *scriptural* dimension is the dynamic process in which people actively engage themselves, the world around them, and the transcendent in, with, and through their inherited texts.[11]

The following eight types of activity are presented as an exploration of the treatment that inherited texts receive at a formative stage in one of the world's great scripturalizing religions.

derived largely from the Bible, Smith lines out quite convincingly that the Qur'an 'represents the notion *par excellence* of scripture' (*What Is Scripture?*, p. 47) and that 'The concept of scripture has not seriously developed since the Qur'an in the seventh century' CE (*What Is Scripture?*, p. 45).

9.   Smith, *What Is Scripture?*, p. 56.

10.   'From Isaiah 61 to Luke 4', in J. Neusner (ed.), *Christianity, Judaism, and Other Greco–Roman Cults: Studies for Morton Smith at Sixty, Part One: New Testament* (SJLA, 12; Leiden: Brill, 1975), p. 93. The present paper takes the 'quest for the question' (Sanders, 'From Isaiah 61', p. 103) a step further to ask what underlies the axioms. Among the most valuable discussions of 'interpretation' and 'hermeneutical techniques' in the scrolls are M. Fishbane, 'Use, Authority and Interpretation of Mikra at Qumran', in M.J. Mulder (ed.), *Mikra: Text, Translation, Reading and Interpretation of the Hebrew Bible in Ancient Judaism and Early Christianity* (Assen/Maastricht: Van Gorcum; Philadelphia: Fortress Press, 1988), pp. 339-37; *idem, Biblical Interpretation in Ancient Israel* (Oxford: Oxford University Press, 1985); G.J. Brooke, *Exegesis at Qumran: 4QFlorilegium in its Jewish Context* (JSOTSup, 29; Sheffield: JSOT Press, 1985), pp. 1-44; D. Patte, *Early Jewish Hermeneutic in Palestine* (SBLDS, 22; Missoula, MT: Society of Biblical Literature and Scholars Press, 1975), pp. 209-314; and W.H. Brownlee, 'Biblical Interpretation among the Sectaries of the Dead Sea Scrolls', *BA* 14 (1951), pp. 54-76.

11.   In contrast to the typical focus on a bilateral relationship of humans and texts, Smith speaks of a *trilateral* relationship 'referring to a relation—an *engagement*— among humans, the transcendent, and a text' (*What Is Scripture?*, p. 239).

In a first type of activity, *the scripturalist is a conservator preserving an artifact.*[12]

For example, as is widely known, nearly identical texts of the book of Isaiah are preserved in 1QIsa[b] and Codex B19[A], produced nearly a thousand years apart. The divergences between the two are principally variations in orthography and grammar, as well as occasional scribal errors.[13] The virtual identity of these two manuscripts testifies to a type of scripturalizing in which the primary concern is preserving a text precisely—letter by letter—as it is received. This conservatorial activity in the scrolls is also found in the tendency of at least some scripturalists to 'correct' divergent manuscripts, such as 1QIsa[a], which presents a text that frequently diverges from B19[A]. However, 1QIsa[a] contains numerous interlinear 'corrections' that attempt to bring it into closer agreement with the text of Isaiah as attested in B19[A] (and 1QIsa[b]).[14]

12. Fishbane employs the expression 'textual artifact' to refer much more generally to the physical production of manuscripts ('Use, Authority and Interpretation', pp. 342-43).

13. A few examples must suffice (drawn from the list in E.L. Sukenik, *Dead Sea Scrolls of the Hebrew University* [Jerusalem: Magnes, 1955], pp. 31-34). First, variation in orthography is evident in Isa. 54.4 where B19[A] transmits a full spelling *'lmnwtyk* ('your widowhood') where 1QIsa[b] spells with no *matres lectiones*, *'lmntk* ('your widows' or 'your widowhood'). Secondly, the two manuscripts diverge from time to time on the presence or absence of the conjunction 'and' (e.g. 46.6—'they hire' in B19[A], but 'and they hire' in 1QIsa[b]) and in grammatical number (e.g. 59.4—B19[A] 'he brings forth', but 1QIsa[b] 'they bring forth'). Thirdly, other divergences are clearly the result of an interchange of letters, as in Isa. 45.2 where the similar looking ר (*r*) and ד (*d*) have been confused. 1QIsa[b] transmits *hrwrym* ('mountains') where B19[A] reads *hdwrym* ('honored ones' or 'adorned ones'), otherwise unattested in Classical Hebrew and usually interpreted as 'swells (of land)' (see BDB, p. 213) in an attempt to harmonize with the Septuagint's *orē*, 'mountains' (= 1QIsa[b]). Giovanni Garbini's claim ('1QIsa[b] et le texte d'Esaïe', *Henoch* [1984], pp. 17-21) that 1QIsa[b] cannot be reckoned as belonging to the Massoretic tradition because of its numerous textual divergences from MT and because the scroll may have transmitted a shorter text than B19[A] fails on both accounts. First, his analysis does not make the elementary and essential text-critical distinction between the *number* and the *nature* of the variants. The latter is far more significant, and on this point the divergences in 1QIsa[b] are consistently *un*remarkable. Secondly, mere length of text is by no means a clear indicator of textual affiliation. As in the preceding point, Garbini has focused on *quantity* without addressing the more telling matter of the *qualities* of the textual witness.

14. For example, in Isa. 12.6, 1QIsa[a] reads, 'Shout and sing, *daughter* of Zion', where B19[A] reads, 'Shout and sing, *inhabitant* of Zion'. However, 'daughter' in the scroll is marked through and 'inhabitant' is written above it in a later hand. Similarly,

The scripturalist as conservator is concerned above all with 'textual correctness' and is committed to *a* 'standard text', even to the point of altering an existing manuscript to preserve that standard. The standard text is received as 'the accessible form in words' of 'people's awareness of involvement with transcendence', and so it is conserved with the utmost care and diligence.[15]

In a second type of activity, *the scripturalist is a reader understanding written communication.*

This type is widely evident in 1QIsa^a, in which the scripturalist hands on a text as it is *read and understood*. Shemaryahu Talmon calls for an assessment of this scroll 'as a witness to ancient Jewish exegesis and of its writer as an exegete of no mean achievements'.[16] In other words, the

---

in 21.1, 1QIsa^a transmits 'From the wilderness it comes, from a land *distant*' where B19^A contains 'From the wilderness it comes, from a land *terrible*'. In the scroll the final word is marked out, and 'terrible' is written above the line. (See S. Talmon, 'Aspects of the Textual Transmission of the Bible in the Light of Qumran Manuscripts', in F.M. Cross and S. Talmon [eds.], *Qumran and the History of the Biblical Text* [Cambridge, MA: Harvard University Press, 1975], pp. 234-35; a more comprehensive list of 'corrections' is provided in E.Y. Kutscher, *The Language and Linguistic Background of the Isaiah Scroll [1QIsa^a]* [STDJ, 6; Leiden: Brill, 1974], pp. 531-36). A more significant 'correction' occurs in 40.7-8. The body of the scroll agrees with the Septuagint in transmitting simply, 'The grass withers, the flower fades, but the word of our God will stand forever'. A later hand has added (above the line and down the left margin), 'when the breath of the Lord blows on it; surely the people are grass; the grass withers, the flower fades', which brings the scroll into agreement with what is now known as the 'received text' (see J. Koenig, 'Réouverture du débat sur la Première main rédactionnelle du rouleau ancien d'Isaïe de Qumran [1QIs^a] en 40,7-8', *RevQ* 11 [1983], pp. 219-37).

15. Despite Smith's insightful and exclamatory insistence to the contrary, it appears that there are communities for whom, just as emphatically, 'Scriptures are texts!' That these groups may be naively (or studiously) unaware of the shortcomings of such a conception is, for the moment at least, beside the point. An alternative understanding of the role of the text in this approach might recognize it as 'icon' rather than 'artifact', provided one does not appropriate the predictably iconoclastic and secularist prejudices of most western consideration of such items, which mediate the presence of the transcendent to an adherent and vice versa.

16. Talmon, 'DSIa as a Witness to Ancient Exegesis of the Book of Isaiah', in Cross and Talmon (eds.), *Qumran and the History*, p. 126. Talmon's appraisal stands in contrast to H.M. Orlinsky's earlier dismissal of this scroll as 'an unreliable oral variation on the theme of what came to be known as the masoretic text of Isaiah' ('Studies in the St. Mark's Isaiah Scroll', *JBL* 69 [1950], p. 165).

'writer' is no mere copyist but 'an exegete', one who reads and understands in a particular way.

Divergences between 1QIsa[a] and the Massoretic text as attested in B19[A] frequently derive from reading rather than copying. Copyists typically read the text they are copying. Because, as is well known, the oldest manuscripts contain only consonants, because they sometimes preserve linguistic forms and expressions no longer current in the Hebrew of the scripturalist, and because in some scripts some letters are easily interchanged, there was ample opportunity for multiple readings, even of an identical set of letters.[17] Divergences in 'the text' arise because different readers understand what they read differently.

In this type of scripturalizing, 'communication' takes precedence over 'text'. Awareness of transcendence 'reduced to speech or writing' is not reduced to *a* (standard) text. Scripture involves *communication* to be understood more than a text to be preserved. Multiple readings and new understandings are constitutive of the dynamic process that Scripture is.

In a third type of activity, *the scripturalist is a reviser contributing to a living literary tradition.*

This type is evident in 4QpaleoExod[m].[18] The text of Exodus in

17. Sometimes the resulting difference is as small as a single word; at other times several words or entire sentences are at issue. Only one word differs in Isa. 11.6, which begins, 'The wolf shall live with the lamb, the leopard shall lie down with the kid', followed by 'the calf and the lion *and the fatling (ûmĕrî' > wmry')* together' in B19[A], but 'the calf and the lion *shall grow fat (yimĕrû > ymrw)* together' in 1QIsa[a]. The former reads a noun where the latter sees a verb. In 26.16, four words are read differently, with the result that the content and the phrasing of the verse are quite different. B19[A] reads,

> O Lord, in distress *they visited you (pĕqādûkā)*,
> > *they poured out (ṣāqûn) a prayer (laḥaš)*
> > > when *your chastening (mûsārĕkā)* was on them.

1QIsa[a], however, reads,

> O Lord, in distress *they called out (ṣā'āqûn)*
> > *your precepts (piqqûdêkā)*;
> > > *they prayed (lāḥāšû) your commandments (mûsārêkā)* to themselves.

B19[A] transmits three clauses containing verbs but 1QIsa[a] only two. For discussion of these and other examples, see Talmon, 'DSIa as a Witness', esp. pp. 123-25.

18. The critical edition of this scroll appears in P.W. Skehan, E. Ulrich, and J. Sanderson, *Qumran Cave 4. IV. Palaeo–Hebrew and Greek Biblical Manuscripts* (DJD, 9; Oxford: Clarendon Press, 1992), pp. 53-130.

4QpaleoExod^m (and in the Samaritan Pentateuch) exhibits several notable expansions relative to the text of the Massoretic tradition. For example, at least five times in 4QpaleoExod^m the narratives of the plagues
on Egypt are expanded by repeating to Pharaoh the words God spoke to
Moses.[19] In another instance, Deut. 1.9-18 is incorporated into Exod.
18.21-26 in place of Exod. 18.25.[20] The harmonizing tendencies are
clear: Exodus (within itself) and Exodus and Deuteronomy (between
them) should present a complete and unified witness. Patrick W. Skehan,
who pioneered the work on 4QpaleoExod^m, referred to the kind of
activity evident in this scroll as explaining the Bible by the Bible within
the Bible.[21]

4QpaleoExod^m testifies to Scripture that is alive and growing, not
calcified or fossilized. The scripturalist exercises a measure of freedom
in 'improving' an inherited text as it is passed along.[22] The scriptural
form of 'a people's symbolizing of the transcendent' is a living literary
tradition to be nurtured and developed.

In a fourth type of activity, *the scripturalist is an elaborator spinning
a variation on a theme.*

This type is evident in the 'Genesis Apocryphon' (1QapGen). In
places, 1QapGen offers a literal translation of the book of Genesis into
Aramaic; sometimes, however, it paraphrases; sometimes it harmonizes

---

19. For instance, after Yahweh addresses Moses and Aaron in Exod. 8.16-19
(Eng. 8.20-23), 4QpaleoExod^m (with the Samaritan Pentateuch) adds, 'So Moses and
Aaron came to Pharaoh, and they said to him', followed by an exact repetition of the
words of Yahweh in vv. 16-19. The narrative then picks up again with v. 20 (Eng.
v. 24) 'And Yahweh did so. . . ' (other instances are following Exod. 7.18; 7.29; 9.5;
9.19). After 10.2 the scroll (with the Samaritan Pentateuch) supplies a command from
Yahweh for the 'plague' of locusts (for a discussion of these and similar expansions
see J.E. Sanderson, *An Exodus Scroll from Qumran: 4QpaleoExod^m and the Samaritan Tradition* [HSS, 30; Atlanta: Scholars Press, 1986], pp. 196-207; and E. Tov,
'The Nature and Background of Harmonizations in Biblical Manuscripts', *JSOT* 31
[1985], pp. 7, 13-14).

20. Skehan, Ulrich, and Sanderson, *Qumran Cave 4*, pp. 67, 97-98. See also J.H.
Tigay, 'An Empirical Basis for the Documentary Hypothesis', *JBL* (1975), pp. 329-
42.

21. P.W. Skehan, 'The Biblical Scrolls from Qumran and the Text of the Old
Testament', in Cross and Talmon (eds.), *Qumran and the History*, p. 277.

22. Sanderson speaks of the 'strictly limited freedom' evident in 4QpaleoExod^m,
since the scripturalist employs only existing biblical material for the expansions
(*Exodus Scroll*, p. 274). Such apparent limitations distinguish the 'reviser' from the
'elaborator', the next type identified.

to diminish tensions, ambiguities, and contradictions; and frequently it strikes out on its own in highly imaginative directions. For instance, in 1QapGen the relatively straightforward biblical account of the promise to Abram of progeny and land in Gen. 13.14-18 is transposed into a marvelous autobiographical reminiscence on the part of Abram.[23]

In this type of activity, an element in an inherited text becomes a theme for variation. 1QapGen testifies to a type of scripturalizing that embellishes freely and imaginatively. A scriptural 'awareness of involvement with transcendence' is made new, is 'given accessible form in words' that invigorate and embellish old forms for a new audience.

In a fifth type of activity, *the scripturalist is a liturgist enacting the drama of worship.*

23. Col. 21.8-20 reads,

> God appeared to me in a vision of the night and said to me, 'Go up to Ramoth-hazor, which is to the north of Bethel, the place where you are dwelling; lift up your eyes and look to the east, west, south, and north, and see all this land which I am giving to you and to your descendants forever'.
>
> The next day I climbed up to Ramoth-hazor and I looked at the land from this height, from the River of Egypt to Lebanon and Senir, and from the Great Sea to Hauran, and all the land of Gebal as far as Kadesh, and at all the Great Desert which is (to the) east of Hauran and Senir as far as the Euphrates. And he said to me, 'To your descendants I shall give all this land; they will inherit it forever. I shall make your descendants as numerous as the dust of the earth which no man can number; so too your descendants will be without number. Rise, walk about, and go (around) to see how great is its length and how great is its width. For I shall give it to you and to your descendants after you for all ages.'
>
> So I, Abram, set out to go around and look at the land. I started going about from the Gihon River, moving along the Sea until I reached the Mount of the Ox. I journeyed from [the coast] of this Great Salt Sea and moved along the Mount of the Ox toward the east through the breadth of the land, until I reached the Euphrates River. I travelled along the Euphrates, until I came to the Red Sea in the east. (Then) I moved along the Red Sea, until I reached the tongue of the Reed Sea, which goes forth from the Red Sea. (From there) I journeyed to the south, until I reached the Gihon River. Then I returned, came home safely and found all my household safe and sound. I went and dwelt at the oaks of Mamre, which are in Hebron, to the northeast of Hebron. There I built an altar and offered on it a holocaust and an offering to God Most High.

Among the more telling elements of this embellishment and elaboration of the biblical story are the first-person narration by Abram; the depiction of the communication between the deity and Abram being initiated by a vision in the night; the instruction in the vision for Abram to go up to higher ground to receive the promise of land as far as he can see; the specific itinerary for Abram's walk through the entire land; and the consummation of his construction of an altar with appropriate offerings. (The translation is from J.A. Fitzmyer, *The Genesis Apocryphon of Qumran Cave 1: A Commentary* [BibOr, 18; Rome: Pontifical Biblical Institute, 1966], p. 61).

Here Scripture is *performed* in worship.[24] The fragment 4Q504 preserves a corporate prayer in which the congregation is taken up into
the narratives of Torah as the people carried on eagles' wings (Exod.
19.4; Deut. 32.11) and as those with whom the deity is present in a
pillar of fire and cloud (Exod. 13.21-22).[25] Through the scripturalizing
of the liturgist, the worshiping community becomes the community in
Scripture. A different sort of example is found in 1QS, the 'Rule of
the Community', where the structure of the covenant ceremony is an
adaptation of the basic outline for worship presented in Deut. 27.11-
26 and carried out in Josh. 8.33-34.[26] Through its form of worship,

24. Unfortunately, the liturgical role of Scripture in the Qumran community is an
area of relatively limited knowledge (see Fishbane, 'Use, Authority and Interpretation', pp. 344, 346). Only recently has the state of the investigation begun to
move beyond the assessment of L. Schiffman: 'the study of Qumran liturgy is in its
infancy' ('The Dead Sea Scrolls and the Early History of Jewish Liturgy', in L.I.
Levine (ed.), *The Synagogue in Late Antiquity* [Philadelphia: American Schools of
Oriental Research, 1987], p. 44).

25. As translated by G. Vermes (*The Dead Sea Scrolls in English* [London:
Penguin, 3rd edn, 1987], p. 220), the text reads,

> Remember, pray, that we are Thy people and that Thou has carried us marvellously [on
> the wings of] eagles and have brought us towards Thee. And like an eagle which rouses
> its nestlings and hovers over [its young], spreads out its wings, takes one and carries it
> on [its pinions], so we dwell apart and are not reckoned among the nations and . . . Thou
> art in our midst in the pillar of fire and the cloud [of] Thy [holi]ness walking before us,
> and as it were Thy glory in our mid[st].

This prayer is one in 'a series of daily supplications for liturgical use' (L. Schiffman,
'Liturgical Texts from Qumran Cave IV', *Proceedings of the Ninth World Congress
of Jewish Studies, Jerusalem, August 4–12, 1985, Division A: The Period of the
Bible* [Jerusalem: World Union of Jewish Studies, 1986], p. 187; see also E.G.
Chazon, '*Divrei Ha-Me'orot*: Liturgy or Literature', *Proceedings of the Tenth World
Congress of Jewish Studies, Jerusalem, August 16–24, 1989, Division A: The Bible
and its World* [Jerusalem: World Union of Jewish Studies, 1990]; M. Baillet, 'Un
recueil liturgique de Qumrân, grotte 4: "Les paroles des luminaires"', *RB* 68 [1961],
pp. 195-250 [+ plates XXIV–XXVIII]); and *idem*, *Qumran Grotte 4* [DJD, 7;
Oxford: Clarendon Press, 1982], III, pp. 137-68 [+ plates XLIX–LIII]).

26. 1QS 2.1-4, 11-18 reads,

> Then the priests shall bless all the men of God's lot who walk perfectly in all his ways,
> and say, 'May he bless you with all good and keep you from all evil; may he enlighten
> your heart with insight for living, may he favor you with eternal knowledge! May he
> lift up his merciful countenance toward you for eternal peace . . . And the priests and
> Levites shall continue and say: 'Because of the idols of his heart which he worships
> cursed be he who enters into this covenant and puts the stumbling-block of his iniquity

the present community is the community in Scripture.

In this type of activity, involvement with transcendence is a present and immediate reality. Through the drama of worship, the scripturalizing community participates in its inherited texts through the powerful combination of its identification with the community in the text and its awareness of the immediacy of transcendence. In no other type of activity is Smith's trilateral *engagement* 'among humans, the transcendent, and a text' accomplished more profoundly and completely.[27] Thus, Scripture as liturgical performance is central to the concept of Scripture as a human activity.

In a sixth type of activity, *the scripturalist is a codifier devising a rule for faith and practice.*

No mere listing of laws or doctrines, this creative manner of scripturalizing is crucial for establishing and maintaining the identity of a community whose faith and practice are grounded in its inherited

> before him so that he backslides, (stumbling) over it . . . May his spirit be destroyed, (suffering) thirst along with saturation, without forgiveness. May God's wrath and his angry judgments flare up against him for everlasting destruction, and may all the curses of this covenant stick to him. May God set him apart for evil that he may be cut off from all the Sons of Light because of his backsliding from God through his idols and the stumbling block of his iniquity. May he put his lot among those who are cursed forever. And all those who enter the covenant shall respond and say after them: 'Amen, Amen!'

The essential features here are the proclamation of blessings and curses to which the congregation responds, 'Amen!' (The translation is from J.H. Charlesworth (ed.), *The Dead Sea Scrolls: Hebrew, Aramaic, and Greek Texts with English Translations*. I. *Rule of the Community and Related Documents* [Tübingen: Mohr (Paul Siebeck); Louisville: Westminster/John Knox, 1994], pp. 9-11). Patte discusses this occurrence as 'a structural use of Scripture' (*Early Jewish Hermeneutic*, p. 274); Fishbane notes it under the rubric, 'Mikra as Model for Practices or Procedures' ('Use, Authority and Interpretation', p. 359).

27. Smith observes that the designation of Scripture as *miqrā'* denotes 'not a written form but a (liturgically) oral' form (*What Is Scripture?*, p. 244 n. 6) by means of which people have garnered 'snatches from it, or phrases, verses, or even large sections, accompanying them as they went about their affairs' (Smith, *What Is Scripture?*, p. 120). Thus, the recitation of Scripture in worship plays 'the dominant role of personalizing it inwardly in memory' (Smith, *What Is Scripture?*, p. 120). Indeed, Smith suggests,

> One could almost ask whether perhaps 'scripture' is a name not for what is read so much as for the ceremonial reading of it, and for the process of personalizing it—as a cosmic relation; or of the complex formed by both the cause and the result of that process (*What Is Scripture?*, p. 120).

texts.[28] For example, the first quotation of a biblical injunction in the 'code of behavior' in 1QS is Exod. 23.7 ('You shall keep far from every false thing'), followed by Isa. 2.22 ('Turn away from humans, who have only breath in their nostrils, for of what account are they?'). These two unlikely citations are employed early in the code to support an essential aspect of the community's identity: separation 'from all the men of deceit who walk in the way of wickedness'.[29]

This creative combination of injunctions from Torah and Prophets is also evident when specific behaviors are at issue. In the 'Damascus Rule', Lev. 19.18 ('You shall not take vengeance or bear a grudge against any of your people') and Nah. 1.2 ('the LORD takes vengeance on his adversaries and rages against his enemies') are joined to curtail rash accusations among members of the community.[30] In a more predictable example, the Sabbath commandment in Deut. 5.12 is invoked and developed throughout the community's life.[31]

---

28. Fishbane provides an excellent analysis of the literary techniques involved in 'Use, Authority and Interpretation', pp. 347-56.

29. 1QS 5.10-11. 1QS 5.14-18 reads,

> for (he remains) impure among all those who transgress his words. No one must be united with him in his duty or his property, lest he burden him (with) guilty iniquity. But he shall keep far away from him in everything, for thus it is written, 'Keep far away from everything that is false'. No man of the men of the Community shall respond to their utterance with respect to any law or judgment. No one must either eat or drink anything of their property, or accept anything from their hand without payment, as it is written, 'Have nothing to do with the man whose breath is in his nostrils, for wherein can he be accounted?' For all those who are not accounted within his covenant, they and everything they have must be excluded.

The translation is Charlesworth's (*Dead Sea Scrolls*, p. 23).

30. As translated by C. Rabin (*The Zadokite Documents* [Oxford: Clarendon Press, 2nd rev. edn, 1958], p. 44), CD 9.2-5 reads,

> And as to that which He said: 'Thou shalt not take vengeance nor bear rancour against the children of thy people'—every man of the members of the covenant who brings against his neighbour an accusation without reproving before witnesses and brings it up when he grows angry or tells his elders to make him contemptible, he is one who takes vengeance and bears rancour—although it is expressly written: 'HE taketh vengeance on HIS adversaries, and HE reserveth wrath to HIS enemies'.

The catchwords 'vengeance' and 'rancor' (/'reserveth wrath') are obviously the basis of the association.

31. More than a third of leaf 10 and almost all of 11 is concerned with the Sabbath. The section begins (CD 10.15-19),

In these creative appropriations, the community's Rules become as of a piece with Scripture so that its codes of conduct and constructions of faith are indisputably anchored in transcendence.

In a seventh type of activity, *the scripturalist is a commentator gazing in a mirror on the present.*[32]

In the hands of a commentator, inherited texts reflect the world of the present community.[33] So, for instance, in 1QS 8.12-16, the 'mission statement' of the community appears in Isa. 40.3.[34] The mirror of

> Let no man do work on the Friday from the time when the orb of the sun is distant from the gate by its own fulness; for this is what He said, 'Guard the Sabbath day to keep it holy'. And on the Sabbath day, let no man speak a lewd or villainous word. Let him not lend anything to his neighbour (or: press his neighbour for repayment of anything). Let him not shed blood for (or: dispute about) property and gain. Let him not speak of matters of labour and work to be done on the morrow.

The translation is Rabin's (*Zadokite Documents*, p. 52).

32. E. Jucci employs the image of a mirror in 'Interpretazione e Storia nei *Pesharim Qumranici*', *Bibbia e Oriente* 29 (1987), pp. 163-77.

33. On the basis of study of the *pesharim*, it has become axiomatic among commentators to refer to the eschatological orientation of the Qumran community as the key to understanding the hermeneutical principles at work in the scrolls. As K. Elliger put it early on, at Qumran '1. Prophetic proclamation has for its content the End, and 2. the present is the End Time' (*Studien zum Habakuk–Kommentar vom Toten Meer* [BHT, 15; Tübingen: Mohr–Siebeck, 1953], p. 275); therefore, biblical prophecy (i.e. Scripture) speaks of the present. As important as eschatology appears to be in many of the scrolls, some qualification is in order where Scripture is concerned. First, it is a common error to assume that the scrolls depict 'a relatively brief "pre-eschatological" era'; in fact, 'it is considerably longer than often thought' (P.R. Davies, 'The Ideology of the Temple in the Damascus Document', *JJS* 33 [1982], p. 298). Secondly, a 'pan-eschatological' perspective tends toward an implicit assumption of typically Christian and Protestant biases that the prophets were predictors of the End (/Messiah); but it is at least as often the case that the prophets are presented in the scrolls 'not as predictors but as preachers of the law' (Davies, 'The Ideology of the Temple', p. 300; see also the examples in type six above). And finally, as J. Sanders has pointed out, eschatology is not the only interpretative axiom operant in the scrolls. He identifies in addition what he calls a 'constitutive' axiom that 'marshalled scriptural authority in service of Qumran ideology' ('From Isaiah 61', p. 95). It is undoubtedly an error to generalize from the distinctive perspectives of the *pesharim* and assume that *all* scripturalizing in the scrolls follows their lead. The variety of types isolated in this paper indicates quite clearly that scripturalizing in the scrolls cannot be reduced to eschatology.

34. The text is as follows:

> When these become the Community in Israel they shall separate themselves from the session of the men of deceit in order to depart into the wilderness to prepare there the

Scripture also contains far wider reflections. For example, the famous commentary on Habakkuk from cave 1 explains that the Romans (the 'Kittim') are the 'Chaldeans' (Babylonians) mentioned in Hab. 1.6-8.[35] Furthermore, because Scripture is a 'full-length mirror', it includes events in the history of the community (and beyond) that are of continuing significance.[36]

> Way of the Lord (?); as it is written: 'In the wilderness prepare the way of the Lord, make level in the desert a highway for our God'. This (alludes to) the study of the Torah wh[ic]h he commanded through Moses to do, according to everything which has been revealed (from) time to time, and according to that which the prophets have revealed by his Holy Spirit.

The translation is Charlesworth's (*Dead Sea Scrolls*, pp. 36-37).

    35. With the biblical text in upper case letters, 1QpHab 2.10–3.6 reads in part,

> FOR BEHOLD I AM RAISING UP THE CHALDEANS, THAT BITTER [AND HA]STY NATION.
> The interpretation of it concerns the Kittim wh[o ar]e swift and vigorous in battle, so as to destroy many
>
> . . .
>
> . . . for this is what it says: TO TAKE POSSESSION OF DWELLING PLACES NOT THEIR OWN. FEARFUL AND TERRIBLE ARE THEY. A CLAIM TO DIGNITY GOES OUT FROM THEM.
> The interpretation of it concerns the Kittim, fear and dread of whom are upon all the nations. By design all their plans are to do evil, and with cunning and deceit they associate with all the peoples.

The translation is from M.P. Horgan, *Pesharim: Qumran Interpretation of Biblical Books* (CBQMS, 8; Washington: Catholic Biblical Association, 1979), p. 13.

    36. 1QpHab 11.2-8 recounts the persecution of the Teacher of Righteousness by the Wicked Priest (Hos. 2.15 is in upper case in the translation by Horgan, *Pesharim*, p. 19):

> WOE TO HIM WHO GIVES HIS NEIGHBORS TO DRINK MIXING IN HIS POISON, INDEED, MAKING (THEM) DRUNK IN ORDER THAT HE MIGHT LOOK UPON THEIR FEASTS. The interpretation of it concerns the Wicked Priest, who pursued the Teacher of Righteousness—to swallow him up with his poisonous vexation—to his place of exile. And at the end of the feast, (during) the repose of the Day of Atonement, he appeared to them to swallow them up and to make them stumble on the fast day, their restful sabbath.

In 4QpNah (frags. 3–4, col. 1.1-3), Nah. 2.12 reflects the incursion of Demetrius III Eukerus (95–88 BCE) into Judah against Alexander Jannaeus (103–76 BCE):

> [The interpretation of it concerns Deme]trius, King of Greece, who sought to enter Jerusalem on the advice of the Seekers-After-Smooth-Things, [but God did not give Jerusalem] into the power of the kings of Greece from Antiochus until the rise of the rulers of the Kittim.

The translation is by Horgan (*Pesharim*, p. 163).

The world reflected in Scripture *is* the world of the commentator, and Scripture makes it possible to understand the world and one's place in it. It is important to note that this type of scripturalizing does not involve 'commenting on the text' as much as it does 'commenting on the *world*'. This distinction is crucial for understanding the nature of Scriptures and their roles in communities. Where scripturalizing is a vital component in the life of a community, one *interprets the world* (and one's self) in light of Scripture, not vice versa.[37] By seeing its own world and itself through its Scriptures, the scripturalizing community participates in transcendence 'brought down to earth', not only in the holy and eternal now of worship but also in the community's concrete place and activity in the wider natural, social, and political contexts of its existence.

Finally, in an eighth type of activity, *the scripturalist is a visionary peering through a window on the future.*

Although the community of the scrolls understood itself to be living in the 'latter days', the End had not yet arrived. So, for instance, 4QFlorilegium (4Q174) envisions the appearance of the Coming One in a collocation of 2 Sam. 7.11-14 and Amos 9.11.[38] Similarly, Nah. 3.7 is understood to describe a future event, the demise of opponents of the visionary's community.[39]

---

37. That the categories and presuppositions of the commentator's world are brought (in)to the text in the process goes without saying. But it is only with the rise of historical–critical analysis that Scriptures are removed from the world of the present to be treated instead as *historical objects* for interpretation in their own time and place, understood quite narrowly as the time and place of their origin. H. Frei describes the transition this way: 'the biblical story began to fade as the inclusive world whose depiction allowed the reader at the same time to locate himself and his era in the real world rendered by the depiction' (*The Eclipse of Biblical Narrative: A Study in Eighteenth and Nineteenth Century Hermeneutics* [New Haven: Yale University Press, 1974], p. 50).

38. With the biblical material in quotation marks, 4QFlor 1.10-13 reads,

> 'And the Lord declares to you that he will build you a house. And I will raise up your seed after you, I will establish the throne of his kingdom for ever. I will be to him as a father, and he will be to me as a son': he is the shoot of David who will stand with the Interpreter of the Law, who [will rule] in Zion in the latter days as it is written, 'And I will raise up the booth of David which is fallen': he is the booth (or, branch) of David which was fallen, who will take office to save Israel.

The translation is from Brooke, *Exegesis*, p. 92.

39. 1QpNah (fragments 3–4, column 3.6-8) reads,

In this manner of scripturalizing, wherever the text speaks of the future, it may serve as a window on whatever is future to the scripturalist. Thus, the implications of 'involvement with transcendence' are by no means limited to the present but extend as far as the vision of the scripturalist permits.

Implications

The scrolls from Qumran contain important cues for understanding the human activity that is Scripture prior to the consolidation of the 'Scripture movement' in Judaism, Christianity, and Islam. The following four points pursue implications of the scripturalizing activity evident in the scrolls in the light of W.C. Smith's concept of Scripture.

First, the liturgical use of inherited texts is central for understanding Scripture as a human activity. Within the drama of worship Smith's trilateral *engagement* 'among humans, the transcendent, and a text' is accomplished more profoundly and completely than in any other type of scripturalizing. It is in worship in scripturalizing communities that Scriptures most clearly exhibit their character as one form among others 'of a people's symbolizing of the transcendent within and among and around them'. Thus, where worship and liturgy are ignored, Scripture remains unexplored.

Secondly, Scripture as a human activity is multifaceted and varied. Neither communities nor individuals typically scripturalize in the same manner all the time, nor should they be expected to. Dancers and their troupes perform more than one type of dance; so also with scripturalists. Conservatorial and visionary activities may be pursued side-by-side. Reading, revising, elaborating, and commentating are but different degrees on a single arc. Devising a rule for faith and practice and directing the drama of worship are simply alternative modes of *engagement*. These complementary modes of symbolizing the transcendent and cultivating an awareness of involvement with transcendence reveal an ancient and constitutive variety in the treatment that inherited texts receive.

> 'NINEVAH IS DEVASTATED, WHO WILL MOURN FOR HER? WHENCE, INDEED, SHALL I SEEK COMFORTERS FOR YOU?' The interpretation of it [concerns] the Seekers–After–Smooth–Things, whose council will perish, and whose congregation will be dispersed. They will not again lead [the] assembly astray, and the sim[ple ones] will no longer support their policy.

The translation is from Horgan, *Pesharim*, p. 165.

Thirdly, the spectrum of activities identified here would appear to extend across divisions within and between scripturalizing communities and religions, all of which exhibit a shared human propensity in relating to transcendence. Certainly, the types identified above are neither exhaustive nor even necessary within a given scripturalizing community. Nevertheless, the types of activity illustrated above may be played in a dazzling array of keys and on an unlimited variety of instruments. In scripturalizing, in whatever key, in whatever orchestration, in however faulty a manner, the ineffable is articulated and the unsearchable is investigated. The common tonality is a prior commitment to engaging transcendence through inherited texts.

Fourthly and finally, the study of Scripture only secondarily involves attending to literary techniques and conceptual manipulations of texts. Were Scriptures merely texts, the ardent loyalty and sometimes vicious fanaticism (evident in the scrolls, as well as elsewhere) with which people 'defend' their Scriptures or mode of scripturalizing would be inexplicable. But it is not 'texts' that are at stake in this defensiveness. It is people's understanding of themselves and the transcendent in the world that is at issue in divergences of or over Scriptures. For many individuals and communities, altering their scripturalizing activity—or to relinquish it or to admit another's as authentic and efficacious—is tantamount to revisioning their world and reconfiguring themselves.

Paradoxically, then, Scripture deeply divides people and communities one from another and at the same time unites them in a shared human quest to confound chaos, to search out order in the universe, and to discover what it means to be human. To study Scripture is to explore the human engagement of self, world, and the transcendent through inherited texts. The comparative study of Scripture is the effort to explicate the surface fractures and the profound congruences in one distinctive and powerful human effort to fathom the universe and divine a place in it. Nothing less is adequate as an elucidation of the supremely human and transcendent venture that is Scripture.

THE RHETORIC OF QUOTATIONS: AN ESSAY ON METHOD

Christopher D. Stanley

The last few years have seen a growing interest in the way Jews and Christians interpreted Scripture in the Graeco-Roman era. Several monographs and a steady stream of articles have explored the hermeneutical practices of individual authors and offered fresh insights into particular texts. Much of the research in this area has revolved around issues of individual and group self-definition. Hermeneutical questions invariably take center stage in such investigations: What meaning did the author find in the biblical text? What interpretative traditions might have influenced (or determined) this result? What ideological and/or methodological presumptions governed the way the text would be read? How (if at all) does this later meaning relate to the original (contextualized) sense of the text? These are all important questions that arise directly out of the subject matter, and there is ample reason to pursue them, even if the answers remain rather elusive.

But something is missing here. With all of the recent interest in hermeneutical questions, relatively little attention has been paid to the *rhetorical* significance of these appeals to Scripture. Certainly there are places in the literature where a Jewish or Christian author shows a concern to understand the biblical text for its own sake. In most cases, however, the ancient author quotes a passage from Scripture as part of a broader argument designed to convince others to believe or act in a certain way. This is a *rhetorical* act, and it should be investigated as such.

Recent studies of quotations in the fields of rhetoric, linguistics, and literary studies have emphasized that the meaning and/or effect of a quotation arises directly out of its current literary and rhetorical context, regardless of how this relates to the 'original sense' of the quoted passage. A review of some of these studies will point the way toward a more balanced approach to the study of early Jewish and Christian appeals to Scripture.

Rhetorical Approaches

Modern textbooks on rhetoric and speech communication say little about the effect of using quotations in speeches and other rhetorical works.[1] The subject typically receives rather cursory treatment in a section dealing with the use of evidence or testimony to lend credibility to an argument. The purpose of quotations in this framework is to offer authoritative grounding for a statement or position advanced elsewhere in the speaker's own language. The effectiveness of a quotation (as with other forms of evidence) depends for the most part on the perceived authority and/or credibility of the original source, although the credibility of the speaker can also affect the reception of evidence.[2] 'Effectiveness' is defined here as the production of lasting changes in the beliefs and/or attitudes of the immediate audience.[3]

Most rhetoricians have recognized that quotations do more than simply reproduce the ideas of an authority. Quotations can also be used to illustrate or expand a point made by the speaker in ordinary language.

---

1.   The same is true for the ancient handbooks on rhetoric. Aristotle refers briefly to the practice of citing 'ancient witnesses' (defined as 'the poets and all other notable persons whose judgments are known to all', *Rhet.* 1.15) to support an argument, but limits their value to establishing the facts about past events that might be adduced as analogies to support a contemporary legal case (2.23). The use of proverbs and maxims (arguably a special form of quotation) is restricted here to elderly men whose long experience gives them the credibility to cite traditional wisdom (2.21). In the right hands, says Aristotle, maxims can prove helpful to an orator 'due to the want of intelligence in his hearers, who love to hear him succeed in expressing as a universal truth the opinions which they hold themselves about particular cases' (2.21). Quintilian offers similar observations in a brief section where he recommends the use of quotations to lend authority to the orator's pronouncements (*Inst. Orat.* 5.36-44). Pronouncements from the past are valuable because 'they form a sort of testimony, which is rendered all the more impressive by the fact that it was not given to suit special cases, but was the utterance. . . of minds swayed neither by prejudice or influence, simply because it seemed the most honourable or honest thing to say' (5.37). Maxims can also be useful because they have 'carried conviction of their truth to all mankind' (5.41). This is as far as the ancient sources take us.

2.   In his book *Persuasion* (Englewood Cliffs, NJ: Prentice–Hall, 1983), Robert Bostrom describes the detailed experiments of James McCroskey, who demonstrated that appeals to evidence could be quite effective for speakers who were perceived as having low- to medium-credibility by the audience, but were of minimal help for a high-credibility speaker (pp. 146-50).

3.   Bostrom, *Persuasion*, pp. 150-52.

The effect here is less direct, and therefore less predictable. According to one text, 'The value and power of any literary material quoted in a speech depends upon its relevance to the point of the message and upon its strength in saying something—with grace, felicity, and a sense of the poetic or the dramatic—that could not be said as aptly in the speaker's own words'.[4] Here we see a recognition of the poetic dimension of the quotation process. The 'value and power' of a quotation may depend as much on the manner of expression as on the content or source of the statement.

In broad terms, then, rhetorical studies remind us that a direct quotation from a recognized authority can serve to increase the audience's receptivity to a speaker's message. But how? A review of the rhetoric and speech communication literature offers little help with this question. For an answer, we must turn instead to recent developments in the fields of philosophy and linguistics.

Linguistic Approaches

The publication in 1955 of J.L. Austin's *How to Do Things with Words*[5] signaled a paradigm shift in the study of language by philosophers and linguists. According to Austin, language does more than simply make a statement or pass on information. Words are spoken (or written) with the aim of *doing* something to the hearer(s), that is, evoking some sort of response. This is true even when the response is limited to accepting the speaker's words as 'fact'.

Austin identified three distinct aspects of the speech process: (1) the *locutionary act*, the vocalization (or inscription) of a series of words that carry a more or less definite sense and reference in a given language; (2) the *illocutionary act*, the construction of words into a specific form of communication (informing, questioning, commanding, promising, etc.) according to the linguistic conventions of a particular society; and (3) the *perlocutionary act*, the effect (whether intended or not) that these words have on the feelings, thoughts, or conduct of the hearer(s), for example, convincing, persuading, deterring, surprising, or misleading the audience.[6] Even the simplest of statements produces some

4.   K.G. Hance, D.C. Ralph, and M.J. Wiksell, *Principles of Speaking* (Belmont, CA: Wadsworth, 3rd edn, 1989), p. 88.
5.   (Cambridge, MA: Harvard University Press, 2nd edn, 1962).
6.   Austin, *How to Do Things with Words*, pp. 94-120.

perlocutionary effect.[7] As Austin puts it, 'Once we realize that what we have to study is *not* the sentence but the issuing of an utterance in a speech situation, there can hardly be any longer a possibility of not seeing that stating is performing an act'.[8] Every meaningful use of language is in reality a 'speech-act', the term that gives this theory its name.

Austin's 'speech-act theory' laid the groundwork for contemporary studies of language in the fields of philosophy and linguistics. Included here are several studies that have examined the way *quotations* work as part of a broader 'speech-act'. Most of the philosophers who have written on this subject have focused on broader theoretical questions about the meaning and reference of quotations and what it means to place quotation marks around words in a sentence. Questions such as these lie beyond the limits of the present study.[9] The same can be said for several of the linguistic studies that explore the links between direct, indirect, and 'free indirect' quotations.[10] But there are other lines of research that speak directly to the issues under consideration here. The most important of these are the dramaturgical theory of Anna

---

7.   Austin, *How to Do Things with Words*, pp. 133-40.

8.   Austin, *How to Do Things with Words*, p. 139. J.R. Searle, who studied with Austin, makes a similar point: 'The unit of linguistic communication is not, as has generally been supposed, the symbol, word or sentence, or even the token of the symbol, word or sentence, but rather the production or issuance of the symbol or word or sentence in the performance of the speech act' (*Speech Acts: An Essay in the Philosophy of Language* [Cambridge: Cambridge University Press, 1969], p. 16).

9.   See Searle, *Speech Acts*, pp. 72-76; D. Davidson, 'Quotation', in *Inquiries into Truth and Interpretation* (Oxford: Clarendon Press, 1984), pp. 79-92; N. Goodman, 'Some Questions Concerning Quotation', in *Ways of Worldmaking* (Indianapolis, IN: Hackett, 1978), pp. 41-56. The one insight from the philosophical approach that might prove useful in analyzing biblical quotations is the recognition that 'in quotation, the normal referential function of words is suspended, because the words that we utter when we quote are not our own' (F. Coulmas, 'Reported Speech: Some General Issues', in F. Coulmas [ed.], *Direct and Indirect Speech* [Berlin/New York: Mouton/de Gruyter, 1986], p. 12). The significance of this observation will become clear at a later point in the study.

10.   E.g. B. Hall Partee, 'The Syntax and Semantics of Quotations', in S.R. Anderson and P. Kiparsky (eds.), *A Festschrift for Morris Halle* (New York: Holt, Rinehart & Winston, 1973), pp. 410-18; A. Banfield, 'Narrative Style and the Grammar of Direct and Indirect Speech', *Foundations of Language* 10 (1973), pp. 1-39; Y. Hirose, 'Direct and Indirect Speech as Quotations of Public and Private Expression', *Lingua* 95 (1995), pp. 223-38.

Wierzbicka, the 'Proteus Principle' of Meir Sternberg, and the demonstration theory of Herbert Clark and Richard Gerrig.

The Dramaturgical Theory

The dramaturgical theory of Anna Wierzbicka[11] was developed to answer several theoretical questions about the relation between direct, indirect, and 'free indirect' quotations.[12] At the heart of all quotations, says Wierzbicka, lies a concern to 'dramatize' the words of an earlier speaker to a later audience. As Wierzbicka puts it, 'The person who reports another's words by quoting them, temporarily assumes the role of that other person, "plays his part", that is to say, imagines himself as the other person and for a moment behaves in accordance with this counterfactual assumption'.[13] At the moment of quotation, says Wierzbicka, the quoting author takes on the *persona* of the original speaker and dramatically reenacts the original speech-act, so that the two voices merge into one.[14] The reason behind such an imaginary exercise (the 'illocutionary purpose' of the quotation) is to convey not only *what* the original speaker said, but also *how* he said it.[15] The task of communicating *what* was said can be fulfilled through the use of indirect speech ('he said *that*. . . '). The use of a direct quotation therefore signals a concern to lead the later audience into a brief, imaginary reenactment of the original speech-event.[16] When a written text is quoted, the reenactment is limited to hearing the words of the original speaker. In the case

11. A. Wierzbicka, 'The Semantics of Direct and Indirect Discourse', *Papers in Linguistics* 7 (1974), pp. 267-307.

12. The term 'free indirect quotation' is one of several terms used by linguists to refer to a form of speech, found primarily in fictional literature, in which the identity of the speaker appears to shift throughout the course of the passage. As Coulmas puts it, 'the stylistic veil covers the speaker, leaving it up to the reader to determine whether the speaker of a given section of a narrative is the hero or the author' ('Reported Speech', p. 7). For examples, see Banfield, 'Narrative Style', pp. 10-13, 25-33; Wierzbicka, 'Semantics', pp. 294-97; and H.H. Clark and R.R. Gerrig, 'Quotations as Demonstrations', *Language* 66 (1990), pp. 786-88.

13. Wierzbicka, 'Semantics', p. 272. Wierzbicka's more complex discussion of the role of dramatic reenactment in indirect speech (pp. 283-300) is left aside for now, since it contributes nothing to the present investigation.

14. Wierzbicka, 'Semantics', p. 273.

15. Wierzbicka, 'Semantics', pp. 274-77. According to Wierzbicka, the words 'I want to cause you to know. . . ' are always implied in the quotation process.

16. This would be the 'perlocutionary effect' of the direct quotation. Wierzbicka's discussion is laced with references to 'speech-act theory'.

of observed speech, the quoting speaker can also mimic the tone of voice, facial expressions, gestures, and other nonverbal elements of the communicative process.[17]

Unfortunately, Wierzbicka has little to say about why a later speaker would want to create such a momentary reenactment of the original speech-event. The closest she comes is her suggestion that 'a person who quotes another's speech may feel unable to separate the meaning from the form and to state it in his own words... Quoting directly one undertakes to portray the meaning *together* with the form, thus avoiding the responsibility for a correct representation of the meaning as such.'[18] In other words, the speaker who chooses direct quotation purposely leaves to the reader the dual task of interpretation and response.

Wierzbicka's insistence on the imaginative or 'dramatical' quality of direct quotation has found broad support from subsequent investigators.[19] Much of this is due to the fact that linguists have found it a helpful way of explaining some of the similarities and differences between direct, indirect, and 'free indirect' quotations. Its usefulness for the study of ancient biblical quotations, however, is less apparent. Perhaps the greatest value of Wierzbicka's approach is its emphasis on the dynamic interplay between the voice of the quoting author and the voice of the quoted text. In direct quotation, the quoting author temporarily lays aside his own speech to allow the biblical text to speak for (or through) him. Thus the readers are enabled (in theory) to hear for themselves what the quoting author heard in his own earlier encounter with the biblical text. But direct quotation also empowers the readers by opening up the possibility that they might hear something different in the text than what the quoting author intended. To preclude this possibility, authors of argumentative texts routinely embed their quotations in an interpretative context that predisposes the reader toward a

17. The latter point is developed more fully by C.N. Li in 'Direct Speech and Indirect Speech: A Functional Study', in Coulmas (ed.), *Direct and Indirect Speech*, pp. 38-40.

18. Wierzbicka, 'Semantics', p. 279. Wierzbicka says this is only 'one of the reasons why people sometimes prefer to quote rather than to paraphrase the speech of others' (p. 279), but she fails to mention any others.

19. The validity of Wierzbicka's theory is assumed by Coulmas in 'Reported Speech', pp. 2, 6, and affirmed (with qualifications) by Clark and Gerrig in 'Quotations', pp. 801-802. The term 'dramaturgical theory' as a label for Wierzbicka's theory actually comes from the latter study, not from Wierzbicka herself. Wierzbicka's theory is developed further by C.N. Li in 'Direct Speech', pp. 29-45.

particular response to the quoted text.[20] In these cases, direct quotation does not offer the kind of unmediated reenactment of the original speech-event that Wierzbicka thought. Instead, the voice of the original is muffled (in varying degrees) by the voice of the quoting author.

In summary, Wierzbicka is correct in insisting that direct quotation brings the reader into forceful contact with the voice of the original text. In the case of Jewish and Christian quotations from Scripture, this is a voice that speaks with profound authority. But Wierzbicka fails to observe (along with many contemporary students of biblical quotations) that direct quotation can also be used to advance an author's rhetorical agenda. By claiming the voice of Scripture as his own, an author can increase the chances that an audience of Christians or Jews will adopt (or reject) the set of beliefs and/or practices that he recommends (or opposes).

The Proteus Principle
The question that concerns Meir Sternberg[21] is what happens to the meaning of a statement when it is extracted from its original setting and embedded into a new context as part of a quotation. According to Sternberg, 'Quotation brings together at least two discourse-events: that in which things were originally expressed (said, thought, experienced) by one subject (speaker, writer, reflector), and that in which they are cited by another'.[22] The quotation-event differs qualitatively from the original speech-event. Where the original statement is grounded in the subjective experience of an individual speaker, the quotation makes the words themselves (the 'world of discourse') the object of reflection

---

20. In the pre-modern world (including Graeco-Roman antiquity), it was also common practice to reshape the wording of the quotation to reflect the quoting author's understanding of the original text. See C.D. Stanley, *Paul and the Language of Scripture* (SNTSMS, 74; Cambridge: Cambridge University Press, 1992), pp. 338-60. The same phenomenon occurs routinely in oral quotations, as documented in the experiments of E. Wade and H.H. Clark, 'Reproduction and Demonstration in Quotations', *Journal of Memory and Language* 32 (1993), pp. 805-19. According to Clark and Gerrig, the common assumption that quotations strive for verbatim reproduction can be traced to 'the written language bias of linguistics and philosophy' ('Quotations', p. 800). The same authors criticize Wierzbicka for her implicit acceptance of this view ('Quotations', p. 802).

21. M. Sternberg, 'Proteus in Quotation-Land: Mimesis and the Forms of Reported Discourse', *Poetics Today* 3 (1982), pp. 107-56.

22. Sternberg, 'Proteus', p. 107.

and interpretation.[23] The original statement becomes, in functional terms, 'an *inset* within the surrounding *frame* of the context-of-quotation'.[24] This recontextualization can have a profound effect on the meaning of a statement. Sternberg's analysis deserves to be quoted at length:

> What this new mode of existence involves is not just formal restructuring but manifold shifts, if not reversals, of the original meaning and significance. For regardless of the formal relations between inset and frame. . . the framing of an element within a text entails a communicative subordination of the part to the whole that encloses it. However accurate the wording of the quotation and however pure the quoter's motives, tearing a piece of discourse from its original habitat and reconstructing it within a new network of relations cannot but interfere with its effect.[25]

This happens because

> the very extraction of a part from a speech-event must, to a certain degree, modify, if not misrepresent, its role and import within the original whole, where it is qualified and supplemented, defined and substantiated, by a set of other components relating to the various parameters of context. And the resetting of the part within a different whole widens the distance still further by exposing it to the pressure of a new network of relations.[26]

A shift in meaning is inevitable:

> Whatever the units involved, to quote is to mediate, to mediate is to frame, and to frame is to interfere and exploit. Autonomous, nonnarrated, reporter-free, single-voiced quotation: each of these is a contradiction in terms. . . Charged with a different significance and assigned a new role by the whole, the recontextualized discourse proportionately moves away from the original string of words or thoughts.[27]

In the final analysis, says Sternberg,

23. Sternberg, 'Proteus', p. 107. Cf. Coulmas, 'Reported Speech', p. 12: 'The speaker does not claim authorship of for a part of his utterance which he ascribes to another speaker or unspecified source. This part of his utterance does not serve a regular referential function such that words refer to things. Rather, they refer to words, not to any arbitrary words, but purportedly to those words that some other speaker uttered at some other time'.
24. Sternberg, 'Proteus', p. 108.
25. Sternberg, 'Proteus', p. 108.
26. Sternberg, 'Proteus', p. 131.
27. Sternberg, 'Proteus', pp. 145, 150.

each act of quotation serves two masters. One is the original speech or
thought that it represents, pulling in the direction of maximal accuracy.
The other is the frame that encloses and regulates it, pulling in the direction
of maximal efficacy. Reported discourse thus presents a classic case of
divided allegiance, between original-oriented representation (with its face
to the world) and frame-oriented communication (with its face to the
reader).[28]

In sum, every quotation, no matter how faithfully it reproduces the
wording of the original, is a complex speech-event in which 'the quotee
always subserves the global perspective of the quoter, who adapts it to
his own goals and needs'.[29] But the voice of the original is not lost; quotation produces rather 'an expressive repatterning, or in other words,
a perspectival montage between the original subject and the quoting
subject who cites and manipulates his discourse within its new frame:
between quotee and quoter, reportee and reporter, represented and representing voice'.[30] In cases where the later audience has no independent access to the original source, this 'repatterned' version is the
only form of the original that they will encounter, and thus the sole
basis for their construction of its meaning.[31] In this setting, it is the
context-of-quotation, and not the original context, from which the audience obtains the necessary cues for interpreting the text.

The importance of Sternberg's work for the study of biblical quotations should be apparent. While there is much to be gained from looking at the way Jewish and Christian authors interpreted the biblical text,
modern investigators have often failed to ask how much of this interpretative activity would have been apparent to the intended audience.
Questions about how the recontextualized quotation helps to further
the rhetorical purposes of the quoting author have also been ignored.
As Sternberg observes, the effect of a quotation 'depends not so much
on the makeup of the inset vis-à-vis the original as on the strategy

28. Sternberg, 'Proteus', p. 152.

29. Sternberg, 'Proteus', p. 109. It is from this 'many-to-many relationship
between linguistic form and contextual function', the result of a complex interplay between rhetorical, contextual and functional forces, that Sternberg's 'Proteus Principle'
gets its name (p. 154).

30. Sternberg, 'Proteus', p. 109. Cf. p. 131: 'The inset's configuration of point of
view must be different and more complex than the original's, even when composed
of the same words in the same order, for the perspectives of the global speaker and
his audience are superimposed on those of the original participants'.

31. Sternberg, 'Proteus', pp. 140-44.

informing the frame'.[32] Unless the readers were familiar with the original passage (a doubtful assumption for most 'Gentile' Christians, and perhaps for many Jews as well), their experience with the words of Scripture would have been filtered through the interpretative and rhetorical lens of the quoting author.[33] In other words, the author's rhetorical strategy determined how many readers would respond to particular quotations from Scripture. Only a careful rhetorical analysis of specific passages can discover how direct quotations might have affected a particular ancient audience.

The Demonstration Theory

The demonstration theory put forward by Herbert H. Clark and Richard R. Gerrig[34] is currently the fullest and most satisfying account of how quotations work from a linguistic perspective. Like Wierzbicka, Clark and Gerrig insist that a person who quotes the words of another intends not simply to report (or 'describe') what the other person said, but to show (or 'demonstrate') what the person *did* in saying what he said.[35] To 'demonstrate' (that is, selectively repeat an action to show how it was done) is a qualitatively different mode of communication than to 'indicate' (refer to an event still in progress) or 'describe' (report on an event using a verbal narrative). 'Demonstrations', according to Clark and Gerrig, 'work by enabling others to experience what it is like to perceive the things depicted', including 'what in part it looks, sounds, or feels like to a person for an event, state, process, or object to be present'.[36] But no demonstration can reproduce every

32. Sternberg, 'Proteus', p. 153.

33. This is not to deny that there are biblical quotations and allusions that make little sense without a basic familiarity with the biblical text (e.g. Paul's unexplained references to Abraham and his family in Rom. 9.7-13 and Gal. 3.6, 8, 16). In most cases, however, the quoting author supplies enough of an interpretative context to make clear what meaning he expects his audience to derive from the quoted material, which may or may not correspond to its 'original meaning'.

34. Clark and Gerrig, 'Quotations', pp. 764-805.

35. Clark and Gerrig, 'Quotations', p. 764. In a footnote, Clark and Gerrig make it clear that they are using the term 'demonstrate' here 'in its everyday sense of "illustrate by exemplification" and not in its technical linguistic sense of "point to" or "indicate" (as in demonstrative reference)' (n. 2). As with Wierzbicka, the theory propounded by Clark and Gerrig is explicitly grounded in speech-act theory ('Quotations', pp. 778-80, 785).

36. Clark and Gerrig, 'Quotations', pp. 765, 766 (cf. p. 793).

detail of an earlier action, and no demonstrator attempts to do so. Rather all demonstrations are selective, that is, they focus on certain parts of the action that are deemed important in the eyes of the demonstrator. Subsidiary elements may be included to round out the demonstration, but these must be distinguished from the intended point of the demonstration.[37] An effective demonstrator will signal to the observer (using explicit commentary or implicit cues) which parts of the demonstration are meant to be taken as primary, and which are supportive or incidental.[38]

So how does this relate to written quotations? According to Clark and Gerrig, the standard assumption that speakers employ direct quotations only when they feel they can reproduce the wording of the original is invalid.[39] The decision to include direct quotations in a written work depends entirely on the rhetorical aims of the quoting author.[40] Direct quotations can advance an argument in a number of ways. (1) Direct quotations lend vividness and drama to a discourse, since they 'give the audience an experience of what it would be like in certain respects to experience the original event'.[41] The inclusion here

37. Clark and Gerrig, 'Quotations', pp. 767-68, 774-78, 782-85. Clark and Gerrig label those features that serve as the focal point of the demonstration its 'depictive aspects', while the less central features are divided into 'supportive aspects', 'annotative aspects', and 'incidental aspects' (p. 768). This attention to the 'selectivity' of direct quotation helps to explain why quotations are rarely rendered verbatim in common speech. Clark and Gerrig mount a sustained and effective attack against the widespread assumption that speakers (or writers) who incorporate direct quotations into their work are committed to verbatim reproduction of the original source (pp. 795-800). Cf. Wade and Clark, 'Reproduction', p. 808: 'Speakers who remember the exact wording but produce a quotation that is not verbatim aren't lying. They are merely choosing to depict aspects of the original other than its wording.' See also the related comments and materials cited in note 21.

38. Clark and Gerrig, 'Quotations', pp. 768-69. Features that can be 'marked' for audience attention in a written quotation include the language/dialect/register of the original speaker, the original style of delivery (rare), and the linguistic acts of the original (propositional content, illocutionary point, etc.) ('Quotations', pp. 782-86).

39. Alternative theories of quotation are summarized and refuted in Clark and Gerrig, 'Quotations', pp. 795-802, and Wade and Clark, 'Reproduction', pp. 806-808.

40. Cf. Wade and Clark, 'Reproduction', p. 808: 'The wording and demonstration theories contrast, then, in their emphasis on memory versus rhetoric. . . By the demonstration theory, a speaker's choice is a matter of rhetorical purpose.'

41. Wade and Clark, 'Reproduction', p. 808. Cf. Clark and Gerrig, 'Quotations',

of the phrase 'in certain respects' reveals the key difference between Clark and Gerrig's theory and that of Wierzbicka. What the audience experiences in this approach is not a full reenactment (contra Wierzbicka), but an edited version of the original speech-event. The quoting author ultimately decides which aspects of the original event will be re-experienced by the audience. This rhetorical strategy is typically hidden from the view of the audience. (2) Direct quotation also helps to distance the author somewhat from the material being presented. In direct quotation, the author takes responsibility for those parts of the original speech-act that he chooses to emphasize (or 'depict'). The remainder is charged to the original source. Thus quotations allow the speaker 'to convey information implicitly that it might be more awkward to express explicitly'.[42] In other words, an author can use direct quotations to say things to his audience that he would feel uncomfortable stating openly in his own words. (3) Direct quotations also help to create a sense of solidarity between speaker and audience. Where both parties are familiar with the original text, a well-chosen quotation can dispose the audience to respond more favorably to the speaker's message.[43] As Clark and Gerrig put it, 'When speakers demonstrate only a snippet of an event, they tacitly assume that their addressees share the right background to interpret it the same way they do. In essence, they are asserting, "I am demonstrating something we both can interpret correctly", and that implies solidarity.'[44]

Clark and Gerrig's proposal offers a helpful theoretical framework for the study of biblical quotations. In particular, it helps us to understand why authors include direct quotations in their texts, and why quotations affect readers in the way they do. For Jewish and Christian audiences in antiquity, biblical quotations spoke more powerfully than many interpreters have recognized. Direct appeals to a community's

---

p. 793: 'When we hear an event quoted, it is as if we directly experience the depicted aspects of the original event. We perceive the depicted aspects partly as we would the aspects they are intended to depict.'

42. Clark and Gerrig, 'Quotations', p. 792, citing R.K.S. Macaulay, 'Polyphonic Monologues: Quoted Direct Speech in Oral Narratives', *International Pragmatics Association Papers in Pragmatics* 1 (1987), p. 2.

43. The problem of how to create a well-disposed audience has been a central concern of rhetoricians at least since Aristotle's treatment of the subject (*Rhet.* 1.2, 2.1-17, 3.14-15, 3.19).

44. Clark and Gerrig, 'Quotations', p. 793.

Scriptures do more than simply reinforce a point or settle a dispute. Quotations increase the likelihood of a favorable response to the speaker's message by recalling the common bond that unites speaker and audience. Quotations also allow the speaker to shape the hearers' response by highlighting certain aspects of the authoritative text and minimizing others. Most importantly, quotations lead the audience into a personal encounter with the original text, where a second, more powerful voice speaks on behalf of the quoting author. In short, biblical quotations bring the audience into the presence of God, who typically stands firmly on the side of the speaker.

The chief weakness of Clark and Gerrig's study is that it says little about the kinds of 'markers' that an author might use to signal to an audience which aspects of a quotation are meant to be 'depicted' (that is, made the basis of a response) and which are merely supportive or incidental. More is also needed on the many ways in which quotations can advance the rhetorical strategies of a later author. On the whole, however, Clark and Gerrig's theory provides a solid foundation for a truly rhetorical approach to the study of biblical quotations.

Literary Approaches

Both linguists and literary theorists are concerned with the uses of language. But it was the linguists who developed the theoretical framework currently used to study quotations in literature. All of the linguistic studies examined above quote heavily from literary sources, and all devote substantial attention to the phenomenon of literary quotation.[45] We should not expect to find a distinctively 'literary' approach to the study of quotations.

There is, however, an important current in contemporary literary criticism that could prove helpful (if only indirectly) in the study of biblical quotations. This is the school of 'reader response criticism'.[46] Reader response criticism analyzes (among other things) how readers construct 'meaning' out of written symbols as they move through a document from beginning to end. The locus of 'meaning' in this ap-

---

45. Unlike the literary scholar, however, the linguist seeks to understand how quotations work in both oral and written speech.

46. For a helpful survey of the various types of reader response criticism, see the collection of essays edited by J. Tompkins, *Reader Response Criticism* (Baltimore: The Johns Hopkins University Press, 1980).

proach lies not in the text itself, but in the dynamic interplay between the reader's consciousness and the progression of symbols on the page.

The 'reader' whose experience is under investigation here is not a specific individual (whether ancient or modern), since the experiences of individual readers will vary and are in any event beyond the reach of the investigator. The focal point of reader response criticism is the 'implied reader', an artificial construct inferred from the various interpretational demands that a text imposes on its readers as it unfolds from beginning to end. More specifically, the 'implied reader' is 'the reader whose education, opinions, concerns, linguistic competence, etc., make him capable of having the experience the author wished to provide'.[47] The proximity of this implied reader to any 'original readers' of the text will vary with the situation, depending on the specificity of the original address, the reliability of the author's information about the intended audience, the skill (and transparency) with which the author uses that information, and the interpretative abilities of the modern critic.

What makes the 'implied reader' construct so useful is not what it says (if anything) about the original readers of a text, but rather what it reveals about the author's *perception* of the intended audience, including how that perception shaped the author's strategies for communicating with this audience. By examining the author's cumulative assumptions about how the reader ought to respond to the unfolding argument, we can develop a better understanding of what the author hoped to accomplish and how the author meant to achieve these goals.

It is here that the author's use of quotations becomes relevant. As should be clear by now, the decision to introduce a direct quotation into a piece of discourse is a rhetorical act, reflecting not only the author's understanding of the source text, but also certain assumptions about the likely responses of the intended audience. A judicious combination of reader response criticism and rhetorical analysis can help to illuminate this process. Both approaches focus on the linear unfolding of the text, and both attend to the way the text affects the reader. The difference between them is largely a matter of emphasis.

47. S. Fish, 'Interpreting the Variorum', in Tompkins (ed.), *Reader Response*, p. 174. The term Fish actually uses here is 'optimal reader', but the intention is the same. For a helpful analysis of the various types of 'readers' and 'authors' encountered in the diverse literature of reader response criticism, see R. Fowler, 'Who Is "the Reader" in Reader Response Criticism?', *Semeia* 31 (1985), pp. 6-20.

Rhetorical analysis uses the canons of persuasion to isolate the author's presumed rhetorical strategy. Reader response criticism examines the unfolding argument from the reader's point of view. Both approaches are necessary, since we cannot assume that the reader's step-by-step response to a developing argument corresponds precisely to the author's rhetorical strategy in a given passage.[48]

In the case of biblical quotations, a rhetorical approach will ask how a particular citation furthers the author's persuasive strategy in a given passage. A reader response approach, on the other hand, will ask how the 'implied reader' might respond to the sudden intrusion of material from an outside source at this point in the argument. Observations about the author's prior reflection on the quoted text could prove useful in the former method, but would be wholly out of place in the second. In both approaches, it is the surface structure of the text that is deemed to merit attention and explanation, not the interpretative activity behind the text. This is a significant departure from most modern studies of Jewish and Christian uses of Scripture.

Conclusions

Recent studies of biblical quotations in early Judaism and Christianity have focused rather one-sidedly on the interpretative process that lies behind the present text. In the process, the rhetorical dimension of the quotation process has been largely overlooked. Quotations are typically embedded into an argumentative discourse in which the author's prior interpretative activity is largely hidden from view. While there is much to be gained from studying early Jewish and Christian hermeneutical techniques, this should not be confused with an investigation of how the Bible was actually *used* in early Jewish and Christian literature. For this, a truly rhetorical analysis of biblical quotations is needed, one that examines how quotations function in their present argumentative context.

---

48. For example, the apostle Paul included biblical quotations at certain points in his letters to heighten the persuasive effect of his own statements. For the many readers who lacked the background to comprehend these references, however, the effectiveness of such argumentation would have been limited, if not lost altogether.

To Invert or Not to Invert:
The Pharisaic Canon in the Gospels

Wolfgang Roth

How do 'the Law and the Prophets', the Pharisaic canon in the formative period of Judaism and Christianity, play a role in the compositional
layout of the New Testament Gospels? The following examination of
their partly varying, partly correlating structures suggests that in the
narrative strategies of John, Matthew and Luke different uses of that
canon are discernible. Whether Jesus' mission is portrayed as inversion
of that canon's storyline (John) or as its continuation (Matthew, Luke,
by implication Mark), the evangelists' differing but partly overlapping
employment of that canon generates two Gospel types: Johannine and
'synoptic'. Furthermore, each evangelist's 'canon reading' generates the
narrative strategy characteristic of each Gospel. In conclusion, the findings are related to issues in contemporary research.

1. 'The Law and the Prophets' in John, Matthew, Mark, and Luke–Acts

The Fourth Gospel informs its readers by what standard claims it makes
on behalf of Jesus are to be measured. When the newly called Philip
meets Nathanael, he says to him, 'The one of whom Moses has written
in the Law and (of whom) the Prophets (wrote), we have found! It is
Jesus, Joseph's son, the one from Nazareth.' Nathanael's initial scep-
ticism is countered by Philip's response 'Come and see!' and overcome
by his confession to Jesus that he is both 'son of God and king of
Israel' (Jn 1.45-49).

This is the only reference to 'the Law and the Prophets' in the
Johannine Jesus story. What is the significance of its appearance in the
opening paragraphs? In the ensuing exchange between Nathanael and
Jesus no explicit reference is made to the standard to which Philip had
appealed, and the phrase does not appear again. On the other hand, the

Johannine work points in this scene to the future in the sense that once persons 'come' to Jesus, they 'will' eventually 'see' or 'gain insight' (1.46, 50); in the Farewell Discourses the promised Comforter will similarly provide insight not yet available (14.25-26 and 16.12-14). Does this reference to 'the Law and the Prophets' imply that in the future it will be evident how the stated norm supports Philip's claims on behalf of Jesus' mission? Or is that insight already discernible within John's work for those for whom 'Law and Prophets' are 'Scripture' or 'canon'?

The first Gospel has Jesus make reference to 'the Law and the Prophets' in the opening discourse, in the Sermon on the Mount (Mt. 5–7). After calling out blessings on nine groups of persons of seemingly little esteem as represented by his disciples and honoring them with the titles 'the salt of the earth' and 'the light of creation', Jesus begins his further teaching with an affirmation. 'Think not that I came to undo the "Law and the Prophets"! On the contrary, I did not come to undo them but to put them into full force' (Mt. 5.17). He then explains the continuing validity of 'the Law' and concludes with this point: You, my disciples, need to exceed the scripture interpreters and the Pharisees in the quality of observance (5.20). The rest of the discourse spells this out in detail, and not without returning to the topic in its concluding paragraphs: 'Therefore all that which you wish that human beings do to you, do you also do to them! After all, it is this (way of life) which is (the gist of) "The Law and the Prophets"' (7.12).

Matthew's composition returns to this standard in its closing sections. After Jesus has responded to test questions put to him by both Sadducees and Pharisees, he concludes with a summary reference to 'the Law and the Prophets'. He affirms with reference to the commandments to 'worship God alone' (Deut. 6.4) and to 'love one's fellow (human being) as oneself' (Lev. 19.18), that 'on these two commandments hang all the Law and the Prophets' (Mt. 22.23-33/34-40). In short, the (formal) canon of 'the Law and the Prophets' demands (in essence) love of God and of one's fellow.

The only other reference to that standard is found in the middle of Matthew's composition. There the mission of John the Baptizer is the topic. His preaching marks the end of the period of 'the Prophets and the Law'. His appearance may be interpreted as the return of Elijah with the promise of which 'the Law and the Prophets' look to their future (Mt. 11.2-14, compare Mal. 4.4-5). In short, the form which the legacy of Israel's past assumes is that of 'the Prophets and the Law'. The order of the two parts is here inverted because John the Baptist's mission picks up where 'the Prophets', as it were, conclude by looking both backward to Moses' teaching and forward to Elijah's return.

In short, Matthew's Jesus is portrayed with more emphasis than in John's composition as conforming to 'the Law and the Prophets'. In fact, Jesus and his followers are the only ones who really, fully do so—in contrast to Scripture scholars and Pharisees who also hold to that standard but do not meet it in terms of their obedience (Mt. 23). What is in dispute is not the canon itself but the degree to which it is honored. In other words, both Matthew's and John's 'canon' are 'the Law and the Prophets'.

What can be said about the canons of the other two Gospels? Mark does not formally identify a 'canon' in the way John and Matthew do. However, I will later show that 'the Prophets', represented by the Elijah/Elisha narrative (1 Kgs 17–2 Kgs 13), are in fact 'canon'.

Luke, on the other hand, repeatedly mentions a 'canon' in both Gospel and Acts. There are four references in the context of Paul's mission-ary activity: 'the Law and the Prophets' (Acts 13.15; 24.14) or 'the Prophets and Moses' (26.22) or 'the Law of Moses and the Prophets' (28.23). All identify summarily the collection of holy writings which both the apostle and his audience share. From them the readings in the sabbath service of his hosts' synagogues are drawn, and Paul himself is at pains not to preach anything but which 'the Law and the Prophets' say will happen. The apostle writes as much in one of his letters when he argues that in Christ God's righteousness has been made manifest as attested by 'the Law and the Prophets' (Rom. 3.21; the only occurrence of the term in his letters).

As for the third Gospel, two related references to a 'canon' appear in the Emmaeus story (Lk. 24.13-49). They are complex in relation to those noted so far. We are told that the risen Jesus hears the two disci-ples' puzzled report of their female fellow disciples' visit of Jesus' empty tomb. There they had seen a vision of angels who said that Jesus is alive. In response, Jesus affirms that the Christ's suffering and glory are prophetically foretold and then, 'beginning with Moses and all the Prophets he interpreted for them in all the Scriptures the references concerning himself' (24.27). Later in the same story Jesus returns to this more comprehensive 'canon' of 'all the Scriptures', now identifying it as 'the Law of Moses and the Prophets and the Psalms' (Lk. 27.44).

Evidently, in Luke's view, 'the Law and the Prophets' are the two basic parts of a wider but not yet fully defined canon.

2. *'The Law and the Prophets'—Canon of the Pharisees*

The canon of John's and Matthew's Jesus and Luke's Paul is also the canon of their Pharisaic contemporaries. As for the latter, Paul claims that he is, in the manner of his interpretation of 'the Law', a Pharisee (Phil. 3.5). According to Luke, when Paul is brought before the synhedrion, composed of both Sadducees and Pharisees, he claims his Pharisaic identity and thus succeeds in avoiding a condemnation (Acts 22.30–23.11). On the other hand, when he later in Rome meets with several persons, he attests to them the kingdom of God, 'seeking to persuade them concerning Jesus on the basis of "the Law of Moses and the Prophets"' (Acts 28.23).

According to Matthew's work, when Jesus addresses the crowds and his disciples, he affirms as valid all which 'Scripture interpreters and Pharisees... say to you'. His hearers are to observe and to act in accord with Pharisaic teaching but not to do as they do (Mt. 23.1-3).

In the Johannine Gospel, a connection between 'the Law and the Prophets' and the Pharisaic canon is not explicitly made. Thus when Jesus converses with Nicodemus, a distinguished Pharisee (Jn 3.1-13), 'canon' is not the topic nor is it mentioned. But the discussion indirectly deals with the canonical rank of 'the Prophets'. The issue is Nicodemus's inability to recognize the scriptural ground for Jesus' assertion that 'unless someone is born out of water and spirit, that person cannot enter the Kingdom of God'. The scriptural basis is the story of Elisha's commissioning, 'out of the Jordan and with spirit', so that he is empowered to initiate the series of actions which will lead to the overthrow of apostasy and the initiation of a divinely sanctioned royal rule (2 Kgs 2–13). Whatever else this exchange signifies, it is also a discussion on this section of the Pharisaic canon.

My description of the Pharisaic 'canon' on the basis of the writings of the New Testament evangelists agrees with the familiar outline of the emergence of the three parts of the Hebrew Bible during the last century BCE and the first century CE. By contrast, the Sadducean and the Samaritan canon are made up of the five 'books' Genesis–Deuteronomy. Jesus, as portrayed by the first and fourth evangelists, as well as Luke's Paul, assume 'the Law and the Prophets' as their own and their interlocutors' recognized canon. In addition, the third evangelist's (risen)

Jesus illustrates the (gradual) appearance of 'the Writings', which came to be the third and last part of the Jewish Scriptures.

A quasi-canonical status of 'The Law and the Prophets' is attested at the end of the second century BCE in the prologue with which Sirach's grandson prefaces the translation of his grandfather's work. He observes that the sage ventured to write what amounts to a textbook on Judaism only after he had given himself to the reading especially of 'the Law and of the Prophets and of the other writings'. The point is illustrated by the grandfather's own review of Israel's famous ancestors which concludes his book (44–49); it is basically co-extensive with 'the Law and the Prophets'.

Sometime during the first century BCE the writer of 2 Maccabees tells of Judas Maccabaeus encouraging his fellow fighters 'out of the Law and the Prophets' (15.9). A similar reference comes from the first half of the first century CE. According to *4 Macc.* 18.10, the mother of the seven martyrs reminds them that their father, while still alive, taught them 'the Law and the Prophets'. Finally, the Mishnah tractate *Megilla* offers detailed instructions concerning the Sabbath reading from 'the Law and the Prophets' (4.1-5). These directives show that the lections are taken exclusively from this 'canon' in such a fashion that the first and basic portion, derived from the Law of Moses, is 'closed' with a selection from the Prophets.

3. *'The Law and the Prophets'—Canon as Narrative Strategy?*

The role of 'The Law and the Prophets' as 'canon' during the formative period of Judaism and Christianity readily explains the appearance of Scripture quotations and allusions on almost every page of the New Testament. This 'anthological use' of quotations is discussed by Patte in *Early Jewish Hermeneutic in Palestine* (1975) under the heading 'The Use of Broad Biblical Patterns to Structure Apocalyptic Writings' (169-77). He differentiates the anthological use of quotations from a structural use of Scripture. While the former provides for the new composition, as it were, 'a mere *language*', the latter draws on 'broad biblical patterns' in order to provide for it a 'general framework' (Patte 1975: 171-72, author's italics). Patte illustrates his thesis by showing how an apocalyptic pattern, such as the one underlying the Book of Daniel, generates works based on that compositional framework (Patte 1975: 169-71).

Biblical research during the last two generations has explored how the Hebrew Scriptures serve as the primary matrix of early (Jewish–) Christian literary activity. Thus Leo Baeck published, in 1938 in Germany (!), an essay titled 'The Gospel as a Document of the History of the Jewish Faith' (English translation 1958). The evangelists, like their fellow Jewish writers, gave meaning and shape to their works through the lens of the Hebrew Scriptures. He concludes that 'whatever was said or written was, in spite of all peculiarities and distinctions, presented in terms of a traditional genre, *within the outlines of some ancient model*' (Baeck 1938: 59; my italics).

More recently, in a paper on 'Literary Typologies and Biblical Interpretation in the Hellenistic–Roman Period', Devorah Dimant discussed the 'compositional' use of biblical text units as 'models' for Jewish literary activity. She notes that such use 'relies, for achieving the desired effect, on the understanding and active participation of the reader, who is assumed to have the necessary background of knowledge to detect the allusion' (Dimant 1991: 74). She observes that '[t]he compositional mode of employing biblical elements... used extensively... is especially prevalent in the various genres of the Apocrypha and Pseudepigrapha'. Important for our perspective is that 'these elements are never explicitly signalled in the compositional mode, but rather are integrated into the fabric of the work as elements of style or form, or else serve as models' (Dimant 1991: 77).

This observation casts light not only on the parabolic dimension of all New Testament Gospels but also on the evocative allusions to the 'secret(s)' of the Kingdom of God in Luke's, Matthew's and Mark's narratives about Jesus' mission. In what manner are John's readers 'to search the Scriptures' so that they discover how 'they bear witness concerning' him (Jn 5.39)? Given the comprehensive parameters of such search, it is necessary to keep in mind the possibility that also the accepted 'canon' in its entirety provided compositional frameworks and narrative strategies to those seeking to present their understanding of Jesus as story.

Moreover, the evangelists composed in Greek and so can be expected to have also been heirs to the Greek rhetorical tradition. Thus Luke Timothy Johnson, in his introduction to the New Testament, observes: 'To an extent we can scarcely appreciate, Greek culture was built *on the imitation of models from the past*... Novelty was not a virtue' (Johnson 1986: 37; my italics). In sum, the enquiry into how the canon of 'the Law and the Prophets' provided as such an 'ancient genre' of which Baeck spoke, is suggested by what is known about the literary creativity of emerging Judaism.

In the following four sections I will briefly deal with each of the Gospels. First, the narrative layout of the Johannine 'Book of Signs' will be shown to follow the sequence of the five parts of 'the Law' and, as sixth, 'the Prophets', but doing so by way of reversing their order. Then it will be argued that Mark's and Matthew's 'Gospels' continue the canonical narrative from where 'the Prophets' and 'the Law' leave off, that is, with the expectation of Elijah's return. Finally, attention will be given to Luke's 'ordered narrative'; its two-part narrative layout broadly echoes the 'Law–Prophets' sequence. Fuller reports of these studies were published in a series of six articles on the narrative strategies of the Gospels in *The Bible Today* 30.3–31.2 (Roth 1992–93) and in 'John and the Synoptics' (Roth 1992); for the second and the fourth Gospels see the still fuller discussions in Roth 1988 and 1987 respectively.

4. *The Johannine Inversion of 'The Law and the Prophets'*

The six Judean festivals which John mentions are without parallel in the other Gospels. Their formulaic nature and distribution across the narration (2.13; 5.1; 6.4; 7.2; 10.22; 11.55) serves to mark six sections, each telling of a 'sign' which symbolizes a spiritual gift conveyed by Jesus. Moreover, each of the sections is connected through notable words, phrases and themes to sequentially linked units of the Hebrew Scriptures. Prologue (1.1-18), book title (20.30-31) and epilogue (21.1-15) apart, the correlation of the Johannine units, their gift themes, and their Old Testament 'text' may be tabulated as follows:

John 1.19–4.54	Water of Eternal Life	1 Kings 17–2 Kings 13
John 5.1-47	Health after Weakness	Deuteronomy 1–34
John 6.1-71	Heavenly Food	Numbers 1–36
John 7.1–10.21	Spiritual Sight	Leviticus 1–27
John 10.22–11.54	Life out of Death	Exodus 1–40
John 11.55–20.29	Holy Spirit	Genesis 1–50

Jesus' solemn affirmation addressed to Nicodemus programmatically brackets this sixfold schema: 'Except anyone is born out of *water and spirit*, that person cannot enter the Kingdom of God' (Jn 3.5).

The sequence of the six gifts is evidently based on the Johannine manner of reading 'the Law and the Prophets'. To begin with, the

Elijah/ Elisha narrative (1 Kgs 17–2 Kgs 13) here represents 'the Prophets'. As such it is the scriptural backdrop for the first section and provides the theme 'life-giving water' in the story of Elisha's commissioning (2 Kgs 2.1-18). The third Johannine section derives its theme from the manna story as found in Numbers 11. The sixth and final section uses selected motifs from Genesis as its foil, used in inverted sequence, and comes to its climax in Jesus' gift of holy spirit (Jn 20.22/Gen. 2.7).

Notable words or phrases serve to connect each Johannine unit to its scriptural base text. For example, as in Num. 11.9, so also repeatedly in John 6, the manna 'descends' from heaven, and that for 'thousands to be fed'—a numerical term not appearing qualified in this manner elsewhere either in John's work or in 'the Law and the Prophets'. Or, in the fifth section which correlates with Exodus, two unusual words stand out: Lazarus already 'stinks' and Jesus 'wept' (Jn 11.39, 35). Both verbs also stand out in Exodus (8.14; 2.6). Finally, in the sixth Johannine section, the motif sequence 'embalming–farewell–footwashing–vine–preservation from evil-decision in the garden-spirit gift' inverts the ordering of its counterparts in Genesis (Jn 12.3-7/Gen. 50.2, 26; Jn 13–17/Gen. 49.1-27; Jn 13.1-20; Jn 15.1-10/Gen. 9.20-27; Jn 17.15/Gen. 6.5 and 8.21/Gen. 18.3-4 and 19.2; Jn 18.1-11/Gen. 2.4b–3.24; Jn 20.22/Gen. 2.7).

The unusual feature of compositional, selective reversal calls for comment. Beginning with the Temple reform motif found in 2 Kgs 12.5-17, the evangelist's motif sequence moves backwards to the beginning of the Elijah/Elisha narrative (1 Kgs 17), thence through Deuteronomy, Numbers, Leviticus, and Exodus to Genesis. There some seven motifs follow each other so as to culminate with the 're-creation through inbreathing of holy spirit' theme.

The narrative strategy of inversion suggests that Jesus' mission undoes step by step, representatively and in inverse order, the gradual breakdown of the wholeness of God's creation as told in 'the Law and the Prophets'. The reversal is, as it were, a healing process in which the goal is complete restoration. Moreover, the Johannine portrayal of Jesus' mission turns six dominant motifs of Genesis 2–3 into as many spiritual gifts: water of life/eternal water (Gen. 2.6 and 10/Jn 4.14); bodily life/health instead of weakness (Gen. 2.6 and 17/Jn 5.6); food for daily sustenance/heavenly manna (Gen. 2.9, 16/Jn 6.32); physical sight/spiritual discernment (Gen. 2.9 and 3.6/Jn 9.37-38); life leading to death/death leading to life (Gen. 2.17 and 3.19/Jn 11.39-44), and life giving breath/holy spirit (Gen. 2.7/Jn 20.22).

The story of the wedding at Cana (Jn 2.1-11) is the 'master sign' because it is a parabolic preview of the Johannine work in its entirety: the water of 'the Law and the Prophets', filled into six (!) jars, is transformed into the 'wine' which Jesus' six gifts offer.

5. *Mark's Extension of ('the Law and) the Prophets'*

Contradicting John, Mark shows that in the person of the Baptist Prophet Elijah has returned as the anticipated harbinger of God's great intervention perceived to be happening in Jesus' mission (Mk 9.11-13/1.6/6.17-29; contrast Jn 1.21). After all, it is with this anticipation that the sustained storyline of 'the Law and the Prophets' (Genesis–Malachi, as ordered in the Hebrew Bible) concludes (Mal. 4.5; MT 3.23). In this prophetic word is shown how the narration begun in 'the Law and the Prophets' is expected to be continued, and that at whatever time is deemed proper by Israel's God. In short, this Gospel continues where 'Law and Prophets' leave off. Its evangelist sets out to supply the still missing next part: the story of Jesus' mission. Thus Mark's narrative strategy employs a continuity model.

If the storyline begins with Elijah's return in John the Baptist, how is it to continue? Does the Elijah/Elisha narrative (1 Kgs 17–2 Kgs 13) offer a clue? For Mark, it does. As Elisha was commissioned at the Jordan by Elijah, so now Jesus is commissioned by John at that same canonical river crossing into the land of promise. As Elisha then proceeded in stages to carry out the mission of overthrowing apostasy and initiating a divinely sanctioned rule in both Israel and Judah, so Jesus' mission will follow that progression. As Elisha, having received a double portion of his master's spirit, carried out twice as many powerful deeds, so Jesus will in turn exceed the quantitative and qualitative standards which Elisha's activity had set. As Elisha's mission leads to fateful encounters in the capitals of Israel and Judah, so does that of Jesus. And as Elisha's mission had concluded with the resurrection motif, so will that of Jesus.

It has been noted that the Elisha story cycle in the Hebrew Scriptures provides in several respects the model for the Markan Jesus story (Brown 1971). Going beyond this observation, one observes that it is only in Mark's work that halfway through the Gospel a powerful deed of Jesus is greeted with the people's surprise that now 'he had done all (miracles) well' (Mk 7.37). Why is this said at this point in the narrative? Why not after earlier miracles? Why not after some of the following deeds of power? Does the evangelist imply a standard according to which both the number and power of Jesus' miracles are measured?

A count of the preceding miracle units in Mark 1–7 adds up to 16 (collective healing texts, for instance, 1.32-34, are counted as one). What is noteworthy is that medieval Jewish storytellers noted that this is the number of Elisha's deeds of power, and that this number is to be compared with his predecessor Elijah's eight deeds of power (Ginzberg 1909-38: IV, 239). If this quantitative standard is applied to Mark's Jesus, the second Gospel in fact signals that with this miracle—and only with this, the 16th one—Jesus has satisfied the Elisha standard. Also, Jesus will immediately go beyond that total with further deeds of power, exceeding the Elisha standard as the latter had exceeded that of his master. As for the quality of Jesus' deeds of power in relation to those of Elisha, the multiplication of loaves and fishes (Mk 6.32-45) illustrates how Jesus does 'well' what Elisha in his feeding of one hundred people with 20 barley loaves had done on a lesser scale (2 Kgs 4.42-44): the master from Nazareth feeds thousands, not a hundred, and that with only five loaves. Both Jesus and Elisha had all their people sated and food left over; in Jesus' case not fewer than twelve baskets. These observations illustrate how the second evangelist draws on 1 Kings 17–2 Kings 13 as a model in a broad sense, reminiscent of the way in which the Elijah/Elisha story cycle draws itself on the Moses/ Joshua narrative sequence in Deuteronomy/Joshua. In both Mark and 1 Kings 17–2 Kings 13 the plot is that of the re-establishment of the rule of Israel's God over the people of the covenant at a time when reformation was needed. The main stages of the narrative execution may be tabulated in this way:

Mark 1.1-15	Announcement and Commissioning	1 Kings 17–2 Kings 2
Mark 1.16–13.37	Attestation through Deeds of Power	2 Kings 2–8
Mark 14.1–15.39	Fateful Encounter(s) in the Capital(s)	2 Kings 9–12
Mark 15.40–16.20	Vindication through Resurrection	2 Kings 13

Can this hypothesis throw light on the different placement of the

Temple cleansing in Mark and John? Why does it appear in Mark toward the end of the narration, but in John close to its beginning?

On the assumption that the Temple 'cleansing' episode of 2 Kgs 12.5-17 supplies the scriptural model for John's as well as Mark's version, the contradictory placements become understandable. John used 1 Kings 17–2 Kings 13 as a framework for the first of the Gospel's six sections (1.19–4.54); and since it inverts the motif sequence, it is constrained to place the Temple unit which appears toward the end of the Elisha story, as close to its own beginning as feasible. Thus it comes to be placed after the programmatic 'master sign' story of the wedding at Cana. On the other hand, Mark does not invert the storyline of its model and thus places the episode toward the end of Jesus' mission. In other words, the puzzling contradictory placements are the result of the evangelists' different manners of drawing on motif sequences in the scriptural master story they share.

6. *Matthew's Fulfillment of 'the Law and the Prophets'*

For Matthew's Gospel, Moses and his 'Law' must come first. This accords well with this evangelist's repeated and explicit references to the Pharisaic canon of his time, 'the Law and the Prophets'. The first Gospel's version of Jesus' transfiguration illustrates the point in its own way: while Mark writes that Peter, James and John saw 'Elijah with Moses' conversing with their master, Matthew says that 'Moses and Elijah' were talking with Jesus (Mk 9.4/Mt. 17.3). Thus Mark's perspective needs to be balanced in keeping with the two constitutive components of the canon; hence, 'the Law *and* Moses' must receive their due. Jesus came not only to fulfil the prophetic expectation with which the second part of the canon concludes, but also to do the same for 'the Law'. I will now explore how Matthew overlays Mark's Jesus portrayal of a greater Elisha with that of a new Moses.

How does the first Gospel echo its explicitly canonical orientation? Before I explore this, an observation on the relationship of Matthew to Mark is in order. There can be little question that Matthew exhibits basically Mark's storyline—as does Luke. Hence the grouping of Matthew's, Mark's and Luke's works as 'synoptic' Gospels. Whether or not their relationships are primarily or partly of a literary nature, is a question not pursued here but touched upon in a concluding section below when the Gospels' narrative strategies and their practitioners are discussed.

What is assumed here is that the Elijah/Elisha cycle is shared by the three first New Testament evangelists as their narrative base model. This generates their commonality or, put differently, what has come to be known as 'the synoptic Gospel' type, in distinction from the Johannine storyline. In other words, the two New Testament Gospel types are the result of different ways of reading the same canon, 'the Law and the Prophets'.

What distinguishes Matthew's from Mark's Gospel are thorough-going compositional differences. To begin with, the identification of John the Baptist as Elijah Returned is made optional (Mt. 11.14), and with it Mark's use of the Elijah/Elisha cycle as the only foundational structure. The considerable difference introduces the casting of Jesus as a new Moses and the use of the Markan layout as narrative framing of five teaching discourses (Mt. 5–7; 10.1–11.1; 13.1-53; 18.1–19.1; 24.3–26.1). In keeping with this perspective, the first Gospel partly groups Jesus' deeds of power into a Moses pattern in support of the programmatic Sermon on the Mount (Mt. 8–9). There the evangelist narrates ten miracles, authenticating this teacher's claim in the way in which the 'ten wonders [which] were wrought for our fathers in Egypt' (Mishnah, *Ab.* 5.4) support Moses' mission. Finally, throughout the narration Matthew intersperses 'prophecies' with explicit or implied 'fulfilments' (for instance, 1.22-23; 2.5-6), in keeping with the view of 'the Law' that fulfilment is the criterion of valid prophecy (Deut. 18.21-22).

Closer study shows that the first evangelist is a freely working composer indeed. The five instructional discourses are the most characteristic, structural feature of this Gospel, but they do not use the five-fifths of the Law of Moses as their foil in the manner of the fourth Gospel writer. Many of the teaching units pointedly go beyond or even against what Moses teaches (notably the antitheses in 5.21-48), others are primarily vessels of the (Christian–) Pharisaic theology which informs the first Gospel, such as the mission of the disciples or pictures of the judgment to come (10.1–11.1; 24.3–26.1). In the third instruction, not fewer than seven parabolic stories illuminate the nature of 'the Kingdom of the Heavens' (13.1-50). In its conclusion, the listeners affirm that they have understood the parables, and are then told by the teacher that Scripture teachers 'discipled to the Kingdom of the Heavens. . . bring out of their treasures both what is old and what is new' (13.51-52). Clearly, Matthew measured up to this standard!

In conclusion I turn to the manner in which Matthew appropriates and newly focuses 'the Law'. It has been proposed that Matthew's work, 'as a Second Testament Deuteronomy', was written 'to be read perpetually as the living voice of the Son of God' (Grassi 1989: 29). To begin with, the Sermon on the Mount as the first and longest discourse, resembles Moses' last will (Deut. 1–30) in both formal layout and interpretative approach. As far as the latter is concerned, the tenor in which Matthew's Jesus draws on the legacy of 'the Law (and the Prophets)' is reminiscent of that in which Deuteronomy's Moses encompasses and focuses the many and varied ordinances given at Sinai and in the wilderness (Deut. 6.4-9/Mt. 22.34-40).

Neither teacher merely reiterates the tradition; both reconceive it into a coherent whole and proceed to internalize it. Both have only Israel in view (Mt. 7.6/Deut. 23.3-8). Each stresses that God is neither far removed from the people nor to be acknowledged merely with words. Rather, the LORD is near Israel, and doing of the divine will through internal motivation is decisive (Mt. 7.21-23/Deut. 30.11-14). In sum, Matthew travels further on the road that Deuteronomy opened; its Jesus promulgates, as it were, a third law: 'Tritonomy'.

Given the complex layering of this Gospel's relation to its foils in 'the Law and the Prophets' and in Mark's composition, a tabulation of correlations as offered above for the fourth and the second Gospels would not do justice to what has been found. My exploration of Luke's extensive two part narrative now shows how it moves beyond both Matthew and John in its attempt to be more comprehensive and inclusive still. Its horizons and periods covered are yet more inclusive, as are its 'canon' and its coverage of its predecessors, John, Mark and Matthew.

8. *'Moses and the Prophets' and Luke's 'Jesus and the Apostles'*

Already the prefaces (Lk. 1.1-4; Acts 1.1-8) show that Luke embarks on an ambitious enterprise: a definitive description of the rise of the Christian movement. The existence of narratives of Jesus' words and deeds is explicitly acknowledged. On the basis of the broad layout of the Lukan Gospel narrative along the lines of Mark and Matthew, one must assume that the third evangelist follows the Elijah/Elisha story outline, comparable to Matthew, with comprehensive adaptations. Hence the long-standing recognition that Luke's Gospel parallels Mark's and Matthew's to an extent that calls for the kind of synoptic tabulation which already 'Eusebius' Canons' represent.

Moreover, on the basis of certain shared unique topics such as 'Mary and Martha', 'Lazarus' or 'future recapitulation of all (creation)', one must assume that Luke also knows the Johannine work or the circles in which its inversion hermeneutic would or could generate in narrative form a presentation of Jesus' mission. Finally, Luke was acquainted with a similar reversal perspective expressed by Paul in the latter's affirmation that 'in Christ... there is neither Jew nor Greek, neither slave nor free, neither male nor female' (Gal. 3.27-28). This sequencing, after all, inverts the sequence in which Genesis tells of these representative fractures of the wholeness of creation (Gen. 2; 16; 29-30/35) and posits 'a new creation' as Jesus' mission (2 Cor. 5.17).

What do earlier portrayals of Jesus' mission lack that Luke will supply in order to demonstrate to Theophilus the certainty of all that he has already been told by others? To write such a work is a tall order. For Luke, it covers the span of some two generations from the announcements of John's and Jesus' births to Paul's final days in Rome. Moreover, that story is set in a comprehensive 'creation–re-creation' horizon (Lk. 3.23-38/Act 3.17-21). The spatial setting is equally encompassing: after 'the Law and the Prophets' had narrowed their storyline to a birth in the family of a priest serving in the Temple, Luke's narration will center Jesus' mission in Jerusalem in order to take the apostles from that center through Judea and Samaria outward 'to the ends of the earth' (Lk. 3.16/Acts 1.8; compare Lk. 16.16).

Finally, what is meant by the promised arrangement of the sustained narrative 'in order'? Is sequence in time the principle of arrangement? Or does the risen Jesus' interpreting that which concerns him in the Scriptures 'beginning from Moses and all the prophets' indicate that the sequence of the narrative units follows a canonical order? The latter seems to be the case because already Luke's two part design echoes the layout of 'Moses and the Prophets' in that it focuses in the first part on Jesus, in the second on the apostles. Therefore Jesus' life journey and its place of destiny must broadly correspond to those of Moses; the movement of the apostle Paul from Israel to the nations cannot but correlate with a similar one of the prophet Jeremiah from rejection by his own people to his mission as 'prophet to the nations'. Both Paul and Jeremiah are portrayed as letter writers in the service of their mission; both Acts and deuteronomistic work end with a guardedly positive scene in Rome and Babylon respectively (Acts 28.30-31/2 Kgs 25.27-31).

Luke's re-investment of 'Moses and the Prophets' (Gen./Exod./Lev./ Num./Deut./Jos./Judg./1–2 Sam./1–2 Kgs/Isa./Jer./Ezek./The Twelve) in 'Luke–Acts' thus follows a canonical macro-model. Recent studies of the third evangelist's use of Scripture have illuminated various aspects of this compositional technique, such as the role of the rhetorical use of '*imitatio*' as a generative principle (and demonstrations of such analysis in relation to Lukan texts; Brodie 1983, 1986), of casting major figures in the image of their scriptural model, for instance, Luke's Hannah portrayed as a new Sarah (Goulder 1989), and correlations in the Lukan 'travel narrative' (9.51–19.27) with corresponding features in Moses' journey as told in Numbers and Deuteronomy (C.F. Evans 1955; C.A. Evans 1993; Sanders 1993). Range and complexity of such studies in various ways reflect the double layering of Scripture appropriation described by Luke: 'the Law and all the Prophets' are, as it were, the primary canon within the wider canon of 'all the Scriptures' (Lk. 24.27).

The comprehensive perspective of Luke's 'Jesus and the Apostles' has won for this work the role of the organizing center for the emerging canon of the New Testament. The work is also in this respect a counterpart to the deuteronomistic work, its model in the Hebrew Bible. Both function as extensive, orienting prefaces to clusters of varied, older and in perspective partly diverging writings: as 'Moses and the (Former) Prophets' presents an introduction to three longer prophetic books, followed by 'the Twelve Minor Prophets', so in a similar manner 'Jesus and the Apostles' is followed by three longer letters of Paul as well as shorter ones by him and by Pauline writers.

On the other hand, as the Deuteronomistic work incorporates and partly frames the three variant narrative traditions of the Priestly, the Elohist and the Yahwist strands, making them co-constituents of its comprehensive perspective, so the Lukan composition eventually drew the three variant portrayals of Jesus' mission by Matthew, Mark and John into its constituency. In sum, Luke played in the evolution of the New Testament canon a role comparable to that of Deuteronomy in the emergence of the canon of the Hebrew Bible.

Even though Luke's work does not employ the reversal approach of the Johannine circle, it incorporates the latter's perspective: re-creation through the divine spirit (comp. Acts 3.21). Thus 'Jesus and the Apostles' is conceived within horizons as encompassing as those of the fourth evangelist and, for that matter, of Paul of Tarsus: 'new creation' is their lodestar. Thus it is only consistent when in New Testament editions Matthew and Mark came to be placed before Luke–Acts, like steps leading to Luke's full unfolding of the continuity of Jesus' mission with 'the Law and the Prophets'. The Johannine portrayal of Jesus' mission, on the other hand, comes to stand between Luke's Gospel and Luke's Acts and is through such framing both affirmed and relativized. The reversal perspective of Paul's letters is similarly fitted into the third evangelist's mediating religious philosophy: Luke's work now functions as its interpretative introduction. The history of biblical interpretation shows that while Luke's comprehensive philosophy continued to provide the basic framework for most churches, both the Johannine and the Pauline canon reversals were from time to time the basis for challenges to Luke's (ecclesiastical) middle way and to the church at large—the emerging religious institution for which it prepared the way.

8. *Conclusion: To Invert or Not to Invert?*

This enquiry explains the difference between the Johannine and the synoptic Gospel type on the basis of their mutually exclusive readings of 'the Law and the Prophets', the canon the evangelists share with Pharisees. While the compositions of Mark (by implication), Matthew and Luke begin at the point where the basic storyline of the canon had ended with its anticipation of how the narrative thread will continue, John's inversion of a six-part sequence of that same canon generates a reversal model.

Both Gospel types, however, present Jesus' mission as a heightening of divine action portrayed in their canon, whether by his changing the 'water' of the Scriptures into the 'wine' of the gospel or by his deeds of power exceeding in number and strength those of Elisha, his biblical foil. In short, the Gospel writers derive their basic compositional layout from 'the Law and the Prophets', but distinguish themselves from each other through their differing as well as partly overlapping ways of appropriating that canon.

The 'synoptic problem' appears now in a different light. It is the Elijah/Elisha narrative (1 Kgs 17–2 Kgs 13) that provides Mark with the primary foil for Jesus' mission. Matthew and Luke also employ it as base models, but considerably modified and combined with further scriptural compositional models. Given the existence of other models such as John's or that of the *Gospel of Thomas*, why did Mark, Matthew and Luke choose this option? Was there a constraint to do so? Luke's Acts may provide the answer: when Peter is about to receive celestial confirmation that Jesus' mission goes beyond Israel to the nations, he begins with a review of the divine word to Israel, that is, Jesus' earthly mission. The manner in which Peter summarizes it, is in fact a precis of Mark's storyline (Acts 10.37-41). Does Luke here preserve the gist of Peter's own conceptualization of Jesus' mission? If this is the case, did the apostle's prominence lead to the employment of the Elijah/Elisha model by the first, second and third evangelists? If so, does also John's work attest as much by way of contradiction when it values the beloved disciple's faith higher then that of Peter and portrays the former, not Peter, as the disciple closest to Jesus (Jn 20.1-10)?

There is a further indication that the synoptic evangelists affirmed in veiled fashion both congruence and difference in terms of their conceptual and narrative models of Jesus' mission. According to Mark, when Jesus had told the lead parable of the Kingdom of God, that of the sower, those close to him ask in private about the parables. Jesus responds that to them 'the secret of the Kingdom of God has already been given', while to those outside the parabolic veil will remain impenetrable (Mk 4.11). Both Matthew and Luke tell of the same question addressed to Jesus, and of his like answer, except for a detail: these two evangelists have Jesus speak of the Kingdom's secret*s*, that is, in the plural (Mt. 13.11/Lk. 8.10). In other words, for Mark, Jesus' (one) secret is that he both meets and exceeds the scriptural standard set by Elisha as ultimate initiator of God's royal rule through a chosen king, but for Matthew and Luke this would at best be one of two or even several secrets, notably that of Jesus' mission as new Moses.

What social-communal settings does this enquiry suggest for the Gospel writers? Except for Luke, they do not explicitly claim to be authors creating literature as individuals. They, their close followers and their audiences are comparable to the circles of disciples and wider constituencies of teachers such as Rabbi Hillel or Rabbi Shammai or, for that matter, similar to how the evangelists themselves portray Jesus, his associates and audiences. Such groups draw on local theologies with unique, already established expectations of how God will act. These groups interact with each other in a competitive and usually friendly manner and may remain active beyond their teachers' deaths. Their debates and polemics generate, clarify and defend their own positions; the presence of sections later added to Mark (16.9-20 and its variants) or John (21.1-25; 7.53b–8.11) probably originated in these continuing interchanges. Given the tolerant mood of Judaism before (and briefly beyond) the destruction of the Temple, the various positions encountered in the early Christian writings (both within and outside the soon emerging New Testament canon) co-existed and could be brought together, selectively, under the wings of Luke's inclusiveness.

Moreover, the compositions of Mark, John, Matthew and Luke did not all originate with the label 'Gospel'. Mark's and (probably) Matthew's work's are indeed so identified (Mk 1.1; 14.9/Mt. 24.14), but John's composition is by implication a 'Book of Jesus' Signs' and that of Luke, a sustained 'researched and ordered disquisition' (Jn 20.30-31; Lk. 1.1-4). Neither this variety of names nor that of apocryphal Jesus books argues for a fixed genre; their constituent groups were quite varied in outlook and social location.

Given the cosmopolitan nature of the Roman–Hellenistic world and the universal accessibility of 'the Law and the Prophets', adherents to this or that position were found in many cities. The Scriptures provided a center as well as horizons, especially in the period following the destruction of the unifying symbol of the Temple. Does this loss at the center not signal both an end and a beginning, as Assyrian and Babylonian conquests and exiles had done several centuries ago? Now, after 70 CE 'the Law and the Prophets' remained Judaism's primary symbol of continuity and basis of observance. Also, for the New Testament Gospels, the loss of the Temple is the new situation in Judaism to which they respond with their claims for Jesus' mission: his community is a new Temple (Jn 2.18-23; Mk 14.58; Mt. 26.6).

We may think of Luke as a person of letters and student of the Greek Bible who in the first decades of the second century writes for a Diaspora-wide Judaism of both Pharisaic and incipient Patristic persuasions. The other evangelists wrote more directly in the wake of 70 CE; it seems that for Mark the destruction of the Temple provided the setting for the coming of the Kingdom of God 'in power' (Mk 13.1-37; 9.1). One seeks Matthew among Jesus-affirming Pharisees, much like Saul of Tarsus or Nicodemus of Jerusalem. His (still intra-Pharisaic) polemic is at times stinging, betraying a passionate involvement comparable to that of some vituperations found in the Dead Sea Scrolls.

The writer of the Johannine work, whose voice we also recognize in the letters of John, was a Scripture mystic whose meditative immersion in the holy writings opened to him 'marvels out of God's Law' (Ps. 119.18). The 'Healers' whom the Hellenistic philosopher of religion Philo of Alexandria describes, were his kin, as was the writer of the letter to the Hebrews. Finally, Mark relates to (Northern?) groups among whom the legacy of migrant prophets is alive and who, like councilor Joseph of Arimathea, are 'awaiting the reign of God' (Mk 15.43). Mary and Martha of Judean Bethany and Simon Peter, Philip and Andrew of Galilean Bethsaida similarly held that Israel's God will ensure his sovereignty through divinely approved men of power. For them, the story of Elijah's and Elisha's overthrow of apostasy was programmatic for whatever Israel's God will do with Israel.

Saint Augustine once observed that 'the New Testament lies hidden in the Old, the Old Testament lies open in the New' (*Quaestiones in Heptateuchum* LXXIII, on Exod. 20.19, adapted). The suggestive formulation may also be used in relation to this enquiry into the way in which each Gospel is narrated according to a storyline that lies both hidden and ready in the canon shared by evangelist and audience. Readers steeped in the Scriptures can discern, as through a veil, master plots and telling motifs that guide the strategy of each Gospel writer.

I noted in the introductory discussions that in early Judaism and Christianity, literary activity was based on scriptural prototypes. Hence my hypothesis that each of the four Jesus narratives in the New Testament conceives and presents Jesus' mission 'within the outlines of some ancient model' (Baeck 1958: 59) and that it is discovered by 'detecting the allusion' (Dimant 1991: 74). In sum, my findings introduce a dimension of the Gospels' scriptural depth. Through the exploration of each evangelist's narrative strategy one catches glimpses of each Gospel's unique ways of reading and appropriating the canon of 'the Law and the Prophets', the Scriptures that emerging Christianity and Judaism shared.

BIBLIOGRAPHY

Baeck, L.
1958   'The Gospel as Document of the History of the Jewish Faith', *Judaism and Christianity* (trans; Philadelphia: Jewish Publication Society of America [1938]): 41-84.
Brodie, T.L.
1983   'Greco–Roman Imitation of Texts as Partial Guide to Luke's Use of Sources', *Essays in Luke/Acts* (ed. C.H. Talbert; New York: Crossroad): 17-46.

1986   'Towards Unravelling Luke's Use of the Old Testament: Luke 7:11-17 as
             an *Imitatio* of 1 Kings 17:17-24', *NTS* 32: 247-67.

Brown, R.E.
1971   'Jesus and Elisha', *Perspective* 12: 85-104.

Dimant, D.
1991   'Literary Typologies and Biblical Interpretation in the Hellenistic–Roman
             Period', *Jewish Civilization in the Hellenistic–Roman Period* (ed. S.
             Talmon; Philadelphia: Trinity Press): 73-80.

Evans, C.F.
1955   'The Central Section of St. Luke's Gospel', *Studies in the Gospels* (ed.
             D.E. Nineham; Oxford: Basil Blackwell): 37-53.

Evans, C.A.
1993   'Luke 16:1-18 and the Deuteronomy Hypothesis', in C.A. Evans and J.A.
             Sanders, *Luke and Scripture: The Function of Sacred Tradition in Luke–
             Acts* (Minneapolis: Fortress Press): 121-39.

Ginzberg, L. (ed.)
1909–38   *The Legends of the Jews* (7 vols.; Philadelphia: Jewish Publication Society
             of America).

Goulder, M.D.
1989   *Luke: A New Paradigm*, I (Sheffield: Sheffield Academic Press).

Grassi, J.A.
1989   'Matthew as a Second Testament Deuteronomy', *BTB* 19: 23-29.

Johnson, L.T.
1986   *The Writings of the New Testament* (Philadelphia: Fortress Press)

Patte, D.
1975   *Early Jewish Hermeneutic in Palestine* (SBLDS, 22; Missoula: Scholars
             Press).

Roth, W.
1987   'Scriptural Coding in the Fourth Gospel', *BR* 32: 6-29.
1988   *Hebrew Gospel: Cracking the Code of Mark* (Oak Park, IL: Meyer–
             Stone).
1992   'Mark, John and their Old Testament Codes', *John and the Synoptics* (ed.
             A. Denaux; Leuven: Leuven University Press): 458-65.
1992–93   'The Old Testament and the Gospels 1–6', *TTB* 30.3–31.2 (1992–
             93/1993).

Sanders, J.A.
1993   'The Ethic of Election in Luke's Great Banquet Parable', in C.A. Evans
             and J.A. Sanders, *Luke and Scripture: The Function of Sacred Tradition
             in Luke–Acts* (Minneapolis: Fortress Press): 106-20.

THE USE OF THE OLD TESTAMENT IN THE NEW TESTAMENT: A BRIEF COMMENT ON METHOD AND TERMINOLOGY

Stanley E. Porter

1. *Introduction*

The use of the Old Testament and related texts in the New Testament[1] is an active area of contemporary New Testament research.[2] Its significance is related to a number of factors important to the wider field of New Testament studies. One of these is its perceived ability to unite under a single rubric the investigation of the whole of the Christian Bible. Another is the attention it pays to the Jewish background of the New Testament (although there have been a few investigations of the use of non-biblical Greek texts, to which the comments of this paper may also at least in part apply).[3] A third is the utilization of modern interpretative methodology, especially literary criticism, in biblical studies, something thought to be important in this eclectic methodological age. Other matters of significance could be cited as well. Each dimension of this investigation, however, raises a number of related questions that must also be asked. It seems to me that, in the fervor of contemporary study, a number of fundamental questions regarding the use of the Old Testament in the New have been overlooked. This brief paper is not an investigation of how particular texts of the Old Testament are used in the New. Instead, it has the modest purpose of raising

1.   As this paper unfolds, it will become obvious why I use this rather archaic-sounding terminology to refer to this very contemporary discussion. The major reason is that the recent terminology is the issue under discussion.

2.   Although I do not treat the question in a systematic way here, much of what I say below applies to the closely related topic of the use of Jesus material in other writers of the New Testament, especially Paul. I do draw into the discussion some secondary literature on that topic that shares some of the difficulties being discussed in this paper.

3.   See, for example, C.D. Stanley, 'Paul and Homer: Greco-Roman Citation Practice in the First Century C.E.', *NovT* 32 (1990), pp. 48-78.

two interrelated methodological questions that apply to discussion of
the use of the Old Testament (or any other extra-biblical text) in the
New. The first question is this: how does one define the various terms
used to label use of the Old Testament in the New Testament, and why
is the matter of definition important? The second question follows on
from it: what is the relation between direct quotation and other kinds
of use of the Old Testament in the New Testament, and how do these
categories figure into estimations of the influence of the Old Testament
upon a given New Testament writer? After discussing these issues, I
will attempt to outline briefly a set of considerations for future discussion of the use of the Old Testament in the New.

2. Defining the Categories Used to Describe the Use of the Old Testament in the New

The range of terminology used to speak of the way that a New Testament writer may use the Old Testament or a related text is simply
astounding. Without attempting to be comprehensive, at least the following terms have been used with some regularity or in important
works on the topic: citation, direct quotation, formal quotation, indirect
quotation, allusive quotation, allusion (whether conscious or unconscious), paraphrase, exegesis (such as inner-biblical exegesis), midrash,
typology, reminiscence, echo (whether conscious or unconscious),
intertextuality, influence (either direct or indirect), and even tradition,
among other terms.[4] Sometimes all instances that are not direct
quotation are subsumed under one of the above (or another) terms.
Other times fine distinctions in meaning are made between many of
the above terms. It is this situation that needs to be addressed.

It would appear *prima facie* that the concept of direct quotation
would be rather straightforward to define and utilize as an interpretative category. Nevertheless, a recent, and in many respects excellent,
study of Paul's use of the Old Testament illustrates the problem even
with the term direct quotation (and others similar to it, arguably). In

---

4. Bibliographic references can be found in numerous sources. For a recent
brief list, see C.A. Evans, '"It Is Not as though the Word of God had Failed": An
Introduction to Paul and the Scriptures of Israel', in C.A. Evans and J.A. Sanders
(eds.), *Paul and the Scriptures of Israel* (JSNTSup, 83; SSEJC, 1; Sheffield: JSOT
Press, 1992), pp. 13-14 nn. 1, 2. My survey does not attempt to refer to the wealth
of secondary literature, but often illustrates its points by reference to recent work.

Paul and the Language of Scripture,[5] recognizing that 'Only rarely, however, does one find even a brief discussion of such technical questions as: what differentiates a "citation" from other levels of engagement with the biblical text',[6] Christopher Stanley claims that it was not until a study by Dietrich-Alex Koch in 1986[7] that any scholar had set forth in a methodologically precise way the criteria used to determine a direct quotation.[8] Even if not everyone would agree with his historical reconstruction, it appears to be the case that the vast majority of those discussing the issue do not bother to define their terms. For example, Earle Ellis simply states, 'Paul quotes the OT ninety-three times', and then adds a list of the number of reminiscences. He also includes an appendix of direct quotations and an appendix of allusions.[9] Better perhaps is Robert Gundry, who at least offers a footnote in defense of his distinction between formal quotations and allusive quotations, although he seems simply to assume what constitutes a quotation.[10] Early in his study, Stanley shares the concern of Koch and attempts to address the issue of definition. His own study reveals the problems of defining the terms mentioned above, however. On the one hand, he begins by discussing the concept of 'citation', although it soon becomes clear that what he means by citation is direct and explicit quotation.

---

5. C.D. Stanley, *Paul and the Language of Scripture: Citation Technique in the Pauline Epistles and Contemporary Literature* (SNTSMS, 74; Cambridge: Cambridge University Press, 1992).

6. Stanley, *Paul and the Language of Scripture*, p. 8.

7. D.-A. Koch, *Die Schrift als Zeuge des Evangeliums: Untersuchungen zur Verwendung und zum Verständnis der Schrift bei Paulus* (BHT, 69; Tübingen: Mohr [Paul Siebeck], 1986), pp. 11-23.

8. Stanley, *Paul and the Language of Scripture*, pp. 34-35.

9. E.E. Ellis, *Paul's Use of the Old Testament* (repr. Grand Rapids: Baker, 1981 [1957]), p. 1, and appendixes on pp. 150-52 and 153-54. Cf. also *idem*, 'How the New Testament Uses the Old', in I.H. Marshall (ed.), *New Testament Interpretation: Essays on Principles and Methods* (Grand Rapids: Eerdmans, 1977), pp. 199-219.

10. R.H. Gundry, *The Use of the Old Testament in St Matthew's Gospel: With Special Reference to the Messianic Hope* (NovTSup, 8; Leiden: Brill, 1975), p. 9: 'the distinction between formal and allusive quotations is not always easily made. I have tried to judge by whether the quoted words flow from and into the context (allusive) or stand apart (formal). With this criterion, an allusive quotation may be of some length, i.e., more than a fleeting phrase or two.' Similar is T. Moritz, *A Profound Mystery: The Use of the Old Testament in Ephesians* (NovTSup, 85; Leiden: Brill, 1996), esp. p. 2, but who fails to cite the work of Thompson (see n. 26 below).

On the other hand, after discussing Koch's seven criteria for determining a direct quotation, Stanley settles on three for a direct quotation: introduction of the quotation by an explicit quotation formula, an interpretative gloss accompanies the quotation, and syntactical tension is found between the quotation and its context in Paul. As a result, Stanley must admit that a number of passages that others would consider direct quotations must be excluded[11] (see below for discussion of this and its implications). In other words, Stanley has not found a method for defining direct quotation, and certainly not a method for distinguishing direct quotation from other forms of citation, even though he recognizes the problem. What he has done is simply cut the proverbial Gordian knot and found what he considers a critical minimum with which he can undertake his investigation of Paul's technique in using these quoted texts. This procedure does not bode well for defining other terms in the discussion.

If direct quotation seems difficult, other terms prove to be even more problematic. A few examples must suffice here. In a recent article on Paul's use of Jesus tradition, James Dunn repeatedly uses the words 'echo' and 'allusion'. His use of these terms is instructive for the purposes of this article. Sometimes they seem to be distinguished, as when he dismisses various early attempts to find allusions to Jesus tradition in Paul.[12] At other times, however, they seem to be equated, as when he discusses allusions to Jesus. In other places, however, it appears that echo is the superordinate term, of which allusions of varying strengths are subordinate terms. It is difficult to get a precise sense of the meanings of Dunn's terminology.

For the terminology of echo, Dunn seems to be highly dependent upon the work of Richard Hays.[13] Relying upon the work of the literary

---

11. Stanley, *Paul and the Language of Scripture*, p. 37. E.g., Rom. 10.13; 11.34-35; 12.20; 1 Cor. 2.16; 5.13; 10.26; 15.32; 2 Cor. 9.7; 10.17; 13.1; Gal. 3.11.

12. J.D.G. Dunn, 'Jesus Tradition in Paul', in B. Chilton and C.A. Evans (eds.), *Studying the Historical Jesus: Evaluations of the State of Current Research* (NTTS, 19; Leiden: Brill, 1994), p. 159.

13. R.B. Hays, *Echoes of Scripture in the Letters of Paul* (New Haven: Yale University Press, 1989). For a review of Hays's work, see 'Part I: Echoes of Scripture in Paul—Some Reverberations', pp. 42-96, in Evans and Sanders (eds.), *Paul and the Scriptures of Israel*. The only essay that raises questions regarding determining echoes is J.C. Beker, 'Echoes and Intertextuality: On the Role of Scripture in Paul's Theology', pp. 64-65, responded to by Hays in 'On the Rebound: A Response to

critic John Hollander, whom he cites,[14] Hays is concerned to define the concept of echo and develops seven tests to enable one to do so. The first, 'availability', asks the question of whether the source of an echo was available to the author and/or original readers. Stanley also rightly distinguishes between authors and readers, although neither concept is without problems (see below).[15] For example, if one is writing to an uninformed audience who does not know the source text, does that mean that the echoes are no longer present? If they are clear to another audience, does that mean that the text itself is now different, or only the audience? Apart from audience perception, what means are available to recognize an author's echo? Clearly this criterion is inadequate. The second of Hays's criteria is 'volume'. Defining a metaphor with another metaphor is often dangerous, and this is no exception. Among other criteria, Hays defines volume in terms of explicit repetition, which appears to be a separate issue related to verbal coherence, unmentioned by Hays. The third is 'recurrence', which applies a statistical test to determine echoes. This may work to determine more or less frequent echoes, but it does not seem to be able to determine a singular echo. The fourth to seventh criteria are 'thematic coherence', 'historical plausibility', 'history of interpretation' and 'satisfaction'. As Hays admits, these last four are less criteria for determining echoes than they are attempts to establish the interpretation of these echoes. In other words, Hays has offered only three criteria for determining echoes, all problematic. As Hays says of the last, 'satisfaction', 'This criterion is difficult to articulate precisely without falling into the affective fallacy, but it is finally the most important test: it is in fact another way of asking whether the proposed reading offers a good account of the experience of a contemporary community of competent readers'.[16] It is perplexing that the most important criterion is not in fact a criterion for discovering echoes, but only for interpreting them, leaving the question of definition and determination unresolved. As a result, it is not clear that the term

Critiques of *Echoes of Scripture in the Letters of Paul'*, p. 85, both in Evans and Sanders (eds.), *Paul and the Scriptures of Israel*.

14. J. Hollander, *The Figure of Echo: A Mode of Allusion in Milton and After* (Berkeley: University of California Press, 1981), cited in Hays, *Echoes of Scripture*, p. 31.

15. Stanley, *Paul and the Language of Scripture*, p. 34.

16. Hays, *Echoes of Scripture*, pp. 31-32.

echo provides a way forward in understanding the way that the Old Testament may be used in the New.

A word that is bandied about very frequently in recent discussion of this issue is the term 'intertextuality'. Hays uses it frequently in his volume, often in the phrase 'intertextual echo',[17] and it has been adopted by many others. Foregoing the problem of whether such a compound phrase can be used when one of the terms can only be defined with great difficulty, the term 'intertextuality' deserves consideration in the light of its frequent use. Whereas many of the other terms used in discussion of the use of the Old Testament—such as allusion and quotation—are longstanding, with many of them being part of non-technical parlance, the term intertextuality is a fairly recent term that was first used as a technical term in literary-critical discussion.[18] Intertextuality originated as a philosophically bolstered theory of language relations, distinguished from simpler concepts such as influence. It has rarely if ever been picked up in this way in New Testament studies, however.[19]

17. See Hays, *Echoes of Scripture*, esp. pp. 14-21, although he is criticized for his minimalist approach by W.S. Green, 'Doing the Text's Work for it: Richard Hays on Paul's Use of Scripture', pp. 59-61, in Evans and Sanders (eds.), *Paul and the Scriptures of Israel*, responded to by Hays, 'On the Rebound', pp. 79-81. Interestingly, Hays states that he can surrender his use of the term intertextuality, since nothing is at stake for him in its use. This odd response, in the light of how much importance is given to using the term in his book, seems to illustrate my point that, in New Testament studies, the term is being used in a way different from that in literary studies, and is perhaps an unnecessary, if not unstable, usage.

18. For a fine summary, with bibliography of the principal players, see S.D. Moore, *Poststructuralism and the New Testament: Derrida and Foucault at the Foot of the Cross* (Minneapolis: Fortress Press, 1994), p. 130 for definition, and pp. 123-24 for bibliography. Major sources include: J. Kristeva, *Desire in Language: A Semiotic Approach to Literature and Art* (New York: Columbia University Press, 1980); J. Clayton and E. Rothstein (eds.), *Influence and Intertextuality in Literary History* (Madison: University of Wisconsin Press, 1991). This is not to say that literary-critical discussion has necessarily been coherent or well-defined, but that is another matter.

19. Cf. K.M. Heim, 'The Perfect King of Psalm 72: An "Intertextual" Inquiry', in R.S. Hess, P.E. Satterthwaite, and G.J. Wenham (eds.), *The Lord's Anointed: Interpretation of Old Testament Messianic Texts* (Carlisle: Paternoster Press, 1995), pp. 231-34, for work on the Old Testament, in which he attempts to utilize G. Genette's categories of intertextuality, paratextuality, metatextuality, hypertextuality and architextuality (G. Gennette, *Palimpseste: Die Literatur auf zweiter Stufe* [Frankfurt: Suhrkamp, 1993], pp. 9-21). I cannot help but think that this results in nontextuality.

For the most part, it seems that intertextuality is being used in the way that others of the terms mentioned above are used, such as echo or allusion. For example, Gail O'Day, although offering the proper references to those who developed the term intertextuality, equates it with M. Fishbane's 'inner biblical exegesis', which she utilizes in her study.[20] Sylvia Keesmaat defines intertextuality in terms of recent literary theory, seeing it as concerned with the ongoing dialogue that texts in a culture have in creating social and ideological systems. Nevertheless, when Keesmaat applies intertextuality to discussion of the New Testament, she employs an only very slightly modified set of the seven criteria used by Hays.[21] In other words, intertextuality appears to be the same as echo, which closely resembles allusion. Robert Brawley seems to use the term intertextuality as an inclusive term, at times to be equated with allusion, echo and a host of other relations.[22] As a final example, William Kurz simply uses 'intertextual' to describe how the plot of Luke–Acts was influenced by the structure of Sir. 48.1-16.[23] He admits: 'My use of intertextuality is that of traditional literary studies, not a poststructural deconstruction'.[24] As Stephen Moore rightly observes in his discussion of poststructuralism, 'Intertextuality is not what it used to be; the term now trips off the tongues even of conservative biblical scholars discussing the Synoptic problem'.[25]

One must turn to discussion of allusion for the most rigorous recent discussions of these kinds of categories in New Testament studies, however. In a study of Jesus material in Paul, Michael Thompson has attempted to come to terms with the problem of allusion in a way that

20. G.R. O'Day, 'Jeremiah 9:22-23 and 1 Corinthians 1:26-31: A Study in Intertextuality', *JBL* 109 (1990), pp. 259-67, citing M. Fishbane, *Biblical Interpretation in Ancient Israel* (Oxford: Clarendon Press, 1985).

21. S.C. Keesmaat, 'Exodus and the Intertextual Transformation of Tradition in Romans 8.14-30', *JSNT* 54 (1994), pp. 29-56, esp. 34-35.

22. R.L. Brawley, 'An Absent Complement and Intertextuality in John 19:28-29', *JBL* 112 (1993), pp. 427-43, esp. 428-30.

23. W.S. Kurz, 'Intertextual Use of Sirach 48.1-16 in Plotting Luke–Acts', in C.A. Evans and W.R. Stegner (eds.), *The Gospels and the Scriptures of Israel* (JSNTSup, 104; SSEJC, 3; Sheffield: JSOT Press, 1994), pp. 308-24.

24. Kurz, 'Intertextual Use', p. 309 n. 2.

25. Moore, *Poststructuralism and the New Testament*, p. 123. A possible exception is T. Pippin, 'Peering into the Abyss: A Postmodern Reading of the Biblical Bottomless Pit', in E.S. Malbon and E.V. McKnight (eds.), *The New Literary Criticism and the New Testament* (JSNTSup, 109; Sheffield: JSOT Press, 1994), pp. 251-68.

few have done.[26] The way he discusses the question merits attention. First, he draws upon recent work in literary criticism. Although at least one literary critic has expressed disappointment in the past that there is not a precise definition of what constitutes an allusion,[27] Thompson states that literary critics 'concur that allusion involves (1) the use of a sign or marker that (2) calls to the reader's mind another known text (3) for a specific purpose'.[28] Secondly, Thompson points out that this kind of precise definition has eluded New Testament scholars. As a result, he outlines an amazing eleven criteria for determining allusion! There are questions that need to be raised about a number of them, especially those of direct relevance for the larger question of the use of the Old Testament in the New. The first is 'verbal agreement'. Thompson states that 'the greater the number of significant shared words in [the Gospel] and [Epistle]. . . the higher the probability that there exists some kind of shared tradition'.[29] Although this may well be true, this criterion does not distinguish allusion or echo from direct quotation. In fact, it may well establish a direct relationship. This raises the question of whether echo and quotation are being confused in Thompson's analysis. The second criterion, 'conceptual agreement', is also said to be a requirement for establishing allusion/echo. However, Thompson must admit that it is also possible for an author 'deliberately to use the same language in a different sense (i.e. an antithetical or contrastive allusion)'.[30] Is this or is this not a necessary criterion? The third, 'formal agreement', is treated as self-evident, and defined only by asking the question of the extent of parallelism. Thompson does not say how much is necessary. The fifth criterion is 'common motivation' or 'rationale'. It is treated like the third, simply by means of a question, asking whether a similar rationale is given or implied. What of a case where material might be used in a different way? The sixth criterion, 'dissimilarity to Graeco–Roman and Jewish traditions', returns, as Thompson

---

26. M. Thompson, *Clothed with Christ: The Example and Teaching of Jesus in Romans 12.1–15.13* (JSNTSup, 59; Sheffield: JSOT Press, 1991), esp. pp. 28-36. This has apparently been accepted by D. Wenham, *Paul: Follower of Jesus or Founder of Christianity?* (Grand Rapids: Eerdmans, 1995), esp. pp. 25-26.

27. See C. Perri, 'On Alluding', *Poetics* 7 (1978), p. 289; cf. also C. Perri *et al.*, 'Allusion Studies: An International Annotated Bibliography, 1921–1977', *Style* 13 (1979), pp. 178-224.

28. Thompson, *Clothed with Christ*, p. 29.

29. Thompson, *Clothed with Christ*, p. 31.

30. Thompson, *Clothed with Christ*, p. 32.

recognizes, to the minimalist results of Gospel criticism. Allusions or echoes become not references to known texts but the explanation of last resort when all else has failed. The eighth criterion, 'presence of tradition indicators', may be, as Thompson admits, simply the result of the author's redactional style. The ninth criterion claims that the presence of other echoes in the immediate context helps to establish the presence of further echoes. This form of statistical argument does little to establish the presence of individual echoes or allusions. The tenth criterion, the likelihood of the author knowing the alluded to material, may well be circular, assuming its conclusion, as Thompson admits. The last criterion, 'exegetical value', is clearly more concerned with interpretation than with determination. Thompson's one of eleven criteria appears to be actually a much smaller and more negligible one than he at first posits. Although Dunn says that Thompson has 'attempted a more scientific analysis', Dunn's subsequent statement is more to the point: Thompson admits that 'in most cases the judgment of the scholar is subjective'.[31] One might also point out that not only does his method appear to be subjective, but it also proves to be virtually unworkable.

As Dunn rightly states, discussion of allusion and related terminology has reached something of a stalemate for those who engage at all in the debate. For those who do not raise the issues, the discussion seems to continue unabated. In fact, that is how it continues for Dunn and his treatment of Jesus tradition in Paul. He depends upon the consensus—that Paul cites dominical tradition at two places (1 Cor. 7.10-22 and 9.14), that he alludes to or echoes Jesus tradition in a handful of other places, and that there are a few other passages where there may be some common elements—as the starting point for his discussion of the passages. Brian Rosner rather surprisingly claims that 'Objective criteria for the identification and evaluation of evidence for Paul's dependence upon the Scriptures are not difficult to list'. He then presents six criteria similar to those discussed above. However, he states that, although these criteria are necessary to avoid 'parallelomania', and claims that the six criteria undergird his study, 'to run through them in each isolated case would be wearisome and is unnecessary'.[32] It is clear

---

31. Thompson, *Clothed with Christ*, p. 31; cf. Dunn, 'Jesus Tradition', p. 160.

32. B.S. Rosner, *Paul, Scripture and Ethics: A Study of 1 Corinthians 5–7* (AGJU, 22; Leiden: Brill, 1994), p. 19. Two of the three scholars he cites as most helpful in discussion of the supposedly objective criteria for identification of evidence

from what has been said above that the criteria for determining and labeling the use of Old Testament and related texts in the New Testament are far from being resolved and even further from providing objective tests. On the one hand, many simply do not define their terms, and most attempts to do so fail to provide the kind of definitions necessary. On the other hand, research continues unabated, occasionally with a passing nod to the idea that there is a problem, but certainly not one that impedes the discussion.

3. *The Relation between Direct Quotation and Other Kinds of Use of the Old Testament in the New*

A brief survey of a number of sources illustrates that various scholars through the history of discussion have found varying numbers of instances of use of the Old Testament or similar kinds of texts in the New Testament. For example, in his discussion of Mark, Howard Kee states that there are 'hundreds of allusions to and quotations from scripture' in Mark.[33] He does not give the exact figure, but, taking a conservative estimate that 217 (on the basis of his subsequent reference to direct quotations and allusions) approximates the figure he is working with, there are roughly fourteen 'quotations and allusions' in each chapter of Mark. Kee goes on to state that in 'Mark 11–16 alone there are more than 57 quotations',[34] an average of almost ten *direct* quotations per chapter. The significance of Kee's numbers is seen when one compares them with the classic 'whipping boy' in discussing incorporated material. Adolf Resch purported to find over 1100 instances of parallels of the Synoptic Gospels in the Pauline letters, with an average of about 12.5 per chapter.[35] Despite the fact that his work is rather quickly dismissed by most scholars today (such as Dunn, Thompson and Neirynck), and is only concerned with parallels in the Synoptic Gospels and Paul, he is not the only one to posit significant numbers of instances of

are Hays's *Echoes of Scripture* and Thompson's *Clothed with Christ* (the third is two pages in a doctoral thesis).

33. H.C. Kee, *Community of the New Age: Studies in Mark's Gospel* (London: SCM Press, 1977), p. 45, referring to his 'The Function of Scriptural Quotations and Allusions in Mark 11–16', in E. Grässer and E.E. Ellis (eds.), *Festschrift für Werner Georg Kümmel* (Göttingen: Vandenhoeck & Ruprecht, 1975), pp. 165-88.

34. Kee, *Community of the New Age*, p. 45.

35. A. Resch, *Der Paulinismus und die Logia Jesu in ihrem gegenseitigen Verhältnis untersucht* (TU, 12; Leipzig: Hinrichs, 1904), esp. pp. 35-122.

material incorporated into the New Testament. For example, Hans Hübner estimates that there are more than a hundred allusions and quotations to the Old Testament in only three Pauline chapters, Romans 9–11.[36] The *UBSGNT*[1, 2] had what they called a list of quotations, which was revised radically downward in subsequent editions, so much so that it is only one-eighth of its former size. The list that the *UBSGNT* presents is a reasonable approximation of the kind of list found in a number of discussions. For example, Silva uses O. Michel, Ellis and Koch to formulate a list of around 100 Old Testament citations in all of Paul.[37]

With such an abundance of material, it is not unusual when Rosner states, 'Most studies of the use of the Old Testament in the New Testament concentrate upon explicit usage, looking only at quotations of and perhaps allusions to Scripture'.[38] Exceptions to this are to be found, but even in a work such as Hays's, the tendency is to dwell upon passages where there is some form of explicit quotation. Passages with explicit quotation still have priority in the discussion. But is this correct? Several reasons indicate that in order to offer a complete assessment of the use of the Old Testament and related texts in the New Testament, one must consider all of the available evidence. One example is sufficient to make this point.

A book with purportedly no direct quotations of the Old Testament is Philippians, although in the Pauline corpus alone, according to the *UBSGNT*[3] listing, one could also cite Philemon, Colossians, 1 and 2 Thessalonians, and Titus. To my knowledge, there have been no recent major monographs on the use of the Old Testament in Philippians. This may be because there is not enough for a monograph, but studies of the use of the Old Testament in the New have long acknowledged uses other than direct quotation.[39] In his discussion of the Old Testament in Paul, perhaps in the light of his having written a useful commentary on Philippians, Silva discusses a number of significant uses of the Old Testament in Philippians. Included in his list are Phil. 4.18, which

36. H. Hübner, *Gottes Ich und Israel, zum Schriftgebrach des Paulus in Römer 9–11* (FRLANT, 136; Göttingen: Vandenhoeck & Ruprecht, 1984), pp. 149-60, according to M. Silva, 'Old Testament in Paul', in G.F. Hawthorne and R.P. Martin (eds.), *Dictionary of Paul and his Letters* (Downers Grove, IL: Inter-Varsity Press, 1993), p. 634.

37. Silva, 'Old Testament in Paul', p. 631.

38. Rosner, *Paul, Scripture and Ethics*, p. 17.

39. Ellis, *Paul's Use of the Old Testament*, appendix 2. See also A.T. Lincoln, 'The Use of the OT in Ephesians', *JSNT* 14 (1982), pp. 16-57.

reflects various ceremonial passages in the Old Testament (e.g. Exod. 29.18; Ezek. 20.41), and Phil. 2.9-11, which may reflect Isaiah 45, among a number of other examples.[40]

Perhaps most instructive for our purposes, however, is Phil. 1.19.[41] In Phil. 1.19, Paul states that he knows that τούτῳ μοι ἀποβήσεται εἰς σωτηρίαν, which five words are found in Job 13.16 LXX. Even though the same five words are cited in this order, this passage is not listed as an explicit quotation by the *UBSGNT*³, Silva, Ellis (who lists it as an allusion), Koch, or Stanley. This is despite the fact that a significant number of commentaries seem to treat the passage as a quotation, not as an allusion as does Silva,[42] whether they see the contexts or use of the quotation to be similar or not. For example, Alfred Plummer states that 'Here we have a quotation from Job xiii. 16; cf. xv. 3. Quotations from Job are rare in N.T. Cf. I Thess. v. 22; Rom. xi. 35; Lk. i. 52.'[43] Where discussion of this passage is found in works other than commentaries, several interesting comments are worth noting. For example, Silva states that 'Philippians, for example, is conspicuously absent from the list of explicit citations', although he rightly admits that 'it would be a grave mistake to infer that this letter shows no OT influence'.[44] But later he states, 'Another allusion which is easy to miss unless one refers specifically to the LXX text is at Philippians 1:19, "what has happened to me will turn out for my deliverance"... a

40. Silva, 'Old Testament in Paul', pp. 634-35.

41. This is not the only example of this sort that could be cited. See Stanley, *Paul and the Language of Scripture*, p. 34 n. 7 for a list of others.

42. M. Silva, *Philippians* (Wycliffe; Chicago: Moody, 1988), p. 77.

43. A. Plummer, *A Commentary on St Paul's Epistle to the Philippians* (London: Robert Scott, 1919), pp. 25-26. See also H.A.A. Kennedy, 'The Letter to the Philippians', in *The Expositor's Greek Testament* (5 vols.; repr. Grand Rapids: Eerdmans, n.d.), III, p. 426; E. Lohmeyer, *Die Briefe an die Philipper, Kolosser und an Philemon* (MeyerK; Göttingen: Vandenhoeck & Ruprecht, 13th edn, 1964), pp. 50-51; P. Bonnard, *L'épitre de Saint Paul aux Philippiens* (CNT, 10; Paris: Delachaux & Niestlé, 1950), p. 26; F.W. Beare, *A Commentary on the Epistle to the Philippians* (repr. Peabody, MA: Hendrickson, 1987 [1959]), p. 62; R.P. Martin, *Philippians* (NCB; Grand Rapids: Eerdmans, 1976), p. 75 following J.H. Michael; J.-F. Collange, *The Epistle of Saint Paul to the Philippians* (trans. A.W. Heathcote; London: Epworth Press, 1979), p. 59; G.F. Hawthorne, *Philippians* (WBC, 43; Waco, TX: Word Books, 1983), p. 39; P.T. O'Brien, *The Epistle to the Philippians* (NIGTC; Grand Rapids: Eerdmans, 1991), pp. 108-109.

44. Silva, 'Old Testament in Paul', p. 634.

verbatim quotation from Job 13:16 LXX'.[45] Apart from the confusion of allusion and quotation, there appears to be some tension between 'explicit citation' and 'verbatim quotation' in Silva's reasoning. Stanley, after distinguishing between 'reader-centered' and 'author-centered' approaches to determining citations, and claiming that author-centered approaches run the risk of being too diffuse, questions what to do with Phil. 1.19.[46] Three pages later, however, he comes to a conclusion. His study uses three criteria (see above), including the use of an explicit quotation formula, which Phil. 1.19 lacks, to circumscribe his body of data, 'on the grounds that the un-informed reader could readily take any or all of them as Pauline formulations'.[47] Later still, Stanley claims that 'In a few cases the question has been raised as to whether the phrase or clause in question might already have evolved into a common Jewish idiom, such that no explicit citation is to be posited. . .'[48] As noted above, Stanley's criteria for direct quotation are very narrow. There is the further difficulty that he has clearly opted for the audience-oriented approach, although, to be honest, there is little or no substantiation for his hypothesis of the use of Job 13.16 at Phil. 1.19 being some kind of Jewish idiom.

Hays recognizes the pivotal nature of Phil. 1.19. As he admits, this text is 'rarely treated in the critical literature on Paul's use of the Old Testament'. As noted above, 'In Philippians, exegetical exposition of the Old Testament plays no explicit role. Indeed, if we limit our consideration to quotations introduced with an explicit citation formula and exclude the instances of allusion and echo, this epistle of thanks and exhortation would appear to contain no Old Testament references at all.'[49] Hays then notes that, in Phil 1.19, Paul gives 'a verbatim citation of words lifted from Job 13:16 (LXX). . . ' However, he then says 'The echo is fleeting, and Paul's sentence is entirely comprehensible to a reader who has never heard of Job'.[50] Hays goes on to discuss how the quoted words function in the Pauline and Jobian contexts.

These comments present enough information to raise a number of

---

45. Silva, 'Old Testament in Paul', p. 634.

46. Stanley, *Paul and the Language of Scripture*, p. 34.

47. Stanley, *Paul and the Language of Scripture*, p. 37. In n. 14 he says that he will examine Phil. 1.19 and other passages at a later date.

48. Stanley, *Paul and the Language of Scripture*, p. 67 n. 8.

49. Hays, *Echoes of Scripture*, p. 21.

50. Hays, *Echoes of Scripture*, p. 21.

questions regarding discussion of the use of the Old Testament in the New. It appears clear from the evidence, as well as the discussion in the commentaries on the topic, that five words from Job 13.16 are found in exactly the same order and arrangement in Phil. 1.19. Why is it then that, even though many commentators recognize this as a quotation by Paul of the Old Testament, so many who write explicitly on this topic do not?

The first is that there is persistent confusion over terminology, including what appears to be confusion over echo, allusion and quotation or citation. The difficulty with these terms has been discussed above, but the confusion has particular relevance for the discussion here, as the label has a way of placing the given use into a particular interpretative category. Several further comments need to be made. It appears that there is a particularly restrictive understanding of quotation being used. Stanley explicitly endorses it for his study, and Hays, as well as Silva, seems to acknowledge, if not endorse, it. This definition is that quotation is confined to texts explicitly marked by some kind of a citation formula. If this is one's definition, then one must apparently label all else 'allusion' or the like, especially since (as indicated above) there has been no general agreement on what to call that which is not quotation. It is no wonder that the result is that many discussions of Philippians (and other New Testament books as well, one can easily presume) end up stating that there is no explicit quotation of the Old Testament in Philippians. The labels have a heuristic value, and end up shaping the interpretation of the evidence at hand, even if the admitted facts run contrary to this. Labeling the passage from Job 13.16 as an allusion makes it seem to be something different from a direct quotation, especially one introduced by an explicit quotation formula. In the light of what has been said above, I find it difficult to accept this, at least in the case of Phil. 1.19. To limit oneself to discussion of those passages that are introduced by an explicit quotation formula clearly skews the evidence. In fact, I would say that it makes the evidence arbitrarily and unjustifiably narrow if one is seeking to discuss the use of the Old Testament in Paul. This limitation is, of course, legitimate if one simply wishes to discuss passages introduced by quotation formulas or the like, but this is different from discussing the topic of Paul's use of the Old Testament, which is, according to the ostensible purpose and explicit statements of those discussing the issue, the goal.

The second difficulty is with the audience-oriented approach to the use of the Old Testament. This perhaps indicates a fundamental difference in orientation to the issue. Specialist studies and monographs on the use of the Old Testament, perhaps daunted by the potential amount of data to discuss, yet wanting to make something resembling a comprehensive statement, often adopt the audience-oriented approach. As noted above, Stanley adopts this approach, as does Hays. As Hays states regarding the possible quotation of Job 13.16 in Phil. 1.19, 'a reader nurtured on the LXX might, without consciously marking the allusion, sense a momentary ripple of elevated diction in the phrase, producing a heightened dramatic emphasis. The reader whose ear is able, however, not only to discern the echo but also to locate the source of the original voice will discover a number of intriguing resonances.'[51] On the other hand, the commentators do not raise the issue of how the audience will hear, respond to or relate to the quotation, but instead raise such issues as the similarity in the actual wording of the texts and how the Pauline context relates to the one in Job. The commentaries seem more oriented to reflecting, at least in the first instance, what it is that the author is attempting to do, rather than reconstructing the author through how the audience may have perceived him or his writings. There are, however, several questions to raise regarding the audience-oriented approach. The major one is the fact that, as Stanley admits, there 'is the exclusion of a number of passages whose closeness to a particular biblical passage reveals a clear intent to reproduce the wording of that passage within the later Pauline context...'[52] Can a method that excludes such passages purport to be anything representing a comprehensive or even representative view of Paul's use of the Old Testament? If, as appears to be the case, the result is that many scholars end up working from the premise that there is no quotation of the Old Testament in Philippians, even when there are explicit words from the Old Testament, then the method has apparently failed. The reasonable solution would appear to be to adopt the author-centered approach reflected in the commentaries, in which each set of words is assessed on its own merits.

The third issue relates to the question of what is intended by such analyses of the use of the Old Testament. As stated above, it appears that many are trying to create a solid base for a comprehensive analysis

51. Hays, *Echoes of Scripture*, pp. 21-22.
52. Stanley, *Paul and the Language of Scripture*, p. 34.

of the use of the Old Testament in one of the corpora of the New Testament, especially the Pauline letters. It is doubtful that such a picture can be created given the difficulties mentioned above. Nevertheless, this does not preclude analysis of smaller units, even as portions of the total picture of the use of the Old Testament in the New, but one must not think that the smaller pictures approximate to the whole. As has been illustrated with the example of Phil. 1.19, only consideration of all of the possible uses within recognizably well-defined categories (without drawing arbitrary lines of demarcation), can begin the process of formulating a comprehensive picture. As illustrated above, the arbitrary definition of quotation has severely curtailed discussion of the use of the Old Testament in Philippians, arguably in an unjustified way.

4. *Conclusion*

In the light of the issues raised above, I suggest that the following definitional and methodological points be kept in mind when discussing the use of the Old Testament in the New.[53]

1. One must know the goal of the investigation. Is one attempting a comprehensive discussion of the use of the Old Testament in all of the New Testament, in one author, or simply in one book or passage? Or, is one attempting a discussion of one particular kind of use of the Old Testament in a given body of material? There is also the possibility that one is examining how certain kinds of texts were used or understood in various contexts. Before investigation can proceed very far, the essential question must be formulated. My impression is that many previous studies, despite their apparent intentions, have not come to terms with the essential issue of this investigation.

2. In order to undertake any such investigation it is imperative that one define the categories under discussion, and then apply them rigorously. Ideally, a common language would be found that all could willingly use, but this is an unreasonable expectation. Therefore, short of a common language, interpreters should be clear in their own

53. Although he simply invokes the terms quotation and allusion without definition (pp. 423-25), K. Snodgrass offers useful guidelines for determining use of the Old Testament in the New in 'The Use of the Old Testament in the New', in D.A. Black and D.S. Dockery (eds.), *New Testament Criticism and Interpretation* (Grand Rapids: Zondervan, 1991), pp. 425-26.

terminology and the application thereof. This would allow categories of usage to be compared and discussed. Two terms would appear to constitute the starting point of discussion. One of the obvious terms that requires definition is explicit or direct quotation or citation. I would suggest that this term needs a larger definition than is often found in monographs discussing the topic, such as Stanley's, and more in line with how quotation is apparently handled in commentary discussion. The focus would be upon formal correspondence with actual words found in antecedent texts. Although there would of course be the question of how many words would qualify as a quotation, at least there is now debate over data, as opposed to hypotheses about reconstructed competencies.[54] Another difficult term is allusion. Perhaps the best way of handling this is not in terms of large and complex categories that prove unworkable, but rather in terms of a streamlined definition (resembling those in literary criticism) that covers the material not found in quotation. Allusions (or 'echoes', if one must) could refer to the nonformal invocation by an author of a text (or person, event, etc.) that the author could reasonably have been expected to know (for example, the Old Testament in the case of Paul).[55] With these two basic definitions in mind, it appears that much of the material under discussion could be usefully discussed.

3. Although investigation of an audience-oriented approach has merit in establishing the shared assumptions and biblical knowledge of the audience (in fact, much more could and should be done in this area), it is questionable whether it provides the proper basis for establishing the author's use of the Old Testament. If one is interested in establishing a given author's use of the Old Testament, it would appear imperative to orient one's discussion to the language of the author, rather than supposed, reconstructed 'knowledge' of the audience. The difference in orientation appears to revolve around whether formal means are invoked to analyze the specific uses of language, or whether

54. See J.D.G. Dunn, '"Righteousness from the Law" and "Righteousness from Faith": Paul's Interpretation of Scripture in Romans 10:1-10', in G.F. Hawthorne with O. Betz (eds.), *Tradition and Interpretation in the New Testament: Essays in Honor of E. Earle Ellis for his 60th Birthday* (Grand Rapids: Eerdmans, 1987), p. 217.

55. For a recent definition using H.P. Grice's conversational implicatures ('Logic and Conversation' [1975], repr. in *Studies in the Way of Words* [Cambridge, MA: Harvard University Press, 1989], pp. 22-40), see J.H. Coombs, 'Allusion Defined and Explained', *Poetics* 13 (1984), pp. 475-88.

one is engaging in historical-sociological reconstruction. Both are valid, although the former seems to be the means necessary when one is attempting to understand the use of the Old Testament within a given corpus.

4. Although there is merit in investigating the various kinds and types of use of the Old Testament and related texts in the New Testament, one cannot claim to provide an accurate study of a given New Testament author's use of the Old Testament unless all of the types of usage and influence are discussed. As the example from Phil. 1.19 illustrates, failure to be explicit in defining terms, or defining terms in overly restrictive ways for the task which is being undertaken, has pre-empted full and complete analysis of the use of the Old Testament in Philippians. This procedure has serious implications. For example, it is a commonplace to have scholars state that Paul's use of the Old Testament occurs predominantly in the *Hauptbriefe*. A check of the standard lists (such as Ellis's) confirms this. If Paul does cite Job 13.16 at Phil. 1.19, and similarly cites Isa. 45.23 at Phil. 2.10-11 and Deut. 32.5 at Phil. 2.15 (these can be established along similar lines of argumentation), suddenly we have three direct quotations in Philippians. A book that before had no quotations can now be defined as having three explicit quotations, besides a number of possible allusions (Ellis cites eight in all, including several of those mentioned above as quotations). This evidence would need to be taken into account, and could well change our view of Paul's general confinement of his quotations of the Old Testament to the *Hauptbriefe*.

Although this article has not arrived at firm conclusions, it has tried to raise questions that need to be addressed, or at least those which have not been addressed to the extent that they need to be, in recent work on the use of the Old Testament in the New Testament. This is not to say that the task will be an easy one. It may well mean that some of the work that has purported to speak for the whole on the basis of a small part will need to be re-thought. However, a thorough examination of the issues raised seems to be in order.

Part II

THE GOSPELS

THE USE OF SCRIPTURE IN TWO NARRATIVES
OF EARLY JEWISH CHRISTIANITY (MATTHEW 4.1-11; MARK 9.2-8)

William Richard Stegner

Fortunately, for those interested in the use of Scripture in early Jewish Christianity, there is a growing consensus that certain narratives in the Gospels were formulated by Jewish Christians. Among such narratives are The Temptation and The Transfiguration. Let me begin this study with the narrative of The Temptation.

In his *History of the Synoptic Tradition*, Rudolf Bultmann noted its Jewish Christian origin. He described the narrative as 'scribal Haggada' in that 'the dialogue between Jesus and the devil reflects Rabbinic disputations'. Two pages later he wrote that 'Christian scribes made the story in Q and gave it the form of a controversy dialogue on the Jewish model'.[1] Accordingly, he assigned the origin of the story to 'the sphere of the Palestinian Tradition', although he felt the phrase 'Son of God' was a 'Hellenistic concept'.[2] In his significant study of the narrative, Jacques Dupont also assigned the origin of the story to a Jewish Christian milieu.[3] He argued that the account reflected a Jewish mentality and that the typological use of Old Testament quotations to point to the significance of Jesus can only be conceived among Jewish Christians. (These two points will be developed later in the paper.) In addition, attempts to classify the narrative as a Christian midrash point to the same milieu.[4]

---

1. R. Bultmann, *History of the Synoptic Tradition* (trans. J. Marsh; New York: Harper & Row, 1963), pp. 254 and 256.

2. Bultmann, *History*, p. 257.

3. J. Dupont, 'L' Arrière-fond biblique du récit des tentations de Jésus', *NTS* 3 (1956–57), p. 299. He uses the phrase 'dans des milieux judéo-chrétiens'. So also his later monograph, *Les tentations de Jésus au désert* (StudNeot, 4; Bruges: Desclée de Brouwer, 1958).

4. B. Gerhardsson, *The Testing of God's Son: An Analysis of an Early Christian*

However, before examining the use of Scripture in the narrative of The Temptation, I will clarify which narrative is meant since accounts of The Temptation are found in Mt. 4.1-11, Mk 1.12-13, and Lk. 4.1-13. In actuality, there are two narratives of The Temptation—the brief Markan narrative and the Q narrative which lies behind both the Matthean and Lukan accounts. Since the Markan narrative contains no quotations (that is, words in sequence or a passage) and, perhaps, quotes only a few individual words and a phrase from Scripture, I will mention it only briefly. (Further, there is no scholarly agreement concerning the relationship between the Markan narrative and the Q narrative.) Hence, the primary concern lies with the Q narrative which contains four well-known quotations from the Old Testament, as well as individual words and phrases quoted from the context of those quotations and from other stories about Moses.

An additional difficulty remains: which account—the Matthean or the Lukan—more faithfully reproduces the Q narrative? Here most scholars hold that Matthew more faithfully reproduces Q and cite the *order* of the temptations as an example.

While Q apparently gave the order of the temptations as Israel experienced them in the wilderness (Matthew's order), Luke changed the order of the second and third temptations for a theological reason. According to Luke's view of salvation history, Jerusalem plays a central role: thus the third and last temptation takes place at the Temple in Jerusalem. Consequently, in the following pages I will first discuss the Matthean account and, secondarily, mention the Lukan agreements and disagreements with Matthew. The Markan narrative will be brought into the discussion only incidentally.

However, while Matthew apparently reproduced Q more faithfully than did Luke, the issue of words found only in Matthew's account still remains. Specifically, the words in Mt. 4.2, 'and forty nights' and the words in Mt. 4.8, 'to a very high mountain' are not found in Luke's account. Several of these words seem to be quoted from the Old Testament. Do these words reflect the underlying Q narrative or Matthew's redactional activity? Is Matthew or Q drawing a secondary comparison between Jesus and Moses?

Since most of the critical issues that bear on the narrative of The

---

Midrash (Lund: Gleerup, 1966). See also, M.D. Goulder, *Midrash and Lection in Matthew* (London: SPCK, 1974), p. 245.

Temptation have been reviewed, let me start this analysis by examining the four quotations from Scripture that Matthew and Luke share.

The Four Quotations

Three of the four quotations are cited from Deuteronomy: they are so integral to the narrative, it is appropriate to begin with them. The first quotation is found in Mt. 4.4 and Lk. 4.4: Matthew and Luke agree exactly in the words they have in common, and they have reproduced the Septuagint (LXX) exactly. They differ in that Matthew quotes eight additional words from the LXX: 'but by every word that proceeds from the mouth of God'. The second quotation, found in Mt. 4.7 and Lk. 4.12, is the same in both and follows the LXX exactly. The third quotation, found in Mt. 4.10 and Lk. 4.8, again is the same in both. The quotation is also the same as in Manuscript A of the LXX. Manuscript B of the LXX, on the other hand, reads 'fear' rather than 'worship' and lacks the word 'only'. In the fourth quotation the devil cites Ps. 91.11-12 (LXX 90.11-12). Again, Matthew and Luke agree in the words quoted and follow the LXX. Only here the situation is reversed from the first quotation (Mt. 4.4) cited from Deut. 8.3: Luke's quotation contains more words from the LXX than does Matthew's. These quotations have been studied extensively and Krister Stendahl succinctly summarizes the results:

> In any case the quotations are without influence from texts other than the LXX and their LXX character is almost a literal one. In spite of the lesser differences between Matthew's and Luke's passages on the temptation, even in their quotations, they presuppose a common source and not merely material from an oral tradition or a framework consisting only of the four quotations as testimonies.[5]

Thus it is concluded that early (that is, before CE 70) Jewish Christians used explicit quotations from the LXX version of the Old Testament in a narrative that they formulated.

However, the dependence of this narrative upon the Old Testament is much more extensive than the words of these four quotations. In addition, individual words and phrases are quoted. Some of these words and phrases are quoted from the context of at least one of the quotations

---

5.   K. Stendahl, *The School of St Matthew and its Use of the Old Testament* (Lund: Gleerup, 2nd edn, n.d.), p. 89.

and some are quoted from other Old Testament stories. Let us now turn our attention to these quoted words.

Quoted Words and Phrases

In Jewish exegetical practice of the time, the use of such quotations as have been discussed above sometimes pointed to the context or surrounding passage from which they were taken. The Temptation narrative itself shows that the formulators of the story had the context of Deut. 8.3b in mind. The first temptation (Mt. 4.3-4) culminates in the quotation from Deut. 8.3b; however, the 'setting' of the narrative (Mt. 4.1-2) also quotes several important words from the context of Deut. 8.3b. Thus the Greek words for 'was led', 'the wilderness', 'to be tempted' (tested), and 'forty' are all found in the LXX of Deut. 8.2: '...the Lord your God *has led* you these *forty* years in the *wilderness...testing* you to know what was in your heart...' To these should be added the Greek word for 'loaves of bread' and, probably, 'was hungry'. These same six words are found in the Lukan version of the Q narrative.

The word for 'was hungry' is not found in the immediate context (although a synonym is), but is used in Deut. 25.18 to describe the same wilderness sojourn. Moreover, the same word is found twice in the classic description of the wilderness wanderings in Ps. 107.4-9. Also, Isa. 49.10 uses the word when it describes the redemptive return through the wilderness in the eschatological future. The word for 'loaves of bread' (Luke has the singular) seems to be cited from the quotation in 8.3b rather than the context.

In describing a homiletical pattern found in the sermon in Jn 6.31-58 and in Philo, and in the later Palestinian midrashim, Peder Borgen notes:

> It is apparent, then, that the homily in John 6 reflects a pericope rather than a single verse from the Old Testament, just as the homilies in Leg. all. III 162–168 and Mut. 253–263 reflect the pericopes from which the Old Testament texts are taken.[6]

It is not surprising then that Jewish Christians should cite words from the context of their quotations. They were simply following the exegetical practice of the times.

---

6. P. Borgen, *Bread from Heaven* (NovTSup, 10; Leiden: Brill, 1965), p. 42.

Like Matthew and Luke, the brief Markan narrative also contains the words 'forty' and 'tempted' and the phrase 'in the wilderness'. While it is possible that the later Evangelists copied these words from Mark, they could not have copied 'was led' from Mark and the brief Markan narrative does not speak of Jesus' 'hunger' or of 'bread'. Thus the more likely conclusion is that Mark's narrative, like the Q narrative, is also quoting these three words from Deut. 8.2. However, this line of investigation leads us astray.

In addition to the words quoted from the context of Deut. 8.3b, Matthew's account quotes words from two other stories associated with the wilderness wanderings of Israel. For example, both Matthew and Luke mention 'forty days' but Matthew alone records 'and forty nights'. Thus, Jesus 'fasted forty days and forty nights' (Mt. 4.2). Jesus' fast recalls Moses' fast on Mt Sinai, recorded both in Deut. 9.9 and Deut. 9.18. 'I remained on the mountain forty days and forty nights; I neither ate bread nor drank water' (Deut. 9.9).

The other story is associated with the third temptation. Mt. 4.8 reads: 'Again, the devil took him up to a very high mountain...' Luke's account does not mention a mountain, but reads: 'And the devil took him up...' (Lk. 4.6a). The 'mountain' in Matthew's account recalls Moses' ascent to Mount Nebo in Deut. 34.1-4 because of the words that immediately follow. After taking Jesus to the 'mountain', the devil 'showed him all the kingdoms of the world... and he said to him, "All these I will give you..." ' (Mt. 4.8b-9a). The Greek words for 'showed him all the... I will give' are the same words found in Deuteronomy, where the Lord 'showed him all the land...' (Deut. 34.1b), 'And the Lord said to Moses... I will give...' (Deut. 34.4b).

Are the words 'and forty nights' and 'very high mountain' Matthew's redactional inserts into the Q narrative? Here one must first examine the latter story and then consider the first story in the context of the whole narrative of The Temptation. There seems little doubt that Luke's account is alluding to the story of Moses on Mount Nebo for it contains the same words from Deuteronomy as does Matthew's account. Indeed, it is closer to Deuteronomy for the verb tense of 'showed' is the same as that found in Deuteronomy, and Luke's account quotes two additional words from the context—'all' and 'this'—found in Deut. 34.1b and 4a, respectively. Although Q alludes to the story of Mount Nebo, it seems impossible to know whether Q contained the word 'mountain' or the more enigmatic 'And leading him up'.

Now let us view the allusion to Moses' fast in the context of the whole narrative. In Matthew's account each of the quotations from Deuteronomy refers to a temptation of Israel in the wilderness. Also, each of the three temptations carries a secondary reference to another Old Testament passage. In the first temptation, Jesus' fast recalls Moses' fast. In the third, the high mountain recalls Mount Nebo. In the second, the devil quotes Psalm 91 which speaks of God's protection for him 'who dwells in the shelter of the Most High. . . ' (Ps. 91.1a). The devil infers that the Psalmist was speaking of Jesus! Accordingly, the two secondary references to Moses bracket the secondary reference to Jesus in the Psalm. However, Luke's account contains only two secondary references: God's showing Moses all the land and Psalm 91. So the three major references to Old Testament stories in the quotations from Deuteronomy are balanced or unbalanced by two secondary references. The symmetry of a secondary reference for each of the primary references is broken. Consequently, it is more likely that Luke omitted a secondary reference to Moses than that Matthew added the secondary reference. Nevertheless, certainty does not seem possible.

The quotations and additional quoted words from the larger context of Deuteronomy still do not exhaust the influence of the Old Testament on the narrative of The Temptation. Indeed, the very structure of the narrative shows the interplay between the activity of Jesus and Old Testament stories.

The Structure of the Narrative and Typology

Three times in this narrative the devil tempts Jesus to be disobedient to God. Three times Jesus turns aside the temptation with a quotation from Deuteronomy. These three quotations have the same theme—the temptations of Israel in the desert. The situation of Jesus is like that of Israel. So parallel are the situations that Jesus may be said to be reliving the temptations of his ancestors.

Let us look in detail at the interplay between the situation of Jesus and that of the generation under Moses. In Deut. 6.13 Moses warns the people about idolatry, lest they 'go after. . . the gods of the people who are round about you' (Deut. 6.14). In the third temptation, the devil invites Jesus to worship him in order to receive 'all the kingdoms of the world. . . ' (Mt. 4.8). The situation is closer than the word 'idolatry' indicates, for essentially the same false god is involved. In the Judaism of the time, idols were commonly regarded as manifestations of demons. As the prince of demons the same demonic power sought worship in both cases. The second temptation recalls the incident at Massah (Exod. 17.1-7) where Israel demanded to know whether God was with them by seeking a miracle. Similarly, the devil tempts Jesus to throw himself down from the temple so God can prove by a miracle that he is with him. In the first temptation, Jesus fasts and is hungry. Similarly, Israel, early in the wilderness wanderings, experiences hunger.

In addition, there is a similar interplay between the situations of Jesus and Moses. As Moses fasts forty days and forty nights, so Jesus fasts forty days and forty nights. As Moses ascends Mount Nebo and is shown 'all the land', so Jesus is shown 'all the kingdoms of the world'.

In view of the parallel situation between Jesus and the wilderness generation, and in view of the fact that the first quotation from Deuteronomy is cited from Deut. 8.3b, one might infer that the point of the testing is the same. According to Deut. 8.2, Moses recalls to Israel that 'God has led you. . . in the wilderness. . . testing you to know what was in your heart, whether you would keep his commandments or not'. The inference is strengthened by the fact that four words quoted in the setting of the narrative of The Temptation are cited from this very sentence, one of those words being the key verb for testing/tempting!

Pointing out the similarities in the situations of Jesus and the generation under Moses is simply another way of speaking of typology. Typology is an ancient method of biblical interpretation by which New Testament writers sought to relate Jesus to persons, situations, and events recorded in their Bible (our Old Testament).

According to this method, Old Testament persons, situations, and events are 'types' or foreshadowings of similar persons, situations, and events in the New Testament. St Paul gives another example of typology in 1 Cor. 10.1-2 where Israel's passing through the cloud and the Red Sea is a type or foreshadowing of baptism. Typology relates two historical persons, events, or situations because it assumes that God acts in history. God's actions through persons, situations, and events in one age foreshadow his actions in another age.

Typology may be compared to some symphonic music: a theme or melody which is sounded at the beginning (prelude) of a work will be repeated on a higher and grander level later on in the work. Perhaps this musical analogy enables one to understand what the formulators of the narrative of The Temptation were trying to say. Moses' fast foreshadows Jesus' fast, but God's activity in Jesus is repeated on a higher and grander level than the foreshadowing in Moses. Whereas Moses was shown 'all the land' (that is, the promised land of Canaan) from Mount Nebo, from 'a very high mountain' Jesus is shown 'all the kingdoms of the world and the glory of them'. Indeed, the relationship between Israel and Jesus is a special kind of typology in which one serves as an anti-type to the other. Israel failed the test: Israel was disobedient to God. On the other hand, Jesus was obedient to God. He withstood the temptations posed by the devil and remained faithful to God. God tested him in order to know what was in his heart and found him obedient. While the situation is much the same, Israel's failure is an 'anti-type' to Jesus' obedience.

The early Jewish Christians' use of typology tells us much about their use of Scripture and their view of history. They believed that the Mosaic age, as well as other past ages, foreshadowed the end of history or this age as we understand it. In this narrative, the Mosaic age foreshadows, and in some way parallels, the coming time of God's final deliverance. Where Israel failed, Jesus succeeded: consequently, Jesus is completing and fulfilling the history of Israel. Indeed, his obedience to God has in some sense broken the power of the devil: his career heralds the time of deliverance.

Let us pause a moment in this quest to understand the use of Scripture among some early Jewish Christians. They used quotations from the Old Testament. They quoted isolated words from the contexts of their quotations and also from other Old Testament stories. They used typology. However, this does not exhaust their understanding and use of Scripture. We may naively blame them for reading their Bible with uncritical eyes, or else think that they read the Old Testament in as literal a manner as we read it. We seldom realize that they read an interpreted Bible. Already in the first century there were exegetical traditions which enabled them to read passages in a certain way and with a certain understanding. This discussion of the use of Scripture among early Jewish Christians would not be complete without investigating the exegetical traditions—the glasses, so to speak—which enabled them to see and understand the passages from Deuteronomy in a certain way.

An Interpreted Bible: First-Century Exegetical Traditions

In discussing an interpreted Bible in relationship to The Temptation, two exegetical traditions come to mind at once. The first is associated with the term 'wilderness' as it is used in the Dead Sea Scrolls. The second is associated with Deut. 1.1. Let us turn to the Dead Sea Scrolls first.

The Scrolls provide a logical place to begin since the Qumran Community, located in the same wilderness in which Jesus was tempted, was flourishing during the time of Jesus' temptation, as well as the time in which the narrative of The Temptation was formulated. In the Scrolls, the term 'wilderness' was understood eschatologically.[7] The sect believed they were living at the end of this evil age and even during the beginning of God's new age of deliverance. They, too, believed in typology and thought that the Mosaic age foreshadowed the coming deliverance. As Israel in the wilderness was destined to inherit the promised land, so they in the wilderness were preparing the way for inheriting the land in the new age. So close was the time of salvation that they were already being warmed by its dawning rays. The term 'wilderness' also designated the devil's primary area of activity. Hence, the term 'wilderness' meant a place and time of testing. They were preparing the way for the coming of God's final deliverance by keeping the Law as perfectly and properly as they could. Belial (the devil) tried to prevent their obedience to God's law by tempting them to disobedience. Finally, the term 'wilderness' designated a particular geographical area. Robert Funk seeks to determine whether the wilderness 'was localized in proximity to the holy land and the holy mountain, Zion'. He finds that the temptation narratives in the New Testament reflect the usage of the Dead Sea Scrolls:

> ... nominal *eremos* [the wilderness] in the NT is usually localized as the wilderness of Sinai or the wilderness of Judea (not just Judah), the latter including the lower Jordan valley and possibly the eastern slopes of the valley. There is precedent for this usage in the LXX and Qumran literature.[8]

If Funk is correct, the second and third temptations were also located in the wilderness: the temple borders the wilderness and the 'high mountain', echoing Moses' ascent to Nebo, was located among 'the eastern slopes of the valley'.

---

7.   The following material has been widely discussed for years. For a convenient summary of the exegetical traditions clustered around the term 'wilderness', see W.R. Stegner, *Narrative Theology in Early Christianity* (Louisville: Westminster/John Knox, 1989), pp. 37-40.

8.   R. Funk, 'The Wilderness', *JBL* 77 (1959), p. 214. The first quotation is found on page 206.

Since the Jewish Christian formulators of the narrative used the LXX and were familiar with the thought-world of the Dead Sea Scrolls, they presupposed these same exegetical traditions.

The exegetical tradition associated with Deut. 1.1 also seems to have been known by the Jewish Christian formulators of the narrative. This tradition maintains that the words Moses spoke to Israel in Deut. 1.1 were words of rebuke for their failures in the wilderness. According to this exegetical tradition, specific failures and the accompanying rebuke are associated with each place-name listed in Deut. 1.1: 'beyond the Jordan in the wilderness, in the Arabah over against Suph, between Paran and Tophel, Laban, Hazeroth, and Di-zahab'.

The tradition is found in later rabbinic works, such as *Sifre Deuteronomy*, the *Midrash Rabbah to Deuteronomy*, the Targums, the Mishna, and the Babylonian Talmud. It is also found in the book of Jubilees and the Dead Sea Scrolls.[9]

This exegetical tradition has never before been associated with the temptation narrative. However, this tradition answers questions that have plagued exegetes of this narrative over the years. Why, for example, does Jesus quote from Deuteronomy and not cite the primary accounts located in Exodus 16 and 17? Why were Israel's numerous failures in the wilderness summarized by three temptations? and why these three?

Note how the rebuke tradition addresses these questions. In the rabbinic literature, where the rebuke tradition is fully explicated, the words from Deuteronomy are primary and the original accounts of the incidents are quoted only to add specificity. For example, in *Sifre Deuteronomy*, Israel's grumbling preceding the giving of the Manna is connected with the phrase 'in the wilderness'. First, the place-name is mentioned, then the following: 'teaches that he rebuked them concerning what they did'. Next the place-name is repeated and, last of all, *Sifre* quotes Exod. 16.3: 'Would that we had died by the hand of the Lord in the land of Egypt, when we sat by the fleshpots and ate bread to the full'. Apparently Jesus quotes from Deuteronomy because only these words were regarded as rebukes for Israel's sins.

Why does the temptation narrative reduce Israel's failures in the wilderness to three? The two Targums—*Neofiti* 1 and *the Fragmentary Targum*—agree both in listing three wilderness sins as the cause of

---

9.   For an extensive discussion of this tradition in relationship to the narrative of The Temptation, see Stegner, *Narrative Theology*, pp. 40-44.

God's anger and in naming those sins: sending out the spies from
Paran, grumbling about the manna, and making the golden calf. The
Midrash Rabbah to Deut. 1.2 also knows of the tradition of three sins.
In attempting to reconcile God and Israel over the sin of the golden
calf, Moses compares Israel to a wife who continually provokes her
husband. Israel has provoked God 'in the wilderness, in the Arabah,
over against Suph'. Other works cite three sins of Israel in the wilderness. This may be a case where an oral exegetical tradition, known in
the first century by Jewish Christians, later surfaced in written form
in rabbinic works.[10] An analogous case is found in Paul in 1 Cor. 10.4
where Paul maintains that the rock from which water gushed in the
temptation at Massah was peripatetic. This same tradition is found in a
later rabbinic work.

The rebuke tradition also helps us understand why two of these three
temptations are cited. Nearly every rabbinic exposition of the rebuke
tradition (that I found) cites an act of idolatry involving either the
golden calf or some other incident. The act of idolatry is the climactic
sin according to *Sifre Deuteronomy* and *Midrash Rabbah to Deuteronomy*. Almost as often the same sources cite the grumbling concerning
the giving of the Manna. What other factors besides the rebuke tradition, such as the experiences of Jesus, influenced the Christian scribes
who formulated the rebuke tradition are not known.

Now that we have reviewed the use of Scripture in the temptation
narrative, let us assess what we have learned. The use of quotations
from the Old Testament is not surprising. Nor is the use of quoted
words from the context of the quotations and from other Old Testament
stories, although the extensive use of such quoted words is surprising.
In addition, the use of typology and the related theology of history is
familiar from other New Testament passages as well as from the Dead
Sea Scrolls. Very surprising, however, is the sophisticated use of typology. In contrast to Paul, for example, who directly stated the types in
1 Cor. 10.1-4, this narrative relies on the more allusive approach of
quoting words from the Old Testament stories that furnish the types
and anti-types. Moreover, three anti-types involving the wilderness
generation are coupled with two secondary types from the life of Moses.
Remarkable balance is achieved in juxtaposing the failures of Israel
against the faithfulness of Jesus. The formulators were, so to speak,

10. G. Vermes, *Jesus and the World of Judaism* (Philadelphia: Fortress Press,
1983), pp. 84-85.

weaving a tapestry in which the background of exegetical tradition—particularly the rebuke tradition—causes the remarkable obedience of Jesus to stand out. The intricacy, balance, and unity of the narrative is a stunning achievement.

Conclusions

Up to this point I have focused on the mechanics of Jewish Christian use of Scripture. The use of Scripture to form a theological message is equally impressive. First, the selection of types from Moses and the wilderness generation shows us they were working with an *Urzeit/ Endzeit* (beginning time/end time) theology of history. Of the six passages of Scripture which they utilize, only the quotation from the Psalms lies outside the Pentateuch. Secondly, and more importantly, they were preoccupied with Christology, although apologetic and, perhaps, polemical interests were also present.

Let us look more closely at the Christology that this narrative portrays. Here we really see what is meant by Jewish Christians. These people were working exclusively with Jewish exegetical traditions, Jewish methods of exegesis, and more importantly, the Jewish Bible of the time. They were making their new-found faith in Jesus intelligible out of their own background and Scripture. They focused on the *obedience* of the Son of God and pointed to his victory over the devil. Since 'Son of God' is the key term in the narrative,[11] Jesus *demonstrates* that sonship by obedience to the Word of God (Deut. 8.3b) and by his consequent triumph over the prince of this world. He binds the 'strong man'.

How different is this Christology from that which we find in other passages in the New Testament! Yet the question of high or low Christology does not 'fit' this narrative because early Jewish Christians were working out of a different mindset and with a different ontology from other New Testament writers. Nevertheless, in terms of their categories, their Christology approaches a high Christology. According to the world-view of the time the devil was the 'ruler of this world' (Jn 12.31). In this narrative Jesus overcomes 'the ruler of this world'. He bound the 'strong man' by resisting sin. Who else could accomplish such a feat except the strong Son of God!

In addition to its major focus on Christology, this narrative shows

---

11. Gerhardsson, *The Testing of God's Son*, p. 20.

an apologetic thrust in its exploitation of the aspirations of contemporary Judaism. Both the Dead Sea Scrolls and Josephus witness to the strength of the wilderness motif. In view of the intense eschatological expectations of the time, the message of the fulfillment of the expectations of wilderness theology in Jesus would exert a powerful attraction on Jews outside the Jewish Christian circle.

There may be two polemical thrusts in the narrative as well. First, Moses is subordinate to the Son of God. In the secondary parallel to the third temptation, Moses ascends Mt Nebo and views 'all the land'. In contrast, Jesus is led up 'a very high mountain' and sees 'all the kingdoms'. Possibly the use of the rebuke tradition is a polemical thrust against the larger Jewish community. God's anger was directed at their failures in the wilderness while Jesus was faithful. Do their earlier failures in the wilderness foreshadow their contemporary failure to believe in the Son? On the basis of wilderness failures, St Paul warned the Corinthians: 'Now these things happened to them as a warning, but they were written down for our instruction. . . ' (1 Cor. 10.11). Could Paul have learned that warning from Jewish Christians?

The many facets of this narrative are like a finely cut diamond which glitters as it is turned in the light. The narrative shows how early Jewish Christians used Scripture; it gives a glimpse of their Christology; it hints at their situation in life. Let us now look at another Jewish Christian narrative to determine whether the results of this research are confirmed and enlarged.

The Narrative of The Transfiguration

As in the case of the previous narrative, certain critical issues concerning The Transfiguration must be addressed before the use of Scripture in it can be explained. Also here, three accounts of The Transfiguration appear in the Gospels—Mt. 17.1-8, Mk 9.2-8, and Lk. 9.28-36. Again, there is a scholarly consensus: Matthew and Luke have used the earlier Markan account and edited it for their own purposes. Mark's version, then, deserves primary attention. A fourth account is found in the second letter of Pet. 1.16-18. While this account differs markedly from the Synoptic accounts, it does not seem to be independent, but, rather, seems to depend upon the earlier Synoptic Gospels.[12]

---

12. J. Neyrey, 'The Apologetic Use of the Transfiguration in 2nd Peter 1:16-21', *CBQ* 42 (1980), p. 509.

The unity of this Markan narrative is still a matter of debate. Some earlier critics thought the narrative was composed of two originally separate parts, one part being modeled on the theophany on Mt Sinai (Exod. 24) and the other part being modeled on the shining of Moses' face as a result of his nearness to God. However, the failure to find a seam in the story where the two parts were sewn together has greatly weakened that theory. More recent redaction critics have tried to separate Markan redactional additions from an original pre-Markan story. Unfortunately, there is very little agreement among the critics. One of the few points on which redaction critics do agree is the existence of a pre-Markan narrative that Mark incorporated into his Gospel.

Today, most critics do agree that the Markan narrative possesses a certain unity and a definite focus—the focus being the message of the heavenly voice:

> In the text of Mark, the climax of the narrative is not in the metamorphosis of Jesus and the radiance of his clothing, but in the heavenly voice.[13]

Consequently, I will treat the story as a literary unity in the following analysis.

Another critical issue that continues to divide scholars is the proper classification of the *form* of the narrative. The form of a story is important because form and meaning are closely related. Hence, it makes a difference whether the narrative is a resurrection story projected back into the ministry of Jesus, or an epiphany that reveals the divine essence of Jesus, or an apocalyptic vision that unveils the future.

Recent scholarship has tended to reject the classification that The Transfiguration is a resurrection story and that it is an epiphany story[14] in favor of the view that in some way it portrays the future. I hold the view that the narrative in form is an apocalyptic vision: it is, so to speak, a preview of coming attractions. The narrative shares certain characteristics with other visions such as the sudden fading away of Moses and Elijah (Mk 9.8) and the use of the same Greek term translated as 'there appeared' (Mk 9.4a).[15] It also shares certain characteristics with

13. H. Kee, 'The Transfiguration in Mark', in J. Reumann (ed.), *Understanding the Sacred Text* (Valley Forge, PA: Judson, 1972), p. 139.

14. R.H. Stein, 'Is the Transfiguration (Mark 9:2-8) a Misplaced Resurrection-Account?', *JBL* 95 (1976). Howard Kee argues that it is not an epiphany story. See Kee, 'The Transfiguration in Mark'.

15. C. Rowland, *The Open Heaven: A Study of Apocalyptic in Judaism and Early Christianity* (New York: Crossroads, 1982), pp. 366-67 and n. 40.

that literary stereotype of an apocalyptic vision in Daniel 10.[16]

Another reason for classifying the narrative as an apocalyptic vision is the exegetical tradition associated with Mt Sinai, the literary archetype of The Transfiguration. Mt Sinai came to be interpreted apocalyptically and figured in some descriptions of the approaching end-of-the-world drama. Thus Mt Sinai became a proper vehicle for conveying an apocalyptic vision. This will become clearer in working with the tradition associated with Mt Sinai.

The Transfiguration—A Jewish–Christian Narrative

Critics have been so preoccupied by matters of form and redaction criticism that they have not focused on the Jewish Christian origins of the pre-Markan narrative. Actually, three lines of evidence lead us to Jewish Christianity. They are the literary form of the narrative, the use of the narrative as a validating formula for church leaders, and the use of the Mt Sinai narrative as a literary archetype. Let me briefly examine each of these lines of evidence.

Apocalyptic visions are primarily found in late Old Testament books (such as Daniel), in some intertestamental Jewish works, and in some New Testament books. Apocalyptic presupposes a certain view of history which Christianity inherited from Judaism. Therefore, if The Transfiguration is a piece of apocalyptic, its formulators must be sought either in Judaism or Jewish Christianity.

The view that this narrative performed a validating function in primitive Christianity is modern and has gained acceptance as scholars have investigated the social function of pieces of literature.[17] The three witnesses, Peter and James and John, occupy an important place in the narrative. The statement in 9.2b, 'he was transfigured before them', further illustrates their importance. They correspond to Aaron, Nadab, and Abihu in the literary archetype. These three formed an inner circle

---

16. M. Sabbé, 'La rédaction du récit de la transfiguration', in *La venue du messie* (RechBib, 6; Leuven: Leuven University Press, 1962), p. 67. Both Sabbé and Kee identify The Transfiguration as an apocalyptic vision. See Sabbé, p. 70 and Kee, 'The Transfiguration', pp. 149-50.

17. B.D. Chilton, 'The Transfiguration: Dominical Assurance and Apostolic Vision', *NTS* 27 (1980–81), pp. 115-24. See also, J.A. McGuckin, *The Transfiguration of Christ in Scripture and Tradition* (Lewiston, NY: Edwin Mellen, 1986), pp. 53-57.

among the twelve and Paul later mentions them as three 'pillars' of the Jerusalem church in Gal. 2.9. They were leaders of Jewish Christianity, and, as a secondary function, this narrative validated their role by mentioning their names in connection with this significant event. Similarly, the pre-Pauline list of witnesses of the Resurrection in 1 Cor. 15.3-7 played a validating function for leaders of the primitive church.

The third line of evidence pointing to Jewish Christianity is the reinterpretation of Exodus 24 in intertestamental Judaism. Like many other stories in Scripture, the story of Mt Sinai was embellished and changed in its many retellings. And like other stories about the wilderness generation, this story too was understood eschatologically and apocalyptically. Sinai becomes the place where the future is revealed. The book of *Jubilees* offers a good example of this retelling. *Jubilees* opens by recalling Exodus 24. Then, the angel of the presence receives tablets recording history 'from the day of creation until the day of the new creation. . .'[18] Who else would know about the apocalyptic reinterpretation of Mt Sinai but Jews and Jewish Christians?

Since critical issues concerning The Transfiguration have been reviewed, we should now turn to the use of Scripture in this narrative.

The Use of Scripture in The Transfiguration

In the above study of the narrative of The Temptation, it was found that typology played a key role in the use of Scripture. There, Old Testament persons, situations, or events foreshadowed similar persons, situations or events in the New Testament. However, the narrative of The Transfiguration does not exemplify typology as I have defined it. The narrative is not comparing *parallel* situations between the life of Jesus and that of the wilderness generation in that Mt Sinai foreshadows an event in the ministry of Jesus. For example, Mt Sinai foreshadows the Sermon on the Mount for Matthew. Rather, this apocalyptic vision was portraying a future event that had not yet happened. Further, an eschatological and apocalyptic understanding of Exodus 24 is used to picture 'the eschatological end. . . being enacted in the conclave of Moses, Elijah, and Jesus'.[19] Rather than speak of Mt Sinai as a *type* foreshadowing The Transfiguration, it is preferable to say The

18. *Jub.* 1.29, *The Old Testament Pseudepigrapha* (ed. J.H. Charlesworth; Garden City, NY: Doubleday, 1985), II, p. 54.
19. Kee, 'The Transfiguration in Mark', p. 147.

Transfiguration was modeled upon the apocalyptic understanding of Exodus 24. In this sense I previously spoke of Mt Sinai as the literary archetype of The Transfiguration.

Even the statement that The Transfiguration was modeled upon the apocalyptic understanding of Exodus 24 needs further qualification. The relationship between the two stories is complicated by the presence of words from other Old Testament stories, most of which were related to Mt Sinai and were also interpreted eschatologically. Thus, the apocalyptically interpreted Mt Sinai story in Exodus 24 acted as a kind of literary magnet that attracted other stories associated with it. The picture will become clearer if we first examine the relationship between Exodus 24 and The Transfiguration and then turn to the words and phrases from other Old Testament stories.

Words, Phrases and Details from Exodus 24

Let me begin by citing details that are common to both stories. It is noteworthy that most of these details function in a similar manner. For example, both Mark and Exodus use the detail 'six days'. Moses waited on Sinai for six days (Exod. 24.16), and 'after six days' Jesus led Peter, James, and John up the mount (Mk 9.2). In both the six days precede the encounter with God.

Another detail is the three witnesses. Peter and James and John correspond to Aaron, Nadab, and Abihu (Exod. 24.1). In both stories they see what happened but participate only as witnesses. In both stories the voice of God comes out of a cloud (Exod. 24.16, Mk 9.7) and the participants are covered by that cloud.

Two details which may be the same, but function differently, are Moses and the booths/sanctuary. While Moses appears in both stories, he plays different roles. In the Sinai story he is the primary human actor. In The Transfiguration he is subordinate to Jesus and in 9.4 even to Elijah. In Mk 9.5 Peter says, 'let us make three booths', apparently referring to the feast of Succoth (Lev. 23.43). On the top of Sinai in Exod. 25.8 God says, 'And let them make me a sanctuary' (the same Greek word), and then in Exodus 26 and 27 God gives detailed directions for the sanctuary.

In addition to the above details, the two narratives share many significant words. Of course, the words for 'six days', 'Moses', 'make', 'booths/sanctuary', 'cloud', and the preposition 'out of' are the same.

The words for 'only/alone' and 'saw' are common. In Mk 9.8 the witnesses 'saw' Jesus 'only', whereas in Exod. 24.10 'they saw the God of Israel', and Moses 'alone' comes near the Lord (24.2). In Exod. 20.18 the people 'feared' the theophany on Sinai and in Mk 9.6 the disciples were 'afraid'. The LXX uses the verb while Mark uses the cognate adjective plus a preposition for emphasis.

Most significant of all are three words, *hapax legomena* found in Mark, but also found in Exodus 24 and 25. They are 'beheld/appeared' (in Mk 9.4 and Exod. 24.11), 'led' (Mk 9.2), and 'booths'. On Sinai they 'beheld God': in Mark, Elijah with Moses 'appeared'. After a similar discussion of the relationship of The Transfiguration and Exodus 24 Bruce Chilton writes:

> At the level of tradition and redaction, it is beyond reasonable doubt that the Transfiguration is fundamentally a visionary representation of the Sinai motif of Exod. 24.[20]

Words from Other Old Testament Stories

In addition to Exodus 24, words from other Old Testament stories are found in the narrative of The Transfiguration. Deut. 18.15 is the probable source of the words 'listen to him' that the voice directs to the witnesses. The Greek words are the same. Further, the eschatological significance of Moses is probably derived from this passage. Also, another story about Moses may be involved here. According to many interpreters, the story of the shining of Moses' face after 'talking with God' (Exod. 34.29-35) lies behind Jesus' transfiguration and his glistening white garments. Significantly, Paul uses the same Greek word for 'transfigured' while telling the story of the shining of Moses' face in 2 Cor. 3.7-18. Here the word is used in an eschatological sense, although Paul applies it to believers rather than to Jesus. Another word in Mark's account points to this story: in 9.4 'Elijah and Moses. . . were talking to Jesus'. This word, which occurs only here in Mark's Gospel, is also found in Exod. 34.35 in describing Moses' talking to God. In Exod. 34.29-34 the root (*laleo*) without the preposition is found six times; the summary statement in verse 35—as in Mark—contains the preposition. There, too, the reaction of the people of Israel to Moses' shining face is 'fear'. Thus two stories about Moses, both associated with Mt Sinai and both interpreted eschatologically, were attracted to the literary archetype.

20. Chilton, 'The Transfiguration', p. 119.

Like Moses, Elijah, too, encountered God on Mt Sinai. Elijah also figured prominently in the eschatological expectations of first-century Judaism.[21] According to Malachi 3 and 4, Elijah will be the 'messenger' of 'the great and terrible day of the Lord' (Mal. 4.5). His appearance in The Transfiguration signals that the end-time has arrived. Indeed, his appearance 'fits' the eschatological and apocalyptic interpretation of Exodus 24.

Even Peter's suggestion to make three booths 'fits' the eschatological thrust of the narrative. The later prophet Zechariah predicted that the rule of God would be demonstrated during the feast of booths or Succoth: 'Then every one that survives of all the nations that have come against Jerusalem shall go up year after year to worship the King, the Lord of hosts, and to keep the feast of booths' (Zech. 14.16).[22]

Perhaps the most controversial words from Scripture are those spoken by a voice from the cloud: 'This is my beloved Son. . . ' Most interpreters argue that these words, like those at the Baptism, are quoted from Ps. 2.7 and designate the messiah. On the other hand, Joseph Fitzmyer argues that the words 'beloved Son' are 'a title that is pre-Pauline and has connotations other than messiah'.[23] Elsewhere I have argued that the words 'beloved Son' are words spoken by another voice from heaven recorded in Gen. 22.2, 12, and 16.[24] The presence of 'beloved Son' in Genesis 22, the absence of the word 'beloved' in the LXX of Ps. 2.7, the inappropriateness of the term 'beloved' as a description for the Messiah, and the uncertain date of the Targum which might account for the term—these four points support the thesis that the voice from the clouds is quoting Genesis 22.

If the above survey is correct, I have accounted for most of the words quoted from Scripture and perhaps all of the Old Testament stories from which they were quoted. Let me review the use of Scripture in the narrative of The Transfiguration.

In several ways The Transfiguration is both like and unlike The Temptation. Unlike The Temptation, this narrative does not contain a quotation from the Old Testament, unless the words 'beloved Son' and

21. Kee, 'The Transfiguration', p. 146.

22. Kee, 'The Transfiguration', p. 147. Kee's summary of the scholarship concerning booths is very helpful.

23. J. Fitzmyer, *The Gospel according to Luke* (AB, 28; Garden City, NY: Doubleday, 1981), p. 793.

24. Stegner, *Narrative Theology*, pp. 17-20.

'listen to him' be regarded as such. Whereas typology largely determined the use of Scripture in The Temptation, here only the words that allude to Isaac, to the prophet-like Moses, and to the feast of booths approach typology. The use of Scripture in The Transfiguration is determined primarily by its being modeled upon one Old Testament passage—Exodus 24—as a literary archetype.

Both narratives are alike in the extensive use of quoted words from Old Testament stories. The Transfiguration alludes to five other Old Testament stories in addition to the literary archetype, if my research is correct. Interestingly enough, The Temptation contains quotations about three Old Testament stories, from one Psalm, and words allude to two stories about Moses. Hence, each story contains references to six Old Testament passages in addition to its primary thrust about Jesus. This is certainly an extensive use of Scripture within the compass of such brief narratives. There may also be a hint of numerology in that each narrative refers to six Old Testament passages as part of its primary message about Jesus.

Heretofore, the focus has been on the mechanics of the Jewish Christian use of Scripture; now it is on the theological message that this narrative sets forth. Again we find that Jewish Christians were preoccupied with Christology and articulated that Christology in terms of their background and Scripture. In addition, apologetic and polemical interests seem to be present.

The Use of Scripture and its Theological Message

If Sabbé and Kee are correct and the climax of the narrative is found in the words of the voice out of the cloud, the central christological thrust of the passage is found in the words: 'This is my beloved Son; listen to him'. However, what freight or meaning did the title 'beloved Son' convey for Jewish Christians? Fitzmyer seems to be on the right track in saying: 'Here the Synoptic tradition has made use of a title that is pre-Pauline and has connotations other than messiah'.[25] I have previously shown that the voice is quoting Genesis 22 rather than Ps. 2.7. Accordingly, the passage is citing an Isaac/Jesus typology. As Isaac was the beloved son of Abraham, so Jesus is the beloved Son of God. Also, in Jewish Christian ears the the words 'beloved Son' possibly

---

25. Fitzmyer, *Luke*, p. 793. In this regard the work of Geza Vermes is extremely important. See G. Vermes, *Jesus the Jew* (New York: Macmillan, 1973), pp. 192-213.

echoed Jesus' prayer life (Abba) and consciousness of an intimate relationship to God.

In addition, the title 'beloved Son' is partially defined by the context
in which it is set. In the previous narrative, the title 'Son of God'
depicted one whose obedience to God enabled him to overcome the
devil and, consequently, demonstrate his Sonship. Here, the Son of God
is pictured in another role. In form, the narrative is an apocalyptic
vision. In its apocalyptic re-interpretation, Sinai is the place where the
future is revealed. In this scene the Father assigns to the Son the role
of 'spokesman for the end-time' by telling the audience to 'listen to
him'. In his discussion of the final phrase 'listen to him', Kee wrote:
'The Son of God, in this proleptic vision of Jesus' eschatological vindication, is God's spokesman for the end-time'.[26]

The interpretation that Jesus 'is God's spokesman for the end-time'
admittedly differs from the more traditional view of this narrative.
According to the traditional view, The Transfiguration previews Jesus'
second coming. While these two interpretations are not far apart, the
narrative probably does not depict two different scenes from the eschatological drama, given its literary unity. Which view is correct? The
words of the narrative do not favor the traditional view. Note the
absence of words and phrases such as 'Son of Man', 'comes in glory',
'with the holy angels' (Mk 8.38b). Such words and phrases are usually
associated with the second coming. Further, the words 'This is my
beloved Son' and 'listen to him' do not picture the second coming of
Jesus; rather, they point to the authority of his words.

Indeed, the picture of Jesus as 'spokesman for the end-time' is closer
to another Jewish Christian picture of the Son's eschatological authority
than that of the Parousia. In Mt. 7.21-23 Jesus testifies on behalf of his
followers in the last judgment: 'Not everyone who says to me, "Lord,
Lord", shall enter the kingdom of heaven. . . ' (7.21). The Transfiguration emphasizes the authority of Jesus' words and the Matthean scene
pictures Jesus as advocate.[27]

A secondary thrust of the words 'listen to him' is probably polemical.
In Deut. 18.15 Moses speaks these same words to the people con-

---

26. H. Kee, *Community of the New Age: Studies in Mark's Gospel* (Philadelphia:
Westminster Press, 1977), p. 123.

27. H.D. Betz, *Essays on the Sermon on the Mount* (Philadelphia: Fortress Press,
1985), pp. 151-54. Betz finds that Matthew redacted an early Jewish Christian source
in composing his Sermon on the Mount.

cerning the prophet like himself whom God will raise up in the latter days. In this narrative the function of the prophet-like Moses has been given to the Son. This elimination of the role of the prophet-like Moses in the eschatological drama, together with the subordination of Moses to Jesus in the rest of the narrative, probably reflects a theological purpose of early Jewish Christianity. We see the same subordination of Moses to the Son both in 2 Cor. 3.7-14 and in Heb. 3.1-6, where Jesus is greater than Moses just as a 'son' is greater than a 'servant'.

In addition to serving a christological function, a polemical function, and a validating function, this narrative probably also served an apologetic function. The century in which Jesus lived was a time of heightened eschatological expectations. In this narrative one aspect of the end itself is depicted. By gathering together and exploiting the common symbols/expectations of the end-time—Mt Sinai, Elijah, the prophet-like Moses, the Feast of Booths—the story would appeal to the hopes not only of Jewish Christians, but also of the wider Jewish audience.

The Use of Scripture and Early Jewish Christianity

The use of Scripture in these two narratives not only reveals the theological reflections of Jewish Christians, but also reveals something about the hopes and life-styles of these same people. For example, if these two narratives are typical, they show that early Jewish Christians understood themselves to be an eschatological community-in-waiting. In The Temptation, Jesus' obedience in some sense broke the power of the devil and inaugurated the time of deliverance. In The Transfiguration a scene from the very end itself is pictured. This same scene points Jewish Christians to their not-too-distant future destiny. We can only imagine the excitement such a narrative engendered.

As in The Temptation, the primary types and stories depicting the end-time come from the Exodus/Sinai/Wilderness cycle of stories. Yet, The Transfiguration reflects a broader sampling of types and stories than the first narrative. Isaac, Elijah, the Feast of Booths supplement the primary emphasis upon Mt Sinai and Moses.

This story also points us to one aspect of the spirituality of early Jewish Christianity. The narrative is an apocalyptic vision in form. Certainly, a literary form reveals something about the people who use it. Let us remember that not only Jesus and Paul, but also Peter and Stephen beheld visions. Visions were an integral part of the apocalyptic mindset and milieu of Jewish Christianity. Perhaps visions were one form of listening to the Son.

While most modern biblical scholars tend to regard this narrative as a conscious literary creation—a kind of scissors and paste creation of an ancient editor—this modern view does not 'fit' the ancient milieu so well as the minority report. Accordingly, the narrative is the result of an actual vision.[28]

28. C. Rowland, 'The Open Heavens', p. 368, and esp. n. 47. Rowland posits Peter as the original recipient of the vision.

THE WOMAN WITH A BLOOD-FLOW (MARK 5.24-34) REVISITED: MENSTRUAL LAWS AND JEWISH CULTURE IN CHRISTIAN FEMINIST HERMENEUTICS

Charlotte Fonrobert

In the third century the anonymous Christian author of the *Didascalia Apostolorum*[1] in Syria attempts to persuade the newly converted, formerly Jewish women in his community to abolish their observance of menstrual separation from prayer, eucharist and study. The document is unique in the cultural history of Christianity and Judaism in that it provides us with an extended and elaborate argument of the women *on behalf of* their practice of menstrual separation which they maintain against the objection of the author of the document.[2] Hence, he summons his power of authority and persuasion against the practice of these women. As one of his arguments he introduces the story of the woman with a blood-flow of twelve years who is healed by Jesus (Mk 5.24-34 and parr.). Addressing the husbands of the women in his community the *Didascalia* states:

> And again you shall not separate those (women) who have their period.
> For she also who had the flow of blood when she touched the border of

---

1. For a discussion of the dating of the document, see the introduction of A. Vööbus (1979) to his translation, which is used for this essay, as well as R.H. Connolly's translation (1929) and G. Strecker's extensive analysis (1971: 244). Of the Greek original only remnants are preserved, primarily in the Apostolic Constitutions, a fourth-century compilation of ecclesiastic rules (Vööbus 1979: 23; Connolly 1929: xi). Two early translations of the work exist. The Syriac translation on which Vööbus relies for his English rendition, stems from the fourth century, and is deemed to be older than the Latin translation (Vööbus: 28 and Connolly: xvii). The Latin text has been edited by E. Tidner (1963). For important passages I have compared both the Syriac and the Latin version of the text.

2. Though the *Didascalia* is written presumably by a male author, it is possible to reconstruct the woman's argument by analyzing the rhetorics of the text, as I argue in my dissertation.

our Savior's cloak, was not censured but was even esteemed worthy for
the forgiveness of all her sins. And when (your wives) have those issues
which are according to nature, take care, as is right, that you cleave to them,
for you know that they are your members (*Vööbus* 1979: 244).

In this use of the story which appears in all three Synoptic Gospels,
the author of the *Didascalia* advances an argument which bears remarkable resemblance to some recent Christian feminist interpretations of
the same Gospel story. The concurrence of those feminist interpretations with the argument of the *Didascalia*'s author who did not have
liberatory goals in mind compels me to consider the polemics of some
of the recent interpretations of this Gospel story.

The Study of the Woman with a Blood-Flow of Twelve Years

Of the three versions of the story (Mk 5.25-34; Mt. 9.20-22; Lk. 8.42-
48), Mark's is the most elaborate, of which Matthew presents a radical
abbreviation,[3] while Luke remains closer to the *Vorlage* of Mark. All
three start out with the fact that the woman had a flow of blood for
twelve years. According to Mark and some manuscripts of Luke she
had spent all she had on doctors and yet none of them could heal her.[4]
According to all three she comes to Jesus from behind to touch his garment, for—according to Mark and Matthew—she tells herself that if
she can only touch his garment she will be made well.[5] She is instantly

---

3. Jesus and the woman seem to be alone: both the crowds and the disciples
disappear from the narrative stage. Matthew leaves out Mark's commentaries on the
narrative development (Theissen 1974: 137).

4. Mk 5.26: καὶ πολλὰ παθοῦσα ὑπὸ πολλῶν ἰατρῶν καὶ δαπανήσασα
τὰ παρ' αὐτῆς πάντα καὶ μηδὲν ὠφεληθεῖσα ἀλλὰ μᾶλλον εἰς τὸ χεῖρον
ἐλθοῦσα—'She had endured much under many physicians, and had spent all that she
had; and she was no better, but rather grew worse' (NRSV). Lk. 8.43: [ἰατροῖς
προσαναλώσασα ὅλον τὸν βίον] οὐκ ἴσχυσεν ἀπ' οὐδενὸς θεραπευθῆναι
'[and though she had spent all she had on physicians], no one could cure her' (NRSV).

5. Mk 5.28: ἐὰν ἄψωμαι κᾶν τῶν ἱματίων αὐτοῦ σωθήσομαι—'If I but
touch his cloak, I will be made well'. Mt. 9.21 ἐὰν μόνον ἄψωμαι τοῦ ἱματίου
αὐτοῦ σωθήσομαι—'If I only touch his cloak I will be made well'. On the meaning
of σωθήσομαι as getting well in the physical as well as the spiritual sense in the
Synoptic Gospels see G. Fohrer in *TDNT* (1979: 7), Luke and Matthew further
specify the part of Jesus' garment which the woman touches, that is ἥψατο τοῦ
κρασπέδου τοῦ ἱματίου αὐτοῦ (Mt. 9.20; Lk. 8.44). The κράσπεδον can mean
the hem of his garment, but is used by LXX for the fringes which the Israelites are commanded to wear at the corner of their garments (Num. 15.38-39; Deut. 22.12). The

healed.[6] According to Mark and Luke, Jesus asks who touched him, because he feels that something has happened to him, that power has gone out from him.[7] The disciples disqualify the question, since in the midst of the crowd around them anybody might have touched him.[8] But Jesus glances upon the crowd. According to Mark and Luke she comes forward on her own, whereas according to Matthew he sees her. Both the former gospel writers emphasize her fear and trembling while she comes forward to tell her deed.[9] Jesus' answer is the same in all three gospels: θυγάτηρ, ἡ πίστις σου σέσωκέν σε—'daughter, your faith has made you well' (Mk 5.34; Lk. 8.48; Mt. 9.22).

The narrative has been dealt with in two recent monographs (Selvidge 1990; Trummer 1991), in numerous articles,[10] and, of course, in all the major New Testament commentaries series. Most of this literature discusses the Jewish milieu of the narrative. The story of the woman with a blood-flow becomes for New Testament scholars the occasion to reflect not just on this particular incident in which Jesus is said to heal

---

distinction is important only for those who use this narrative to make an argument with respect to how strictly Jesus followed Mosaic law. However, it has only minor relevance for the following reading.

6. Matthew puts the healing at the end of the story, after Jesus' pronouncement to the woman.

7. Lk. 8.46: ἥψατό μού τις ἐγὼ γὰρ ἔγνων δύναμιν ἐξεληλυθυῖαν ἀπ' ἐμοῦ—'Someone touched me; for I noticed that power had gone out from me' (NRSV).

8. Mk 5.31 καὶ ἔλεγον αὐτῷ οἱ μαθηταὶ αὐτοῦ βλέπεις τὸν ὄχλον συνθλίβοντά σε καὶ λέγεις τίς μου ἥψατο—'And his disciples said to him: You see the crowd pressing in on you; how can you say, "Who touched me?"' (NRSV). Lk. 8.45: εἶπεν ὁ Πέτρος (MSS: καὶ οἱ σὺν αὐτῷ) ἐπιστάτα οἱ ὄχλοι συνέχουσίν σε καὶ ἀποθλίβουσιν—'Peter (some manuscripts add: and those who were with him) said: Master, the crowds surround you and press in on you' (NRSV).

9. Mk 5.33: ἡ δὲ γυνὴ φοβηθεῖσα καὶ τρέμουσα, εἰδυῖα ὃ γέγονεν αὐτῇ—'But the woman, knowing what had happened to her, came in fear and trembling, fell down before him, and told him the whole truth'. Lk. 8.47: ἰδοῦσα δὲ ἡ γυνὴ ὅτι οὐκ ἔλαθεν, τρέμουσα ἦλθεν καὶ προσπεσοῦσα αὐτῷ δι' ἣν αἰτίαν ἥψατο αὐτοῦ ἀπήγγειλεν ἐνώπιον παντὸς τοῦ λαοῦ καὶ ὡς ἰάθη παραχρῆμα—'When the woman saw that she could not remain hidden, she came trembling; and falling down before him, she declared in the presence of all the people why she had touched him, and how she had been immediately healed' (NRSV).

10. The articles are too numerous to be listed here. For a survey, however, see the first chapter in Selvidge 1990. In addition to Selvidge's survey see also von Kellenbach's list of references (1993: 112), mostly to West German Christian feminist New Testament scholars.

a woman from her sickness, but on what some call 'jüdische Blutriten' (Jewish blood-rites) or 'jüdische Blutscheu' (Jewish fear of blood), others 'jüdische Kautelen mit dem Menstruationsblut' (Jewish precautionary anxieties about the blood of menstruation) and again others women's 'restrictive cultic roles in society' (Selvidge 1990: 83) and most often the 'menstrual taboo'. Such terms indicate, at best, the persisting lack of understanding with which New Testament scholars reconstruct the presumed Jewish milieu of the story.

Based on such reconstructions the narrative has become a 'banner for equality of women within church and society' (Selvidge 1990: 30) for many Christian feminists. Selvidge herself claims that 'this story was written to free early Christian women from the social bonds of *niddah*, "banishment"[11] during a woman's menstrual period' (1990: 30). However, one may argue that this approach falls right under what Daum and McCauley have called 'Jesus-was-a-feminist strategy' (quoted in von Kellenbach 1994: 30). Such a hermeneutic strategy and the implied anti-Judaism often running alongside it, has been extensively criticized from a feminist critical perspective by von Kellenbach in her recent book on *Anti-Judaism in Religious Feminist Writings*. She builds on the work of other feminist critics of feminist readings of New Testament literature. My intent here is not to condemn of anti-Judaism all those feminist New Testament scholars who are engaged in the work of retrieving the meaningfulness of New Testament literature or the work of Jesus as the central figure of the Christian religion for contemporary women.

Nonetheless, this narrative of Jesus' healing of the woman with a blood-flow turns out to be particularly difficult. Its interpretation by both feminist and non-feminist Christian New Testament scholars more often than not proves to be part of what von Kellenbach has described as 'the unself-conscious, small and seemingly innocent distortions of Judaism which add up and sustain more pernicious forms of prejudice'

11. This rendering of the Hebrew term with its sociological implications is not adequate. Rather, the biblical term niddah should be rendered as 'menstrual condition'. It can either be derived from the root n–d–h, 'to cast, hurl, throw' (Levine 1989: 97), or from the root n–d–h, 'to expel' (Milgrom 1991: 745). In both cases the verbal roots describe 'the physiological process of the flow of blood' (Levine 1989: 97) rather than the sociological process of banishing the woman. This rendering is strengthened by the medieval Jewish commentator Rashi who connects it to the root n–z–h 'to spatter' (*Rashi ad Num.* 19.9).

(1994: 13). For by passing a judgment on the suffering and oppression of the woman not only in this particular narrative, but by implication on Jewish traditions surrounding menstruation in general, and by making her the emblematic Jewish woman whom Jesus comes not only to heal but presumably also to liberate from the oppressive rituals of her culture, such hermeneutic approaches in New Testament scholarship also pass a judgment on Jewish women today, who choose to observe menstrual separation[12] as a part of living their Jewishly-defined lives. Such hermeneutic approaches, therefore, do the salvage work of their own religious tradition by turning Jewish women's lives in the first century (and by implication in our own century) into the negative background of this salvage work, or, as von Kellenbach has so aptly formulated: 'By equating the (Jewish) foes of Jesus with the (patriarchal) enemies of feminism, some scholars arrive at the conclusion that Christianity and feminism are fighting the same battle' (1994: 74).

The challenge then is to determine or at least to speculate how the story would be read from the position of a woman who is committed to the observation of menstrual separation as a meaningful part of her tradition, who regards this observation as part of what it means to live her life in relation to the biblical God. The challenge is to think how the women against whom the *Didascalia* writes would have read the story.[13] Such a perspective would refuse to regard the traditions surrounding menstruation exclusively as a patriarchal tool, invented by men in the service of patriarchy in order to keep women in a subordinate position, from which they need to be liberated.[14] To deliberately imagine the position of the *Didascalia*'s women then could show that most New Testament critics not only misrepresent the complex of *Niddah* in either the biblical text or in rabbinic literature, but it could also reveal that most Christian readings choose to exaggerate the general conditions of Jewish woman in the first century, in order to

12. It should be emphasized here, that a woman separates herself from marital intimacy only, and not from entering the synagogue or any other public activities.

13. From the *Didascalia* we do not learn the counter-argument of the women as in the preceding arguments. The citation of the story by the author against the women's practice of mentrual separation is the author's concluding remark on the issue.

14. How would those feminist critics who read this story as a narrative of women's liberation from their indigenous culture respond to Jewish women who insist on maintaining the observance of Niddah, or to the women of the *Didascalia*? Is not the only answer to them then that they have been co-opted into some outmoded patriarchal practice?

make the contrast between Jesus and his Jewish cultural environment all the more poignant. What, then, does the miracle as part of the canonical literature for Christians really achieve for Christian attitudes towards menstruation, and regulation of menstruation?

The Narrative as a Miracle Story

This story is one among the many in which Jesus appears as a miraculous healer. It underlines the contrast between Jesus' power to heal and that of regular doctors. In an early classic article, Rudolf and Martin Hengel treated this story in the context of attitudes toward medical treatment of illness in Jewish and Graeco–Roman culture. They choose as the literary context or cultural intertexts of this story the genre of miraculous healings (Weinreich 1909), which circulated in the world of late antiquity in various cultures, and elaborate on the typical narrative elements of such stories. Hence, they note that 'as far as the remarks on the extent of the suffering and the failure of the doctors are concerned, these are typical characteristics of miraculous healing stories in- and outside the New Testament' (1980: 346, my translation).[15] Similarly, the instantaneous healing at the end of the story represents 'a characteristic typical of miraculous healings' (1980: 347). As the Hengels point out, the narrative element of touch as a means of healing does not appear only in this story, but in others in the Synoptic Gospels, most significantly perhaps in Mark's summary of Jesus' fame as a healer:

> When [Jesus and the disciples] had crossed over, they came to land at Gennesaret and moored the boat. When they got out of the boat, people at once recognized him, and rushed about that whole region and began to bring the sick on mats to wherever they heard he was. And wherever he went, into villages or cities or farms, they laid the sick in the marketplaces, and begged him that they might touch even the fringe of his garment;[16]

---

15. Similarly, Gnilka (1986: 215): 'Gemäss dem hier vorliegenden Wunderverständnis, das hellenistisch konzipiert ist, kam das Wunder durch eine von Jesus ausgehende Kraft zustande'. Witherington takes the narrative elements that are typical for stories of miraculous healings in antiquity as an incentive to reflect on whether the story is merely a fictional account composed from such literary means, or whether it has a historical kernel. He insists on the latter, i.e. he accepts 'the nucleus of the story as revealing something of Jesus' views of women' (1986: 72), whereas the genre elements are merely Mark's embellishments of the historical account in front of him.

16. καὶ παρεκάλουν αὐτὸν ἵνα κἂν τοῦ κρασπέδου τοῦ ἱματίου αὐτοῦ

and all who touched it were healed (Mk 6.53-56; cf. also Mk 3.10, Lk. 6.19; see Hengel and Hengel 1980: 347).

In these other incidents, it is mostly people with undefined illnesses who are healed by touch. Hence the semantic weight of the woman's touching of Jesus' garment lies in the healing-power of his touch:[17] after the doctors have tried whatever medical treatments, a mere touch of Jesus suffices to heal her. As a miraculous healing, then, the story became popular and lived on in the popular religious imagination in later centuries.[18] At the beginning of the fourth century Eusebius describes in great detail in his *Ecclesiastical History* a bronze statue

---

ἅψωνται. The term for the fringe of his garment here—τοῦ κρασπέδου τοῦ ἱματίου—appears in the story of the woman with a blood-flow only in Matthew's and Luke's version, whereas Mark there only knows about her touching of his garment.

17. R. Hengel and M. Hengel again refer to O. Weinreich's analysis of ancient legends of healing, who observes that healing by touch is also a common element in hellenistic healing stories (1980: 347). New Testament scholars often make the point that the story intends to differentiate between some 'magic touch' and the woman's touching of Jesus as an act of faith. When Jesus tells the woman at the end of the story that 'your faith has made you well' he is understood as reinterpreting her act. Thus, the readers of the story are supposed to understand that it was not the touch in and by itself which healed the woman, but her faith (Guelich 1989: 299; Kertelge 1994: 115; Gnilka 1986: 1.213). Other New Testament commentaries also seem to recognize the magical element of a healing by touch, but here faith and magic are not competitors, but the trust in the healing magic of the touch enhances her faith (Schmithals 1979: 294).

18. One is tempted to say, against the readings of New Testament scholars especially from the form-critical school, who attempt to isolate the pre-Markan collection of stories about Jesus' miraculous healings part of which this story (Pesch 1976: 306). This collection can presumably be isolated by its ideology or Christology of representing Jesus as one thaumaturg or 'charismatic healer' among many roaming around in the world of late antiquity. Not surprisingly this collection of stories with its low Christology is then attributed to a Jewish–Christian milieu. But even this Jewish–Christian milieu from which the story is said to emerge is not slave to a concept of the 'man of God', however special he might be for '. . . mit einer solchen Konzeption unterwerfen sich die [judenchristlichen] Missionare des Urchristentums noch nicht der Konzeption von einem "göttlichen Menschen", solange klar bleibt, dass von diesem Jesus aus Nazaret die Rede ist, den Jahwe als seinen eschatologischen Boten gesandt und als Gekreuzigten in seiner Auerweckung gerechtfertigt hat' (Pesch 1976: 281). The integration of the pre-Markan collection of stories into the Gospel then finally resolves any doubts as to the appropriate Christology. Clearly, such an attribution is determined by a theological concern, one which attempts to ascertain the christological orthodoxy of New Testament literature.

erected as a memorial of her 'who had an issue of blood, and who, as we learn from the sacred Gospels, found at the hands of our Saviour relief from her affliction [τὴν γὰρ αἱμορροοῦσαν, ἣν ἐκ τῶν ἱερῶν εὐαγγελίων πρὸς τοῦ σωτῆρος ἡμῶν τοῦ πάθους ἀπαλλαγὴν εὕρασθαι μεμαθήκαμεν]' (Eusebius, *H.E.* 7.18 [LCL]). The statue, which Eusebius claims to have seen with his own eyes, apparently represented the scene of the woman's healing and stood in front of a house in Caeserea Philippi (in northern Palestine), which had been identified as the woman's house. Eusebius notes that the statue itself had certain healing powers by virtue of an herb which 'climbed up to the border of the double cloak of brass [μέχρι τοῦ κρασπέδου τῆς τοῦ χαλκοῦ διπλοΐδος], and acted as an antidote to all kinds of diseases' (Eusebius, *H.E.* 7.18 [LCL]; cf. Selvidge 1990: 20). Similarly, Athanasius relates in his *Vita St Antonii*, of the latter half of the fourth century, the story of a paralyzed young girl who had 'a terrible and very hideous disorder. For the runnings of her eyes, nose and ears fell to the ground and immediately became worms.' Not only that, she was also 'paralyzed and squinted'. Her parents 'having heard of monks going to Anthony, and believing on the Lord who healed the woman with the issue of blood [πιστεύσαντες τῷ Κυρίῳ τῷ τὴν αἱμορροοῦσαν θεραπεύσαντι], asked to be allowed, together, with the daughter to journey with them'. They allowed her to participate in the pilgrimage and the girl was eventually healed.[19]

The Narrative Read in the Context of Jewish Culture

However, in spite of the context in Mark's Gospel and the later wide reception of the story as a narrative of a miraculous healing which enhanced the powers of Jesus in folkloric imagination, the story comes to be read on the background of biblical impurity regulations and by extension also on the 'background' of the misnaic discourse of impurity. Indeed, the woman's sickness is identified mostly as what could be

19. PG XXVI: 925-28. The English translation of the *Life of Anthony*, from which I quote here, is published in *Nicene and Post-Nicene Fathers* (2nd series; ed. Ph. Schaff and H. Wace, 1891), IV: 211-12. For questions of identifying the date and the author of this work, see *Nicene and Post-Nicene Fathers*, IV: 188-93 (see also Selvidge 1990: 20). The story of how Constantine's daughter Constantina became a virgin begins with recounting how she was advised by St Agnes to believe in 'Jesus Christ, the son of God, who grants health', whereupon she was healed from her leprosy instantaneously (Salisbury 1991: 61).

called specifically a 'Jewish sickness'. It is not only a physical ailment from which she suffers, but she also suffers from the μάστιξ[20] of her own Jewish culture. Jesus then comes to heal her from both.

First of all she is identified unquestioningly by almost every commentator as a Jewish woman. By 'Jewish' woman then commentators mean a woman whose life is unquestionably defined and circumscribed by the biblical text on the one side, and the mishnaic text on the other. But even if the narrators indeed imagined her as a Jewish woman, one would still have to ask what kind of Jewish woman, since the Jewish community in first century Palestine turns out to be so vastly diverse. The biblical text on menstrual regulations, which is prescriptive and not descriptive, requires interpretation in order to be applied to the regulation of daily life. Hence, would she be a woman in whose community purity laws were more strictly or more leniently interpreted and observed? Be that as it may, the fact remains that the Gospel narrators leave her ethnic identity unspecified.[21] This keeps the possibility open that the woman's status of impurity according to the priestly regulation in Leviticus is of no interest to them, since they are primarily concerned about the healing miracle.

Secondly, her sickness is identified as a 'Jewish sickness' by choosing Leviticus 15 as Mark's (and pars.) inter-text. Hence the woman is identified as a *zavah*, or a woman with an irregular or extended blood-flow. The connection with Leviticus 15 is established primarily linguistically.[22] The linguistic similarity between the description of the woman's sickness in the Gospels and the Septuagint appears to identify Leviticus 15 as an intertext which the narrators, and if not the nar-

20. The term that Mark employs to describe the woman's affliction (Mk 5.29). The term can be used both in a physical and in a spiritual sense, and would best be rendered as affliction in English.

21. It is this narrative openness that facilitates those allegorical interpretations in early church literature which take this woman as a type of Gentile and take her to be representative of the Gentile church such as Jerome and Augustine. Selvidge comments on Jerome's allegorization that 'as a type of gentile, the heroine lost her identity. Jerome ignored the meaning and significance of this passage for Mark's earliest auditing and reading publics' (1990: 18). However, in this judgment she ignores the fact that the story does precisely allow for such a reading, because the woman with the blood-flow remains ethnically undefined.

22. In this Septuagint rendition of Lev. 15.25 the woman with a discharge of blood for many days is described as γυνὴ ἐὰν δὲ ἐν τῇ ῥέῃ ῥύσει αἵματος ἡμέρας πλείους. Cf. Mk 5.25 γυνὴ οὖσα ἐν ῥύσει αἵματος δώδεκα ἔτη (= Lk. 8.43).

rators of the pre-literary story, so at least writers of the Gospels, had in mind. Commentators point out the suffering of the woman from her 'Jewish illness'.[23] But even here it is important to keep in mind that this linguistic connection is not a necessary one,[24] for as M. Hengel has pointed out, 'the verb αἱμοῤῥεῖν exists already in the hippocratic corpus' (Hengel and Hengel 1980: 346 n. 35) and is a component of medical vocabulary.

However, most important to this reading of the story as a repudiation of Jewish traditions surrounding menstruation, is the narrative moment of the woman's touching of Jesus. Identified as a *zavah*, she is bracketed between Leviticus 15 on the on hand, and mishnaic law, on the other. At the one end of the spectrum stands Leviticus 15, according to which supposedly the *zavah* transfers the status of impurity by touch. Surprisingly enough, however, none of the New Testament commentators take note of the fact that as far as the *zavah* is concerned, the masoretic text does not include an explication that she communicates impurity by *being touched*, as does the menstrous woman (Lev. 15.19). Nor is there any mention that either she or the menstruant woman communicate impurity by *touching anyone*. The difference between *being touched and touching* is more significant than it seems. The menstruant woman does transfer impurity by being touched (Lev. 15.19). However, Leviticus does not mention that she communicates impurity by touching. Milgrom comments that this 'can only mean that in fact her hands do not transmit impurity. The consequence is that she is not banished but remains at home. Neither is she isolated from her family. She is free to prepare their meals and perform household chores. They, in

23. 'Die Krankheit selbst war in dem vorliegenden Falle für eine Jüdin deshalb so schwerwiegend, weil sie in den Zustand ständiger kultischer Unreinheit versetzte, das Betreten des Heiligtums, die Teilnahme an religiösen Festen, z.b. dem Passahfest, unmöglich machte, ja überhaupt, ähnlich dem Aussatz, aus der menschlichen Gesellschaft ausschloss' (Hengel and Hengel 1980: 346-47; cited by Pesch 1976: 301; Guelich 1989: 296).

24. Selvidge's method notwithstanding. She argues that the predominance of the term for blood flow in Leviticus indicates that 'the Greek translation of Leviticus seems to exhibit a preference of the vocabulary used in Mark to describe or diagnose the condition of the woman in Mark 5:24-34' (1990: 48). Her point that of the seventeen times ῥύσις is used in the LXX, fifteen are found only in Lev' (1990: 48) seems to work with the assumption that intertextual or linguistic connections are quantifiable. More convincing is her point that the term for 'the source of her blood' (Mk 5.29) is found in LXX only in Leviticus, that is Lev. 12.7 and Lev. 20.18.

turn, merely have to avoid lying in her bed, sitting in her chair, and touching her' (1991: 936). This could all the more apply to the *zavah*, who could even be touched, according to the masoretic text. The *zavah*, then, communicates impurity only indirectly: if somebody touches her bedding or anything on which she sat, 'whoever touches *them* shall be impure; he shall launder his clothes, bathe in water, and remain impure until the evening' (Lev. 15.27). Nonetheless, two manuscripts and the Septuagint translation of Lev. 15.27 read: 'whoever touches *her*, shall launder his clothes. . . ' (Milgrom 1991: 943).[25] Only if we accept with Milgrom the latter reading, the *zavah*—similar to the *zav*, that is, the man with an irregular discharge—communicates impurity by *being touched* (Milgrom 1991: 943).

However, at the other end of the spectrum stands the mishnaic ruling in *m. Zab.* 5.1: 'He who touches a *zav*, or he whom a *zav* touches, transfers a status of impurity to food, drink and vessels that (can be purified by immersion)'.[26] *M. Zab.* 5.1 extends Leviticus 15, for according to the biblical text, as we have just seen, only the person who touches (somebody in the status of impurity) becomes impure, but presumably not the one who is touched (by somebody in the status of impurity). As a mishnaic *zavah* the woman in our story is then compared to the status of a leprous person (Schottroff 1990: 113; Schmithals 1979: 293). Selvidge goes as far as to write that 'the woman in the miracle story was beaten because of her physical ailment. She was taboo to all. She could have no intimate relations with men,[27] nor could she, as a responsible Jewess, with a good conscience, be milling about among the masses' (1990: 88).[28]

Consequently, the presumption is often that the woman, deliberately

25. Milgrom prefers the former reading. The difference of the Hebrew versions lies between the use of either בה or בם.

26. Ever since Billerbeck's collection of rabbinic sources as a 'background' for the Gospels, the reference to this passage has made its entry into the New Testament commentary literature (Gnilka 1986; Pesch 1976: 301). The problem of this treatment of mishnaic law, both in terms of historical methodology and cultural–political terms, is of course, an old one and will not be rehearsed here.

27. I am tempted to ask: Who says that she wanted to have intimate relations with men?

28. Compare also Trummer who writes that the woman 'hat überdies noch die besonderen Kautelen mit dem Menstruationsblut zu beachten, die sie fast völlig gesellschaftsunfähig machen, und das auf Dauer' (1991: 84).

or not, would have rendered Jesus impure (Selvidge 1990: 92; Luz 1989: 52; Mann 1986: 286). Or she touched Jesus only secretly, because she knew that she really should not touch Jesus, since a status of impurity would be transferred to him: 'Coming from the rear of the crowd, the appropriate place for the defiled, she risked defiling others by approaching and deliberately touching Jesus' clothes' (Guelich 1989: 297; see also Witherington 1984: 73; Kertelge 1994: 58).[29] Further, her fear and trembling at the end of the story is often explained as being caused by her guilt-complex about having rendered Jesus deliberately impure (Kertelge 1994: 59) or revealing 'her awareness of having violated a taboo' (Ruether 1975: 65).[30]

29. Trummer even argues that she does not merely render Jesus impure, but that she makes him guilty: 'Jedenfalls mutet diese Frau mit ihren Blutungen Jesus sehr viel zu, zu viel sogar, denn sie setzt auch ihn der Gefahr ihrer Unreinheit aus, macht auch ihn mitschuldig, selbst schuldig' (1991: 85). This infection of guilt he explains based on Lev. 5.3 (1991: 121). However, he completely misunderstands the verse. For the verse sets up a case in which someone 'who touches human impurity [such as the *niddah* or a *zavah*]—any such impurity whereby one becomes impure—and, though he has known it the fact escapes him but (thereafter) he feels guilt' as a consequence of which such a person would have to bring an offering of purification to the Temple (Lev. 5.6). In his careful analysis of this text Milgrom explains this case as referring to someone who 'has contracted impurity knowingly, even deliberately, but has forgotten to purify himself within the prescribed time limits. If he subsequently remembers and feels guilt, he must confess his wrong and expiate it by a purification offering' (1991: 313). Thus Trummer is wrong when he confuses the incurrence of a status of impurity with the rhetorics of transgression or guilt. In our story, Jesus would only be obligated to bring a sacrifice if he neglected to purify himself, of which we learn nothing in the story. But he certainly does not incur any form of guilt merely by being touched.

30. Many New Testament scholars, however, reject the interpretation of the woman's fear as a sign of her guilt-complex. Theissen considers that she might have been afraid that her act could be misinterpreted as either the intent to rid herself of her sickness by transferring it to Jesus, or as some love magic (1974: 137; cited by Pesch 1976: 304 and Gnilka 1986: 216), which seems an unlikely interpretation to me. Guelich rejects all these suggestions and proposes that 'this description expresses her reaction of awe at what had happened to her' (1989: 298; also Schmithals 1979: 294). Most convincing I find Trummer's reference to the only other use of this pairing of fear and trembling at the end of Mark's Gospel where it describes the woman's reaction when they are told that Jesus has risen from the dead (Mk 16.8). Thus, fear is in the gospel of Mark always the reaction when the significance of Jesus is recognized. Hence, Trummer argues, 'die erfolgte Heilung bringt der Frau

Finally, and perhaps most significantly, Jesus is regarded as having abolished the levitical impurity regulations concerning women by not only disregarding the fact that she committed the dreadful act of touching him, but by even praising her for her faith: 'Dass die Frau weder abgewiesen noch getadelt, sondern wegen ihres Glauben anerkannt und geheilt wird, macht deutlich, dass hier auch ein Stück der jüdischen Blutscheu überwunden ist' (Sand 1985: 201).[31]

However, even if we accept Leviticus 15 and by extension its mishnaic elaboration as the intertexts of the story, and even if we assume that the woman is Jewish, what is disregarded in all these speculations is the fact that the woman does not commit a transgression by touching Jesus, neither according to the priestly writings nor according to mishnaic law. Thus Jacob Milgrom points out that in Leviticus 15 'there is no prohibition barring the menstruant from touching anyone' (1991: 936). That is, neither Leviticus 15, nor the mishnaic expansion of biblical im/purity regulations, ever prohibit to touch, and thus do not treat the event of touch as a transgression, as opposed to, for example, forbidden sexual relationships. The latter, including the sexual relationship with a menstruous woman, are indeed a matter of transgression, whereas the biblical and rabbinic discourse of im/purity is not a punitive discourse.[32] If it should so happen that someone touches, and that might

zum Bewusstsein, dass sie sich in der Person Jesu nicht getäuscht hatte, sondern dass sie sogar noch Grösseres erwarten konnte, als sie vermuten durfte' (1991: 98).

31. Selvidge writes, 'The woman had touched him. According to Jewish tradition, she had potentially defiled him. "He shows no indignation at the ritual defilement, but ignores it; for the woman is seen not as an unclean object but as a human being suffering... He does not attack the demands of the cult worship directly, he merely ignores them as irrelevant when they distract from the essential relationship between man and God"' (1990: 92). The quotation stems from I. Breannan, 'Women in the Gospels' (*New Blackfriars* 52 [1971], p. 296). This is the center of Selvidge's argument that this story was written to free early Christian women from the social bonds of *niddah*. Similarly Ruether who contends that 'Jesus' reaction to the woman with a hemorrhage shows his deliberate discarding of this taboo' (1975: 65).

32. Professor D. Schmidt kindly called my attention to P. Fredriksen's recent discussion of M. Borg's work on the historical Jesus. Her criticism in her article, 'Did Jesus Oppose the Purity Laws?' (1995a: 19-47), underlines my current claim here, though she does not specifically deal with the story of the woman with a blood-flow. She refutes Borg's contention that Jesus imagines 'a community shaped not by ethos and politics of purity, but by the ethos and politics of compassion' (quoted in 1995a: 20). Frederiksen notes that 'the opposition between compassion (Jesus) and purity (first-century Judaism, especially as associated with Jerusalem) is a leitmotif

even be quite often, then the person who touches the *zav/ah* or the woman with a regular menstrual blood-flow (or is touched by such a person in the mishnaic view), is simply also rendered impure until the evening of that day.

The woman in the Gospel story, therefore, never commits a transgression when she touches Jesus' garment. Neither biblical nor mishnaic law consider the case of a person in a status of impurity who deliberately touches somebody else. Hence, rabbinically speaking, the woman of our narrative would only have committed a transgression had she done anything that might lead to or initiate sexual contact, which is clearly not the point of the story.[33] But otherwise, she does not commit an act of transgression. Further, as far as I know, there is not a single *case story* in talmudic literature of someone in the status of impurity touching somebody else.[34] Thus, in spite of the *halakhic theory* expressed in *m. Zab.* 5.1 the concern about touch remains at the very most subdued in rabbinic literature. Selvidge's contention that 'a responsible Jewess with a good conscience' would not have been milling around in

of Borg's scholarship' (1995a: 45 n. 1). Borg's effort, while to be commended for its effort to present a Jesus in his Jewish cultural environment, thus repeats the majority of New Testament scholarship with respect to our story, i.e., the confusion of impurity with sin or transgression. Refuting Borg's confusion of impurity with social distinctions Frederiksen then emphasizes that first, impurity is not sin, secondly, it does not correspond to social class, and thirdly, that it is gender-blind (1995a: 23), the latter meaning that both men and women can contract a status of impurity vis à vis the Temple.

33. Gnilka's commentary that the woman's fear and trembling is caused by the thought that her act might have been misunderstood as wanting to approach or come on to Jesus as a beautiful woman (1986: 216), has no basis in the story whatsoever. Where does the presumed beauty of the woman come from all of a sudden, if not from the commentator's imagination?

34. There are several factors that account for that. First of all, of course, the fact that for most of the *Order of Purities*, including the mishnaic tractate that deals with the impurity of irregular discharges, we do not have a Talmud. Secondly, the main concern of the tractate for which we do have a Talmud, i.e., Tractate Niddah, is about the biblical prohibition of sexual contact between a woman in her menstruation and her husband. Here the transfer of impurity by touch (of something and not of somebody) comes into play only concerning the priestly share of food, which the menstruant woman, as well as other people in a status of impurity, would invalidate. The third factor is, of course, that in post-Temple times the transfer of the status of impurity becomes irrelevant.

the masses[35] is, therefore, unfounded aside from having slightly polemic undertones. For, again, there is no indication that rabbinic literature expresses any concern about milling around in the masses, for either those who are in the status of impurity because of a regular or irregular discharge, or those who are concerned about remaining in the status of purity. We might have expected such an indication had there been hermeneutic or practical concern about being touched by a person with such an invisible impurity.

The case for impurity according to either biblical or rabbinic law as a primary concern of the narrative cannot therefore be consistently argued. The attempt to read this story as abrogation of biblical traditions concerning menstruation and irregular discharges of blood remains unsuccessful. The Jesus of this narrative appears as someone who has the powers to heal a woman with a severe sickness, where others have failed. It is because of the open and unclear relationship of this narrative with the biblical text in Leviticus that Christian writers already in the early period can use the story for whatever purpose they want to use it for. Hence, the *Didascalia*, as the only text in early Christian literature that I am aware of, uses the story in a way similar to how contemporary Christian feminists have used it. Its author is, of course, not concerned about the liberation of the women converts from a Jewish background in his community from their old oppression. Rather, he attempts to persuade them to turn away completely from that which gave them meaning in their previous lives, in order to conform to his interpretation of what it means to be Christian.

At the same time, the same story could be used to achieve the complete opposite end. In the mid-third century, at approximately the same time in which the *Didascalia* was composed in Syria, Dionysius, the bishop of Alexandria and a student of Origen, wrote in response to the inquiry of Basilides, a colleague in rank:

> The question concerning women in the time of their [menstrual] separation, whether it is proper for them when in such a condition to enter the house of God, I consider a superfluous inquiry. For I do not think, that, if they are believing and pious women, they will themselves be rash enough in

---

35. Ironically the very fact that she was milling around in the masses could also be read as an indication that (Jewish) women who were *zavot* could move around freely in the streets (von Kellenbach 1994: 62). I have already mentioned elsewhere that women with a regular menstruation were not subjected to ostracization or banishment from public life, except from the Temple, as long as it still stood.

such a condition either to approach the holy table or to touch the body and blood of the Lord. Certainly the woman who had the discharge of blood of twelve years' standing did not touch (the Lord) Himself, but only the hem of His garment, with a view to her cure (Kraemer 1988: 43).

Whereas the *Didascalia* tried to convince women in its community to partake in the Eucharist while they are menstruating, Dionysius attempts to keep them away from it, as well as from the altar and the church altogether. Again the woman with the twelve-year flow of blood is representative of any woman who has her menstruation. But now she becomes exemplary for barely having touched Jesus, since in fact she never touched Jesus himself, his body that is, and her touch is not really any touch at all. The priestly terminology and regulation of Leviticus has sunk into oblivion.[36] The rhetoric is a different one, and in a way a more misogynist one, because he is no longer arguing about the validity or abolishment of a tradition, be it a legal or practical tradition. Rather, he seems to consider menstruation to be essentially and inherently forbidding, so much so that the very question about it should be regarded as superfluous, so much so that 'good' women, that is, pious women, would never even get such a horrendous idea as to partake in the Eucharist 'in such a condition'.

It is this discourse of menstrual repugnance which subsequently predominates in Christian legal literature[37] over and against such an

36. S. Cohen, however, argues that 'Dionysisus is transferring to Christianity the pollution categories of Leviticus 15', based on Dionysius' application of Temple terminology to the church, since the woman who is not 'pure in both soul and body shall be prevented from approaching the holy and the holy of holies' (1991: 288). Nonetheless, Dionysius does not reason that the menstruous woman should not do that because Leviticus 15 rules in that manner. They should not do so as 'pious and faithful' women. He might perhaps allude to concerns that stem from the traditions based on Leviticus 15, but he certainly treats them rather discriminately: 'as to those who are overtaken by an involuntary flux in the night-time, let such follow the testimony of their own conscience, and consider themselves as to whether they are doubtfully minded in this matter or not' (Kraemer 1988: 43). As far as the man and his 'impurity' is concerned, he should act according to his own conscience, whereas the woman and her 'impurity' are not given such a choice. Hence, his motivation to exclude the women from the Eucharist and from church must lie elsewhere than in his attachment to the regulations of Leviticus 15.

37. For the regulations concerning sexual behavior in general, and the prohibition of sexual relations during the wife's menstrual period in medieval Christian literature, see the comprehensive work of J. Bundage (1991). He discusses the origin of the prohibition, that is in the context of the penitential literature: 'This prohibition was based

argument as the *Didascalia* had advanced. That might seem to be logical, since the *Didascalia* reacted and responded to a merely local situation. Dionysius, on the other hand, responded to the question of a colleague, who wanted to know the Christian *principle* or ruling regarding menstruous women in their relationship to the Christian public. Nonetheless, the *Didascalia*'s argument would seem to be the more consistent one in a Christianity in which Pauline theology won the day. For if in Christ the 'law' as that which set the Israelites apart from other cultures was fulfilled and no longer the basis of that which made a Christian a Christian, then the regulations concerning menstruation should also have been abolished. Thus it seems that Dionysius's opinion persisted not because it seemed consistent. Rather, it persisted because Christian thought, by virtue of its 'westernization', that is, by its ever deepening permeation by Greek metaphysics and ontology, and its accompanying dualistic pattern which bred the contempt of the physical world, of the body, and in particular of the female body, could allow for such an 'inconsistency'.[38]

on the purity rules of the Mosaic law, perhaps augmented by a belief in the terrifying physical effects of contact with menstrual fluid described in the Natural History of the elder Pliny' (1991: 156). But Bundage here only speculates on the origins. An exception seems to be the opinion of one Huguccio at the end of the 12th century who considers the possibility of menstrual sex. Huguccio writes during a period when canon law began to come into its own, independent from theology. He notes that if the wife sought sexual intercourse during her menstruation, her husband could refuse, unless there was imminent danger that she might commit fornication (1991: 283).

38. In this I would argue in particular against those Christian feminist approaches which consider Dionysius's opinion to represent a revival of 'old Testament laws of purity' (Ruether 1975: 65), and hence blame the church's Jewish past for the separation of menstruous women from the Eucharist. Thus Leonard Swidler, who was one of the first scholars to write a monograph on *Women in Judaism* (1976) which serves as one of the main sources for many Christian feminists, unfamiliar with rabbinic literature, argued that 'Dionysius forbade Christian women from entering a church during their menstruation' because he held on 'to the Hebraic laws of ritual impurity, which Jesus rejected' (1979: 343). Again, here I wish to follow von Kellenbach's brilliant critique of this 'Jewish-cultural-lag-theory', who contends that 'Christianity is depicted as a powerless and innocent victim of a sexist Jewish past rather than active and responsible shaper of a new patriarchal tradition. The power of sexism is underestimated; Christianity's choices, mistakes and failures are glossed over' (1994: 113).

Conclusion

My argument is not that the menstrual regulation and separation in and by itself is necessarily affirming of women, for we have seen that in the mouth of a Dionysius from Alexandria the prohibition to enter the church and partake in the Eucharist while menstruating becomes a tool of repression of women's embodied lives. Nor is the opposite position any more affirming of women, in which the *Didascalia* wants to get rid of any menstrual regulation that is being passed down from biblical tradition. Since the author of the *Didascalia* enacts a discursive repression of what women do with their bodies, his rhetorics in the end is almost equal to Dionysius's prohibiting discourse, only in the opposite direction. Hence, the position of contemporary feminists who want to argue that Jesus liberated (Jewish) women from their rootedness in biblical culture, and that the 'reintroduction' of a menstrual taboo by Dionysius in the third century represented a fall-back into patriarchy in Christianity, amounts to similar discursive repression of women's life-choices, who do not go the Christian path. Christian feminists who desire to reread the Gospels as meaningful for women today have to develop an awareness of their concurrence with early Christian anti-Jewish polemics. A feminist reading of the Gospels which is developed at the expense of women's life within the Jewish cultural context does not fulfill its promise of women's liberation.

BIBLIOGRAPHY

Bundage, J.
    1991   *Law, Sex, and Christian Society in Medieval Europe* (Chicago and London).
Cohen, S.
    1984–85   'Solomon and the Daughter of Pharaoh: Intermarrage, Conversion and the Impurity of Woman', *Journal of Ancient Near East Society* 16–17: 23-37.
    1991   'Menstruants and the Sacred in Judaism and Christianity', in S.B. Pomeroy (ed.), *Women's History and Ancient History* (Chapel Hill and London: University of North Carolina Press): 273-99.
Connolly, R.H.
    1929   *Didascalia Apostolorum: Syriac Version Translated and Accompanied by the Verona Latin Fragments* (Oxford: Clarendon Press).
Dinari, Y.
    1979–80   'Customs Relating to the Impurity of the Menstruant: Their Origin and Development', *Tarbiz* 49: 302-24 [Hebrew].

Frederiksen, P.
    1995a   'Did Jesus Oppose the Purity Laws?', *Biblical Review*, pp. 19-47.
    1995b   'What you See is What you Get: Context and Content in Current Research on the Historical Jesus', *TTod* 52.1: 75-98.

Gnilka, J.
    1986   *Das Matthäusevangelium I. Teil (1:1–13:58)* (HTKNT; Freiburg and Basel: Herder).

Guelich, R.A.
    1989   *Mark 1–8:26* (WBC, 34A; Dallas: Word Books).

Hengel, M., and R. Hengel
    1980   'Die Heilungen Jesu und medizinische Denken', in A. Suhl (ed.), *Der Wunderbegriff im Neuen Testament* (Darmstadt: Wissenschaftliche Buchgesellschaft [1959]): 338-74.

Kellenbach, K. von
    1994   *Anti-Judaism in Feminist Religious Writings* (Atlanta: Scholars Press).

Kertelge, K.
    1994   *Das Markusevangelium* (Die Neue Echter Bibel; Wurzburg: Echter Verlag).

Kraemer, R. (ed.)
    1988   *Maenads, Martyrs, Matrons, Monastics: A Sourcebook on Women's Religions in the Greco–Roman World* (Philadelphia: Fortress Press).

Levine, B.
    1989   *Leviticus* (JPS Commentary; Philadelphia and New York: Jewish Publication Society of America).

Luz, U.
    1989   *Das Evangelium nach Matthäus 8–17* (EKKNT; Gütersloh: Neukirchener Verlag).

Mann, C.S.
    1986   *Mark: A New Translation with Introduction and Commentary* (AB, 27; New York: Doubleday).

Milgrom, J.
    1986   'The Priestly Impurity System', in *Proceedings of the Ninth World Congress of Jewish Studies* (Jerusalem: World Union of Jewish Studies): 121-27.
    1991   *Leviticus 1–16: A New Translation with Introduction and Commentary* (AB; New York/London: Doubleday).

Pesch, R.
    1976   *Das Markusevangelium I. Teil: Einleitung und Kommentar zu Kapitel 1,1–8, 26* (HTKNT; Freiburg and Basel: Herder).

Ruether, R.R.
    1974   'Misogynism and Virginal Feminism in the Fathers of the Church', in R.R. Ruether (ed.), *Religion and Sexism* (New York: Simon & Schuster): 150-83.
    1975   *New Woman New Earth* (New York: Seabury Press).
    1979   'Mothers of the Church: Ascetic Women in the Later Patristic Age', in R.R. Ruether and E. McLaughlin (eds.), *Women of Spirit: Female Leadership in the Jewish and Christian Traditions* (New York: Simon & Schuster): 71-99.
    1990   'Women's Body and Blood: The Sacred and the Impure', in A. Joseph (ed.), *Through the Devil's Gateway: Women, Religion and Taboo* (London: SPCK): 7-22.

Salisbury, J.
1991   *Churchfathers, Independent Virgins* (London and New York: Verso).
Sand, A.
1985   *Das Evangelium nach Matthäus* (Regensburg: Verlag Friedrich Pustet).
Schmithals, W.
1979   *Das Evangelium nach Markus, Kapitel 1–9,1* (Ökumenischer Taschenbuch–
            Kommentar zum Neuen Testament 2.1; Gütersloh: Gütersloher Velagshaus/
            Gerd Mohn).
Schottroff, L.
1990   *Befreiungserfahrung: Studien zur Sozialgeschichte des Neuen Testaments*
            (TBü, 82; Munich: Chr. Kaiser Verlag).
Selvidge, M.
1990   *Woman, Cult and Miracle Recital: A Redactional Critical Investigation on
            Mark 5:24-34* (London and Toronto: Associated University Presses).
Strecker, G.
1971   'On the Problem of Jewish Christianity', Appendix, in W. Bauer (ed.),
            Orthodoxy and Heresy in Earliest Christianity (Philadelphia: Fortress
            Press): 241-85.
1988   'Judenchristentum', *TRE* 17: 310-25.
Swidler, L.
1976   *Women in Judaism: The Status of Women in Formative Judaism* (Metuchen:
            The Scarecrow Press).
1979   *Biblical Affirmations of Women* (Philadelphia: Fortress Press).
Theissen, G.
1974   *Urchristliche Wundergeschichten: Ein Beitrag zur formgeschichtlichen
            Erforschung der synoptischen Evangelien* (Gütersloh: Gerd Mohn).
Tidner, E.
1963   *Didascaliae Apostolorum Canonum Ecclesiasticorum Traditionis
            Apostolicae Versiones Latinae* (Berlin: Akademie Verlag).
Trummer, P.
1991   *Die blutende Frau: Wunderheilung im Neuen Testament* (Freiburg and
            Basel: Herder).
Vööbus, A.
1979   *The Didascalia Apostolorum in Syriac* (CSCO, 401-402, 407-408; 2 vols.;
            Louvain [with English translation]).
Weinreich, O.
1909   *Antike Heilungswunder: Untersuchungen zum Wunderglauben der
            Griechen und Romer* (Religionsgeschichtliche Versuche und Vorarbeiten;
            Giessen: Töpelmann).
Witherington, B.
1984   *Women in the Ministry of Jesus: A Study of Jesus' Attitudes to Women and
            their Roles as Reflected in his Earthly Life* (Cambridge: Cambridge
            University Press).
1988   *Women in the Earliest Church* (Cambridge: Cambridge University Press).
1990   *Women and the Genesis of Christianity* (Cambridge: Cambridge University
            Press).

THE ONE WHO COMES UNBINDING THE BLESSING OF JUDAH: MARK 11.1-10 AS A MIDRASH ON GENESIS 49.11, ZECHARIAH 9.9, AND PSALM 118.25-26

Deborah Krause

1. *Introduction*

Traditionally, Jesus' entry into Jerusalem is interpreted as the fulfillment of Zech. 9.9. He enacts the role of the victorious yet humble King approaching Jerusalem, riding on a colt. And the crowd enacts the role of rejoicing daughters of Jerusalem and Zion as they go before and follow behind acclaiming Jesus with words from Ps. 118.25-26. The whole event, to one degree or another, constitutes a prophetic enactment of Jesus' identity as the peaceful, Messiah–King.[1]

In this stream of interpretation, the story of the colt that precedes the entry in the Synoptic Gospels has received scant attention.[2] At the least it provides a scenario in which Jesus secures a ride for the enactment of Zech. 9.9,[3] and at the most it underscores the entry's prophetic

---

1. C.F.D. Moule, *The Gospel according to Mark* (Cambridge: Cambridge University Press, 1965), pp. 86-87. Citing a point made by G.A. Smith, *The Book of the Twelve Prophets* (1928), II, p. 456, that asses are used by high officials, but only for civil, not military duty, Moule concludes: 'Jesus seemed to his friends, as they recollected the scene, to have ridden into Jerusalem like that: as Messiah, as Deliverer, but as a peaceful one, not in the guise of a warrior. "I am Messiah" he had to say, "but not the warrior-Messiah whom you are looking for"', p. 87.

2. The form-critical assessment of the story of securing the colt focuses on Jesus' foreknowledge of events in Mk 11.2-3, and the fairy-tale motif that everything happened just as he said (R. Bultmann, *The History of the Synoptic Tradition* [trans. J. Marsh; New York: Harper & Row, 1963], p. 261). This emphasis detects the important formal parallel between Mk 11.1-6 and Mk 14.12-16, but at the expense of considering each story in its own immediate context.

3. E.g. V. Taylor, *The Gospel according to St. Mark* (London: Macmillan, 1952), p. 452.

character, namely that Jesus can discern and direct future events.[4]

With regard to Mark's particular presentation of the entry into Jerusalem, there are several significant problems with emphasizing Jesus' fulfillment of Zech. 9.9.[5] First, the simple assumption that Jesus is a peaceful Messiah does not cohere with Mark's overall characterization of Jesus in Jerusalem.[6] Disrupting Temple services, and teaching that the Temple will be destroyed, seem less than peaceful behavior, and less than positive regarding the central institution of traditional messianic expectation.[7]

Secondly, Mark's presentation of the entry, unlike Matthew and John, alludes to, but does not does not directly quote the Zech. 9.9 oracle.[8]

---

4.   E.g. L. Williamson, *Mark* (Atlanta: John Knox, 1983), p. 203. J. Blenkinsopp, 'The Oracle of Judah and the Messianic Entry', *JBL* 80 (1961), pp. 55-65; H. Patsch, 'Der Einzug Jesu in Jerusalem', *ZTK* 68 (1971), pp. 1-26; J.D. Crossan, 'Redaction and Citation in Mark 11:9 and Mark 11:17', *BR* 17 (1972), pp. 35-41; and J.A. Sanders, 'A New Testament Hermeneutic Fabric: Psalm 118 in the Entrance Narrative', in C.A. Evans and W.F. Stinespring (eds.), *Early Jewish and Christian Exegesis: Studies in Memory of William Hugh Brownlee* (Atlanta: Scholars Press, 1987), p. 185.

5.   This essay addresses issues in Mark's presentation of the Zech. 9.9 tradition. It is not concerned primarily with the potential historical background of the event. A thorough treatment of the historical background of the story can be found in D. Catchpole, 'The "Triumphal" Entry', in E. Bammel and C.F.D. Moule (eds.), *Jesus and the Politics of his Day* (Cambridge: Cambridge University Press, 1984), pp. 319-34.

6.   Immediately following the entry, Jesus curses a fig tree to die (Mk 11.12-14). After that, he expels money changers and dove sellers from the Jerusalem temple (Mk 11.15-16). Later in the temple, he challenges traditional Davidic messianic expectations (12.35-37). And in chapter 13.1-2 he teaches the temple's violent end (Mk 13.2).

7.   In his redaction-critical investigation of Mark's Gospel, W. Kelber (*The Kingdom in Mark: A New Place and a New Time* [Philadelphia: Fortress Press, 1974], p. 97), argues against interpretations of Mark's entry narrative as 'messianic'. In fact, he argues, the scene is ironic: '11:1-10 does not depict Jesus' triumphal, messianic entry into Jerusalem, but the rejection of Davidic messianism outside of Jerusalem'.

8.   M.D. Hooker, *The Gospel according to St. Mark* (Peabody, MA: Hendrickson, 1991), p. 257. The fact that Mark does not quote Zech. 9.9, however, does not prove that he is unconcerned with the tradition in Mk 11.1-10 (cf. M.C. Black, 'The Rejected and Slain Messiah who is Coming with his Angels: The Messianic Exegesis of Zech 9–14 in the Passion Narratives' [PhD dissertation; Emory University, 1990], p. 163 n. 2). Such a delineation between quotation and allusion does not take into account the highly allusive character of many of Mark's Scripture references, particularly in chs. 11–16. Cf. H.C. Kee, 'The Function of Scripture

Instead, Mark offers the most protracted version in all the Gospels of the legend of attaining the colt. In Mark's account, the description of the colt as 'bound' (δέω) is repeated twice, and the command to unbind it (λύω) is repeated three times. In light of Mark's generally sparse narrative, might this legend bear more significance than mere preparation for the enactment of Zech. 9.9 in Mk 11.7-10?

This paper argues that Mark's story of the colt (Mk 11.1-6) is integrally related to Mark's presentation of the entry tradition. The paper claims that the Scripture allusions and quotations which inform these traditions (Gen. 49.11; Zech. 9.9; and Ps. 118.25-26) are more than a symbolic backdrop that imbue Jesus' actions in the entry with prophetic or messianic significance. Rather, these texts have an exegetical function in Mark's narrative. The Scripture allusions of Gen. 49.11 in the story of the colt is widely noted. And the entry proper (Mk 11.7-10) has always been read in relationship with Zech. 9.9 and Ps. 118.25-26. A closer look at these texts, however, suggests that they are not disparate allusions, but an assembly of traditions that Mark appropriates in order to frame his presentation of Jesus' entry into Jerusalem. Finally, a reading of Mark's entry narrative sensitive to this scriptural framework, and the role of Mk 11.1-6, provides an interpretation of Jesus' entrance to Jerusalem which coheres with Mark's overall presentation of Jesus' actions and teachings in Mark 11–13.

2. *Mark and Scripture*

The assertion that Scripture references in Mk 11.1-10 have an exegetical function can only be made in the debt of research on Mark's use of Scripture in recent years. In light of the general advances of redaction criticism, J.D. Crossan and H.C. Kee have shown that instances of Scripture citation heretofore understood as examples of Mark's ignorance or editorial sloppiness, are in truth combinations and alterations of Scripture texts that cohere with Mark's redactional schema.[9] Of late, J. Marcus has noted that these quotations are often surrounded by related, narratively embedded allusions which also serve Mark's

Quotations and Allusions in Mark 11–16', in E.E. Ellis and E. Gräßer (eds.), *Jesus und Paulus: Festschrift für Werner Georg Kümmel zum 70 Geburtstag* (Göttingen: Vandenhoeck & Ruprecht, 1975), p. 177.

9.   Crossan, 'Redaction and Citation', pp. 33-50; Kee, 'The Function of Scripture Quotations', pp. 165-88.

particular story of Jesus.[10] As Juel claims regarding Mark 11–16 in general, Scripture allusions and quotations are so frequent as to suggest a sensible framework for interpreting Mark's narrative.[11] The problem, Juel notes, comes in discerning what are actual allusions, and how they are organized into a sensible interpretive framework.

3. *A Scriptural Framework in Mark 11.1-10—The One who Comes*

In the case of Mk 11.1-10 establishing Mark's Scripture references is not complicated. They have long been observed. The legend of attaining the colt (Mk 11.1-6) has been associated with Jacob's blessing on Judah in Gen. 49.11 since the earliest patristic exegetes.[12] And Matthew and John directly quote Zech. 9.9 in the parallel to Mark's allusion of Jesus riding a colt in Mk 11.7-10.[13] Finally, Mark himself quotes a portion of Ps. 118.25-26 in Mk 11.10. Establishing these references as a framework for interpreting Mark's entry, however, demands that they be *connected* in some meaningful way. I will argue that these Scripture references are connected with one another on several levels: (1) lexically, in that all of the traditions, in Hebrew and Greek, share a catch word connection: the verb בוא/ἔρχομαι; (2) traditionally, as within the interpretative tradition of Royal Messianism; and (3) intertextually, in that one of the texts (Zech. 9.9) is literarily dependent on another (Gen. 49.10-11). These three levels of connection indicate that Mark intends the Scripture references to function as a framework for interpreting Jesus' entry into Jerusalem, specifically, a framework that comments upon the traditional connections between the Scripture references, and the traditional assumptions that they hold about to whom and for what reasons the Messiah comes.

---

10. J. Marcus, 'Mark 9:11-13: As it has been Written', *ZNW* 80 (1989), pp. 42-63; *The Way of the Lord: Christological Exegesis of the Old Testament in the Gospel of Mark* (Louisville, KT: Westminster/John Knox, 1992); cf. pp. 8-10.

11. D. Juel, *Mark* (Minneapolis: Augsburg, 1990), p. 152.

12. Patristic exegetes often meditate on the entry tradition in light of Jacob's blessing on Joseph Gen. 49.8-12. Cf. Justin, *Apol.* 1.32; *Trypho* 42; Clement of Alexandria, *Paed.* 5; Hippolytus, *Treatise on the Christ and Anti-Christ* 9; Methodius, *Oration on the Psalms* 2. All texts found within *The Ante-Nicene Fathers: Translations to the Writings of the Fathers Down to AD 325* (10 vols.; ed. R. and J. Donaldson; Buffalo: Christian Literature Publishing, 1885–96).

13. Mt. 21.5; Jn 12.15.

a. *Lexical Connections*

In their Hebrew and Greek versions Gen. 49.11, Zech. 9.9 and Ps. 118.25-26 each contain some reference to a concrete term, namely the verb בוא2ᵇ/ἔρχομαι (see Appendix). Such a collection of Scripture references around a shared catch word suggests that Mark has intentionally assembled these traditions into his entry narrative. Mark employs this method of combining Scripture allusion and quotation in several other places (for example, Mk 1.2-3; 9.11-13; 12.1-11).[14] In light of this assembly, it becomes clear that the legend of attaining the colt in Mk 11.1-6 and the entry tradition proper in Mk 11.7-10 are connected as a whole commentary about who Jesus is, and in what ways and for what purposes he comes to Jerusalem. But these catch words point to an even broader connection between these texts, namely their collective place within early Jewish and Christian messianic exegesis.

b. *Connections within the Interpretive Tradition of Royal Messianism*

In studies of the entry tradition across all the Gospels Eduard Lohse and James Sanders have shown that Zech. 9.9 and Psalm 118 share a common tradition in Royal Davidic theology and messianic interpretation.[15] Sanders argues that Mark's quotation of Psalm 118, particularly in association with the royal oracle of Zech. 9.9, transcends its first-century function as part of the Hallel, and evokes its pre-exilic function in the ritual throning and dethroning of the king.[16] Furthermore, Joseph Blenkinsopp has demonstrated that Gen. 49.11, far from some obscure reference to an ancient tribal blessing in the legend of attaining the colt, has a tremendous legacy of Royal-messianic interpretation in both early Jewish and Christian exegesis which focuses on the unclear Hebrew phrase: עד כי־יבא שילה.[17]

---

14. J. Marcus offers analyses of the catch word exegesis in these texts, *The Way of the Lord*, pp. 12-47, 95-110, and 111-29.

15. E. Lohse, 'Hosianna', *NovT* 6 (1963), pp. 113-19; Sanders, 'A New Testament Hermeneutic Fabric', pp. 177-90.

16. Sanders, 'A New Testament Hermeneutic Fabric', pp. 179-85.

17. The origin of the problem is the uncertain Hebrew phrase: עד כי־יבא שילה. As Skinner has demonstrated, the heart of the problem is the interpretation of the final term שילה; J. Skinner, *Genesis* (New York: Scribners, 1917), pp. 521-24. Elsewhere in the Hebrew Bible this term refers to the place name Shiloh. On this basis, the phrase has been variously interpreted as 'until he (namely Judah) comes to Shiloh' or 'until Shiloh comes'. Within this interpretation the text received much attention in the early Jewish and Christian exegetical milieu in terms of its messianic significance.

Lohse, Sanders and Blenkinsopp all advance over the 'peaceful Messiah' interpretation in that they acknowledge how the Gospel writers
employ Scripture in the context of first-century Jewish exegetical traditions, not merely as isolated proof texts (for example the image of a
humble king). In their reading, the image of the colt and Jesus riding the
colt is significant not simply because it proves Jesus to be Messiah,
prince of peace, but because it portrays him enacting an oracle of
Israel's national hope, and stakes a claim to his identity as Messiah–
king and savior. Most importantly their studies suggest that the legend
of attaining the colt (which is informed by Gen. 49.11) provides more
than a necessary preliminary step to the enactment of Zech. 9.9 and Ps.
118.25-26, that of getting Jesus a ride. Rather, it is integrally related to
the entry tradition through its place in the Royal-messianic interpretive tradition.

c. An Exegetical Connection between Zech. 9.9 and Gen. 49.8-12
The traditional relationships between Gen. 49.8-12, Zech. 9.9 and Ps.
118.25-26 demonstrated by Lohse, Sanders and Blenkinsopp suggest
that these texts share a common exegetical milieu. But in one case,
scholars have noted that this transcends shared milieu, and becomes literary relationship in the connections between Gen. 49.8-12 and Zech.
9.9.[18] This relationship stems back to Gen. 49.8-12, and its core exegetical problem: the unclear description of the one to come in the blessing
of Jacob on Judah, Gen. 49.10 עד כי־יבוא שילה. As many scholars have
shown, this phrase provided fertile ground for messianic utilization in
Israel's later prophets and early Jewish and Christian exegesis in the
description of Israel's ideal King. In early Jewish exegesis, the place

Blenkinsopp shows that Shiloh was understood in early Judaism and Christianity as
'the ideal king'. In particular, *Targum Onqelos* and the *Jerusalem Targum* render
Shiloh as 'messiah'. Blenkinsopp, 'The Oracle of Judah', pp. 58-59. A thorough discussion of the verse and its messianic interpretation is found in A. Poznanski, *Schiloh:
Ein Beitrag zur Geschichte der Messiaslehre. I. Die Auslegung von Genesis 49,10
im Altertume bis zu Ende des Mittelalters* (Leipzig: Hinrichs, 1904), cited by
M. Fishbane, *Biblical Interpretation in Ancient Israel* (Oxford: Clarendon Press,
1985), p. 501 n. 4.
    18. E.G.H. Kraeling, 'The Historical Situation in Zech. 9:1-10', *AJSL* 41
(1924), p. 30; Blenkinsopp, 'The Oracle of Judah', p. 57; K. Seybold, 'Spet-
prophetische Hoffnungen auf die Wiederkunft des Davidischen Zeitalters in Sach. 9–
14', *Judaica* 29 (1973), p. 105; Fishbane, *Biblical Interpretation*, pp. 501-502.

name Shiloh was often personified as the ideal King/Messiah (*Pseudo-Jonathan*; *Targum Onqelos*; *Jerusalem Targum*). Zech. 9.9 is a part of this interpretation about the ideal King. And the phrase in the Zechariach oracle: מלכך יבוא לך is a direct interpretation of Gen. 49.10: עד כי־יבוא שילה.[19]

4. *The Rationale Behind the Royal-Messianic Traditions in Mark 11.1-10*

Thus far this analysis has shown that rather than disparate allusions to messianic imagery, Mk 11.1-10 presents a complex web of organically related Scripture traditions. In order to discern how these references function as a framework of interpretation for Mark's narrative, it is necessary to delineate the relationships between the texts, and Mark's presentation of them. In his recent study of early Jewish biblical interpretation, J. Kugel describes this kind of analysis as 'reverse engineering'.[20] This process begins with the finished product (in this case Mk 11.1-10) and then discerns its exegetical components, and how they are related to one another.

In the case of Mark's assembly of traditions around the shared theme of ἔρχομαι, it is perhaps best to start with an analysis of the root of the problem, the ancient blessing of Jacob on Judah, and assess toward what ends Zechariah appropriated the blessing, and finally toward what ends Mark may have appropriated it in relationship to Zech. 9.9.

a. *Genesis 49.8-12: The Blessing of Jacob on Judah*
Prior to his death in Gen. 49.33, Jacob is portrayed as offering a last testimony to his twelve sons. Overall the oracles are a mixture of curse and blessing, but the verses which comprise the address to Judah are unmitigated blessing.[21] The address begins in 49.8 with an affirmation of Judah's prowess among his brothers, v. 9 dwells upon the image of a lion to describe Judah's power and wit, and finally, vv. 10-12 describe

19. Following Gressmann, Skinner, *Genesis*, p. 524; E.A. Speiser, *Genesis* (Garden City, NY: Doubleday, 1964), p. 366.

20. J.L. Kugel, *In Potiphar's House: The Interpretive Life of Biblical Texts* (Cambridge, MA: Harvard University Press, 1994), p. 251.

21. Both Skinner, *Genesis*, p. 520, and Fishbane, *Biblical Interpretation*, p. 501, note that the blessing most probably bears a post facto legitimization of Judean hegemony.

the abiding power and blessing of Judah into the future: 'The scepter shall not depart from Judah, nor the ruler's staff from between his feet, until what is stored for him comes, and the obedience of the peoples is his. Binding his foal to the vine and his ass's foal to the choice vine; He washes his raiment in wine, and his clothes in the blood of the grape! With eyes made dull by wine, and teeth whitened with milk.' The imagery in v. 10 concerns itself primarily with Judah's stability and power. The objects of the scepter and the staff denote his primacy and leadership. The promise is that Judah's reign will be enduring. But the imagery in vv. 11-12 shifts. Rather than stalwart objects of rule, the verses whimsically describe abundant wealth and resources. The agricultural production of Judah will be so great that young animals can be hitched to the choice vines, and clothing laundered in wine.[22] Jacob's blessing announces that Judah's provision from God will be so abundant that Judah can live without a care, all his needs will be fulfilled.

b. *Zechariah 9.9 Interprets Genesis as an Oracle of National Hope*
In the interpretative life of Jacob's blessings on his sons, the blessing on Judah provided a powerful topos for commentary on Judean hegemony and God's providential care for Jerusalem. Blenkinsopp demonstrates that the interpretative tradition of Gen. 49.8-12 developed the image of the scepter not departing from Judah into a Davidic-dynastic claim of divine favor and blessing. He argues that this can be seen in the LXX personifying the Hebrew metaphorical phrase: לֹא יָסוּר שֵׁבֶט מִיהוּדָה with οὐκ ἐκλείψει ἄρχων ἐξ Ιουδα. In addition to this, the text was important in establishing nationalist–Zionist eschatological claims. LXX renders the generic vision of וְלוֹ יִקְּהַת עַמִּים with the specifically Zionist vision of καὶ αὐτὸς προσδοκία ἐθνῶν.

According to M. Fishbane, it was the notion of an abiding Davidic-dynastic power that attracted Zechariah to the blessing of Jacob on Judah. Fishbane argues that Zechariah renders the lexical ideas of coming and the colt found in Judah's blessing into his oracle of nationalistic pride: 'Rejoice O Daughter of Zion, shout aloud O daughter of Jerusalem, lo your King *comes* to you, triumphant, his victory won, humble and riding on an *ass, the foal of a she-ass*'.[23] Here Zechariah collapses the images of stalwart rule in Gen. 49.10 (the scepter will not depart from Judah) with a portion of the image of abundant blessing

22. Skinner, *Genesis*, p. 524.
23. Fishbane, *Biblical Interpretation*, pp. 501-502.

in Gen. 49.11 (the foal of a she-ass). The one who comes and the colt he rides (described in poetic parallelism) fulfill Judah's blessing in the person of a victorious king, and in the peaceful prosperity he brings to Jerusalem. In sum, Zechariah transforms the future sense of this ancient clan blessing, with its varied imagery, into a proclamation of Davidic-dynastic prominence and Judah's confident assurance of God's abiding favor.

c. *Mark's Appropriation of Genesis 49.11 and Zechariah 9.9*

In light of the presence of Gen. 49.10-11 in Zech. 9.9, Mark's allusion to the Genesis oracle is intriguing. Why, if the colt already resides within the imagery of Zechariah, does Mark return to Genesis? Mark's association of the Zech. 9.9 oracle with the Gen. 49.11 blessing is best understood by examining the motif of the colt in each text. In Zech. 9.9 the colt appears as the mount of the king. Its original condition in Gen. 49.11, 'bound to the choice vine', is not mentioned. In fact, the preponderance of imagery, other than the colt, in Zechariah is drawn from Gen. 49.10: the imagery of rule, and abiding power. In Mk 11.1-6, however, (prior to the enactment of Zech. 9.9) the original condition of the colt in Gen. 49.11 receives exhaustive attention.[24] In Mk 11.2 Jesus tells two of his disciples that they will find a colt bound (δεδεμένον) in a neighboring village. He then commands them to unbind (λύετε) it and bring it to him. After this command, the narrative details again that the colt is bound (Mk 11.4), and the necessity of unbinding it (Mk 11.4, 5). These repetitions of δέω/λύω contrast the colt's current status as bound and Jesus' desire that it should be unbound. In light of the Genesis blessing, this protracted description of attaining the colt does more than merely set up the enact ment Zech. 9.9. It takes Mark's audience back

---

24. The repetition of the 'bound' condition of the colt in Mk 11.2, 4 so colored Justin's reading of the entry tradition with Gen. 49.11 that he remembers that in the Gospel tradition the colt is bound to a vine outside the neighboring town (*Apology I* 32): Τὸ δὲ, Δεσμεύων πρὸς ἄμπελον τὸν πῶλον αὐτοῦ, καὶ πλύνων τὴν στολὴν αὐτου ἐν αἵματι σταφυλῆς σύμβολον δηλωτικὸν ἦν τῶν γενησομένων τῷ Χριστῷ καὶ τῶν ὑπ' αὐτοῦ πραχθησομένων. Πῶλος γάρ τις ὄνου εἰστήκει ἔν τινι εἰσόδῳ κώημς ἄμπελον δεδεμένος, ὅν ἐκέλευσεν αγαγεῖν αὐτῷ τότε τοὺς γνωρίμους αὐτοῦ. Greek text found in J.P. Migne (ed.), *Patrologiae Cursus Completus Series Graeca* (Paris: J.P. Migne, 1857), VI. L. Williamson's critique of Justin's interpretation as 'contrary to Mark 11:4', and 'but the beginning of patristic extravagances concerning the colt', *Mark*, p. 202, misses the opportunity to note the power of the Gospels' allusive use of Scripture in the mind of an early exegete.

to an original image of blessing which the Zechariahan oracle associated with Davidic-dynastic power, and reverses it, more specifically, destroys it.[25] By returning to the image of the colt bound to a vine, Mark shows that in Jerusalem the condition for abundant blessing no longer exists.

Read in the context of Mark's midrash on the one who comes, the repeated demand to unbind the colt prepares Mark's readers to hear the confident scriptural claims regarding Judah/Jerusalem's place in divine providence critically: Zech. 9.9 (Rejoice Jerusalem/Zion, YOUR king comes to you); and the Markan addition to Ps. 118.25-26 ('Blessed is the kingdom of our ancestor David which is coming'). In the whole of Mk 11.1-10, the crowd's affirmation of Jesus as the one who comes to restore the Kingdom of David is in no way a misunderstanding of what they have witnessed. For them, Jesus enacts Zech. 9.9, a tremendous display of Davidic-dynastic chauvinm. But here, as in so many places, Mark privileges his readers. He has prefaced the public symbolic act with a private symbolic act which erodes the very basis of the Zechariahan claims.[26] In the story of the colt, Mark returns to the image of the bound colt, an image of Judah's blessing and abundance, and repeatedly establishes that it has been reversed, even destroyed.

25. The verb λύω bears two uses in koine: unbind, and destroy. Mark employs ἀπόλυμμι in contexts which depict the destruction of people (e.g. Mk 3.6, 11.18 or 12.9); however, in direct reference to the destruction of the Jerusalem Temple Mark portrays Jesus using καταλύω (Mk 13.2).

26. Kelber, *The Kingdom in Mark*, p. 96: 'The "un-Markan" nature of the redactional 11:10a finds its explanation in Mark's putting the wrong confession on the lips of the acclaimers. The sheer foreignness of the Davidic acclamation is to catch the attention of the reader and to question its validity.' While I agree with Kelber that Mark's accommodation of the psalm citation (Ps. 118.25-26, with the phrase: εὐλογημένη ἡ ἐρχομένη βασιλεία τοῦ πατρὸς ἡμῶν Δαυίδ) is critical of Davidic messianic expectation, I disagree that the matter is simply that the mistaken crowd serves as a foil for Mark's readers. The Davidic acclamation is not foreign to Mark's narrative. In great proximity to the entry, Mark has presented a not wholly unflattering portrait of one who acclaims Jesus, 'υἱὲ Δαυίδ' (Mk 10.47, 48). Rather, the careful combination of messianic tradition, through both the legend of attaining the colt (Mk 11.1-6) and the entry proper (Mk 11.7-10) prepare Mark's reader, in a way the crowd is not prepared, to evaluate critically the hope that Jesus comes to restore Jerusalem to its Davidic glory.

5. *Conclusion*

A reading of Mk 11.1-10 attentive to the function of Mark's Scripture appropriations prepares for Mark's portrayal of Jesus in Jerusalem as less than peaceful and less than traditionally messianic. The reversal of an image of abundance in Jacob's blessing on Judah coheres with Mark's reversal of other images of fruit production associated with the blessing of Jerusalem and its central institution of the Temple. The image of the fig tree is widely understood to stand as a symbol of Israel's golden age, and the proper functioning of the cult.[27] In Mk 11.12-14, prior to disrupting the Temple's function, Jesus approaches a fig tree in full leaf, and curses it to die for not bearing fruit. The image of the vineyard is employed by Israel's prophets to describe God's careful planting and blessing of Jerusalem. In Mk 12.1-10, Jesus teaches out of the Isaiah 5 image of the vineyard, and describes how, rather than producing abundant harvests, it has become a place of death.[28]

The story of the colt (Mk 11.1-6), read in light of Mark's appropriations of Gen. 49.11, Zech. 9.9, and Ps. 118.25-26, provides Mark the opportunity to initiate the dislocation of traditional confidences that no longer bear the weight of his community's experience. As chs. 11–13 progress, Mark in turn relocates these confidences through reconfigured Scripture tradition. In Mk 11.12-25, the cursed and cleared house of prayer is relocated in the community's practice of faith and prayer.[29] In Mk 12.1-11 the 'vineyard' is ultimately given to 'others' (Mk 12.9).[30]

27. For a review of the image of the fig tree in Hebrew Biblical and early Jewish literature, see W. Telford, *The Barren Temple and the Withered Tree: A Redaction-Critical Analysis of the Cursing of the Fig-Tree Pericope in Mark's Gospel and its Relation to the Cleansing of the Temple Tradition* (Sheffield: JSOT Press, 1980), pp. 128-204. See also D. Krause, 'Narrated Prophecy in Mark 11: The Divine Authorization of Judgment', in C.A. Evans and W.R. Stegner (eds.), *The Gospels and the Scriptures of Israel* (JSNTSup, 104; SSEJC, 3; Sheffield: JSOT Press, 1994), pp. 235-48.

28. Marcus, *The Way of the Lord*, pp. 115-18, demonstrates that Mk 12.1-11 engages exegetical traditions and issues contemporary with the Jewish War.

29. S.E. Dowd, *Prayer, Power, and the Problem of Suffering: Mark 11:22-25 in the Context of Markan Theology* (Atlanta: Scholars Press, 1988), pp. 37-55.

30. Marcus, *The Way of the Lord*, p. 127: 'Mark's community knows that it owes its very existence as part of God's Israel to the vindication of the rejected stone, that stone's exaltation to the head of the corner. In a very real way, the members of the community share in the stone's reversal. They too know what it means to be rejected

The scriptural framework of the 'one who comes' in Mk 11.1-10 coheres with Mark's larger program in chs. 11–13 of engaging the problem of Jerusalem, the Temple, and the location of the Markan community under God's abiding care.

APPENDIX

Gen. 49.10-11 LXX
οὐκ ἐκλείψει ἄρχων ἐξ Ιουδα
καὶ ἡγούμενος ἐκ τῶν μηρῶν αὐτοῦ,
ἕως ἂν ἔλθῃ τὰ ἀποκείμενα αὐτῷ,
καὶ αὐτὸς προσδοκία ἐθνῶν.
δεσμεύων πρὸς ἄμπελον τὸν πῶλον αὐτοῦ
καὶ τῇ ἕλικι τὸν πῶλον τῆς ὄνου αὐτοῦ
πλυνεῖ ἐν οἴνῳ τὴν στολὴν αὐτοῦ
καὶ ἐν αἵματι σταφυλῆς τὴν περιβολὴν αὐτοῦ

Gen. 49.10-11 MT
10לא־יסור שבט מידה ומחקק מבין רגליו
עד כי־יבא שילה ולו יקהת עמים
11אסרי לגפן עירה ולשרקה בני אתנו
כבס ביין לבשו ובדם־ענבים סותה

Zech. 9.9 LXX
Χαῖρε σφόδρα, θύγατερ Σιων κήρυσσε, θύγατερ Ιερουσαλημ
ἰδοὺ ὁ βασιλεύς σου ἔρχεταί σοι, δίκαιος καὶ σῴζων αὐτός, πραΰς καὶ
ἐπιβεβηκὼς ἐπὶ ὑποζύγιον καὶ πῶλον νέον.

Zech. 9.9 MT
9גילי מאד בת־ציון הריעי בת ירושלם
הנה מלכך יבוא לך צדיק ונושע‏a הוא
עני ורכב על־חמור ועל־עיר בן־אתנות

Ps. 117.25-26 LXX
ὦ κύριε, σῶσον δή,
ὦ κύριε, εὐόδωσον δή.
εὐλογημένος ὁ ἐρχόμενος ἐν ὀνόματι κυρίου
εὐλογήκαμεν ὑμᾶς ἐξ οἴκου κυρίου.

by Israel's scribal builders, relegated to the status of "others". . . . They too have been rejected stones, but contrary to all expectation they now find themselves incorporated into a living sanctuary that pulses with the very life of God.'

Ps. 118.25-26 MT

25אָנָּא יהוה הוֹשִׁיעָה נָּא אָנָּא יהוה הַצְלִיחָה נָּא
26בָּרוּךְ הַבָּא בְּשֵׁם יהוה בֵּרַכְנוּכֶם מִבֵּית יהוה

Hebrew Text: *BHS* (DBS, 1967/77, 1983)
Greek Text: A. Rahlfs, *Septuaginta* (Stuttgart: Deutsche Bibelgesellschaft, 1935, 1979)

PSALM 118 IN LUKE–ACTS: TRACING A NARRATIVE THREAD*

J. Ross Wagner

Luke's account of Jesus' post-Resurrection appearance to his disciples provides an intriguing window into the world of early Christian hermeneutics (Lk. 24.44-47 NRSV):

> Then Jesus said to them, 'These are my words that I spoke to you while I was still with you—that everything written about me in the law of Moses, the prophets, and the psalms must be fulfilled'. Then he opened their minds to understand the scriptures, and he said to them, 'Thus it is written, that the Messiah is to suffer and to rise from the dead on the third day, and that repentance and forgiveness of sins is to be proclaimed in his name to all nations, beginning from Jerusalem'.

These words serve not merely to summarize the events narrated in the Gospel of Luke and to foreshadow the plot of Acts. They also indicate the way in which Luke and other Christians believe that they have been transformed in their reading of Scripture so that they now recognize its true nature as a witness to God's climactic act to redeem the world in and through his Messiah.[1] One would naturally expect that Luke's own use of Scripture would reveal the influence of this post-resurrection

---

*   I am indebted to the New Testament Seminar at Duke University (Fall, 1994), led by Richard B. Hays, for stimulating discussion and criticism of an earlier version of this essay.

1.   That Luke did not view this new understanding of the Scriptures as confined to the small group of original followers of Jesus is suggested in Acts by the descriptions of the preaching of Philip (Acts 8.35), Paul (Acts 9.20-22; 13.16-41) and Apollos (Acts 18.24-28), by the believing response of multitudes to Christian preaching, and by the gift of the Holy Spirit to all Christians. One is reminded of Paul's view that turning to the Lord (the Spirit) in faith removes the veil that lies over Scripture and reveals Scripture's true *telos* to be Christ (2 Cor. 3.12-18; cf. the discussion by R.B. Hays, *Echoes of Scripture in the Letters of Paul* [New Haven: Yale University Press, 1989], pp. 122-53).

hermeneutic.[2] Indeed, the early Christian preaching in Acts finds in Torah, Prophets, and Psalms clear prefigurations of the Messiah and of the Christian mission.[3]

Luke's use of Scripture in the Gospel, however, is more difficult to characterize both because of the complications involved in sorting out source from redaction and because explicit quotations of the Old Testament are fewer. Moreover, for the greater part of the narrative of the Gospel, the resurrection—for Luke, the decisive moment for understanding the true significance of Scripture—has not yet occurred. Nevertheless, a careful reading of the Gospel shows that here also Scripture plays an essential role. Although direct quotations are not as common as in Acts, Luke weaves Scripture tightly into the fabric of

2.   Important studies of the use of Scripture in Luke–Acts include: T. Holtz, on the form of Old Testament text used by Luke (*Untersuchungen über die alttestament-lichen Zitate bei Lukas* [TU, 104; Berlin: Akademie Verlag, 1968]); P. Schubert, whose essay provides the classic description of Luke's hermeneutic as 'proof from prophecy' ('The Structure and Significance of Luke 24', in W. Eltester [ed.], *Neutestamentliche Studien für Rudolf Bultmann* [BZNW, 21; Berlin: Töpelmann, 1957], pp. 165-86); and M. Rese, whose major study poses a serious challenge to this view (*Alttestamentliche Motive in der Christologie des Lukas* [SNT, 1; Gütersloh: Mohn/Gütersloher Verlagshaus, 1969]). More recently, D.L. Bock has challenged Rese's methodology and conclusions and defended a modified form of Schubert's thesis. Bock emphasizes the importance of both prophecy and typology for Luke and conceives of Luke's primary purpose as proclamation of Christ rather than as apologetic (*Proclamation from Prophecy and Pattern: Lucan Old Testament Christology* [JSNTSup, 12; Sheffield: JSOT Press, 1987]). See also the articles by C.K. Barrett ('Luke/Acts', in D.A. Carson and H.G.M. Williamson [eds.], *It is Written: Scripture Citing Scripture* [Cambridge: Cambridge University Press, 1988], pp. 231-44), and the collection of studies by C.A. Evans and J.A. Sanders (*Luke and Scripture* [Minneapolis: Fortress Press, 1993]). In addition, several recent monographs touch on important aspects of Luke's use of Scripture: C.A. Kimball, *Jesus' Exposition of the Old Testament in Luke's Gospel* (JSNTSup, 94; Sheffield: JSOT Press, 1994); B. Kinman, *Jesus' Entry into Jerusalem in the Context of Lukan Theology and the Politics of his Day* (AGJV, 28; Leiden: Brill, 1995); M.L. Strauss, *The Davidic Messiah in Luke–Acts* (JSNTSup, 110; Sheffield: JSOT Press, 1995).

3.   See Barrett, 'Luke/Acts', pp. 238-49, for a listing of Scripture quotations in the sermons in Acts. For a discussion of the importance of Luke's use of Scripture in his conception of the Christian mission, see D.L. Bock, 'The Use of the OT in Luke–Acts; Christology and Mission', *SBLSP* 1990, pp. 494-511; *idem*, 'Proclamation from Prophecy and Pattern: Luke's Use of the Old Testament for Christology and Mission', in C.A. Evans and W.R. Stegner (eds.), *The Gospels and the Scriptures of Israel* (JSNTSup, 104; SSEJC, 3; Sheffield: JSOT Press, 1994), pp. 280-307.

his Gospel narrative through quotations and allusions at crucial points in the story.

One striking example of the way in which Luke utilizes Scripture as an integral part of the narrative structure of the Gospel and Acts is his frequent reference, by quotation and by allusive echo, to Psalm 118. Major studies of Luke's use of Scripture have examined Psalm 118 within the context of larger issues such as the question of the Old Testament text form(s) utilized by Luke or the problem of Luke's hermeneutics, particularly the role of Scripture in the presentation of his Christology.[4] In general, however, they have tended to treat Luke's uses of Psalm 118 in isolation from one another, without adequately illuminating the significance of the connections *among* the references to Psalm 118 within Luke's narrative. Similarly, shorter studies of particular Lukan pericopes that have touched on one or two of Luke's quotations of Psalm 118 have not examined all of the quotations of and allusions to this psalm together.[5]

The present study seeks to approach the question of Luke's use of Scripture by tracing Psalm 118 through Luke–Acts, showing that Luke uses this psalm in his narrative more extensively and in a more subtle and sophisticated manner than has heretofore been recognized. Psalm 118 runs like a thread through Luke–Acts, helping to structure and advance the narrative (for example, by foreshadowing events, creating dramatic tension, heightening irony) and, in the process, serving to further Luke's theological agenda. The net effect is that Luke's narrative itself, rather than isolated quotations within it, points to the fulfillment of Israel's Scriptures in the ministry of Jesus and the mission of the Church.

Methodologically, I begin with explicit quotations as the place where the Old Testament text is most firmly stitched to the narrative and then work from there to discern further allusions and echoes that may be woven into the text. Luke quotes from Psalm 118 four times in Luke–Acts. The quotations appear at Lk. 13.35 (Ps. 118.26), Lk. 19.38 (Ps. 118.26), Lk. 20.17 (Ps. 118.22), and Acts 4.11 (Ps. 118.22). The second and fourth quotations are uniquely Lukan while the first appears

---

4.　Note the debate surrounding Schubert's description of Luke's hermeneutic as 'proof from prophecy' (n. 2 above). A more detailed history of the discussion is offered by Bock (*Proclamation*, pp. 13-53).

5.　There will be occasion to refer to many of these studies in the notes that follow.

in a different location in Matthew's Gospel. In the third quotation, shared with Mark and Matthew, Luke has highlighted the royal connotations of the Psalm, identifying 'the one who comes' as 'the king'. These quotations evince Lukan interest in Psalm 118 and suggest that the search for further allusions to and echoes of Psalm 118 may be fruitful.[6] The following discussion highlights possible allusions and echoes in Luke's narrative from Psalm 118 and also from several texts (Zech. 9.9-10; Isa. 8.14; Dan. 2.35, 44; Ps. 110.5-6) that may be related thematically to Psalm 118. Careful attention to these quotations and echoes suggests a pattern to Luke's use of Psalm 118. The recurrence of Psalm 118 throughout Luke and the early part of Acts functions as one thread that Luke employs to weave the story of Jesus and the Church into a tapestry illustrating the salvific purpose of God in history.

Psalm 118

Before looking at Luke's use of Psalm 118 in detail, it will be helpful to examine the psalm and its interpretation outside Luke–Acts. The structure of Psalm 118 may be analyzed as follows:

1-4	Call to thanksgiving
5-18	Description of divine rescue
19-20	Entrance into the Temple ('gates', cf. Ps. 24.7-10)
21-28	Celebration of rescue
29	Closing call to thanksgiving (inclusion with v. 1)

Psalm 118 appears to be the thanksgiving song of a king who returns to the Temple after experiencing divine deliverance from death at the hands of his enemies.[7] The hymn may be divided among several voices,

---

6. The results of this search are displayed graphically in the table following this paper. For the concept of 'allusive echo' in biblical texts, see Hays, *Echoes of Scripture*. This paper maintains no systematic distinction between allusion and echo. Following Hays (*Echoes of Scripture*, p. 29), 'allusion' generally indicates a more obvious reference to another text, while 'echo' denotes a subtler intertextual reference. Both terms presuppose some degree of both verbal and thematic correspondence between two texts.

7. Psalm 118 is 'a king's hymn of thanksgiving for delivery from death and for a military victory' (M. Dahood, *Psalms III (101–150)* [AB, 17A; Garden City, NY: Doubleday, 1970], p. 155). The psalm is classified as royal by many scholars, including J.H. Eaton, A. Weiser, A.A. Anderson, and L.C. Allen.

including those of the king (the 'I' of the psalm), the people, and probably the priests.[8]

J. Jeremias and others have argued that this royal psalm (and, in fact,
the entire *Hallel*) was understood as having eschatological and messianic
connotations by the time of Jesus.[9] However, the rabbinic evidence traditionally used to support this contention is problematic.[10] None of the
rabbinic eschatological interpretations of the psalm can be placed in the
first century with any degree of certainty. The earliest authorities cited
for eschatological interpretations of the *Hallel* or of Psalm 118 are
R. Jose (late 2nd century CE; *b. Pes*. 118b [Ps. 117.1]), R. Johanan (3rd
century CE; *b. Pes*. 118a [Ps. 115.1]; *Midr. Ps*. 36 §6 [Ps. 118.27]),
R. Hama b. Hanina (late 3rd century CE; *Pes. K*. 17.5 [Ps. 118.15]) and
R. Abin (4th century CE; *y. Ber*. 4d (2.4) [Ps. 118.27-28]).[11] The eschatological interpretations preserved in the *Midrash on Psalms* do not
carry attributions with them.[12] Although much of the material may date
from the Talmudic period, it is difficult to be more precise than this.[13]

8.   For one way of dividing the voices, see J.A. Sanders, 'A Hermeneutic
Fabric: Psalm 118 in Luke's Entrance Narrative', in Evans and Sanders (eds.), *Luke
and Scripture*, pp. 146-47. Rabbinic literature also offers schemes for dividing the
voices. *B. Pes*. 119a divides Ps. 118.21-28 among David, his brothers, Jesse and
Samuel. *Midr. Ps*. 118 §14 and 118 §22 suggest an antiphonal call and response in
Ps. 118.15-16, 25-29 between singers within and without the walls of Jerusalem. The
Targum to Ps. 118.23-29 divides the voices among David and his contemporaries.

9.   J. Jeremias, *The Eucharistic Words of Jesus* (London: SCM Press, 1966),
pp. 255-61; B. Lindars, *New Testament Apologetic* (London: SCM Press, 1961),
pp. 169-85; E. Werner, 'Hosanna in the Gospels', *JBL* 65 (1946), pp. 97-122 (114-
17); H.-J. Kraus, *Theology of the Psalms* (Minneapolis: Augsburg, 1986), p. 193.
Several more recent scholars of Luke have followed Jeremias without questioning the
evidence, including Bock (*Proclamation*, p. 325 n. 109), Kimball (*Jesus' Exposition*,
p. 159 n. 46) and Kinman (*Jesus' Entry*, p. 57 n. 45).

10.   Jeremias appeals to texts from the *Midrash on Psalms*, *Pesiqta de Rab
Kahana*, *Exodus Rabbah*, *Talmud Yerushalmi* and *Talmud Babli*.

11.   The interpretation of R. Abin is also preserved (with slight variations) in *y.
Meg*. 73a (2.1); *Lev. Rab*. 30.5; *Pes. K*. 27.5; *Midr. Ps*. 26 §6.

12.   Eschatological interpretations of Psalm 118 are found in *Midr. Ps*. 26 §6; 27
§1; 36 §6; 118 §§8, 12-14, 22.

13.   The Midrash on Psalms consists of two parts: Psalms 1–118 and Psalms 119–
50. The material in the first part developed over many centuries, although Strack–
Stemberger argue that 'most of the material certainly dates back to the Talmudic
period' (H.L. Strack and G. Stemberger, *Introduction to the Talmud and Midrash*
[Minneapolis: Fortress Press, 1992], p. 351). The second part (Pss. 119–50) is normally dated to the 13th century (p. 351).

The earliest date proposed by W.G. Braude for the *Midrash on Psalms* is the third century, and he recognized that the material probably continued to grow for the next ten centuries.[14] Consequently, the rabbinic material itself provides no sure indication that these interpretations of Psalm 118 were current in the first century.

The problem of the late date of the rabbinic material is compounded by the fact that there appear to be no references to Psalm 118 in any of the extant extra-biblical Jewish literature from the centuries preceding the *Mishnah* that would provide evidence of a trajectory of interpretation extending from the first century to these later rabbinic texts.[15] Consequently, although many of the rabbinic uses of Psalm 118 appear to have a Palestinian provenance, there is no evidence for the existence of these interpretations at the time of the writing of the New Testament.[16]

That Psalm 118 may have been read messianically within some circles in first century Judaism is suggested, however, by several other lines of evidence. First, as B.S. Childs observes concerning the canonical form of the Psalter, the post-exilic editors' arrangement of the psalms is 'highly eschatological in nature'.[17] Accordingly, royal psalms become witnesses to the messianic hope of Israel: 'At the time of the final redaction, when the institution of kingship had long been destroyed, what earthly king would have come to mind other than God's Messiah?'[18] P.D. Miller offers a contextual reading of Book Five of the Psalter that appears to support this line of argumentation. In a paper delivered at the 1995 Annual Meeting of the Society of Biblical Literature, Miller argued that Psalms 111–18 are presented as the song

14. W.G. Braude, *The Midrash on Psalms* (2 vols.; New Haven: Yale University Press, 1959), I, p. xxxi.

15. For the importance of evidence of a pre-rabbinic history for alleged rabbinic parallels to the New Testament, see C.A. Evans, 'Early Rabbinic Sources and Jesus Research', *SBLSP 1995* (ed. E.H. Lovering, pp. 53-76; Atlanta: Scholars Press, 1995), p. 55. My own search of extra-biblical Jewish texts has turned up no quotations of Psalm 118 in Philo, Josephus, the DSS, the Apocrypha or in Pseudepigraphical works. In addition, I am not aware of any secondary literature that has found reference to Psalm 118 in this body of literature.

16. For the probable Palestinian origin of the *Midrash on Psalms*, see Strack–Stemberger, *Introduction to the Talmud and Midrash*, p. 351.

17. B.S. Childs, *Introduction to the Old Testament as Scripture* (Philadelphia: Fortress Press, 1979), p. 518.

18. Childs, *Introduction*, p. 516.

of praise promised by the king/Messiah in Ps. 109.30 and offered up after his deliverance by God in Psalm 110.[19]

A second line of evidence that may suggest an eschatological inter-pretation of Psalm 118 in first-century Jewish circles is found in the interpretation of the psalm by its Greek translators.[20] The Septuagint translation of Psalm 118 may reflect a sharpening of the individual focus of the psalm. In v. 16a, the LXX reads, δεξιὰ κυρίου ὕψωσέν με ('the right hand of the Lord has exalted me') for the MT's ימין יהוה רוממה ('the right hand of the Lord is exalted'). Although this evidence alone is inadequate to establish that an interpretation of Psalm 118 along indi-vidual, messianic lines was intended by the translators, the wording is certainly consonant with such an interpretation. If Acts 2.33 and 5.31 are identified as allusions to Ps. 118.16, it is clear that the rendering of the LXX would have been essential for such a messianic interpretation of this verse by Luke.[21]

It is also possible that the use of Psalm 118 in the Jewish liturgy may have facilitated its interpretation in an eschatological sense.[22] Accord-ing to the *Mishnah*, Psalm 118 was sung as part of the *Hallel* at Taber-nacles (*m. Suk.* 3.9, 4.1, 5, 8), Hanukkah (*m. Ta'an.* 4.4-5) and at Passover, both at the sacrificing of the Passover (*m. Pes.* 5.7) and at the meal (*m. Pes.* 10.5-7; cf. *t. Pes.* 10.8-9; Mk 14.26//Mt. 26.30).[23] The association of Psalm 118 with the acts of divine deliverance celebrated at Tabernacles, Hanukkah and Passover may have encouraged readings of the psalm that focused on the hope of God's future deliverance of Israel through the agency of his Anointed One. Interestingly, the end of Psalm 118 was emphasized in the liturgy by repetition of vv. 21-29

19. Paper delivered to the Book of Psalms Group of the SBL (11/18/95) during the 1995 Annual Meeting in Philadelphia.

20. On the presence of eschatology in the LXX Psalter, see J. Schaper, 'Die Septuaginta-Psalter als Dokument jüdischer Eschatologie', in M. Hengel and A.M. Schwemer (eds.), *Die Septuaginta zwischen Judentum und Christentum* (WUNT, 72; Tübingen: Mohr [Paul Siebeck], 1994), pp. 38-61; *idem*, *Eschatology in the Greek Psalter* (WUNT, 2nd series, 76; Tübingen: Mohr [Paul Siebeck], 1995).

21. See below, n. 63.

22. I assume here that liturgical practice is relatively more stable than exegetical practice and thus that there is no reason to doubt the basic veracity of the witness of the *Mishnah* and *Tosefta* to the use of the *Hallel* at major feasts such as Passover. See Evans, 'Early Rabbinic Sources', p. 56.

23. The *Tosefta* adds that the Hallel was also sung on the first day of the Feast of Weeks (*t. Suk.* 3.2).

(*m. Suk.* 3.11; cf. *b. Suk.* 39a; *b. Pes.* 119b). This is just the section of the psalm that Luke and the other evangelists quote directly.

While the evidence for a first-century messianic reading of Psalm 118 outside Christian circles is relatively slight, the widespread use of Psalm 118 in the New Testament suggests that the convention of inter- preting the psalm messianically pre-dates the writing of the Gospels. Psalm 118 is quoted in the Synoptics—in both double and triple tradi- tion and in Luke's unique material—in Acts, in John, and in 1 Peter.[24] In all of these instances, the psalm is used by the writers as a reference to Jesus.[25] Luke's use of Psalm 118, then, fits within the New Testament pattern of reading this psalm with reference to the Messiah. The impor- tance of Psalm 118 for Luke becomes clear as one follows the thread of quotation and echo of this psalm through the fabric of Luke's narrative.

Psalm 118 in the Narrative of Luke–Acts

a. *John the Baptist's Question (Luke 7.18-23)*
Luke first evokes Psalm 118 by means of allusion. Languishing in Herod's prison, John sends his disciples to ask Jesus: 'Are you the one who comes (ὁ ἐρχόμενος) or do we await another?' (7.19). The phrase ὁ ἐρχόμενος recalls the Baptist's messianic preaching (Lk. 3.16: 'The one stronger than me comes [ἔρχεται]')[26] but also seems to allude to Ps. 118.26 (εὐλογημένος ὁ ἐρχόμενος ἐν ὀνόματι κυρίου). In John's question, ὁ ἐρχόμενος functions as a designation of the Messiah.[27] Note

24. Ps. 118.22-23 is quoted in Mk 12.10-11//Mt. 21.42. Ps. 118.22 is quoted in Lk. 20.17, in Acts 4.11 and in 1 Pet. 2.7. Allusions to this verse appear in Mk 8.31// Lk. 9.22, in Lk. 17.25 and in 1 Pet. 2.4 (combined with Isa. 28.16; 8.14). Ps. 118.25-26 is quoted in Mk 11.9//Mt. 21.9 and in Jn 12.13. Ps. 118.26 is quoted in Mt. 23.39//Lk. 13.35 and in Lk. 19.38. It is alluded to in Mt. 11.3//Lk. 7.19. Further allusions in Luke–Acts will be noted below.

25. In addition to these citations, Ps. 118.6 is quoted in Heb. 13.6 and alluded to in Rom. 8.31, but not as words about Christ. Other possible allusions include Ps. 118.17 (2 Cor. 6.9); Ps. 118.19 (Rev. 22.14); Ps. 118.20 (Jn 10.9); Ps. 118.24 (Rev. 19.7).

26. Cf. Mt. 3.11: 'The one coming after me [ὁ δὲ ὀπίσω μου ἐρχόμενος] is stronger than me'.

27. Bock remarks, 'It seems clear from the Lucan usage that [John's] question is messianic in force' (*Proclamation*, p. 112); he later says, 'ὁ ἐρχόμενος has become a formal title for Luke' (p. 118). V. Taylor observes that ὁ ἐρχόμενος is used as a designation of the Messiah in Mt. 11.3//Lk. 7.19; Mt. 23.39//Lk. 13.35; Jn 1.15, 27; 6.14 (with 'the prophet'); 11.27; Acts 19.4; Heb. 10.37. Taylor concludes that the

that Jesus' answer evokes a chain of messianic prophecies from Isa.
29.18; 35.5-6; 61.1; 42.18; and 26.19. Although Mt. 11.3 reports the
Baptist's question with virtually the same wording, suggesting a common source for the pericope, Luke alone repeats the question (7.20).
This Lukan repetition emphasizes Jesus' identification with ὁ
ἐρχόμενος.

b. *Jesus' Prediction of his Passion (Luke 9.22)*

The confession of Peter that Jesus is 'the Messiah of God' is followed
by Jesus' warning to tell no one and his announcement that 'the Son of
Man must undergo great suffering, and be rejected by the elders, chief
priests, and scribes, and be killed, and on the third day be raised'
(NRSV). The word Luke uses (in common with Mk 8.31) for 'be rejected', ἀποδοκιμασθῆναι, echoes Ps. 118.22: 'The stone the builders
rejected' (λίθον, ὃν ἀπεδοκίμασαν οἱ οἰκοδομοῦντες).[28] In all but
one occurrence in the New Testament, this verb appears in quotations
of or allusions to Psalm 118 (Mk 8.31//Lk. 9.22; Lk. 17.25; 1 Pet. 2.4,
7). The sole exception is Heb. 12.17, which describes the rejection of
Esau after he forfeited his blessing.[29] This evidence strongly suggests
that the verb in Lk. 9.22 should be understood as a reference to Ps.
118.22. Although Luke has here adopted the wording from Mark, his
repetition of ἀποδοκιμασθῆναι in the context of the passion prediction of 17.25 suggests both a recognition of and further exploitation
of this intertextual echo of Psalm 118. In the context of Jesus' (and
later the Church's) conflict with the leaders of Israel, this faint echo of
Ps. 118.22 will be amplified into a triumphant fanfare announcing that
the words of the psalm find their fulfillment in Jesus' death and resurrection (Lk. 20.17; Acts 4.11).

c. *Jesus' Lament over Jerusalem (Luke 13.34-35)*

The first explicit quotation of Psalm 118 comes as Jesus responds to the
Pharisees' warning that Herod is seeking his life (Lk. 13.31), a warning

phrase (under the influence of Ps. 118.26 and possibly Dan. 7.13) may have circulated
as a messianic designation in 'Baptist and Christian circles' (*The Gospel according
to St Mark* [Grand Rapids: Baker, 2nd edn, 1966], p. 457).

    28. This link is noted by K. Snodgrass, *The Parable of the Wicked Tenants*
(WUNT, 27; Tübingen: Mohr [Paul Siebeck], 1983), p. 100 (see his n. 126 for other
scholars who hold this view).

    29. The verb ἀποδοκιμάζω does not appear in the LXX version of the Genesis
narrative.

that carries some weight in light of Herod's execution of John the Baptist (Lk. 9.9). The mention of Herod reminds the reader of the setting of the first allusion to Psalm 118 (where John is in Herod's prison) and subtly underlines the connection between the two uses of Ps. 118.26. Jesus' remark that it is not fitting for a prophet to perish outside of Jerusalem leads to his prophetic complaint concerning the city's murderous resistance to God's messengers.

Although Luke's wording is close to Mt. 23.37-39 in this pericope, Luke situates the lament in a different context from Matthew's. Matthew places the lament after Jesus has entered Jerusalem, between his pronouncement of Woes (23.1-36) and the Apocalyptic Discourse (24.1–25.46). In this context, Ps. 118.26 refers to the *parousia*. Luke, however, incorporates the pericope into his long travel narrative (9.51–19.27), *before* Jesus' entry into Jerusalem. As a result, the language of Ps. 118.26 most naturally refers to Jesus' anticipated arrival in Jerusalem.[30] Luke's placement of this quotation of Ps. 118.26 plays a significant role in the unfolding of his narrative. It creates dramatic tension by evoking images of the hostility awaiting Jesus in Jerusalem and builds suspense as the possibility is held open that Jerusalem will receive him as Messiah.

The complaint ends with a prophetic pronouncement of judgment on the Temple (v. 35a): 'Your house is left to you' (cf. Jer. 12.7; 22.5; Ezek. 10.18-19).[31] Verse 35b follows the warning of imminent judgment with a conditional prophecy that holds out hope that Jesus will be welcomed in Jerusalem and the judgment averted: 'You will not see me until you say, "Blessed is the one who comes in the name of the Lord"'.[32] D.C. Allison has shown that the syntactical pattern of this prophecy is paralleled in later rabbinic sources which address the conditions necessary for the coming of the Messiah. For example, *b. Sanh.* 98b reads: 'Rab said: "The Son of David will not come until (עד) the [Roman] power enfolds Israel for nine months"'.[33] In Lk. 13.35b, the

30. See below, n. 44.

31. An alternative explanation is proposed by F.D. Weinert, who sees here judgment on the leaders in Jerusalem rather than on the Temple: Jesus declares that he will leave them alone for now; the final conflict between them awaits his arrival in Jerusalem ('Luke, the Temple and Jesus' Sayings about Jerusalem's Abandoned House', *CBQ* 44 [1982], pp. 68-76 [76]).

32. Cf. C.H. Giblin, *The Destruction of Jerusalem according to Luke's Gospel* (An Bib, 105; Rome: Biblical Institute Press, 1985), p. 38.

33. For this and other examples, see D.C. Allison, 'Matt 23:39 = Luke 13.35b as

condition for Jerusalem 'seeing' Jesus is their acclamation of him as the Messiah, 'the one who comes in the name of the Lord' (Ps. 118.26). With this quotation, then, Luke raises the possibility that at the end of Jesus' journey, Jerusalem will welcome its Messiah. This expectation creates tension with Jesus' repeated prophecy of his imminent rejection and death. In addition, it heightens the irony and tragedy of Jerusalem's eventual refusal to 'see' him.[34]

d. *Another Prediction of the Passion (Luke 17.25)*

In the context of teaching on the kingdom of God (Lk. 17.20-21), Jesus speaks of the coming of the day of the son of man (17.22-37). Before this event occurs, however, the son of man must suffer much and be rejected (ἀποδοκιμασθῆναι) by this generation (17.25). As suggested above in the discussion of the first passion prediction, the verb 'rejected' appears to echo Ps. 118.22. This time, however, the guilt of rejecting the Messiah falls not just on the leaders of the people (cf. 9.22), but also on the people as a whole ('this generation'). The note of imminent judgment on those who reject the son of man is sounded by the comparison of 'the days of the son of man' both with the time of Noah and the judgment of the flood and with the time of Lot and the judgment on Sodom. The use of Ps. 118.22 in this pericope corresponds to the manner in which Luke elsewhere employs Psalm 118 to speak of the rejection of the Messiah and his subsequent vindication. Here, the vindication seems to come at the *parousia*, although elsewhere it is connected with the resurrection (Lk. 20.17; Acts 4.11).

e. *The Entry into Jerusalem (Luke 19.28-40)*

The second quotation of Psalm 118 occurs in the context of Jesus' entry

a Conditional Prophecy', *JSNT* 18 (1983), pp. 75-84 (79). Allison's interpretation is adopted by Kinman (*Jesus' Entry*, p. 97).

34. Note Lk. 19.42, where 'the things that make for peace. . . are now hid from your eyes'. Allison argues that the conditional nature of the prophecy in Lk. 13.35b holds open the possibility of Israel's future acceptance of Jesus as Messiah. While agreeing with Allison that Luke does not argue for God's abandonment of Israel, I am less sure that 13.35 functions in the narrative in the way he suggests. It appears significant that, after Jesus' entry into Jerusalem, there are no more allusions to or quotations of Ps. 118.26. Instead, Ps. 118.22 becomes dominant, and the emphasis in Luke's references to Psalm 118 shifts from a focus on the 'coming' of Jesus to a celebration of his vindication by God. Later references to the *parousia* in Luke–Acts are not linked verbally either to Lk. 13.35 or to Psalm 118.

into Jerusalem. The journey which began in 9.51 has been darkened by foreshadowings of the suffering and rejection that await Jesus in Jerusalem (9.22, 44; 13.33-34; 17.25). To the Passion prediction of 18.31-34 (cf. Mk 10.32-34; Mt. 20.17-19), Luke adds the phrase: 'And all the things written through the prophets concerning the son of man will be completed' (18.31). Luke thus sets the stage for Scripture's prophecies of Messiah to play a major role in the unfolding of events. Prominent among those prophecies that interpret and shape Luke's narrative is Psalm 118.

After the healing of Bartimaeus in Jericho (18.35-43) and the encounter with Zacchaeus (19.1-10), Luke narrates the Parable of the Pounds. Luke's introduction to the parable shows its relevance in the narrative: Jesus tells it because they were close to Jerusalem, and some thought the kingdom was going to appear immediately. The parable is loaded with kingship terminology (βασιλεία occurs in 19:11, 12, 15; βασιλεύω in 19.14, 27).[35] This kingship language prepares for the acted parable of kingship by Jesus in the Triumphal Entry (cf. Zech. 9.9) and for the acclamation of Jesus as king (Lk. 19.38). The parable also portends the rejection of Jesus' kingship by the people. In the Lukan context, Jesus' story teaches the unexpected nature of the coming of the kingdom (rejection of the king followed by vindication) and promises judgment on Jesus' opponents.

The fact that in Luke this is Jesus' first journey to Jerusalem during his ministry heightens the significance and the drama of his arrival, especially in light of his prophecy in 13.35 and his forewarnings of the conflict that awaits him in the city. Jesus' riding on the donkey dramatizes the prophecy of Zech. 9.9, 'Rejoice greatly, O daughter Zion! Shout aloud, O daughter Jerusalem! Lo, your king comes to you; triumphant and victorious is he, humble and riding on a donkey, on a colt, the foal of a donkey' (NRSV). Luke appears to recognize the reverberations of Zechariah 9 in Mark's narrative, for he turns up the volume a bit by adding a direct reference to the colt in place of Mark's pronoun (19.35; cf. Mk 11.7) and by using the verb ἐπεβίβασαν (from ἐπιβιβάζω), similar in sound and meaning to the ἐπιβεβηκώς (from ἐπιβαίνω) used in Zech. 9.9 (LXX).[36]The πῶλον νέον of Zech. 9.9

---

35. This is one of the striking differences from Matthew's Parable of the Talents. It is unclear whether, or in what way, the two parables are related.

36. Bock, 'The Use of the OT in Luke–Acts', p. 501. Contra J.A. Fitzmyer, who asserts, 'Luke has not the slightest reference to [Zech. 9:9], apart from the use of

seems to be paralleled by Luke's description of the animal as 'a colt upon whom no one has ever sat' (19.30; cf. Mk 11.2).

As presented by Luke, Jesus' action functions as a powerful claim to kingship. The association of a colt with the Messiah is seen in Jacob's blessing of Judah in Gen. 49.11, where the messianic figure ties his πῶλον to a vine (cf. Lk. 19.30, πῶλον δεδεμένον).[37] Solomon's riding on David's mule (ἡμίονος) plays an important symbolic role in his claim to succeed his father as king in the face of Adonijah's bid to take over the throne (1 Kgs 1.28-53). It may be that Jesus' ride into Jerusalem would have evoked images of the accession of David's heir to the throne.[38]

In Luke's description of the rejoicing of the crowd one can detect further reverberations of Zech. 9.9 (Lk. 19.37: ἤρξαντο...χαίροντες αἰνεῖν τὸν θεὸν; Zech. 9.9: Χαῖρε σφόδρα) as well as echoes of Psalm 118 (Lk. 19.37: χαίροντες αἰνεῖν τὸν θεὸν φωνῇ μεγάλῃ περὶ πασῶν ὧν εἶδον δυναμεων; Ps. 118.15: φωνὴ ἀγαλλιάσεως... δεξιὰ κυρίου ἐποίησεν δύναμιν). To the quotation of Ps. 118.26 Luke adds the interpretative gloss, 'the king' (19.38). This title is especially significant in Luke's narrative, for although Luke has had much to say about the kingdom, Jesus has not yet been named 'king'.[39] In light of the presence of Zech. 9.9 as a subtext for Jesus' entry into the city, it is probable that Luke has borrowed the appellation from Zech. 9.9 and that he intends here to conflate the acclamation of Ps. 118.26 with the call to rejoice at the coming of 'the king' in Zechariah. This conflation makes it clear that the coming one is the Messiah.[40] It also

---

pōlos for the animal' (*The Gospel according to Luke X–XXIV* [AB, 28a; New York: Doubleday, 1985], p. 1244).

37. J. Blenkinsopp argues that Zech. 9.9 is one of several later interpretations of Gen. 49.11 found within the Hebrew Bible ('The Oracle of Judah and the Messianic Entry', *JBL* 80 [1961], pp. 55-64 [57]).

38. For possible parallels between the narrative in 1 Kings and Jesus' entry into Jerusalem, see Giblin, *The Destruction of Jerusalem*, p. 50; A. George, *Etudes sur l'oeuvre de Luc* (SB; Paris: Gabalda, 1978), p. 275; and most recently, Kinman, *Jesus' Entry*, pp. 91-95, 110.

39. Ironically, as Luke makes clear, Jesus suffers trial as a false king (χριστὸν βασιλέα; Lk. 23.2) and endures shameful mocking as a pitiful pretender to royalty (Lk. 23.38).

40. Further messianic associations are evoked by the comment, unique to Luke, that the crowd's acclamation breaks forth as they reach the top of the Mount of Olives (cf. Zech. 14.4), just as they are preparing to descend to the city.

serves to weave together these two Old Testament prophecies into a complex motif that thickens the texture of Luke's narrative of Jesus' arrival in Jerusalem.[41]

Luke alone reports the final part of the acclamation: 'Peace in heaven and glory in the highest (heavens)!' (Lk. 19.38). This may reflect Luke's understanding of Mark's 'hosanna' as a word of praise. It seems to function at a narrative level, however, by linking the triumphal entry with the announcement to the shepherds in Lk. 2.8-14 of the birth of the Messiah, the Savior.[42] At this moment, Jesus enters into Jerusalem to fulfill his role as savior and to take up his kingship. Tannehill elucidates in detail the many verbal links between the Triumphal Entry and the Birth Narratives and suggests that Luke draws these connections to highlight the tragic reversal of Israel's hope, as they now reject the one sent to save them.[43] In light of the expectation for Jesus' reception in Jerusalem aroused by Luke's first quotation of Ps. 118.26 in the prophecy of 13.35b, it is significant that it is 'the whole company of the disciples' (Luke's phrase) who sing the welcome of Ps. 118.26, rather than the residents of Jerusalem.[44] As the unfolding of the story will make clear, Jesus has *not* been received as Messiah, with disastrous consequences for the city.

Opposition to Jesus' claim to kingship comes quickly (Lk. 19.39-40). This scene is unique to Luke (but cf. Mt. 21.14-16). 'Some of the Pharisees in the crowd', scandalized by the messianic acclamation of the disciples, do not join in but instead demand that Jesus, the 'teacher', rebuke his disciples (v. 39). Whereas Jesus 'rebuked' the disciples after

41. Should a reference to Zech. 9.9 be deemed unlikely here, Luke's gloss still shows that he understands the crowd's shouting of Ps. 118.26 as their welcome of the Messiah.

42. For Messiah as 'saviour', cf. Zech. 9.9; Ps. 118.25; 'Peace' may be a further link with Zech. 9.10.

43. R.C. Tannehill, *The Narrative Unity of Luke–Acts* (2 vols.; Philadelphia: Fortress Press, 1986), I, pp. 159-60.

44. R.C. Tannehill, 'Israel in Luke–Acts: A Tragic Story', *JBL* 104 (1985), pp. 69-85 (85); Fitzmyer, *Luke X–XXIV*, p. 1035. Several scholars argue that Lk. 13.35 must refer to the *parousia* because the prophecy is not fulfilled at Jesus' entry into Jerusalem (E.E. Ellis, *The Gospel of Luke* [NCB; Grand Rapids: Eerdmans, 2nd edn, 1974], p. 191; C.A. Evans, 'Prophecy and Polemic: Jews in Luke's Scriptural Apologetic', in Evans and Sanders, *Luke and Scripture*, pp. 171-211 (178). However, this view appears to overlook the irony in Luke's narrative. Lk. 19.37-38 *is* a fulfillment of 13.35, but in an unexpected and tragic manner.

Peter's confession in 9.20, he now refuses to 'rebuke' them: the time for public revelation has come.[45] Jesus claims that if the disciples were to become silent, the stones would cry out the welcome for the king. Jesus' reply is in the form of a 'future more vivid' construction.[46] This emphatic assertion that the stones *will* cry out if the disciples are silenced underlines the fact that this is the crucial moment of decision for Jerusalem. It further hints at the coming destruction of Jerusalem in which no stone will be left upon another (19.44) because of the city's failure to receive him.[47] E.E. Ellis suggests that Jesus' words echo Hab. 2.11, where the stones of a house cry out against the iniquity committed within its walls.[48] The reference to judgment evoked by this allusion is jarring in the context of the disciples' rejoicing, yet it is consistent with Luke's ironic tone throughout this passage; furthermore, it coheres with Jesus' prediction of the destruction of Jerusalem that follows his exchange with the Pharisees.

J.A. Sanders argues that the stones of the Temple are in view (cf. Ps. 118.26b, 'We bless you from the house of the Lord'). This appears to be confirmed by Luke's continued play on the word 'stone' in the Temple scenes (19.44; 20.6; 20.17-18; 21.5-6) and by the fact that, upon his arrival in the city, Jesus immediately enters the Temple to cleanse it (19.45-46).[49] Through his subsequent references to Ps. 118.22, Luke will subtly contrast these Temple 'stones', destined for destruction, with Jesus, the chosen 'cornerstone'. In the midst of the rejoicing surrounding Jesus' arrival in Jerusalem, the Pharisees' opposition sounds an ominously discordant note that foreshadows the rejection of Jesus that will culminate in his death.

---

45. Tannehill, *The Narrative Unity of Luke–Acts*, I, p. 158.

46. According to H.W. Smyth, conditional clauses of this form 'vividly anticipate the realization of a future event' (*Greek Grammar* [rev. G.M. Messing; Cambridge, MA: Harvard University Press, 1956], §2565).

47. 'In Luke's narrative, these words render a verdict as severe as that of the king in the "parable" [19:27]' (D.L. Tiede, *Prophecy and History in Luke–Acts* [Philadelphia: Fortress Press, 1980], p. 81).

48. *The Gospel of Luke*, p. 226. Cf. 2 Esd. 5.5 for stones crying out during the eschatological judgment.

49. Sanders, 'A Hermeneutic Fabric', p. 150. Note that Luke omits Mk 11.11-14 (cf. Mt. 21.10), so that Jesus proceeds immediately into the Temple.

f. *Jesus Weeps over Jerusalem/Cleansing of the Temple*
(Luke 19.41-48)

Jesus' words make it clear that he has not been 'seen' and welcomed as king (cf. 13.35). The echoes of Psalm 118 intensify the irony and pain of the scene. Jesus weeps over the blindness of Jerusalem; the city has not recognized 'this day' (19.42), 'the time of your visitation' (19.44), perhaps an ironic reference to 'the day' of God's deliverance which is celebrated in Ps. 118.24.[50] The rejection of Jesus brings about a reversal in Jerusalem's situation. Her failure to recognize the time of visitation for deliverance calls forth a prophecy of imminent visitation for punishment. They have refused peace (19.42), which the king would have brought to them (19.38; cf. Zech. 9.10). In response, Jesus predicts the destruction of Jerusalem. In a striking reversal of the holy war image of Ps. 118.10-12, in which encircling enemies (κυκλώσαντες ἐκύκλωσάν με) are warded off by the aid of the Lord, Jerusalem will be encircled (περικυκλώσουσίν σε) and destroyed. God now fights not for them (Ps. 118.6-7), but against them. Jesus prophesies a destruction of the city so complete that no stone will be left upon another (Lk. 19.44). This prophecy, repeated in the introduction to the Apocalyptic Discourse (Lk. 21.6, paralleled in Mk 13.2//Mt. 24.2), continues the play on the stone theme of Ps. 118.22 first introduced in Lk. 19.40.

The cleansing of the Temple (Lk. 19.45-46) functions as a harbinger of God's judgment on the leaders of Israel who have turned it into a 'den of robbers' (Lk. 19.46, quoting Jer. 7.11, a warning of judgment on the Temple).[51] In 19.47-48, Luke shows Jesus teaching daily in the Temple. He is opposed by the chief priests, scribes, and the first among the people, but 'the people' (ὁ λαός) listen to him intently. Throughout the passion narrative, Luke distinguishes between the culpable leaders

---

50. Note the Zacchaeus story in which 'today' is a day of salvation (Lk. 19.1-10): 'Today [σήμερον] salvation has come to this house'. 'Visitation', while often used in the sense of visitation for judgment (Isa. 10.3; Jer. 6.15; Sir. 18.20), may also refer to God's visitation to save. The latter sense is common in Luke's use of the word (Lk. 1.68, 78; 7.16; Acts 15.14; cf. Acts 7.23; 15.36).

51. Several scholars have seen in the Temple-cleansing echoes of Zech. 14.21. For references see S. Kim, 'Jesus—the Son of God, the Stone, the Son of Man, and the Servant: The Role of Zechariah in the Self-Identification of Jesus', in G.F. Hawthorne and O. Betz (eds.), *Tradition and Interpretation in the New Testament* (Grand Rapids: Eerdmans, 1987), pp. 134-45 (147 n. 37).

and 'the people' who are favorable to Jesus.[52] This distinction reaches its climax at the cross, where the people stand by and watch (in sympathy?) while the leaders mock Jesus (Lk. 23.35).

g. *Parable of the Wicked Tenants (Luke 20.9-19)*

From this point on in the narrative, Ps. 118.22 becomes the focal point of Luke's interest in Psalm 118. The 'coming' of Jesus (Ps. 118.26) is no longer in view; he has come, and he has been met with rejection. Luke's remaining quotations of and allusions to Psalm 118 focus on Jesus' vindication by God in the face of this rejection.

Immediately prior to this parable, the chief priests, scribes and elders question Jesus' authority (20.1-8). Jesus outwits his adversaries because they are afraid to answer his counter-question concerning John's authority. Only Luke mentions the specific reason for their fear of the crowd: they believe the crowd will reward their answer that John was a false prophet by stoning them. Luke's verb for stoning, καταλιθάζω, is a New Testament hapax and does not occur in the LXX. It is tempting to see here one more of Luke's mutations of the 'stone' theme of Ps. 118.22.[53]

Jesus tells the parable 'to the people' (20.9), but the leaders are his specific target (20.19). Luke brings the parable closer to the vineyard oracle of Isa. 5.1-7 (which Jesus' parable self-consciously echoes) by adding in v. 13 the question the Lord asks when faced with Israel's unfruitfulness, τί ποιήσω. Luke also shows more closely the correspondence between the son of the parable and Jesus. In v. 15, Luke (with Matthew) changes Mark's order of events so that the tenants cast the son out of the vineyard before killing him.

The quotation of Ps. 118.22 'acts as an explosive postscript to the parable'.[54] The citation unambiguously interprets the parable as a reference to the rejection and vindication of the Messiah. The parable itself says nothing to prefigure Jesus' resurrection; it merely promises judgment on the opponents. The quotation of the psalm, however,

---

52. Cf. J. Kodell, 'Luke's Use of LAOS, "People", Especially in the Jerusalem Narrative (Lk 19, 28-24, 53)', *CBQ* 31 (1969), pp. 327-43.

53. Cf. the similar suggestion by Tiede, *Prophecy and History*, p. 81.

54. A.A. Milavec, 'A Fresh Analysis of the Parable of the Wicked Husbandmen in the Light of Jewish–Catholic Dialogue', in C. Thoma and M. Wyschogrod (eds.), *Parable and Story in Judaism and Christianity* (New York: Paulist Press, 1989), pp. 81-117 (109). It is widely thought that the quotation and parable were originally linked by means of paronomasia: הבן/אבן (Snodgrass, *Wicked Tenants*, p. 63 n. 79).

foreshadows the resurrection of Jesus and his vindication by God.[55] The designation 'cornerstone' recalls other uses of this metaphor for royalty, such as that in Zech. 10.4 (See also Isa. 28.16; Judg. 20.2; 1 Sam. 14.38; Isa. 19.13; Jer. 51.26).[56] In Psalm 118, the cornerstone appears to refer to part of the Temple.[57]

Luke follows the quotation of Ps. 118.22 with a second 'stone' saying (Lk. 20.18), found also in Mt. 21.44.[58] In Luke, this second saying is tied closely to the quotation of Psalm 118 both by its asyndetic juxtaposition to the quotation[59] and by the demonstrative pronoun *'that* stone'. The saying appears to be a combination of Isa. 8.14; Dan. 2.35, 44; and possibly Ps. 110.5-6. All three Old Testament passages speak of God's judgment and of the vindication of his rule. The verbs λικμάω and συνθλάω occur only here (and in the parallel in Matthew) in the New Testament. λικμάω is rare in the LXX and occurs in collocation with 'stone' only in Dan. 2.44. συνθλάω likewise is rare, but it occurs twice in Psalm 110. Daniel 2 vividly pictures the everlasting kingdom

55. It is tempting to make a further connection between Luke's Passion narrative and the confident statement of Ps. 118.17, 'I shall not die, but shall live' (cf. C.H. Dodd, *According to the Scriptures* [London: Nisbet, 1952], p. 99). The vindication spoken of in the psalm finds unexpected fulfillment in the Messiah's experience of death and preservation *through* death rather than in his preservation *from* death (cf. Ps. 118.18).

56. Explicit combination of Ps. 118.22 with Isa. 28.16 and Isa. 8.14 (cf. Lk. 20.18) occurs in 1 Pet. 2.4-7 in reference to Jesus' rejection and vindication.

57. J. Marcus, *The Way of the Lord* (Louisville, KY: Westminster/John Knox, 1992), p. 119. The association of Messiah with the Temple building and with the designation 'stone' seems to be a further echo of Zechariah. Kim notes that in Zechariah, Zerubbabel, the Davidic prince, is presented as builder of the Temple (4.7-10). This function is apparently reapplied to the Messiah: Zech. 6.12-13 presents the 'branch' as builder of the Temple. Further, in Zech. 3.8-9, the 'branch' is linked with the 'stone' (cf. the 'top stone' of 4.7). The Targum interprets 'branch', 'stone' and 'top stone' here messianically (Kim, 'Jesus', p. 138).

58. The saying appears in brackets in the UBSGNT[4]/Nestle–Aland[27] text of Matthew, indicating the editors' opinion that the reading is an early interpolation from Luke. See B.M. Metzger, *A Textual Commentary on the Greek New Testament* (Stuttgart; UBS, 2nd edn, 1994), p. 47.

59. Contrast Matthew, where an extra verse of Psalm 118 (v. 23) and an interpretation of the parable by Jesus intervene between the quotation and saying (Mt. 21.43). Luke's omission of Ps. 118.23, found in both Mark and Matthew, concentrates attention on the rejection of the stone and its consequences—vindication and judgment (cf. L.T. Johnson, *The Gospel of Luke* [Collegeville, MN: Liturgical Press, 1991], p. 306).

of the Messiah that will crush all other kingdoms (cf. Lk. 1.33: 'his kingdom will have no end'). Psalm 110 likewise depicts the destruction of the Messiah's enemies by the Lord, who will shatter kings (v. 5) as he makes Messiah's enemies a footstool for his feet (v. 1).[60] The opponents of Jesus are in danger of occupying the place of the Gentile kings (Psalm 110) and kingdoms (Daniel 2) and so being crushed and shattered by the 'Stone'.[61]

h. *Prediction of the Destruction of the Temple (Luke 21.5-6)*

This passage, which introduces Luke's version of the Apocalyptic Discourse, is linked with the previous quotations of Psalm 118 by the word 'stone' in both v. 5 and v. 6. The prediction of destruction recalls the prophecy of Lk. 19.44 and seems to be a further example of Luke's technique of using repetition for emphasis.[62] Following the conflict narratives in which opposition to Jesus has intensified, this prediction further heightens the note of judgment and reversal sounded by previous citations of Ps. 118.22. After the Apocalyptic Discourse (21.7-36), Luke's narrative moves swiftly on to the crucifixion of Jesus and his resurrection. It is from a post-resurrection perspective that the final citation of Psalm 118 in Luke–Acts unequivocally interprets these events as the fulfillment of Ps. 118.22.

i. *Peter and John before the Sanhedrin (Acts 4.1-12)*

The early preaching in Acts makes generous use of psalm texts, although Psalm 118 appears only twice (2.33; 5.31), in fairly subtle allusions that have often been identified with Psalm 110. Luke's previous use of Psalm 118 in the Gospel makes allusions to Ps. 118.16 likely here, however, in view of the strong verbal links (ὑψόω and δεξία in the dative).[63] The decisive quotation for this study, however, occurs in Acts 4.11.

---

60. The echo of Psalm 110 here is admittedly extremely faint and perhaps non-existent; it is made slightly more plausible by the quotation of Ps. 110.1 in 20.42-43.

61. A rabbinic proverb often cited in the secondary literature captures well the sense of Jesus' words: 'If a pot falls on a stone, woe to the pot! If the stone falls on the pot, woe to the pot! Either way, woe to the pot!' (*Est. R.* 3.6).

62. See the comments above on Lk. 7.19//7.20; 9.22//17.25.

63. Though most commentators see in Acts 2.33 and 5.31 an allusion to Ps. 110.1, Dodd has suggested that τῇ δεξιᾷ οὖν τοῦ θεοῦ ὑψωθείς be heard as an echo of Ps. 118.16, with the dative understood as instrumental rather than locative. This reading is supported by F.F. Bruce (*The Acts of the Apostles* [Grand Rapids:

At last Luke lays all his cards out on the table, as it were, making explicit the connections between Psalm 118 and the story of Jesus that up to now have been implied in the narrative rather than clearly stated. The faint echoes of Psalm 118 found in the Gospel are amplified in Acts 4 to a triumphant fanfare announcing that the words of the psalm find their fulfillment in Jesus' death and resurrection. Acts 4.11 thus serves as the hermeneutical key to Luke's use of Psalm 118 throughout the Gospel.[64] For Luke, the psalm clearly prefigures the rejection and vindication of God's Messiah.

There are a great number of similarities between this passage and Lk. 20.1-19, suggesting that Luke intends the passages to be read in light of one another.[65] The vindication of Jesus that was a promise in Luke 20 has now become a reality through the resurrection. What was insinuated indirectly in Lk. 20.17, the identification of the 'cornerstone' of Ps. 118.22 as Jesus and the 'builders' as the leaders of Israel, is now proclaimed boldly in Acts 4.11.[66] The fulfillment of the psalm undergirds Luke's theology that all that happened to Jesus was in accordance with the Scriptures (Lk. 24.25-27; 44-47).

Moreover, the reversal motif of Psalm 118 encourages a Church whose conflict with Jesus' opponents, the 'rulers' of Israel (ἄρχοντες, Acts 4.5), continues throughout the narrative of Acts and beyond.

Eerdmans, 3rd edn, 1990], p. 126) and G. Voss (*Die Christologie der lukanischen Schriften in Grundzügen* [StudNeot, 2; Paris: Desclée de Brouwer, 1965], p. 133). In view of Luke's other uses of Psalm 118, perhaps Dodd's suggestion deserves reconsideration (Dodd, *According to the Scriptures*, p. 99).

64. That Acts functions to interpret the Gospel of Luke has been argued in a different context by L.T. Johnson ('The Lukan Kingship Parable', *NovT* 24 [1982], pp. 139-59 [42]).

65. Compare in each scene the opponents (scribes, chief priests, elders: Lk. 20.1, 19; rulers, elders, scribes, high priest and his family: Acts 4.5-6), the occasion of the conflict (Jesus cleanses the Temple, teaches in the Temple: Lk. 19.45-48; disciples heal in the Temple, teach in the Temple: Acts 3.1–4.2), the question of authority (Lk. 20.2; Acts 4.7) and the quotation of Ps. 118.22 (Lk. 20.17; Acts 4.11).

66. In Acts 4.11, the quotation of Ps. 118.22 reads ἐξουθενέω for ἀποδοκιμάζω (LXX and Luke's other quotations). Bruce notes that in the LXX ἐξουθενέω translates מאס (the Hebrew verb in Ps. 118.22) in 1 Kgdms 8.17; 10.19 (Bruce, *The Acts of the Apostles*, pp. 151-52). The variation in the quotation of Ps. 118.22 in Acts 4.11 may stem from Luke's source. For the suggestion that Luke draws on a traditional midrash, see E.E. Ellis, *Prophecy and Hermeutic in Early Christianity* (WUNT, 18; Tübingen: Mohr–Siebeck, 1978), p. 208.

Even as it points to God's foreordination of Jesus' sufferings and vindication, Psalm 118 exhorts Jesus' followers to trust and hope in the Lord
rather than in 'rulers' (ἄρχοντες, Ps. 118.8-9).[67] Although crucified
as a messianic pretender, Jesus has been exalted by God's right hand
(Acts 2.33; 5.31) and made the cornerstone of a new Temple (Acts
4.11). The leaders of Israel who opposed him, and who continue to
oppose the Church, have been displaced and their 'vineyard' given to
others (Lk. 20.16). It is the Church (in Acts clearly made up of both Jew
and Gentile), united to the vindicated Messiah, which represents the
true Israel, even as many Jews continue to reject the message. In Acts,
the vindication of Jesus gives his followers confidence that they too
will share in his vindication.[68]

Conclusion: Luke's Use of Psalm 118

Luke repeatedly appeals to Psalm 118 at important points in the narrative of Luke–Acts. Allusions to this psalm figure prominently in the
identification of Jesus as Messiah by John the Baptist (Lk. 7.19-20; cf.
3.16). The quotation of Ps. 118.26 in Jesus' prophecy in Lk. 13.35 plays
a crucial role in building suspense during Luke's travel narrative, all
the more since it falls between two allusions to Ps. 118.22 in Passion
Predictions (Lk. 9.22; 17.25). Similarly, Psalm 118 is the major Old
Testament text utilized by Luke at the climax of the travel narrative,
when Jesus finally enters Jerusalem. The acclamation of Ps. 118.26 by
the disciples rather than by the inhabitants of Jerusalem (Lk. 19.38)
signals that Jesus has not been received as Messiah, while the clus-
tering of allusions to and echoes of Psalm 118 in the aftermath of the
Triumphal Entry portends imminent judgment on the city (Lk. 19.40,
42, 43, 44; 20.18, 21.5-6). The two quotations of Ps. 118.22 form an
inclusio of sorts around the Passion Narrative; the first (Lk. 20.17)
foreshadows the resurrection and pronounces judgment on Jesus'
opponents, while the second (Acts 4.11) triumphantly declares the

---

67. For this point, see J.T. Carroll, 'The Uses of Scripture in Acts', *SBLSP* 29
(1990), pp. 512-28 (518). Carroll also notes the following links between Psalm 118
and Acts 3–5: (1) 'The name of the Lord' (Ps. 118.10-11; 26), 'the name of Jesus'
(Acts 3.6, 16; 4.7, 10, 12, 17); (2) 'The Lord has become my salvation' (Ps.
118.14), 'salvation is found in no one else. . . no other name' (Acts 4.12).

68. Compare the similar use of the cornerstone images from Ps. 118.22 and Isa.
8.14; 28.16 in 1 Pet. 2.4-8.

vindication of Jesus and the rejection of Israel's leaders, who continue
to persecute Jesus' followers.

Throughout most of Luke–Acts, references to Psalm 118 are fairly
subtle. Luke does not highlight the Old Testament text through the use
of explicit citation formulas (as Matthew often does), but by weaving
quotations of and allusions to the psalm into the very fabric of the
text. An explicit interpretation of Psalm 118 occurs only in its final
citation (Acts 4.11). This technique carries with it surprising rhetorical
power. As Bock has observed, Luke's style 'heightens the prophetic
emphasis, since it is not the narrator, but the narrative itself which
points to fulfillment'.[69]

In addition to the occurrence of Psalm 118 at crucial points in Luke's
narrative, a second feature of Luke's use of the psalm is noteworthy.
This is the shift in focus from Ps. 118.26 to Ps. 118.22 that takes place
after Jesus' entry into Jerusalem. Luke's shift from Ps. 118.26 to Ps.
118.22 not only coheres with the flow of his narrative, it becomes one
of the tools Luke uses to create dramatic tension and movement in his
story. In the first part of the Gospel, Ps. 118.26 functions to establish
Jesus' messianic identity as 'the one who comes'. This title creates a
sense of expectation and tension as Jesus' lament and prophecy in
Lk. 13.34-35 raise the question of whether Jerusalem will welcome him
as Messiah. When Jesus enters the city, however, Ps. 118.26 is found
only on the lips of his disciples. From the Jewish leaders he receives
swift opposition.

From this point on in Luke–Acts, Ps. 118.26 disappears from the
narrative, and Luke focuses on Ps. 118.22 in his appeal to the psalm.
Luke employs Psalm 118 to argue that the rejection of Jesus by his
people was within the sovereign purpose of God. The refusal of Israel
to receive God's Messiah was spoken of beforehand in Scripture; in
Luke's theology, this rejection is part of that which the Christ had to
suffer (ἔδει παθεῖν) according to the revelation given through 'Moses
and all the prophets' (Lk. 24.26-27; cf. 18.31) and according to 'all
that was written in the law of Moses and in the prophets and in the
psalms' (Lk. 24.44).

At the same time, Psalm 118 promises that God will vindicate the
Messiah. Luke alludes to this vindication even before the crucifixion by

69. Bock, 'The Use of the OT in Luke–Acts', p. 502. Bock describes Luke's
technique of juxtaposing narrative and Old Testament text as being similar to the
manner in which 'a title is placed under a master painting' (p. 502).

placing Ps. 118.22 on Jesus' lips in his conflict with Israel's leaders (Lk. 20.17). The juxtaposition of Dan. 2.44 in the second 'stone' saying (Lk. 20.18) with the cornerstone passage from Ps. 118.22 emphasizes the eternality of Messiah's reign and identifies the inauguration of the kingdom of God with the resurrection of Jesus. The quotation of Ps. 118.22 in Acts 4.11 makes unmistakable the identification of the vindication of Jesus with the resurrection. This final quotation clearly condemns the leaders of Israel for their rejection of the Messiah and designates Jesus as the cornerstone of God's people, defined in Acts as those (Jew and Gentile) who confess Jesus' name.

The results of this study suggest that the use of Scripture in the narrative of Luke–Acts is more complex than has generally been recognized. The method followed here of tracing the connections *among* Luke's references to Psalm 118 has proven to be illuminating.[70] Luke's repeated reference to Psalm 118 by means of quotation, allusion and echo contributes to the dramatic tension of the narrative at the same time as it enriches the theological message of Luke's opus. The narrative thread created by Luke's repeated quotation of and allusion to Psalm 118 anchors the story of Jesus and the unfolding experience of the Church firmly within the larger story of God's saving acts revealed in Scripture.

TABLE OF QUOTATIONS OF AND ALLUSIONS TO PSALM 118 IN LUKE–ACTS

Key: A = allusion/echo Q = quotation + = unique to Luke
~ different position in Matthew † = text in Matthew disputed

Luke				Psalm 118
7.19	John the Baptist's Question:			
	σὺ εἶ ὁ ἐρχόμενος;		A	118.26
7.20	σὺ εἶ ὁ ἐρχόμενος;		A	118.26+
9.22	First Passion Prediction:			
	δεῖ τὸν υἱὸν τοῦ ἀνθρώπου πολλὰ παθεῖν			
	καὶ ἀποδοκιμασθῆναι ἀπὸ τῶν			
	πρεσβυτέρων καὶ ἀρχιερέων καὶ			
	γραμματέων		A	118.22

70. It remains to be seen whether other Old Testament texts quoted in Luke–Acts function in a similar way in the narrative.

13.35	Lament over Jerusalem:		
	<u>εὐλογημένος ὁ ἐρχόμενος ἐν ὀνόματι</u>		
	<u>κυρίου</u>	Q	118.26~

17.25	Day of the Son of Man:		
	δεῖ αὐτὸν πολλὰ παθεῖν καὶ		
	<u>ἀποδοκιμασθῆναι</u> ἀπὸ τῆς γενεᾶς ταύτης	A	118.22+

19.37a	Entry into Jerusalem:		
	ἤρξαντο ἅπαν τὸ πλῆθος τῶν μαθητῶν		
	<u>χαίροντες</u> <u>αἰνεῖν</u> τὸν θεὸν <u>φωνῇ</u> μεγάλῃ	A	118.15a+
19.37b	περὶ πασῶν ὧν εἶδον <u>δυνάμεων,</u>	A	118.15b+
19.38	λέγοντες· <u>εὐλογημένος ὁ ἐρχόμενος,</u> ὁ		
	βασιλεὺς <u>ἐν</u> <u>ὀνόματι</u> <u>κυρίου</u>	Q	118.26
			(cf. Zech. 9.9)

19.40	Jesus Answers the Pharisees:		
	ἐὰν οὗτοι σιωπήσουσιν, <u>οἱ</u> <u>λίθοι</u> κράξουσιν	A	118.22+

19.42	Jesus Weeps over Jerusalem:		
	εἰ ἔγνως ἐν <u>τῇ</u> <u>ἡμέρᾳ</u> <u>ταύτῃ</u>	A	118.24+
19.44	ἀνθ’ ὧν οὐκ ἔγνως <u>τὸν</u> <u>καιρόν</u>	A	118.24+
19.43	οἱ ἐχθροί σου... <u>περικυκλώσουσίν</u> σε	A	118.10-12+
19.44	οὐκ ἀφήσουσιν <u>λίθον</u> ἐπὶ <u>λίθον</u> ἐν σοί	A	118.22+

20.6	Question about Authority:		
	ὁ λαὸς ἅπας <u>καταλιθάσει</u> ἡμᾶς	A	118.22+

20.17	Parable of Wicked Tenants		
	<u>λίθον</u> <u>ὃν</u> <u>ἀπεδοκίμασαν</u> <u>οἱ</u> <u>οἰκοδομοῦντες,</u>		
	<u>οὗτος</u> <u>ἐγενήθη</u> <u>εἰς</u> <u>κεφαλὴν</u> <u>γωνίας</u>	Q	118.22
20.18	πᾶς ὁ πεσὼν ἐπ’ ἐκεῖνον <u>τὸν</u> <u>λίθον</u>	A	118.22†

21.5	Prediction of Destruction of Temple:		
	Καί τινων λεγόντων περὶ τοῦ ἱεροῦ ὅτι <u>λίθοις</u>		
	καλοῖς... κεκόσμηται	A	118.22
21.6	οὐκ ἀφεθήσεται <u>λίθος</u> ἐπὶ <u>λίθῳ</u>	A	118.22

Acts

2.33	Peter's Pentecost Sermon:		
	<u>τῇ</u> <u>δεξιᾷ</u> οὖν τοῦ θεοῦ <u>ὑψωθείς</u>	A	118.16+

4.11   Peter and John before Jewish Leaders:
οὗτός ἐστιν <u>ὁ λίθος ὁ ἐξουθενηθεὶς</u> ὑφ᾽ ὑμῶν
<u>τῶν οἰκοδόμων, ὁ γενόμενος εἰς κεφαλὴν</u>
<u>γωνίας</u>   Q   118.22+

5.31   Peter's Speech to Sanhedrin
τοῦτον ὁ θεὸς ἀρχηγὸν καὶ σωτῆρα <u>ὕψωσεν</u>
<u>τῇ δεξιᾷ</u> αὐτοῦ   A   118.16+

INTERTEXTUAL PERMUTATIONS OF THE GENESIS WORD
IN THE JOHANNINE PROLOGUES

William S. Kurz, SJ

Introduction

The reinterpretation by the Fourth Gospel's prologue of LXX Genesis 1 is well known.[1] As shown especially by Peder Borgen, Thomas Tobin and Craig Evans, the Fourth Gospel shares in a long history of interpretation of the Genesis creation story, not only within later biblical writings, including books found only in the Septuagint, and within targumic and exegetical traditions, but also in Hellenistic Jewish writers like Philo. Most scholars see this reinterpretation by Genesis in the Fourth Gospel prologue as somehow or at some time taking place in a

---

1. See a helpful series of Peder Borgen's closely related articles: P. Borgen, 'Observations on the Targumic Character of the Prologue of John', *NTS* 16 (1970), pp. 288-95 (as a special illustration of this, see the comparison between Targum Neophiti on Gen. 1.1 and 2.2a and Jn 1.1a and 1.3a in G. Schwarz, 'Gen 1:1, 2:2a und Joh 1:1a.3—ein Vergleich', *ZNW* 73 [1982], pp. 136-37); P. Borgen, 'Logos was the True Light: Contribution to the Interpretation of the Prologue of John', *NovT* 14 (1972), pp. 115-30; *idem*, 'Chapter Four: The Prologue of John—As Exposition of the Old Testament', in P. Borgen, *Philo, John and Paul: New Perspectives on Judaism and Early Christianity* (BJS, 131; Atlanta: Scholars Press, 1987), pp. 75-101. See esp. his conclusion, pp. 92-93. The close comparisons of the kind of interpretations of Genesis in the Fourth Gospel's prologue and the targumic materials are the most enlightening aspects of these articles. Note, however, the important methodological cautions by C.A. Evans, *Word and Glory: On the Exegetical and Theological Background of John's Prologue* (JSNTSup, 89; Sheffield: JSOT Press, 1993), esp. pp. 114-34. See also M. Rissi, 'John 1:1-18 (The Eternal Word)', *Int* 31 (1977), pp. 394-401; R. Kieffer, *Le monde symbolique de Saint Jean* (Lectio Divina, 137; Latour-Maubourg: Cerf, 1989), pp. 35-38; J. Painter, 'Theology, Eschatology, and the Prologue of John', *SJT* 46 (1993), pp. 27-42. Cf. T. Tobin, 'The Prologue of John and Hellenistic Jewish Speculation', *CBQ* 52 (1990), pp. 252-69; J. Ashton, *Understanding the Fourth Gospel* (Oxford: Clarendon Press, 1991), pp. 527-29.

hymnic context.[2] Recently, scholars have focused more explicitly on the literary critical aspects of intertextuality in this reinterpretation.[3]

After briefly retracing the main lines of the Fourth Gospel's reinterpretation of Genesis 1, this article will describe how the prologue of 1 John further reinterprets the Fourth Gospel prologue, and finally how it too relates to Genesis 1, sometimes through the interpretative filter of the Fourth Gospel prologue. It will try to show that whereas the Fourth Gospel had applied Genesis allusions primarily to revelation of God by 'the Word' become flesh, 1 John applies the same Genesis backdrop to salvation as 'eternal life' through 'the life' who has appeared to us.

2. For the hermeneutical implications of this hymnic context, see H. Weder, 'Der Raum der Lieder: Zur Hermeneutik des Hymnischen im Neuen Testament', *EvT* 53 (1993), pp. 328-41. He reminds us how hymns are grateful celebrations of unambiguous faith and leave out doubt and complications.

3. E.g., J. Painter, 'Theology, Eschatology and the Prologue of John', *SJT* 46 (1993), pp. 27-42. He summarizes and reapplies many previous insights under two rubrics—1. 'inter-textual resonances': treating cosmologies, the λόγος, 'in the beginning', and 'wisdom'; and 2. 'inter-textual transforming strategies': dealing with the λόγος, dualism, antithetical Johannine language, apocalyptic ideology, and how eschatology affects the incarnation, ministry of signs, death/exaltation, being born of God and ongoing judgment, and future judgment. See also my approaches to intertextuality in W.S. Kurz, SJ, 'Intertextual Use of Sirach 48:1-16 in Plotting Luke–Acts', in C.A. Evans and W.R. Stegner (eds.), *The Gospels and the Scriptures of Israel* (JSNTSup, 104; SSEJC, 3; Sheffield: Sheffield Academic Press, 1994), pp. 308-24, esp. pp. 310-14. For canonical intertextality, see, e.g., R.L. Brawley, 'Canon and Community: Intertextuality, Canon, Interpretation, Christology, Theology, and Persuasive Rhetoric in Luke 4:1-13', in E.H. Lovering (ed.), *Society of Biblical Literature 1992 Seminar Papers* (SBLSP, 31; Atlanta: Scholars Press, 1992), pp. 419-34; D. Boyarin, 'Old Wine in New Bottles: Intertextuality and Midrash', *Poetics Today* 8 (1987), pp. 539-56; and S. Draisma (ed.), *Intertextuality in Biblical Writings: Essays in Honour of Bas van Iersel* (Kampen: Kok, 1989).

For the valuable notion of 'writing with Scripture', see J. Neusner and W.S. Green, *Writing with Scripture: The Authority and Uses of the Hebrew Bible in the Torah of Formative Judaism* (Minneapolis: Fortress Press, 1989), esp. Green's title article, 'Writing with Scripture: The Rabbinic Uses of the Hebrew Bible', pp. 7-23, and Neusner's article, 'Judaic and Christian Uses of Scripture: "As it is said" or "The Old Testament in the New"', pp. 1-6. For a useful treatment of literary allusion, see C. Petri, 'On Alluding', *Poetics* 7 (1978), pp. 289-307.

Reinterpretation of Genesis 1 in the Fourth Gospel Prologue

As is widely acknowledged, the Fourth Gospel's beginning echoes that in LXX Genesis: both start with ἐν ἀρχῇ, referring to cosmic origins. Within this cosmic setting, Genesis opens simply with God's creating the heaven and earth (ἐν ἀρχῇ ἐποίησεν ὁ θεὸς τὸν οὐρανὸν καὶ τὴν γῆν). Only later does it refer to God speaking a word that creates (καὶ εἶπεν ὁ θεός Γενηθήτω φῶς. καὶ ἐγένετο φῶς).

Interpreting this simple Genesis narrative, the Fourth Gospel first hypostasizes and personalizes the verbal command in Gen. 1.3, 'Let there be light' into 'the Word' through whom God creates. With this personification of the Word, the prologue sets the stage for all that follows, showing God and the hypostastized Word existing before creation (v. 1: ἐν ἀρχῇ ἦν ὁ λόγος).[4]

Next it claims that everything was created through this Word (v. 3: πάντα δι' αὐτοῦ ἐγένετο). Tobin alerts us to how this use of the preposition διά is like Philo's treatment of the Logos as that through (διά) which the universe was framed. Both Philo and the Johannine prologue are commenting on Genesis, and both are using a 'metaphysics of prepositions' as in emerging Middle Platonism, which stresses different propositions for different kinds of causality. It was a widespread *topos* in Middle Platonism taken up by Jewish interpreters.[5]

Whereas the main concentration in Genesis 1 was on creation, the reinterpretation by the Fourth Gospel prologue focuses especially on the creative Word as *revelation* of God. In itself the use of 'Word' implies communication or revelation by God (Jn 1.1). Verses 4-5 further emphasize the revelatory aspects of the Word by locating life in the

---

4. Cf. M.D. Goulder, 'Exegesis of Genesis 1–3 in the New Testament', *JJS* 43 (1992), pp. 226-29, esp. p. 227; and A. Reinhartz, *The Word in the World: The Cosmological Tale in the Fourth Gospel* (SBLMS, 45; Atlanta: Scholars Press, 1992).

5. Tobin, 'Prologue', pp. 257-60, esp. pp. 259-60. Cf. the further reflections on Philo's exegesis, on the prologue of the Fourth Gospel, and on Tobin's article in Evans, *Word and Glory*, pp. 100-14. A different but complementary perspective on the Johannine διά with the genitive as expressing the Son's mediation of all God's activity *ad extra* is offered by T.E. Pollard, 'The Father–Son and God–Believer Relationships according to St John: A Brief Study of John's Use of Prepositions', in M. de Jonge (ed.), *L'évangile de Jean: Sources, rédaction, théologie* (BETL, 44; Gembloux: Duculot; Leuven: Leuven University Press, 1977), pp. 363-69, esp. p. 366.

Word, and stating that 'the life was the *light* of humans, and the light shines in the darkness, and the darkness did not grasp it'. The emphasis on (revelatory) light continues in the contrast between the Baptist, who is not the light but only a witness to the light (vv. 6-8), as distinguished from the true light that enlightens every human (v. 9). Verse 10 goes on to stress the world's failure to know this revelation. Verse 14 continues the emphasis on revelation when it stresses that when the Word became flesh, 'we have seen his glory'. Finally the concluding v. 18 clearly portrays the Word, now identified as the 'only-begotten God', as making the Father known, with the final and climactic word being ἐξηγήσατο.[6]

Reinterpretation of the Fourth Gospel Prologue by that of 1 John

In turn, with most scholars, I find that the prologue to the First Letter of John (1 John) reworks the Fourth Gospel's prologue.[7] It reinterprets

6. On the focus of the Fourth Gospel's prologue on the Word as revelation, see R. Bergmeier, 'Weihnachten mit und ohne Glanz: Notizen zu Johannesprolog und Philipperhymnus', *ZNW* 85 (1994), pp. 47-68, esp. pp. 56-59. Cf. R. Schnackenburg, *The Gospel according to St John* (HTKNT; 3 vols.; New York: Herder & Herder, 1968–82), esp. I, pp. 277-81; W. Bindemann, 'Der Johannesprolog: Ein Versuch, ihn zu verstehen', *NovT* 37 (1995), pp. 330-54, esp. pp. 347-48 on Christ as 'exegete' or 'interpreter' of the Father. J.P. Louw, 'Narrator of the Father— EXĒGEISTHAI and related terms in Johannine Christology', *Neot* 2 (1968), pp. 32-40, suggests the sense of narration of the Father for ἐξηγήσατο, which would still qualify as a form of revelation.

7. A. Feuillet, 'The Structure of 1 John: Comparison with the Fourth Gospel: The pattern of Christian life', *BTB* 3 (1973), pp. 194-216; I. de la Potterie, 'La notion de "commencement" dans les écrits johanniques', in R. Schnackenburg *et al.* (eds.), *Die Kirche des Anfangs: Festschrift für Heinz Schürmann zum 65. Geburtstag* (Leipzig: St Benno, 1977), pp. 379-403; R.E. Brown, *Epistles of John* (AB, 30; Garden City, NY: Doubleday, 1982), pp. 176-80. For early articulations of how the concept of 'beginning' was reinterpreted in 1 John, see H.H. Wendt, 'Der "Anfang" am Beginne des I Johannesbriefes', *ZNW* 21 (1922), pp. 38-42; and É. Tobac, 'La notion du Christ-Logos dans la littérature johannique', *RHE* 25 (1929), pp. 213-38. Cf. F.O. Francis, 'The Form and Function of the Opening and Closing Paragraphs of James and 1 John', *ZNW* 61 (1970), pp. 110-26.

An important dissenting voice to the notion of 1 John reinterpreting the Fourth Gospel prologue is W.E. Sproston, 'Witnesses to What Was ἀπ' ἀρχῆς: 1 John's Contribution to our Knowledge of Tradition in the Fourth Gospel', *JSNT* 48 (1992), pp. 43-65. She argues that each writer is utilizing common Johannine tradition. Cf. C.H. Talbert's treatment of 1 John as *prior* to the Fourth Gospel in his commentary, 'the beginning' from the cosmic event in the Fourth Gospel to Christian experience (v. 1: ὃ ἦν ἀπ᾽ ἀρχῆς, ὃ ἀκηκόαμεν, ὃ ἑωρά-καμεν τοῖς ὀφθαλμοῖς ἡμῶν, ὃ ἐθεασάμεθα καὶ αἱ χεῖρες ἡμῶν ἐψηλάφησαν περὶ τοῦ λόγου τῆς ζωῆς). The indefinite pronoun ὅ is the subject of the first verb ἦν ('what was from the beginning') and is the object of several verbs in subordinate clauses (v. 1: ὃ ἀκηκόαμεν, ὃ ἑωράκαμεν... ὃ ἐθεασάμεθα...; v. 3: ὃ ἑωράκαμεν καὶ ἀκηκόαμεν...) in this massive four-verse initial sentence: '*What* was from the beginning, *what* we have heard, *what* we have seen with our own eyes, *what* we have gazed upon and our own hands have touched...' In the main clause, the object that is correlative to this relative pronoun ὅ is an understood demonstrative pronoun like τοῦτο, as in '[τοῦτο understood +] ἀπαγγέλλομεν καὶ ὑμῖν': '[*this*] we announce to you also'. The sentence is notoriously awkward in its grammar.[8] There is nothing obviously corresponding to this succession of neuter singular pronouns, as that which was from the beginning and what we have seen, heard, and announced; perhaps these pronouns are interpreted by the phrase περὶ τοῦ λόγου τῆς ζωῆς (v. 1), or are a generalized reference to Jesus' whole career.[9]

Whereas the prologue of the Fourth Gospel proclaims, 'In the beginning was the Word, and the Word was with God... all things were made through him...', that of the first Johannine letter announces to its audience 'What was from the beginning, what we have heard... seen... gazed upon and... touched...' In both prologues, the referent is to either the pre-incarnate Word and/or [incarnate] Jesus. However, whereas the Fourth Gospel begins with the pre-incarnate Word at the

---

Reading John: A Literary and Theological Commentary on the Fourth Gospel and the Johannine Epistles (Reading the New Testament Series; New York: Crossroad, 1992), esp. pp. 3-4, 56-57.

8. Brown, *Epistles of John*, pp. 152-54; S.S. Smalley, *1, 2, 3 John* (WBC, 57; Waco: WordBooks, 1984), p. 4, both with bibliographical discussion referring to C.H. Dodd, *The Johannine Epistles* (MNTC; London: Hodder & Stoughton, 1946), pp. 1-3; and J.L. Houlden, *A Commentary on the Johannine Epistles* (BNTC; London: A. & C. Black; New York: Harper & Row, 1973), pp. 45-46.

9. Cf. the suggestion by Smalley, *1, 2, 3 John*, p. 6, that this περί phrase may be construed as yet another object of 'declare'; but Brown, *Epistles of John*, p. 154, appealing to BDF, p. 138, argues that the neuter functions comprehensively to cover Jesus' whole career: person, words, and works. He cites from this letter a similar unusual neuter construction in 1 Jn 5.4, ὅτι πᾶν τὸ γεγεννημένον ἐκ τοῦ θεοῦ νικᾷ τὸν κόσμον.

cosmic origins as in Genesis, and only later focuses on eyewitness testimony to the incarnate Word, the letter focuses more quickly on this witness to fleshly realities seen, heard, and touched.

The letter also adapts the Fourth Gospel's treatment of the Word and Life. The consensus about the hypostasized meaning of 'the Word' in the Fourth Gospel's prologue (as pre-existent, later incarnate Son of God) does not extend to the enigmatic expression in 1 Jn 1.1, 'about the word of life' (περὶ τοῦ λόγου τῆς ζωῆς). If the word of life is construed as the life-bringing gospel, and if the letter prologue is understood as resignifying the Fourth Gospel prologue, then 'word' (λόγος) has mutated from meaning a pre-existent divine person in the Fourth Gospel to meaning a message proclaimed, 'the word of life'. This is a reversion of λόγος from its form and sense as a hypostasis in the Fourth Gospel to its more normal form as a non-hypostasized noun with an ordinary meaning of 'message'.[10]

Even though the *meaning* of 'the Word' in the letter is different from that in the Gospel, most of its *functions* in the Gospel prologue are not lost in the letter prologue but are transferred to 'the Life'. In 1 Jn 1.1, the noun *life* in the phrase 'the word of life' could refer to Jesus as 'the Life' (cf. 1.2a: καὶ ἡ ζωὴ ἐφανερώθη); or it could be a simple epexegetical genitive (the word 'which is life'), or qualifying genitive (the 'life-giving' word), or objective genitive (the word 'about life').[11]

One does not have to settle definitively for 1 Jn 1.1 the question whether or not 'the life' in the expression 'about the word of the life' is a personified reference to Jesus, because 'the Life' clearly *is* personified in the immediately following mention in 1 Jn 1.2ab that 'the Life appeared'. In fact, the letter prologue seems to imitate for 'the Life' the development of 'the Word' in the Fourth Gospel prologue, namely, from pre-incarnate existence with God to incarnate appearance among us. Thus we find in the letter prologue a somewhat unusual transition from the enigmatic expression 'the word of life' to 'the life was made manifest' to the further explanation 'the eternal life, which was in the presence of [πρός] the Father and made manifest to us'. Whatever import the word *life* had in the phrase 'word of life', the following statements about the life becoming manifest to us after being in the presence of the Father clearly parallel the progression in the Fourth Gospel prologue from the Word being in the presence of God and

10. So Sproston, 'Witnesses', p. 49, esp. n. 14, with many other scholars.
11. Brown, *Epistles of John*, p. 165; cf. Smalley, *1, 2, 3 John*, pp. 6-7.

then becoming flesh and dwelling among us (cf. 1 Jn 1.1-2 and Jn 1.1-5, 9-14).

Accordingly, 'the Life' in 1 John takes on many of the same forms and functions as 'the Word' in the Fourth Gospel. The parallel structure and function between 1 Jn 1.2 and both Jn 1.1 and Jn 1.14 are striking:[12]

> τὴν ζωὴν τὴν αἰώνιον ἥτις ἦν πρὸς τὸν πατέρα καὶ ἐφανερώθη ἡμῖν—ὃ ἑωράκαμεν καὶ ἀκηκόαμεν (1 Jn 1.2b, as well as 1 Jn 1.2a noted above) parallels καὶ ὁ λόγος ἦν πρὸς τὸν θεόν (Jn 1.1b) and καὶ ὁ λόγος σὰρξ ἐγένετο καὶ ἐσκήνωσεν ἐν ἡμῖν, καὶ ἐθεασάμεθα τὴν δόξαν αὐτοῦ (Jn 1.14).

Both the Word and the Life were with 'the God'/with 'the Father' initially (in the beginning Jn 1.1, eternal Life 1 Jn 1.2). Both the Word and the Life subsequently become visible: the Word became flesh and dwelt among us, and the eternal Life which was with the Father was made manifest to us. In each case 'we' have seen (ἐθεασάμεθα) this Word or Life now visible among us (Jn 1.14; 1 Jn 1.1, cf. ἑωράκαμεν in 1.1, 2, 3).

Thus this prologue of 1 John reinterprets that of the Fourth Gospel, abandoning the Fourth Gospel prologue's personification of *word* to allow *word* in 'word of life' to refer more naturally to the message, and instead applying the Fourth Gospel's functions of the hypostasized Word to a hypostasized Life.

Reinterpretation of Genesis 1 by 1 John 1 through the Fourth Gospel Prologue

Not many scholars have addressed to what extent and how the letter's prologue also relates to the beginning of Genesis. More needs to be said about how these permutations regarding the Word and Life in 1 John likewise relate to the LXX Genesis matrix.

The Fourth Gospel had reinterpreted Genesis by personalizing the Word at creation, and narrating how this creating Word became flesh among us. In turn, 1 John reinterpreted the Gospel prologue with several different emphases. Regarding 'the beginning', 1 John put more stress on community origins than on cosmic origins, though it still alluded to the latter (in v. 2b, 'the eternal life which was in the presence

---

12. See the chart in Brown, *Epistles of John*, p. 179.

of the Father also appeared to us'). Secondly, it reinvested 'the word' with its more usual sense of 'message'. Thirdly, it transferred to the personalized Life most functions that the Word had in the Fourth Gospel. The Fourth Gospel prologue had prepared the way for this transfer from Word to Life in v. 4: ἐν αὐτῷ [τῷ λόγῳ] ζωὴ ἦν, καὶ ἡ ζωὴ ἦν τὸ φῶς τῶν ἀνθρώπων. There life is ascribed to the Word, and this life is identified as the revelatory light of humans.

In Genesis 1, God had created by his word both light (v. 3) and life (vv. 11-12, especially vv. 20-30). Corresponding to this, the Fourth Gospel states that life was ἐν αὐτῷ (τῷ λόγῳ), either in the sense that the Word was the means of life or was the place where life was. Not only does the Fourth Gospel indicate that life was 'in/by the Word', but also that 'the life [that was in/by the Word] was the light of humans'.

The Fourth Gospel statement that life was in/by the Word grounds the transfer in 1 John of forms and functions from Word to personified Life. This Fourth Gospel precedent permits 1 John to transfer to the Life the Fourth Gospel's kinds of interpretative applications of the Genesis creation account for the Word.

Evidence for such a transfer from Word to Life of applications of Genesis are the following close parallelisms between seeing the Word in the Fourth Gospel and seeing the Life in the first letter. In the Fourth Gospel, 'we' have seen the glory of the Word who created the universe, and who has now been made flesh and dwelt 'among us'. In 1 Jn 1.2b 'we' have seen the Life, which was with/in the presence of the Father and has been made manifest 'to us'. The reinterpretation of the Genesis creation account by the Fourth Gospel prologue had identified the light of humans with the life that was in/by the Word, and asserted that this light (of the Word) shone in the darkness as revelation, which the darkness did not grasp (that is, in either sense of 'understand' or 'overcome').[13]

The creation account had treated the creation of light and its division from the darkness (which was over the abyss) in Gen. 1.2 as an etiological narrative explaining the origin of day and night. The Fourth Gospel saw in this etiological account the primeval symbolism of light against darkness in the senses of revelation vs. unbelief and of the moral dualism of light vs. darkness, good vs. evil: 'And the life was the light of humans, and the light shines in the darkness, and the darkness

13. On the Fourth Gospel Word as revelation, see esp. Bergmeier, 'Weihnachten', pp. 56-59.

did not grasp it' (Jn 1.4-5).

1 John maintains the Fourth Gospel's interpreted senses of the light in Genesis as revelation vs. unbelief and as a moral light–darkness dualism, but applies them differently than the Fourth Gospel. In v. 5, which acts as a transition between the prologue and first section of the letter, 1 John identifies the light with God, rather than with the Word as the Fourth Gospel had done. 'And this is the message (or gospel)[14]. . . that God is light, and in him there is no darkness at all' (1 Jn 1.5). The following verses immediately focus on the moral implications of this light–darkness dualism. 'If we say we have fellowship with him [God] while we walk in [moral] darkness, we lie and do not live according to the truth; but if we walk in the light, as he [God] is in the light, we have fellowship with one another, and the blood of his son Jesus cleanses us from every sin' (vv. 6-7).

Thus the relationship of 1 Jn 1.1-7 to the Genesis creation account is mediated through the moral symbolism by which the Fourth Gospel had interpreted light and darkness in Genesis, as well as through the respective uses of ἀρχή and the Word/Life parallels already mentioned. It takes the 'missing link' of the Fourth Gospel prologue to demonstrate an unambiguous claim for allusion to Genesis in 1 John.[15]

Yet one can point to evidence from Genesis and 1 John that Genesis (as interpreted in the first century) does actually remain in the background of 1 Jn 1.1-5. First, although the 1 John prologue places more of its immediate focus on community origins (v. 1-2a), it retains allusion to Genesis cosmic origins (v. 2b). Secondly, along with the Fourth Gospel (Jn 1.18b) but putting even more emphasis upon it, 1 John explicitly names the God of Genesis 1 as the Father (1 Jn 1.2) and explicitly correlates the Father with the Son (v. 3b), as well as the implicit correlation (v. 2b) treated next. Thirdly, 1 John has a sense of pre-existent (because eternal) life which/who was with the Father at the Genesis origins (at least as mediated by being in/by the Fourth Gospel's pre-existent Word), and has now been made manifest 'to us' (v. 2). In both the Fourth Gospel and 1 John, the *textual grounding* for identifying some personified being with God before creation is

---

14. See Brown, *Epistles of John*, pp. 191-93, on the functional equivalence of ἀγγελία with 'gospel' in 1 John, as in LXX Isa. 28.9 and 52.7 (p. 193).

15. However, J.M. Lieu, 'What Was from the Beginning: Scripture and Tradition in the Johannine Epistles', *NTS* 39 (1993), pp. 458-77, argues for a general allusive use of the Scriptures of Israel by 1 John through three other examples.

probably the plural statement by the creating God in Gen. 1.26 (both LXX and MT): 'Let *us* make man in *our* image and likeness' (LXX: Ποιήσωμεν ἄνθρωπον κατ' εἰκόνα ἡμετέραν καὶ καθ' ὁμοίωσιν). It is common knowledge that both rabbis and Christian fathers noticed and tried to interpret this strange plural for their one God. Philo's speculation of the logos being with God at creation seems to point to a similar pre-existing Jewish tradition of exegesis which tried to identify who was with 'the [one] God' who proposed, 'Let us' make humans 'in our image'.[16] Fourthly, 1 John further retains a light–darkness contrast as in Genesis, but with the Fourth Gospel reinterprets it as a moral dualism (1 Jn 1.5-7).

Conclusions

From the perspective of life rather than of revelation or word, 1 John makes a use of the Genesis creation account similar to that found in the Fourth Gospel prologue, sometimes employing the Fourth Gospel prologue as an intermediate interpretative filter for reading Genesis. 1 John highlights community origins against the background of allusions to Genesis cosmic origins by further reinterpreting the Fourth Gospel's earlier reinterpretation of Genesis 1. Whereas the Fourth Gospel had hypostasized God's verbal command in Gen. 1.3, 'Let there be light', into a pre-existent Word with/in the presence of God in the beginning, 1 John reverts back to the more normal meaning of 'word' as 'message' and instead hypostasizes Life, who is similarly with/in the presence of God, for whom 1 John emphasizes the personal name of Father.

In v. 14 of the Fourth Gospel prologue, the hypostasized creating Word from Genesis 'became flesh and tented among us and we have seen his glory' (Jn 1.14). In 1 Jn 1.2, the hypostasized Life (from Genesis via the Fourth Gospel prologue) 'was made manifest to us' and 'we have seen and we witness and we announce to you [this] eternal life'.

Although the Fourth Gospel prologue had a strong emphasis on salvation (e.g. v. 12: 'As many as received him, he gave them power to become children of God. . . '; and v. 16 plus v. 17: 'from his fullness we have all received, grace upon grace), it had put special focus on

---

16. E.g. Philo, *Conf. Ling.* 146-47, on logos as first-born in this Genesis context, and *Cher.* 125-27, on logos as instrument of creation, and the discussions in Tobin, 'Prologue', esp. pp. 255-62; and Evans, *Word and Glory*, pp. 100-14.

revelation. It had emphasized the creating Word of Genesis as the light of humans (vv. 4-5, 9), but whom the world did not know (v. 10). The same creating Word of Genesis revealed the unseen God by becoming flesh and tenting 'among us' (Jn 1.14). This 'only begotten God [μονογενὴς θεός], who is in the bosom of the Father [ὁ ὢν εἰς τὸν κόλπον τοῦ πατρὸς, both 'in the beginning' (see v. 1) and after returning there from earth], has made him known' [ἐξηγήσατο] (v. 18).

Although the prologue of 1 John retains much of the Fourth Gospel's regard for revelation (as in the focus on what we have seen, etc. [vv. 1, 3, cf. v. 5], and that 'the Life has been made manifest' [twice in v. 2]), it focuses more on *salvation*, especially in the form of *'eternal life'* (which of course is also a major theme in the Fourth Gospel, if not explicitly mentioned in its prologue). After the enigmatic reference to 'the word of the life' (1 Jn 1.1), v. 2 of the prologue clarifies that the life that has been manifested to us is 'the eternal life'. 'We' announce what we have seen and heard 'also to you, so that you may have fellowship [κοινωνία] with us; and our fellowship is with the Father and with his Son Jesus Christ' (v. 3 RSV). The desired result of our writing this is 'that our joy may be complete' (v. 4).

The letter's ending, 1 Jn 5.11-13, 20, confirms the emphasis in its prologue on salvific eternal life to be found in Jesus: those who have the Son have eternal life. 'And this is the testimony, that God gave us eternal life, and this life is in his Son. Whoever has the Son has life; whoever has not the Son of God has not life' (RSV modified).[17] The letter writer's concluding statement of purpose further substantiates this emphasis in focusing on eternal life from knowing God's Son: 'I write this to you who believe in the name of the Son of God, that you may know that you have eternal life' (5.13 RSV).[18]

This focus on life rather than Word relates to the background of Genesis allusions more in relation to salvation (our eternal life from the Life which had been with God and has made manifest to us) than to the Fourth Gospel emphasis on revelation ('The only begotten God. . . he has made him known', Jn 1.18). As with most first-century

---

17. καὶ αὕτη ἐστὶν ἡ μαρτυρία, ὅτι ζωὴν αἰώνιον ἔδωκεν ἡμῖν ὁ θεός, καὶ αὕτη ἡ ζωὴ ἐν τῷ υἱῷ αὐτοῦ ἐστιν. ὁ ἔχων τὸν υἱὸν ἔχει τὴν ζωήν· ὁ μὴ ἔχων τὸν υἱὸν τοῦ θεοῦ τὴν ζωὴν οὐκ ἔχει.

18. ταῦτα ἔγραψα ὑμῖν ἵνα εἰδῆτε ὅτι ζωὴν ἔχετε αἰώνιον, τοῖς πιστεύουσιν εἰς τὸ ὄνομα τοῦ υἱοῦ τοῦ θεοῦ.

authors in the biblical tradition, 1 John treats salvation against the backdrop of the Genesis creation account, reinterpreting and applying the creation of life in Genesis to the granting of eternal life, the favorite Johannine expression of salvation.

THREATS ANSWERED BY ENTHRONEMENT:
DEATH/RESURRECTION AND THE DIVINE WARRIOR MYTH
IN JOHN 5.17-29, PSALM 2 AND DANIEL 7

Mary R. Huie-Jolly

Introduction: Presuppositions and Points of Departure

The relationship between the divine father and the son is set forth in Jn 5.21-23.[1] The opening affirmation of the son's utter dependence upon God the father is developed into an argument demonstrating the son's equality with God: he has been given the powers of creation and judgment. The relationship is so exalted that no down to earth analogy is adequate to explain it, it pushes beyond familiarity with father and son relationships to a godlike image of divine sonship, which cannot be communicated except through myth.

Others have looked for a particular mythic frame of reference to explain the extraordinary sonship claim. Bultmann includes Jn 5.19-23 in his famous proposal that the Johannine conception is linked to a Gnostic Redeemer myth.[2] Ashton modifies Bultmann's proposal; assembling more recent research on the same question, he points to revealer figures of Jewish apocalyptic as a meaningful framework for the Johannine claim of the son's equality with God.[3] In this paper I will explore the possibility that a version of the divine warrior myth is the mythic framework for the divine sonship in John 5; the divine warrior

---

1. The limits of the text are set at Jn 5.18-29 to preserve the juxtaposition of conflict in exalted speech. However, as is appropriate to the development of the proposal, I focus here on Jn 5.17-23, and later on Jn 5.1-29.

2. See R. Bultmann, *The Gospel of John: A Commentary* (Oxford: Blackwell, 1971), p. 261; and *idem*, 'Die Bedeutung der neuerschlossenen mandaischen und manichaischen Quellen fur das Verstandnis des Johannesevangeliums', *ZNW* 24 (1925), pp. 100-101.

3. See J. Ashton, *Understanding the Fourth Gospel* (Oxford: Clarendon Press, 1991), pp. 337-68.

myth links John 5 to the form of early Christian death and resurrection speech. (The death and resurrection speech sequence is
formed in reference to testimonia that are expressions of the divine
warrior myth in Israel's Scriptures. Thus the sonship speech in John 5
is interpreted within the framework of an early Christian version of
the divine warrior myth. Thus the divine warrior myth is, I will
propose, the framework not only for John 5 but also for a significant
group of early Christian death-and-resurrection testimonia.

These linked assumptions will be explained only briefly in this
proposal. The limited scope of this paper allows me only to introduce
the hypothesis with the hope that it will generate further research and
discussion.[4]

> *The rationale: John 5.18-29 as death-and-resurrection speech*
> Jn 5.18-29 juxtaposes a death threat with enthronement-like speech which
> reflects a resurrection perspective.

> *Threat*
> Jn 5.18 They sought to kill him.

> *Resurrection perspective: enthronement speech concerning the son*
> Jn 5.19-27 The son acts as does the father. The father has given him the
> power to create life and to judge in order that they will honor the son as
> the father. Just as the father raises the dead, in the same way also the son.
> He has been given the power to execute judgment because he is the son of

---

4.   My unpublished PhD dissertation contains a more detailed rationale for the
methodological assumptions made in this paper; see M.R. Huie-Jolly, 'The Son
Enthroned in Conflict: A Socio-Rhetorical Interpretation of John 5:17-23' (Dunedin,
New Zealand: University of Otago, 1994).

I will not attempt to demonstrate, within the limited scope of this paper, that
early Christian death-and-resurrection speech is built upon the scaffolding of the
divine warrior myth, rather, I simply assume that this is the case. Scholars of the
divine warrior myth in New Testament writings have not to my knowledge
formulated the question in these terms before. (Notes 22–27 refer to recent research
on the divine warrior myth in the New Testament.) Accordingly I merely assume as a
working hypothesis that the death-and-resurrection form of speech was shaped by
testimonia from dw texts (such as Psalm 2 and Dan. 7.9-14) which provided a link
between the myth and early Christian expression of the significance of Jesus. In
future research I aim to bring more substance to these claims. They function in this
paper as foundational assumptions, though admittedly they are, as yet, assertions
which lend coherence to the whole picture. If, by a circular form of reasoning, this
hypothesis can make sense of John 5, then perhaps the gestalt proposed herein may
give support to the assertions that construct it.

man. All in their graves will hear the voice of the son of God. (Selectively
abbreviated from 5.18-29)

The rejection or killing or crucifixion of Jesus is one part of a pattern
in early Christian writing. Mention of the persecution, rejection or
death of Jesus is frequently juxtaposed with an affirmation of his
exalted status. In some early Christian traditions the resurrection was
synonymous with the enthronement of Jesus at the right hand of the
throne of God. The summary of the kerygma (1 Cor. 15.3-5) 'he died
according to Scripture and rose according to Scripture' is a notable
abbreviated example of the speech pattern juxtaposing death and resurrection within a scriptural frame of meaning. The pattern links, as if
in one breathless sequence, the death with the resurrection of Jesus.
The death and resurrection 'according to' an unstated frame of scriptural meaning in 1 Cor. 15.3-4 may presuppose a particular type of
scriptural explanation of the resurrection. A comparable pattern
joining death-and-resurrection speech with an explicitly stated scriptural frame of meaning is found in Acts 2.32-35 and 13.33 where
resurrection is mythically explained as enthronement at the right hand
of God.

I assume that the exalted sonship speech in Jn 5.19-29 is understood
within the primitive Christian tradition of the heavenly enthronement
of the son. Certain New Testament texts which cite testimonia such as
Psalm 2 (Acts 13.33), Dan. 7.13-14, and Ps. 110.1 (Mk 14.62) can be
seen to share common elements when they are read in light of this
mythic tradition of death and resurrection. Dodd argued that a primitive exegetical tradition based on interpretation of testimonia formed
the substructure of New Testament theology.[5] Building upon one
aspect of Dodd's thesis, I believe that early preachers of the resurrection of Jesus understood some significant testimonia, such as Psalm
2 and Dan. 7.9-14, as various scriptural expressions of a common
scriptural sequence of enthronement in response to threats.[6] 'Threats
answered by enthronement' summarizes a foundational early Christian
story or plot line; it supported the retelling of the story of Jesus' rejection, death and vindication in terms of the mythic significance of

---

5. C.H. Dodd, *According to the Scriptures: The Substructure of New Testament
Theology* (London: Nisbet, 1952), p. 11.

6. A comparable view is expressed by B. Lindars, *New Testament Apologetic:
The Doctrinal Significance of the Old Testament Quotations* (London: SCM Press,
1961), pp. 169-74.

these events. The threat/enthronement sequence links these otherwise divergent testimonia, such as Dan. 7.9-14 and Psalm 2. It is the framework for the proclamation linking, as if in one breath, the death with the resurrection of Jesus.

The only clear scriptural citation in John 5 υἱὸς ἀνθρώπου (Jn 5.27) is from Dan. 7.13.[7] However, it is typical for John to proceed by allusion rather than direct citation.[8] I make the assumption that the earlier oral tradition of Jesus' enthroned resurrected status is tacit within Jn 5.19-29.

The Rationale for a Death Threat/Enthronement Connection in John 5
Noting the division between narrative and discourse beginning in 5.19, traditionally interpreters have treated 5.19-30 as a christological discourse, as if it could stand on its own.[9] If the text is viewed solely from a source-critical perspective, such a division is reasonable; but it fails to ask whether the death threat in 5:18 is connected with the meaning of the exalted sonship speech. Similarly, Bultmann and Ashton, while insisting that god-like sonship speech can only be understood within the framework of a myth, fail to look for a myth that

---

7.   As shown by Ashton, *Understanding the Fourth Gospel*, p. 357.

8.   See C.K. Barrett, 'The Old Testament in the Fourth Gospel', *JTS* 48 (1947), pp. 155-60; and M. Hengel, 'The Old Testament in the Fourth Gospel', *HBT* 12 (1990), pp. 19-41, here p. 32.

9.   For example, S. Freyne ('Vilifying the Other and Defining the Self: Matthew's and John's Anti-Jewish polemic in Focus', in J. Neusner and E. Frerichs [eds.], *'To See Ourselves as Others See Us': Christians, Jews and Others in Late Antiquity* [Chico, CA: Scholars Press, 1985], p. 123) notes that a conflict over the Sabbath triggers a dispute that quickly passes over to the one theme central to the whole of the Fourth Gospel: Jesus' authority and his claim to be equal to God. W. Bauer's discussion (*Das Johannesevangelium* [Tubingen: Mohr (Paul Siebeck), 1933], p. 84) of the discourse section which in his commentary begins at 5.19-47 is entitled the 'Christological Rede'. Likewise in G.R. Beasley-Murray, *John* (WBC, 36; Waco, TX: Word, 1987), pp. 75-76; C.K. Barrett, *The Gospel according to John* (Philadelphia: Westminster Press, 2nd edn, 1978), p. 257; and F.-M. Braun, *Jean le théologien: Les grandes traditions d'Israel l'accord des écritures d'après le quatrième évangile* (Paris: Librairie Lecoffre, 1964), p. 107, the relationship of conflict in 5.18 is not considered integral to discourse on the father–son relationship. Although R. Schnackenburg (*The Gospel according to St John* [London: Burns & Oates, 1980], II, pp. 98-113) divides the passage at 5.15-30, he does not the see the claim to unique sonship in close connection with the threat of death.

encompasses both the death threat (5.18) and the god-like language of sonship (5.19-29).[10]

Others following the work of J.L. Martyn do acknowledge an integral link between the death threat (5.18) and the high Christology of (5.19-23) at the level of the Johannine community's experience of persecution. For Martyn, and others building upon the same assumptions, the accusations in John 5 echo the accusations which were experienced by John's community. The text retrojects onto the story of Jesus the persecution of Johannine Christians; they are charged with ditheism for confessing that Jesus the son is 'just like' God the father.[11] Martyn's approach rightly perceives a social link between the death threat and the christological discourse in John 5, though he fails to explore another possibility: John 5 may also reflect a socially understood *pattern* that is not limited to Johannine experience.

Could the juxtaposition of conflict and enthronement-like speech in Jn 5.18-29 signal an already widely understood mythic pattern? I propose that a scripturally coded myth used for retelling Jesus' death (and the threats foreshadowing it as in Jn 5.15-18) was typically retold within the formal structure of the scripturally attested myth. Thus the mythic pattern of conflict/enthronement speech, was widely used in early Christian preaching. John 5 does not simply reflect Johannine community conflict. Rather, via a form of mythic speech, it links the

10. See Bultmann, *Gospel of John*, p. 261; Ashton, *Understanding the Fourth Gospel*, pp. 337-68.

11. J.L. Martyn (*History and Theology in the Fourth Gospel* [Nashville: Abingdon Press, 2nd edn, 1979 (1968)], p. 70) interprets John 5 as part of a 'two-level drama', in which the pervasive conflict with 'the Jews' is to be interpreted primarily in terms of contemporary Johannine experience of conflict. See also pp. 29-37. L. Schenke, 'Joh 7–10: Ein Dramatische Szene', *ZNW* 80 (1989), pp. 172-92; R.A. Whitacre, *Johannine Polemic: The Role of Tradition and Authority* (SBLDS, 67; Chico: Scholars Press, 1982), p. 10; B.J. Malina, *The Gospel of John in Sociolinguistic Perspective: Protocol of the Forty-Eighth Colloquy* (Center for Hermeneutical Studies in Hellenistic and Modern Culture; Berkeley: Graduate Theological Union and the University of California, 1985); J.H. Neyrey, *An Ideology of Revolt: John's Christology and Social Science* (Philadelphia: Fortress Press, 1988); and D. Rensberger, *Overcoming the World: Politics and Community in the Gospel of John* (London: SPCK, 1989). These books are representative of scholarship which builds upon Martyn's methodological assumptions concerning reconstruction of the social situation of the Johannine community.

death threat in 5.18 with god-like enthronement speech concerning the son in 5.18-27.

The divine sonship claims (5.19-23) are found within the literary context of conflict: a sabbath healing that leads to charges against Jesus. He answers the first charge concerning improper Sabbath action by saying 'My father is working still and I am working' (5.17). His claim to a filial relationship with God provokes a second accusation against Jesus, 'he calls God his own father making himself equal with God' (5.18). The accusation reflects a distinctive Johannine emphasis.[12] But it is prefaced by a statement that is more common in early Christian writings 'they sought to kill him'.

Mention of persecution, rejection, or crucifixion of Jesus signals one part of an early Christian speech pattern, which was typically linked with an affirmation of his resurrected status. It is not difficult to see that Jn 5.18 foreshadows the 'killing' of Jesus and thus relates to one element in this early Christian pattern of speech. Less obvious is the relation between resurrection, the second part of the early Christian pattern, and the amazing claims that follow the mention of the killing of Jesus.

Threat
Jn 5.18 They sought to kill him

Resurrection perspective: enthronement speech concerning the son
Jn 5.19-27 The son acts as does the Father. The Father has given him the power to create life and to judge in order that they will honor the son as the Father. All in their graves will hear the voice of the son of God. He has been given the power to execute judgment because he is the son of man[13] (selectively abbreviated from 5.18-29).

Though it is not immediately obvious the distinctive Johannine account of a death threat answered by speech concerning the son in relation to the father does conform to a typical early Christian speech pattern, as suggested above. The analysis assumes that the various narrative elements associated with Jesus' death—threats, rejection, forensic

---

12. See W.A. Meeks, 'Equal to God', in R.T. Fortna and B.R. Gaventa (eds.), *The Conversation Continues: Studies in Paul and John: In Honor of J. Louis Martyn* (Nashville: Abingdon Press, 1990), pp. 309-21.

13. In Jn 20.31 the kingly title 'messiah' is placed in apposition to the title 'son of God' indicating that in John the use of the title 'son of God' is sometimes consistent with messianic use of sonship language. I presume that the use of 'son of God' and 'son' in 5.25, 26 has messianic connotations.

trials, and crucifixion—are identified under the single formal heading of 'threat'. The rejection, trial, and crucifixion of Jesus all would have counted as threats to the honor of Jesus according to conventional social values.[14] Similarly the images and language associated with resurrection—transfiguration, glorification, and enthronement—are all treated under the one single formal heading 'enthronement', for all represent a resurrection proclamation; all speak of the identity of Jesus from the heavenly perspective of the son enthroned.

In conventional social terms, crucifixion and enthronement are opposites. Why has a death threat formally become linked with enthronement-like speech? Why are they juxtaposed within one single speech pattern? Why would early Christians see them as one form of speech, one single sequence?

Death by crucifixion would ordinarily define Jesus as a man who had publicly and finally been shamed.[15] The crucifixion posed a problem. Scripture attests to the link between death threats with enthronement and provides a pattern that answers the problem. It expresses the conviction that the divine empowerment of Jesus continues even more after his death. Further, the claim 'Jesus is enthroned' vindicates his honor: it refutes the shame conventionally linked to one judged worthy of death by public execution.[16] By linking his death in the same breath with his exalted status as son of God, the death-and-enthronement pattern of early Christian speech reverses the social shame of crucifixion and makes Jesus the judge of any who question his honor.

However, the juxtaposition which reverses the shame of crucifixion would not have been widely accepted if it had no cultural precedent, if it was an interpretation meaningful to the followers of Jesus alone.[17]

14. See A.E. Harvey, *Jesus on Trial: A Study in the Fourth Gospel* (London: SPCK, 1976); B.J. Malina and J.H. Neyrey, *Calling Jesus Names: The Social Value of Labels in Matthew* (Sonoma, CA: Polebridge Press, 1988); M. Hengel, *Crucifixion in the Ancient World and the Folly of the Message of the Cross* (London: SCM Press, 1977); and J. Gager, *Kingdom and Community: The Social World of Early Christianity* (Englewood Cliffs, NJ: Prentice–Hall, 1975).

15. J.H. Neyrey, 'Despising the Shame of the Cross: Honor and Shame in the Johannine Passion Narrative', *Semeia*, forthcoming.

16. Malina and Neyrey, *Calling Jesus Names*. See also Lindars, *New Testament Apologetic*.

17. M. Barker (*The Older Testament: The Survival of Themes from the Ancient Royal Cult in Sectarian Judaism and Early Christianity* [London: SPCK, 1987]) argues that early Christian proclamation caught on quickly because it relied upon an

Would they themselves have made the connection between resurrection experience and exaltation apart from the conceptual framework of scriptural narratives? These had already carved out a publicly understandable link between death threats and exaltation as king.[18]

Points of departure for my proposal can be summarized as follows:

1.   Jn 5.18-29 is understandable within a typical Christian pattern that links mention of Jesus' death with mention of his exaltation in resurrection.

2.   If Jn 5.18-27 conforms to a threat/enthronement speech pattern, then the formal significance of christological speech in 5.19-29 cannot be understood in isolation from the death threat in 5.18.

3.   In the remainder of this paper I will argue that early Christian speech juxtaposing the sequence of 'threat' and 'enthronement' is fruitfully interpreted within the framework of the divine warrior myth. The myth links John 5 with other early Christian texts which cite testimonia taken from divine warrior myth texts. Further, it intertextually interprets the forensic context of John 5 within the scriptural tradition of testimonia used in forensic contexts, for example Mk 14.61-64, and Acts 4.25 in the context of the arrest and imprisonment scene in Acts 4.3-23. The threat/enthronement (death/resurrection) form of Christian speech follows a pre-Christian pattern of scriptural testimony; it links the threat of death with enthronement in one continuous sequence of meaning. The link between threat and kingly enthronement is related to the pattern: 'he died according to Scripture, rose according to Scripture'. Further such early Christian proclamation attests a version of the myth which resonates with popular traditions current within first century Jewish culture.[19] (While not excluding the possibility of influences from non-Jewish thought, this paper will discuss the Hebraic background and sources of the divine warrior myth myth.)

already existing mythology; via the mythology within which the Jesus events were framed, they were made publicly understandable and meaningful to a wide audience.

18. Following Dodd, *According to the Scriptures*, I presume that 'common plots' based upon familiar scriptural narratives undergird early Christian use of primary testimonia. The quoted material recalls the entire wider context from which it is derived. According to H. Koester, *Ancient Christian Gospels: Their History and Development* (London: SCM Press, 1990), and J.D. Crossan, *The Cross that Spoke: The Origins of the Passion Narrative* (San Francisco: Harper & Row, 1988), the source of the testimony shaped the narrative about Jesus.

19. See Barker, *The Older Testament*.

Death/Resurrection and the Divine Warrior Myth:
A Framework for John 5

A widely accepted analysis of the motif variously described as the divine warrior myth, or the combat myth or chaos motif, is presented by Frank Cross. It is abstracted from Northwest semitic descriptions of battles between various gods, which follow a recognizable mythic plot. Cross identifies the following sequence of images as the divine warrior myth. Few texts contain every element of the myth; and in some expressions the sequence is altered:[20]

(1) the march of the divine warrior
(2) the convulsing of nature as the divine warrior manifests his power
(3) the return of the divine warrior to his holy mountain to assume divine kingship
(4) the utterance of the divine warrior's voice (thunder) from his palace, which provides rains to fertilize the earth.

The divine warrior myth has been identified also in specific early Christian texts. A.Y. Collins[21] and Day[22] trace it within the book of Revelation; Duff[23] finds it in the triumphal entry. Ricoeur in very general terms relates it to the Christian celebrations of Jesus' death and resurrection in baptism and eucharist.[24] McCurley's more extensive study links the divine warrior myth to elements in Gospel narratives; for example the divine warrior motif of victory over the waters is echoed when Jesus walks upon water.[25] J.L. Kovac identifies the cosmic battle in John with the divine warrior myth motif as it is found in texts

---

20. F.M. Cross, *Canaanite Myth and Hebrew Epic: Essays in the History of the Religion of Israel* (Cambridge, MA: Harvard University Press, 1973), pp. 162-63. This work continues to be the standard treatment of the myth.

21. A.Y. Collins, *The Combat Myth in the Book of Revelation* (Missoula, MT: Scholars Press, 1976).

22. J. Day, *God's Conflict with the Dragon and the Sea: Echoes of a Canaanite Myth in the Old Testament* (Cambridge: Cambridge University Press, 1985).

23. P.B. Duff, 'The March of the Divine Warrior and the Advent of the Greco–Roman King: Mark's Account of Jesus' Entry into Jerusalem', *JBL* 111 (1992), pp. 55-71.

24. P. Ricoeur, *The Symbolism of Evil* (Boston: Beacon Press, 1967).

25. F.R. McCurley, *Ancient Myths and Biblical Faith: Scriptural Transformations* (Philadelphia: Fortress Press, 1983). McCurley also attempts to identify Christian echoes of the themes of cosmic mountain, divine reign, and fertility.

from the Second Temple period.[26] While it is coherent with these earlier studies, my approach focuses upon the evidence of citation from testimonia which are themselves expressions of divine warrior myth.[27] I suggest that a version of the divine warrior myth based on early Christian exegesis of Scripture was foundational for death-and-resurrection speech patterns. It undergirds the form of early Christian speech that juxtaposes images of threats to the life of Jesus with speech exalting him as son.

Thus I will read John 5 as a retelling of the story of Jesus according to the scriptural plot of the divine warrior myth. Even in testimonia as diverse as Dan. 7.9-14 and Psalm 2 the threat/enthronement pattern is consistent. The common myth is suggestive of the common significance of a widely understood scriptural interpretation of the rejection and crucifixion of Jesus. It allows for a glorious retelling of the rejection and death of Jesus from a resurrection point of view; the mythic structure juxtaposes the threat to Jesus' integrity and life, with sonship that vindicated his status as the one enthroned who now has power to judge his accusers claims. The divine warrior myth appears to link divine warrior myth Scriptures, such as Psalm 2 and Daniel 7, and the early Christian threat/enthronement speech pattern. This observation provides a hermeneutic for texts such as John 5, which juxtapose threats with exalted sonship speech. Just as the significance of one piece of a puzzle becomes clear when it is placed in relation to the overall frame within which it belongs, so the myth of the divine warrior, which underlies the metaphor that God is king, makes sense of the pattern of speech in Jn 5.18-29.

The Divine Warrior King, a Motif Linking Various Texts
The title 'king' is given unexpected and relatively extensive prominence in the Fourth Gospel, though the concept of the Davidic messiah recedes in comparison with John's use of the royal title 'Son of God'[28] (see Jn 5.25). The motif of kingship in John draws upon the heavenly

26. See J.L. Kovac, '"Now shall the Ruler of this World be Driven Out": Jesus' Death as Cosmic Battle in John 12:20-36', *JBL* 114 (1995), pp. 236-47.

27. For example the divine warrior myth is recognizable in Zechariah 9–14; Dan. 7.9-14; Psalms 2; 110; and, less obviously, 118. The myth common to these primary testimonia may have constructed scripturally derived plot-lines within which the death of Jesus was retold in light of scriptural interpretation of his resurrection.

28. W.A. Meeks, *The Prophet King, Moses Traditions and the Johannine Christology* (NovTSup, 14; Leiden: Brill, 1976), pp. 16-17.

enthronement of the god-like υἱὸς ἀνθρώπου[29] of Dan. 7.13-14.[30]

The mythic concept YHWH is king, is reflected in monarchic images of the earthly king as God's son. In Psalms 2 and 89, the son (victorious over threats from enemies and exalted to reign over all) belongs within the larger sequence of the divine warrior myth.[31] Psalms 2 and 89 relate to the Davidic monarchy. However, they employ a mythic structure and imagery derived from the earlier myth of the enthronement of YHWH. The same structure of myth appears, quite apart from Davidic associations inscribed within apocalyptic texts, such as Dan. 7.9-14. The root metaphor associated with divine enthronement is the focus of my attention, rather than one specific text concerning either Davidic or heavenly enthronement.

Though the divine warrior myth is found in a variety of ANE texts the earliest source of it, and the one closest to the earlier adaption of the myth in Israel is the Ba'al cycle of Canaanite myths from Ras Shamra. J.J. Collins[32] commenting upon the use of these myths in Daniel 7 argues that the ancient traditions shaped by the Canaanite myth act as paradigms; they interpret the new situation in terms of another level of meaning that is related to a myth. Often the relationship is apparent 'only in its outline and a few key details'.[33] The relationship between the situation depicted in the text and the pattern of an ancient myth is,

29. Jn 5.27 uses the term υἱὸς ἀνθρώπου—the term is identical to the LXX of Dan. 7.13.

30. See P. Borgen, 'Some Jewish Exegetical Traditions as Background for Son of Man Sayings in John's Gospel (Jn 3,13-14 and context)', in M. de Jonge (ed.), *L'évangile de Jean: Sources, rédaction, théologie* (BETL, 44; Gembloux: Duculot, 1977), pp. 243-59. Ashton, *Understanding the Fourth Gospel*, p. 357; Meeks, 'Equal to God', pp. 317-18.

31. G. von Rad (*Holy War in Ancient Israel* [Grand Rapids: Eerdmans, 1991], p. 70) says that to look at YHWH and his way of ruling is the method proper to reconstruction of the conceptual world associated with the cult in Israel.

32. Collins, *The Apocalyptic Vision of the Book of Daniel* (Missoula, MT: Scholars Press, 1977), pp. 111, 115.

33. J.J. Collins, *The Apocalyptic Vision*, p. 113. In the context of exploring the root metaphors that underlie Israelite expressions of God, T.N.D. Mettinger (*In Search of God: The Meaning and Message of the Everlasting Names* [trans. F.H. Cryer; Philadelphia: Fortress Press, 1988], p. 97) remarks that in the light of the ancient myth from which expressions that YHWH is king derives, 'We are on the trail of a conceptual deep structure that endows certain Old Testament texts with a surprising internal coherence'.

in words Collins borrows from Edwin Honig, speech that is allegorical in 'quality', like

> a twice-told tale written in rhetorical, or figurative, language and expressing a vital belief. . . The twice-told aspect of the tale indicates that some venerated or proverbial antecedent (old) story has become a pat- tern for another (the new) story.[34]

As Collins observes, 'the word pattern is of crucial importance in this definition; for at issue is not' a set of isolated correspondences, but telling a story in a way that 'reflects the pattern of a venerated older story', a form of expression that is a typical characteristic of myth.[35]

The basic mythic structure persists in early Christian speech. To show this I will focus on two moods in the structure of the divine warrior myth. 'Conflict' and 'victory' persist as the framework for Israelite and early Christian acclamation of divine kingship.

CONFLICT
Threats assail the status and authority of the son.
Battle: writhing of nature as divine warrior manifests his power.

VICTORY
Victory: He manifests power over chaos, enemies and death, signaled by the voice of divine warrior.
Triumphant procession: with shouts of witnesses who proclaim him king.
Enthronement: dominion over all things is handed over to the kingly son.
Manifestation of kingly reign: fertility and abundance of life for those who honor the king; judgment, wrath, death for those who do not honor the king.

The mood of 'conflict' is developed in the derivative elements of threat, battle. The writhing of nature creates a bridge linking conflict with victory.

The mood of victory is developed through derivative elements: the voice of the divine warrior signals victory, the triumphant procession is accompanied by shouts of witnesses who acclaim the victor as king; when he is enthroned all dominion is handed over to him. The mood of victory is double-edged: its outcome is an outpouring of fertility and

---

34. The quotation is from E. Honig, *Dark Conceit* (Evanston, IL: Northwestern University Press, 1959), p. 12; it is cited by J.J. Collins, *The Apocalyptic Vision of the Book of Daniel*, p. 113.

35. J.J. Collins, *The Apocalyptic Vision*, pp. 113-14. Collins relies upon M. Eliade's [*The Myth of Eternal Return* (New York: Pantheon, 1954], pp. 3-4) exposition of myth.

abundance to those who honor the king, but wrath and judgment are the lot of all who do not willingly submit to his reign.

I will introduce this analysis of the myth by paraphrasing John Day's translation of the Canaanite myth of Ba'al's kingship.[36]

Threat/Conflict

Yamm the sea god (also known as judge river) challenges the entire divine council to hand over El's son Ba'al the storm god. While the other gods are intimidated into submission, Ba'al moves as to attack the envoy of Yamm and then shouts to the council:[37]

> Lift up, o gods, your heads!
> From the top of your princely knees.
> Take your ease on your princely thrones.
> And I will answer the messengers of the Sea,
> Even the witnesses of Judge River. . .

Battle

In the next discernible scene *CTA* 2.IV (= *KTU* 1.2.IV), Ba'al and Yamm are at war. The battle is in 'full flight' and, according to Day's description, 'Yam is clearly in the ascendant, for we read that Ba'al sank under the throne of Prince Yamm'.[38] Kothar-and-Hasis (the craftsperson god) exhorts Ba'al:

> Truly I say to you, O Prince Baal,
> I repeat (to you), O Rider of the Clouds:
> Now your enemy, Baal,
> now your enemy you will smite,
> You will take your everlasting kingdom,
> your dominion for ever and ever.[39]

36. I have inserted material from my unpublished dissertation (pp. 194-95) in the summary of Day's translation of the Ba'al myth. My summary below follows Day's account of the myth and, except where otherwise noted, the material quoted is from his translation, *God's Conflict*, pp. 7-9. The account is from the Ugaritic text concerning Ba'al's defeat of the sea god in *CTA* 2.I and 2.IV (= *KTU* 1.2.I and IV).

37. Gordon, *UH* 137, pp. 39-40, cited in J. Gray, *The Legacy of Canaan: The Ras Shamra Texts and their Relevance to the Old Testament* (Leiden: Brill, 1957), p. 27.

38. Day, *God's Conflict*, p. 8; so also P. Craigie, *Ugarit and the Old Testament* (Grand Rapids: Eerdmans, 1983), p. 62.

39. Compare Dan. 7.12-14.

Kothar-and-Hasis, the craftsperson god, arms Ba'al with a magic club which lethally strikes prince Yamm. The mythic element is seen in the writhing of nature.

Writhing of Nature

> Yam collapsed, he fell to the earth;
> his joints quivered
> and his form crumpled.
> Ba'al dragged out Yam and put him down,
> he made an end of Judge River.

Next the victor is acclaimed as king: 'Yam is indeed dead! Ba'al shall be king!'

The account that follows concerns the construction of Ba'al's palace. The building of the palace appears to be a consequence of Ba'al having defeated Yamm and gained kingship.[40] While Ba'al is constructing his palace, conflict breaks out again. This time the enemy is Mot (Death). Ba'al is eventually victorious in this conflict as well. He re-establishes his rule.

The basic structure of the Ba'al myth survived intact in diverse expressions of the victorious reign of YHWH.[41] In the Israelite metaphor of God as King reference to a past victory over the threat of the chaotic waters is seen from the perspective of enthronement: 'The YHWH sits enthroned over the flood (reminiscent of Yamm the sea god). The YHWH sits as king forever' (Ps. 29.10).

In Psalm 89 the divine warrior myth occurs twice: first as the mythic enthronement of God is recounted; next as the king is installed after the manner of YHWH's enthronement. The primal battle of YHWH is described first:

Battle/Victory

YHWH you rule the raging of the sea
You crushed Rahab like a carcass
You scattered your enemies with your mighty arm (89.9-10).

---

40. Day, *God's Conflict*, p. 9.

41. See Mettinger, *In Search of God*, and P.D. Hanson, *The Dawn of Apocalyptic: The Historical and Sociological Roots of Jewish Apocalyptic Eschatology* (Philadelphia: Fortress Press, 1979), p. 302. I borrow elements from Hanson as well as from Cross, *Canaanite Myth and Hebrew Epic*, in my own construction of a Christian version of the divine warrior myth.

Manifestation of Reign
Righteousness and justice are the
foundation of your throne (89.14).

Victory Shout-Procession
Happy are the people who know the festal shout (89.15).

Next the Davidic king is presented after the pattern of God's primal victory over the waters and enthronement.

Battle
God will crush [the Davidic king's] foes before him and strike down those who hate him (89.23).

Victory
I will set his hand on the sea and his right hand on the rivers [recalling God's power over the waters] (89.25).

Enthronement
He shall cry to me, 'You are my Father, my God, and the Rock of my salvation'. . . . I will establish his line forever and his throne as long as the heavens endure (89.26-29).

The account of the son's coronation above is intentionally modeled after the familiar pattern of the enthronement of God over the waters. Sonship after the manner of God's enthronement is, I suggest, the version of the divine warrior myth that shapes early Christian accounts which present Jesus' death and resurrection, according to the scriptural myth, as enthronement at the right hand of God.

In this 'sonship version' of the myth, the primal enthronement of God is understood to be the pattern behind the coronation ritual; the root metaphor of divine kingship, victory over the waters, establishes the legitimacy of the throne of the Davidic king. The Davidic king's reign is a type of the YHWH's victory over the deep in Psalm 89. As God is exalted over the waters, so is the king with his hand over the rivers; he is exalted to rule over the chaotic rage of his enemies (Ps. 89.25). Likewise, via this myth, Jesus the son is exalted by God to reign even over the chaos of crucifixion at the hands of enemies.

The derivative 'sonship version' expression of the myth, which I have reconstructed above, places the human king in the framework that already signifies God's enthronement. The version of the myth that Psalm 89 displays offers a coherent background for death and resurrection speech.

Though Psalm 89 is not quoted in the New Testament,[42] some significant Christian testimonia are quotations from other Israelite texts
which reflect the divine warrior myth. Two which are quoted as testimony to Jesus' crucifixion and enthronement, Psalm 2 and Dan.
7.13-14, support an interpretation of John 5 within a divine warrior
myth framework. The υἱὸς ἀνθρώπου of Dan. 7.13-14 is clearly
cited in Jn 5.29. Though Psalm 2 is not cited in John 5, its mood—
those who challenge the son's authority are resisted by speech concerning the divine authority of his sonship speech—is replicated in the plot
of Jn 5.16-29.

Psalm 2 expresses the divine warrior myth by a sonship pattern
similar to that in Psalm 89.

> *Threat*
> Rage and plots against the LORD and his messiah (2.1-4).
>
> *Enthronement*
> God enthroned in heaven rebukes his enemies. The son answers enemies
> by recounting the coronation decree: God said to me, 'You are my son'.
> Dominion of the nations is given to son (2.4-9).
>
> *Judgment*
> Submit to the dominion of the son or perish (2.9-12).

In the New Testament, quotation from Psalm 2 attests the messianic
status of Jesus. A voice from heaven at baptism and transfiguration
addresses him: 'You are my son'; the acclamation from Ps. 2.7 foreshadows his enthroned status in resurrection. Other parts of Psalm 2
are quoted as evidence of his enthronement in the context of Jesus'
ascension and resurrection.[43]

A more exceptional use of quotation from Psalm 2 is found in Acts
4. Following a forensic encounter Peter and John pray by quoting Ps.
2.1: 'Why do the Gentiles rage, the people lay their plots, the kings of
the earth take their stand and the rulers against the Lord and against

---

42. W.C. van Unnik ('The Quotation from the Old Testament in John 12:34',
NovT 3 [1959], pp. 174-79) maintains that there is a citation from Psalm 89 in John
12, but his view is not widely held.

43. Psalm 2 is quoted concerning baptism in Mt. 3.17 and parallels, concerning
the transfiguration in 2 Pet. 1.17. The sonship of Jesus in contrast with the rebellion
of hostile forces is emphasized in testimonies from Psalm 2 in Acts 4.25; 13.33; Heb.
1.5; 5.5; 7.28; and Rev. 2.26; 6.15; 11.15, 18, 17, 18; 19.19. See H.-J. Kraus,
Theology of the Psalms (Minneapolis: Augsburg, 1986), p. 180.

his Messiah?' and now in this city kings. . . Herod and Pilate were gathered against your child Jesus (Acts 4.25-29). Their prayer uses Psalm 2 as the prototype of the trial of Jesus.

In light of the widespread use of Psalm 2 to attest Jesus' resurrected status, this single quotation linking Psalm 2 to his trial and death is highly significant. It suggests that while the sonship theme was associated with Psalm 2, this association included the whole mythic sequence, including the death threat posed in Ps. 2.1-4.[44] Van Iersel maintains that certain sermon summaries in Acts follow an outline based on Psalm 2; the summaries proclaim the election, death, enthronement of Jesus and they call for submission to Jesus in a way that is structurally similar to Psalm 2.[45] More recently, Crossan's study of the extra-canonical *Gospel of Peter* concludes that the earliest strata of that trial narrative was a 'narrativization of Psalm 2'.[46]

The plot of Psalm 2 coheres with the mood of the speech in John 5, as the chart below aims to show.

Threat
Rage and plots against his messiah (Ps. 2.1-4).
They sought to kill him (Jn 5.16-18).

Reply from superior perspective of throne (repels threat)
The son answers enemies (Ps. 2.4-8) by recounting the coronation decree: God said to me, 'You are my son'. Dominion of the nations is given to son (Ps. 2.4-9).
'My father' gives divine powers to create and to judge (Jn 5.19-23).

Judgment for all who do not honor the son
Submit to the rule of the son or perish (Ps. 2.9-12).
That all may honor son just as they honor the father, any who do not honor the son do not honor the father (Jn 5.23, 27).

The independent use of the various parts of Psalm 2 for testimonia in the New Testament would support trying out Psalm 2 as a conceptual frame for John 5, even though it is not cited in John 5. However, its

44. Relying on the method set out by Dodd (*According to the Scriptures*), I assume that early Christian quotation of one verse of a primary testimony represents the whole narrative from which the quotation is derived, and that the audience already knows the wider literary context from which the testimony has been taken.

45. The work of van Iersel is described by W.W. Weren, 'Psalms 2 in Luke–Acts: An Intertextual Study', in *Intertextuality in Biblical Writings* (Kampen: Kok, 1989, pp. 189-203.

46. Crossan, *The Cross that Spoke*.

apparent coherence with the plot of trial/sonship speech in John 5 and Psalm 2 may not signal a simple one-to-one relationship between them, or between Psalm 2 and any other single early Christian text. Rather, it may hint of a mythic coherence between certain testimonia (not limited to Psalm 2) and the plot line of the gospel story as a whole.

Daniel 7 also includes elements of threat, not from vassals but from beasts, symbolic of a primal battle (unlike Ps. 2.1 where the threat comes from plots by people, kings, and rulers). Psalm 2 and Daniel 7 were variously used to interpret the resurrection of Jesus via the divine warrior pattern. The enemy 'plots' from Psalm 2 overlap with 'primal beasts' in Daniel in the 'threat' element of the structures of the divine warrior myth. The element of heavenly enthronement overlaps with the image messianic earthly enthronement, compare the Synoptic trial accounts, Mk 14.61-64 (Mt. 26.64, Lk. 22.69): imagery from Dan. 7.14 conflates with Ps. 110.1 in a scene which can be interpreted in light of the coronation drama of Ps. 2.1-4.

The Plot of the Early Christian Divine Warrior Myth

Early Christian quotation from divine warrior texts serves as one strong form of evidence that the myth provided a framework for interpretation of Jesus. Less explicit but no less pervasive as evidence is the dramatic story-line surrounding Jesus' death and resurrection. Below I tentatively propose a version of the divine warrior myth which coheres with the early Christian gospel.

Elements in the Christian Version of the Divine Warrior Myth

The following elements constitute the Christian version of the divine warrior myth: (1) *divine decree*—Jesus acts according to decree from the throne of God in heaven; (2) *conflict* with authorities who put him on trial and do not recognize him as the son; (3) *threats* of death foreshadowing his execution; (4) *battle*—Jesus is mocked, surrounded by enemies, crucified, and buried; he remains three days in the jaws of death; (5) the *writhing of nature*, as seen in the darkness of a solar eclipse, earthquake and tearing of the door to the Temple attend the climatic battle that is associated with Jesus' death; (6) *victory*, as seen when God raises Jesus from the dead, vindicating him as the son of God; he rises in triumph from the cosmic battle; (7) *victory procession*—the victorious voice of the son of God calls the dead into a victory procession to the throne of God in heaven. His triumphal entry to Jerusalem foreshadows this procession; (8) *enthronement*—the son is seated at the right hand of the throne of his father who gives him dominion over all; (9) *fertility of restored order*—the spirit of life is poured out from the presence of the son to reconcile and restore the divine order of life; and (10) *judgment* is upon those who do not honor the son, they will not see life.

The elements of the myth do not always follow a rigid sequence, and they can occur in ways that anticipate later elements within the plot of the story.[47] A more detailed discussion follows.

Divine Decree

Jesus' actions are ordained by decree from the throne of God. The early Christian version of the myth assumes that God the Father is already King, victoriously enthroned in heaven, from whence he decrees every divinely inspired event on earth.[48]

Significant events in Jesus' life correspond on earth to the mythic action that has already taken place in heaven. God has already asserted his power over the raging sea and established his throne above all rule and authority. Jesus' life, lived according to kingly decree, follows the primal drama associated with the creating and ruling actions of God. On earth Jesus rebukes demonic forces. He thereby asserts rule over the chaos of sickness, the unruly wind and sea of Galilee.

Threat, Conflict, Battle

Jesus enters into conflict with religious authorities. Conflict in the myth is associated with chaos and enemies; thus opponents are typecast by the myth. They threaten to undermine him by refusing to recognize his messianic authority.[49] They threaten him with public execution, a

47. For instance, an account such as the acclamation of Jesus as God's son, at baptism and transfiguration, quoting the monarchic coronation statement in Psalm 2, may anticipate his exalted enthroned status, which is to be fully realized at a later point in the narrative. Similarly a speech that belongs in a vision associated with the throne in heaven, can flash back to an earlier stage in the plot of the divine warrior myth. For example, in Revelation 1, John in a vision of the heavenly throne recalls 'everyone who pierced him', an earlier event, by quoting Zech. 12.10.

48. M. Black, 'Christological Use of the Old Testament in the New Testament', *NTS* 18 (1971), pp. 1-14, on the divine decree.

49. A mythic reading of the conflict experienced by Jesus may have led to a more rigid typecasting of his opponents as 'enemies' of mythic proportions, planting the

threat which foreshadows his final battle.

All the forces of chaos and enemies are gathered against him in Jerusalem where he is betrayed, tried, mocked, crucified. He is buried and remains three days in the grave where he enters the jaws of death.

The Convulsing of Nature as the Divine Warrior Manifests his Power
The darkness of a solar eclipse, an earthquake, and the ripping of the curtain of the Temple attend the climactic battle that is associated with Jesus' crucifixion.

Victory
God raises Jesus from the dead, vindicating him as the son of God, victorious in the cosmic battle.

Victory Procession
The triumphal entry to Jerusalem foreshadows the procession in victory to heaven when he leads captivity captive (Ps. 68.17-18). He brings the righteous with him as he ascends to his throne on high. The triumphant voice of the son of God calls those who were in their graves to eternal life (Jn 5.25, 28-29).

Enthronement, Manifestation of Reign
After the manner of God's enthronement above the waters, he ascends on high and is seated at the right hand of the father in heaven. The son shares with the father the role of heavenly king. Early Christians saw themselves as heralds of and witnesses concerning the festival of Jesus' enthronement, as they cited Scripture relating to the enthronement of the son (Psalm 2; Dan. 7.13-14).

Fertility of Restored Order
In the Christian version of the divine warrior myth, the element of new life replaces the abundant blessings of fertility. Jesus judges the living and dead and pours out his life-giving spirit upon the earth. Those who honor him receive new birth and eternal life through the outpouring of God's spirit.

---

potential for an anti-Jewish view of Jesus' death within the mythic structure of the Gospel narratives themselves.

Judgment

The kingly order is enforced in judgment when those who do not honor him as king are cast out of the presence of God.

My Christian version of the divine warrior myth sketched above is a composite and ahistorical. Derived from conflation of many texts, it represents a process of selection and abstraction. John 5 is not an obvious example of the divine warrior myth; but, as I will argue below, the dramatic plot of the myth brings a new coherence to otherwise disparate elements in John 5.

John 5 in Light of the Christian Divine Warrior Myth

The extraordinary speech concerning sonship, and its link to the threat of execution in John 5 acquire new significance when they are interpreted as part of the plot of the Christian version of the myth. Details such as the festival location take on another meaning in light of the divine warrior myth.

Festival Location

John 5.1 is set within an unnamed feast of the Jews. Jesus 'goes up' ἀνέβη to Jerusalem. The timing and geography are appropriate for a festival of enthronement, recalling the mythic return of the divine warrior to the cosmic mountain.[50] The place [possibly the Shepherd's gate] on the north side near the Temple[51] was traditionally associated with the entrance of the king. A combination of imagery specific to John 5 leads me to link this unnamed feast with New Year, *Rosh ha Shanah*.[52] The Mishnah describes it as 'the festival of kings'.[53] A pool

---

50. I am indebted to Dr Arthur Walker-Jones of Pacific Theological College, Fiji, for this suggestion. McCurley (*Ancient Myths*) also develops the theme of the cosmic mountain extensively in relation to Gospel texts.

51. R.E. Brown, *The Gospel according to John* (AB, 29; Garden City, NY: Doubleday, 2nd edn, 1986), p. 206.

52. The Mishnah tractate Rosh ha-Shanah (the new year festival of kings) describes court proceedings. The elders adjudicate over the testimony of people who claim to have seen the sign (the new moon) signifying that it is time to hallow the festival. Witnesses who must travel to testify are allowed to violate customary Sabbath rule, they can carry objects (like a mat?) to come to the Temple to witness for the hallowing of *Rosh ha Shanah*. Further research is needed if a connection with either the Sabbath breaking on the charge of carrying a mat in Jn 5.9-16, or the court of (festival?) witnesses in Jn 5.31-47 is to be established.

is the location for the healing.It is named Bethesda. Milke translates the word as 'house of flowing'. It could recall the apocalyptic festival of enthronement in Zech. 14.8-9 in which living waters shall flow out from Jerusalem and '. . . the LORD will become king over all the earth, in that day the Lord will be one and his name one'. The coronation-like speech which follows in 5.21-23 demonstrates the oneness of Jesus with God. Zechariah 9–14 was used by John as a major source of testimonia.[54]

Power Superior to the Stirred-Up Waters
A more tentative suggestion relates to the pool in John 5. When troubled it was assumed to contain curative power. Might the pool recall the chaotic sea? The connection is questionable because the text itself associates the pool with healing. A lame man thought he could have been healed if he entered this troubled water, but with this attitude he had lain by the pool thirty eight years without deliverance from his affliction (5.7). In contrast, at the word of Jesus, 'rise take your mat and walk', power over the affliction is established: The victorious voice is more powerful than the cure associated with these waters.

Threat—Jesus' Claim to Sonship is Rejected
John 5 functions concretely as an informal trial of Jesus.[55] His mention of God as father provokes a threat of execution, for 'he calls God his own father making himself equal with God' (5.18). The accusation and reply format, the forensic aspect of the speech has some counterpart in Psalm 2. The anointed one is at the center of conspiracy.

The question concerning sonship in the Synoptic trial accounts is similar to the sonship question in Jn 5.17-29; further, the Synoptic accounts follow a trial sequence similar to that of Jn 5.16-29 and Jn 10.30-39.[56] (In Acts 4.25-29 the trial of Jesus is described by his dis-

53. In this I concur with the observations of A. Guilding, *The Fourth Gospel and Jewish Worship* (Oxford: Clarendon Press, 1960), and M.J. Moreton, 'Feast, Sign, and Discourse in John 5', in F.L. Cross (ed.), *Studia Evangelica* (Berlin: Akademie Verlag, 1968), IV, pp. 209-13.

54. D.J. Moo, *The Old Testament in the Gospel Passion Narratives* (Sheffield: Almond Press, 1983).

55. A.E. Harvey, *Jesus on Trial: A Study in the Fourth Gospel* (London: SPCK, 1976).

56. Noting similarity in pattern, Meeks (*The Prophet King*, p. 56) and Brown (*John*, 1.408-409) consider that the material in John 5 and 10 may derive originally

ciples through scriptural testimony from Ps. 2.1: Why do the people set themselves against the Lord and against his Messiah?) In both the Johannine and the Synoptic trial traditions, Jesus responds to a challenge concerning his sonship. (This resonates with the general plot-line of Psalm 2 where the son responds to rebels who question his status as God's anointed.)

By reading John 5 within the frame of the myth, a legitimate complaint concerning Sabbath action changes into a conspiracy, a plot, a counsel to destroy. When the memory of forensic action against Jesus is placed within a concrete expression of the divine warrior myth, such as Psalm 2, the structure of the myth channels interpretation of the event. On a mythic level Jesus is identified with God by virtue of his claim to sonship. His opponents are linked with the role of enemy of God in the myth.

Enthronement Affirms the Superior Power of the Son

Jesus answers the challenge to his sonship with language evocative of the divine warrior myth expressed in the coronation scene of Ps. 89.26-27, '[the kingly son] shall cry to [God], 'you are my father. . . I [God] will make him the firstborn, the highest of the kings of the earth'.

As in Psalm 2, when the king is threatened by enemies he recounts to them the decree of the Lord, 'God said to me, "this is my son, I give you dominion"'. Similarly, in John 5 the mention of the god-like powers of creation and judgment is coronation-like speech declaring the powers decreed by the father to the son. However, the transfer in John 5 evokes a heavenly—not any earthly—enthronement setting. The son is given the power in order that they honor the son as the father.

The divine warrior pattern of God's dominion is replicated in the son. The myth is used to legitimate the authority of the son. Anyone who does not honor the son thus does not honor the father (Jn 5.23). It also is designed to draw lines between those who will worship the enthroned son as God, and those who refuse. The heavenly language evokes the divine warrior myth setting of heavenly enthronement of the god-like human one in Dan. 7.13-14.

from a passion trial of some sort. Furthermore, E.D. Freed (*Old Testament Quotations in the Gospel of John* [NovTSup, 11; Leiden: Brill, 1965], pp. 60-65) also detects similarities between the synoptic trials sonship theme and Jesus' claim to sonship in Jn 5.17-23 and 10.39.

Let me digress briefly to the plot of the divine warrior myth in Dan. 7.1-14.

Threat
First devouring beasts come up out of the sea (Dan. 7.3).

Manifestation of Reign
Thrones are set in place. The enthroned one the ancient of Days, judges and the great beast is destroyed. Next, on the clouds comes one like 'a son of man'. He is presented before the ancient of Days. To him is given dominion, glory and a kingship that all should serve him (Dan. 7.9-14).[57]

John 5.27 is the only citation in New Testament of υἱὸς ἀνθρώπου, that exactly reproduces the Greek of Dan. 7.13; elsewhere the New Testament uses (ὁ) υἱὸς τοῦ ἀνθρώπου.[58] The citation also demonstrates a connection between the Synoptic trial accounts and Jn 5.17-23. A question concerning sonship is found in both John 5 (an 'informal' trial scene) and the Synoptic accounts of a trial before the Sanhedrin; in both the trial question on sonship is answered with enthronement imagery and citation from Dan. 7.13-14.

Though Dan. 7.9-14 is cited in John 5 and appears to shape its imagery, my focus is upon the plot of the myth, not upon one single divine warrior myth testimony. The early Christian divine warrior myth pattern of threat/enthronement appears in Psalm 2 which is not quoted in John 5, the same pattern appears in Dan. 7.13-14, which is cited in John 5. I read the narrative mythically, not simply against the background of the one text that is cited but against other divine warrior texts commonly associated death and resurrection speech. Within this mythic framework, the element of threat is associated with the trial and crucifixion of Jesus. It may be applied to threat of dishonor from enemies as in Ps. 2.1, or the threat may be symbolized by conflict of beastly proportions as in Dan. 7.3. Concretely, Jn 5.15-19 narrates a forensic situation. However the whole of John 5 in its final form have

57. Collins (*The Apocalyptic Vision*, p. 144) identifies the υἱὸς ἀνθρώπου as a variant of heavenly angelic savior figures represented in *1 En*. 46.1, the Qumran War Scroll (1QM 17.7-8) and the Melchizedek Scroll (11QMelch 2.10). Collins (*The Apocalyptic Vision*, pp. 100-101) relates the figure of the Ancient of Days to El who in the imagery of Canaanite myth is the high god who presides over the divine council of the gods.

58. Ashton (*Understanding the Fourth Gospel*, p. 357) notes that it is the only occurrence in the Gospels of the anarthrous form υἱὸς ἀνθρώπου that duplicates the Greek of Dan. 7.13 in both the Septuagint and Theodotion's version.

been redacted to evoke echoes of the myth. On a second level of abstraction the myth resonates with the story of Jesus' rejection, trial, death and resurrection. The whole mythic narrative proves adequate to deal with the conventional attitude of the ancient world that anyone who had been crucified was shamed and cursed by God. Thus it frames the trial that threatens Jesus with the death penalty in Jn 5.16-18. With the Christian divine warrior myth the concrete trial is transformed when in Jn 5.16-29 the trial is made to fit within the familiar sequence of threat and battle followed by victory and enthronement. The divine warrior myth lent coherence and publicly significant meaning to the story of this trial scene. The mythic presentation of the trial confirmed and reinforced the experience of vindication through the living presence of Jesus even after his death.

The Voice of the Son Brings Eternal Life
Following enthronement the utterance of the divine warrior's voice (thunder) from his palace provides rains to fertilize the earth, in Cross's description of the divine warrior myth. In the version of the myth expressed in John 5, fertility translates into eternal life.[59] Those who hear the voice of the son and believe in his enthroned status have eternal life (Jn 5.24).

Victory Procession
The mythic scenario continues with a victory procession in Jn 5.28-29, when the dead in their graves hear the voice of the son of God and come out. It recalls the image of the son who preaches to those in Hades and leads them out in the victory procession of resurrection for the last judgment before his throne. Those who do good proceed forth ἐκπορεύσονται to share the victory of the enthroned son's life; those who do evil proceed forth to judgment. Jn 5.29 evokes the resurrection scene in the divine warrior text Dan. 12.1-2.

The above discussion of Jn 5.1-29 in terms of the divine warrior myth is summarized briefly as follows:

59. I am indebted to Dr Arthur Walker-Jones for this observation concerning Jn 5.24-26, 29. In my dissertation, the analysis of the divine warrior myth in Jn 1.1-18 also equates the traditional element of fertility with new birth in Jn 1.12-13. McCurley, *Ancient Myths*, also develops the divine warrior theme of fertility in relation to New Testament motifs.

Festival—location near Temple in Jerusalem (5.1-2).

Threat—Jesus' honor is threatened and his claim to sonship rejected (5.16-18).

Enthronement—The son declares that God has given him all power that they might honor the son just as they honor the father (Jn 5.21-23; compare the trial in Mk 14.61-62, which alludes to Dan. 7.13 and Ps. 110.1).

Voice of the son brings the dead to life (5.24-26).

Judgment—God has given him the power of judgment because he is υἱὸς ἀνθρώπου (citation of the Septuagint Dan. 7.13).

Victory Procession—Those in their tombs hear his voice and proceed forth to life or to judgment (5.9).

As is characteristic of the Christian divine warrior myth, the son is identified by following the pattern of God's enthronement. Thus the son is placed within the divine drama of the ancient divine warrior myth myth of YHWH's enthronement above enemies and chaos. The emphasis on divine sonship is the primary message of the early Christian version of the myth. The mythic pattern was already known and did not need to be emphasized in early Christian divine warrior myth. However, the point that did need to be demonstrated for the earliest Christians was that the son is identified as Jesus. John 5 builds upon this well established early Christian point to create a distinctive Johannine tautology: the meaning of the son becomes one with the meaning of the father. The son is to be honored just as God the father already is honored.

Myth both reflects and creates social reality. By definition, the divine warrior myth projects a structure of conflict resolved by the absolute power of one over all others. Jn 5.17-23 sets forth the mythic relationship between divine father and son. The relationship demands that divine honor be given to the son in exchange for life. Early Christians identified their experience of Jesus with the myth. It provided a framework for retelling the story of forensic threats to his life. Further, it proclaimed that the outcome of the story is not that conventionally expected of a crucified criminal or slave; his life continues one with God, in the face of death.

The myth itself is not God, but if unrecognized as myth, it supplants the person it frames. It frames Jesus as son in the overpowering, dominating, either/or character of the divine warrior myth. Thus when uncritically embraced as confession of faith the father/son relationship that is shaped by the myth recreates its divine warrior mythic structure in social and ecclesial reality. It projects authoritarian, patriarchal and exclusive structures. The tale is twice told, after the same pattern, for its adherents.

HUNGERS ASSUAGED BY THE BREAD FROM HEAVEN: 'EATING JESUS' AS ISAIAN CALL TO BELIEF: THE CONFLUENCE OF ISAIAH 55 AND PSALM 78(77) IN JOHN 6.22-71

Diana M. Swancutt

John 6.22-71 is a thematically rich pericope, a plate full of intermingled foods that, when consumed, leave the reader stuffed and drowsy. Historical, form, and source critics have long recognized this richness, analyzing, dividing, and reconstituting the text.[1] Adding a literary perspective to theirs may only give the reader indigestion, but at this point a little upset is desirable: the rhetorical power of Jn 6.22-71 is clarified not through ingenious textual rearrangements, but by noting the ways scriptural intertexts move the narrative and substantiate its characters.[2] Even the most careful studies of the function of Scripture in John 6, such as the impressive works of Freed (1965), Reim (1974), and Schuchard (1992), focus on explicit citations.[3] While illuminative

---

1. Cf. n. 13 below. Andreas Obermann's *Die christologische Erfüllung der Schrift im Johannesevangelium: Eine Untersuchung zur johanneischen Hermeneutik anhand der Schriftzitate* (WUNT, 83; Tübingen: Mohr, 1996) came to my attention as this essay went to press. I have therefore not been able to incorporate his findings here.

2. Cf. Hays 1989: 14. Intertextuality is 'the imbedding of fragments of an earlier text within a later one' as scriptural echo or allusion. The reader must decide whether an earlier text is a proof-text, or whether (and how) the meaning or context of the earlier text (A) has been taken up, used, and/or changed in a later text (B). If the latter is the case, 'text B should be understood in light of a broad interplay with text A, encompassing aspects of A beyond those explicitly echoed' (p. 20). In other words, when a literary echo links a text to an earlier text, the echo's 'figurative effect can lie in the unstated or suppressed points of resonance between the two texts'. This interplay, called *metalepsis*, 'places the reader within a field of whispered or unstated correspondences' with an earlier text (p. 20). The reader's task becomes (1) naming an echo so that others may hear it and (2) discussing how the intertext is refigured in the later text.

3. Menken (1988a; 1988b), who has produced a series of articles on explicit

of the Gospel's quotations of Torah, Psalms, and prophets, these studies deal thoroughly with its more deeply embedded scriptural allusions.

To be clearer, critics have long recognized Exodus 16, Psalm 78 (77), and Isaiah 54 as possible sources for the explicit quotations in Jn 6.31 and 6.45. But few notice the allusive play of Isa. 55.2-3 in 6.27.[4] To my knowledge, none has adequately explained the remarkable influence of Isaiah 55 on Jn 6.22-71 generally, and on its explicit quotations particularly.[5] Language and themes from Isaiah 55 intertwine with those of

Johannine citations, should also be listed among these scholars. Menken's essays have recently been collected in a helpful and accessible volume entitled *Old Testament Quotations in the Fourth Gospel: Studies in Textual Form* (Contributions to Biblical Exegesis and Theology, 18; Kampen: Kok, 1996). Throughout this essay, I refer to his original articles.

4. The oft-referenced Guilding (1960) notes that Isa. 54.9–55.3 provides 'interesting parallels' to Jn 6.27 and 45 (p. 63), and correctly sees a connection between feeding and being taught by God (p. 64). However, she fails to discuss the extensive allusion to Isa. 55.1-13 in John 6. She also asserts that Isa. 54.9-17 is the Passover haphtorah reading for Gen. 6.9. While interesting, her conclusions are based on a somewhat tenuous reconstruction of the Jewish lectionary cycle (should we take our lectionary information from Babylonian or Palestinian sources? Will we begin with Nisan or Tishri? How will we use the Mishnah for reconstruction?) Cf. Mulden 1990: 136-52; and D.M. Smith 1965: 102-105. Her focus on that cycle leads her away from seeing textual and thematic parallels in Jn 6 later than 55.3 or from seeing how language and themes from Isa. 54 resurface in the rest of John's Gospel.

Dahms 1981 and Lausberg 1979, who independently trace the Johannine coming–going and descent–ascent motifs to Isa. 55.10-11, do not consider the broader influence of Isa. 55 in Jn 6. Feuillet (1965) presents an intriguing argument that Jn 6 reflects a creative synthesis of the Old Testament's messianic banquet (Isa. 25.6-8, 49.9-10, 55.1-3, 65.13) and banquet of Woman Wisdom (Prov. 9.1-6, Sir. 24.19-22) motifs. While Feuillet correctly identifies the messianic banquet imagery echoed here, he is incorrect in asserting that all these texts are featured together in John. This discussion will show that it is explicit linguistic links with Isa. 55 that help form the backbone of this dialogue. Finally, Young suggests linkages between Isa. 55.1-11 and Jn 6, especially 6.33 and 6.38 (1955: 228). However, he does not discuss the full intertextual interplay of the passage in John. Further, his notice has been dismissed. Cf. Bultmann 1971: 228, n. 2. Cf. also Lindars 1987: 254-55, and Brown 1966: 273-74.

5. I divide intertextual references into three main categories (quotations, allusions, and thematic fields). First is quotations, which can be explicit or implicit. Explicit quotations are preceded by citation formulae. Implicit quotations lack such formulae, but can be clearly recognized, since they are set off by an implicit 'comma' or pause in the verse (e.g. 12.15 and 12.13). Second is allusions, which are more difficult to recognize and cannot be separated easily into explicit and implicit categories. Rather,

Psalm 78(77) and Isaiah 54 to form a complex, playful weaving that supports and colors the thematic and rhetorical movements in Jn 6.22-71. Together these scriptural allusions drive the discourse toward its undeniable conclusion, that Jesus alone is the life-giving bread from heaven.

'Redaction', Unity, Structure

Perhaps scholars overlook the allusive potential of Isaiah 55 because they have been interested primarily in the structural unity or thematic flow of the 'surface' text; that is, they determine the authenticity of portions of a pericope by their thematic and linguistic continuity with it or explicate the meaning of quotations only in terms of their immediate contexts. Critics consequently ignore the import of both scriptural echoes and apparent redactions for the text's description. Of course, this practice is problematic if so-called redactions are really logical outgrowths of scriptural allusions and are, therefore, integral to the text.

In his magisterial *The Gospel of John*, for example, Rudolf Bultmann asserts that an ecclesiastical redactor unhappy with the lack of sacramental imagery in John (ch. 13) added to a sapiential discourse vv. 51b-58 and the clause ἀναστήσω αὐτὸ [ἐν] τῇ ἐσχάτῃ ἡμέρᾳ (6.39, 40, 44). He also thinks the intensive verb τρώγων, 'to consume' or 'to munch', which appears only in Jn 6.54, 56, 57, 68 and 13.18, signals the work of another hand since ἔσθιων ('to eat') would normally be expected.[6] G. Richter also suggests that 6.51b-58 is an interpolation, albeit for different reasons.[7] One of the first scholars to argue for

their recognizability is marked by linguistic, syntactical, structural, and thematic parallels between texts. Thus, pinpointing their actual textual source (MT or OG?) is more difficult than in the case of quotations. Sometimes sources (which book?, which verse?) themselves cannot be located (e.g. 7.37). Third, a thematic field is the extent to which a work assumes an entire narrative (like the Exodus or the figure of Moses). Jn. 6.2-71 displays each of these three types.

6.   Bultmann 1971: 219, 234-37. His other reasons include thematic shifts (he thinks ὁ υἱὸς τοῦ ἀνθρώπου in 6.27 is inconsistent with other Johannine portraits of the Son of Man as divine revealer and judge, 6.62) and differences in theology generally (sapiential v. sacramental). See my discussion of τρώγων below.

7.   Richter 1969: 35-39. Because of futuristic eschatology (vv. 54, 39, 40, 44), the application of the immanence formulae to Christians' relation to Christ (ἐν ἐμοὶ μένει κἀγὼ ἐν αὐτῷ 6.56) and the phrase οὐκ ἔχετε ζωὴν ἐν ἑαυτοῖς in 6.54

textual unity based on the role of scriptural allusion,[8] Peder Borgen counters their claims by arguing that 6.31-58 is an extended exegesis of Exodus 16 (vv. 4, 15), which the evangelist quotes in 6.31. For example, Borgen demonstrates that by changing parts of that central quotation in אל תקרי form,[9] the evangelist immediately alters 6.31 in 6.32-33 as follows:

6.31		ἔδωκεν	ἄρτον ἐκ τοῦ οὐρανοῦ	φαγεῖν
6.32	<u>οὐ Μωϋσῆς</u>	<u>δέδωκεν</u>	τὸν ἄρτον ἐκ τοῦ οὐρανοῦ	
			τὸν ἄρτον ἐκ τοῦ οὐρανοῦ <u>τὸν</u>	
	ἀλλ'	<u>ὁ δίδωσιν</u>	<u>ἀληθινόν</u>	
	<u>πατήρ μου</u>			
6.33			ὁ γὰρ ἄρτος <u>τοῦ θεοῦ</u> εστιν	
			<u>ὁ καταβαίνων</u> ἐκ τοῦ	
			οὐρανοῦ καὶ	
		<u>ζωὴν διδοὺς</u>		
		<u>τῷ κόσμῳ</u>		

Borgen understands 6.51-58 as a Johannine re-reading of φαγεῖν, the last word of 6.31, and notes further references to v. 31 in v. 58.[10] He therefore believes 6.51b-58 to be the final section of the evangelist's ongoing exegesis of Exodus 16.[11] While some of his findings require

(which he thought the evangelist reserved exclusively for Christ and Christ's relation to God [1.4, 5.26]), Richter thought 6.51b-58 was a secondary addition reflecting the changed concerns of the Johannine community. As Schnackenburg notes, 'Richter makes the purpose of the gospel as announced in 20.31 the criterion for deciding which sections of the present gospel are to be attributed to this author. In his view, only the metaphorical discourse fulfills this aim, which is to show that Jesus is the Messiah and Son of God' (1990: II, 57).

8. D.M. Smith (1965: 141-52), provides the best explication of the unity of 6.25-71 without describing the role of scriptural echo. In truth, his trenchant literary observations are largely complementary to my own and those of Borgen.

9. According to Borgen (1981: 40), אל תקרי is a method of Jewish exegesis that replaces or alters original pieces of one text in a 'do not read this (Moses has given), but instead read this (God gives)' fashion. Alterations include verbal repointing, haggadic variations of verbs, and adding a negation before the subject. Often a pentateuchal text is interpreted in light of a prophetic passage. Cf. Barrett 1978: 290.

10. E.g. the Jews 'ancestors *ate* and died', the 'bread *descended* from heaven', and the one who eats '*lives forever*' (cf. 6.33) (cf. Borgen 1981: 59).

11. He states, 'If John 6:51-58 is regarded as an interpolation, the term φαγεῖν (v. 31b) is mentioned only in vv. 49, 50, 51, and it does not receive a treatment comparable to the discussion of the other words in the quotation from Scripture. Vv. 51ff. develop the needed interpretation of the term, and thus repeat the term and its synonym

review,[12] his emphasis on the unity of vv. 31-58 based on the extended exegesis of an intertext is compelling. Any discussion of the integrity of vv. 51b-58 must take place in light of a full examination of scriptural echoes in the text.

Verses 51b-58 is not the only section of the discourse whose integrity scholars question. Bultmann, Barrett, and others consider all or part of vv. 22-26 and 60-71 additions to the pericope. Bultmann assigns vv. 22-26 to the 'water miracle' (vv. 16-21) and vv. 60-71 to the end of Jesus' public ministry (ch. 12).[13] Although he keeps vv. 22-71 in its present order, Barrett (1978: 301-302) also regards vv. 60-71 and vv. 22-59 as two distinct pericopes. Whereas he does not discuss Synoptic parallels to vv. 22-24, and vv. 25-59 have none, he thinks vv. 60-71 are influenced by Synoptic accounts of the confession of Peter and rejections of Jesus in synagogues. Peder Borgen's excellent study (1981) cannot account for 6.60-71 as continued midrash on v. 31 or for the textually difficult introduction (vv. 22-25). Even G.H. Macgregor and A.Q. Morton, who

again and again. Jn 6.32ff. therefore deal mainly with the giving of bread, as said in v. 31b, while vv. 49ff. move into the theme of the eating, which also comes from the quotation in v. 31b. The conclusion seems obvious. The discourse in John 6 certainly draws on different oral and written sources, but it is composed as a unity to interpret the quotation from the Old Testament source found in John 6:31' (Borgen 1983: 22). Borgen (1983: 32) answers criticisms raised by G. Richter about his under-standing of the function of τρώγων and the repetition of the paraphrased quotation in 6.49, 58. Cf. also Borgen 1987: 131-44.

12. Martyn (1979: 108-19) finds Borgen's description of the exegetical methods used in this discourse basically accurate but disagrees with his assumption that the main thrust of the argument is antidocetic. Martyn thinks the evangelist has Jesus telling the Jews that 'the issue is not to be defined as an argument about an ancient text. It is not a midrashic issue. By arguing asbout texts you seek to evade the present crisis (God's present gift in Christ)' (p. 118). Cf. Barrett 1978: 289. Of course, Scripture could also be interpreted as functioning as God's testimony to 'true bread', which Jews cannot 'see' to accept because they are blind (cf. Jn 9). I should add that the methodological connection (midrashic exegesis of 6.31) is not the only type of scriptural interplay in 6.22-71. I also disagree that Exodus 16 is the scriptural text cited in 6.31. See below.

13. Bultmann (1971: 216-37, 443-52) thinks 6.60-71 sums up so beautifully the separation of believers from unbelieving 'Jews' and 'Pharisees' that it belongs at the end of Jesus' public ministry (12.20-33, 8.30-40, 6.60-71), immediately before 12.37-43.

Dodd (1963: 219-22) views the discourse (and vv. 60-65) as an original Johannine composition, but separates 6.66-70 from 6.22-59. Cf. Schnackenburg (1990: II, 1-33), who notes scholars' disagreement about the pericope's boundaries and discusses the variety of variants in vv. 22-24, a testimony to the difficulty copyists had reading it.

some thirty years ago described 6.22-71 as a unity composed by J^2,[14] note minor redactional activity in vv. 22-23 and 66-71 (1961: 93).

Despite these (variously apparent and real) textual dilemmas, the clarification of scriptural allusions' extensive play in 6.22-71 will support my contention that the discourse on the 'bread from heaven' is best read as a textual unity extending from v. 22 through v. 71, and that the discourse's structural divisions should follow changes of speaker within the dialogue, changes simultaneously indicating the thematic shifts the dialogue addresses.[15] Support for this approach derives from contextual evidence; elsewhere the evangelist constructed narratives analogously to 6.22-71 (e.g. chs. 3, 4, 5, 9) and within them employed dialogues as springboards for didactic discourse. Both 4.1-6 and 6.22-25a are extended introductions describing the geographical setting for dialogues. Like 3.1-21, 4.1-42, and (to some extent) 9.1-41, 6.22-71 is composed as a series of question–response conversations between various people (the crowds, the Jews, the Samaritan woman, some of the disciples, the twelve) and Jesus. Finally, chs. 5 and 6 both contain a 'sign' (5.1-18, 6.1-21) and a discourse (5.19-47, 6.22-71), in which the 'sign' provides the opportunity for Jesus to discuss his identity with the audience.[16] Thus, while 6.22-71 is unique in so far as the dialogue (and the theological explanation of the feeding of the multitude) springs from an exegesis of a scriptural quotation (6.31),[17] 6.22-71 is constructed similarly to other Johannine pericopes.

Structurally, a geographical transition 'across the sea' (vv. 22-24)

14. The hypothesized author of 4.1-42, 6.22-71, 10.19-29, 1-18, 30-42, 11.1-52, 14.1–16.24, and 17.1-26.

15. Schackenburg (1990: II, 31) notes scholars' various unsatisfactory structural divisions of the pericope. Sometimes it is arranged by strophes, elsewhere by 'frameworks', which divide the discourse into the request for a sign (vv. 27-36 [+ 37-40 loosely]), the Jews' murmuring and Jesus' second discourse (vv. 41-51), and the eucharistic section (vv. 51b-58). His own structure (II, 32) is also unacceptable.

16. Ch. 9 functions similarly, culminating in the healed man's confession of the 'Lord as the Son of Man' and the Pharisees' lack of sight. Ch. 9 is less a discourse arising from questions than a dialogue about Jesus, however.

17. Ch. 12 ends with scriptural quotations from Isaiah, and scriptures punctuate theologically important parts of the book. However, only in 6.22-71 is the dialogue so focused on the explanation on a scriptural text. The one possible exception to this rule occurs in ch. 4, both with reference to the importance to the Genesis 'woman at the well' motif and Isa. 44.1-5 and Isaiah 55. But the lack of quotation formulae requires these possible allusions to be background, not foreground, for the dialogue.

sets the scene of the bread discourse in the metaphorical wilderness of Capernaum. A quick exchange (vv. 25-33) between the crowd and Jesus follows immediately, introducing the main themes of the pericope (vv. 26-27, 32-33) and the central scriptural quotation (v. 31). Jesus then gives three longer speeches concerning the meaning of the quotation. These speeches address, thematically, the giver of bread (ἄρτον ἔδωκεν, vv. 34-40), the origin of the gift (ἐκ τοῦ οὐρανοῦ, vv. 41-51), and the quality of the gift (αὐτοῖς φαγεῖν, vv. 52-58). Another dialogue of approximately the same length as the first follows (vv. 60-71), clarifying proper and improper responses to the gift (vv. 60-69) and pointing forward to its giving (vv. 62, 70-71).

6.22-24	Geographical Transition	
6.25-33	Thematic Introduction	
	6.31	The Quotation
		(ἄρτον ἐκ τοῦ οὐρανοῦ ἔδωκεν αὐτοῖς φαγεῖν)
	6.32-33	First Clarification
		אל תקרי Thematic Restatement
6.34-40	The Giver of the Bread (ἄρτον ἔδωκεν)	
6.41-51	The Origin of the Gift (ἐκ τοῦ οὐρανοῦ)	
6.52-59	The Quality of the Gift (αὐτοῖς φαγεῖν) as Offense to the Jews	
6.60-71	Responses of Jesus' Followers to the Gift	
	6.60-66	Response of Many Disciples
	6.67-71	Response of the Twelve

Provocative transitional questions or remarks (6.25, 6.34, 6.42, 6.52, 6.60, 6.67) demand responses from Jesus, leading each of these sections ineluctably to the next.

Discerning Sources

As Borgen demonstrates, this dialogical structure turns rhetorically on the v. 31 quotation, ἄρτον ἐκ τοῦ οὐρανοῦ ἔδωκεν αὐτοῖς φαγεῖν.[18]

---

18. Borgen 1981: 59-98. In 6.31 ℵ W Θ *f*[13] *pc* read δέδωκεν for ἔδωκεν, probably as an accommodation to 6.32. In 6.32, B D L W *al* Clement change ἔδωκεν to δέδωκεν, accommodating to 6.31. Cf. Menken 1988b: 41. While most texts read ἔδωκεν in 6.31 and δέδωκεν in 6.32 (thereby establishing this reading), ℵ Θ *f*[13] read δέδωκεν in both verses while W *switches* tenses, so that 6.31 contains δέδωκεν and 6.32, ἔδωκεν. Perhaps significantly, the Hebrew *qal* of נתן can be translated with either the Greek aorist or perfect of δίδωμι.

But the clarity with which 6.32 is set out as a scriptural citation[19] is off-set by scholars' difficulty discerning its source. Their identifications of its origin range from being impossible to locate,[20] clearly Exodus 16,[21] Exodus according to a targum,[22] Psalm 78(77),[23] or Jewish haggadah,[24] various combinations of Exodus or Psalm 78(77) and another text or texts.[25] All is not lost, however. While Psalm 105(104).40, Neh. 9.15, Exod. 16.4, 15, and Ps. 78(77).24 each contain portions of the quotation, (the combined) Exod. 16.4, 15 and Psalm 78(77) resemble Jn 6.31 most closely.[26]

John 6.31

Borgen's claim that its source is Exodus 16 (MT) at first appears obvious, since the combination of Exod. 16.4 and 15 contains most of the quotation's elements. The figure of Moses (v. 32), murmuring (vv. 41, 43, 61),[27] satisfaction with food (v. 26),[28] and the metaphorical leap to the wilderness, suggested both by v. 31's introduction ('Our fathers

19. Cf. Schuchard 1992: 34; Menken 1988b: 40; and Evans 1982: 79-84.

20. Schnackenburg 1990: II, 40-41.

21. Cf. the review in Menken 1988b: 39-40, and Richter 1972: 197-208. Cf. also Reim 1974: 13-15, 90, 96, who agrees with Borgen that Exodus 16 is quoted in 6.31.

22. M.E. Boismard–A. Lamouille with G. Rochais (*L'evangile de Jean*, p. 196) attribute the quotation to Exodus according to a targum that replaces 'to make rain' with 'to make come down'. Cited in Menken 1988b: 39-40.

23. Freed 1965: 15; Schuchard 1992: 36; Menken 1988b: 39-59; Pancaro 1975: 461 n. 29; Geiger 1984: 449-64, and others listed by Schuchard 1992: 36 n. 13.

24. Richter 1972: 208-31.

25. Cf. Schuchard 1992: 35 n. 11, 36 n. 12.

26. Cf. Menken 1988b: 43, Schuchard 1990: 34-35. Ps. 105(104).40 lacks φαγεῖν, ἔδωκεν, and ἐκ τοῦ, and αὐτούς is accusative rather than dative. Neh. 9.15 reflects the Exodus narrative as Psalm 78(77) does, but lacks Jn 6.31's φαγεῖν, has ἐξ rather than ἐκ τοῦ, and the subject of ἔδωκας varies. Menken (p. 43) hypothesizes that the evangelist's φαγεῖν might be a variant of Nehemiah's εἰς σιτοδείαν αὐτῶν. But if that were true, we might have expected to have seen the phrase more prominently featured in John, perhaps (for example) as a replacement of ἐχορτάσθητε (6.26).

27. Cf. Exod. 16.2, 7-9, 12. The evangelist's γογγύζω differs slightly from the OG's διαγογγύζω but both mean to 'complain or 'grumble'. Cf. BAGD: 164, and Jn 7.12, 32.

28. Exod. 16.3: The people sat by fleshpots in Egypt and ate bread to the full (εἰς πλησμονήν/לשבע). Cf. also 16.8 (εἰς πληομονήν/לשבע) and 16.12 (πλησθή-σεσθε ἄρτων/תשבעו-לחם).

ate the manna in the wilderness, as it is written') and by the disciples' trip 'across the sea' (6.16-22), further facilitate the hearer's transportation to Israel's primitive past. But these carefully crafted pointers, no doubt intended to place the hearer symbolically in that wilderness, are betrayed by the quotation itself.

Taken separately Exod. 16.4 and 16.15 vary markedly from Jn 6.31. Only if read together could they possibly be Jn 6.31's source, and even, then, two important differences remain:[29]

Exod. 16.4 (OG)	ἰδοὺ ἐγὼ ὕω ὑμῖν ἄρτους ἐκ τοῦ οὐρανοῦ
Exod. 16.4 (MT)	הִנְנִי מַמְטִיר לָכֶם לֶחֶם מִן־הַשָּׁמָיִם
Exod. 16.15 (OG)	οὗτος ὁ ἄρτος, ὃν ἔδωκεν κύριος ὑμῖν φαγεῖν
Exod. 16.15 (MT)	הוּא הַלֶּחֶם אֲשֶׁר נָתַן יְהוָה לָכֶם לְאָכְלָה

Exodus 16 includes the indirect object ὑμῖν/לכם rather than αὐτοῖς and the explicit subjects ἐγώ/הנני and κύριος/יהוה, whereas the subject of Jn 6.31 is unclear. These two incongruities are hard to explain if Exodus 16 is v. 31's source. It is precisely the ambiguous subject of ἔδωκεν that makes the אל־תקרי juxtaposition of 'Moses' and 'my father' in 6.32 so effective; since the Exodus narrative clearly identifies God as the giver of bread, the evangelist would have had to remove its divine subject to create the crowd's misunderstanding, which Jesus then corrects in 6.32-33. It makes even less sense for the evangelist to have removed the ὑμῖν in the Exodus quotation from 6.31, since it served his purposes nicely in 6.32.[30]

29. Cf. Menken 1988b: 42-43. The accusative plural ἄρτους is also different. The OG is a nearly literal translation of MT Exodus. The one exception is Exod. 16.4, where לחם is translated ἄρτους. The Hebrew לחם permits the English translation 'loaves' (i.e., 'bread' generally, rather than 'one loaf of bread') which is the sense the Greek translator delivers with ἄρτους. The Greek translation probably anticipates 16.4b, in which many people over several days' time gather לחם. Cf. Menken 1988b: 42, and Schuchard 1992: 35.

30. Borgen 1981: 40-41, 51-52, 65-66, maintains that Exod. 16 (MT) is the quotation's source because (1) in both Philo and John, he sees a homiletical pattern in which a prophetic or other text (cf. Jn 6.45) follows a quoted pentateuchal text; (2) an אל־תקרי exegesis of Exod. 16.15 (MT) best explains vv. 32-33; and (3) 'bread' and 'murmuring' only occur together in Exod. 16. But as Barrett (1978: 284) and Schnackenburg (1990: II, 31-32, 41) show, the evangelist could mold homiletical patterns to his purposes, just as elsewhere he crafted quotations in the same way (cf. 1.23, 12.40). The writer's freedom also explains why the existence of אל־תקרי in vv. 32-33 need not imply a Hebrew text. Although the shift from the *qal* perfect נָתַן ('he gave/has given') to the active participle נֹתֵן ('he gives/is giving') is clear in

Unlike Exodus 16, Ps. 78(77).24 contains almost every element of the Johannine quotation (only differing from Jn 6.31 in its lack of φαγεῖν and ἐκ τοῦ[31]):

Ps. 78(77).24   καὶ ἔβρεξεν αὐτοῖς μαννα φαγεῖν
                 καὶ ἄρτον οὐρανοῦ ἔδωκεν αὐτοῖς
Jn 6.31   ἄρτον ἐκ τοῦ οὐρανοῦ ἔδωκεν αὐτοῖς φαγεῖν

The psalm's lack of an explicit subject for ἔδωκεν therefore facilitates the Johannine crowd's confusion about the giver of the bread from heaven; likewise, the psalm's dative plural αὐτοῖς accounts for the Johannine shift from first- (ἡμῶν) to third- (αὐτοῖς) and then second-person (ὑμῖν) speech in 6.30-32. As for the absence of φαγεῖν and ἐκ τοῦ in Ps. 78(77).24b, since φαγεῖν is the last word of the synonymously parallel line in v. 24a, the evangelist could have lifted this theologically important word (cf. 6.48-58) from v. 24a to complete the sense of v. 24b.[32]

Thus, the main problem with Psalm 78(77) being the source for v. 31 is its lack of ἐκ τοῦ, clearly important since the Johannine context demands that Jesus be bread *from* heaven, not ἄρτον οὐρανοῦ, 'heavenly bread'.[33] Because Exod. 16.4 or ἐξ οὐρανοῦ in Ps. 78(77).26a could have inspired ἐκ τοῦ, a number of legitimate resolutions to this problem are possible.[34] However, I contend that ἐκ τοῦ is a Johannine addition (perhaps prompted by Ps. 78[77].26a's ἐξ οὐρανοῦ) aligning

Hebrew, the verb change is just as effective rhetorically in Greek, 'not Moses δέδωκεν but my Father δίδωσιν'. The choice of δέδωκε rather than ἔδωκε in 6.32 may have arisen from the evangelist's attempt to mimic the haggadic practice of repointing verbs with his own alliteration and vowel changes (δέδωκεν. . . δίδωσιν); however, mimicry necessarily implies only an awareness of method, not indisputable use of a particular text. Finally, the murmuring of 'the Jews' and 'some of the disciples' in Jn 6 is surely intended to guide the reader back to the Exodus narrative, the thematic field in which Jesus' words should be understood. But the use of γογγύζω alone cannot favor Exod. 16 as the quotation's source. As we will see, Ps. 78(77) contains the concept of 'murmuring', although not the verbal parallel (77.17-22, 32-43). Cf. Menken 1988b: 43.

31. Menken 1988b: 41, and Schuchard 1992: 35.

32. Barrett 1978: 289, Schnackenburg 1990: II, 41, Menken 1988b: 44, Schuchard 1992: 36, and those he cites, p. 36 n. 14.

33. Schuchard 1992: 36-37, and Menken 1988b: 44-45.

34. Cf. Schuchard 1992: 37, and Menken 1988b: 44-55. As Schuchard points out, the parallelism between Ps. 78(77).24 and 26-27 (ἀπῆρεν νότον ἐξ οὐρανοῦ) is conspicuous.

Ps. 78(77).24b with the descent–ascent motif seen especially in John 3. The evangelist's fondness for the preposition ἐκ plus the article in 6.22-71 (vv. 31, 32 [3×], 33, 41, 42, 50, 51, 60, 65, 66, 71) and elsewhere is undisputable.[35] In fact, of the twenty-one occurrences of οὐρανοῦ in John, twenty are prefixed by prepositions, of which fourteen are ἐκ τοῦ. Only the allusion to Gen. 28.12 in Jn 1.51 does not attach a preposition to οὐρανοῦ. Each of the other six occurrences refer either to descent from, or ascent into, heaven.[36] One should therefore find instructive Dahms's (1981) and Lausberg's (1979) independent recognition that Isa. 55.10-11 is the impetus for the Johannine coming–going and ascent–descent motifs (and therefore, for the addition of ἐκ τοῦ in v. 31).[37] Εκ τοῦ in Jn 6.31 is one indication of the larger influence of Isaiah 55 on Jn 6.22-71.

But let's not look too far ahead yet. For now, it is enough to say that Ps. 77.24b—that is, the Greek translation[38]—is the source of Jn 6.31. Further linguistic parallels between Jn 6.22-71 and the psalm only support this assessment.[39] The clause 'our fathers ate the manna in the wilderness' (v. 31), which directs the audience's attention to the thematic field of the Exodus story, is actually tied more closely to Psalm 77 than to the Exodus text. Never mentioned in Exodus 16, 'our fathers' is used repeatedly in the psalm (Ps. 77.18-19, 24) to refer to discontented Israel eating manna in the wilderness; those who saw God's

35. Jn 1.16, 24, 35, 40, 44; 2.15; 3.1, 13, 27, 31; 8.23, 42, 47; 13.3; 16.28, 30, etc. Cf. Schnackenburg 1990: II, 41, and Menken 1988b: 44.

36. ἐξ οὐρανοῦ occurs in 1.32 and 6.58; ἀπο τοῦ οὐρανοῦ in 6.38; and εἰς τοῦ οὐρανοῦ in 3.13 (2×) and 17.1.

37. However, Dahms (1981: 82) incorrectly separates the two motifs and asserts that the descent–ascent motif could not be traced to Isa. 55.10-11. While he specifically acknowledges Isa. 55.11 (OG's) ἐξέρχομαι–ἀποστρέφω pairing, he fails to account for the repetition and pairing of ἀποστρέφω with καταβαίνω in 55.10. Not coincidentally, in Isa. 55.10, καταβαίνω ἐκ τοῦ οὐρανοῦ is the logeme of importance. Therefore, καταβαίνω ἐκ τοῦ οὐρανοῦ and ἐξέρχομαι are functional synonyms, which together with ἀποστρέφω form a conceptual unit in Isa. 55.10-11.

38. As Menken (1988b: 41) astutely notes, the Greek should be favored because the Hebrew's דגן (78.24b) is rendered by ἄρτος rather than σίτος. Otherwise the Greek translation is relatively literal. Cf. also Freed 1965: 15; and Schuchard 1992: 36, who agree that the Greek is in view.

39. I disagree with Schuchard 1992: 37 n. 21, who opposes Geiger's assessment (1984: 459-64) that the larger psalm influences John 6. Schuchard's important criticism that 'Geiger fails to show why the features which he finds in both the psalm and John 6 could not just as easily have come from, e.g., Exod. 16' will be answered below.

mighty signs in Egypt and elsewhere (77.12) yet disobeyed God (77.8); and those commanded by God to teach their children God's ways (77.3, 5).[40] In Jn 6.22-71 the crowd's 'fathers' (vv. 31, 49, 58)—and Jesus' earthly father (v. 42)—stand in exquisite opposition to Jesus' Father (vv. 27, 32, 37, 40, 44, 45, 57), the ever-faithful Giver of the gift of life. The phrase 'they ate of the loaves and were satisfied' is also a clearer parallel to Ps. 77.29a than to Exodus 16; Exod. 16.3 and 16.8 contain prepositional phrases, whereas Ps. 77.29a includes two successive aorists. Only Exod. 16.12 with its future passive πλησθήσεσθε even approximates Jn 6.26. While it also contains ἄρτων, absent from the psalm (cf. Jn 6.11-12), only Ps. 77.29a (ἐφάγοσαν καὶ ἐνεπλήσθησθησαν) has the same verbal construction as Jn 6.26 (ἐφάγετε... καὶ ἐχορτάσθητε), two aorist indicatives connected by καὶ, with the second an aorist passive indicative.[41]

In addition to these parallels, Psalm 77 contains important references to 'believing' (vv. 22, 32; cf. Jn 6.29, 35), God 'sending' food/provisions (v. 25; cf. Jn 6.38), and (in a parallel line to 24a) 'flesh' (v. 26; cf. Jn 6.54). Also interesting is the psalmist's imperative to Israel's 'fathers' to educate (τοῦ γνωρίσαι) its children in order that they might hope in God and not forget his 'works' (τῶν ἔργων τοῦ θεοῦ, Ps. 77.5-7; cf. Jn 6.28). Τῶν ἔργων τοῦ θεοῦ is yet another phrase found in Psalm 77 but not in Exodus 16. Ps. 77.20c is also strikingly similar to Jn 6.52, where the Jews ask Jesus πῶς δύναται οὗτος ἡμῖν δοῦναι τὴν σάρκα αὐτοῦ φαγεῖν? The psalmist's question, μὴ

---

40. Freed 1965: 15.

41. Interestingly, the Johannine ἐχορτάσθητε is not present in Exodus or Psalm 77. BAGD: 883-84 notes that the passive has both a literal ('be filled') and figurative sense, so that the eaters were both full and craved nothing *better*. Understanding ἐχορτάσθητε in this way is enhanced by the repeated psalmic line (77.18b, 29b), 'he gave them what they craved'. This connection is also supported by my contention that the Johannine ἐχορτάσθητε can be traced to Ps. 106.9 (OG), where the empty soul is filled (ἐχόρτασεν) and the hungry soul satisfied with good things (ψυχὴν πεινῶσιν ἐνέπλησεν ἀγαθῶν). Recall that this is the same verb used in Ps. 77.29a (ἐφάγοσαν καὶ ἐνεπλήσθησαν). Cf. Jn 6.12. I am presently working on an article arguing that Psalm 106 (OG) was used to compose Jn 6.16-21 and that *gezara shewa* connections between Ps. 106 (OG) and other scriptural allusions in John 6 (cf. Isa. 55.2-3 OG) support the assertion that John 6 was written as a unity. On the unity of John 6, cf. again D.M. Smith 1965: 141-52.

καὶ ἄρτον δύναται δουναῖ?, is stunning, especially if 77.24 and 77.27a are to be considered God's answers.[42]

Together these observations indicate that Ps. 77.24 (OG) is the source of Jn 6.31 and that other psalmic themes and language envelop the audience of John 6 in the story it tells, the Exodus story of God's provision of bread and flesh to faithless Israel during their journey in the wilderness. This kind of metalepsis occurs elsewhere in John, especially when Jesus' death is in view.[43] In John 6, it enables Jesus to provide a proper perspective on the crowd's request for a sign and to raise the dialogue's fundamental question:[44] Psalm 77 both introduces the theme of a faithless Israel testing God ('They tested God in their hearts by demanding food they craved', Ps. 77.18) and asks whether God is faithful, able to spread a table in the wilderness and provide his people with bread and meat (Ps. 77.19-20). These themes fit nicely in the context of Jn 6.31, where the people demand—of Jesus—a feeding sign that will certify his worth as ὅν ἀπέστειλεν ἐκεῖνος (6.29), and they help forecast Jesus' answer to perceptive questers, the provision of an eschatological banquet for those who are taught by God.

John 6.45

Although some scholars worry over its introductory formula ἔστιν γεγραμμένον ἐν τοῖς προφήταις, John 6's second explicit quotation (v. 45) certainly comes from only one source.[45] Multiple instances of

42. Vaticanus of Ps. 77.20c reads δυνήσεται, a clear attempt to conform the Greek to 77.19b. δύναται is the best reading.

43. That is, the evangelist employs psalms similarly in Jn 19.24 and 19.36. Jn 19.24 is a direct quotation from Ps. 22.16, but it is paired with a description of Aaron's priestly robe in Exod. 28.32. Jn 19.36 is a quotation of a non-existent Old Testament referent, much like Jn 6.31. The verb is clearly from Ps. 34.20, but the referent is intended to direct the listening audience to the story of the Passover (Exod. 12.46), which also contributes language to the quotation. On the other hand, psalms are also often used without a pentateuchal parallel (e.g. Jn 19.28).

44. Thus, the psalm is cited not simply because its ambiguous verbal subject 'lends itself best to the crowd's desire to attribute the giving of the manna to Moses'. Contra Menken 1988b: 54-56, and Schuchard 1992: 45, following him.

45. Cf. Schuchard's excellent discussion of 'in the prophets', pp. 48-49; based on the work of Menken (1988a), he also incorporates the insights of Richter 1972: 253. For those who would not want to narrow the source possibilities, cf. Freed 1965: 17-18; Brown 1996: 271; Schuchard 1992: 48 n. 5; and Richter 1972: 254-62, for a listing.

God's eschatological teaching (e.g. Isa. 54.13, Jer. 24.7, 31.33-34, Joel 2.27, and Hab. 2.14) notwithstanding, the phrase 'in the prophets' should be understood in its technical sense, common to both Jewish and early Christian usage, where it denotes the second division of the Tanakh.[46] In Jn 6.45, 'the prophets' represents the collection (the other being 'law', cf. Jn 1.45 and 10.34) from which a textual witness is adduced to support Jesus' messiahship.

The quotation itself, which has only two close parallels (Isa. 54.13, Jer. 31.34), supports this hypothesis. While Jer. 31.34's πάντες εἰδήσουσίν με corresponds to its thematic thrust, only Isa. 54.13 is sufficiently close to the actual citation:[47]

Isa. 54.13 (OG)   καὶ πάντας <u>τοὺς υἱούς</u> σου διδακτοὺς <u>θεοῦ</u>
Isa. 54.13 (MT)   וכל <u>בניך</u> למדי <u>יהוה</u>
Jn 6.45   καὶ ἔσονται πάντες διδακτοὶ θεοῦ

But which textual tradition is quoted in John? As Schuchard has outlined (1992: 51-52), the only significant difference between the Hebrew and Greek is the divine name (יהוה/θεός), troubling a quick judgment about source language. Whereas John's sentence structure (use of the nominatives πάντες and διδακτοὶ rather than accusatives) seems to support the assertion that 6.45 is a translation of a Hebrew original,[48] the occurrence of διδακτοὶ (a Johannine *hapax legomenon* [Barrett 1978: 296]) and θεοῦ better mirror the Greek text. Taking the evidence for the Greek source first, we find that διδακτός occurs in the New Testament only here and in 1 Cor. 2.13 and, in the Old Greek, only in Isa. 54.13 and 1 Macc. 4.7 (Schnackenburg 1990: II, 51). Despite Schuchard's assertion that διδακτός is a 'natural rendering of למד' (Schuchard 1992: 52), it is a terribly infrequent one. Further, although septuagintal translators sometimes rendered יהוה with θεός,[49] most employed

---

46. Cf. Sir. 1.1; 2 Macc. 15.9; *Mek.* Amelek 2 on Exod. 17.14; *b. Sanh.* 90b; Philo, *Fug.* 197 and *Mut. Nom.* 169; Josephus, *Ant.* 11.3-4; Justin Martyr, *Dial.* 89.3, 119.3; and Acts 7.42, 13.40, and 15.15. Cf. also Mt. 5.17, 22.40, Rom. 3.21, Jn 1.45.

47. Concurring with this assessment are Reim 1974: 16-18; Pancaro 1975: 279; Lindars 1987: 264; Evans 1982: 80; Kysar 1986: 105; Menken 1988a: 164-72; Schuchard 1992: 51, and others he mentions (p. 51 n. 5).

48. The Greek seems to attach the accusative clause to the verb θήσω from Isa. 54.12. Cf. Freed 1965: 18; Reim 1974: 16-17; and Schuchard 1992: 51.

49. As, of course, Isaiah did here. Freed 1965: 19 and Schuchard 1992: 52.

κύριος.[50] When a preponderance of evidence is lacking, arguments about sources must rely on what is probable, not on what is possible.

Probability suggests that both διδακτός and θεός came from a source, Isa. 54.13 OG. Believing that Jn 6.45 is a Hebrew translation, however, Reim reasons that the evangelist does not call God κύριος and so changes יהוה to θεός (1974: 168). While Reim rightly recognizes that the evangelist reserves the title κύριος for Jesus, calling God θεός or πατήρ instead, he fails to account for the evangelist's different use of κύριος and θεός in narratives and quotations. In narration, the evangelist saves κύριος as an epithet for Jesus. In citations of Scripture, on the other hand, he seems to preserve the source text. For example, in Jn 1.23, a quotation of Isa. 40.3 OG, κύριος probably refers to Jesus; in 12.13 and 12.38, however, it alludes to God the Father (Menken 1968a: 169). The evangelist did not change titles within quotations.[51] Thus, θεός probably derives from his source.

So what should one make of the nominatives in Jn 6.45? Why would the evangelist, reading the Greek, change accusatives to nominatives?[52] This question assumes that the Hebrew must be read nominatively, when it (like the Greek) can be read accusatively, the fourth of a series of

50. יהוה and phrases including יהוה are translated by thirteen different words, many of which were only used once. The most frequently employed translational equivalents were κύριος and θεός. κύριος was the overwhelming favorite. Hatch and Redpath 1954: 800-39, indicate that κύριος translates thirty-two different words or phrases, but the vast majority are יהוה or phrases including יהוה. In fact, κύριος is used 6156 times as an equivalent for יהוה and 'only by way of exception is (it) used for other terms for God' (Quell 1965b: 1059). θεός translates thirty words or phrases, including יהוה or phrases of which יהוה is a part. However, according to Quell (1965a: 79) θεός is used as an equivalent for יהוה only 330 times. Thus, if we can assume he knew both Hebrew and Greek Scriptures, the evangelist could have been familiar with the יהוה–θεός equivalency. But he would also have known the far more prevalent equivalency, κύριος for יהוה.

51. Further, in every citation in which a title occurs and the Greek source is appreciably different than the Hebrew, the quotation is closer to the Old Greek than to the Hebrew. Cf. Jn 1.23 (Isa. 40.3) (Gen. 28.12—no הנני); 10.34 (Ps. 81.6); 12.13 (Ps. 118.25-26); 12.38 (Isa. 53.1). Jn 12.13 (Ps. 118.25-26) *may* be the exception. Whereas the Hebrew reads 'save us' and the Greek translates that faithfully, John reads 'Hosanna'. The rest of the quotation is the same in both Greek and Hebrew. While some have argued that the Hebrew text is in view, the transliterated shout 'Hosanna!' is probably early Christian tradition (cf. Mt. 23.39). Therefore, 'Hosanna' is not helpful in adjudicating the source of Jn 12.13.

52. Cf. Menken 1988a: 170 for this discussion.

promises God will 'establish' (שמתי/θήσω, 54.12). *BHS* understands 13a in precisely this way, placing it on the same line as its parallel, 12c. Of course, the Greek is not ambiguous, even if the Hebrew is. But if the evangelist were using Greek, changing the accusatives to nominatives would fit his contextual needs nicely. The quotation requires an additional verb, and 54.13b OG καὶ ἐν πολλῇ εἰρήνῃ τὰ τέκνα σου suggests that an addition of 'to be' fits the sense of the whole verse better than would θήσω. With the addition of ἔσονται, the evangelist's shift to the nominatives πάντες and διδακτοὶ makes perfect sense. Those who doubt that the evangelist would have changed the text in this way need look no further than Jn 1.51, where he altered to τοὺς ἀγγέλους τοῦ θεοῦ his source, Gen. 28.12 OG, which (following the Hebrew) reads οἱ ἄγγελοι τοῦ θεου. Changing the nominatives to accusatives to suit his purposes, the evangelist made 'angels of God' parallel to 'heaven', and treated them both as objects of what 'you will see'.

Thus, while pinpointing the source language of Jn 6.45 is difficult, both the rare διδακτός and the occurrence of θεός rather than κύριος suggest that Isa. 54.13 OG is in view. As both Menken (1988: 168, 171) and Schuchard (1992: 52-53) maintain, one contextual feature of the Greek may lean the evidence even further in its favor. John's citation eliminates בניך/τοὺς υἱούς σου[53] from the quotation, perhaps emphasizing the inclusion of Gentiles among those who are 'able to come' to Christ (6.44). The inclusions of the nations is certainly a Johannine emphasis (cf. 12.19-20), but here the removal of τοὺς υἱούς σου may have been prompted by Isa. 54.15 OG, 'Behold, proselytes will come to you through me, and will flee to you for protection'. The Hebrew text lacks this verse entirely.[54]

Read in its Johannine context, Isa. 54.13a OG asserts that no one can come to Jesus unless first drawn by God (6.44), and conversely, that

53. 1QIsa[a] reads 'builders' for 'sons', a reading followed by Westermann (1969: 277-78), who thinks that the builders of New Jerusalem will be taught by God.

54. Schuchard 1992: 52, puts it succinctly, 'The OG translator apparently understood the Hebrew גור יגור ("He will stir up strife") in Isa. 54.15 in terms of the noun גר ("proselyte"; cf. the verb גור "to dwell as a stranger", or, in the middle Hebrew and Jewish Aramaic in the pi'el or pa'el, "to make a proselyte") and translated Isaiah accordingly: "behold proselytes will come to you through me, and will flee to you for protection". The OG's indications that proselytes too will be numbered among the citizens of the new Jerusalem could easily have been regarded by John as sufficient justification for his omission of "your sons" from John 6.45.'

anyone who has heard God's voice, who has been taught by God, will come to Jesus (6.45b). Schnackenburg (1990: II, 51) observes that ancient Jews thought of Torah instruction as direct divine teaching, and that the eschatological time would bring perfect, inward divine instruction. Isa. 54.13 OG, which looks forward to the consummation of Israel's return from exile in Babylon, alludes to this sort of eschatological teaching, and in John 6, it indicates that the eschatological time is now. Thus, we see the significance of the quotation's role in Jesus' rebuke of 'Jews' for believing that a man with earthly parents (6.42) could not be bread from heaven: the absent Isaian υἱούς σου shouts loudly not only the necessity of believers' heavenly origin (Schuchard 1992: 57), but also the reality that eschatological instruction comes only through υἱὸς μου (Jn 1.34). That is, only Jesus, the one who has alone seen the Father and descended from heaven (6.46) as one sent by him (6.44), possesses the divine eschatological instruction expected by Isaiah. In this way, Isaiah reconfigures the promised psalmic feast God is asked to provide Israel (Ps. 77.5-8) in terms of Jesus' words and the rebuke he levels against 'the Jews'. On the one hand, Jesus' words are precious stones, God's promised eschatological teaching. On the other, Israel's sons seem not to have recognized them and so, seem not to have been taught by God. Thus, with Isaiah's help, Jesus' heavenly Father is again contrasted with the psalmic 'fathers', who had been wildly unsuccessful in teaching Israel's children—or themselves—to remember God's saving works (6.49).

Isaiah 55
Taken together, the quotations from Psalm 77 and Isaiah 54 infuse John 6 with whispers of voices past: those living in the wilderness, craving food and drink; those chronicling their history with celebration and sadness; and those looking forward to Israel's restoration. The thematic and linguistic traces of Ps. 77.24a and Isa. 54.13a in Jn 6.22-71 provide a suggestive background for Jesus' teachng about the bread from heaven. In their conjunction the psalmic dilemmas (Will Israel see? Will God provide?) are answered not in earthly but eschatological terms. Thus, Israel's prophet re-speaks its Torah story.[55] But even here, the Johannine eschatological re-telling is refigured with the help of Isaiah 55, an

---

55. In this sense, Borgen is right on track when, as part of the Johannine homiletical pattern, he sees the prophetic passage used to illuminate a Torah (pentateuchal) text.

unsurprising event given that it describes God's eschatological feast[56] and follows directly the citation of Isaiah 54 (cf. Brown 1966: 274). In the passage just examined, for example, we are told that only the heavenly knows heavenly things, only 'the one who is from the Father' has seen the Father (Jn 6.46). On the one hand, Isa. 54.13 is used to apply this truth to Jesus' listeners (Jn 6.44): those taught by God (that is, those belonging to heaven) know heavenly words when they hear them. But it is Isa. 55.8-9 that whispers Jn 6.46. '"For my plans are not yours, neither are your ways my ways", says the Lord, "For just as the heaven is far removed from the earth, so also is my way far removed from yours and my thoughts from your thoughts"'. It is not a coincidence that the next verses, Isa. 55.10-11, describe 'my word' (τὸ ῥῆμά μου, 55.11) going forth like rain and snow 'descending from heaven' (καταβῇ. . . ἐκ τοῦ οὐρανοῦ, 55.10). In this manner, Jesus answers Jews who ask πῶς νῦν λέγει ὅτι ἐκ τοῦ οὐρανοῦ καταβέβηκα? (Jn 6.42).

To the hearer attuned to Isaian echoes, this move is not surprising. But I introduce the Isaian allusion to adjust the ears to their subtle resonances in John 6. Few words of Isaiah 55 are the same in the text, and one not already aware of its echoes might miss them here. But reinterpreted, Isaiah 55 actually controls Jesus' exegesis of Psalm 77 by answering eschatologically the two questions it poses. Indeed, in the first thematically crucial verse of the dialogue, Jn 6.27, the evangelist assumes and modifies Isa. 55.2-3 in order to contrast godly activity with the ungodly actions foreshadowed in v. 26 and to introduce the fundamental themes in 6.22-71 without detracting from the importance of 6.31 (D.M. Smith 1965: 143). Isaiah's injunction (55.2-3) not to spend one's money (MT: for what is not bread/food, בלוא־לחם) or one's labor for that which does not satisfy (εἰς πλησμονήν/לשבע בלוא), but to

---

56. A prophetic description of God's messianic banquet, Isaiah 55 begins with a call to the hungry and thirsty to come to God for free food and drink (55.1). The oracle continues in vv. 2-3, 'Why do you spend your money or labor for that which does not satisfy? Hear me and eat good things. . . listen so that you may live.' The question and imperatives of these verses thus reframe free food and drink as the 'good things' God will teach his children in the age to come. Sustenance thus becomes the content of a new covenant promise given by God (δέδωκα) to David's offspring (τὰ ὅσια Δάυιδ τὰ πιστά). The effecting of that covenant, to be celebrated with a great banquet in Israel's return from exile, is described in vv. 10-11 with a natural comparison. Like the rain and snow that comes down from heaven and returns only after the earth is watered and there's bread for food, God's word will be sent from heaven to accomplish his will, Israel's salvation.

listen to God and eat good things becomes the Johannine imperative to work not for good which perishes but for that which abides to eternal life.

A close review of Jn 6.27, which Bultmann (1971: 222 n. 5) attributed to his revelation-discourse source, reveals significant thematic parallels with Isa. 55.2-3:

Isa. 55.2-3 (OG)   ἵνα τί τιμᾶσθε ἀργυρίου, καὶ τὸν μόχθον ὑμῶν οὐκ
                   εἰς πλησμονήν; ἀκούσατέ μου καὶ <u>φάγεσθε</u> ἀγαθά,
                   καὶ ἐντρυφήσει ἐν ἀγαθοῖς ἡ ψυχὴ ὑμῶν. προσέχετε
                   τοῖς ὠτίοις ὑμῶν καὶ ἐπακολουθήσατε ταῖς ὁδοῖς
                   μου· ἐπακούσατε μου, καὶ ζήσεται ἐκ ἀγαθοῖς ἡ
                   ψυχὴ ὑμῶν· καὶ διαθήσομαι <u>ὑμῖν</u> διαθήκην <u>αἰώνιον</u>,
                   τὸ ὅσια Δάυιδ τὰ πιστά. ἰδοὺ μαρτύριον ἐν ἔθνεσιν
                   <u>δέδωκα</u> αὐτόν. . .
Isa. 55.2 (MT)   למה תשקלו־כסף בלוא־<u>לחם</u> ויגיעכם בלוא לשבעה
                   שמעו שמוע אלי <u>ואכלו־</u>טוב ותתענג בדשן נפשכם
Jn 6.27   ἐργάζεσθε μὴ τὴν βρῶσιν τὴν ἀπολλυμένην ἀλλὰ
                   τὴν βρῶσιν τὴν μένουσαν εἰς ζωὴν
                   αἰώνιον, ἥν ὁ μιὸς τοῦ ἀνθρώπου ὑμῖν δώσει.

The only linguistic links are φάγεσθε, ὑμῖν, αἰώνιον, δέδωκα, possibly לחם,[57] and the similarity between working (ἐργάζεσθε) and labor (τὸν μόχθον/יגיע).[58] However, Jn 6.26 retains Isaiah's imperative ἀκούσατέ μου καὶ φάγεσθε ἀγαθά in ἐργάζεσθε and the opposition of worthless and worthwhile labor. It also reflects two key themes—with grammatical parallels—present in Psalm 77 and Isaiah 55.

---

57. Hebrew only. See my discussion of 'bread for food' below.

58. Used repeatedly in John, ἐργάζεσθε is an entirely positive term referring to the work people of God must do while 'it is still light' (Jn 9.4). This work includes both believing (Jn 6.29) and harvesting other believers (Jn 4.31). It is instructive that ἐργάζομαι occurs eight times in John to four occurrences in Matthew and one each in Mark and Luke. Likewise ἔργον occurs twenty-seven times in John to six in Matthew, and two in both Mark and Luke. This means two things: the evangelist could have used ἐργάζεσθε without being influenced by any source. On the other hand, it also means that if he were working with Isaiah 55, he would have translated τὸν μόχθον/יגיע with ἐργάζομαι and ἔργον, the very words used to discuss what the crowd must do to receive truly satisfying bread. μόχθος itself only occurs three times in the New Testament (2 Cor. 11.27, 1 Thess. 2.9, 2 Thess. 3.8). In the Old Greek, it also occurs infrequently, almost always translating עמל. Only three times (Isa. 55.2, Jer. 3.24, Ezek. 23.29) does it translate יגיע. In other words ἐργάζομαι and ἔργον are natural Johannine substitutes for τὸν μόχθον or יגיע.

The first of these, the literal and figurative satisfaction that accompanies eating, is seen in the phrase εἰς πλησμονήν and its equivalents ('for satisfaction', Exod. 16.3, 6, 12, Ps. 77.25b, 29a and Isa. 55.2). In Psalm 77 it applies to never-sated Israelites who gorged themselves on the food they craved (esp. 77.25b) yet doubted God's power, and in Isa. 55.2, to that which cannot satisfy eternally. The motif of satisfaction is taken up in Jesus' accusations of the crowd in Jn 6.26, 'You sought me because you ate of the loaves and were sated'. The crowd's foolishness is then encapsulated in 6.27 and their working for βρῶσιν τὴν ἀπολλυμένην. Thus, contrasted with laboring for βρῶσιν τὴν μένουσαν, their fickle satisfaction not only refers back to Jesus' unseen sign of feeding the five thousand (6.11-12), but also to the wilderness narrative, so that the crowds are equated with murmuring Israelites. The evangelist's brilliant move could not have been made so well without Isa. 55.2-3. For while Psalm 77 provides the negative attitude toward such satisfaction, only Isa. 55.2 provides the solution: 'Listen to God and eat good things, and your soul will revel in them'. Picking up this thought, the evangelist contrasts that which does not satisfy (οὐκ εἰς πλησμονήν, 55.2) with what endures to eternal life (εἰς ζωὴν αἰώνιον, 6.27). True satisfaction seems not to accompany eating earthly food, no matter how filling.

'Eating' is the second and related unifying theme, obviously playing a key role in Psalm 77 and Jn 6.22-71. In Isaiah, as well, only the eating equated with listening (ἀκούσατε μου καὶ φάγεσθε ἀγαθά, 55.2b) brings permanent satisfaction, quieting all past and future hungers.[59] Westermann (1969: 281) notes that the metaphorical imperatives beginning Isaiah 55—come, buy, eat (MT), and drink (OG)—flow directly into literal imperatives—hear, eat, incline, follow—that summon the hearer to both a saving event and a new eschatological condition of deliverance and blessing. This condition promised in Isaiah is continued and concretized in Jn 6.27, where the 'object to be attained' is lasting food and the giver (δώσει) is the Son of Man, who is certified or consecrated by God the Father.[60] The abiding nature of the gift

---

59. Isa. 55.1 MT and OG vary considerably. MT reads 'Everyone who thirsts, come to the waters; and the one without money, come, buy and *eat*; *come*, *buy* wine and milk without money and without price'. OG reads 'Those who thirst, come to water; and those without money, go, guy, and *drink* wine and fat without money and price'. Vaticanus replaces 'drink' with 'eat', aligning the text with MT.

60. Jesus does not really replace God, since God is the one initiating and desiring

mentioned in 6.27 will be divulged fully only later in the dialogue.

The evangelist's use of 'food' hints at the nature of the eternal gift given by the Son of Man. The substance of the Son's gift introduced in 6.27, βρῶσις represents a linguistic shift from the ἄρτος in John's preceding and subsequent dialogue. This shift is curious, given the thematic importance of ἄρτος in John 6. Bultmann thinks βρῶσις and ἄρτος are interchangeable, and the shift in 6.27, insignificant (1971: 225). But why shift from 'bread' (6.23, 26) to 'food' (6.27) then back to 'bread' (6.31) when you want to emphasize that Jesus is the 'bread' from heaven? Of the intertexts known in 6.22-71, only Isaiah 55 mentions βρῶσις. In both the Hebrew and Greek texts of vv. 1-2, the object to be eaten varies. The MT reads לחם (55.2, 10). The Greek (55.2) does not name what should be eaten,[61] but ἄρτον εἰς βρῶσιν appears in 55.10. While the evangelist might have (1) translated לחם, which means both 'bread' and 'food', as 'food' or (2) used Isaiah from memory, he probably (3) employed the OG's βρῶσις (55.10) when he did not find ἄρτος in Isa. 55.1-2 OG.[62] We have already seen the possible influence of

Jesus' action. God certifies or consecrates Jesus as the giver. This theological move is typically Johannine. In John 5, for example, Jesus is portrayed as not initiating judgment, but judging nonetheless, since God made the Son of Man judge (5.27).

61. Although neither food nor bread are mentioned in Isa. 55.1 OG, φάγεσθε does appear in 55.2, implying the consumption of food. However, like the Hebrew שבר which means 'to buy grain' (BDB: 991), the Greek ἀγοράσατε (55.1) can imply an object. Of the occasions in which שבר is translated by ἀγοράζω, the implied or explicit direct object is food or grain. This makes more understandable the non-translation of לחם. Gen. 41.57, 42.5, and Isa. 55.1 lack the direct object. Gen. 42.7, 43.4, 43.22, 44.25, 47.14, and Deut. 2.6 have it. Various amendments have been made to OG versions (B *LC*) bring them into line with MT. Haplography of שברו ולכו (in OG, Syriac and 1QIsaᵃ) may be responsible for the difference. OG's additional πίετε would then be understood as an addition after haplography.

62. Cf. the recurrence of βρῶσις in 6.55 and especially 4.32. Cf. also 4.8, where the disciples go to town to buy (ἀγοράσωσιν) food supplies (τροφάς). John could have used βρῶσις, a term he was already familiar with, when he did not find 'bread' in Isa. 55.1. If they are both dependent on Isaiah 55 (as I believe), βρῶσις in both ch. 4 and 6 derives from Isa. 55.10.

βρῶσις is the best piece of evidence for prioritizing the Greek, rather than majority Hebrew version of Isaiah 55. Because it is not a theologically important Johannine word and was used rather than σίτος or τροφάς, it provides the only linguistic evidence favoring the OG. Despite the many variations between the versions, overwhelming evidence for the evangelist's use of one version is missing, however. For example, John's ἔρχομαι might reflect a Hebrew translation of הלך, or the evangelist

Isa. 55.10-11 on 6.31 (ἐκ τοῦ) and 6.44-46 (καταβαίνω ἐκ τοῦ οὐρανοῦ), where it is correlated with the knowledge of God only the heavenly possesses (6.46, Isa. 55.8-9). Here, too, we see that Isa. 55.10-11's ἄρτον εἰς βρῶσιν ('bread for food'), the result of the rain and snow *coming down from heaven*, is linked with the Johannine phrase 'food that abides for eternal life' through καταβαίνω and ἐκ τοῦ οὐρανοῦ, thereby establishing the evangelist's Isaian-Psalmic manna connection.

The implications of this connection are astounding. In the ὡς... οὕτως structure of Isa. 55.10-11, 'bread for food' is likened to the work of God's word, which 'coming down' out of God's mouth, accomplishes God's will. In John, the leap from word of God to Jesus is very small (ch. 1, 6.60, 63, 68), thus the connections are large. Since in John it is Isaiah 55 that defines that which satisfies over against that which does not, and since that definition is made in terms of what is 'eaten', the logical movement from Jn 6.27, the call to work for food that satisfies, to 6.33, where Jesus says the bread of God descends from heaven and gives life to the world, becomes clear. Only Jesus, God's word, is truly 'from heaven'. Thus, only Jesus, who is from God, can truly satisfy. In terms of the giving of the manna, only Jesus can be true manna—or true bread. Laboring for food which abides to eternal life is therefore laboring for Jesus, whom he as Son of Man will give. In this way, Jesus becomes both the giver (v. 27) and the gift of life (cf. 6.51), and 'eating good things', or believing in Jesus (Jn 6.29; Ps. 77.22, 32; Isa. 55.5), is the labor realizing Isaiah 55's eschatological promise. Lest we forget, 'eating good things' is also listening to God, the consumption of end-time instruction (Isa. 54.13). Thus, 'eating' is multivalent, the assent to the Sent One, the reception of divine instruction, and the gobbling (τρώγων) of abiding bread. Jn 6.27, the recast Isaiah imperative, thereby forecasts the τέλος of the Johannine discourse.

could have substituted his favorite, theologically-loaded ἔρχομαι for πορεύομαι, which he used infrequently and only for the physical act of walking. Jn 6.24-25 may reflect Isa. 55.6 OG, which links 55.6c to 55.7 so as to highlight the series seek–find–call, rather than the Hebrew. On the other hand, John's 'sending' language (e.g. 6.38-39) better reflects the Hebrew Isa. 55.11, which has שלח, than the Greek, which has no equivalent; still, because πέμπω is another favorite Johannine word, the evangelist may have used it even if there were no equivalent. In short, a preponderance of evidence for one version is lacking. The evidence for βρῶσις and my determination that the quotation of Isa. 54.13 is from the OG slightly favors the use of Isaiah 55 OG.

Eating Good Things: 'Consuming Jesus' in the Johannine Dialogue

The remarkable Johannine eating–believing–listening and Jesus–word–bread equations enabled by Isaiah 55 suggest that its language and themes permeate Jn 6.22-71, interacting with Psalm 77 to transport the listener back to the wilderness and forward again in and through Jesus' words of eschatological promise. As early as the pericope's introductory verses, the narrative begun with Jesus' Passover feeding (6.1-15) moves to Capernaum and tells the reader that the feeding's witnesses were not aware of Jesus' water walk (vv. 16-21). With 'on the other side of the sea' (6.1, 22, 25), however, the narrative shifts not to an explanation of the sea crossing, but to that of the feeding. Together with the introduction of 'where they ate the bread after the Lord gave thanks for it' (v. 23), a clear reference to 6.11-15, this seeming oversight foreshadows the subject matter of the subsequent dialogue—the ability of the already-satisfied to truly 'eat' the Bread from Heaven.

Further anticipating this upcoming discussion, as early as Jn 6.24 the evangelist deploys Isa. 55.6. After moving the crowd 'across the sea', 6.24-25 says, 'and they came into Capernaum seeking Jesus, and finding him across the sea, they said to him, "Rabbi, when did you (be)come here?"':

Isa. 55.6	<u>Ζητήσατε</u> τὸν θεὸν καὶ ἐν τῷ <u>εὑρίσκειν αὐτὸν</u> ἐπι καλέσασθε
Jn 6.24-25	ὅτε οὖν εἶδεν ὁ ὄχλος ὅτι Ἰησοῦς οὐκ ἔστιν ἐκεῖ... ἦλθον εἰς Καφαρναοὺμ <u>ζητοῦντες</u> τον Ἰησοῦν, καὶ <u>εὑρόντες αὐτὸν</u> πέραν τῆς θαλάσσης εἶπον αὐτῷ· ῥαββί, πότε ὧδε γέγονας;

Once echoed, Isa. 55.6 underscores the disjunction between the actions of people who know, and do not know, the Lord when they see him. Rather than calling upon his name, as Isaiah implores, the people who had just seen both a feeding and sea miracle call Jesus teacher. Naming them an unperceiving people, Jesus rebukes their lack of vision, saying, 'You seek me not because you saw signs, but because you ate of the loaves and were satisfied' (6.26). Jesus' real identity is thereby linked with his σημεῖα. Of course, we know from Isa. 55.6 that if his now-sated followers had truly seen signs, they would have called him Lord; the irony here is only deepened in 6.33, when the crowds finally call Jesus κύριος, but do not know what they have said.

Then, subsuming Isa. 55.2 in the language of Jn 6.27, Jesus contrasts pursuit of lasting food which he as Son of Man will give with the earthly satisfaction just condemned. His response, introduced by the Johannine ἐργάζεσθε,[63] deepens the irony of the crowds' question (6.25). Indicating both physical and moral labor, ἐργάζεσθε is a synonym for ζητεῖτε just as the imperatives in Isa. 55.2-3 (hear–eat–listen–come) were. In his appropriation of Isa. 55.2-3, therefore, Jesus equates 'seeing signs' with 'laboring' for abiding bread and 'missing' them with laboring after wind. Rightly rebuked, the crowd asks Jesus how to labor after abiding bread (v. 28). Jesus' answer, 'believe in the One God sent' (v. 29) shows that the people, while understanding that they have been asked to respond, have not seen the imperative's Source. Their lack of insight deepens with their demand for a sign (vv. 30-31). For while they have understood Jesus' self-identification as the Son of Man, they want a proof—a test passed—that he is who he claims to be. Psalm 77 shouts in the background, 'They tested God in their heart... they did not believe in him, or trust his saving power!' The quotation of Psalm 77 in v. 31 reveals their utter blindness to Jesus' authority and, thus, to the point he has been trying to make. Jesus responds to their ignorance *by repeating what he said in 6.27*, only now in terms they can understand. In אל־תקרי form, he corrects them:

Not Moses	gave	bread from heaven
but *My Father*	*gives*	*true* bread from heaven
For the bread *of God*		*descends* from heaven
	and *gives* life *to the world*	

The assumed parallel between Moses and the prophet-Christ, which Meeks describes in *The Prophet-King* (1967), comes clearly to the forefront here. Being called to believe, the crowd wants proof that Jesus is 'as good as' Moses. Jesus answers that only God gives true bread from heaven; that even God's mighty work through Moses left Israelites murmuring (Exod. 17.3); and that the God who gave manna is the same Father who certified the Son of Man to give abiding food. The evangelist's haggadic addition of ὁ καταβαίνων, absorbed from Isa. 55.10, solidifies the intimate connection between the Father and the Son, thereby allowing the Father to give the Son and the Son to give sustenance. The final phrase of this subsection, ζωὴν διδοὺς τῷ κόσμῳ, not only indicates that such sustenance is available to ἔθνη (Isa. 54.15,

---

63. Versus von Wahlde (1980). This verb does not imply a contrast between faith and works in the Pauline sense.

55.4-5), but that God's sustaining bread (ὁ ἄρτος τοῦ θεοῦ ἐστιν ὁ καταβαίνων ἐκ τοῦ οὐρανοῦ) is emphatically also God's word (τὸ ῥῆμά μου) sent to accomplish his will (Isa. 55.11).

The crowd's response (6.34), which mirrors that of the Samaritan woman (4.15), is a repeated misunderstanding of Jesus' words. Hearing adjectivally an ambiguous Greek ὁ καταβαίνων, which can be substantival (bread 'who') or adjectival (bread 'that'), the crowd requests a continual feeding of earthly—albeit special—bread. Failing to see that the true bread *is* Jesus (vv. 32, 35),[64] they are also blind to the two crucial Isaian themes to which Jesus already alluded, that the earthly cannot satisfy and that eating—or believing—is listening to God. The audience should not be surprised, then, when the crowd fails to understand Jesus' words of instruction.

In the first of four ἐγώ εἰμι sayings,[65] Jesus corrects the crowd's linguistic misunderstanding, emphasizing himself as the bread *who* gives life, and renews God's offer of Isa. 55.1's eschatological food (v. 35b) with reference to himself.[66] Then playing the crowd's own imperative, δός, off of elements of Isaiah 55 (coming, believing, descending from heaven to do God's will), Jesus describes God as the giver of true bread and reaffirms the intimate relationship between the Father and the Son (vv. 36-39). Only the one whom the Father gives can come to, and believe in, the Son. Again clearly paraphrasing Isa. 55.10-11, he references the Father's will as the reason for the crowd's failure to see Jesus' signs or hear his words. With the same breath he answers the psalmic query. Will they believe? It appears the called are few. But for those who believe—who eat what is good—a twice-phrased promise to eternal life is given.

After shifting the exegesis of 6.31 away from the giver to the origin of the bread from heaven, which is introduced by murmuring Jews who contrast Jesus' earthly origin with the heavenly origin of true bread

64. D.M. Smith 1965: 149.
65. Cf. Bultmann 1971: 225-26.
66. Thus, Feuillet (1965: 66-80) wrongly asserts that 6.35 alludes specifically to Sir. 24.21, despite 6.35's wisdom overtones. The context of Sir. 24.21 contributes nothing to Jn 6.22-71, while Isaiah 55 does. Further, Sir. 24.21 suggests that people will never be sated (as does the Psalmic reflection on ancient Israelites!) whereas both Isa. 55.1-3 and Jn 6.27-58 say that if they 'eat' Jesus, they will be truly satisfied. The complex come–not hunger/believe–not thirst answers Isaiah 55's thirst?–come/hungry?–believe (55.3).

(vv. 41-51),[67] the dialogue turns to the most important section of the Johannine discourse. Rebuffing Jews who because they are not 'taught by God' fail to see his origin ἐκ τοῦ οὐρανοῦ, Jesus again contrasts himself as bread that gives life with the earthly bread their long-dead ancestors ate (vv. 49-50). The theme of 'eating Jesus', so long a subtext in this pericope, now becomes explicit:

6.27	food that abides	which Son of Man will give	into eternal life	
6.33	The bread of God is the one descending from heaven	and gives	life to the world	
6.51	The bread	which I will give	for the life of the world	*is my flesh*

Exhausting his haggadic play of Isaiah 55 on every other part of the crowd's psalmic quotation, Jesus turns now to φαγεῖν and unleashes upon it the full power of Isaiah's ὁ ἄρτος ὁ καταβαίνων ἐκ τοῦ οὐρανοῦ. If—as Isaiah says—only those who eat can hear and only those who hear can believe, and Jesus is true bread from heaven, then his hearers must eat him to accomplish God's will. This is precisely what Jesus says in 6.53, where he reintroduces the Son of Man from 6.27 and reiterates the themes set out there. By mixing the metaphors of flesh and eschatological food (and drink, Isa. 55.1), Jesus not only affirms the offensive belief that only those eating the Son of Man have life, but increases that offense by saying, to a people who do not eat blood, that they must drink his. Utterly amazed by Jesus' demand for consumption, the Jews echo Ps. 77.20, 'How can he give us (his) flesh to eat?' (6.52). Unaware of having enacted their 'fathers' words, they fail also to hear the psalm's own response (77.27): God rained down flesh (σάρξ) upon them (6.58).

Thus, the 'eating' discussed in this final dialogue is not the product of an ecclesiastical redactor, but the inevitable, logical result of the evangelist's exegesis of Psalm 77 in light of Isaiah 55's eschatological thrust. Eating *means* believing, coming, and listening to God. That is why Jesus' flesh can be 'true food' (6.55), or in the language of the verse that set out the term, 'food that abides to eternal life' given by the Son of Man (6.27). The repetition of the intensive τρώγων ('munching') in vv. 54-58 should therefore not be viewed as the work of a second hand

---

67. I have discussed this section above.

but as a rhetorically effective method of increasing the offense of 'eating Jesus' (cf. 6.52).[68]

This effect is confirmed not only by offended 'Jews' but by 'many of his disciples' who—also murmuring (6.61)—find this 'word' too hard to hear (6.60). They hear (ἀκούσαντες, cf. Isa. 55.2 ἀκούσατέ μου...), but do not eat (τίς δύναται αὐτοῦ ἀκούειν [ὁ λόγος οὗτος]; cf. Isa. 55.2... καὶ φάγεσθε ἀγαθά). Thus, despite his self-described heavenly instruction (6.62-63), many of his own 'pupils' (ἐκ τῶν μαθητῶν αὐτοῦ) cannot believe. At this level, the importance of 'eating Jesus' lies not in any reference to the eucharistic communion of Christians with the Lord, but to the necessity of *confessing* God's offensive eschatological word, that the Son of Man who has descended from heaven must have his flesh ripped and his blood spilled in order to give life to the world (Isa. 55.11). The repetition of τρώγων in Jn 13.18 indicates that 'eating' is a metaphorical pointer to Jesus' death. There, quoting Ps. 41.9 but replacing the psalm's ἔσθιων ('eating') with the more intensive τρώγων, Jesus reveals Judas as his betrayer by saying, 'he who consumed (τρώγων) my bread has lifted his heel against me'. One of his own now seeks his death. The evangelist's use of τρώγων in 6.54-58 and his reference to Judas in 6.64 and 6.71 are therefore crucial clues foreshadowing (for those who can hear) the sacrificial death that must consume the word of God.

It is indicative of the Johannine narrator's pessimism about people's ability to understand this word (cf. Jn 12) that the Isaian command to 'seek the Lord and finding him, to call on his name', failed to be effected by any with whom Jesus spoke. The essentiality of vv. 60-71 to the bread discourse is proven not only by the references to Jesus' death provided in the character of Judas or by important thematic parallels between 6.60-71 and vv. 22-59,[69] but especially by the refusal of Jesus' followers to accept his hard saying. It is only after all others deny his words, that Peter, in v. 68, calls Jesus Lord and confesses his

---

68. With good reason, D.M. Smith (1965: 147) and Barrett (1978: 247) hypothesize that it may merely reflect the verbal shift to the present tense. Until now the evangelist has employed the aorist φαγεῖν. Needing a present participle he eschews the expected ἔσθιων in favor of τρώγων. Since ἔσθιων never occurs in John, despite the popularity of φαγεῖν, τρώγων may represent the evangelist's small vocabulary. While not contesting that it might, I am emphasizing its rhetorical effect, an effect 'felt' by almost all the discourse's characters.

69. D.M. Smith (1965: 151 nn. 93-94) does a good job of describing parallels. 6.65 clearly refers to vv. 37 and 44. 6.62 presupposes vv. 33, 38, and 50.

sole possession of the words of life. It is only Peter, who has—in the language of Isa. 55.6—sought the Lord, and finding him, called upon his name.

In so doing, Simon Peter confesses two important things on behalf of the twelve; that Jesus has the words of eternal life and that he is the Holy One of God. The second confession confirms the intimate divine relation between the Son and the Father, a theme deployed throughout John 6 to explain the source of Jesus' authority and the reason for people's failure to 'see' it. The first is an entirely Johannine reference to Jesus' nature as logos-became-flesh. As the word of God (Isa. 55.10), he also teaches the eschatological words of God. Isaiah 55 therefore sums up the sense in which Jesus is both word and word-giver, sign and sign-giver, life and life-giver. As the word that proceeds from God's mouth, he both represents and is the essence of God, and through him alone is God's will accomplished. Thus, when Jesus says that the crowds have not seen signs, he means that they have not seen him, since he is God's sign. Isa. 55.13 can be understood to say just this: 'And it (my word) will be for the Lord[70] for a name and an eternal sign and it will not be cut off'. This word brings us to John 6's shattering conclusion, that only the eleven are taught by God.[71]

Hungers Assuaged by the Bread from Heaven

The Johannine discourse on the bread from heaven, a commentary on Jesus' feeding of the five thousand and crossing of the sea, entwines themes of wilderness manna-giving and the descent of the eschato-logical word of God. This intricate weave of words and themes from Psalm 77 and Isaiah 54–55 results in an astonishing discourse demanding that both actors and audience eat the flesh of the Son of Man and drink his blood. For obvious reasons, not the least of which is the existence of other early Christian accounts describing a communal Christian Supper, sapientialists and sacramentalists have long debated the meaning of these words. What does it mean to devour Jesus' flesh and drink his blood?

---

70. While Rahlf's *Septuaginta* places κύριος in the text of Isa. 55.13 OG, his choice is only supported by Eusebius of Ceasarea and Cyril of Alexandria. The Göttingen edition of Greek Isaiah (p. 329) correctly prefers the majority κυρίῳ.

71. This is, of course, the thrust of John 13–17.

Isaiah 55 provides one metaphorical clue to help unlock this interpretative puzzle. Its call to free food and drink is the call to seek God, to listen, to believe. In its Johannine conjunction with psalmic questions (Is God faithful? Will people believe?), Isaiah therefore demonstrates *how* God is faithful and *on what basis* people must believe. If you hear Isa. 55.2 behind Jn 6.60, for example, the Isaian equation of listening and eating is realized in the Johannine call to believe, and then confess, a σκάνδαλον. 'Eating' *is* believing. 'Eating' *is* heeding divine instruction. And here's the catch: 'eating' *is* confessing the divine origin of the Word who points forward to his self-sacrifice as the scroll upon which he is written. That is the σκάνδαλον. That is why his disciples' query ('This word is harsh. Who can hear it?', v. 60) stings so.

Uttered in unison with Psalm 77, the re-spoken Isaian word suggests that God's faithfulness to the crowd, the 'Jews', Jesus' disciples, and especially the Israelite 'fathers', is a new Exodus promise for hungry wilderness-wanderers. The Johannine interweaving of Psalm 77's wilderness narrative and the Isaian new Exodus prophecy results in the recombination of past and present covenant promises that explains Jesus' soteriological significance. While he spoke from a mountain, fed the people, and crossed the sea, Jesus was more than Israel's Redeemer-like Moses. The word of God's mouth, he was sent like bread from heaven and, like God's manna, will be consumed in order to give life to the world (Isa. 55.12-13). Thus, because his kingship was based on death, not on his giving of a new law (6.15, 6.31), only those who hear and believe in Jesus see that by his self-sacrifice he ends believers' wandering and transforms into eternal life Isaiah's promise of an eschatological homecoming. Only then can thirst truly be quenched and hunger be assuaged.

He is then, in a very special sense, a Passover sign. The substance of safety from death, his consumption is the Once for all, the abiding sign for which we should labor. But, answering the psalm's second question (will people believe?), the narrative suggests that such work is only accepted by the few who trust that the offense of eating and drinking God's salvation is believing in the death of his only Son. The doubt rebuked is not only that an earthly man could be true bread from heaven, but that God's eschatological teaching could include vanquishing the Teacher–Son. Jn 6.22-71 therefore looks proleptically toward Jesus' Isaian lament, 'Lord who has believed our report?' (John 12) and to his Passover self-offering in fulfillment of the Scriptures

(John 19). It is there, with pierced side but unbroken bones, that the Son of Man becomes the banquet-bread awaiting those have truly heard God.

Jn 6.22 is therefore a play on words and Word employing Isaian images to describe both God's promise to those who see the sign and the reason for others' blindness. Jn 6.22-71 deploys Isaian banquet metaphors ironically to foreshadow Jesus' Passover death and link it with divine instruction, thereby reminding early Christian 'insiders' of the eschatological knowledge they already possess. The narrative uses Isaiah to instruct them that they are 'taught by God'; that God's 'good food' is found in their communities' shared belief and confession that Jesus is the crucified, glorified Son of God (cf. 12.42), and that others will refuse their testimony because they are not so taught. Thus, the bread discourse also teaches them that Jesus' call to be consumed is the call to believe the unbelievable (a belief they already share) and that those who disbelieve have not been called by God (6.44). In this way, Jn 6.22-71 sustains believers already conversant in a communal language of salvation by confirming that they know the truth they are called to confess in the face of 'earthly' logic and hostile outside pressure.[72] In short, the discourse's language of consumption does not demand a sacramentalist interpretation.

At the same time, *if* Johannine communities shared a supper of remembrance (a hypothesis unprovable based on internal evidence), then John 6 is an exquisite piece of double entendre. Even more thickly layered with dramatic irony, the insider audience simultaneously hears Jesus' teaching as the demand for belief and the awareness of his offensive death, and it experiences the common meal as a consum(e/m)ation of the divine promise. Not simply a remembrance, it would then be an inheritance and enactment of Isaian new covenant promises.

By answering the questions raised in the crowd's psalmic challenge of Jn 6.31, therefore, Isaiah 55 provides a critical interpretive key to the discourse on the bread from heaven. It unifies vv. 22-71 by linking

---

72. Cf. Martyn (1979) for a now-classic explanation of perceived hostile pressures that fostered this insider–outsider perspective. D.M. Smith (1984: 1-36), Culpepper (1983: 211-227), and those Culpepper cites (p. 211) have offered insightful criticisms, refinements, and alternatives to this position. This reading neither requires nor assumes the complete applicability of Martyn's hypothesis, but it does support one of its general findings: the most likely early function of this text was support for a believing community or communities facing perceived hostilities from outsiders.

the geographical setting in the wilderness (vv. 22-24), the eating of the bread from heaven (vv. 51-58), and people's varying acceptance of Jesus (vv. 60-71), to the evangelist's אל־תקרי exposition of Ps. 77.24. It promises eternal life to those who come, hear, eat, and believe, simultaneously naming as wilderness-mumblers those unseeing crowds who demand a sign of the one sent by God (6.29). To the psalmist who wonders whether God can spread a table for his people, Isaiah also answers with a banquet for the instructed. Finally, it teaches early Christians the character of God's Son and sustains their participation in community life. In these ways, John's Isaian discourse spreads a feast of eschatological food and drink, assuaging every hunger of those few who are truly 'taught by God'.

BIBLIOGRAPHY

Barrett, C.K.
    1978   *The Gospel according to St John* (Philadelphia: Westminster Press).
    1989   *The New Testament Background: Selected Documents* (San Francisco: Harper & Row).

Borgen, P.
    1981   *Bread from Heaven: An Exegetical Study of the Concept of Manna in the Gospel of John and the Writing of Philo* (Leiden: Brill).
    1983   *LOGOS was the True Light* (Tepir: University of Trondheim).
    1987   *Philo, John and Paul: New Perspectives on Judaism and Early Christianity* (BJS, 131; Atlanta: Scholars Press).

Brown, R.E.
    1966   *The Gospel according to John* (New York: Doubleday).

Bultmann, R.
    1971   *The Gospel of John* (Philadelphia: Westminster Press).

Cartlidge, D.R., and D.L. Dungan
    1980   *Documents for the Study of the Gospels* (Philadelphia: Fortress Press).

Charlesworth, J.H.
    1990   *John and the Dead Sea Scrolls* (New York: Crossroad).

Crossan, J.D.
    1983   'It is Written: A Structuralist Analysis of John 6', *Semeia* 26: 3-21.

Culpepper, R.A.
    1983   *Anatomy of the Fourth Gospel: A Study in Literary Design* (Philadelphia: Fortress Press).

Dahms, J.V.
    1981   'Isaiah 55:11 and the Gospel of John', *EvQ* 53: 78-88.

Dodd, C.H.
    1963   *Historical Tradition in the Fourth Gospel* (Cambridge: Cambridge University Press).

Evans, C.
    1982   'On the Quotation Formulas in the Fourth Gospel', *BZ* 26: 79-83.
Feuillet, A.
    1965   *Johannine Studies* (Staten Island, NY: Alba House).
Fortna, R.T.
    1970   *The Gospel of Signs: A Reconstruction of the Narrative Source Underlying the Fourth Gospel* (Cambridge: Cambridge University Press).
Freed, E.D.
    1965   *Old Testament Quotations in the Gospel of John* (Leiden: Brill).
Geiger, G.
    1984   'Aufruf an rückkehrende: zum Sinn des Zitats von Ps. 78:24b in Joh 6:31', *Bib* 65(4): 449-64.
Giblin, C.H.
    1983   'The Miraculous Crossing of the Sea (John 6:16-21)', *NTS* 29: 96-103.
Goulder, M.D.
    1983   'From Ministry to Passion in John and Luke', *NTS* 29: 561-68.
Guilding, A.
    1960   *The Fourth Gospel and Jewish Worship* (Oxford: Clarendon Press).
Hatch, E., and H.A. Redpath
    1991   *A Concordance to the Septuagint* (Grand Rapids: Baker Book House).
Hays, R.B.
    1989   *Echoes of Scripture in the Letters of Paul* (New Haven: Yale University Press).
Krodel, G.
    1983   'John 6.63', *Int* 37: 283-88.
Kysar, R.
    1986   *John* (Augsburg Commentary on the New Testament; Minneapolis: Augsburg).
Lausberg, H.
    1979   'Jesaja 55:10-11 im Evangelium nach Johannes', in *Miniscule Philologia* (Nachrichten der Academie der Wissenschaften im Göttingen, 7; Göttingen: Vandenhoeck & Ruprecht): 131-44.
Lindars, B.
    1987   *The Gospel of John* (NCB Commentary; Grand Rapids, MI: Eerdmans).
Macgregor, G.H., and A.Q. Morton
    1961   *The Structure of the Fourth Gospel* (London: Oliver & Boyd).
Martyn, J.L.
    1979   *History and Theology in the Fourth Gospel* (Nashville: Abingdon Press).
Meeks, W.A.
    1967   *The Prophet-King: Moses Traditions and the Johannine Christology* (Leiden: Brill).
Menken, M.J.J.
    1988a   'The Old Testament Quotation in John 6:45: Source and Redaction', *ETL* 64.1: 164-72.
    1988b   'The Provenance and Meaning of the Old Testament Quotation in John 6:31', *NovT* 30: 39-56.

Minear, P.
    1982   '*Logos* Ecclesiology in John's Gospel', in R. Berkey and S. Edwards
                (eds.), *Christological Perspectives* (New York: Pilgrim Press).
Mulden, M.J. (ed.)
    1990   *Mikra* (Minneapolis: Fortress Press).
Painter, J.
    1989   'Tradition and Interpretation in John 6', *NTS* 35.3: 421-50.
Pancaro, S.
    1975   *The Law in the Fourth Gospel* (Leiden: Brill).
Phillips, G.A.
    1983   '"This is a Hard Saying, who can be Listener to it?"': Creating a Reader in
                John 6', *Semeia* 26: 23-56.
Quell, G.
    1965a   'θεός—El and Elohim in the OT', *TDNT*, III: 79-89.
    1965b   'Κύριος—The Old Testament Name for God', *TDNT*, III: 1058-81.
Reim, G.
    1974   *Studien zum alttestamentlichen Hintergrund des Johannesevangeliums*
                (SNTSMS, 22; Cambridge: Cambridge University Press).
Richard, E.
    1985   'Expressions of Double Meaning and their Function in the Gospel of
                John', *NTS* 3: 96-112.
Richter, G.
    1969   'Zur Formgeschicht und literarischen Einheit von Joh 6, 31-58', *ZNW* 60:
                21-55.
    1972   'Die alttestamentlichen Zitate in der Rede vom Himmelsbrot Joh 6,26-51a',
                in J. Ernst (ed.), *Schriftauslegung: Beiträge zur Hermeneutik des Neuen
                Testaments und im Neuen Testament* (Munich: F. Schöningh).
Schenke, L.
    1985   'Die literarische Vorgeschichte von Joh 6:26-58', *BZ* 29(1): 68-89.
Schnackenburg, R.
    1990   *The Gospel according to St John* (3 vols.; New York: Crossroad).
Schuchard, B.G.
    1992   *Scripture within Scripture: The Interrelationship of Form and Function in
                the Explicit Old Testament Citations in the Gospel of John* (SBLDS, 133;
                Atlanta: Scholars Press).
Sproston, W.E.
    1985   '"Is not this Jesus, the son of Joseph?" (Jn 6:42): Johannine Christology
                as a Challenge to Faith', *JSNT* 24: 77-97.
Smith, D.M., Jr
    1965   *Composition and Order of the Fourth Gospel: Bultmann's Literary Theory*
                (New Haven: Yale University Press).
    1976   *John* (Philadelphia: Fortress Press).
    1984   *Johannine Christianity: Essays on its Setting, Sources, and Theology*
                (Columbia, SC: University of South Carolina Press).
Smith, M.H.
    1978   'Mark 6:32–15:47 and John 6:1–19:42', *SBLSP* 14: 281-87.
    1979   'Collected Fragments: On the Priority of John 6 to Mark 6–8', *SBLSP* 16:
                105-108.

Wahlde, U.C. von
    1980   'Faith and Works in John 6:28-29: Exegesis or Eisegesis?', *NovT* 22: 304-15.
    1983   '*Weideraufnahme* as a Marker of Redaction in John 6.51-58', *Bib* 64.4: 542-49.
Westermann, C.
    1969   *Isaiah 40–66: A Commentary* (Philadelphia: Westminster Press).
Whybray, R.N.
    1975   *Isaiah 40–66* (NCB; Grand Rapids, MI: Eerdmans).
Young, F.W.
    1955   'A Study of the Relation of Isaiah to the Fourth Gospel', *ZNW* 46: 215-33.

EZEKIEL'S SHEPHERD AND JOHN'S JESUS:
A CASE STUDY IN THE APPROPRIATION OF BIBLICAL TEXTS

Mary Katharine Deeley

One of the most enduring images in Christian iconography and mythology is that of Jesus as the Good Shepherd. Jesus' self-revelation as narrated by John is filled with images of a shepherd who 'lays down his life for his sheep' and gathers into one flock both his own sheep and those who are not of this fold (10.16). But as compelling or comforting as this image is, its presence in John's text poses something of a mystery. It appears to be out of place in its present position between the healing of the blind man and the raising of Lazarus. Certainly a later hand attempted to smooth the abrupt passage from ch. 9 to ch. 10 with the overheard remark of one of the crowd: 'These are not the sayings of one who has a demon. Can a demon open the eyes of the blind?' (10.21).[1] One could also make a case for the eternal life which Jesus offers the sheep (10.28) being dramatically enacted in the raising of Lazarus. But the overall chapter still raises questions as to its placement and arrangement, particularly since the imagery, unlike much of John's writing, is not found elsewhere in the Gospel.[2]

Traditionally, scholars consider the shepherd imagery of John 10 in general to draw on the 'world of ideas of the Hebrew Bible, particularly on the post-exilic prophets and their texts about the coming eschatological shepherd'.[3] Specifically, they cite John's use of Ezekiel

1. P. Perkins suggests several places where the chapter might be edited including the conflation of the 'door' and 'shepherd' parables and the literary complexity of the chapter as a whole. See 'The Gospel According to John', in R.E. Brown, *et al.* (eds.), *The New Jerome Biblical Commentary* (Englewood Cliffs, NJ: Prentice–Hall, 1990), p. 968.

2. R. Schnackenburg, *The Gospel according to St John* (trans. C. Hastings, *et al.*; New York: Seabury, 1980), II, p. 275.

3. J. Beutler, and R. Fortna, 'Introduction', in J. Beutler, and R. Fortna (eds.), *The Shepherd Discourse of John 10 and its Context: Studies by Members of the*

34 in which Yahweh is the shepherd of the sheep. Flanagan, for instance considers this most important:

> Crucial to the identification of the author's purpose at this point is the necessary realization that he is writing about Jesus with the text of Ezekiel 34 in clear view.[4]

But while many have cited John's use of Ezekiel 34, few have asked why this particular imagery should appeal to John at this point in the Gospel. While it is true that shepherd is a traditional analogical term for ruler in the ancient Near East, it is used sparingly in the Hebrew Text as a complimentary term for a good ruler and is limited to David, Cyrus, and Yahweh. The few references to unworthy or faithless shepherds come during and after the exile (for example, Zech. 11.16, 10.3, 11.5; Isa. 56.11; Jer. 2.8) and there are not many of those. That Ezekiel's text speaks of faithless shepherds as well as the One who is faithful, points to John's purposeful selection of this text as one which helped to articulate his own understanding of the significance of Jesus in the world. That John's analogy occurs in a larger context of signs and self-identifications in the Gospel may be indicative that John borrowed more from Ezekiel than is generally recognized. This paper will show that Ezekiel not only provides a model for John's text but, in the process, provides also a rationale for the context and placement of John 10 in the Gospel as a whole.

A short overview of Ezekiel 34 and its context provides us with a starting point. While some of the finer details of textual interpretation remain disputed, virtually every commentator recognizes Ezekiel 34 as the beginning of the prophecies of hope in the book of Ezekiel.[5] Chapter 33 provides the transition from the oracles of doom, involving Israel and the foreign nations, to the vision of restoration. Here we find

---

Johannine Writings Seminar (Cambridge: Cambridge University Press, 1991), p. 3.

4. N.M. Flanagan, 'John' in D. Bergant and R. Karris (eds.), *The Collegeville Bible Commentary* (Collegeville, MN: Liturgical Press, 1989), p. 998. See also A.T. Hanson, *The Prophetic Gospel: A Study of John and the Old Testament* (Edinburgh: T. & T. Clark, 1991), p. 137. Hanson also considers Jer. 23.44-45 to be of equal importance in John's use of shepherd imagery. This may be so, but I do not see the overarching development of Jeremiah's prophecy in John's Gospel.

5. See, for example, P. Ackroyd, 'Ezekiel', in B. Anderson (ed.), *The Books of the Bible* (New York: Charles Scribner's Sons, 1989), I, pp. 319-32; J. Blenkinsopp, *Ezekiel* (Louisville, KT: John Knox, 1990); and W. Zimmerli, *Ezekiel 2* (trans. J.D. Martin; Philadelphia: Fortress Press, 1983).

a recommissioning of Ezekiel as a watchman and the prophecies of signs that are coming so that all 'may know that I am the LORD' (for example, 33.29). The LORD wastes no time in informing Ezekiel that people will be judged individually. Those who do what is right shall live; those who do evil shall die. In an unexpected twist, God makes clear that the righteous shall not be able to hide behind their righteousness if they commit iniquity, nor are the wicked condemned by their wickedness if they do right (33.10-19). Werner Lemke, writing about this chapter in 1984, voices the opinion that

> the life and death of which Ezekiel speaks refer not simply to physical life and death. . . but to life lived qualitatively in the presence of God and as a faithful member of his people.[6]

This is in keeping with the overall Jewish concern for faithfulness to the covenant and the spiritual life that it brings. The vision of his mission is immediately followed by Ezekiel's own account of his healing. Where he had been unable to speak, he is now able to speak—a sign of the power of God and the importance of the message (33.21-22).

After the healing, the LORD informs Ezekiel that the people keep asking why they do not possess the land. After all, they say, 'Abraham was only one man, yet he got possession of the land; but we are many; the land is surely given to us to possess' (33.24). Ezekiel speaks for God in pointing out that their reasoning is faulty since Abraham did what was right and they kill and destroy. In short they have no claim to the land on the basis of kinship or analogy to Abraham. The fact that they do not use inheritance from Abraham as an argument for possession might indicate that they themselves recognized some of the differences (33.23-29). In this context, the first prophecy of devastation to the people bursts forth with a promise that the devastation itself will be a sign so that 'they will know that I am the LORD'. It will come not only to those who expect to inherit the land, but also to those who sit at the feet of Ezekiel hearing the prophet's words, but not doing what the prophet says (33.30-33). When they see this sign they will know that a prophet has been among them.

In ch. 34, the prophecy moves its focus from the inhabitants of the land to the leaders. Using the traditional Near Eastern term, Ezekiel chastises the rulers of Israel as shepherds who neglect all their duties

6. W. Lemke, 'Life in the Present and Hope for the Future', in *Int* 38 (1984), p. 169.

toward their flock. They have not strengthened the weak, healed the sick, or bound up the crippled. They have not fed the sheep. In short, they have not cared at all for the physical well-being of the sheep, let alone for any spiritual well-being.[7] God replies that he will seek out the lost sheep *like a shepherd* (34.12) and later says: 'I myself will be the shepherd of the sheep. The primary job of this shepherd is seeking out the lost and feeding the flock. God does not use a descriptive term for the shepherding. God is not a 'good' shepherd opposed to 'bad' shepherds.[8] Rather God will carry out the duty of a shepherd for a flock which has been neglected by others. In one sense, God will provide the model for any future shepherds and, at the same time, expose the faults of the previous shepherds. Thus, as Klein writes,

> The effects of Yahweh seeking the flock in this way are three-fold: he will remove the bad shepherds; he will free the sheep from control of the shepherds; he will liberate the sheep from exile.[9]

In feeding the flock and gathering those that are scattered, God fulfills all these goals, caring for both spiritual and physical needs. But, having done this, Yahweh goes on to sit in judgment against the flock (34.17-22), turning briefly from the leaders to the people in general who must be responsible for their own actions. Here Ezekiel echoes one of the themes of 33.10-19, that each person is answerable for his or her actions. Yahweh then announces the return of David who will serve as shepherd and who will feed the flock as God's human counterpart and with the understanding of God's sovereign rule. A covenant of peace between God and the people will ensue. In that era of prosperity, they will know that God is with them (34.30).

---

7. Blenkinsopp attributes the development of the metaphor in Ezekiel to the preaching of Jeremiah (23.1-8). 'Both begin with a woe oracle, rulers are condemned for much the same reasons, there is a promise of a descendent of David ruling over a reunited Israel. . . ', *Ezekiel*, p. 155. It is beyond the scope of this paper to explore all the ramifications of Ezekiel's possible dependence on Jeremiah, but it would be well worth studying the possible effects of such a dependence on John's text.

8. It seems to be a tendency of Christian interpreters (e.g. Blenkinsopp and Cody) to insert the qualifying adjective, good, into Ezekiel's text or the interpretation of it. In fact, Ezekiel does not use the term, which makes its addition in John that much more intriguing and revealing.

9. R. Klein, *Ezekiel, the Prophet and his Message* (Columbia, SC: University of South Carolina, 1988), p. 122.

In chs. 35–36, the LORD announces judgment on the enemies of Israel, particularly Edom, in preparation for the triumphant regeneration of the land and the people, an act of God done for the sake of the Divine name (36.22). The regeneration is symbolized by a gathering, a cleansing, and a giving of the Spirit after which the desolated land becomes like Eden (36.35). The climax of these hope-filled prophecies is the vision of dry bones in 37.1-14, which graphically illustrates God's commitment to bring Israel back to life from spiritual death and back from exile to the promised land. Lemke states

> The day would come when God would open the tombs of their exile and, by the power of his spirit, bring the people back to full life in their own homeland.[10]

The prophecy closes with a return to the shepherd imagery and a vision of unity in nation (37.22), in king (37.24), and in shepherd (37.24). Important to note is the 'prophetic word of command uttered by Ezekiel which actually effects the reconstitution of bodies around the bones and which summons the breath by which the bodies come to life'.[11] Moreover the promise of a covenant of peace is repeated, apparently intimately connected with the themes of unity and shepherding.[12]

The development of Ezekiel 33–37 is characterized by prophecies and signs designed to reveal the true nature of Yahweh's sovereign rule in Israel's life both during and after the Exile. That role is presented in the prophetic exchanges between Yahweh and the people in 33.23-33 and in 34.17-24 and in the comparison between Yahweh and the leaders in 34.1-16. The prophecies and signs speak of restoration in terms of regeneration in land and people,[13] and they connect this regeneration with the notion of a covenant of peace and a oneness or unity of the land and the people.[14] Finally, in this era, Yahweh promises to 'raise up an ideal earthly counterpart shepherd to rule with him' (34.23-24; 37.24-

---

10. Lemke, 'Life in the Present', p. 179.

11. A. Cody, *Ezekiel: With an Excursus on Old Testament Priesthood* (Wilmington, DE: Michael Glazier, 1984), p. 176.

12. For a further discussion of this, see B. Batto, 'The Covenant of Peace: A Neglected Ancient Near-Eastern Motif', in *CBQ* 49 (1987), pp. 188-89.

13. T. Craven, 'Ezekiel', in Bergant and Karris (eds.), *The Collegeville Bible Commentary*, p. 554.

14. P. Joyce, *Divine Initiative and Human Response in Ezekiel* (JSOTSup, 51; Sheffield: JSOT Press, 1989), p. 113.

25).[15] Ultimately, all this activity is to be accomplished so that every nation will know that the LORD is in the midst of Israel (37.28).[16]

For many scholars, John's passage on the Good Shepherd forms the conclusion of a larger section whose beginning point is disputed. Kysar begins the section at 7.1 and ends it at 10.42. He justifies the division because the section 'describes the conflict and opposition which Jesus met in Jerusalem'.[17] Flanagan, on the other hand, considers the immediate context to start at 9.1 and to include images of light, sight, and blindness.[18] Schnackenburg maintains that ch. 10 is part of the 'I am' passages which begin in 6.35 and end in 15.5.[19] Finally, Painter believes that chs. 5–10 form an important part of the Gospel in which the great debates and disputes take place.[20] All of these theories deal in some measure with ch. 10 and its rather abrupt entry into the flow of the Gospel, but none have given an adequate explanation for the placement, context, and arrangement of the chapter. By contrast, almost all have acknowledged at least some dependence on Ezekiel 34. As pointed out previously, Flanagan considers the link crucial; Pheme Perkins adds that chapter 34 of Ezekiel 'may have been particularly attractive to John because it concludes with the affirmation that the people will know God in this activity'.[21] Schnackenburg considers the link valid, but puts forth the problem that God, in Ezekiel, never uses the definite article to describe himself as shepherd, and certainly does not use the adjective 'good'.[22] Finally, Hanson credits both Ezekiel 34 and Jer. 23.4-5 as equally important.[23] What answers, then, can the reader obtain regarding these observations and the questions of contextual appropriateness of ch. 10?

Leaving aside for the moment the question of the beginning of the section, there is reason for considering John 8–11 as a narrative unit building to a climax in ch. 11 in which Jesus gives a definitive sign of his authority and mission and the Pharisees give the order to kill him.

15. Klein, *Ezekiel, the Prophet*, pp. 121, 123.

16. Joyce, *Divine Initiative*, p. 129.

17. R. Kysar, 'John 10.22-30', in *Int* 43 (1989), p. 66.

18. Flanagan, 'John', p. 988.

19. Schnackenburg, *The Gospel according to St John*, p. 79.

20. J. Painter, 'Tradition, History, and Interpretation in John 10', in Beutler and Fortna (eds.), *The Shepherd Discourse of John 10*, p. 53.

21. Perkins, *The Gospel according to John*, p. 968.

22. Schnackenburg, *The Gospel according to St John*, p. 84.

23. Hanson, *The Prophetic Gospel*, p. 137.

There exists within the story John tells in these chapters a liberal use of both the images and the narrative shape of Ezekiel 33–37. John appropriates the elements of Ezekiel's prophecy and makes them his own. The evidence begins in 8.1-30 with the episode of the woman caught in adultery and Jesus' self-identification as the 'light of the world' (8.12). In its broader perspective, the passage deals with two issues, the true judgment of God and the mission of Jesus to speak 'as the Father taught me' (8.28). The Jews are caught by surprise when Jesus does not condemn the woman; they are confused when he talks of the Father and their own fate (10.21). The beginning of ch. 33 in Ezekiel covers both these issues in reverse order. Ezekiel's mission as the watchman who warns of God's judgment gives way to an extended discussion on God's true judgment both on sinners and the righteous. Some sinners may well be saved; some righteous may well perish. The Israelites do not like the message of Ezekiel any more than the Jews like the message of Jesus in John's Gospel. After warning of impending doom unless the Jews believe that Jesus is the one who is to come (8.24), Jesus then engages the Jews in a conversation about freedom. The Jews bring up the fact that they are Abraham's descendants and, therefore, are not slaves to anyone (8.33). Jesus refutes their logic by calling them slaves to sin. Further, he denies them the right to invoke Abraham's name, saying instead that their father is the devil (8.31-47). When the Jews point out that Abraham died, they ask of Jesus the question: 'Are you greater than our Father Abraham who died?' (8.53). In this conversation, John continues his appropriation of Ezekiel's text, using 33.23-29 for his own purposes. Where the claim to connection with Abraham is implicit in Ezekiel; here it is overt. In both cases, such a claim is denied, but in John that denial is enhanced with an identification of the 'true' father of the people. In John, the devil is a murderer and a liar and those who follow him do the same; the people of Ezekiel murder and defile the land as well (33.23-29). Even the argument the people of Ezekiel use is turned on its head. In Ezekiel they claim the land because they are so much greater in number than the one man Abraham (33.24). John's Jews project a similar claim on Jesus (8.53). When Jesus answers cryptically their questions about his identity, invoking Abraham in a new way, they take up stones to throw at him. Like the people who sit at Ezekiel's feet, they hear what Jesus has said, but rather than passively rejecting the word, they actively try to stop it. Thus begins a pattern of appropriation and enhancement in which John bends the shape of Ezekiel to fit his own theology and message and to provide the reader with a heightened sense of the conflict between Jesus and the Jews and the understanding of the true nature of Jesus' authority.

Within the context of the Abraham discussion in Ezekiel, there is a prophecy of great desolation that will come over the land. Brought about by the hand of the LORD, it is the sign by which the people will know that Yahweh is the LORD and that a prophet has been among them (33.29, 33). John follows his Abraham passage with the story of the man born blind. This story functions as the same kind of a sign in John. Where Ezekiel's prophecy was to take place in the narrative future, however, John's story occurs in the narrative present. It is a sign which is already happening and with similar results. Jesus' initial answer to the question of sin makes clear the first: 'It was not this man that sinned, or his parents, but that the works of God might be made manifest in him' (9.3).[24] The statement is similar in tone to Ezekiel's 'that they may know that I am the LORD'. It is the blind man whose sight has been restored that points to the second: 'What do you say about him since he has opened your eyes?'. He said, 'He is a prophet' (9.17). The identification of Jesus as a prophet in a statement of simple conviction recalls the Lord's words in Ezekiel: 'they will know a prophet has been among them' (33.33).

As he did with the discussion regarding Abraham, John first appropriates and then enhances and adds to Ezekiel's context by following the sign with a detailed look at the reaction of the Jews and their leaders, the Pharisees. Significantly, Jesus does not confront either group, but deals only with the man he healed, telling him: 'For judgment I came into the world. . . ' (9.39). Only then does Jesus focus on the Pharisees as the recipient of his remarks: 'If you were blind you would have no guilt; but now that you say, "we see", your guilt remains' (9.41). This sets up the next portion of John which deals with false leaders, following closely Ezekiel's move to discuss the unfaithful shepherds of God's sheep. John makes a change, however, in order to support his claims about Jesus. John introduces the Pharisees as a sub-group of those who questioned Jesus' works in ch. 9. Nowhere in Ezekiel 33 are the leaders specifically designated, though they are certainly implied.[25] Rather

24. Joyce, *Divine Initiative*, p. 129.
25. Cf. Blenkinsopp, *Ezekiel*, p. 157; Cody, *Ezekiel*, p. 163; Ackroyd, *Ezekiel*, p. 320.

Ezekiel opens ch. 34 with a separate prophecy about the shepherds. There was no need to tell those who heard the prophecy whom he meant. When he used the word shepherd, they knew. John has a different agenda and he sets it up accordingly. Moving from the castigation of the Pharisees in 9.39-41, John uses the imagery of shepherd to speak only of Jesus. Those who come in Jesus' place are thieves and robbers and, later, hirelings who care nothing for the sheep. It is clear in the context that Jesus refers to the leaders whom he has just confronted in ch. 9. In his efforts to point to Jesus as the way, John eliminates any reference to leaders when speaking of the Pharisees. They are not bad or unfaithful shepherds; they are not shepherds at all.[26] Moreover, Jesus' claim to be both the door (10.7) through which the sheep go in and out and the good shepherd (10.11) effectively dismantles any claim the Pharisees or anyone else may have made to the flock.[27] They come to steal and kill and destroy, precisely the charge leveled at the Israelites in Ezek. 33.23-29. Jesus comes that the flock may have life (10.10).

As Ezekiel portrays God doing everything that the unfaithful shepherds did not, John contrasts the work of the Pharisees with the work of Jesus. Indeed, 'the shepherd can only represent Jesus or, at a secondary level, the leader (the evangelist) or leaders of the Johannine community'.[28] John's imagery of Jesus, however, tends to use Ezekiel's description of Yahweh as a starting point. Yahweh is a shepherd; Jesus is the *Good* Shepherd. John's Jesus is pointedly concerned about the spiritual life of his flock in comparison with Ezekiel's shepherd. In this regard, Jesus builds on Yahweh's concern. Where Yahweh gathers those that are scattered, Jesus gathers the scattered and then searches for other sheep who are 'not of this fold' (10.16). Yahweh binds the crippled and feeds the flock in safety, a basic concern at least on the surface for physical well-being; Jesus offers his flock eternal life, a spiritual well-being which cannot perish. In Ezekiel, the distinction between God's role and David's is sometimes blurred. At one point

26. Painter gives a more thorough discussion of the contrasts between the shepherd and those who are merely hired or, worse, come to rob the sheep, 'Tradition', pp. 62-63.

27. Schnackenburg, *The Gospel according to St John*, p. 289. On a deeper level of meaning, the door becomes a fitting image of the prophet through whom the word of life comes. In Ezekiel, the prophet is the one through whom God restores Israel to life (Ezek. 37.1-14). If the people listen to the prophet and hear what he says, they will live. The prophet becomes the 'door', through which they enter life.

28. Painter, 'Tradition', p. 73.

God is the shepherd; at another David is the shepherd and God is the covenant LORD of the people who has set David over them (34.15, 23), but there is never a confusion regarding their relationship. In John, Jesus, too, is given power as a shepherd, but Jesus makes no attempt to distinguish between his role and his Father's. Rather he refers to their relationship in surprising and disturbing terms: 'The Father knows me and I know the Father' (10.18) and 'I and the Father are One' (10.30). John's use of shepherd to describe only Jesus and his use of Ezekiel's imagery and shape as a springboard allows the reader to see Jesus both in the role of God as Divine Shepherd and in the role of David as human shepherd appointed to pasture the sheep in Yahweh's place. As such, he can make the claim to oneness with the Father, a unity which has its earthly balance in the unity of the flock.

The goal of providing 'one flock and one shepherd' becomes a focal point of both Jesus' and Yahweh's ingathering. The act itself invites criticism. Some will be chosen; some will be left out. In Ezekiel, the faithful remnant becomes the one flock under David's capable leadership. In John, it is those who follow Jesus' voice and those others whom Jesus seeks out who form the flock (10.16). At this point John lets the readers overhear the reaction of the Jews who heard this. For now Jesus is finished with the Pharisees; John does not need them to provide the link between this section and the next. The Jews, however, argue among themselves. Aside from immediately drawing a link to the sign of the blind man, the arguments all center on the issue of identity. Perhaps Jesus is a possessed man (10.20); no, he is a miracle man (10.21). Is he the Christ (10.24)? Jesus' answer judges them harshly: 'I told you and you do not believe... because you do not belong to my sheep' (10.26). Jesus invokes both the sheep's obedience and God's own authority in refuting them. The sheep have been given to Jesus by the Father and they know and follow him. Furthermore, no one can snatch the sheep from Jesus' because no one can snatch them from the Father's hand. In this authority Jesus and the Father are one. The argument continues with the controversy over Jesus' claims to unity with the Father and the Jews seek to arrest him.

Jesus' controversy with the Jews throughout chs. 8–11 becomes, in part, John's adaptation of the two judgment sections located in Ezekiel 34–36. In using Ezekiel, John recognized that even in the midst of hope for one flock, there is recognition of those who do harm to the flock whether it is from within because they have a self-centered outlook or from outside because of a genuine enmity toward the flock. Ezekiel addresses the two groups in two separate passages (34.17-24 and 35.1–36.7) and calls them out for punishment. Ezekiel implies in the first that those within the flock who injure it are in some way subject to punishment; in the second he prophesies a terrible judgment to outsiders so that 'I may make myself known among them when I judge them' (35.11). John uses the Jews in general and the Pharisees specifically as a substitute for both groups. In their appearance in 8.13-33, John assumes at first that they are or want to be part of the flock: to the Pharisees, Jesus says: 'You will die in your sins, unless you believe that I am he. . . As he spoke thus many believed in him' (8.24, 30). To the Jews in general, he states: 'If you continue in my word. . . you will know the truth (8.31-32). The impending doom if they do not believe is implied, but not announced. Here and in his discussion with the Pharisees in 9.39-41, John parallels Ezekiel's chastisement of the fat sheep (variously translated as rams or cattle) in 34.17-22. These are part of the flock who take for themselves and leave nothing for the rest. By 10.26, however, the connection with the flock is no longer assumed. Rather, a terrible indictment is handed down: 'You do not believe because you do not belong to my sheep'. But where Ezekiel described the judgment of desolation to fall on those outsiders who did harm to the flock of Israel in 35.1–36.7, John chooses to emphasize what the outsiders will not have. They will not have the eternal life which Jesus is offering. Ezekiel, of course, understood that it is those who remain faithful who will enter into the covenant of peace as the flock of the LORD and will rejoice in the restoration of the land and the people. But John deliberately focuses the reader's attention on the faithful remnant/flock by avoiding a description of a specific punishment. John does not dismiss Ezekiel's understanding of God's judgment on these outsiders, however. His use of Psalm 82 subtly supports the concept of the judgment of God. Not only does the psalm refute the Jewish argument against Jesus' identification with Yahweh, specifically in the Greek text, but the reader who recalls it in its entirety knows it also contains the psalmist's own prayer that Yahweh should judge the earth as he judges the heavens (82.1, 8). Just as Ezekiel observes that a remnant will become the covenant people of God in the new age, John writes that those who hear Jesus' voice and follow him will be given eternal life. Jesus' plea that the Jews believe the works so that 'you may know and understand that the Father is in me and I am in the Father' (10.38) echoes Yahweh's consistent refrain that He acts so that 'you may know that I am the LORD' (Ezek. 35.4, 9, 12, 15). When Jesus escapes arrest and goes across the Jordan, John draws a conclusion to ch. 10 and gives the reader some relief from tension by stating simply that 'many believed in him there (10.42).

John's appropriation of Ezekiel does not stop with the judging of the Jews. In his own vision there is a glimpse of the restoration that will happen. There is also a symmetry in the way he chooses to use Ezekiel. The first prophecy of Ezekiel 33 is the desolation which will be a sign of the LORD and his prophet; the last prophecies are sign-visions of the restoration and coming together that the LORD will effect. In John, the sign by which the works of God were made manifest and by which Jesus was known as a prophet is balanced by the sign by which Jesus is known as life, an illustration of his claim to bring eternal life to the flock. The raising of Lazarus (11.1-44) represents John's adaptation of the regeneration visions in Ezekiel. It is a work done for the glory of God and the glorification of the Son (11.4, 40), a reason which is similar to that of Yahweh in Ezekiel: 'It is not for your sake, O Israel, that I am about to act, but for the sake of my Holy Name... and I will vindicate the holiness of my great name...' (36.22-23). The desolation which God has brought gives way to the cleansing, restoration and unity of the flock (37.1-28). Ezekiel's vision is a climax, speaking of the resurrection of a land and nation thought to be buried in the Exile. It closes with a reference to the gathering of the people into one flock with one shepherd. Chapter 11 of John forms a climax as well by bringing the controversy between Jesus and the Jews to a crucial peak. It also stands at an emotional moment of truth when Mary confesses her belief in Jesus as the resurrection and the life. Finally, it foreshadows the terrible desolation that will be present when Jesus leaves.[29] John shares the vision of unity with Ezekiel, but not as an altogether happy one. The prophecy of Caiaphas predicts 'Jesus should die for the nation, and not for the nation only, but to gather into one the children of God who are scattered abroad' (11.49-52). John ends the chapter with an ominous reference to the Pharisees who seek

---

29. Sandra Schneider speaks of ch. 11 as 'the compositional zenith of the fourth gospel and a way for the evangelist to deal with the question of death confronting his community. See 'Death in the Community of Eternal Life: History, Theology, and Spirituality in John 11', in *Int* 41 (1987), p. 47.

to arrest Jesus and put him to death. At this point John leaves Ezekiel's framework and begins his own narrative once again.

Ezekiel 33–37 presents the reader with a broad plot outline which reads as follows: mission, prophesied sign, shepherd imagery, judgment, and restoration. While he refines and enhances some of these elements, John 8–11 follows closely Ezekiel's outline. The appropriation of Ezekiel 33–37 makes it possible for John to speak of Jesus as the 'good shepherd' in such a way and in such a context that he emphasizes Jesus' unity with the Father as well as his authority to rule and his rightful place as Davidic descendant. It is around Jesus that the ideas of mission, sign, and vision operate. In one sense, Jesus takes on Ezekiel's role as prophet as well as the roles of Yahweh and David. He warns, admonishes, encourages, and speaks for the Father. John concentrates on recasting the language and images of Ezekiel to make them more appropriate to his message and his time. He also enhances those images to direct the focus of the reader toward his understanding of the events surrounding Jesus. By the end of ch. 11, John has done much to convince his audience that Jesus is the only one worthy of being called *shepherd* and that all others who claim the title for themselves are frauds. The recognition of the broader outlines of Ezekiel's plot allows the scholar to understand the context in which John places the shepherd analogy and to follow through from beginning to climax John's articulation of Jesus' unique identity and authority in chs. 8–11.

Part III

ACTS, EPISTLES AND REVELATION

VINDICATING THE REJECTED ONE:
STEPHEN'S SPEECH AS A CRITIQUE OF THE JEWISH LEADERS

H. Alan Brehm

If Luke and Acts have constituted a 'storm-center' of New Testament scholarship, Stephen's speech in Acts 7 has been one of the 'atmospheric conditions' that caused and sustained the storm. Stephen's speech touches upon issues central to the debate surrounding Luke and Acts, including issues of composition, theology, and overall reconstructions of New Testament history. Two questions from this text have received prominent attention: (1) whether Stephen expressed a radical critique of the Law and the Temple that set him apart from the Jerusalem Apostles, thus paving the way for Paul and Gentile Christianity in general, and (2) whether the 'speech' constitutes a unity and relates to the immediate context of the book.

Unfortunately, none of the typical approaches to Stephen's speech take adequate account of its traditio-historical background in the summaries of Israelite history, like the confession of sin led by the Levites (or Ezra) in Neh. 9.5-37. Against this background, Stephen's speech constitutes a critique of the Jewish leaders for their affliction of a righteous person (Stephen), for their rejection and execution of 'the Righteous One' (Jesus), and for their stubborn and continual disobedience toward God. In contrast to the Jewish leaders' rejection of Stephen and Jesus, the speech implicitly claims God's vindication for them by emphasizing the vindication of Joseph and Moses, who were also rejected but vindicated by God.

The speech combines several themes from the Old Testament and Second-Temple literature. Stephen's speech begins with Joseph as the example *par excellence* of a righteous sufferer whom God vindicated (Gen. 39.2, 21, 23; *T. Reub.* 4.8-10; *T. Jos.* 1.2-7), implying that God had vindicated Stephen by the 'grace' and 'wisdom' he gave to him before his opponents. The speech highlights Moses as the paradigm for the prophets whom the 'ancestors' had rejected and especially for the Jewish leaders' rejection of Jesus. Nevertheless, as God vindicated Moses as the Israelites' redeemer, so the speech implies that God has vindicated Jesus. It alludes to the prophetic critiques of the Israelites for their disobedience (esp. Amos 5.21-27; Jer. 7.1–8.3; Isa. 66.1-4), which focus on their worship at the Temple, as does Jesus' Temple cleansing. The speech concludes with a pointed rebuke against the Jewish leaders for their stubborn disobedience in a way that resembles the Chronicler's rebuke of the priesthood in 2 Chron. 36.13-16. Thus a traditio-historical analysis of Stephen's speech in Acts 7 indicates that it constitutes a critique of the Jewish leaders for their affliction of Stephen, for their rejection and execution of Jesus, and for their stubborn and continual disobedience toward God. It also implicitly claims God's vindication for Jesus and Stephen.

Reconstructing a 'Hellenist' Theology?

Many claim to be able to reconstruct a 'theology' of the 'Hellenists' from Stephen's speech that is critical of the Law and the Temple and that paved the way for the view that the Temple had been rejected and/or replaced. This view was popular among scholars working in the tradition of F.C. Baur.[1] Walter Grundmann most clearly drew out

1. See F.C. Baur, *The Church History of the First Three Centuries* (trans. A. Menzies; London: Williams & Norgate, 3rd edn, 1878), I, pp. 44-47; C.A. Witz, 'Stephanus und seine Vertheidigungsrede', *Jahrbücher für Deutsche Theologie* 20 (1875), pp. 604-605; G. Hilgenfeld, 'Die Apostelgeschichte nach ihren Quellenschriften untersucht: Die Septemvirn Stephanus und Philippus, Apg. C. 6-8', *ZWT* 38 (1895), p. 401; H.J. Holtzmann, 'Forschungen über die Apostelgeschichte', *ZWT* 28 (1885), pp. 437-38; W. Heitmüller, 'Zum Problem Paulus und Jesus', *ZNW* 13 (1912), pp. 134-35; W. Bousset, *Kyrios Christos: Geschichte des Christusglaubens von den Anfängen des Christentums bis Irenaeus* (Göttingen: Vandenhoeck & Ruprecht, 6th edn, 1967), p. 75; W. Grundmann, 'Das Problem des hellenistischen Christentums innerhalb der Jerusalemer Urgemeinde', *ZNW* 38 (1939), pp. 59-60, 64-65, 73; R. Bultmann, *Theology of the New Testament* (trans. K. Grobel; New York: Charles Scribner's Sons, 1951), I, p. 56. Cf. similarly J. Weiss, *The History of Primitive Christianity* (ed. R. Knopf; trans. F.C. Grant; New York: Wilson–Erickson, 1937), I, p. 167, who claims that Stephen's preaching aroused opposition because he proclaimed an alteration of the Mosaic code in light of Jesus' parousia; J. Bihler, *Die Stephanusgeschichte im Zusammenhang der Apostelgeschichte* (Munich: Huebner, 1963), pp. 71, 169; A. Weiser, *Die Apostelgeschichte* (Gütersloh: Mohn, 1981), p. 187; J. Roloff, *Die Apostelgeschichte* (NTD; Göttingen: Vandenhoeck &

the implications of this viewpoint. He portrayed the 'Hellenists' as the 'channel' of true Christianity from Jesus to Paul and John in contrast to the 'judaizing' Jerusalem congregation, and called Stephen the 'theologian' of the characteristic form of Christianity which took root at Antioch.[2] A number of scholars who do not follow the Baur tradition have nevertheless also accepted this position.[3]

Ruprecht, 1981), pp. 188-19, 124-25. Cf. further H.-W. Neudorfer, *Der Stephanuskreis in der Forschungsgeschichte seit F.C. Baur* (Giessen: Brunnen Verlag, 1983), pp. 146-47, 166, 253, 256, 258.

2.   See Grundmann, 'Das Problem', pp. 65, 69-71, 73. Cf. G. Lüdemann, *Opposition to Paul in Jewish Christianity* (trans. M.E. Boring; Minneapolis: Fortress Press, 1989), pp. 60-61, 114, where he argues that the Jerusalem congregation became dominated by 'judaizing' Christians. Although an argument *ad hominem* should be avoided, Grundmann's strong deprecation of the 'judaizing' element in the Jerusalem congregation should be taken in light of the fact that the article was published in 1939. Compare Neudorfer, *Stephanuskreis*, p. 53 n. 220, where he says that 'der Geist der spätere dreißige Jahre' can be detected in Grundmann's argument.

3.   See, for example, A. Neander, *History of the Planting and Training of the Christian Church by the Apostles* (trans. J.E. Ryland; London: George Bell & Sons, 1889), I, pp. 49, 50; II, pp. 74-75, where he surmises that Stephen addressed the issue of the necessity of the Law for salvation and the destruction of the Temple symbolizing that Judaism was obsolete. Compare also J.B. Lightfoot, 'St. Paul and the Three', in *St. Paul's Epistle to the Galatians* (London: Macmillan, rev. edn, 1892), pp. 296-97, where he says that the role of the 'Hellenists' was to 'emancipate' the Gospel from the trappings of Judaism in order to prepare the way for the Gentile mission; L. Goppelt, *Apostolic and Post-Apostolic Times* (trans. by R.A. Guelich; London: A. & C. Black, 1970; repr. Grand Rapids: Baker, 1980), p. 53, where he speaks of a 'new theological element' with the Hellenists; E.E. Ellis, 'The Circumcision Party and the Early Christian Mission', in *Prophecy and Hermeneutic in Early Christianity: New Testament Essays* (WUNT, 1.18; Tübingen: Mohr–Siebeck, 1978), pp. 122 n. 27, where he speaks of their emphasis on 'freedom from the law'; and M. Hengel, 'Between Jesus and Paul: The "Hellenists", the "Seven" and Stephen (Acts 6.1-15; 7.54–8.3)', in M. Hengel, *Between Jesus and Paul: Studies in the Earliest History of Christianity* (trans. by J. Bowden; London: SCM Press, 1983; repr. Philadelphia: Fortress Press, 1983), p. 21, where he says that Stephen anticipates Paul's critique of the Law. Cf. further O. Cullmann, 'L'Opposition contre le Temple de Jerusalem', *NTS* 5 (1958–59), pp. 161, 162; D. Juel, *Messiah and Temple* (Missoula, MT: Scholars Press, 1977), pp. 148, 149 [replacement] ; R. le Déaut, 'Actes 7:48 et Matthieu 17:4 (par) à lumière du targum palestinien', *RSR* 52 (1964), p. 85; L. Barnard, 'Saint Stephen and Early Alexandrian Christianity', *NTS* 7 (1960–61), p. 32; M. Simon, 'Saint Stephen and the Jerusalem Temple', *JEH* 1–2 (1950–51), p. 127 [rejection]. For a recent discussion of this issue, see D.D. Sylva, 'The Meaning and Function of Acts 7:46-50', *JBL* 106 (1987), pp. 261-75.

Some who attempt to reconstruct a critique of the Law and the Temple from Stephen's speech do so against the backdrop of Stephen's debates with the Jews of the Hellenist Synagogues (Acts 6.9).[4] In this context, Stephen's opponents accuse him of speaking 'blasphemous words against Moses and God' (Acts 6.11). They also bring forward 'false witnesses' who accuse him of speaking words 'against this holy place and against the Law' (Acts 6.13).[5] Finally Stephen's accusers charge him with saying that Jesus would destroy 'this place' and 'change the customs which Moses delivered to us' (Acts 6.14).[6] These scholars,

---

4.   P. Feine, *Die vorkanonische Überlieferung des Lukas in Evangelium und Apostelgeschichte: Eine Untersuchung* (Gotha: F.A. Perthes, 1891), p. 23; cf. also A. Schlatter, *Die Geschichte der ersten Christenheit* (intro. by R. Riesner; Stuttgart: Calwer Verlag, 6th edn, 1984), p. 27, where he argues that the accusations against Stephen reflect the fact that the Jewish 'Hellenists' adhered to the Law and the Temple just as fervently as their 'Hebrew' counterparts. See also G. Stählin, *Die Apostelgeschichte* (NTD; Göttingen: Vandenhoeck & Ruprecht, 10th edn, 1962), p. 102. Cf. H.J. Cadbury, 'The Hellenists', in *The Beginnings of Christianity* (ed. K. Lake and H.J. Cadbury; London: Macmillan, 1933), V, p. 41, where he cautions against pressing the 'loose connexions' of the text too far by identifying Stephen's opponents with the Jewish 'Hellenists' of Acts 9.29 who disputed with Paul. While the connection is admittedly a loose one, it is nevertheless arguably there.

5.   It is clear that the 'holy place' against which they accused Stephen of speaking was the Temple. See F. Blass, *Acta Apostolorum sive Lucae ad Theophilum Liber Alter* (Göttingen: Vandenhoeck & Ruprecht, 1895), p. 95; H.H. Wendt, *Die Apostelgeschichte* (MeyerK; Göttingen: Vandenhoeck & Ruprecht, 8th edn, 1899), p. 149; E. Haenchen, *The Acts of the Apostles: A Commentary* (trans. by R. McL. Wilson, *et al.*; Philadelphia: Westminster Press, 1971), pp. 271-72 n. 6; R. Pesch, *Die Apostelgeschichte* (EKKNT; Zürich: Benziger; Neukirchen–Vluyn: Neukirchener Verlag, 1986), I, p. 238; H. Conzelmann, *The Acts of the Apostles: A Commentary on the Acts of the Apostles* (Hermeneia; trans. J. Limburg, A.T. Kraabel, D.H. Juel; ed. E.J. Epp, C.R. Matthews; Philadelphia: Fortress Press, 1987), p. 48 (cf. Acts 21.28; 2 Macc. 5.17-20). Cf. T. Zahn, *Die Apostelgeschichte des Lukas* (Leipzig: Deichert, 3rd edn, 1922), I, pp. 244-45, who explores the possibility that this might have been the case, objects to this interpretation on the grounds that it would have Stephen's accusers calling the Temple a τόπος rather than an οἶκος. Thus he argues that the accusation must refer to a statement regarding Jerusalem. But the similarity with the accusations made against Jesus at his trial argues in favor of identifying τοῦ τόπου τοῦ ἁγίου [τούτου] (Acts 6.13) and τὸν τόπον τοῦτον (Acts 6.14) with the Temple.

6.   Wendt, *Apostelgeschichte*, p. 147; A.F. Loisy, *Les actes des apôtres* (Paris: E. Nourry, 1920), p. 309; and Stählin, *Apostelgeschichte*, p. 102 suggest that both accusations are but different forms of the same accusation. Contrast H.J. Holtzmann,

despite Luke's protest that the witnesses against Stephen were false ones, take the accusations against Stephen in Acts 6.11, 13-14 as the hermeneutical key to his speech.[7]

On the other hand, nothing Stephen says can be construed as 'against' Moses and God, nor against the Law. While he does express a critique of the Temple, that is not the main point of the speech.[8] Rather Stephen's speech is a critique of the Jewish leaders in light of the fact

Die Apostelgeschichte (HKNT; Freiburg: Mohr–Siebeck, 1889), p. 347; and who identifies the accusation in Acts 6.11 with that in 6.14 rather than 6.13. On the other hand, Pesch, *Apostelgeschichte*, I, p. 237 argues that the charge in 6.11 relates entirely to the Law, since it was given by Moses and was revealed to him by God.

7.   Cf. F.C. Baur, *Paul, The Apostle of Jesus Christ: His Life and Work, his Epistles and his Doctrine* (trans. and ed. E. Zeller; rev. by A. Menzies; London: Williams & Norgate, 2nd edn, 1876), I, pp. 52-53, 57-60. Because he argues that the contents of Acts 7.2-53 cannot be attributed to Luke, he therefore reconstructs Stephen's 'theology' on the basis of the accusations alone. For further examples of those who interpret Stephen's Speech in light of the accusations, see Grotius, *Annotationes in Novum Testamentum* (repr. Gronigae: W. Zuidema, 1828), V, p. 45; J.A. Bengel, *Gnomon of the New Testament* (ed. A.R. Fausset; Edinburgh: T. & T. Clark, 1860), II, p. 568; Wendt, *Apostelgeschichte*, p. 148; G.P. Wetter, 'Das älteste hellenistische Christentum nach der Apostelgeschichte', *ARW* 21 (1922), pp. 414-17; Loisy, *Les actes des apôtres*, pp. 313-17; Grundmann, 'Das Problem', pp. 63-65; and R. Schumacher, *Der Diakon Stephanus* (NTAbh, 3.4; Münster: Aschendorff, 1910), pp. 89-90, 93, where he supposes that Stephen had contradicted the enduring validity of the Jewish cultus and Mosaic customs on the basis of Jesus' teaching. The problem with this is that Stephen says nothing in his speech to suggest that this was his belief, and Jesus never makes any statement implying a limited validity to the cultus. For a similar critique of this position, compare Neudorfer, *Stephanuskreis*, p. 165, where he says that Baur 'distilled' the theology of the speech from the accusations against Stephen. Others who utilize the accusations in order to interpret the Speech include Neander, *Planting and Training*, I, pp. 49-50; II, pp. 74-75; Hengel, 'Between Jesus and Paul', pp. 22, 24; Ellis, 'Circumcision Party', p. 119 n. 14; Pesch, *Apostelgeschichte*, I, pp. 238, 239. He suggests that the 'Hellenists' drew their critique of the Temple and the Law from Jesus' statement at the Last Supper that his death was to be 'for the many' (Mk 14.24), i.e., that it was to have redemptive significance.

8.   Cf. Pesch, *Apostelgeschichte*, I, p. 247; J.B. Polhill, *Acts* (New American Commentary; Nashville: Broadman Press, 1992), p. 206. This is not to say that the speech is totally unrelated to its context in Acts. For examples of that opinion, see E. Trocmé, *Le 'Livre des actes' et l'histoire* (Etudes d'histoire et de philosophie religieuse, 45; Paris: Presses Universitaires de France, 1957), p. 208; Haenchen, *Acts of the Apostles*, p. 288; Loisy, *Les actes des apôtres*, p. 318; Holtzmann, *Apostelgeschichte*, p. 55.

that they had rejected Jesus and Stephen, they were 'stiff-necked' and 'uncircumcised in heart and ears', and they had disobeyed the Law.[9] It is more likely that the accusations constitute misrepresentations of something Stephen said and have more to do with the 'Hellenist' Jews' devotion to the Law and the Temple than any supposed Hellenist 'theology' that is critical of the Law and the Temple.[10]

Unity of the Speech

The debate about the unity of the speech arises from questions about source[s] and the relationship of the parts to one another. Dibelius's view that the source of the speech was a Hellenistic–Jewish recapitulation of Israelite history led him to conclude that Luke re-worked the overview of Israelite history and added Acts 7.51-53 to give the resulting speech a more polemical tone and make it fit the context of Acts.[11] Dibelius's proposal led to the consensus view that the speech

9. The fact that Stephen is critiquing the Jewish leaders ought not to be construed as an example of 'anti-Semitism'. While it is true that texts like this in the New Testament can be used in a modern context to marginalize the Jewish people, one must remember who was marginalizing whom in the first-century context. In this context, Stephen the Christian Jew was confronting his oppressors from among the Jewish leaders. Thus Stephen's speech ought to be construed as no more 'anti-Semitic' than the prophets' critiques of the people in the Old Testament. Cf. similarly C.A. Evans, 'Prophecy and Polemic: Jews in Luke's Scriptural Apologetic', in *Luke and Scripture: The Function of Sacred Tradition in Luke–Acts* (Minneapolis: Augsburg–Fortress, 1993), pp. 210-11.

10. In this regard cf. Schlatter, *Geschichte*, p. 105 who argues, 'Den angeblichen Antinomismus des Stephanus hat Lukas "ein falsches Zeugnis" genannt, ganz so, wie auch Paulus solche Vorwürfe immer als grundlos abgewiesen hat'. See G. Schneider, 'Stephanus, die Hellenisten und Samaria', in *Les actes des apôtres: Traditions, rédaction, théologie* (BETL, 48; ed. J. Kremer; Leuven: Leuven University Press, 1979), p. 220. Cf. Conzelmann, *Acts of the Apostles*, p. 48.

11. M. Dibelius, 'The Speeches in Acts and Ancient Historiography', in *Studies in the Acts of the Apostles* (ed. H. Greeven; trans. M. Ling, P. Schubert; London: SCM Press; New York: Charles Scribner's Sons, 1956), p. 167; cf. further C.K. Barrett, 'Submerged Christology in Acts', in *Anfänge der Christologie: Festschrift für Ferdinand Hahn* (ed. C. Breytenback and H. Paulsen; Göttingen: Vandenhoeck & Ruprecht, 1991), pp. 239-40; E.J. Richard, 'The Polemical Character of the Joseph Episode in Acts 7', *JBL* 98 (1979), pp. 255-57; M.L. Soards, *The Speeches in Acts: Their Content, Context, and Concerns* (Louisville, KY: Westminster/John Knox, 1994), pp. 1-17.

attributed to Stephen actually originated with 'Luke'.[12] The common ground in the varying expressions of this viewpoint is the opinion that the body of the speech, which concerns the summary of Israelite history, has nothing at all to do with the accusations against Stephen.[13] In spite of widespread agreement that Stephen's speech in Acts 7.2-53 combines 'tradition' and 'redaction', the attempt to separate the two has not been entirely successful.

In one sense, this approach is flawed by design. It is ultimately self-defeating to reconstruct a 'Hellenist' theology in Acts 7 if the speech was written by 'Luke'.[14] This places research in a position of being entirely dependent on the accusations, which do not in and of themselves present evidence for any unique theological position. For example, Christoph Burchard argues that 'a coherent account of the life and

---

12. Cf. Baur, *Paul*, I, pp. 57-58, who argues that the form of the Speech in Acts 7.2-53 cannot be attributed to Stephen. J. Wellhausen, *Kritische Analyse der Apostelgeschichte* (Abhandlungen der königlichen Gesellschaft der Wissenschaften zu Göttingen, 15.2; Berlin: Weidmann, 1914), p. 12, argues that the speech as a whole was composed by the 'Redactor'. Cf. also F. Spitta, *Die Apostelgeschichte: Ihre Quellen und deren Geschichtswert* (Halle: Waisenhauses, 1891), p. 115, who believed that the only firmly historical kernel of truth was that Stephen, who was a leader in the congregation, came to a martyr's death by means of stoning. G. Schneider, 'Stephanus', p. 224, assumes as a consensus the view that the speech comes from 'Luke'. See further Schumacher, *Der Diakon Stephanus*, pp. 81-87; Wendt, *Apostelgeschichte*, p. 152; H.W. Beyer, *Die Apostelgeschichte* (NTD; Göttingen: Vandenhoeck & Ruprecht, 7/8th edn, 1956), pp. 50-51; Haenchen, *Acts*, p. 289; R. Scroggs, 'The Earliest Hellenistic Christianity', in *Religions in Antiquity: Essays in Memory of Erwin Ramsdell Goodenough* (Studies in the History of Religions, 14; ed. J. Neusner; Leiden: Brill, 1968), pp. 182-84; Grundmann, 'Das Problem', pp. 60-65; and F.J. Foakes-Jackson, 'Stephen's Speech in Acts', *JBL* 49 (1930), pp. 283-86.

13. It is precisely for this reason that Haenchen criticizes Dibelius's idea that 'Luke, has inserted the Speech into the episode of Stephen's martyrdom (*Acts*, pp. 287-88). On the other hand, Dibelius was aware of this problem ('The Speeches in Acts', pp. 167-70).

14. Compare the cautions Pesch expresses about the effort to separate tradition from redaction in Stephen's speech in *Apostelgeschichte*, I, pp. 246 47. See also J. Munck, *Paul and the Salvation of Mankind* (trans. F. Clark; London: SCM Press, 1959), p. 221, where he says, 'If we have the writer of Acts to thank for Stephen's Speech, we have only his opponents' words to judge by, and their accusations against Stephen (6.11, 13f.) are in no way different from the accusation against Jesus'. This then makes it impossible to know anything at all about Stephen and the 'Hellenists', assuming he had some relationship to them.

works of Paul, let alone a history of Christian origins, may not be written on the basis of the Acts of the Apostles any more than a life of Jesus on the basis of the Gospels—and that means it may not be written at all' (my translation).[15] While Burchard's point about the limitations of historical reconstructions is certainly well-taken, this undercuts the effort to derive a particularly 'Hellenist' theology from Stephen's speech. On the other hand, it is only on the assumption that Stephen's speech at least represents 'old traditions that merely owe their present form to the writer of Acts' that it is possible to know anything at all about the Hellenists' theology.[16]

Perhaps the view that the body of the speech and its conclusion do not come from the same hand has caused the impasse. Yet a comparison with the pattern of summaries of Israelite history in the Old Testament and other Jewish literature provides important evidence in favor of maintaining the unity of the speech and its conclusion in Acts 7.51-53.[17] Such a comparison of these summaries also supports the

15. 'Eine zusammenhängende Darstellung auch nur der Wirksamkeit des Paulus, geschweige denn eine Geschichte des Urchristentums, läßt sich auf Grund der Apostelgeschichte ebenso wenig schreiben wie ein Leben Jesu auf Grund der Evangelien—und das heißt sie läßt sich überhaupt nicht schreiben.' C. Burchard, *Der dreizehnte Zeuge: Traditions- und kompositions-geschichtliche Untersuchungen zu Lukas' Darstellung der Frühzeit des Paulus* (FRLANT, 103; Göttingen: Vandenhoeck & Ruprecht, 1970), p. 173.

16. Cf. Munck, *Paul and Salvation*, p. 221.

17. See also Conzelmann, *Acts of the Apostles*, pp. 56, 57. He refers as well to *Mart. Isa.*, Lk. 13.34; 1 Thess. 2.15; Heb. 11.36-38; Justin, *Dial.* 16.4; and Josephus, *Ant.* 9.265-66; 10.3-4. Conzelmann comes to a much different conclusion, however, arguing that Luke is responsible for the speech and that the verses which carry the emphasis on Israel's disobedience and rejection of the prophets were Luke's literary 'seams'. Cf. M. Noth on the 'great speeches' of the Deuteronomistic History in *The Deuteronomistic History* (JSOTSup, 15; trans. D.J.A. Clines, *et al.*; Sheffield: JSOT Press, 1981), pp. 4-6, 26-74, 75-78; O.H. Steck, *Israel und das gewaltsame Geschick der Propheten: Untersuchungen zur Überlieferung des deuteronomistischen Geschichtsbildes im Alten Testament, Spätjudentum und Urchristentum* (Neukirchen–Vluyn: Neukirchener Verlag, 1967). Soards (*The Speeches in Acts*, pp. 143-48) compares the pattern of preaching in the Deuteronomistic History that recounted Israel's disobedience, God's sending of prophets, Israel's rejection of the prophets, the threat of judgment, and a call to repentance with the Speeches in Acts. On the other hand, the 'speeches' in the Deuteronomistic History, according to Noth, serve to unify the overall composition and mark off periods of time. This is not only quite different from the perspective of the Speeches in Acts (as Soards recognizes), but also from the perspective of the summaries of Israelite

conclusion that the theme of Stephen's speech is a critique against the Jewish leaders.[18]

The comparison for this study was based on nine summaries of Israelite history (Josh. 24.2-15, Neh. 9.6-37, Ps. 78, Ps. 105, Ps. 106, Ezek. 20, Wis. 10–19, Sir. 44–50, and Jdt. 5.6-21).[19] Though none of the summaries contain all of the elements enumerated in the table, it may nevertheless be possible to speak of this as a 'pattern'. The table demonstrates that such a summary usually begins with Abraham, though the summaries in Nehemiah 9 and Wisdom of Solomon 10 begin with creation. It is also common to find an emphasis on Israel's sojourn in Egypt and God's deliverance from the Egyptians through plagues and especially at the Red Sea. The wilderness wanderings occur regularly, with an emphasis on God's care for his people and their repeated rebellion against him. The conquest also plays a role in the summaries, along with an emphasis on God's continuing grace in spite of Israel's ongoing disobedience.

On the other hand, some of the elements occur in only a few of the summaries. Surprisingly, the calling of Abraham from Ur of the Chaldees is one of these elements. It might seem equally surprising that Stephen's speech is not alone in relating Joseph's experience in Egypt,

history. Cf. similarly U. Wilckens, *Die Missionsreden* (WMANT, 5; Neukirchen–Vluyn: Neukirchener Verlag, 3rd edn, 1974), p. 203. Contrast M. Rese, 'Einige Überlegungen zu Lukas XIII, 31–33', in *Jésus aux origines de la christologie* (BETL, 40; ed. J. Dupont; Leuven: Leuven University Press, 1975), pp. 201-25; and G. Schneider, *Die Apostelgeschichte* (HTKNT; Freiburg: Herder, 1980), I, pp. 100-101, who criticize Noth's theory.

18. Cf. Richard, 'Joseph Episode', pp. 264-65. Others who maintain the unity of the speech and its conclusion in Acts 7.51-53 include Bihler, *Stephanusgeschichte*, pp. 34-35, 77-81 (he says [p. 35] 'Die Aussagen in V 51 53 sind aber ganz eindeutig mit den vorausgehenden Ausführungen verknüpft:. . . "wie eure Väter, so auch ihr". Der Ungehorsam und die Verstockung der Juden gegenüber dem Willen Gottes haben ihre eigene Geschichte.') ; J.J. Kilgallen, *The Stephen Speech: A Literary and Redactional Study of Acts 7,2-53* (AnBib, 67; Rome: Pontifical Biblical Institute, 1976), pp. 101-102; Pesch, *Apostelgeschichte*, I, pp. 237-38; G. Krodel, *Acts* (Philadelphia: Fortress Press, 1981), pp. 32-36; Schneider, *Apostelgeschichte*, I, pp. 446-52. See also the discussion in Soards, *The Speeches in Acts*, pp. 58-60 n. 138.

19. Other summaries of Israelite history include Deut. 6.20-24; 26.5-9; Ps. 136; 1 Macc. 2.52-60; 3 Macc. 2.2-12; CD 2.14–3.9; 4 Ezra 14.19-31; and Josephus, *Ant.* 3.84-88; 4.40-49. All of these summaries are either shorter than Stephen's speech or lack its extensive scope. See the table at the end of this article for a comparison of these summaries.

but it does not occur in most of the summaries (cf. Ps. 105.16-22 and Wis. 10.13-14). The story of Israel at Sinai and the sin of the Golden Calf (cf. Ps. 106.19-20; Neh. 9.18; Ezek. 20.8), God's provision of the judges as 'saviors', the prophets' mission to rebuke Israel, the covenant with David, and Solomon's building the Temple all occur in only a few of the summaries. The concluding exhortation in Stephen's speech occurs only infrequently (cf. Josh. 24.14-15; Ezek. 20.27-31). Perhaps any supposed 'pattern' in the summaries of Israelite history should be seen as general.

It is interesting to note how this 'pattern' could be used by different authors toward differing ends. In Josh. 24.2-15 the summary recounts God's act of redemption at the Exodus and his conquest of the land for Israel as a basis for a call to renew the covenant. The summary in Neh. 9.6-37 occurs in the context of a prayer of confession and repentance, praising God for his constant love and recounting the disobedience of the ancestors. Psalm 78 commemorates the sins of the wilderness generation to reinforce the importance of remembering God's miraculous deeds in the past in order urge the people to obey him, keep his covenant, and trust his saving power. The summary in Psalm 105 praises God's miraculous works on behalf of Israel and exhorts God's people to remember them. By contrast, Psalm 106 appeals to God to be gracious to his people in spite of the fact that they did not remember his miraculous works, but instead sinned, rebelled, grumbled against God, and turned to idolatry. In Ezekiel 20 God declares his patience toward his rebellious and disobedient people and commands the prophet to rebuke them for their idolatry. The summary in Wisdom of Solomon 10–19, an extended reflection on the Exodus experience, contrasts God's discipline of his people with his destruction of their enemies. Sirach 44–50 constitutes a hymn extolling the righteous ancestors from Enoch to Simon son of Onias. In Jdt. 5.6-21 an Ammonite warns Nebuchadnezzar's general that when the Israelites have obeyed God, he has defended them against their enemies, but when the Israelites disobeyed they were defeated.

The closest parallel with Stephen's summary of Israelite history is found in the prayer of confession and repentance recorded in Neh. 9.6-37.[20] In general, they both share the tenor of the rebellion of the ancestors. A number of specific elements in the summary of Israelite history occur in both. The Levites' confession in Neh. 9.5-37 begins with the

20. Cf. similarly Soards, *The Speeches in Acts*, pp. 148-54.

call of Abram (Neh. 9.7-8; cf. Acts 7.2-8), and recounts the Exodus (Neh. 9.9-11; cf. Acts 7.36), the giving of the Law at Sinai (Neh. 9.13; cf. Acts 7.38), the sin of the golden calf (Neh. 9.18; cf. Acts 7.41), the wilderness wanderings (Neh. 9.12, 15, 19-21; cf. Acts 7.44), the Israelites' desire to return to Egypt (Neh. 9.17; cf. Acts 7.39), the multiplication of the people (Neh. 9.23; cf. Acts 7.17) and the conquest of Palestine (Neh. 9.22-5; cf. Acts 7.45).

The similarity between Neh. 9.5-37 and Acts 7.51-53 is strengthened considerably by their verbal and conceptual similarities. The confession of sin led by the Levites in Neh. 9.5-37 (or by Ezra according to the Septuagint) praises God for demonstrating that he has been gracious and compassionate (Neh. 9.17, 19, 27, 28, 31) time and again in the face of the disobedience of the πατέρες (Neh. 9.16, 32, 34; cf. Acts 7.52). They acted arrogantly and 'stiffened their neck' (ἐσκλήρυναν τὸν τράχηλον αὐτῶν), refusing to listen to God's commandments (Neh. 9.16, 17, 29; cf. Acts 7.51).[21] Although God admonished them by his Spirit through the prophets, the ancestors did not listen (Neh. 9.30), thus effectively resisting the Spirit (Acts 7.51; cf. also Isa. 63.10; Zech. 7.12). Beyond that, they killed the prophets whom God sent to admonish them to obey the Law and cast the Law behind their backs (Neh. 9.26; cf. Acts 7.52). Finally the ancestors, along with the kings, leaders, and priests, did not practice the Law, and did not pay attention to God's commandments and testimonies (Neh. 9.34; cf. Acts 7.53).

It is tempting to claim that these verbal links support the proposal that Stephen's speech is framed on the basis of biblical summaries of Israelite history like Neh. 9.5-37.[22] But direct influence between the two cannot be demonstrated. Rather the comparison simply supports the thesis that the speech is coherent, including 7.51-53 as an integral part of the speech, and that the theme is a critique against the Jewish leaders. It also suggests that the speech is relevant to the context in Acts because

21. Cf. Jer. 6.10, where the essence of having ἀπερίτμητα ὦτα is a refusal to hear. On the phrase ἀπερίτμητοι καρδίαις καὶ τοῖς ὠσίν, see further Lev. 26.41. The context of Lev. 26.14-45 contains similar topics, including an emphasis on the 'sins of the ancestors' (Lev. 26.39, 40), on the exile as punishment for sin (Lev. 26.31-33, 38-39), on disobedience (Lev. 26.14, 21, 23, 27, 40), and on idolatry (Lev. 26.30); cf. also Isa. 6.9-10.

22. Cf. Soards, *The Speeches in Acts*, p. 155, where he says that a comparison between Acts 7 and Nehemiah 9 'does not account for all the matters of form, style, content, and function' of Stephen's speech, but 'there are sufficient parallels to suggest some relationship between the two'.

it serves as a counter accusation in reply to Jewish leaders' accusations against Stephen.

Tracing the Themes of Stephen's Speech

On the basis of the comparison between Stephen's speech in Acts 7.2-53 and the summaries of Israelite history, it is possible to demonstrate that the problem of rejecting the prophets and disobeying God reflected in the concluding rebuke constitutes the theme of the speech as a whole.[23] In addition, the speech calls attention to God's vindication of Joseph and Moses as redeemers for Israel, thus implying that God had vindicated Jesus and Stephen. Beginning with Abraham's call, which served as the beginning point for Israelite history in several of the summaries of Israelite History, it continues by citing Joseph as the one who brought Jacob's descendants to Egypt and as an example of one of God's messengers whom the 'ancestors' had rejected. The speech then moves to the account of the Israelites' rejection and denial of Moses, which sets up a comparison with the fact that the Jewish leaders had rejected and killed the 'Righteous One' (Acts 7.52). It proceeds to call attention to the Israelites continuing disobedience as demonstrated by the incident with the Golden Calf and their problem with idolatry. Stephen's speech concludes by launching a rebuke against his opponents as 'stiff-necked' and 'uncircumcised in heart and ears'.

The speech 'begins at the beginning' by introducing the call of Abraham. From a narrative perspective, it would seem that this is the logical starting point for the story of God's dealings with Israel. Stephen particularly emphasizes Abraham's call and the promise that his descendants would inherit the promised land (Acts 7.5). The promise of progeny is, of course, implied in this context also. More specifically, God's prediction to Abraham of his descendants' sojourn in Egypt and their deliverance (Acts 7.6-7) serves to introduce the stories of Joseph and Moses, which occupy the bulk of the speech.

In Jewish tradition, Abraham stood as a paradigm for his faith and obedience; he was the one who received the promise; in response to God's call he abandoned the idolatry of the Babylonians. Some argue that Abraham introduces the motif of promise and fulfillment as the

---

23. See J.J. Kilgallen, 'The Function of Stephen's Speech (Acts 7, 2-53)', *Bib* 70 (1989), pp. 174-76; Pesch, *Apostelgeschichte*, I, p. 247; Polhill, *Acts*, p. 206.

theme of the speech.[24] On the other hand, aside from an off-handed reference in Acts 7.17, nothing more is made of the promise–fulfillment schema. Others suggest that the point of recounting Abraham's call *in Mesopotamia* emphasizes that God is present with and active on behalf of his people outside the 'land'.[25] While this theme may be implied in the speech, it is not explicitly drawn out. Rather Stephen's speech stresses God's intention that Abraham's seed would serve God 'in this place' (Acts 7.7; cf. Gen. 15.13 14; Exod. 3.12).[26] This might provide a point for the counterpoint that the 'ancestors' had not obeyed God in the conclusion to the speech.

Joseph as an Example of Vindication

Stephen's speech recalls Joseph as the one who led Jacob and his descendants to Egypt. Aside from this obvious role of Joseph in the narrative, the speech also appeals to Joseph in an ironical fashion as an example of one of the messengers whom the 'ancestors' rejected.[27] The fact that the πατριάρχαι became jealous of Joseph and sold him as a slave

24. See Bihler, *Stephanusgeschichte*, pp. 38-46. He seems to overplay the emphasis on 'promise' in the context of Stephen's speech. Although it is clearly brought out, the primary emphasis in this context is on the prediction of Israel's sojourn in Egypt and their later deliverance. In the context of the speech, however, this serves a narrative function rather than a thematic one. Bihler's overemphasis on the theme of 'promise' in Stephen's speech causes him to miss the point of the appeal to Joseph on Stephen's part. See also N. Dahl, 'The Story of Abraham in Luke–Acts', in *Studies in Luke–Acts* (ed. L.E. Keck, J.L. Martyn; Philadelphia: Fortress Press, 1966), pp. 139-58; Pesch, *Apostelgeschichte*, I, p. 258; Polhill, *Acts*, p. 190.

25. See Richard, 'Joseph Episode', pp. 144, 158; F.F. Bruce, *The Acts of the Apostles: Greek Text with Introduction and Commentary* (Grand Rapids: Eerdmans, 3rd rev. edn, 1990), p. 263; Polhill, *Acts*, p. 189; E. Larsson, 'Temple-Criticism and the Jewish Heritage: Some Reflections on Acts 6–7', *NTS* 39 (1993), p. 388.

26. See Kilgallen, *The Stephen Speech*, pp. 36-42, where he argues that the prediction of Israel's sojourn in Egypt and the intention that Abraham's seed would serve God in Acts 7.6-7 serves as the climax of the Abraham episode and points to important themes in the rest of the speech. Cf. similarly, J. Dupont, 'La structure oratoire du discours d'Etienne [Actes 7]', *Bib* 66 (1985), pp. 153-66. Soards, *The Speeches in Acts*, p. 62, rightfully criticizes this approach for reading too much into the text. Nevertheless, he overlooks the function of these verses in the overall context of Stephen's speech.

27. See Kilgallen, 'Stephen's Speech', p. 181; Richard, 'Joseph Episode', pp. 255-67.

(Acts 7.9) could provide an analogy for the fact that the πατέρες had persecuted the prophets and had killed those who delivered God's word (Acts 7.52).[28] This thesis finds confirmation in the traditio-historical background of the figure of Joseph in Second Temple literature. The fact that Joseph appears as the messenger of God against idolatry in *Joseph and Aseneth* could support the interpretation that Stephen compares Joseph, as one of the prophets whom the ancestors persecuted, with the 'Righteous One', Jesus.[29] But the emphasis in Acts 7 is not on the fact that the 'ancestors' rejected Joseph, as is the case with the portion of the speech that relates to Moses, but rather that Joseph found χάριν before Pharaoh because God was with him (Acts 7.9-10). Thus it would seem more likely that Stephen recounts Joseph's story in order to introduce the theme of vindication by God.[30]

The motif of Joseph as a good man who suffered and whom God delivered from his afflictions is clearly attested in Jewish tradition, especially in the *Testaments of the Twelve Patriarchs*. For example,

28. Contrast Conzelmann, *Acts of the Apostles*, p. 52, who claims that Acts 7.9 does not constitute a rebuke of the patriarchs. He makes this argument on the basis of Ps. 105.17, which makes no mention of their role in selling Joseph into slavery, and 4 Macc. 7.19; 16.25, which praises the patriarchs. This ignores the thrust of Stephen's speech which is brought out clearly in the conclusion.

29. See especially *Jos. et As.* 23.10, where Joseph's brother Levi says to Pharoah's son that 'our brother Joseph is like the firstborn son of God' ('Ιωσὴφ ὁ ἀδελφὸς ἡμῶν ἐστίν ᾧ υἱὸς τοῦ θεοῦ πρωτότοκος). For this text, see C. Burchard, 'Ein vorläufiger griechischer Text von Joseph und Aseneth', *Dielheimer Blätter zum Alten Testament* 14 (1979), pp. 2-53. For the English translation, see C. Burchard, 'Joseph and Aseneth', in *The Old Testament Pseudepigrapha* (ed. J.H. Charlesworth; Garden City, NY: Doubleday, 1985), II, p. 240. Contrast the text of this passage in Philonenko's edition: 'Joseph, notre frère, est aimé de Dieu' ('Ιωσὴφ ὁ ἀδελφὸς ἡμῶν ἐστιν ἀγαπητὸς τῷ θεῷ). See M. Philonenko, *Joseph et Aséneth: Introduction, Texte Critique, Traduction et Notes* (SPB, 13; Leiden: Brill, 1968), pp. 202-203. Another support for the interpretation cited above may be found in *T. Benj.* 3.8, where Joseph is the prefigurement of the one who would die for the sake of impious men. This text, however, seems to bear more of a resemblance to patristic traditions that connected Joseph with Christ. See M. de Jonge, 'Joseph in Test. Benjamin 3:8', in *Jewish Eschatology, Early Christian Christology and the Testaments of the Twelve Patriarchs: Collected Essays of Marinus de Jonge* (NovTSup, 63; Leiden: Brill, 1991), pp. 297-99.

30. Cf. similarly Kilgallen, *The Stephen Speech*, pp. 47-54. Kilgallen also argues (pp. 62-63) that the account of Joseph's role in bringing Israel to Egypt during the famine not only reinforces God's deliverance of Joseph but also highlights Joseph as the agent of God's deliverance of Israel.

Reuben (*T. Reub.* 4.8 10) commends Joseph as an example of one who 'found favor with God and men' (εὗρεν χάριν ἐνώπιον θεοῦ καὶ ἀνθρώπων)³¹ because he avoided promiscuity, and thus 'the God of our ancestors rescued him from every visible or hidden death' (διὰ τοῦτο ὁ θεὸς τῶν πατέρων ὑμῶν ἐρρύσατο αὐτὸν ἀπὸ παντὸς ὁρατοῦ καὶ κεκρυμμένου θανάτου).³² In similar fashion, Simeon says (*T. Sim.* 4.4) that Joseph was a good man who had the spirit of God in him ('Ιωσὴφ δὲ ἦν ἀνὴρ ἀγαθὸς καὶ ἔχων πνεῦμα θεοῦ ἐν ἑαυτῷ).³³ The theme of Joseph as a man possessing σοφίαν, the πνεῦμα of God, and χάριν is also reflected elsewhere in Jewish tradition. For example, in *Joseph and Aseneth*, Aseneth's father Pentephres says (*Jos. et As.* 4.7) that 'Joseph is (also) a man powerful in wisdom and experience, and the spirit of God is upon him, and the grace of the Lord (is) with him' (καὶ ἔστιν 'Ιωσὴφ ἀνὴρ δυνατὸς ἐν σοφίᾳ καὶ ἐπιστήμῃ καὶ πνεῦμα θεοῦ ἐστιν ἐπ' αὐτῷ καὶ χάρις κυρίου μετ' αὐτοῦ). In similar fashion Philo attributes to Joseph the fact that he 'has a divine spirit in him' (ἔχει πνεῦμα θεῖον ἐν ἑαυτῷ).³⁴

---

31. See also *T. Jos.* 11.6; 12.3. For the text of the Testaments of the Twelve Patriarchs, see R.H. Charles, *The Greek Versions of the Testaments of the Twelve Patriarchs* (Oxford: Clarendon Press, 1908), and M. de Jonge *et al.*, *The Testaments of the Twelve Patriarchs: A Critical Edition of the Greek Text* (PVTG, 1; Leiden: Brill, 1978). The text cited follows Charles, *Greek Versions*, p. 9. Cf. the similar phrases in Lk. 2.40: καὶ χάρις θεοῦ ἦν ἐπ' αὐτό; and Lk. 2.52: καὶ 'Ιησοῦς προέκοπτεν ἐν τῇ σοφίᾳ καὶ ἡλικίᾳ καὶ χάριτι παρὰ θεῷ καὶ ἀνθρώποις.

32. The Greek version follows De Jonge, *Testaments*, p. 9. For the English translation, see H.C. Kee, 'Testaments of the Twelve Patriarchs', in J.H. Charlesworth (ed.), *The Old Testament Pseudepigrapha* (Garden City, NY: Doubleday, 1983), I, p. 784.

33. See also *T. Dan* 1.4; and *T. Benj.* 3.1, where Benjamin exhorts his progeny to 'pattern your life after the good and pious man Joseph'; see Kee, 'Testaments', p. 825. Cf. also Acts 11.24, where Luke describes Barnabas as ἀνὴρ ἀγαθὸς καὶ πλήρης πνεύματος ἁγίου καὶ πίστεως, in fashion both similar to the description of Joseph in *T. Sim.* 4.4 and to the description of Stephen in Acts 6.3, 5. Cf. also *T. Sim.* 4.5, which says that Simeon's descendents had observed χάριν, δόξα, and εὐλογίαν in Joseph. For a discussion of these texts from the *Testaments of the Twelve Patriarchs*, see H.W. Hollander, 'The Ethical Character of the Patriarch Joseph: A Study in the Ethics of *The Testaments of the XII Patriarchs*', in *Studies on the Testament of Joseph* (SBLSCS, 5; ed. G.W.E. Nickelsburg, Jr; Missoula, MT: Scholars Press, 1975), pp. 73-80; and *idem*, *Joseph as an Ethical Model in the Testaments of the Twelve Patriarchs* (SVTP, 6; Leiden: Brill, 1981), pp. 51-57.

34. Philo, *De Jos.* 116, cited by Philonenko, *Joseph et Aséneth*, p. 144.

The portrait of Joseph as the example *par excellence* of a righteous man who suffered affliction but was vindicated by God stands out especially in the *Testament of Joseph*.[35] At the very outset of his testament, Joseph pronounces a poetic piece which constitutes an extended contrast between the fact that Joseph's brothers oppressed him but God delivered him (*T. Jos.* 1.2-7):[36]

> My brothers and my children.
> Listen to Joseph, the one beloved of Israel.
> Give ear to the words of my mouth.
> In my life I have seen envy and death.
> But I have not gone astray: I continued in the truth of the Lord.
> These, my brothers, hated me but the Lord loved me.
> They wanted to kill me, but the God of my fathers preserved me.
> Into a cistern they lowered me; the Most High raised me up.
> They sold me into slavery; the Lord of all set me free.

35. See further 1 Macc. 2.53, where Joseph is included among the 'ancestors' who 'received great honor and an everlasting name'; see also Philo, *Jos.* 246-48; Josephus, *Ant.* 2.43, 50, 69; and *Apoc. Pauli*, p. 47. See also Hollander, 'Ethical Character', pp. 57-58, where he cites a number of these texts in support of the conclusion that the motif of the righteous who endure affliction 'was traditionally connected with Joseph'. See also *ibid.*, p. 67, where he says that in the Testaments 'Joseph is the person par excellence who—after a time of distress in which he kept faithful to God—is saved from his oppression and exalted and honored'. He also argues that the pattern of vindicating the rejected one is reflected generally in the Old Testament and Septuagint, citing examples from 1 Maccabees, but also Ps. 105 (104).17-22 and Wis. 10.13-14. Cf. also Hollander, *Joseph*, pp. 48-49; and H.W. Hollander and M. de Jonge, *The Testaments of the Twelve Patriarchs: A Commentary* (SVTP, 8; Leiden: Brill), pp. 363-65. Contrast J. Thomas, 'Aktuelles im Zeugnis der zwölf Väter', in *Studien zu den Testamenten der Zwölf Patriarchen* (BZNW, 36; ed. W. Eltester; Berlin: Töpelmann, 1969), pp. 88-92, 106-111; and K.H. Rengstorf, 'Herkunft und Sinn der Patriarchen-Reden in den Testamenten der Zwölf Patriarchen', in *La littérature juive entre Tenach et Mischna: Quelques problèmes* (RechBib, 9; ed. W.C. van Unnik; Leiden: Brill, 1974), pp. 38-39, 40-41, 43. Both Thomas and Rengstorf stress the role of Joseph as an ideal Jew of the Diaspora in the *Testaments*. On this, see also M. de Jonge, 'The Interpretation of the Testaments of the Twelve Patriarchs in Recent Years', in *Studies on the Testaments of the Twelve Patriarchs: Text and Interpretation* (SVTP, 3; ed. M. de Jonge; Leiden: Brill, 1975), pp. 191-92. Contrast also Richard, 'Joseph Episode', p. 264 n. 30, who suggests that the idea that Joseph served as the prime example of a righteous man who suffered affliction and was delivered by God is unique to Stephen's speech.

36. On the form of *T. Jos.* 1.2-7, see Hollander, 'Ethical Character', pp. 47-50; *idem, Joseph*, pp. 16-21.

I was taken into captivity; the strength of his hand came to my aid.
I was overtaken by hunger; the Lord himself fed me generously.
I was alone, and God came to help me.
I was in weakness, and the Lord showed his concern for me.
I was in prison, and the Savior acted graciously in my behalf.
I was in bonds, and he loosened me;
falsely accused, and he testified in my behalf.
Assaulted by bitter words of the Egyptians, and he rescued me.
A slave, and he exalted me.[37]

Along these lines the *Testament of Joseph* repeatedly emphasizes the fact that God rescued Joseph from his temptations and afflictions.[38] In sum, Joseph serves as the example of the fact that 'if anyone wishes to do you harm, you should pray for him, along with doing good, and you will be rescued by the Lord from every evil' (*T. Jos.* 18.2).[39]

Thus the traditio-historical background of the concept of Joseph as a man possessing σοφία, χάριν, and the πνεῦμα of God, along with his

---

37. For the English translation quoted above, see Kee, 'Testaments', p. 819. Charles cites the Greek text as follows (Charles, *Greek Versions*, pp. 182-84):

Ἀδελφοί μου καὶ τέκνα μου,
Ἀκούσατε Ἰωσὴφ τοῦ ἠγαπημένου ὑπὸ Ἰσραήλ,
Ἐνωτίσασθε ῥήματα τοῦ στόματός μου.
Ἐγὼ εἶδον ἐν τῇ ζωῇ μου τὸν φθόνον καὶ τὸν θάνατον
Καὶ οὐκ ἐπλανήθην ἀλλ' ἔμεινα ἐν τῇ ἀληθείᾳ Κυρίου.
Οἱ ἀδελφοί μου οὗτοι ἐμίσησάν με, Ὁ δὲ Κύριος ἠγάπησέ με
Αὐτοὶ ἤθελόν με ἀνελεῖν, Ὁ δὲ Θεὸς τῶν πατέρων μου ἐφύλαξέν με·
Εἰς λάκκον με ἐχάλασάν, Καὶ ὁ ὕψιστος ἀνήγαγέν με·
Ἐπράθην εἰς δουλείαν, Καὶ ὁ πάντων δεσπότης ἠλευθέρωσέν με·
Εἰς αἰχμαλωσίαν ἐλήφθην, Καὶ ἡ κραταιὰ αὐτοῦ χεὶρ ἐβοήθησέ μοι·
Ἐν λιμῷ συνεσχέθην, Καὶ αὐτὸς ὁ Κύριος διέθρεψέ με·
Μόνος ἤμην, καὶ ὁ Θεὸς παρεκάλεσέ με·
Ἐν ἀσθενείᾳ ἤμην, καὶ ὁ Κύριος ἐπεσκέψατό με·
Ἐν φυλακῇ ἤμην, καὶ ὁ σωτὴρ ἐχαρίτωσέ με·
Ἐν δεσμοῖς καὶ ἔλυσέ με.
Ἐν διαβολαῖς καὶ συνηγόρησέ μοι.
Ἐν λόγοις ἐνυπνίων πικροῖς καὶ ἐρρύσατό με.
Δοῦλος καὶ ὕψωσέ με.

The one difference between the English translation and the Greek text is that instead of 'bitter words of the Egyptians' the text reads λόγοις ἐνυπνίων πικροῖς. Charles, however, cites Αἰγυπτίων as a variant for ἐνυπνίων.

38. See *T. Jos.* 2.2, 4.3, 8. See also *T. Gad* 2.5; and *T. Benj.* 3.4, where Benjamin says God watched over Joseph, even though many wanted to destroy him (cf. also 4.3).

39. See Kee, 'Testaments', p. 823. Cf. also *T. Benj.* 5.4-5.

role as an example of a rejected one whom God vindicated, raises the possibility that Stephen's speech related Joseph's story as a parallel for his own affliction by the Jews. This is plausible particularly since Stephen emphasizes that God rescued Joseph from all his afflictions and gave him χάριν καὶ σοφίαν before Pharoah (Acts 7.10), which compares with the descriptions of Stephen in the previous chapter.[40] There Luke includes Stephen as one of the 'Seven' who were πλήρεις πνεύματος καὶ σοφίας (Acts 6.3), and describes him as a man who was πλήρης χάριτος καὶ δυνάμεως (Acts 6.8). The statement in Acts 7.10 about Joseph's σοφία also corresponds to the fact that the Jews were unable to withstand Stephen's σοφίαν (Acts 6.10), even though they accused him of blasphemy.

Therefore Stephen's speech does answer the accusations against him. In a sense, the speech turns the accusations against Stephen's opponents. By citing the example of Joseph, the speech implies that just as God had vindicated Joseph by giving him χάριν and σοφίαν before Pharoah so God had vindicated Stephen by the χάριν and σοφίαν he gave to him before the Jews.[41] While it is true that Stephen does not explicitly draw this point from the Joseph narrative, he does refer to the motif of vindication by calling attention to the fact that 'God was with him' (Acts 7.9) and by citing the account of Joseph's brothers returning to Egypt to buy grain, in which he was vindicated before them.[42] The motif that 'God was with' Joseph is clear in the Genesis narrative, and the fact that it occurs repeatedly (Gen. 39.2, 21, 23) marks it as one of the main themes of Joseph's story.[43]

40. See Charles, *Testaments*, p. lxxxiv, where he remarks that the similarity between Acts 7.10 and *T. Reub.* 4.8 is 'remarkable'. See also *ibid.*, pp. lxxxii-lxxxv, where he traces what he believes is the influence of the Testaments on Luke–Acts. Cf. esp. ibid., p. xc, where Charles remarks on the large number of common words between the Testaments and Luke–Acts. This alone cannot establish a literary relationship between the two, but it can serve to support the observation of the similarity between Stephen's reference to Joseph and the themes in the Testaments. See also Kilgallen, *The Stephen Speech*, pp. 49-50; Polhill, *Acts*, p. 191.

41. See Krodel, *Acts*, pp. 32-33; Richard, 'Joseph Episode', p. 265; G. Stanton, 'Stephen in Lucan Perspective', *StudBib* 10 (1980), pp. 345-60; P. Dschulnigg, 'Die Rede des Stephanus im Rahmen des Berichtes über sein Martyrium (Apg 6,8-8,3)', *Judaica* 44 (1988), p. 205.

42. Contrast Conzelmann, *Acts of the Apostles*, p. 53, where he claims that the sufferings of Joseph are 'all but ignored'.

43. See also *T. Jos.* 6.8, where Joseph says he prayed for the angel of Abraham

This interpretation has the advantage of relating the significance of Joseph in Stephen's speech to the Joseph narrative in the Old Testament and its motif of vindication. Furthermore it has the advantage of drawing on the image of Joseph in the mainstream of Jewish tradition, which was an image of the example *par excellence* of a righteous person who was afflicted, and yet God delivered and vindicated him. This view would also address the question of why the speech does not appear to fit the historical setting of Stephen's martyrdom. If the interpretation suggested above is plausible, then Stephen may have cited the Joseph narrative in order to imply that, just as Joseph was rejected by the 'ancestors' but vindicated by God, so Stephen expected to be vindicated before his accusers.

Israel's Paradigmatic Rejection of Moses

Stephen's speech moves from Joseph to the story of Moses as a rejected λυτρωτής and depicts him as a paradigmatic example of the fact that the 'ancestors' had persecuted the prophets (Acts 7.52). In the account of Moses' killing the Egyptian, the speech alludes to the idea that the 'sons of Israel' did not understand that Moses was sent to give them σωτηρίαν (Acts 7.25).[44] Stephen emphasizes this as a foreshadowing of their later rejection of Moses, particularly in light of the phrasing of Exod. 2.14, where the Israelite questions his appointment as ἄρχοντα and δικαστὴν (Acts 7.27).[45] God vindicated Moses, however, by means

to be with him when Potiphar's wife tempted him.

44. See Acts 7.23 for the statement of Moses' intention to 'visit' (ἐπισκέψασθαι) his brothers, which may imply an element of deliverance in light of the meaning of this term in the Septuagint. See also Josephus, *Ant*. 2.331, where Moses declared that God had given the Israelites 'everything that He promised to perform through me for your salvation and deliverance from bondage' (πρὸς σωτηρίαν καὶ τὴν ἀπαλλαγὴν τῆς δουλείας). See Josephus, *Jewish Antiquities* (LCL; trans. H. St. J. Thackeray; London: Heinemann; Cambridge, MA: Harvard University Press, 1930), IV, pp. 310-11 for the text and translation. See also Josephus, *Ant*. 9.10. Cf. further Haenchen, *Acts*, p. 281, where he says, 'For the first time in the speech we hear the theme of the people's incomprehension and their failure to recognize the saviour sent by God'. As noted below, however, Haenchen considers this to be the result of Luke's redaction of the speech. Cf. also Polhill, *Acts*, pp. 195-96.

45. Cf. Acts 7.35 for the phrase ἄρχοντα καὶ λυτρωτὴν. On the idea of Moses as one sent by God to deliver Israel but rejected by them, see Kilgallen, *The Stephen Speech*, pp. 68-73, 75-78, 80-83; Haenchen, *Acts*, p. 282, where he says, 'The leader and redeemer sent by God is rejected by the Jews: this applies both to Moses and to

of the vision of the burning bush, whereby the Lord declared that he
intended to deliver his people from the Egyptians *by sending Moses*
(Acts 7.33-34; citing Exod. 3.5, 7-8, 10). Stephen's speech emphasizes
this in contrast to the Israelite's denial in Acts 7.27 by affirming in Acts
7.35 that God indeed had sent this very Moses to be both ἄρχοντα and
λυτρωτὴν by means of the angel who appeared to him in the burning
bush.[46] Thus Stephen's speech cites Moses as a paradigmatic example
of the fact that the 'ancestors' had rejected the one whom God had sent
as redeemer but God had vindicated him, and relates this to the accusation that Stephen's persecutors had killed the 'Righteous One', Jesus
(Acts 7.52).[47]

Jesus, though the speaker does not come to the theme of Jesus until verse 52'.
Haenchen considers this statement another reflection of Luke's redaction of the passage. See further T.L. Donaldson, 'Moses Typology and the Sectarian Nature of Early
Christian Anti-Judaism: A Study of Acts 7', *JSNT* 12 (1981), pp. 42-43, where he
points out that the idea of Moses as a rejected prophet relates to the theme of the rejection of the prophets by Israel in the speech as a whole.

46. Moses is never called λυτρωτής in the Septuagint; rather the Lord is the
λυτρωτής (Pss. 18[19].14; 77[78].35; cf. also *T. Lev.* 2.10; *T. Zeb.* 9.8). This is
especially the case with reference to the Exodus (Deut. 7.8; 9.26; 13.5[6]; 15.15; 21.8;
24.18; 2 Sam. 7.23; 1 Chron. 17.21). In the Septuagint, Moses is primarily designated
ὁ θεράπων κυρίου (Exod. 14.31; Num. 12.7, 8; Josh. 9.2 [8.33]) and the οἰκέτης
κυρίου (Deut. 34.5). Moses could also be called προφητής (*Vit. Proph.* 2.11; *Mart.
Isa.* 1.3.8; cf. also Eusebius, *Pr. Ev.*, 9.30.1 [citing Eupolemus]), νομοθέτης
(Eusebius, *Pr. Ev.*, 8.10.8 [citing Aristobulus], 9.26.1 [citing Eupolemus]; *Ep. Arist.*
131, 139, 148; cf. also *Ep. Arist.* 144), and διδάσκαλος (Eusebius, *Pr. Ev.*,
9.27.4 [citing Artapanus]). Nevertheless, Stephen's use of the term λυτρωτής with
reference to Moses can be explained easily on the basis of the fact that God sends
Moses into Egypt to effect the deliverance (Exod. 3.7-10; Stephen explicitly quotes
this passage in Acts 7.33-34). In comparison with Stephen's use of the term ἄρχοντα
to describe Moses, which is taken from Exod. 2.14, in Jewish tradition Moses could
be called ἡγητήρ (*Sib. Or.* 3.248-58, esp 3.253), ἡγεμών (Eusebius, *Pr. Ev.*,
9.29.14.32 [citing Ezekiel the Tragedian]; cf. also 9.29.5.1-15, where he depicts
Moses as sitting on the throne of God), and στρατηγός (Eusebius, *Pr. Ev.* 9.27.7
[citing Artapanus]). See further J. Jeremias, 'Μωυσῆς', in *TDNT*, IV, pp. 849-57
on the titles for Moses in Jewish tradition.

47. Despite the fact that Haenchen views the body of Stephen's sermon as an
overview of sacred history with no specific theme, he recognizes the parallel between
the Jews' rejection and denial of Moses and their treatment of Jesus (Acts 7.37). See
Haenchen, *Acts*, pp. 288-89; cf. also Conzelmann, *Acts of the Apostles*, p. 54. On
this parallel between Moses and Jesus, compare also R.B. Rackham, *The Acts of the
Apostles: An Exposition* (London: Methuen, 1939), p. 93, who argues that the theme

Stephen repeatedly emphasizes the fact that it was 'this' Moses, that is, the one whom the Israelites had initially rejected, who led them out of Egypt (Acts 7.36), who predicted the 'prophet like me' whom God would raise up (Acts 7.37), who met with the angel at Sinai and received the 'living oracles' (Acts 7.38).[48] Yet Stephen relates that the 'ancestors' rejected Moses again by requesting Aaron to make a golden calf (Acts 7.39-40), thus introducing the problem of disobedience. Within the overarching theme of their rejection of Moses, Stephen's speech introduces the problem that Israel was 'stiff-necked' and 'uncircumcised in heart and ears' (Acts 7.51) by relating the incident of the golden calf.

It is not without reason that Haenchen considers Acts 7.35, 37, 39-43, and 48-53 to be Lukan additions to the original speech, for those passages carry the substance of the comparison between Moses and Jesus. The primary basis for his argument is the assumption that since Stephen is supposed to have cited Amos 5.25–27 from the Septuagint, 'Nobody will maintain that Stephen sought to persuade the High Council with a LXX text which diverges widely from the Hebrew'.[49] This, however, derives from his view that the speech is 'merely a didactic recapitulation of Israel's relations with God' and thus constitutes 'sacred history told for its own sake and with no other theme'.[50] But if the Speeches of Acts accurately summarize the content of what was said, then the fact that Peter could make a similar comparison between Moses and Jesus (Acts 3.25) would confirm this interpretation

---

of Stephen's speech is that Jesus is Savior, Redeemer, and Ruler, and therefore the true prophet and mediator (like Moses) and that as the 'Righteous One' he fulfills the Law (cf. Rom. 10:4). Cf. also Soards, *The Speeches in Acts*, p. 65; cf. especially Kilgallen, *The Stephen Speech*, pp. 66-67; Pesch, *Apostelgeschichte*, I, p. 246; and Polhill, *Acts*, p. 199, who extends the comparison between Moses and Jesus to include the description of Moses' childhood in Acts 7:20-22. Contrast Bihler, *Stephanusgeschichte*, pp. 59-60, where he designates the Moses episode as the 'time of the fulfillment of the promise' (cf. Acts 7.17) and continues his rather one-sided treatment of Stephen's speech from the perspective of promise–fulfillment, which breaks down after the Moses episode. Nevertheless, he does recognize the comparison between the figure of Moses and the figure of Jesus (cf. pp. 60-62).

48. See Lake and Cadbury, *Beginnings*, IV, p. 77, where they confirm that the repetition of οὗτος emphasizes the theme that Israel had rejected Moses.

49. Haenchen, *Acts*, p. 289.

50. Haenchen, *Acts*, p. 288. Haenchen must strip away what he considers 'Lucan additions' in order to maintain this perspective, for when they are left intact, the speech contains a remarkably consistent critique against his opponents.

and make it a plausible one for Stephen's speech.[51] Even if this is not granted, the case for the unity of the speech supports the thesis that it compares Jesus with Moses as a rejected redeemer who was vindicated by God.

The Continuing Problem of Disobedience in Israel

Stephen's speech proceeds by relating the golden calf to the continuing problem of disobedience in Israel (Acts 7.41), especially in their idolatry, as further evidence that they were 'stiff-necked' and 'uncircumcised in heart and ears' (Acts 7.51) and the fact that although they had received the Law by the command of angels, they did not keep it (Acts 7.53).[52] In this regard Stephen introduces a quotation from the Septuagint version of Amos 5.25-27. In the context of Amos, this passage reminded Israel that even in the wilderness they engaged in idolatry. Specifically according to Amos 5.26 they carried along 'Sikkuth your king' (סִכּוּת מַלְכְּכֶם) and 'Kiyyun' (כִּיּוּן) who were 'your images, the star of your gods which you made for yourselves' צַלְמֵיכֶם כּוֹכַב אֱלֹהֵיכֶם (אֲשֶׁר עֲשִׂיתֶם לָכֶם). In the Septuagint this has been changed somewhat, partially on the basis of the Hebrew text, and perhaps partially on the basis of the setting of the Septuagint. Instead of 'Sikkuth your king' the Septuagint says that the Israelites carried the 'tent of Moloch' (σκηνὴν τοῦ Μολοχ), presumably based on the similarity of סֻכּוֹת with סִכּוּת and the similarity of מֶלֶך (perhaps referring to מֹלֶך or מַלְכּוּ?) with מַלְכְּכֶם.

---

51. See further Jeremias, 'Μωυσῆς', pp. 868-69, where he argues that the comparison between Moses and Jesus 'cannot be regarded as a theologoumenon developed by Lk.', saying that this is demonstrated, apart from Paul's reference to the Israelites' 'baptism into Moses' in 1 Cor. 10.1 2 (which stands in juxtaposition with Christ as the 'spiritual rock that followed'), by the fact that 'in one passage at least the pre-Lucan Gospel tradition is shaped by the Moses/Messiah typology, namely, in the account of the transfiguration', where the heavenly voice in Mk 9.7 contains an allusion to Deut. 18.15. On the role of Deut. 18.15 in Acts 3 and Acts 7, cf. Bihler, *Stephanusgeschichte*, pp. 104-111. On the speeches as accurate summaries of what was said, see M. Hengel, *Acts and the History of Earliest Christianity* (trans. J. Bowden; London: SCM Press, 1979; repr. Philadelphia: Fortress Press, 1980), pp. 60-61; I.H. Marshall, *Luke: Historian and Theologian* (London: Paternoster Press, 1970; repr. Grand Rapids: Zondervan, 1971), pp. 72-73; and Bruce, *Acts of the Apostles: Greek Text*, pp. 34-40.

52. Cf. Kilgallen, *The Stephen Speech*, pp. 84-87, where he draws out the emphasis that the rejection of God's messenger results in false worship. See also Krodel, *Acts*, p. 34; Larsson, 'Temple-Criticism', p. 392.

In addition the Septuagint says that the Israelites carried 'the star of your god 'Ραιφαν' (τὸ ἄστρον τοῦ θεοῦ ὑμῶν 'Ραιφαν) instead of 'Kiyyun'. According to the Septuagint these gods, Μολόχ and 'Ραιφάν, were the Israelites' 'images' (τύποι) which they had made for themselves.

In the larger context of Amos, however, this passage is part of the prophet's critique of the 'house of Joseph' for not practicing justice and righteousness (Amos 5.21-27). In a similar manner Stephen's speech recounts the Israelites' disobedience in order to stress the theme that they were 'stiff-necked' and 'uncircumcised in heart and ears' (Acts 7.51), and that they had not kept the Law (Acts 7.53). In this regard, however, Amos also proclaims in the name of the Lord, 'I hate, I reject your festivals, and I do not delight in your festive assemblies. Even though you offer up to me burnt offerings and your grain offerings, I will not enjoy them, and I will not accept the peace offerings of your fattened cattle' (Amos 5.21-22). While Amos does not explicitly specify his critique of the Israelites' worship in the Temple, it is clearly implied. This may help establish why Stephen could also relate the problem of disobedience, as exemplified by the rejection of God's messengers, to the Temple. He did this not because he saw anything inherently idolatrous with the Temple itself, but on the basis of the precedent which Amos had already set for criticizing the Israelites' Temple worship because of their disobedience.

The fact that Stephen appeals to this Old Testament text supports the view that his speech is not primarily a 'critique of the Temple', but rather a critique of the Jewish leaders.[53] On the other hand, it is clear that the speech criticizes the very notion of the Temple as 'housing' God in view of the fact that it is a house 'made with hands'. Perhaps the

---

53. Cf. similarly C.A. Evans, 'Prophecy and Polemic', pp. 197-908. Contra Bihler, *Stephanusgeschichte*, pp. 146-48. Bihler thinks that the radical critique of the Temple in Stephen's speech differs greatly from the Jewish milieu of the first century, with the exception of the Fourth Sybilline Oracle, and thus concludes that it can scarcely be derived from any 'Temple critique' in Judaism. This results from his overlooking the Temple critiques in the Old Testament, which provide a clear backdrop for Stephen's speech. Contrast also C.K. Barrett, 'Attitudes to the Temple in the Acts of the Apostles', in *Templum Amicitae: Essays on the Second Temple Presented to Ernst Bammel* (JSNTSup, 48; ed. W. Horbury; Sheffield: JSOT Press, 1991), p. 361, where he argues that Stephen's claim that the Most High never desired a permanent house is unparalleled in Judaism.

speech may also at least imply a contrast between the Temple as originating in David's impulse and the tabernacle as given by God's 'living
oracles'.[54] Nevertheless, the primary thrust of the critique relates to the
Israelites and their recurrent disobedience, especially with reference
to the leaders of the Temple establishment. In the course of his speech,
Stephen emphasizes the fact that the Israelites had the 'tent of witness'
the whole time they were engaged in idolatry during the wilderness
wanderings (Acts 7.44).[55] He further calls attention to the fact that they
brought the tent into the land of Canaan with them and had it until the
time of David (Acts 7.45), during which time they continued to engage
in idolatrous practices and to disobey God. This is precisely the impression conveyed by the charges in the speech's conclusion.

A comparison between Stephen's speech and 2 Chron. 36.13-16 may
help to explain why Stephen relates the problem of disobedience to the
Temple. There the Chronicler says that the Israelites, including 'all the
officials of the priests and the people', had defiled the 'house of the
Lord which he had sanctified in Jerusalem' by their idolatry (2 Chron.
36.14).[56] The comparison with Stephen's speech is strengthened by the
fact that in that context the Chronicler rebukes the people of Israel for
being unfaithful, following the abominations of the nations, and defiling
the 'house of the Lord which is in Jerusalem' (οἶκον τοῦ κυρίου τὸν
ἐν Ιερουσαλημ) like Zedekiah who 'stiffened his neck and hardened
his heart' (ἐσκλήρυνεν τὸν τράχηλον αὐτοῦ καὶ τὴν καρδίαν
αὐτοῦ κατίσχυσεν, 2 Chron. 36.13; cf. Acts 7.51). Moreover, the
Chronicler charges the people with 'mocking' God's messengers, 'despising' his words, and 'scoffing' at his προφήταις (2 Chron. 36.16;

---

54. Cf. Simon, 'Stephen and the Temple', pp. 128-31; Haenchen, *Acts*, p. 285;
A.F.J. Klijn, 'Stephen's Speech—Acts vii.2-53', *NTS* 4 (1957), p. 29). Cf. also
Kilgallen, *The Stephen Speech*, p. 92, where he suggests that Stephen's speech com-
pares the Temple to the false worship during the wilderness wanderings because the
Israelites had rejected God's messenger, Jesus.

55. See Conzelmann, *Acts of the Apostles*, pp. 55–56. Contrast Lake and Cadbury,
Beginnings, IV, p. 79, who claim that Amos makes a different point, namely that
God rejected the 'sacerdotal emphasis on sacrifices'.

56. Compare H. Olshausen, *Biblical Commentary on the New Testament* (trans.
A.C. Kendrick; New York: Sheldon, Blakeman, & Co., 1858), III, p. 250, where he
recognizes this as one of Stephen's purposes, but contends it was only one of
several. Contrast Foakes-Jackson, 'Stephen's Speech', pp. 283-86, who says that
this theme was already a commonplace in Judaism, and that it is not relevant to the
situation. As argued below, however, it can be interpreted as a counter-accusation.

cf. Acts 7.52). Therefore, these similarities make it entirely plausible to understand Stephen's speech as a critique against the Israelites, especially their leaders, who had defiled the Temple by their disobedience.

It is true, on the other hand, that Stephen's speech emphasizes the transition from the 'tent of witness', which Moses made according to the pattern that he had seen, to the 'house' that Solomon built for God (Acts 7.45-48).[57] But the point of this transition is clearly not that Solomon's act of building the Temple was another example of Israel's disobedience, for the initiative began with David, whom Stephen clearly emphasizes found χάριν with God (Acts 7.46). Rather, the speech relates the Jewish leaders' disobediencet to the Temple just as Amos and the Chronicler had done.[58]

The fact that the Most High does not dwell in the Temple is then supported by the fact that God himself had declared through Isaiah that no Temple was adequate for the God who made the universe as his throne (Isa. 66.1-2). In one respect, the point of this text is to lay stress on God's transcendence of the Temple.[59] On the other hand, like the other prophets, Isaiah also directs his critique of the Temple against the people, rejecting their worship and rebuking them for not listening when the Lord spoke (Isa. 66.3-4). In similar fashion Stephen's critique could be seen as directed primarily toward the Jewish people, perhaps specifically the leaders themselves, rather than the Temple.

---

57. The strong adversative ἀλλά in Acts 7.48 calls attention to this contrast. A number of scholars have interpreted this transition as support for Stephen's rejection of the Temple. See Conzelmann, *Acts of the Apostles*, p. 56. On the other hand, it is important to note that the text of the speech itself does not make anything of this contrast. The argument that Stephen was interrupted and would have continued with a full-blown critique of the Temple and the Law, much like the content of the Epistle to the Hebrews, while an attractive one, constitutes no more than an argument from silence. The question regarding the antecedent of αὐτῷ in Acts 7.47 is complicated by a textual problem. Although the antecedent would be Jacob according to Acts 7.46, the sense of 7.48 demands that the antecedent be the 'Most High'.

58. If the speech follows the pattern of the critique of Israel by Amos and the Chronicler, then it is plausible to suggest that the contrast in Acts 7.48 implies a reference to the fact that the 'house' which was 'made with hands' had been defiled by their disobedience, and thus the 'Most High' does not dwell there.

59. Cf. Sylva, 'The Meaning and Function of Acts 7:46-50', pp. 261-74; Kilgallen, *The Stephen Speech*, p. 93, argues that this section of the text speaks of the Temple as the symbol of wrong thinking about the nature of God.

This understanding of Stephen's 'critique' of the Temple finds further confirmation in key elements of the history of tradition. Among the prophets Jeremiah demonstrates the same perspective with his call to repentance, which expressed criticism of Israel's disobedience and their false reliance on the Temple.[60] Jeremiah warns the people in the name of the Lord not to think that God would not destroy Jerusalem because the Temple, the οἶκος of the Lord, was located there (Jer. 7.14; cf. also 7.4, 26, 32).[61] In addition, the prophet utters the Lord's complaint that in spite of the fact that he had commanded the πατέρας to obey his voice and walk in his way, they did not listen, they did not 'incline their ears' (οὐ προσέσχεν τὸ οὖς αὐτῶν), but 'they walked in the reflections of their evil heart' (LXX: ἐπορεύθησαν ἐν τοῖς ἐνθυμήμασιν τῆς καρδίας αὐτῶν τῆς κακῆς), or 'in the counsels [and] in the stubbornness of their evil heart' (MT: בְּמֹעֵצוֹת בִּשְׁרִרוּת לִבָּם הָרָע וַיֵּלְכוּ, Jer. 7.23-24). Moreover, he specifically charges that from the days of the Exodus the πατέρες had not listened to 'my servants the prophets' but rather they 'stiffened their neck' (ἐσκλήρυναν τὸν τράχηλον αὐτῶν, Jer. 7.25-26). Furthermore, Jeremiah rebukes the 'sons of Judah' for defiling 'the house which is called by my name' (Jer. 7.30: ἐν τῷ οἴκῳ, οὗ ἐπικέκληται τὸ ὄνομά μου ἐπ' αὐτόν) with their idolatrous practices.[62] In another context, Jeremiah laments that the word of the Lord was a reproach to the people of Jerusalem, and that they could not hear it because their ears were 'uncircumcised' (Jer. 6.10, MT: הִנֵּה עֲרֵלָה אָזְנָם;

60. Cf. M. Baumgarten, *The Acts of the Apostles, or The History of the Church in the Apostolic Age* (trans. A.J.W. Morrison; Edinburgh: T. & T. Clark, 1863), I, pp. 133-36, who argues that Stephen called the Jews to repentance and that he appealed to Old Testament criticism of Israel's disobedience and false faith in the Temple when they excused their complacency on the basis of the Law and the Temple. See also C.A. Witz, 'Stephanus und seine Vertheidigungsrede', *Jahrbücher für Deutsche Theologie* 20 (1875), p. 604, where he calls Stephen 'ein eifriger, lebendiger Schüler der Propheten, eines Jesaias, eines Hezekiel, eines Jeremias'. He makes this argument, however, on the basis of his view that Stephen proclaimed the fulfillment of the Temple service in the New Covenant, a topic which is absent from Acts 7.2-53.

61. Compare the fact that Jeremiah calls the οἶκος 'which is called by my name' the τόπος 'which I gave to you and your ancestors' (Jer. 7.14) with the accusation made against Stephen in Acts 6.13, 14 that he had spoken κατὰ τοῦ τόπου τοῦ ἁγίου [τούτου] and had declared that Jesus would destroy τὸν τόπον τοῦτον.

62. See also Jer. 11.6-13; cf. also Deut. 29.18 where 'stubbornness of heart' is particularly related to idolatry.

LXX: ἰδοὺ ἀπερίτμητα τὰ ὦτα αὐτῶν). Therefore, Jeremiah's critique of the Temple is a critique of the 'sons of Judah' for their stubborn disobedience. The connections with Stephen's accusations against his opponents again suggest that Stephen's speech constitutes a critique of the Jewish leaders for their disobedience, not the Temple.

Jesus' critique of the Temple as expressed in the Temple cleansing supports this perspective on the history of tradition. As with Amos, Isaiah, and Jeremiah, Jesus' 'critique' of the Temple is in fact a critique of the Jewish leaders. In fact, Jesus uses Jeremiah's words in his rebuke of the Jews for turning 'my house' (ὁ οἶκός μου), which should have been a 'house of prayer for all the nations' (οἶκος προσευχῆς πᾶσιν τοῖς ἔθνεσιν; cf. Isa. 56.7), into a 'den of thieves' (σπήλαιον λῃστῶν, Mk. 11.17, citing Jer. 7.11).[63] In light of the testimony at Jesus' trial that he claimed he could destroy the Temple and rebuild it in three days (Mk 14.58), it is possible that the accusation against Stephen in Acts 6.14 reflects Jesus' critique of the Temple. In comparison with the account in John's Gospel, however, it becomes apparent that what Jesus said can neither be construed as a critique of the Temple, nor a prediction that he would destroy the Temple at the parousia.[64] On the contrary, the testimony at Jesus' trial is a misrepresentation of what John reports was the intention of the Temple cleansing—to present a sign of Jesus' own death and resurrection (Jn 2.19, 21).[65]

On the other hand, the testimony at Jesus' trial raises the possibility

63. Once again, the original context for the house of God as a 'den of robbers' in Jer. 7.9-11 concerns the problem of Israel's disobedience to the Law of God and their idolatry. John's Gospel reports the same essential facts, namely that Jesus commanded the Jews to stop making the 'house of my father into a house of market' (Jn 2.16: μὴ ποιεῖτε τὸν οἶκον τοῦ πατρός μου οἶκον εμπορίου).

64. Haenchen suggests (based on Mk 13.2 and parallels) that this refers to an eschatological event by which the earthly Temple is destroyed at the parousia and replaced by the heavenly one (cf. *Acts*, p. 272 n. 1); cf. also 1 En. 90.20; Rev. 21.22. Cf. further Sylva, 'The Meaning and Function of Acts 7:46-50', pp. 270-72, where he argues that Stephen's reference to the Temple as χειροποίητος and his argument that God transcends the Temple (Isa. 66.1) constitutes an answer to the charge against Jesus that he would destroy the Temple χειροποίητον and build another ἀχειροποίητον (Mk 14.58). Cf. Schneider, *Apostelgeschichte*, I, p. 467, who also endorses the idea of transcendence as the point of the passage; see further, Sylva, 'The Meaning and Function of Acts 7:46-50', p. 262 n. 4.

65. Contrast Haenchen's view that this was but one of the 'expedients' by which the Evangelists 'toned down' the concept of the Temple as χειροποίητον. See Haenchen, *Acts*, pp. 273-74.

that Jesus criticized the Temple as χειροποίητος (Mk 14.58). If he had engaged in such a critique, it would have sounded quite radical to ears accustomed to an Old Testament perspective. In the Septuagint the term χειροποίητος is used to translate אלילם.[66] Thus, according to the Old Testament context, along with later Jewish tradition, that which is by definition χειροποίητος is an εἴδωλον.[67] As such they stand under a curse (ἐπικατάρατον) along with their makers (Wis. 14.8). Therefore it would appear that by the very nature of the case it would have caused quite an offense had Jesus called the Temple in Jerusalem χειροποίητος. On the other hand, there is evidence that just such a view of the Temple existed in some circles of Judaism in the first century.[68] The Fourth Sibylline Oracle contains a rejection of the Temple as such as a 'stone set up as a temple' in contrast with the true 'house' of the 'great God', which 'was not fashioned by mortal hand':

> I am not an oracle-monger of false Phoebus, whom vain men call a god, and falsely described as a seer, but of the great God, whom no hands of men fashioned in the likeness of speechless idols of polished stone. For he does not have a house, a stone set up as a temple, dumb and toothless, a bane which brings many woes to men, but one which it is not possible to see from earth nor to measure with mortal eyes, since it was not fashioned by mortal hand (Sib. 4.4-11).[69]

66. See Lev. 26.1; Isa. 2.18; 10.11; 19.1; 31.7; 46.6; cf. also Lev. 26.30; Jdt. 8.18.

67. See Isa. 10.11; 21.9; Dan. 5.4, 23; 6.28 (LXX); Bel 5 (Θ); Sib. 3.606, 618.

68. On the date of book four of the Sibylline Oracles, see J.J. Collins, 'The Place of the Fourth Sibyl in the Development of the Jewish Sibyllina', *JJS* 25 (1974), pp. 367, 379-80. While it is true that the fall of the Temple may have stimulated this view of the Temple in Jewish circles, the tradition-history of the critique against the Temple demonstrates a long tradition, going back several centuries to the major prophets of the Old Testament. Since Isaiah could utter a similar sentiment (Isa. 66.1-2), and Jesus may also have criticized the Temple as χειροποίητος, there is no reason to exclude the possibility that Stephen's speech might have done so, along with certain elements in first-cetury Judaism. Collins himself admits (*ibid.*, p. 380), 'we cannot decisively exclude the possibility' that other Jewish groups rejected Temple worship as such in this manner before 70 CE.

69. See J.J. Collins, 'Sibylline Oracles', in *The Old Testament Pseudepigrapha* (ed. J.H. Charlesworth; Garden City, NY: Doubleday, 1983), I, p. 384. See also Heb. 8.1-5; 9.11-12, 24 on the contrast between the Temple and the true heavenly 'tent', the one not χειροποίητος; and see Acts 17.24 for a similar perspective, namely that 'the God who made the cosmos and everything in it, this one who is Lord of

As a result of this the Sibyl proclaims that those who love God will reject all temples:

> They will reject all temples when they see them; altars too, useless founda-
> tions of dumb stones (and stone statues and handmade images [ἀγάλματα
> χειροποίητα]) defiled with blood of animate creatures, and sacrifices of
> four-footed animals' (Sib. 4.27-30).[70]

It would appear in this context that any temple as such is rejected as idolatrous because it is 'made with hands' and therefore cannot be the true Temple of God.[71] This statement is similar to the charge made against Jesus in Mk. 14.58 and to Stephen's statement in Acts 7.48 but expresses a more radical rejection of all temples. In this regard it is unique in the history of tradition, but not totally without precedent, since Isa. 66.1-2 utters a comparable sentiment.[72]

In contrast to the thrust of the Fourth Sybilline Oracle, the thrust of Jesus' temple cleansing does not constitute a rejection of the Temple per se, but a rebuke against the disobedience of the Jewish leaders. That this is the case may be confirmed by comparing Jesus criticisms against them elsewhere for violating the will of God for the sake of their own traditions (cf. Mt. 15.1-9; 23.13-33; Mk 7.1-13; Lk. 11.37-48). Thus, Jesus' critique at the Temple cleansing differs from the Sibyl's view that

---

heaven and earth does not dwell in temples made with hands' (οὐκ ἐν χειροποιήτοις ναοῖς κατοικεῖ).

70. See Collins, 'Sibylline Oracles', p. 384. On this cf. Isa. 16.12, where the קְדֵשׁ of Moab is translated as χειροποίητα in LXX, presumably on the basis of its associations with idolatry; cf. also Heb. 8.1-5; 9.11-12, 24.

71. The Sibyl also contrasts the behavior of those who love God and reject all temples with the abominations of others. Cf. *Apoc. Abr.* 24–27, which claims that the Temple was destroyed due to idolatry. See M. Himmelfarb, *Ascent to Heaven in Jewish and Christian Apocalypses* (New York: Oxford University Press, 1993), pp. 61-66.

72. While there are some comparable elements in Jewish tradition, this view is quite unique. The sectarians at Qumran rejected the Temple, but on the basis of the fact that they considered it to have been defiled by their opponents. Cf. also H.-J. Schoeps, *Theologie und Geschichte des Judenchristentums* (Tübingen: Mohr–Siebeck, 1949), p. 155, who suggests that Stephen's speech bears resemblances to the teaching of the Ebionites, who rejected the sacrificial Law as such. On the other hand, Stephen's speech has nothing to do with 'eine ganze Theorie über den widergöttlichen Ursprung des Opferkults'. See also, *idem, Jewish Christianity: Factional Disputes in the Early Church* (trans. D.R.A. Hare; Philadelphia: Fortress Press, 1969), pp. 82-84; and Collins, 'Fourth Sibyl', pp. 378-79.

the Temple itself was a 'house made with hands' and therefore idolatrous. Rather, his critique primarily concerns the Jewish leaders' disobedience, and especially the fact that they had defiled the Temple by turning it into a marketplace. On this basis it is possible to understand Stephen's speech as a critique of the Jewish leaders.

To sum up, the history of tradition behind Stephen's speech supports the contention that in reality it does not primarily contain a critique of the Temple but a critique of the Jewish leaders.[73] This tradition is reflected in Amos' rebuke of the 'house of Joseph' for their disobedience and idolatry, and his pronouncement that God had rejected their worship at the Temple. It is developed by Isaiah when he questions whether anyone could build a 'house' for the Lord, and when he also rebukes the people of Judah for their disobedience. It is developed further by Jeremiah in his critique of the 'sons of Judah' for relying on the Temple for protection in the face of their refusal to open their uncircumcised ears, their stiff-necked disobedience, and their idolatrous practices. This served as the basis for Jesus' Temple cleansing, where he again rebuked those who had turned the Temple into a σπήλαιον λῃστῶν. Thus it should come as no surprise if Stephen's speech echoes these ideas. Therefore Stephen does not criticize the Temple itself, and he does not say that building the Temple was an act of idolatry.[74] Rather

---

73. Contrast Conzelmann, *Acts of the Apostles*, p. 56, where he says that 'the quotation from Isaiah. . . is a clear rejection of the temple'. While that sentiment was expressed in the first-century context by the Sibyl, and while χειροποίητος does carry this implication in the Old Testament context, Stephen does not make it explicit in his speech.

74. In light of the fact that Stephen addresses the Temple in the context of recounting the problem that the Jews themselves had continually disobeyed God and engaged in idolatry, some have suggested that he saw the Jewish leaders of his day as turning the Temple into a virtual idol, like the 'ancestors' had done in the days of Jeremiah. See Lake and Cadbury, *Beginnings*, IV, p. 89, who suggest 'the meaning is that in attributing permanent sanctity to the Temple the Jews were verging on idolatry'. See also E.F. Harrison, *Acts: The Expanding Church* (Chicago: Moody Press, 1975), p. 124, where he says that Stephen may have intended to point out that 'by magnifying the Temple and its cultus, the Jewish nation in his time had made the Temple almost an end in itself and were glorifying in it rather than in the God for whose sake it was constructed'. See also J.P.M. Sweet, 'A House not Made with Hands', in *Templum Amicitiae: Essays on the Second Temple Presented to Ernst Bammel* (JSNTSup, 48; ed. W. Horbury; Sheffield: JSOT Press, 1991), pp. 386-90; Kilgallen, *The Stephen Speech*, p. 94; and Polhill, *Acts*, pp. 202-204. This does

he criticizes the Jewish leaders for being 'stiff-necked' and 'uncircumcised in heart and ears' (Acts 7.51) and for manifesting that disobedience most clearly by rejecting the 'Righteous One'.[75]

Stephen's Concluding Rebuke

Stephen concludes his speech by tying together the themes of the
rejection of the prophets and their vindication by God, as well as the
continual problem of the Israelites' disobedience to God, which relate
integrally to the content of the whole.[76] The conclusion refers to the
recurring pattern of disobedience on the part of the 'ancestors' in
Israelite history and relates that pattern to opposing the Holy Spirit and
rejecting God's messengers, the prophets. The conclusion makes explicit the implicit comparison between the ancestor's rejection of Joseph
and Moses as God's messengers and the Jewish leaders' rejection of
Jesus.[77] It also accuses Stephen's Jewish opponents of the same kind of
disobedience to the Law that characterized the wilderness generation.

The critique of the Israelite people for the destruction of Jerusalem in
2 Chron. 36.15-21 has a similar function for the book of 2 Chronicles.
Like the conclusion of Stephen's speech, 2 Chron. 36.13-6 summarizes
the Israelites' rejection of God, leading up to the Babylonian exile, in
terms of being 'stiff-necked' and 'hardening the heart', 'mocking' and
'scoffing' his 'messengers' and 'despising' God's words. The Chronicler's rebuke makes more specific the 'people' who rejected God by
adding the reference to 'all the officials of the priests' (2 Chron. 36.14).
This conclusion to the book of 2 Chronicles serves to drive home the
rebuke against the people and especially their leaders for continually

not seem very likely in view of the primary thrust of Stephen's speech and in light of
the traditio-historical background of prophetic Temple critiques.

75. See L. Goppelt, *Theology of the New Testament* (ed. J. Roloff; trans. R.A.
Guelich; Grand Rapids: Eerdmans, 1982), II, p. 283, where he says that by this act
the Jews 'sealed their opposition to God'.

76. Contrast Haenchen's statement that 'The swift passage to the string of charges
in verses 51-53 which goad the audience into fury can only be explained if the preceding verses form a radical denunciation of the Temple worship'. See Haenchen,
Acts, p. 286. This ignores the possibility that the content of the charges against the
Jewish leaders is precisely the theme of Stephen's speech.

77. Contrast Barrett, 'Submerged Christology', p. 243, where he complains that
Stephen's speech does not draw out the christological analogy in comparison with
Joseph and Moses.

rejecting God's messengers and disobeying God. The conclusion to Stephen's speech serves a similar function.

Conclusion

In contrast to the common interpretation, which insists that Stephen represented a 'theology' of a critique against the Temple that was radically different from the views of the Jerusalem Apostles, the traditio-historical background points to the view that Stephen's speech constitutes a defense against his opponents' charges. In the first place, it contains an implicit claim to God's vindication by the χάρις and σοφία which Stephen had displayed in the context of his debates with the Jews, just as God had vindicated Joseph by giving him χάρις before Pharaoh. In the second place, Stephen's defense consists of a counter-accusation that his accusers were the ones who killed the 'Righteous One', citing Moses in his speech as the example *par excellence* of the fact that the 'ancestors' had persecuted and rejected the prophets. God's vindication of Moses as the λυτρώτης for the people of Israel implies his vindication of Jesus in that role as well. In the third place, Stephen's defense constitutes a rebuke against his accusers for being 'stiff-necked' and 'uncircumcised in heart and ears' just like the 'ancestors' who disobeyed God during the wilderness wanderings, in spite of the fact that they had the 'tent of witness' with them during the whole time. Thus Stephen's speech constitutes a critique of the Jewish leaders for rejecting those whom God had vindicated, including Joseph, Moses, Jesus, and Stephen.

Acts 7.2-53 compared with Summaries of Israelite History

#	Event	Acts	Neh.	Josh.	Ps. 78	Ps. 105/106	Ezek.	Wis.	Sir.	Jdt.
1.	God calls Abraham from Ur of the Chaldees	Acts 7.2-4	Neh. 9.7	Josh. 24.3				[Wis. 10.5]		Jdt. 5.6-9
2.	Covenant/Promise to Abraham	Acts 7.5, 8	Neh. 9.8	Josh. 24.3		Ps. 105.9, 11			Sir. 44.20-21	
3.	God shows his favor to Joseph in Egypt	Acts 7.9-10				Ps. 105.16-22		Wis. 10.13-14		
4.	God sends Jacob's descendents to Egypt	Acts 7.14-15		Josh. 24.4		Ps. 105.23-24				Jdt. 5.10
5.	God sees Israel's distress in Egypt, hears their cry	Acts 7.34	Neh. 9.9							
6.	God sends Moses and afflicts Egypt with plagues	Acts 7.38	Neh. 9.13	Josh. 24.5	Ps. 78.44-51	Ps. 105.26-36		Wis. 10.16, 11.5-17; 18.5, 13; 19.1	Sir. 45.3	Jdt. 5.12
7.	God delivers Israel at the Red Sea by signs and wonders	Acts 7.34, 36	Neh. 9.9-11	Josh. 24.6-7	Ps. 78.11-13, 43, 53	Ps. 106.9-11	Ezek. 20.10	Wis. 10.18-19; 19.7		Jdt. 5.13
8.	God speaks to Israel at Sinai, giving his commands	Acts 7.38	Neh. 9.13				Ezek. 20.11-12		Sir. 45.3, 5	
9.	Israel makes a golden calf	Acts 7.40-41	Neh. 9.18			Ps. 106.19-22	Ezek. 20.8			
10.	God cares for Israel in the wilderness	Acts 7.36	Neh. 9.12-15, 19-21	[Josh. 24.7]	Ps. 78.14-16, 24-29, 52	Ps. 105.39-41		Wis. 11.2-4; 16.2, 20-21; 18.3		Jdt. 5.14
11.	Israel rebels against God in wilderness	Acts 7.39, 42-43	Neh. 9.16-17		[Ps. 78.8, 17-18, 32, 40-41]	Ps. 106.[7], 14-18, 24-25, 28-29, 32	Ezek. 20.8, 13, 21			
12.	God punishes the wilderness	[Acts 7.42]				Ps. 106.26-27	Ezek. 20.15-16, 23-24	[Wis. 11.9-10; 12.20-22; 16.5-6; 18.20]		

#	Description	Acts	Neh.	Josh.	Ps.	Ps.	Ezek.	Sir.	Jdt.
13.	God gives Israel the kingdoms of the Amorites		Neh. 9.22	Josh. 24.8-10		Ps. 105.44			Jdt. 5.15
14.	God gives Israel the rich land of Canaan through the conquest		Neh. 9.23-25 24.11-13	Josh.	Ps. 78.55	Ps. 105.44	Ezek. 20.6, 28	Sir. 46.1-6	Jdt. 5.15-16
15.	Isrel disobeys God repeatedly	Acts 7.51	Neh. 9.26-29, 33-34		Ps. 78.56-57	Ps. 106.43		[Sir. 48.15-16]	[Jdt. 5.18]
16.	God delivers Israel to their enemies		Neh. 9.27-28		Ps. 78.61-64	Ps. 106.40-42		[Sir. 49.5-7]	[Jdt. 5.18]
17.	God sends 'saviors' to deliver Israel		Neh. 9.27-28		[Ps. 78.66]	Ps. 106.43			
18.	Israel turns to other gods	Acts 7.42-43			Ps. 78.58	Ps. 106.34-39			
19.	God sends prophets to rebuke Israel, whom they killed	Acts 7.51-52	Neh. 9.26, 30				Ezek. 20.28-31	Sir. 48.1-14	
20.	God continually shows mercy and grace to Israel		Neh. 9.31	Josh. 24	Ps. 78.38-39	Ps. 106.44-46	Ezek. 20.8-9, 13-14, 17, 21-22	Sir. 47.22, 48.20	
21.	God choses David to lead his people	Acts 7.45-46			Ps. 78.70-72			Sir. 47.2, 11	
22.	God establishes his dwelling in Jerusalem through Solomon	Acts 7.47			Ps. 78.69			Sir. 47.13	
23.	Israel/Israel's leaders disobey God	Acts 7.53	Neh. 9.34					Sir. 47.23-25; 49.4	

PAUL AND HIS STORY:
EXODUS AND TRADITION IN GALATIANS*

Sylvia C. Keesmaat

Introduction

The relation of Paul to his story and tradition has become the topic of
much debate in biblical studies today. This article enters that discussion by way of a study of Paul's use of Scripture in Galatians. The exegesis is then situated in the larger context of Paul's relation to his
tradition and some conclusions are drawn regarding the dynamic between Paul and his Scripture. The way in which Paul's use of the scriptural story speaks to contemporary theological concerns will also be
briefly addressed.

Exodus and Tradition in Galatians

If the central issue for the book of Romans is the question of God's
faithfulness to Israel,[1] it could perhaps be said that the central issue of
Galatians is the question of *how* God is faithful to Israel. *How* does God
fulfill the promises made to Abraham? How does God grant the inheritance? In the words of Galatians, does God grant the inheritance
through the law or through the promise (Gal. 3.18)? Perhaps another
angle on that question concerns how the people of God actually inherit
those promises. Again, did the Galatians receive the Spirit through the
works of the law or by the hearing of faith (3.2)? The issue fundamentally concerns the identity of God, that is, how is this God faithful?
Moreover, this is closely connected to the fundamental issues surrounding the identity of the people of this God, that is, how are the people of this God to be faithful?

---

*   A shorter version of this article appeared in *HBT* 18 (1996): 133-68.
    1.   On the faithfulness of God as the central concern of Romans see Hays 1989a;
Elliott 1990; Wright 1991: 234-35.

As a way into these questions, this paper will discuss a few of the places in Galatians where Paul seems to be alluding to or echoing the exodus tradition.[2] The nature of Paul's use of exodus imagery in Gal. 4.1-7 has recently been argued convincingly by James Scott.[3] Although I believe Scott's case could be strengthened, rather than focus primarily on 4.1-7, I wish to explore how the exodus tradition is echoed elsewhere in chs. 4–6.

A number of recent commentators on Galatians have refocused the scholarly discussion of Galatians dramatically. The consensus that has dominated the study of Galatians for so many years, that is, that the primary focus of Galatians is Paul's discussion of the law and justification by faith, is now being challenged. There is good reason for this. The traditional argument has led to a neglect of the first two chapters of the book, as well as a devaluing of the last two chapters, which were seen as paranetic material not immediately connected to the theological argument of the book.[4] Galatian scholarship has now begun to focus on a number of themes which are found throughout the book. J. Louis Martyn has focused on the apocalyptic nature of the work, with its emphasis on revelation and the contrast between human effort and the invasive action of God.[5] Beverly Roberts Gaventa has explored the issue of Christology and the new creation inaugurated in Jesus Christ as being central to the discussion in Galatians.[6] Similarly, Richard B. Hays has emphasized the importance of the cross in Galatians, and the resultant cruciform character of the community which lives in union with a crucified Messiah.[7]

All of these discussions attempt to understand Galatians in the light of the whole letter, start to finish, and they result in readings of Galatians that are far more integrated than those concerned primarily with the issue of justification by faith.

2.   The methodological framework for this undertaking is informed by the concept of intertextuality, a term used by literary theorists in its broadest sense to designate the structural relations between two or more texts. The most explicit of intertextual relations is quotation; the most implicit is allusion (an intentional reference to a previous text), or echo (an unintentional reference to a previous text). See Morgan 1985: 5; Hays 1989a; Keesmaat 1994a: 31-35; Keesmaat 1994b: 48-54.

3.   Scott 1992: 121-86.

4.   See Gaventa 1991: 148; Barclay 1991: 1-35.

5.   Martyn 1985a, 1991.

6.   Gaventa 1991.

7.   Hays 1991a: esp. p. 242; Hays 1987.

The past concentration on justification by faith has also affected the themes that predominate in Galatian studies. For instance, studies on Abraham or the law are myriad, whereas discussions of what the 'promise' might be, or of the inheritance language are somewhat more rare.[8] A number of other threads have yet to be explored in this letter, such as those related to the exodus tradition. I do not wish to argue that these exodus themes are as central to Paul's concern in this letter as is his contrast between this age and the new creation, or his emphasis on the cross of Christ. However, the exodus motif, as it is used in this letter, contributes to these larger themes in a number of ways; a perusal of this motif might be helpful for a deeper understanding of the letter as a whole.

Slavery and Sonship

Throughout the letter to the Galatians Paul sets up a number of antitheses, or antinomies, as Martyn has put it, which characterize the life in Christ as opposed to the life of the cosmos.[9] One such antithesis is the contrast between being slaves and being sons. This particular antithesis is heavily concentrated in ch. 4. The terminology concerning the Galatians' status as sons and as slaves also occurs throughout the letter in isolation from one another. In addition, the language of slavery functions as part of another antithesis which is found even more extensively in the letter—that of slavery and freedom. References to slavery and freedom and/or sonship are found in Gal. 1.10; 1.15-16; 2.4; 2.20; 3.7; 3.16; 3.19; 3.26; 3.28-29; 4.1; 4.4-9; 4.19; 4.22-26; 4.28; 4.30-31; 5.1; 5.13. As even a quick look at these passages indicates, the issues of who are sons rather than slaves, and if sons, whose sons—sons of freedom or sons of slavery—are evident in much of this letter. I shall first explore the possible background for Paul's use of these images, and then discuss how such images function within the larger argument of the letter to the Galatians.

Scott argues that Paul's language surrounding slavery and sons in 4.1-7 is rooted in the exodus. Part of his reason for thinking this is the vocabulary that forms the context for these terms. Since νήπιος, ἐπιτρόπους, οἰκονόμους and προθεσμίας can all plausibly be rooted

---

8. On the last two see Williams 1988; Hester 1967.

9. This way of framing the antithesis is from Gaventa 1991: 149. On the precise use of 'cosmos' here, see n. 25 below.

in Israel's time of bondage in Egypt and the exodus, it is likely that the language of slavery in these verses refers to the same events. Moreover, Scott notes that the language of sonship was associated with God's restoration of the people in a number of new exodus contexts in Jewish tradition.

There are, however, other indications in this letter which also suggest that the exodus motif informs this imagery. This is evident first of all in the narrative sequence of Paul's argument in 3.23-26 and 4.1-7. Paul outlines a trajectory here that begins with imprisonment and slavery and which ends in sonship—no longer are believers subject to the law, they are sons of God (3.25, 26); believers have been redeemed from the law and have received sonship (4.5).[10] The pattern of redemption from slavery and bondage to become sons of God is found in the exodus event and called upon as the paradigm for the new exodus event in much of Jewish literature.[11] Paul's description of the Galatians' story has the same narrative flow as the story of the exodus.[12] Hence Paul not only echoes the basic motifs of the exodus; he also tells the story of God's salvation of the Galatians in such a way that the exodus of Israel becomes paradigmatic for their redemption in Christ.

Such a narrative background is suggested by the two verses in which Paul warns the Galatians against becoming enslaved again (4.9 and 5.1). These verses seem to refer to the kind of desire in the Galatian

10. According to Longenecker (1990: 145) the feature of constraint is prominent in these verses (3.19-25), especially in Paul's use of συγκλείω. Lull (1986) argues that 'Paul's portrayal of pedagogue implies that the function of law was to *curb* or *prevent* transgressions until the period of bondage to sin came to an end' (p. 489) and that the 'metaphor would also identify the experience of those "under the law" as no different from that of slaves, for as their pedagogue the law would be master over them, keeping them in their custody as long as they were in bondage to sin' (p. 495). Further on 3.23-26 as a portrayal of constraint, see Thielman 1989: 74; Young 1987: 171-73; Gordon 1989: 153-54; Betz 1979: 176; Howard 1990: 61; cf. Biaswell 1991; Belleville 1986: 69; E.P. Sanders 1985: 68-69; Räisänen 1986: 21.

11. See Exod. 4.22; Deut. 32.6, 7, 20, 43 (cf. vv. 10 and 11); Isa. 43.5-7; Jer. 31 (38 LXX).8-9, 20; Hos. 11.1, 10-11; Wis. 12.6, 21; 14.3; 16.10, 26; 18.4, 13; 19.6; Sir. 36.14; *Pss. Sol.* 17.27; cf. Isa. 63.16; Deut. 32.6, 7, 18 where God as father to Israel is emphasized in an Exodus context. Cf. also Hos. 2.1; *Jub.* 1.24, 25; *Sib. Or.* 3.702; *T. Mos.* 10.3. See also Keesmaat 1994b: 65-74; cf. de la Potterie 1976: 225-26.

12. My terminology here is from Stockhausen (1993: 146-54), whose very provocative article shows how Paul uses the Abraham narrative as paradigmatic for the story in Galatians.

community that Israel experienced in the exodus where they became afraid during the wilderness wandering and petitioned Moses to return them to bondage in Egypt.[13] Paul cannot fathom that the Galatian believers would want to be once again enslaved to the 'weak and beggarly elements'. That Paul's thoughts are possibly moving within an exodus context here is also suggested by the echo of 4.3 in 4.9. In 4.3, Paul states that 'we were enslaved (δεδουλωμένοι) to the elements of the cosmos (τὰ στοιχεῖα τοῦ κόσμου)'. As Scott has ably argued, this slavery parallels the slavery of Israel in Egypt of vv. 1-2.[14] In 4.9, Paul asks the Galatians if they again want to be enslaved (δουλεύειν) to these elements (στοιχεῖα). In framing his question this way those hearing this letter are compared to the grumbling Israelites in the desert who wished to return to Egypt; their actions are compared to those of Israel which were deemed to be disobedient. In fact, in the exodus narrative, those who participated in such grumbling were not permitted to receive the inheritance, they did not enter the promised land. Paul's reference to those who will not receive the inheritance in 5.21 would seem to indicate that he has this part of the narrative in mind as well.

The call not to return to bondage is reiterated again by Paul in 5.1, where he writes: 'For freedom Christ has set you free; stand therefore and do not again submit to the yoke of slavery (ζυγῷ δουλείας)'. Not only does Paul urge the Galatians not to return to their former slavery, he does so in language that specifically echoes the tradition about the exodus. For instance Lev. 26.13 reads: 'I am the Lord your God who led (ἐξαγαγὼν) you out of the land of Egypt where you were enslaved (δούλων) and have broken the bars of your yoke (ζυγοῦ)'. The deuteronomic tone of this passage is evident as it continues to outline the blessings and curses that are attendant upon obedience and disobedience to God's commandments.[15]

The language of a yoke figures prominently in Israel's Scriptures in passages that envisage a future deliverance for the people of God, and the breaking of their yoke in such a deliverance. There are a number of other texts that also envisage redemption in terms of the yoke being lifted from the people of Israel. Isa. 9.3 contains such a vision, as do Isa. 10.24-27; 14.5 (referring to the overthrow of Babylon); Isa. 14.25

---

13. So also Bligh (1969: 417): a 'Christian going back to the law is like a follower of Moses going back to slavery'.

14. Scott 1992: 155-57.

15. I explore these themes further in Keesmaat 1994b: 274-86.

(with reference to Assyria); Jer. 37(30).8; and Ezek. 34.27.[16] Two of these passages are noteworthy here.

Ezek. 34.27 particularly links the language of God breaking the yoke and freeing the people from those who enslaved them: 'And they shall know that I am the Lord when I break the bars of their yoke (ζυγὸν) and lead them out from the hand of those who enslave them (καταδουλωσαμένων)'. It is in such a freeing that the people would know that their God is the Lord; this is how the power of their God would be made known to them. Such language of knowing God is used by Paul in Gal. 4.9, the other passage that asks the Galatians why they want to submit again to slavery, now that they know God, or rather are known by him. Moreover, this freeing from the yoke of slavery in Ezek. 34.27 occurs in the larger context of Israel being established in the land safely and securely, in plenty and fruitfulness, ἐν ἐλπίδι εἰρήνης. Israel's yoke is broken only in the context of a creation-wide covenant of peace in which showers come in their seasons, the trees yield their fruit and the earth is bountiful. If, as I am suggesting, Ezek. 34.23-31 contributed to the intertextual matrix on which Paul was drawing, then his emphasis on a new creation at the end of Galatians would be natural; if his thoughts were moving in the context of God's new restoration in the land, then a reference to a new creation would allude to that restoration.[17] As we shall see below, in the light of Paul's emphasis on inheritance in this letter, such an allusion seems likely.

Also of note is Isa. 10.24-27, where God promises to remove the yoke of Assyria from the shoulders of the people and deliver the people in ways that specifically echo the exodus event. The passage also calls Israel to 'be not afraid' (μὴ φοβοῦ), language that is rooted in the intertextual matrix of the exodus, specifically those texts where Israel wanted to go back into slavery.[18] If Paul's call to the Galatians not to submit again to the yoke of slavery echoes this passage in Isaiah (and this seems likely), then it is plausible that the 'fear not' motif may also have been evoked, recalling the whole matrix in which Israel desired to return to slavery. If so, then Paul is in effect comparing the Galatian believers'

16. In the MT, Jer. 30.8 is immediately followed by a new exodus event which includes a call to be not afraid, which, as we shall see below, is central to the exodus tradition. The LXX, however, does not situate these verses in this chapter.

17. On Ezekiel 34 as an intertext of Rom. 8.14-25 see Keesmaat 1994b: 140-41.

18. See Exod. 14.10-12; Num. 14.9; Deut. 1.19-46; cf. Psalm 26 (27); Isa. 41.8-16; 43.1-7; 44.1-5. Also Keesmaat 1994b: 77-86.

desire to be circumcised to the Israelites' desire to return to Egypt. In wanting to 'go back' the Galatians are withdrawing from God's new exodus, God's new act of salvation, enacted through the Son which God sent, the new Moses.[19]

It should be noted that 'yoke' language had also been used to refer to the law throughout Israel's history.[20] When used in such a way, of course, this yoke was perceived to be a joy and delight. In these verses, Paul is specifically telling the Galatians not to submit to a yoke of slavery. In the context of the letter, that yoke of slavery is the law. Not only is Paul evoking a new exodus motif here, he is also subverting a common way of describing the law. The yoke of the law is no longer a delight; it is a yoke of slavery.

The story Paul tells in chs. 4 and 5, therefore, could be read as outlining a movement from slavery to sonship, with the temptation to go back into slavery. God has made God's self known to them in this new liberating event, as God did so long ago in the first liberating event. Such a revelation, especially when linked with the desire to return to slavery, parallels the exodus narrative. As such it provides a comparison which calls the Galatians to recognize their God and continue to participate in this new exodus event, lest they be judged not worthy of the inheritance. To the language of inheritance we now turn.

Promise and Inheritance

The language of inheritance was fraught with connotation for first-century Jews. The inheritance of the land was the goal of the original exodus event (Exod. 3.7-8), and a return to the inheritance of the land was envisioned by the prophets and by intertestamental writers (for example, Ezek. 36.8-12; Sir. 36.10). Moreover, the tradition had widened that inheritance in the intertestamental period so that it applied to

19. In the intertestamental period the connection of the yoke and slavery was still understood to refer to Israel's condition under foreign rule. So, for instance, in 1 Maccabees, Judas Maccabaeus sends delegates to Rome to make a treaty with the Romans, καὶ τοῦ ἆραι τὸν ζυγὸν ἀπ' αὐτῶν, ὅτι εἶδον τὴν βασιλείαν τῶν Ἑλλήνων καταδουλουμένους τὸν Ισραελ δουλείᾳ (1 Macc. 8.18). See also 1 Macc. 8.31; 13.41. On a possible Moses background for Paul's imagery concerning the sending of Jesus see Scott 1992: 165-79.

20. See Dunn 1993: 263; Bruce 1982: 226; J.A. Sanders 1977: 92-94. This may also be the referent for Jesus' words in Mt. 11.29-30: 'Take my yoke (ζυγόν) upon you. . . for my yoke (ζυγός) is easy and my burden is light'.

the whole world. This is evident particularly in the book of *Jubilees* where Abraham's blessing on Jacob reveals the hope that Jacob might receive the whole earth (Jub. 22.14-15), a hope which is answered by Yahweh's promise to Jacob that his descendants will inherit all the earth (*Jub.* 32.19). This promise is also found in *1 En.* 5.7. In Romans 8 these overtones are present in Paul's discussion in 8.18-23, where he emphasized the importance of the children of God for the freeing of the creation. And, of course, Rom. 4.13 also makes clear that this inheritance is the whole world.

Such overtones are present in Galatians as well. Scott points out that the phrase κύριος πάντων (4.1) has overtones of universal sovereignty, and that in the context of 4.1, 2 this phrase is applied to Israel, the heir who was in slavery. The Galatian believers are then portrayed also as those who were in slavery but have now become sons and, more than that, heirs. In 4.1 the one who is κύριος πάντων is expressly said to be the one who is the κληρονόμος. The term κληρονόμος is then explicitly repeated in v. 7. In light of v. 1, it seems quite likely that the heir referred to in v. 7 also has the status of κύριος πάντων. That is to say, the Galatian believers are now the heirs, the ones who as lord of all are to inherit the whole of creation.[21]

The language of inheritance is not limited to 4.1-7, however. Language of both promise and inheritance underlies the discussion in chs. 3–5, specifically in 3.14; 3.16-18; 3.19; 3.21; 3.22; 3.29; 4.1; 4.7; 4.23; 4.28; 4.30 and 5.21. The conjunction of promise/inheritance language in these verses is notable, if only because the two occur three times as the *culmination* of the particular point that Paul is making. So in 3.18 Paul's argument concerning law and promise is summarized in his assertion that the *inheritance* is not from the law, but from the promise, the promise to Abraham. Similarly in 3.29 the chapter-long discussion of who precisely is the son of Abraham culminates in the point that those who are in Christ are Abraham's seed and *heirs* according to the promise. Again in 4.28-30 Paul brings his 'allegory' to a close by emphasizing that the Galatian believers are children of the promise and hence should cast out the slave woman and her son, for the son of the slave woman will not *inherit* with the son of the free woman.

21. So also Williams (1988: 718-19) who lists the following scriptural and intertestamental passages: LXX Ps. 36.9, 11, 22, 29, 34; *Jub.* 22.14-15; 17.3; 22.29-30; 32.18-19; *1 En.* 5.6-7; Sir. 44.21; *4 Ezra* 6.55-59; cf. Mt. 5.5.

In each of these instances the discussion concludes with a reference to the issue that is really at stake: who becomes the recipient of the promise? Who receives the inheritance? The two are so closely linked that one could easily describe the promise as the promise of inheritance.[22] In addition, the reference to Abraham would surely have evoked the actual story in Genesis where God promised the land to Abraham.[23] This promise, moreover, had been interpreted in the tradition to refer to the whole earth. That Paul's thoughts moved within such a tradition is indicated by Rom. 4.13, where Paul interprets the promise to Abraham and his seed in terms of an inheritance, and that inheritance is of the world.[24]

This theme of inheritance, which characterizes what it is to participate with Jesus Christ, the Son, is brought together with another aspect of participation with Jesus at the end of the letter. There Paul emphasizes his participation in the cross of Christ: 'May I never boast about anything except the cross of our Lord Jesus Christ, through whom the cosmos has been crucified to me, and I to the cosmos' (6.14). This is immediately followed by the assertion that neither circumcision nor uncircumcision counts, but a new creation (6.15). Given the close connection between participation in the Son and receiving the inheritance throughout the letter, this linking of participation in the crucified Christ and the new creation reinforces the suggestion that the inheritance is precisely this new creation. In the light of Rom. 4.13, this seems highly probable. In addition, much new creation language occurs in Israelite tradition in the context of a new exodus event. Paul's use of καινὴ κτίσις in 6.15, therefore, could be a soft echo of this tradition, which increases in volume in conjunction with the exodus imagery in 4.1-7.

Within the exodus narrative, the plot culminates with the gaining of the inheritance, the entry into the land. Paul's telling of the Galatian story as such a narrative, from slavery to sonship (3.26–4.7), to the

---

22. Cf. Williams 1988: 71.

23. Gen. 12.7; 13.14-17; 15.7-21; 17.1-8; 24.7; cf. Gen. 26.2-5; 28.1-4, 13-15; 35.9-12; 48.4; 50.24-25. Westermann (1980: 129) notes that 'the most frequent promise in Genesis 12–50 is that of increase; only slightly less frequent is the promise of the land'.

24. Longenecker (1990: 134) has little basis for his assertion that 'The territorial and material features of the Abrahamic inheritance are not mentioned here by Paul, for in Christian thought "inheritance" had become thoroughly spiritualized (cf. 5.21; also Acts 2.32; 1 Cor. 6.9-10; Eph. 5.5; Col. 3.28) and Paul's opponents would undoubtedly have thought along such lines as well'.

desire to return to slavery (4.8–5.1) and the resultant threat of disinheritance (5.21) should rightly end, if they are not enslaved again, with the inheritance itself—the new creation (6.15). The story of a new exodus is complete in Galatians.

Slavery and Freedom

It is clear as early as Gal. 2.4 that Paul situates the specific conflict in the Galatian congregation over circumcision in a wider framework. The issue has larger overtones for Paul. Beverly Gaventa argues that at the widest level those overtones have to do with the new creation in the crucified Christ in antithesis with the cosmos.[25] This is undoubtedly so. However, before that widest level of Christ versus cosmos, Paul sets up another antithesis; he situates the specific Galatian controversy in the wider context of the antithesis of slavery and freedom. His use of 'freedom' and 'slavery' language in 2.4 already links certain 'false brethren' with those who are opposed to freedom, those who wish to enslave. As the letter progresses, Paul continues to use the language of slavery in contrast to those who are sons. I have discussed the importance of this language above. But then in 4.21-31 Paul returns to the slavery/freedom antithesis. Chapters 2 and 3 have set up a contrast that informs the slavery/freedom contrast of ch. 4. On one side is slavery. On the other is freedom = sons.

On the face of it, it would not seem that Paul's use of the Hagar/Sarah allegory to illustrate the contrast between slavery and freedom would have any exodus overtones. It appeals to earlier scriptural tradition, to the Abraham story, to the interplay between the son who was a slave, and born according to the flesh, and the one who was free and born according to the promise. However, Paul does not merely allude to the Hagar/Sarah story here; he identifies Hagar with Mount Sinai, a Mount Sinai which bears children into slavery (δουλείον), a Mount Sinai which corresponds to the present Jerusalem, which is enslaved (δουλεύει; 4.24, 25). Paul's identification here is an offensive one;[26]

---

25. Gaventa 1991: 149. 'Cosmos' here is taken to refer not to the created order as such but to the 'old age' as opposed to the new age or new creation which has been inaugurated in Christ.

26. The adjective here is taken from Meyer (1986: 140-41): 'the most original and offensive feature of Paul's entire retrieval of the history of sin and salvation was this positioning of the law in the line of Adamic impact'; or perhaps I should say, in the

the correspondence of Mt Sinai, and therefore the giving of the law, with slavery completely reverses the story. According to the exodus tradition, the law was part of the event that freed Israel from slavery. In fact, the law was a sign of freedom, the law was the way in which the Israelites could show that they were a people of freedom, the way that they themselves could image the God who had brought them out of slavery and set them free. Paul begins by retelling a part of the story that no first-century Jew would contest, that Isaac is the child of promise and that the sons of the slave woman do not have an inheritance. But he uses that particular part of the story to completely subvert a later event, the giving of the law. In Paul's telling, the giving of the law at Sinai is identified with slavery rather than with freedom. The story of Israel is reinterpreted in a way which totally undermines one of the central features of the exodus event itself.

This subversion becomes all the more striking when Paul ends this section with the appeal not to go back again to the yoke of slavery (5.1). As I have indicated above, this verse has a number of echoes with the exodus tradition, especially those parts of the narrative where Israel expressed a desire to return to Egypt. Paul seems to be making the same sort of appeal to the Galatians here. So in a small number of verses Paul appears to subvert a central aspect of the exodus tradition, the giving of the law, and yet does so precisely by appealing to the exodus tradition as a model for the Galatians' behaviour.

It should be noted that Paul's language of freedom throughout Galatians echoes the language of the Septuagint,[27] where such terminology is closely associated with that of slavery, especially freedom from slavery.[28] In addition, in the intertestamental period this language seems to have gained overtones connected to the freedom of Jerusalem and the Israelites to worship their God.[29] Especially of note in light of Gal. 4.25 is 1 Macc. 2.11 where Mattathias mourns over Jerusalem using these words: πᾶς ὁ κόσμος αὐτῆς ἀφῃρέθη, ἀντὶ ἐλευθέρας

---

light of these verses, 'his positioning of the law in the line of Hagar-like enslavement'.

27. Of the 37 occurrences of ἐλευθερία, ἐλεύθερος and ἐλευθεροῦν in the Septuagint, 18 are connected with slavery. In addition, 7 do not use the slavery term but are related to political freedom and liberation of the city or its inhabitants.

28. See Exod. 21.2, 5, 26, 27; Lev. 19.20; Deut. 14.12, 13, 18; 21.14; Sir. 7.21; 10.25; 30.34 (33.26); Jer. 41(34).9, 14, 16; 1 Macc. 10.33; 2 Macc. 1.27; *3 Macc.* 7.20.

29. See especially: 1 Macc. 2.11; 10.33; 14.27; 15.7; 2 Macc. 1.27; 2.22; 9.14; *3 Macc.* 7.20.

ἐγένετο εἰς δούλην. We have here another instance of Jerusalem regarded as being in slavery. Also of note is the cosmic language used in this verse. Mattathias states 'her whole world (πᾶς ὁ κόσμος) has been taken away'; the captivity of Jerusalem is comparable to the captivity of the whole of the cosmos for first-century Jews.[30] In such a situation of slavery, deliverance was envisaged in terms reminiscent of the exodus. Moreover, where the slavery of Jerusalem is of cosmic import, the redemption of the people is spoken of as a creation wide renewal.

This is a very brief indication of the way in which exodus motifs and the exodus story undergird and underlie much of the letter to the Galatians. The question is, of course, so what? What significance do these themes have for the letter to the Galatians? Do they contribute to the function of the letter, to the 'aural event, as it was intended and actively anticipated by Paul'?[31] When the Galatian believers heard this letter, did Paul's evocation of exodus themes and traditions have any affect on their hearing? Would such themes have enabled them to discern who they were and what that entailed?

I suggest that Paul's exodus language and imagery contributed very strongly to the aural event which Paul anticipated in this community by both subverting and retelling the story that the Galatian believers had inherited. I am assuming here that the Galatians inherited a telling of the exodus tradition. Their desire to be circumcised indicates that the Abraham story had been told to them and it is not only plausible but highly likely that the exodus narrative—as that which explains the giving of the law—had also been related to them. Paul's language seems to simply assume that they have heard this story. But Paul subverts the traditions surrounding the law as he retells the story. Herein is his radical innovation. Yet he also grounds the Galatians in the tradition by telling the story of the Galatians in terms of slavery and sonship and inheritance. Herein is Paul's fidelity to the tradition. What implications would this innovation and fidelity have had for the Galatian context?

The Galatian Context

The degree to which Paul's opponents and the social situation of Galatians has been discussed in scholarly literature indicates how elusive

30. Cf. Pss. 48, 122, 125 with regard to Jerusalem's centrality in the world.
31. Martyn 1991: 161 (emphasis removed).

the Galatian situation actually is.[32] H.D. Betz, in his 1979 commentary, suggests that the Galatian congregation consisted of both legalists and libertines. The former were insisting that the Galatian community be circumcised (5.2-12; 6.12-15); while the latter were allowing their new freedom in the Spirit to result in gratifying the desires of the flesh (5.13-21). Both tendencies were rooted, according to Betz, in a moral confusion about what is the proper way to behave as Christians.[33] Some found certainty in the midst of their confusion by adhering to the law, especially when faced with the excesses of the libertines. The law was something that brought certainty that they were doing all that was necessary to live rightly before God.[34]

Although the above scenario is certainly plausible, it does not attend to everything that Paul indicates about the Galatian situation, particularly his language addressing the problem of community conflict and dissension. As both Hays and Barclay have argued, Paul seems to be concerned with disunity and conflict in the Galatian church. His list of deeds of the flesh is heavily weighted with attitudes and actions that cause dissension:[35] ἔχθραι, ἔρις, ζῆλος, θυμοί, ἐριθεῖαι, διχοστασίαι, αἱρέσεις, φθόνοι... (Gal. 5.20-21). In addition, Hays points out that this list and the list of the fruit of the Spirit that follows it are 'bracketed by clear directives against conflict in the church' (5.13-15 and 5.25-6.5).[36] The Galatian community seems to be characterized by backbiting, provoking and discord occasioned by the desire of some to be circumcised and follow the law. This dissension seems to be rooted in controversy over obedience to the law. Perhaps that is why Paul contrasts their disruptive behaviour with a call to a different law, the law of Christ (6.2).

How might this disagreement over the law have resulted in such animosity in this community? In the first place, it should be noted that within the Israelite story law is closely connected to the inheritance, particularly the inheritance of the land. If one is obedient to the promises, one will be blessed in the land. Moreover, there is evidence that in first-century Judaism a number of groups considered themselves to be in exile, in slavery in their own land (that is, Judas Maccabaeus in

32. Representative works are Brinsmead 1982; Martyn 1987–88, 1985b.
33. Betz 1979: 8-9.
34. Betz 1979: 9; Gaventa 1991: 159.
35. Barclay 1991: 153; Hays 1987: 286.
36. Hays 1987: 286.

1 Macc. 8.18). In such a situation a new exodus was expected, a return of Yahweh to Israel in which God's people would be freed from the foreigners who ruled over them. One way to ensure that this new exodus would take place was by maintaining obedience to the law. It has been argued that this was the expectation of the Pharisees particularly in the first century.[37]

In the face of such an expectation, disobedience to the law had wide-ranging and devastating implications. If one did not obey the law one was threatening the coming of the new exodus; one was jeopardizing the salvation of the people of Israel. The response to such disobedience may well have been persecution. Too much was at stake to let such actions go unpunished.[38]

That this scenario may have contributed to the conflict in Galatia is supported by a number of things. In the first place, Paul's emphasis on what sort of actions result in inheritance would have countered the argument that obedience to Torah results in the inheritance of the land. Paul emphasizes that those who do the works of the flesh, works which are largely described in terms of dissension in the community, are the ones who will not receive the inheritance. Rather than indicating that those who disobey Torah will not receive the inheritance, Paul argues that those who are insisting on obedience to the law, thereby creating division in the community, will be disinherited.

Secondly, W.D. Davies suggests that the redefinition of one of the key words in Galatians, ἐλευθερία, is a central concern for Paul. He points out that ἐλευθερία 'was to appear in its Hebrew form *hêrûth* on the coins minted by Jews in the war against Rome'.[39] 'Freedom' was the battle cry of those who sought liberation from Rome. Paul's concern with precisely defining freedom could have been a response to those who told a story of a new exodus expectation which proclaimed 'freedom' from Roman slavery and stressed the importance of keeping the law as a way of hastening that freedom.[40]

Thirdly, the letter suggests not only that persecution was experienced by the Galatian believers, but also that such persecution was inflicted by those advocating circumcision. This is evident in the climax

37. Cf. Borg 1984: 56-70.
38. I owe this line of reasoning to N.T. Wright.
39. Davies 1984b: 184.
40. Davies (1984b: 184) goes so far as to say that this epistle emerged in the context of a 'messianic-nationalist ferment'.

of Paul's allegory, where the son of the slave woman is described as persecuting the son of the free woman. Paul explicitly says that this is the situation now in the Galatian church (4.28-29). This might also lie behind Paul's comment regarding circumcision as a way to avoid persecution in 6.12.

Although there is no doubt that there were both legalists and libertines in Galatia, my description of the conflict places the law in the context of the larger symbolic framework of first-century Judaism. It also indicates why the exodus imagery is so pervasive in the letter: if the Galatians were hearing a telling of the exodus that promised the new exodus on the basis of faithful Torah-keeping, then Paul's argument in Galatians serves to undermine such a telling. He asserts that the new exodus has already happened in Jesus Christ, the salvation has come, freedom from bondage is here, and the way to participate in this great exodus event is to join with the Son in crying 'Abba, father'.[41]

In the context of debate over the law, and dissension and persecution in the community, Paul's reinterpretation of the exodus tradition would have a very specific effect. In the first instance, his use of motifs and concepts from the exodus, like his use of Abraham, would indicate to the Galatian believers that Paul is working within the same story, that is, the story of Israel. In the face of teachers who may be suggesting that Paul has repudiated the tradition and story of Israel in his lack of insistence on the law, Paul's echoes and allusions to the exodus indicate that he is not abandoning the tradition, nor is he suggesting that the story of Israel is no longer their story (cf. 6.16). Paul is firmly rooting himself in the story of God's faithfulness to God's promises to Israel.

On the other hand, Paul significantly reinterprets the tradition, most startlingly with regard to the law. As I have shown above, Paul uses the Abraham story in 4.21–5.1 to subvert a prominent feature of the exodus story, specifically the giving of the law. In addition, he draws on two central characteristics of the exodus account, Israel's status as sons and Israel's status as heirs to the promise, to emphasize a new identity

---

41. N.T. Wright has suggested to me that the language of principalities and powers could also relate to the opponents' telling of the exodus event. Their expectation was that Yahweh would give a repeat performance of the victory over the gods of Egypt, only this time in relation to Rome. Paul's depiction of the believers' redemption from the principalities and powers, however, insists that such a defeat has already taken place.

for the Galatian believers which does not have the law as its defining element. In the face of those who argue that obedience to the law will bring the kingdom they are anxiously awaiting, Paul insists that such obedience will, in fact, result in disinheritance. Throughout the letter a central element of the tradition, that Israel had been freed in the exodus so that they might obey the law, is redefined. The point is emphasized again and again: obedience to the law is the equivalent of bondage (3.23-25; 4.3-5, 9; 5.1). If the Galatian believers really wish to experience freedom, law will not achieve that. Freedom is found only in the new exodus already enacted in Christ. Any attempt to obey the law will only return them to the slavery they sought to escape. In appealing to exodus motifs to support this redefinition, Paul would have made it clear that he is here talking about the most fundamental identity of the Galatian believers. In depicting the coming of Christ in terms of the new exodus, Paul would be indicating that this event has given new criteria by which the Galatians are now sons of God. As if to nail the lid shut on any suggestions that the law as it was originally given in the first exodus narrative is still valid, Paul makes his new identification clear in 6.2: the law to be obeyed is now the law of Christ.

This law of Christ, moreover, is the clue to how the Galatian believers are now to relate to one another communally. In an epistle to a community torn apart by strife, backbiting (cf Gal. 5.15), and persecution, Paul's call to a new identity in the crucified Christ would have very practical overtones in terms of how the Galatians relate to one another. Rather than a life of obedience to the law in hopes of coming salvation and in which disobedience is not tolerated, they are called to a life of suffering service, a life of bearing one another's burdens,[42] a life most likely of continued persecution in which they would cry out to God their father. In short, they are called to share in the life of the crucified Christ. Paul's use of the exodus tradition and story, therefore, provides the context in which the Galatian believers can ponder their identity. No longer are they the enslaved people of God still awaiting God's new act of salvation. Rather they are those who have been freed from slavery and have become the sons who will inherit the cosmos. This identity can only be maintained, however, if they do not return to

42. Strelan (1975: 266-76) argues that 'bear one another's burdens' is an exhortation to share a common financial obligation. Although it is clear from 2 Corinthians 8 and 9 that generosity in giving is one way in which Paul expects believers to emulate the crucified Christ, it would seem that Paul's concern is much larger than that here.

their bondage but rather reflect the character of their God, who gave himself up for them.

It is in this context that the faithfulness of Christ is important for this community. Paul emphasizes the faithfulness of Christ throughout the letter.[43] In imitating this Christ, the Galatians are also called to the same faithfulness. This would mean that they are called not to abandon their calling, not to submit to the yoke of slavery, but to remain steadfast and faithful. Like the Christ they image, such a life may result in crucifixion. In spite of that, Paul is certain that such a life will result not in devouring one another but in a new creation.

What Sort of Continuity?

Paul's Epistle to the Galatians was written in a situation of crisis, a time of intense change and conflict. The followers of the crucified Jesus of Nazareth were struggling to define and understand themselves in the midst of a Jewish nation that was coming closer and closer to confrontation with the major political power of the day. In addition, the common assumptions concerning the identity of the people of God were profoundly undermined by Jesus' death and resurrection. How were they to be God's people in the world? Were they to continue to tell the story of God and his dealings with his people that had nurtured Israel for centuries? Or was such a story no longer appropriate? Should this tradition be abandoned or maintained? Should the new Christian movement maintain continuity with its Jewish roots? If so, what sort of continuity?

It has been argued that there are three possible responses to tradition in times of crisis and change. They are: (1) Alienation, or abandonment of the tradition; (2) Reversion or entrenched fidelity to the tradition unchanged; and (3) Transformation of the tradition.[44] The first option clearly ends the importance of one tradition, to be replaced by another. And while the second option appears to conserve the tradition, upon closer inspection it is also just a first step toward the end of the tradition, because when tradition is handed on unchanged it loses its potency and has little meaning for the present. Some would go so far

---

43. Further on this see Hays 1983, 1991b; Hooker 1989; cf. Dunn 1991.

44. I have taken these possible responses from Ludwig 1980: 26. Walsh (1992: 22-25), referring to a possible gap between reality and worldview, describes these options as (1) Conversion (alienation), (2) Entrenchment, and (3) Reformation. See also Shils 1981: 275-79. Cf. J.A. Sanders 1987: 28.

as to say that an unchanged tradition is dead, it has been killed.[45]

It would appear that the only way for a tradition to continue to be fertile and alive is for transformation to occur. This is why Fishbane insists that a vibrant tradition must be not only a conserving (conservative) force, but also an innovative one.[46] The past tradition needs to be revivified for a new cultural and historical context. Seerveld makes a similar point: 'Traditioning goes wrong if the inherited wont is passed on dead, dead-to-the-world, without the breath of passionate love infusing its original contribution'.[47] The only hope for survival lies in a tradition's ability to provide a fresh word of hope in a new situation.

As a result of this constant transformation in the face of new historical circumstances, the tradition which is received by the community at any particular time is not the tradition that is then passed on. The community, in effect, shapes a new tradition out of the old, which becomes the established tradition for those coming after.[48] As a result of such transformation the tradition that is passed on is often only a selection of what had been inherited.[49] But this selectivity is not entirely arbitrary; some aspects of the tradition are more important than others. It is possible to speak of a 'core tradition', which, although changed, is central to any reformulation.[50] This is the 'conservative' side of Fishbane's equation. Historical continuity can be maintained, and the tradition revivified, only if there is a fidelity and rootedness to all transformations of the tradition.

This dynamic can be described as the *interpretation of tradition*; what gives a tradition its life is an effective interpretation for a new time and

45. Nyiri 1992: 76; Seerveld 1991: 30; Allan 1986: 194, 237; Neusner 1975: 194.

46. Fishbane 1977: 286. Hollinger (1980: 198) suggests that innovation is actually a conservative instinct, for it seeks to maintain the viability of a tradition in a new situation. Cf. Davies (1984a: 46-47) who describes the tradition in '*Abot* as being marked by 'fixity and pliability'.

47. Seerveld 1991: 30.

48. See Fishbane 1989: 7; Hollinger 1980: 198: 'Change is possible within the terms of an operative tradition. . . insofar as the elements of the tradition are. . . able to expand their implications enough to deal with new experiences while not losing their identity'.

49. Scholem 1974: 285.

50. Allan 1986: 92, 238; Armstrong 1980: 103. Harrelson 1977: 17-18. See also Bailey 1991. Cf. Davies 1984a: 46-47.

context. The success or failure of such interpretation (or re-interpretation) can result in either the life-giving continuation of the tradition, or its lifeless end.

I suggest that these dynamics were alive and well in the Christian community. There were surely some in the early Church who advocated the abandonment of the tradition. Such a desire to jettison the story and the tradition may have been fuelled by the fact that those who affirmed the traditional Jewish categories looked as though they were on a path headed for national destruction. The story did not seem to be doing any earthly good. It is possible that we see evidence of this view in the letter to the Romans. As far as the Roman Christians could see the Jewish heritage resulted in expulsion and persecution. Better to abandon it altogether.[51]

On the other hand, there were others within the Christian community who advocated the second option, entrenchment or fidelity to the tradition unchanged. This may have been fuelled by those within the traditions of Judaism who were persecuting the new believing communities who followed Jesus. In the face of such persecution a strict adherence to the traditions of Israel might have placated those who were persecuting the community for their abandonment or reformation of the tradition. In such a situation entrenchment is the safest way to ensure that there is no trouble. In addition, in a situation of crisis, fraught with uncertainty, entrenchment seems a safe path to walk.[52] Such an unchanging fidelity to the tradition seems to have been the response of some of the Galatian Christians. Yes, they were Christians, but the tradition and story of Israel has not changed for all that.

In response to this kind of entrenchment Paul offers a relationship to the tradition which neither abandons nor blindly accepts what has been passed on. Paul's response to this community follows the third option, transformation of the tradition. To those in the Galatian community, who would revert to the tradition unchanged, Paul emphasizes that this tradition must not be merely mimicked. It cannot be simply passed on unchanged. The community in Galatia needs to hear the word of God's radically new thing, of God's revelation of Jesus, of the end of the old order. For this community Paul 'defines and defends the

---

51. I have argued this at length in Keesmaat 1994b: 175-203.
52. Such a strategy of entrenchment can be readily discerned in the fundamentalist and neo-conservative movements of our own time.

radically new in terms drawn from the old'.[53] The Galatians have a
new identity and are therefore called upon to do a new thing as well.
The story now has a twist that no one could have expected.[54]

For Paul, the exodus tradition and, I suggest, the larger traditions
of Israel continue to have an abiding importance. That is why abandoning the tradition is not an option for him. However, that importance
is evident partly in the ability of the tradition to provide a fresh word
of hope for a new situation. Paul's relationship to the tradition of Israel
is one in which he resurrects that tradition, he 'reconceive[s] it and
nurture[s] it so that it is continually born anew'.[55] By means of allusion
and echo Paul has evoked the tradition in such a way that it continues
to speak to the challenges and problems facing the Christian communities to which he was writing. He transforms the tradition so that it
continues to be a living word.

But Paul does not merely echo and allude to the tradition. This
exploration of Paul's use of his Scriptures by means of intertextuality
has revealed something about the nature of Paul's echoes and allusions:
they occur within a larger matrix of ideas. The verses that Paul echoes
and to which he alludes often contain clusters of images which he has
drawn upon. More than that, these verses and motifs most often occur
in a narrative context themselves, a narrative of exodus or new exodus.
The intertextual matrix upon which Paul draws is not just a cluster of
motifs and themes which jostled around with one another in the collective mind of first-century Judaism. This matrix is actually a larger
story, told and retold in past remembrance and future hope to shape
Israel's identity and future expectation.[56] The reinterpreted memories
of this story provide a vision of the future which revivifies the tradition
in the present.

This reading of exodus and tradition in Galatians, then, independently
confirms two of what Stockhausen describes as 'Paul's most important
exegetical procedures':

53. Meeks 1983: 176.

54. Ricoeur (1981: 277) actually suggests that 'a narrative conclusion can be
neither deduced nor predicted. . . rather than being *predictable* a conclusion must be
acceptable'.

55. Allan 1986: 237.

56. The conclusion that Paul's intertextual dynamic is based upon a story rather
than mere motifs and themes may actually correspond better with Kristeva's definition
of intertextuality as involving the 'transpositions of one or more *systems* of signs into
another' (Roudiez in Kristeva 1980: 15).

> First, Paul takes as the basis of this interpretive task the Torah; that is to say, narrative texts from the Pentateuch are usually (perhaps always) at the core of his arguments. In interpreting selected Pentateuchal narratives, he is usually (perhaps always) extremely concerned with the stories them-selves—that is, with plot-line, character, narrative event and especially the inexplicable, unusual or unmotivated character or action. Secondly, it is Paul's usual procedure to apply prophetic and occasionally sapiential texts to bring the Torah into the proper contemporary focus. These secondary interpreting texts are usually (perhaps always) linked to each other verbally and linked to the fundamental Torah verbally—forming a network of mutually-interpreting texts which creates a new synthetic meaning at once scriptural and Pauline.[57]

My analysis of Paul's intertextual allusions and echoes to the exodus tradition serves to prove Stockhausen's point. This is not to say that the exodus provides the only narrative framework for these chapters: Stockhausen has shown that the Abraham narrative is even more firmly paradigmatic for Galatians.[58]

In addition, I have also indicated that Paul does interpret these narratives in the light of prophetic, sapiential, and other intertesta-mental Jewish texts. The exodus story which Paul tells is one that has been transformed already by Hosea, Isaiah and Jeremiah, the books of Wisdom and Sirach, the traditions found in Baruch, *1 Enoch, 4 Ezra* and *2 Baruch*. That is to say, Paul draws on these narratives not just in terms of their form in the pentateuch but also in the light of their reinterpretation in Israelite tradition. Moreover, he also applies texts that are not usually linked with the exodus narrative to his telling in such a way that they interpret the story that he is retelling. These texts have verbal links to the motifs of the exodus account, hence they provide a thematic enrichment of the narrative as Paul is telling it.

So we return to the question with which I began this section: what sort of continuity does Paul's telling of the Christian story have with its Hebrew antecedents? His telling has, if you will, a transformational continuity. By means of intertextual echo and allusion Paul continues the Jewish practice of reinterpreting, and so revivifying, the tradition of Israel but does so in the light of the story of Jesus and the Church.

---

57. Stockhausen 1993: 144.

58. The narratives of both Adam and Abraham are prominent in Romans as well (Abraham: Rom. 4; 9.6-13; Adam: Rom. 5.12-21; Rom. 8). See Hooker 1990; Keesmaat 1994a.

Of course, my reading of Paul also takes place in the context of a history of interpretation. To this we now must turn.

The Story of Pauline Interpretation

The story within which this study fits is one of ongoing debate concerning the nature of Paul's relationship to his Scriptures. On the one hand are those who suggest that Paul has completely broken with the tradition, that when he cites Scripture it is to answer his opponents, and that his method of scriptural reference is somewhat akin to the proof-texting of North American fundamentalism. The two most notable scholars who have argued this position are Sanders and Räisänen, although many scholars assume such a position in their work.[59] Sanders actually uses the term 'proof-texts' to describe Paul's scriptural references.[60] Although he later says that Paul's use of Scripture is more than clever proof-texting,[61] his description of Paul's 'canon within a canon' as 'those parts of Scripture which mention faith, righteousness, Gentiles and love... [and] those which accuse Israel of disobedience' amounts to little more than a listing of criteria for prooftexts.[62] Similarly, Räisänen describes Paul's use of Scripture as 'ingenious', although he also suggests that Paul's arbitrary use of Scripture is not unique in his time.[63]

The discontinuity between Paul and his traditions is also argued by Martyn, who emphasizes that for Paul there is no continuity between the history of Israel and the people of God in Christ Jesus.[64] Paul refers to Abraham as a punctiliar figure, according to Martyn, and he emphasizes that in Galatians 'there simply is no indication of a covenant-created people of God during the time of the law'.[65] But this judgment seems hardly tenable in the light of Paul's pervasive use of the exodus narrative in the letter. Since the exodus was about the formation of a people and the calling of a community, Paul's evocation of this narrative

---

59. Witness the large number of exegetes who argue that Paul refers to Abraham in Galatians solely in response to his opponents.

60. E.P. Sanders 1985: 21-22, 53 n. 25. Räisänen (1986: 68-69) does the same.

61. E.P. Sanders 1985: 64 n. 144.

62. E.P. Sanders 1985: 162.

63. Räisänen 1986: 72-73.

64. Martyn 1987–88: 6; Martyn 1991: 173-76.

65. Martyn 1991: 173-76, here p. 174.

suggests that the exodus story of Israel is now the story of the Galatian Christians. It is hardly imaginable that Paul used these images without intending them to evoke such communal (even covenantal) overtones.[66]

On the other hand are those who argue that Paul is in fundamental continuity with his tradition; that he is attempting to root present experience in past tradition; that the story of Israel is somehow central to his understanding of the identity of Christian believers. Scholars who come most readily to mind are Hays, Wright and Stockhausen, although Beker, Thielman, and Gaventa also argue for this kind of continuity.[67]

For instance, Wright argues that Paul was working within the categories of first-century Judaism and asking precisely the same questions that his Jewish contemporaries were asking, albeit coming up with different answers.[68] He describes Paul's starting position in this way:

> Paul was a Pharisee who believed that Jesus of Nazareth, who had been crucified as a messianic pretender, had been vindicated by Israel's covenant God in being raised from the dead. He therefore rethought and reimplemented Jewish theology and the Jewish agenda in the light of this new belief, and (he would quickly have added) in the power of the Spirit of the creator God, made known as the Spirit of Jesus and let loose through the new covenant community to the world.[69]

Paul read Scripture, therefore, as story and as prophecy.

> For Paul, the story was always moving towards a climax; it contained within it, at specific and non-arbitrary moments, advance warning and promises about that climax; it contained within it, again at not arbitrary moments, prefigurements of that climax (the story of Isaac, of the Exodus, and so forth); and, most importantly, it was the story whose climax, Paul believed, *had now arrived.*[70]

66. Gaventa (1991: 158) supports this point: 'His [Christ's] birth under law (4.4) means also that he is born into Israel's particular history of relationship with God. Christ is the offspring of Abraham (3.16), and as such he represents God's intervention in a particular history, now radicalized to include all humankind.'

67. Wright 1992: 403-409; Hays 1989a; Stockhausen 1993; Beker 1985; Thielman 1989, 1993; Gaventa 1991. See also Smith 1988; Segal 1990: 75; Davies 1965. It should be noted that not all of these scholars would agree on the degree and kind of continuity. There is, however, a basic sense amongst them that Paul was in actual dialogue with the traditions of Israel. The list of scholars who can be characterized in this way seems to be increasing daily; the ones listed here are representative.

68. See Wright 1991: 258-67.

69. Wright 1991: 260.

70. Wright 1991: 264.

Paul's story is that of Israel, come to its true meaning in Jesus of Nazareth. As we have seen throughout this article, it is indeed the story of Israel told in the exodus narratives that Paul is evoking for the Christian community. He not only evokes the story, however, he claims that the promises connected to it have been and are being fulfilled.

Wright's description of Paul's use of Scripture is one which emphasizes continuity more than discontinuity. Paul reads the Scriptures of Israel as applying directly to his own situation and that of the Christian community.[71] However, this is not to say that scholars (Wright included) who emphasize that Paul was thinking in terms of basic continuity with the traditions of Israel, naively assume that there is simple continuity with the story with no inbreaking. Hays makes clear that there is a profound reinterpretation of Scripture in Paul. He characterizes Paul's thought in this way:

> In Paul we encounter a first century Jewish thinker who, while undergoing a profound disjuncture with his own religious tradition, grappled his way to a vigorous and theologically generative reappropriation of Israel's scriptures.[72]

Paul's echoes and allusions to the texts of Israel's Scriptures mean that 'Paul repeatedly situates his discourse within the symbolic field created by a single great textual precursor: Israel's Scripture'.[73] To put it in somewhat different terms, 'Paul's way of doing theology occurs in the context of a lively dialogue with scripture'.[74] Such a dialogue results in what Stockhausen has called 'a new synthetic meaning at once scriptural and Pauline'.[75]

This means, however, that there is not an unbroken continuity between Paul and the traditions of Israel. As we have seen, Paul does not simply take up the traditions of Israel and assert that they continue unchanged for those who are in Christ Jesus. In the midst of a fundamental

71. See Wright 1991: 264-65; Hays 1989a: 166.

72. Hays 1989a: 2.

73. Hays 1989a: 15.

74. Beker 1985: 360. See also Gaventa (1991: 159): 'Paul constantly uses biblical interpretation and imagery, not only in response to his opponents' claims about the law but in reference to his own apostolic role ([Gal.] 1.15). This absorption in scripture indicates that the gospel's invasion does not negate the place of Israel (see [Gal.] 6.16)'.

75. Stockhausen 1993: 144. This article is an excellent discussion of Paul's use of Scripture.

continuity with the story and Scriptures of Israel Paul introduces what Hays calls a 'surprising discontinuity'. His description of the continuity/discontinuity tension bears repeating:

> In other words, Paul does not interpret the foundation story as a simple linear *Heilsgeschichte* from Abraham to the present moment. Rather, for Paul, Christ's death has introduced a surprising discontinuity in Israel's story, simultaneously necessitating and enabling a new reading of scripture that discloses its witness to the gospel. Christians have become Isaac; Jews have become Ishmael! Paul's revisionary rereading of scripture—worked out in some hermeneutically jarring ways in Gal. 3.6-29 and 4.21-31—fractures traditional Jewish models for discerning the coherence of Scripture's message. At the same time, however, he insists that God's act in Jesus Christ illuminates a previously uncomprehended narrative unity in Scripture.[76]

It is clear that the old way of framing the discussion in terms of whether Paul rejects or affirms the tradition of Israel, is no longer fruitful. Paul was struggling with the question of what it meant to serve God in Jesus Christ and was doing so in fundamental continuity with the traditions and Scriptures of his people, Israel. However, the invasive action of God in Jesus Christ introduced a new element into the story, an unexpected twist in the plot, which meant that Paul's dialogue with Scripture involved a transformation and reappropriation of the tradition for the new communities that had come into being in Jesus Christ. As I have argued, Paul uses the exodus narrative as foundational for his discussion of Christian identity with the Galatians. However, that tradition is both appropriated and reinterpreted by Paul so that the identity of this community is not the same identity of those who participated in the first exodus event. The tradition has been transformed in such a way that it is revivified. Paul is rooted in the scriptural narrative, but that narrative bears new contemporary fruit.

Such conclusions suggest that the precise nature of both Paul's continuity and discontinuity with the tradition is where the discussion now needs to be focused.[77] Perhaps we could say that these questions appear as a new development in the plot of the narrative (drama?) of Pauline studies. Such a twist in this story has seemed to some scholars

76. Hays 1991a: 237.
77. So also Gaventa (1991: 159 n. 34): 'in my judgment this issue in Pauline theology [the relationship between continuity and discontinuity] cries out for extended discussion'.

unexpected and unwarranted. For others, these readings of Paul result in a telling of Paul's story that is more believable, illuminating, and fruitful than the readings of Paul that had come before.

On Telling the Story Today

In this article, I have been talking of three stories. One is the exodus story as told by Paul. The second is the story of Paul's interpretative work, or the story of how Paul is telling his story. The third is the story of Pauline studies. All three of these stories, but particularly the first two, inform the story of the Christian community today. Both the exodus story as told by Paul and the manner in which Paul tells that story provide a paradigm for Christian identity and the continuous telling, retelling, and enacting of the Christian story.

We have seen that Paul was faced both with those who wished to abandon the tradition altogether and with those who wished to revert to the tradition unchanged. In the face of these options Paul affirmed the importance of both hearing the authority of the past story for interpreting present experience and of the innovative transformation of the tradition for a new situation. Moreover, a comparison of Paul's interpretative strategy in Romans compared with Galatians would reveal that Paul can tell this unexpected story in different ways and with slightly different emphases for different communities. He does not repeat the arguments of Galatians in Romans. Paul's telling is new each time he tells the story for a new community.

Heikki Räisänen comments that

> As everyone except for the extreme conservatives admits, Paul's actual reinterpretations of the Old Testament are rather ingenious; no one will today seriously suggest that we should follow Paul in his exegesis.[78]

Many scholars, even conservatives, would agree with his assessment. However, there have been serious suggestions that we should learn to follow Paul in his exegesis. So Richard Hays states:

> Paul's readings are materially normative (in a sense to be specified carefully) for Christian theology and his interpretive methods are paradigmatic for Christian hermeneutics.[79]

Hays interprets the ways in which Paul's hermeneutic is paradigmatic

78. Räisänen 1986: 72.
79. Hays 1989a: 183.

in the light of the intertextual relations he discusses throughout his book. In view of the discussion in this article, however, the challenge, for those who now not only read Paul's Scriptures but also read Paul himself as Scripture, is how to follow Paul as a paradigm in his *retelling of the story*. How can we engage in the sort of retelling that Paul engaged in? How can we read Paul and his Scriptures as a story that provides a vision for us today? How does Paul 'authorize' our retelling of *his* story in a way that is stable yet adaptable, conservative yet innovative, faithful yet creative?[80]

One thing that this study suggests is that if we were to read and interpret Scripture the way that Paul does, we would be involved in tellings of the story that transform the tradition in some way. We would not tell a story that abandons the tradition, but be involved in telling a story in which the faithfulness of God is emphasized. This story would envision how the tradition is actualized in the present, it would show how God's faithfulness is present in the world today. The story of God's continuing faithfulness to the world and to God's people, the story of a God who continues to act to save would be at the heart of such a telling.[81]

Moreover, our telling would not merely repeat the tellings of the story from the past, as though Paul's message to the Galatians is all that believers need to hear today. Indeed, as we have seen, merely asserting the story unchanged gives it no power or force for our own day and age. Telling the story in a way that is alive and powerful today means telling anew what it means for God to save in this century, in this post-modern world, in this context. It means formulating anew what it is for the believing community to show the identity of their God, to bear the image of the crucified Christ. It means expressing again and differently what it is to groan with creation, bear one another's burdens and cry out to God for salvation.[82]

The other challenge facing those who read Paul as Scripture is that of discerning how the story itself, the story of exodus and new exodus, speaks to the crises of our time. The power of a story to create a world and shape reality for people is clear.[83] As we have seen, the exodus

80. Cf. J.A. Sanders 1987.
81. See also Hays 1989a: 183, 191.
82. Middleton and Walsh 1995, provide an example of such a post-modern reading.
83. Ricoeur 1981: 293; Wright 1992: 38-41; Walsh 1989: 10-12; Birch 1991: 51-

story within Israelite history was a narrative that gave identity to a people, revealed the identity of their God and pointed to the kind of world they were to live in themselves. The categories which the western Christian church has for so long accepted have been shown to be leading us down the path to destruction. In a context where our anthropocentric view of the world has led us to environmental disaster, the exodus story as told by Paul calls us to a groaning with creation, to realize our role in its suffering and redemption, and to a hope for its renewal.[84] In a context of extreme individualism which has led to heightened personal alienation and loneliness, the exodus story as told by Paul reminds us that in Christ we are called to be a community with a common identity and a common calling, a calling to suffering compassion with and acceptance of one another. In the context of post-modernity where much of the church has opted for entrenchment in the face of increasing plurality, Paul's telling of the exodus story reminds us that we are on a journey, a journey through the wilderness of trial wherein we can call out to our God. This is a journey of hope, but a journey nonetheless; a retreat to our safe haven will not bring us the inheritance.

Michael Walzer outlines the meaning which the exodus continues to have for us in this way:

> First, that wherever you live, it is probably Egypt; second, that there is a better place, a world more attractive, a promised land; and third, that 'the way to the land is through the wilderness'.[85]

More than anything, however, Paul's account of the exodus story calls us to tell the story afresh in our own time. In a sense the central redefinition that Paul was engaged in, that of a God who suffers and who has now called a people to such suffering, has not changed. However, for western Christianity that redefinition is almost as radical now as it was for the communities to which Paul was writing in the first century CE. Paul, as he wrote to those communities, told the story anew so that the circumstances of the Galatian Christians were intricately identified with the tale he was telling. Paul thus provides a model for those of us who wish to tell the story afresh today. We must be storied communities, continually recounting our origins and exploring their meaning

---

65; Crites 1989: 65-88; Hauerwas and Burrell 1989. On the social function of narrative see Herrnstein Smith 1981; Georges 1969.

84. See Kraftchick 1987: 86-87.

85. Walzer 1985: 149 quoting Davies 1982: 60.

and assurances for today. In the words of Stanley Hauerwas 'the claim that the church is a social ethic is an attempt to remind us that the church is a place where the story of God is enacted, told and heard'.[86]

Paul tells Israel's story of a righteous God who called Abraham, promised him many descendants and the inheritance of the whole world. This God is revealed as a liberator of slaves in the exodus and as faithful throughout Israel's history and in the new exodus in Christ. Paul assured those to whom he wrote that this story was fulfilled, that the promises had come, that God had called them to a life of suffering obedience and groaning with each other on the earth. The history of the early Church suggests that some of Paul's readers heard this story and lived it.

Francis Watson concludes his book on Paul with this question: 'Should Paul's thought still be a major source of inspiration for contemporary theological discussion? Or should it be rejected as a cul-de-sac, and should one seek inspiration elsewhere?'[87] The reading of Paul in this article suggests that both Paul's theology and Paul's hermeneutic lead not to a cul-de-sac but to a life-giving path.

BIBLIOGRAPHY

Allan, G.
    1986   *The Importances of the Past: A Meditation on the Authority of Tradition*
                (Albany: State University of New York Press).
Armstrong, D.M.
    1980   'The Nature of Tradition', in *The Nature of Mind and Other Essays* (St
                Lucia, Queensland: University of Queensland Press): 89-103.
Bailey, K.E.
    1991   'Informal Controlled Oral Tradition and the Synoptic Gospels', *Asian
                Journal of Theology* 5.1: 34-55.
Barclay, J.M.G.
    1991   *Obeying the Truth: A Study of Paul's Ethics in Galatians* (Minneapolis:
                Fortress Press; originally published; Edinburgh: T. & T. Clark, 1988).
Beker, J.C.
    1985   'Paul's Letter to the Romans as a Model for Biblical Theology: Some Pre-
                liminary Observations', in J.T. Butler, E.W. Conrad and B.C. Ollenburger
                (eds.), *Understanding the Word: Essays in Honour of Bernhard W.
                Anderson* (Sheffield: JSOT Press): 359-67.

86. Hauerwas 1985: 181.
87. Watson 1986: 181.

Belleville, L.L.
    1986   '"Under Law": Structural Analysis and the Pauline Concept of Law in Gal.
                3.21–4.11', *JSNT* 26: 53-78.
Betz, H.D.
    1979   *Galatians: A Commentary on Paul's Letter to the Churches in Galatia*
                (Philadelphia: Fortress Press).
Biaswell, J.P.
    1991   'The Blessing of Abraham versus "The Curse of the Law": Another Look
                at Galatians 3.10-13', *WTJ* 53: 73-91.
Birch, B.C.
    1991   *Let Justice Roll Down: The Old Testament, Ethics, and Christian Life*
                (Louisville, KY: Westminster/John Knox).
Bligh, J.
    1969   *Galatians: A Discussion of St Paul's Epistle* (London: St Paul Publications).
Borg, M.J.
    1984   *Conflict, Holiness and Politics in the Teachings of Jesus* (New York and
                Toronto: Edwin Mellen).
Brinsmead, B.H.
    1982   *Galatians—Dialogical Response to Opponents* (SBLDS, 6; Chico, CA:
                Scholars Press).
Bruce, F.F.
    1982   *The Epistle to the Galatians: A Commentary on the Greek Text* (Grand
                Rapids: Eerdmans).
Crites, S.
    1989   'The Narrative Reality of Experience', in S. Hauerwas and L.G. Jones
                (eds.), *Why Narrative? Readings in Narrative Theology* (Grand Rapids:
                Eerdmans): 65-88.
Davies, W.D.
    1965   *Paul and Rabbinic Judaism* (London: SPCK).
    1982   *The Territorial Dimension of Judaism* (Berkeley: University of California
                Press).
    1984a   'Reflections on Tradition: The *'Abot* Revisited' in W.D. Davies, *Jewish
                and Pauline Studies* (Philadelphia: Fortress Press): 27-48.
    1984b   'Galatians: A Commentary on Paul's Letter to the Churches in Galatia', in
                W.D. Davies, *Jewish and Pauline Studies* (Philadelphia: Fortress Press):
                172-88.
Dunn, J.D.G.
    1991   'Once More ΠΙΣΤΙΣ ΧΡΙΣΤΟΥ', *SBLSP* (ed. E.H. Lovering, Jr; Atlanta:
                Scholars Press): 730-44.
    1993   *The Epistle to the Galatians* (London: A. & C. Black).
Elliott, N.
    1990   *The Rhetoric of Romans: Argumentative Constraint and Strategy and
                Paul's Dialogue with Judaism* (JSNTSup, 45; Sheffield: JSOT Press).
Fishbane, M.
    1977   'Torah and Tradition', in D.A. Knight (ed.), *Tradition and Theology in the
                Old Testament* (London: SPCK): 275-300.

1989   'Inner-Biblical Exegesis: Types and Strategies of Interpretation in Ancient
            Israel', in M. Fishbane, *The Garments of Torah: Essays in Biblical
            Hermeneutics* (Bloomington and Indianapolis: Indiana University Press):
            3-18.

Gaventa, B.R.
1991   'The Singularity of the Gospel: A Reading of Galatians', in J.M. Bassler
            (ed.), *Pauline Theology*. I. *Thessalonians, Philippians, Galatians,
            Philemon* (Minneapolis: Fortress Press): 147-59.

Georges, R.A.
1969   'Toward an Understanding of Storytelling Events', *Journal of American
            Folklore* 82: 313-29.

Gordon, D.T.
1989   'A Note on *PAIDAGOGOS* in Gal 3.24-25', *NTS* 35: 150-54.

Harrelson, W.
1977   'Life, Faith and the Emergence of Tradition', in D.A. Knight (ed.), *Tradition
            and Theology in the Old Testament* (Philadelphia: Fortress Press): 11-30.

Hauerwas, S.
1985   'The Gesture of a Truthful Story', *TTod* 42: 181-184.

Hauerwas, S., and D. Burrell
1989   'From System to Story: An Alternative Pattern for Rationality in Ethics', in
            S. Hauerwas and L.G. Jones (eds.), *Why Narrative? Readings in Narrative
            Theology* (Grand Rapids: Eerdmans): 158-90.

Hays, R.B.
1983   *The Faith of Jesus Christ: An Investigation of the Narrative Substructure
            of Galatians 3:1–4:11* (SBLDS, 56; Chico, CA: Scholars Press).
1987   'Christology and Ethics in Galatians: The Law of Christ', *CBQ* 49: 268-
            90.
1989a   *Echoes of Scripture in the Letters of Paul* (New Haven: Yale University
            Press).
1989b   '"The Righteous One" as Eschatological Deliverer: A Case Study in Paul's
            Apocalyptic Hermeneutics', in J. Marcus and M.L. Soards (eds.), *Apoca-
            lyptic and the New Testament: Essays in Honour of J. Louis Martyn*
            (Sheffield: JSOT Press): 191-215.
1991a   'Crucified with Christ: A Synthesis of the Theology of 1 and 2 Thessa-
            lonians, Philemon, Philippians and Galatians', in J.M. Bassler (ed.),
            Pauline Theology. I. *Thessalonians, Philippians, Galatians, Philemon*
            (Minneapolis: Fortress Press): 227-46.
1991b   'ΠΙΣΤΙΣ and Pauline Christology: What is at Stake?', *SBLSP* (ed. E.H.
            Lovering, Jr; Atlanta: Scholars Press): 714-29.

Herrnstein Smith, B.
1981   'Narrative Versions, Narrative Theories', in W.J.T. Mitchell (ed.), *On
            Narrative* (Chicago and London: University of Chicago Press): 209-32.

Hester, J.D.
1967   'The "Heir" and Heilsgeschichte: A Study of Gal 4.1ff', in *Okonomia: FS
            Oscar Cullmann* (Hamburg: Reich): 118-25.

Hollinger, D.S.
1980 'T.S. Kuhn's Theory of Science and its Implications for History', in G. Gutting (ed.), *Paradigms and Revolutions* (Notre Dame/London: University of Notre Dame Press): 195-222.

Hooker, M.D.
1989 'Πίστις Χριστοῦ', *NTS* 35: 321-42.
1990 'Adam in Romans 1', in *From Adam to Christ: Essays on Paul* (Cambridge: Cambridge University Press): 73-84.

Howard, G.
1990 *Paul in Crisis in Galatia: A Study of Early Christian Theology* (Cambridge: Cambridge University Press, 2nd edn).

Keesmaat, S.C.
1994a 'Exodus and the Intertextual Transformation of Tradition in Romans 8.14-30', *JSNT* 54: 29-56.
1994b *Paul's Use of the Exodus Tradition in Romans and Galatians* (Oxford: Unpublished DPhil. dissertation).

Kraftchick, S.
1987 'Paul's Use of Creation themes: A Test of Romans 1–8', *ExAud* 3: 72-87.

Kristeva, J.
1980 *Desire in Language: A Semiotic Approach to Literature and Art* (ed. L.S. Roudiez; New York: Columbia University Press).

Longenecker, R.N.
1990 *Galatians* (Dallas: Word).

Ludwig, T.M.
1980 'Remember Not the Former Things: Disjunction and Transformation in Ancient Israel' in F.E Reynolds and T.M. Ludwig (eds.), *Transitions and Transformations in the History of Religions* (SHR 39; Leiden: Brill): 25-55.

Lull, D.J.
1986 '"The Law was our Pedagogue": A Study in Galatians 3.19-25', *JBL* 105: 481-98.

Martyn, J.L.
1985a 'Apocalyptic Antinomies in Paul's Letter to the Galatians', *NTS* 31: 410-25.
1985b 'A Law-Observant Mission to Gentiles: The Background of Galatians', *SJT* 38: 307-24.
1987–88 'Paul and his Jewish Christian Interpreters', *USQR* 43: 1-15.
1991 'Events in Galatia: Modified Covenantal Nomism versus God's Invasion of the Cosmos in the Singular Gospel: A Response to J.D.G. Dunn and B.R. Gaventa', in J.M. Bassler (ed.), *Pauline Theology*. I. *Thessalonians, Philippians, Galatians, Philemon* (Minneapolis: Fortress Press): 160-79.

Meeks, W.A.
1983 *The First Urban Christians: The Social World of the Apostle Paul* (New Haven and London: Yale University Press).

Meyer, B.F.
1986 *The Early Christians: Their World Mission and Self-Discovery* (Wilmington, DE: Michael Glazier).

Middleton, J.R., and B.J. Walsh
    1995   *Truth is Stranger than it Used to Be: Biblical Faith in a Postmodern Age*
                (Downers Grove, IL: IVP; London: SPCK).
Morgan, T.E.
    1985   'Is there an Intertext in this Text?: Literary and Interdisciplinary Approaches
                to Intertextuality', *American Journal of Semiotics* 3.4: 1-40.
Neusner, J.
    1975   'The Study of Religion as the Study of Tradition: Judaism', *HR* 14: 191-
                206.
Nyiri, J.C.
    1992   *Tradition and Individuality* (Dordrecht/Boston/London: Kluwer Academic
                Publishers).
Potterie, I. de la
    1976   'Le chrétien conduit par l'esprit dans son cheminement eschatologique', in
                L. de Lorenzi (ed.), *The Law of the Spirit in Rom 7 and 8* (Rome: St
                Paul's Abbey): 209-278.
Räisänen, H.
    1986   *Paul and the Law* (Tubingen: Mohr–Siebeck).
Ricoeur, P.
    1981   'Science and Ideology', in P. Ricoeur, *Hermeneutics and the Human
                Sciences* (ed. and trans. J. Thompson; Cambridge: Cambridge University
                Press): 222-46.
Sanders, E.P.
    1977   *Paul and Palestinian Judaism* (London: SCM Press).
    1985   *Paul, the Law, and the Jewish People* (London: SCM Press).
Sanders, J.A.
    1987   *From Sacred Story to Sacred Text* (Philadelphia: Fortress Press).
Scholem, G.
    1974   'Revelation and Tradition as Religious Categories in Judaism', in
                G. Scholem, *The Messianic Idea in Judaism* (New York: Schocken
                Books): 282-90.
Scott, J.M.
    1992   *Adoption as Sons of God: An Exegetical Investigation into the Background
                of UIOTHESIA in the Pauline Corpus* (Tubingen: Mohr–Siebeck).
Seerveld, C.G.
    1991   'Footprints in the Snow', *Philosophia Reformata* 56: 1-34.
Segal, A.F.
    1990   *Paul the Convert: The Apostalate and Apostasy of Saul the Pharisee* (New
                Haven and London: Yale University Press).
Shils, E.
    1981   *Tradition* (London/Boston: Faber & Faber).
Smith, D.M.
    1988   'The Pauline Literature', in D.A. Carson and H.G.M. Williams (eds.), *It is
                Written: Scripture Citing Scripture: Essays in Honour of Barnabas
                Lindars* (Cambridge: Cambridge University Press): 265-91.

Stockhausen, C.
      1993   '2 Cor 3 and the Principles of Pauline Exegesis', in C.A. Evans and J.A.
                  Sanders (eds.), *Paul and the Scriptures of Israel* (Sheffield: JSOT Press):
                  143-64.
Strelan, J.G.
      1975   'Burden-Bearing and the Law of Christ: A Re-Examination of Galatians
                  6.2', *JBL* 94: 266-76.
Thielman, F.
      1989   *From Plight to Solution: A Jewish Framework to Understanding Paul's
                  view of the Law in Galatians and Romans* (Leiden: Brill).
      1993   'The Story of Israel and the Theology of Romans 5–8', *SBLSP* (ed. E.H.
                  Lovering; Atlanta: Scholars Press): 227-49.
Walsh, B.J.
      1989   *Who Turned out the Lights? The Light of the Gospel in a Post-
                  Enlightenment Culture* (Toronto: Institute for Christian Studies).
      1992   'Worldviews, Modernity and the Task of Christian College Education',
                  Faculty Dialogue 18: 13-35.
Walzer, M.
      1985   *Exodus and Revolution* (New York: Basic Books).
Watson, F.
      1986   *Paul, Judaism and the Gentiles: A Sociological Approach* (Cambridge:
                  Cambridge University Press).
Westermann, C.
      1980   *The Promises to the Fathers* (Philadelphia: Fortress Press).

Williams, S.K.
      1988   'Promise in Galatians: A Reading of Paul's Reading of Scripture', *JBL*
                  107: 709-20.
Wright, N.T.
      1991   *The Climax of the Covenant: Christ and Law in Pauline Theology*
                  (Edinburgh: T. & T. Clark).
      1992   *The New Testament and the People of God* (Minneapolis: Fortress Press).
Young, N.H.
      1987   '*Paidagogos*: The Social Setting of a Pauline Metaphor', *NovT* 29: 150-
                  76.

AN INTERPRETATION OF ISAIAH 22.15-25
AND ITS FUNCTION IN THE NEW TESTAMENT

John T. Willis

The primary purpose of this paper is to offer some suggestions as to the meaning of Rev. 3.7 and Mt. 16.19 in light of their use of Isa. 22.22. In order to accomplish this, it is necessary first to set forth an interpretation of Isa. 22.15-25 with a view to ascertaining the meaning of v. 22 in that pericope. Then one must examine Rev. 3.7-13 and Mt. 16.13-23 respectively as the two New Testament contexts in which Isa. 22:22 is cited in order to attempt to determine how this Old Testament text functions in each of these contexts.

1. *An Interpretation of Isaiah 22.15-25*[1]

Isa. 22.15 begins a prophetic oracle addressed to Shebna, who is 'steward' and 'master of the household'. Since Isa. 36.3, 11, 22; 37.2 indicate that Shebna functioned as an official under Hezekiah, this verse assumes that Hezekiah had made Shebna steward and master of his household some time between his succession to the throne (715 BCE) and the Assyrian siege of Jerusalem (701 BCE). *In its present form*, Isa. 22.15-25 contains a doom oracle directed against Shebna (vv. 15-19), an announcement that Eliakim will receive the office Shebna now holds (vv. 20-23), and a doom oracle directed against Eliakim (vv. 24-25). Isaiah vehemently condemns Shebna (1) because he is hewing out a tomb for himself 'on the height' 'in the rock' (v. 16), that is, in that area of Jerusalem set aside for the burial of kings and other dignitaries; and (2) because he is very ostentatious, frequently appearing in public

---

1. For a recent discussion of the text of Isa. 22.15-25, see J.T. Willis, 'Textual and Linguistic Issues in Isaiah 22.15-25', *ZAW* 105 (1993), pp. 377-99. A detailed explanation of the interpretation of Isa. 22.15-25 sketched here appears in J.T. Willis, 'Historical Issues in Isaiah 22.15-25', *Bib* 74 (1993), pp. 60-70.

places riding in one of his 'splendid chariots' of state (v. 18).[2] He declares that Shebna will be taken into Assyrian captivity, die there, and lose his splendid chariots to his captors (vv. 17-18). Eliakim will replace Shebna in his high official position (vv. 19-23). But Eliakim's relatives will pressure him to give them special favors, Eliakim will yield to this pressure, and eventually he will lose his office and both he and his relatives will fall (vv. 24-25).

However, things did not turn out quite like Isaiah envisioned. When the Assyrian army of Sennacherib was besieging Jerusalem in 701 BCE, Hezekiah sent Eliakim who was over the house, Shebna the secretary (or scribe), and Joah the recorder to meet the Tartan, the Rab-saris, and the Rabshakeh, the Assyrian officials delegated by Sennacherib, to discuss the situation (2 Kgs 18.18, 37 = Isa. 36.3, 22). This indicates that before this Assyrian invasion, Hezekiah had removed Shebna from the office of 'steward' or the one 'who is over the house' (Isa. 22.15), had demoted him to the office of 'secretary' or scribe (סֹפֵר), and had elevated Eliakim to the office of 'steward' which Shebna formerly

2.   J. Skinner (*The Book of the Prophet Isaiah Chapters I–XXXIX* [The Cambridge Bible for Schools and Colleges; 4th repr.; Cambridge: Cambridge University Press, 1909], p. 168); A. Condamin (*Le livre d'Isaïe* [EBib; Paris: Lecoffre, 1905], p. 153); J.H. Hayes and S.A. Irvine (*Isaiah the Eighth-Century Prophet: His Times and his Preaching* [Nashville: Abingdon Press, 1987], p. 284); W.J. Wessels, 'Isaiah of Jerusalem and the Royal Court: Isaiah 22:15-25 A Paradigm for Restoring Just Officials?', *Old Testament Essays* 2.2 (1989), pp. 1-13, especially pp. 5, 8-12; and others propose that a major reason Isaiah opposed Shebna is that he was a prominent member, if not the leader, of the pro-Egyptian and anti-Assyrian party in Jerusalem that Isaiah denounced (Isa. 30.1-7; 31.1-3), whose rebellion led to Sennacherib's invasion of Judah and siege of Jerusalem in 701 BCE, or to Sargon II's invasion of the western states in ca. 713–711 BCE. A. Auret ('A different background for Isa. 22.15-25 presents an alternative paradigm: disposing of political and religious opposition?', *Old Testament Essays* 6.1 [1993], pp. 46-56) thinks Eliakim was the one 'who is over the house' under Hezekiah until Sennacherib conquered Hezekiah in 701 BCE. Then Sennacherib forced Hezekiah to demote the anti-Assyrian, Eliakim, and to put the pro-Assyrian, Shebna, in his place. Isa. 22.15-23 preserves an oracle of Isaiah in which he announces that Shebna will be removed from this office and Eliakim re-installed to his former position. While this is a different historical reconstruction than that proposed by most scholars, it still assumes that political issues are involved in the removal of Shebna and the appointment of Eliakim. Some connect Isa. 22.15-25 with the previous pericope, 22.1-14, and suggest that Shebna was one of the rulers mentioned in v. 3. While these proposals are possible, nothing in the oracle in Isa. 22.15-25 states or even implies them.

held. There is nothing to indicate that the Assyrians carried Shebna into captivity with his splendid chariots, or that he died in a foreign land, as Isaiah had announced (Isa. 22.17-18). The Rabshakeh tells the three-man delegation from Hezekiah to surrender or the Assyrians will overthrow Jerusalem and destroy its inhabitants (2 Kgs 18.28-35 = Isa. 36.13-20). Hezekiah's representatives return to the king and relate the Rabshakeh's threat. Fearful, Hezekiah sends Eliakim, Shebna, and Joah to Isaiah to ask him to pray that Yahweh will deliver the city from the invaders. Isaiah assures them that Yahweh will intervene and save Jerusalem (2 Kgs 19.1-7 = Isa. 37.1-7), and this occurs (2 Kgs 19.8-36 = Isa. 37.8-37). After the Assyrians leave Jerusalem, Eliakim's relatives put increasing pressure on him to use his high office to help them gain lucrative and enviable governmental positions, and he yields to this pressure. Isaiah or one of his disciples denounces this nepotism, and affirms that it will become worse and worse until Eliakim cannot bear the burdens his relatives are heaping upon him, and thus will fall, that is, lose his position as 'steward' and he 'who is over the house', or something worse; and his relatives will fall with him (Isa. 22.24-25). The threefold repetition of כֹּל in v. 24 indicates that when Isaiah or his disciple uttered this oracle, some members of his household were already bringing pressure on him to use his influence to elevate them; and now Isaiah foresees that his *whole* house will do the same: 'And they will hang on him (Eliakim) *the whole weight* of his ancestral house, the offspring and issue, *every* small vessel, from the cups to *all* the flagons'. Beyond this, there is no information as to what happened to Eliakim ultimately.

Isa. 22.15-25 preserves an oracle which Yahweh instructed Isaiah to deliver to Shebna. Throughout the oracle, the speaker addresses Shebna in the second person singular and speaks of Eliakim in the third person. This pericope uses four terms to describe the מַצָּב 'office', or מַעֲמָד 'station' (v. 19), held first by Shebna and then by Eliakim under Hezekiah king of Judah: סֹכֵן 'steward'; אֲשֶׁר עַל הַבַּיִת '(he) who (is) over the house' (v. 15); אָב 'father' (v. 21); and מַפְתֵּחַ בֵּית דָּוִד '(bearer of) the key of the house of David' (v. 22).[3] While these terms originated in different milieux, and in the history of Israel and Judah only gradually were applied to the high governmental official under consideration here, their concurrence at this focal point apparently is due to

---

3.   A study of these four terms with extensive bibliography appears in J.T. Willis, 'אָב as an Official Term', forthcoming in *SJOT*.

the fact that there were striking similarities between the function of the person who bore each title originally and the function attached to the official discussed in the present context. The fact that all four terms are applied to the same official indicates that they were understood to be fundamentally synonymous, or at least to share a basic common core meaning. Hence, methodologically one may use any one of these terms to understand the sense of any other of these terms.

The usages of the Akkadian *saknu(m)* in the Alalakh texts, the Nuzi tablets, the Amarna letters, and elsewhere, of the Ugaritic *skn*, of the Phoenician *skn*, of the Aramaic *skn*, and of the Hebrew סֹכֵן and סֹגֵן in the Old Testament indicate that סֹכֵן in Isa. 22.15 means 'substitute' (for the king), 'prefect', 'governor', 'steward', or 'deputy', that is, the person responsible for the care of the royal palace and of the people, thus the highest official in the land under the king.[4] The nineteen occurrences of the title אֲשֶׁר עַל הַבַּיִת, '(he) who (is) over the house(hold)' (sometimes without אֲשֶׁר) in the Old Testament (Gen. 39.4, 16, 19; 41.40; 44.1, 4; 1 Kgs 4.6; 16.9; 18.3; 2 Kgs 10.5; 15.5 = 2 Chron. 26.21; 2 Kgs 18.18, 37; 19.2 = Isa. 36.3, 22; 37.2; Isa. 22.15), and its eight occurrences in Hebrew inscriptions dating from the preexilic period, as well as the usage of synonymous terms in the Old Testament and in Akkadian texts, suggest that in the early period of the Israelite monarchy beginning with Solomon, it referred to a high governmental official who was in charge of the royal palace and its inhabitants, and later to one who held the highest post in the nation under the king and was over the entire royal estate. Accordingly, he held a governmental position similar to that of the 'chief steward' in Egypt and a high official in Canaanite city states.[5] The contexts in which the Hebrew word

4. See especially A. Alt, 'Hohe Beamte in Ugarit', *Studia Orientalia Ioanni Pedersen* (Copenhagen: Einar Munksgaard, 1953), pp. 1-11; R.A. Henshaw, 'The Office of *Saknu* in Neo-Assyrian Times: I', *JAOS* 87 (1967), pp. 517-25; 'The Office of *Saknu* in Neo-Assyrian Times: II', *JAOS* 88 (1968), pp. 461-83; E. Lipiński, '*Skn* et *Sgn* dans le sémitique occidental du nord', *UF* 5 (1973), pp. 191-207; T. Petit, 'L'évolution sémantique des termes hébreux et araméens *phh* et *sgn* et accadiens *pahatu* et *saknu*', *JBL* 107 (1988), pp. 53-67; and M.W. Stolper, 'The *saknu* of Nippur', *JCS* 40 (1988), pp. 127-55.

5. See in particular R. de Vaux, 'Titres et fonctionnaires égyptiens à la cour de David et de Salomon', *Bible et Orient* (Paris: Cerf, 1967 [1939]), pp. 196-98; T.N.D. Mettinger, *Solomonic State Officials: A Study of the Civil Government Officials of the Israelite Monarchy* (ConBOT, 5; Lund: Gleerup, 1971), pp. 70-79, 109-10; and S.C.

אָב 'father' (or its equivalent) appears as a term for a high governmental official in the Old Testament (five times: Gen. 45.8; 1 Sam. 24.12; 2 Kgs 5.13; Isa. 9.6 [Heb. 5]; 22.21), the Ebla tablets (ca. 2500 BCE), an Egyptian text (early 15th century BCE), the Kilamuwa Inscription (9th century BCE, Phoenician), the Karatepe Inscriptions (9th–8th centuries BCE, two in Hittite, one in Phoenician), the Elephantine Papyri (late 5th century BCE, Aramaic), and 1 Macc. 11.32 indicate this individual was 'second in command' under the king, with very widespread administrative responsibilities.[6] 'The key of the house of David' which Yahweh says he will place on Eliakim's shoulder (which, apparently, had been on Shebna's shoulder) evidently refers to an actual large wooden key which the royal 'steward' carried on his shoulder to lock and unlock doors to various public buildings and offices, whose locks were large (cf. Judg. 3:25; 1 Chron. 9.27). Thus it signified his extensive authority in the Judean governmental administration. He was in charge of the governmental offices and royal chambers, and permitted or refused people to go in to the king. From the central governmental complex in the royal capital, he exercised supreme authority over the entire country. There are noteworthy similarities between Isa. 22.22 and the Egyptian inscriptions on the tomb of the vizier Rekh-mi-Re (who lived during the reign of Thut-most III, Eighteenth Dynasty, 1490–1436 BCE) in the report to the treasurer, and in the account of the daily opening of the king's house.

> Then the vizier, he shall report to the chief treasurer, saying: 'All thy affairs are sound and prosperous; every seat of the court is sound and prosperous. There have been reported to me the sealing of the sealed chambers to this hour (and) the opening of them to (this) hour, by every responsible incumbent.'
>
> Now, after each has reported to the other, of the two officials, then the vizier shall send to open every gate of the king's house, to cause to go in all that goes in, (and) to go out all that goes out likewise, by his messenger, who shall cause it to be put in writing.[7]

This suggests that when the Egyptian vizier opened the palace gates the

---

Layton, 'The Steward in Ancient Israel: A Study of Hebrew (*'aser*) *'al-habbayit* in its Near Eastern Setting', *JBL* 109 (1990), pp. 633-49.

  6. See especially W.A. Ward, 'The Egyptian Office of Joseph', *JSS* 5 (1960), pp. 144-50.

  7. J.H. Breasted, *Ancient Records of Egypt* (Chicago: University of Chicago Press, 1906), 2. 679-80, pp. 274-75.

day officially began, and when he closed them the day officially ended. Hence, he was in complete control of the royal palace and the territory under its jurisdiction.[8] The other terms used for the official who carried the key of David on his shoulder in Isa. 22.15-25 (discussed above) indicate he had a very high authoritative role in Israelite (Judean) government. A.S. Wood describes this official's function very well when he writes: 'What Isaiah had in mind no doubt is the grand vizier or majordomo, into whose hands is committed "unlimited authority over the royal household, carrying with it a similar influence in all affairs of state" (J. Skinner, *Isaiah* [1915], I, 170)'.[9]

2. *Isaiah 22.22 and Revelation 3.7-8*

The figure of (Shebna and?) Eliakim carrying 'the key of the house of David' on his shoulder, and opening so that none shall shut, and shutting so that none shall open (Isa. 22.22) stands behind the statements about Jesus in Rev. 3.7-8 and about Peter in Mt. 16.16-19. C.H. Dodd, B. Lindars, and G.K. Beale have argued very persuasively that New Testament quotations of and references to Old Testament texts are intended to call the hearers' or readers' attention to whole Old Testament contexts in which those quotations or references appear, and not to those quotations or references in isolation from their Old Testament contexts.[10] Further, Lindars affirms that the same Old Testament text

8.   See in particular R. Martin-Achard, 'L'oracle contra Shebnâ et le pouvoir des clefs, Es. 22,15-25', *TZ* 24 (1968), pp. 241-54.

9.   A.S. Wood, 'Key', *ISBE* 3. 10.

10.   In describing the early Christian *method* of using the Old Testament, C.H. Dodd (*According to the Scriptures: The Substructure of New Testament Theology* [New York: Scribner's, 1953), p. 126, writes: 'The method included, first the *selection* of certain large sections of the Old Testament scriptures . . . These sections were understood as *wholes*, and particular verses or sentences were quoted from them rather as pointers to the whole context than as constituting testimonies in and for themselves. At the same time, detached sentences from other parts of the Old Testament could be adduced to illustrate or elucidate the meaning of the main section under consideration. But in the fundamental passages it is the *total context* that is in view, and is the basis of the argument.' B. Lindars (*New Testament Apologetic: The Doctrinal Significance of the Old Testament Quotations* [Philadelphia: Westminster Press, 1961], pp. 16-17) applauds Dodd's position on this point: 'By drawing our

may be used in more than one New Testament context, but that the logical sequence of applications of this Old Testament text may not correspond to the chronological sequence of the New Testament books in which it is quoted or mentioned. As an example, he cites the use of Isa. 6.9-10 in Jn 12.39-40 (the oldest logical application in the New Testament); Acts 28.25-28; and Mk 4.11-12 (the latest logical application in the New Testament), where 'the sequence of interpretation is the direct opposite of the presumed order in which the books themselves were written'.[11] Both of these principles are at work in the use of Isa. 22.22 in Rev. 3.7 and Mt. 16.19.

Although the book of Revelation apparently was written later than the Gospel of Matthew, it preserves an application of Isa. 22:22 which is logically earlier than the application of this text in Matthew. Jesus' statement to Peter in Mt. 16.19, 'I will give you the keys of the kingdom of heaven', assumes that Jesus already possesses these keys and thus is in a position to give them to Peter. But Rev. 3.7 describes Jesus as the one 'who has the key of David'. The traditions reflected in these two texts precede the books in which they are preserved. The origin of each tradition must be determined by considerations other than the dates of the books in which it is preserved.

attention to the blocks of material from which the testimonies have been drawn, Professor Dodd has shown that *the primary meaning must be ascertained by reference to the whole passage*. Generally quotations in the New Testament have not been selected with complete disregard of the original context. Their meaning has been already fixed by the process of working over whole passages which seem most relevant to the Church's fundamental doctrines' (emphasis mine—JTW). Lindars reasons that the early Church used a somewhat limited group of Old Testament passages primarily for apologetic reasons, quoting certain lines from them under various circumstances to address particular issues. 'But this is no arbitrary digging out of proof-texts, without taking the context into account. On the contrary, the context with its Christian interpretation has already defined the meaning of them. It is with this definite meaning that they are found to be useful at a particular stage in argument or discussion' (p. 19).

G.K. Beale ('Revelation', in D.A. Carson and H.G.M. Williamson [eds.], *It Is Written: Scripture Citing Scripture: Essays in Honour of Barnabas Lindars, SSF* [Cambridge: Cambridge University Press, 1988], pp. 321-22) argues that in Revelation, John uses Old Testament texts in harmony with their broader contextual meaning, and cautions against confusing disregard for context with change of application.

11. Lindars, *New Testament Apologetic*, p. 18.

The letter which the risen Christ instructs John to write to the church in Philadelphia begins by declaring:

> These are the words of the holy one, the true one,
>> who has the key of David,
>> who opens and no one will shut,
>>> who shuts and no one opens (Rev. 3.7).

Apparently Christ designates himself in this way because he begins his message to the church at Philadelphia by saying: 'I know your works. Look, I have set before you an open door, which no one is able to shut' (v. 8). Scholars have understood the connection between this description of Christ and these initial words in various ways.

1. G.B. Caird argues that in v. 7 John echoes the language of Isa. 22.22, where the 'key of the house of David' symbolizes that Eliakim, the new steward under Hezekiah, has complete control over the royal household, and authority to grant or refuse access to the king's presence. Thus one might expect John to use this text to declare that Christ had the right to grant or refuse access to God. But John develops the imagery of the key in a different direction. In v. 8, Christ declares that he has opened a door of opportunity for the Philadelphian Christians to participate in the conversion of the Jews living in their region. Here he turns upside down the Jewish hope of converting the Gentiles to God, frequently expressed in the Old Testament, especially in the book of Isaiah (cf., for example, Isa. 43.4; 45.14; 60.14), and declares that it is not the Gentile oppressors of Israel, but the Jewish persecutors of the church, who must accept Christ as the true Holy One of Israel, and the church as the true Israel. Human beings cannot accomplish this conversion of Jews to Christ. However, since Christ has opened the door of opportunity for Christians to proclaim the gospel faithfully to the Jews, no one can shut the door, but God will supply the power for the gospel to realize success among the Jews.[12]

2. Several scholars contend that the statement that Christ has the key of David is messianic (cf. Rev. 5.5; 22.16), and that this means that he has complete authority to admit people to or to exclude people from the city of David, the New Jerusalem. In this context, admission pertains primarily to believing Gentiles and exclusion primarily to unbelieving

---

12. G.B. Caird, *A Commentary on the Revelation of St John the Divine* (New York: Harper & Row, 1966), pp. 51-53. On the 'inverted use of the Old Testament' in Rev. 3.9, see Beale, 'Revelation', pp. 330-31.

Jews, but still the scope is universal. Christ has authority in the kingdom of God (Eph. 1.22) essentially analogous to Eliakim's authority in the kingdom of Hezekiah. H.B. Swete refers to Eliakim as the 'antitype' (*sic* Does he mean 'type'?) of the exalted Christ. The 'open door' of v. 8 calls to mind Paul's use of the same figure (1 Cor. 16.19; 2 Cor. 2.12; Col. 4.3), and thus refers to the opportunity for Christian teachers at Philadelphia to preach the gospel, especially to unbelieving Jews (cf. v. 9). The Old Testament expectation that the Gentiles would be converted to God through the missionary efforts of the Jews (cf., for example, Isa. 60.14) is reversed here, so that the expectation expressed in Rev. 3.8-9 is that the Jews would play the role of the heathen and acknowledge Christians to be the true Israel.[13]

3.   A. Farrer calls attention to several connections between the context of Isa. 22.15-25 and the context of Rev. 3.7-13. In Rev. 3.7, John agrees with Mt. 16.19 in taking the key to be the key of life and death, whose possessor has the authority to exclude from or to admit to the messianic kingdom or the New Jerusalem. Just as the unfaithful key-bearer Shebna is demoted and a worthy minister Eliakim put in his position (Isa. 22.15-23), so the elders of the synagogue, who falsely claim they have the authority of David and use that authority to shut the door of access to God to Christians, will be humbled before those who faithfully follow Christ, who has the key of David and opens a door to Christians which none can shut (cf. Jn 9.34–10.9). Christ's admonition, 'hold fast what you have, so that no one may seize your crown' (Rev. 3.11), places the Philadelphian Christians in bold contrast to Shebna, who, in forfeiting the keys, loses his crown (Isa. 22.21, LXX) to faithful Eliakim. Also, just as the Lord promises Eliakim that he will fix him as a nail in a sure place, so Christ promises the victorious Philadelphian Christian that he will make him a pillar in God's temple, and he will never leave it again (Rev. 3.12).[14]

4.   Several scholars reason that John uses the language of Isa. 22.22 in Rev. 3.7 to present Christ as the Davidic Messiah with absolute

13. C.A. Scott, *Revelation* (The Century Bible; Edinburgh: T.C. & E.C. Jack, 1904), p. 152; H.B. Swete, *The Apocalypse of St John* (London: MacMillan, 3rd edn, 1911 [1906]), pp. 53-54; R.H. Charles, *A Critical and Exegetical Commentary on the Revelation of St John* I (ICC; New York: Scribner's, 1920), pp. 86-89; and J.M. Ford, *Revelation* (AB, 38; Garden City: Doubleday, 1975), p. 416.

14. A. Farrer, *The Revelation of St John the Divine* (Oxford: Clarendon Press, 1954), pp. 80-81.

authority to admit persons to or to exclude them from the New Jerusalem, the heavenly kingdom. John's purpose may be to contrast Christ's admitting Jews into God's kingdom, as the only mediator between humanity and God, with the practice of the local synagogue in Philadelphia of excommunicating Christian Jews. Thus the 'open door' refers to the opportunity which Christ has given Christian Jews, who have been excommunicated from the local synagogue (v. 9), to enter into the messianic kingdom, God's eternal kingdom; and not to a great opportunity for missionary activity by Christians at Philadelphia. Christ's announcement that those 'who say that they are Jews and are not' will 'come and bow down before your feet' (v. 9) suggests Christian vindication against Jewish opponents, not the conversion of Jews to Christ.[15] The use of Isa. 22.15-25 here and the context of Rev. 3.7 favor this interpretation.

These considerations yield four conclusions. First, Christ 'has' the key of David (Rev. 3.7) because God the Father has given it to him. Secondly, as a result of this, Christ functions as the major domo under God his Father. In this role, he is like Shebna and Eliakim, both of whom served as major domo under Hezekiah. John draws this analogy by borrowing language from Isa. 22.22, the meaning of which was already well known to his readers.[16] Thirdly, as major domo, Christ has

15. R.H. Preston and A.T. Hanson, *The Revelation of Saint John the Divine* (Torch Bible Commentaries; London: SCM Press, 1949), pp. 66-67; L. Morris, *The Revelation of St. John* (Tyndale New Testament Commentaries; Grand Rapids: Eerdmans, 1969), pp. 78-79; G.R. Beasley-Murray, *The Book of Revelation* (NCB; Grand Rapids: Eerdmans, 1981 [1974]), pp. 100-101; R.H. Mounce, *The Book of Revelation* (Grand Rapids: Eerdmans, 1977), pp. 116-17; J. Sweet, *Revelation* (TPI New Testament Commentaries; Philadelphia: Trinity Press International, 1979), pp. 101-03; and A.Y. Collins, 'The Apocalypse (Revelation)' (NJBC; Englewood Cliffs, NJ: Prentice–Hall, 1990), p. 1003.

The statements of E.H. Plumptre ('The Epistles to the Seven Churches of Asia. VI.–Philadelphia. (Rev. iii.7-13)', *The Expositor*, first series, 3 [1876], pp. 286-87) are confusing. On the one hand, he says that the open door of v. 8 refers to the admission of the Gentiles into the church; but on the other hand, he says it refers to divinely-approved opportunities for mission work by the church. It is difficult to understand how the door Christ opens could be an opportunity for Christian preachers to proclaim the gospel to Gentiles and the admission of the Gentiles into the church at the same time.

16. G. von Rad (*Old Testament Theology* [2 vols.; repr.; Edinburgh: Oliver & Boyd, 1967 (1965)], II, 47-48, p. 373) explains the relationship between Isa. 22.15-

complete authority over the King's (that is, God the Father's) household or kingdom, the church. He has total control over who is admitted into the King's presence and who is excluded from it, like Shebna and Eliakim did under Hezekiah (Isa. 22.22). Fourthly, in contrast to the authorities in the local synagogue at Philadelphia who have excommunicated Christian Jews, the exalted Christ sets before these excommunicated individuals an open door into God's kingdom, where he will make them pillars in the temple of God so that they shall never go out of it (Rev. 3.12). Those who pretend to be Jews, but in reality are of the synagogue of Satan, will then come and bow down before the feet of genuine Jewish Christians whom they had excommunicated, thereby conceding defeat at their hands because of Christ's power (Rev. 3.9).

3. *Isaiah 22.22 and Matthew 16.16-19*

Matthew's description of Peter's great confession of Christ and then opposition to his announcement that he would go to Jerusalem and be crucified there (Mt. 16.13-23) assumes that his readers knew the Old Testament passage concerning Shebna and Eliakim in Isa. 22.15-25. There are three critical issues in this Matthean pericope, the solution to each of which may be illuminated by recognizing the way this Isaianic text provides a background for it.

First, it is important to attempt to determine precisely what Peter was confessing about Jesus' identity (Mt. 16.16). Many scholars believe the expression, 'You are... the Son of the Living God', means Peter was affirming Jesus' divine origin and nature.[17] They cite Mt. 2.15; 3.17; 4.3, 6; 8.29; 11.27; and 14.33, where Jesus is called the 'Son of

---

25 and Rev. 3.7 typologically. First Shebna, then Eliakim, possessed 'almost Messianic full powers', but both of them failed in their God-appointed task. 'Thus, the office of 'the key of David' remained unprovided for until finally it could be laid down at the feet of Christ (Rev. III. 7)' (p. 373).

17. So F.V. Filson, *A Commentary on the Gospel according to St Matthew* (London: A. & C. Black, 1960), p. 185; E.F. Sutcliffe, 'St Peter's Double Confession in Mt 16:16-19', *HeyJ* 3 (1962), pp. 31-41; J.L. McKenzie, SJ, 'The Gospel according to Matthew' (JBC; Englewood Cliffs, NJ: Prentice–Hall, 1968), p. 91; D. Hill, *The Gospel of Matthew* (NCB; Grand Rapids: Eerdmans, 1981 [1972]), p. 260; R.E. Brown, K.P. Donfried, and J. Reumann (eds.), *Peter in the New Testament: A Collaborative Assessment by Protestant and Roman Catholic Scholars* (Minneapolis: Augsburg, 1973), p. 86 (citing Jn 20.31); and B.T. Viviano, 'The Gospel according to Matthew' (NJBC; Englewood Cliffs, NJ: Prentice–Hall, 1990), p. 659.

God', and interpret these texts to mean by this expression that Jesus is divine. Perhaps this meaning could be argued from Jn 5.18, according to which the Jews concluded that because Jesus called God his Father, he made himself equal with God. However, in the context of Mt. 16.16, it seems clear that 'the Son of the Living God' is equivalent to 'the Christ' (Messiah)'.[18] 'Messiah' (1 Sam. 24.6; 26.9, 11; 2 Sam. 1.14; Pss. 20.6; 84.9 [Hebrew 10]; 89.38) and 'Son of God' (2 Sam. 7.14; 1 Chron. 22.10; 28.6; Pss. 2.7; 89.26-27) are two of several titles for the kings of Israel and Judah in the Old Testament. Accordingly, Peter's confession assumes the widely held Jewish belief of his day that God will raise up a king who will sit on David's throne in Jerusalem, and through him will bring about his ideal kingdom on earth, and affirms his personal conviction that Jesus is that king.

Secondly, it is necessary to attempt to determine the meaning of 'binding' and 'loosing' in Mt. 16.19, and how Jesus' statement about Peter's binding and loosing is related to his promise that he would give Peter the keys of the kingdom of heaven. Scholars have interpreted δέω 'bind', and λύω 'loose', in Mt. 16.19 in at least four ways.

1.   On the basis of the use of δέω and λύω in intertestamental Jewish sources and elsewhere in the New Testament (for example, Mk 3.20-27 = Mt. 12.22-29 = Lk. 11.14-22; Mk 7.31-37; Lk. 13.10-17),[19] Hiers argues that the sayings of Jesus now preserved in Mt. 16.19 and 18.18 originally had to do with Jesus authorizing or empowering Peter and the Twelve to exorcise demons, that is, to 'bind' demons and to 'loose' the demon-possessed in order to prepare them for their new life in the kingdom of God. But in their present Matthean contexts, these statements may refer to Jesus authorizing church leaders to make decisions with regard to congregational order or Christian morality. 'Binding' and 'loosing' suggest that Peter and the other apostles would have authority to deal with whatever problems might arise in the continuing years of the church, possibly including matters of doctrine,

18. So also W.F. Albright and C.S. Mann, *Matthew* (AB, 26; Garden City, NY: Doubleday, 1971), pp. 181, 194; H.C. Kee, 'The Gospel according to Matthew', *The Interpreter's One-Volume Commentary on the Bible* (ed. C.M. Laymon; London: Collins, 1971), p. 629.

19. On the use of this terminology in this passage, see H. Welzen, 'Loosening and Binding: Lk. 13.10-21 as Programme and Anti-Programme of the Gospel of Luke', in S. Draisma (ed.), *Intertextuality in Biblical Writings: Essays in honour of Bas van Iersel* (Kampen: Kok, 1989), pp. 175-87.

excommunication, and determining the ultimate destiny of members of the church.[20]

2. Some argue that 'bind' and 'loose' are terms pertaining to discipline in the church, including the right to condemn ('bind') or acquit ('loose') (cf. Mt. 18.18). The meaning of Mt. 16.19 is stated in a different way in Jn 20.23, which speaks of the disciples forgiving and retaining sins, apparently by preaching the gospel. Thus, to 'loose' refers to the divine power to forgive sins, and so to admit converts into and to restore penitent sinners to the church. To 'bind' is to announce God's judgment on unbelievers and impenitent sinners, and to excommunicate offenders from the church.[21] 'Binding' and 'loosing' refer to the broad power of allowing or refusing entrance into the kingdom.[22]

3. Others contend that 'bind' and 'loose' allude to teaching what is forbidden or permitted. In rabbinic literature, these terms are used of the verdict of the teacher of the law who declares an action 'bound' (forbidden, wrong) or 'loosed' (permitted, right), not of retaining sins or forgiving them.[23] Thus, Peter has the authority to declare what laws

---

20. R.H. Hiers, '"Binding" and "Loosing": The Matthean Authorizations', *JBL* 104 (1985), pp. 233-50.

21. So O. Cullmann, *Peter: Disciple, Apostle, Martyr* (Philadelphia: Westminster Press, 2nd edn, 1962), p. 211; J.A. Emerton, 'Binding and Loosing—Forgiving and Retaining', *JTS* 13 (1962), pp. 325-31 (possibly); P.H. Menoud, 'Binding and Loosing', *IDB* 1 (1962), p. 438; P. Bonnard, *L'Évangile selon Saint Matthieu* (CNT, 1; Neuchâtel: Delachaux & Niestlé, 1963), p. 246; H.W. Basser, 'Derrett's "Binding" Reopened', *JBL* 104 (1985), pp. 297-300; and G.W. Bromiley, 'Keys, Power of the', *ISBE*, p. 12. Hill (*The Gospel of Matthew*, p. 262) argues that views (1) and (2) amount to the same thing, namely, Peter has authority to make pronouncements (legislative or disciplinary), and these will be ratified by God in the Last Judgment. Z.W. Falk ('Binding and Loosing', *JJS* 25 [1974], pp. 92-100) proposes that 'binding' refers to holding a person to a vow, while 'loosing' pertains to releasing a person from a vow. This is a type of retaining or forgiving sins, but seems much too limited for the contexts of Mt. 16.19 and 18.18.

22. See Cullmann, *Peter: Disciple, Apostle, Martyr*, pp. 209-10; and Brown, Donfried, and Reumann (eds.), *Peter in the New Testament*, p. 97.

23. A.H. McNeile, *The Gospel according to St Matthew* (London: MacMillan, 1915), p. 243; B.T.D. Smith, *The Gospel according to St Matthew* (Cambridge Greek Testament; repr.; Cambridge: Cambridge University Press, 2nd edn, 1950 [1927]), p. 154; G.E.P. Cox, *The Gospel according to St Matthew* (Torch Bible Commentaries; repr.; London: SCM Press, 1956 [1952]), p. 111; Filson, *A Commentary on the Gospel according to St Matthew*, p. 187; R.V.G. Tasker, *The Gospel according to St Matthew* (TNTC; Grand Rapids: Eerdmans, 1961), p. 158;

in the Mosaic Torah are 'binding' on Christians, and what laws they are 'loosed' from observing.[24] Stated somewhat more broadly, binding and loosing refers to 'the interpretation of the Scriptures and the determination of an appropriate Christian way of life'.[25]

4. It seems best to understand 'binding and loosing' together as a unified concept equivalent to possessing the keys of the kingdom of heaven, and meaning the totality of power entrusted to Peter and the other apostles without being more specific.[26] J.L. McKenzie writes: 'The phrase certainly signifies the exercise of authority; but the nature and use of the authority are not specified'.[27] Accordingly, 'binding' and 'loosing' are ultimately the same as 'shutting' and 'opening', which is the task of the major domo of the palace or nation. In Mt. 23.13, Jesus condemns the Pharisees, saying: 'You lock people out of the kingdom of heaven. For you do not go in yourselves, and when others are going in, you stop them.' They do this by portraying the Law as a heavy burden which is hard to bear (Mt. 23.4), by not practicing what they teach (Mt. 23.3), and by doing their deeds to be seen by men (Mt. 23.5-7). In sharp contrast to this, Jesus instructs Peter to declare that God is anxious to forgive penitent sinners and grant them entrance into his kingdom, but turns away the self-righteous, who are quick to condemn and shut out others.[28] 'Binding and loosing' in Mt. 16.19 and

Emerton, 'Binding and Loosing—Forgiving and Retaining', pp. 325-31 (possibly); Kee, 'The Gospel according to Matthew', p. 630; J.D.M. Derrett, 'Binding and Loosing (Matt 16:19; 18:18; John 20:23)', *JBL* 102 (1983), pp. 112-17; and V. Kesich, 'Peter's Primacy in the New Testament and the Early Tradition', in J. Meyendorff (ed.), *The Primacy of Peter: Essays in Ecclesiology and the Early Church* (Crestwood: St Vladimir's Seminary Press, 1992), pp. 51-52.

24. S.E. Johnson, 'The Gospel according to St Matthew: Introduction and Exegesis', *IB* 7 (Nashville: Abingdon–Cokesbury, 1951), p. 453; and J. Marcus, 'The Gates of Hades and the Keys of the Kingdom (Matt 16:18-19)', *CBQ* 50 (1988), pp. 443-55, esp. pp. 449-55.

25. R.F. Collins, 'Binding and Loosing', *ABD* 1 (1992), p. 744. So also G. Bornkamm, 'The Authority to "Bind" and "Loose" in the Church in Matthew's Gospel', *Perspective* 11 (1970), pp. 37-50; J.R. Mantey, 'Distorted Translations in John 20:23; Matthew 16:18-19 and 18:18', *RevExp* 78 (1981), pp. 409-16; and F. Manns, 'La Halakah dans l'évangile de Matthieu: note sur Mt. 16.16-19', *BibOr* 25 (1983), pp. 129-35.

26. See Menoud, 'Binding and Loosing', p. 439 (who does not accept this view).

27. McKenzie, 'The Gospel according to Matthew', p. 92.

28. See U. Luz, 'The Primacy Text (Mt. 16:18)', *Princeton Seminary Bulletin* NS 12 (1991), pp. 41-55, esp. pp. 46-47. M.A. Powell ('Do and Keep what Moses

18.18 may very well be a case of merismus, a syntactical phenomenon in which two polar terms are used to express the whole reality.[29] J. Krasovec pairs פָּתַח 'to loose', with אָסַר 'to bind'.[30] But there is also good reason to pair פָּתַח with סָגַר. In the piel, פָּתַח means 'to loose, loosen, set free'.[31] And in the hiphil, סָגַר means 'to deliver up to, shut up, imprison'.[32] This calls to mind the merismus 'bind... loose' in Mt. 16.19 and 18.18. In view of this, Mt. 16.19 affirms that 'Peter is... the chief steward, the *major domus*, in the Kingdom; the 'keys' are the symbol of rule and authority, entrusted by the real Holder...; cf. Apoc. iii. 7 (based on Is. xxii.22)'.[33]

> Isa xxii 15ff. undoubtedly lies behind this saying [i.e., Matt 16:19]. The keys are the symbol of authority, and Roland de Vaux... rightly sees here the same authority as that vested in the vizier, the master of the house, the chamberlain, of the royal household in ancient Israel... The role of Peter as steward of the Kingdom is further explained as being the exercise of administrative authority, as was the case of the Old Testament chamberlain who held the 'keys'... Peter's initiative is well illustrated by the admission of a Gentile to the community in Acts x-xi, under the guidance of the Spirit.[34]

The Greek expressions ἔσται δεδεμένον (δεδεμένα) and ἔσται λελυμένον (λελυμένα) are future perfect periphrastics. Since this syntactical form is rare in the New Testament, the force of its meaning must be respected here. Hence, the statements in which these periphrastics appear in Mt. 16.19 and 18.18 should be rendered: 'Whatever you shall bind on earth *shall have been bound* in heaven, and whatever

---

Says [Matthew 23:2-7]', *JBL* 114 [1995], pp. 419-35, esp. pp. 433-34) also calls attention to the contrast between Mt. 16.19; 18.18 and 23.13, but thinks 'binding and loosing' have to do with interpreting the words of Moses for the present day, which inevitably affects determination of membership in the community.

29. 'Die einzelnen Termini besitzen nicht eine realistische Bedeutung, sondern stehen symbolisch-stellvertretend für die gesamte Realität oder Gattung einer gegebenen Ebene.' J. Krasovec, *Der Merismus im Biblisch–Hebräischen und Nordwestsemitischen* (BibOr, 33; Rome: Biblical Institute Press, 1977), p. 3.

30. Krasovec, *Der Merismus*, pp. 134-35 (no. 202), citing Job 12.18 as an example.

31. BDB 835.

32. BDB 689.

33. McNeile, *The Gospel according to St. Matthew*, p. 243.

34. Albright and Mann, *Matthew*, pp. 196-97.

you shall loose on earth *shall have been loosed* in heaven' (so also the Vg). 'It is the Church on earth carrying out heaven's decisions, communicated by the Spirit, and not heaven ratifying the Church's decisions.'[35]

Thirdly, it is somewhat disturbing that the pericope describing Peter's great confession (Mt. 16.13-20) is followed immediately by the pericope in which Peter opposes Jesus when he announces that he must go to Jerusalem and suffer and die there, and Jesus responds by addressing Peter as Satan and by accusing Peter for being on the side of men rather than on the side of God (Mt. 16.21-23). However, Peter is holding to the common Jewish messianic understanding of his day, and thus cannot accept the concept of a 'suffering Messiah'.[36] The sequence of Peter's God-revealed confession of Jesus (Mt. 16.17) followed by Peter's Satan-motivated objection to Jesus' proclamation that he must suffer and die (Mt. 16.21-23) corresponds strikingly to the sequence of God's elevation of Eliakim to Shebna's office (Isa. 22.20-23) followed by a prophetic announcement that he and all his household will fall (Isa. 22.24-25). The language of Jesus' promise to give Peter the keys of the kingdom of heaven calls to mind God's promise to Eliakim in Isa. 22.22. And the sequence of Peter's confession of and opposition to Jesus calls to mind the sequence of Eliakim's rise and fall.

35. Albright and Mann, *Matthew*, p. 197. The advocates of all four of these views usually believe that the 'rock' on which Jesus will build his church is Peter. However, B.D. Chilton ('Shebna, Eliakim, and the Promise to Peter', in J. Neusner, P. Borgen, E.S. Frerichs and R. Horsley [eds.], *The Social World of Formative Christianity and Judaism: Essays in Tribute to Howard Clark Kee* [Philadelphia: Fortress Press, 1988], pp. 311-26) argues that the 'rock' here is Mount Zion, referring to the Temple. The overall framework of the *Targum of Isaiah* centers on the restoration of the house of Israel, at the center of which are the Temple and Jerusalem. This targum speaks to dispersed and disoriented Israel, who has no cult but expects a Messiah who will restore the Temple and the autonomy of Israel, but only for those who repent according to the Law. In Mt. 23.16-22; 5.23-24; 17.24-27; 21.12-13; 24.1-25, Jesus is presented as developing halakoth in respect to the Temple. Similar to the targumic interpretation of Isa. 22.22, in Mt. 16.18-19 Jesus is establishing the mechanism for articulating the cultic halakah. While Chilton's argument is well-presented and worthy of serious consideration, it does not seem to come naturally from the context of Mt. 16.13-20.

36. See McNeile, *The Gospel according to St Matthew*, pp. 244, 245-46; Cox, *The Gospel according to St Matthew*, p. 113; Filson, *A Commentary on the Gospel according to St Matthew*, pp. 188-89; Bonnard, *L'évangile selon Saint Matthieu*, p. 248; Albright and Mann, *Matthew*, p. 200; and Hill, *The Gospel of Matthew*, pp. 263-64.

4. *Conclusions*

This study has led to the following conclusions.

1. Isa. 22.15-23 was addressed to Shebna, the major domo of Hezekiah, some time between 715 and 701 BCE. The prophet condemns Shebna for his arrogance, announces that he will be removed from the office of steward or major domo and carried into exile, and declares that Eliakim will replace him. Shebna was removed from being major domo and replaced by Eliakim, but instead of being carried into exile he was demoted to secretary or scribe.

2. Isa. 22.24-25 is a later oracle by the prophet or one of his disciples when he learned that some of Eliakim's relatives were putting pressure on him to use his office to benefit them. The prophet declares that this problem of nepotism will increase until 'all' of Eliakim's household will be involved; then Eliakim and his whole house will fall. However, vv. 24-25 do not make sense without statements to which they refer in vv. 15-23, so this later oracle could not have circulated independently of vv. 15-23, and is inseparably connected to this earlier oracle.

3. Accordingly, Isa. 22.15-25 should be read as a whole. In this case, four basically synonymous terms for the major domo emerge: 'steward' (v. 15), '(he) who (is) over the house' (v. 15), 'father' (v. 21), and '(he who carries) the key of the house of David' (v. 22). Each of these terms may be used to illuminate the meaning of any of the other terms.

4. Isa. 22.22 provides the background for the description of Christ in Rev. 3.7 as the one who has the key of David, who opens and no one will shut, who shuts and no one opens. In the context of Isa. 22.15-25, the king is Hezekiah and, first Shebna, then Eliakim is his major domo; and, essentially parallel to this, in Rev. 3.7, God is the king and Christ is his major domo. Under God's appointment to this position, Christ has complete authority over God's kingdom; he has the key of David, and he allows or forbids people to enter that kingdom.

5. Mt. 16.13-23 assumes the reader knows the context of Isa. 22.15-25, and in Mt. 16.19 Jesus borrows the language of Isa. 22.22. According to Mt. 16.16, Peter confesses that Jesus is 'the Christ', 'the Son of the living God', that is, that Jesus is king. The expression 'Son of God' is one of the common Old Testament titles for a king, and the context

of Mt. 16.16 shows Peter had that nuance in mind in his confession, not the idea that Jesus is divine as in other New Testament contexts. Jesus commends Peter for the words he used, but not for his understanding of those words. He tells Peter that he (Peter) will be the rock on which his (Jesus') church will be built. Then, in his role as king, Jesus gives Peter the keys of the kingdom of heaven, the authority and responsibility to bind and loose on earth what has already been bound and loosed in heaven, that is, Jesus makes Peter the major domo of his kingdom with all the privileges and responsibilities accruing to that function.

6. The sequence of Peter's confession that Jesus is the Christ, the Son of the living God, that is, that Jesus is king (Mt. 16:13-20), immediately followed by Peter's denunciation of Jesus for announcing that he will go to Jerusalem to suffer and die there, and Jesus' rebuke of Peter for setting his mind on human things rather than divine things (Mt. 16.21-23), is strikingly similar to the sequence of Isaiah's announcement that Shebna will be removed from his position as major domo under Hezekiah and will be replaced by Eliakim (Isa. 22.15-23), immediately followed by the prophet's declaration that Eliakim will fall along with his household because all his household will seek special favors from him as one who holds a high office in the Judean government (Isa. 22.24-25).

THE INTERPRETATION OF PSALM 95 IN HEBREWS 3.1–4.13[*]

Peter Enns

The purpose of this paper is to discuss the theological concerns that motivated the author of Hebrews to interpret Ps. 95.7b-11 the way he did. This part of the psalm deals with the rebellion of the wilderness community at Meribah and Massah, and is quoted in Heb. 3.7b-11. The writer's particular understanding of Psalm 95 is apparently motivated by a desire to recontextualize the psalm for his audience. His handling of the psalm exhibits similarities to *pesher* exegesis in which a particular passage is given an eschatological interpretation, 'relating to the sect's own position in history, and rooted in its peculiar attitude to the biblical text'.[1] It is significant that he does not quote the psalm as a proof-text to support a preceding argument, as is the case for his Old Testament quotations in the first two chapters. The psalm does not provide data to support a theological point. Rather, it is quoted simply 'for the sake of exposition and application'.[2] This tells us something about the writer's understanding of the church's situation in redemptive history. In the same way that the original exodus community, which rebelled at Meribah and Massah, was a community wandering through the wilderness, so too is the church a community of wilderness wanderers living between Egypt and Canaan with the ever present possibility of rebellion. It is already assumed on the basis of 3.1-6 that Israel and the

---

[*] A fuller and slightly revised version of this paper, which includes a discussion on the structure and interpretation of Psalm 95, may be found in P. Enns, 'Creation and Re-Creation: Psalm 95 and its Interpretation in Hebrews 3:1–4:13', *WTJ* 55 (1993), pp. 255-80.

1. D. Dimant, 'Qumran Sectarian Literature', in *Jewish Writings of the Second Temple Period* (CRINT, 2.2; ed. M.E. Stone; Philadelphia: Fortress Press, 1984), p. 507.

2. S. Kistemaker, *The Psalm Citations in the Epistle to the Hebrews* (Amsterdam: Van Soest, 1961), p. 85.

church are in analogous situations.[3] What once applied to Israel now finds its full meaning with respect to the church.

The precise issue before us, however, is the writer's interpretative handling of the psalm. There is little question that the writer is quoting the LXX rather than the MT. Yet, the author's quotation of the psalm is not entirely consistent with the LXX. We might say that in wishing to make this psalm more relevant to his readers, he says things *about* Psalm 95 that are not actually found *in* Psalm 95. The writer's particular understanding of the psalm for his readers is reflected in three significant variations from the LXX. The most significant variation is the insertion of the conjunction διό 'therefore' in v. 10. The second is the prepositional phrase ἐν δοκιμασίᾳ 'with scrutiny', in v. 9, where the LXX and MT both have a verb (LXX ἐδοκίμασεν 'they tried' and MT בְּחָנוּנִי 'they tried me'). The third variation is ταύτῃ 'this' generation, in v. 10, where the LXX reads ἐκείνῃ 'that' generation.

We are given some insight into the author's theological concerns first by his insertion of διό in v. 10. This particle is absent in the LXX and has no corresponding particle in the MT. Neither is there any manuscript evidence for this variant. Verses 9-10a in the LXX read, 'Where your fathers tested, they tried, and saw my works. I was angry with that generation for forty years.' Similarly, the MT reads, 'Where your fathers tested me, they tried me even though they saw my works. I was angry with that[4] generation for forty years.' The point is that both of these texts state that God was angry for forty years. In other words, God's anger was a characteristic of the wilderness period, an observation that a reading of the wilderness narratives quickly bears out. The addition of διό in Heb. 3.10, on the other hand, changes the meaning significantly. The forty-year period refers now not to the period of God's wrath, but to the period of God's activity in the desert. 'Your fathers tested with scrutiny and saw my works for forty years. Therefore [διό] I was angry with this generation.' God was not angry for

---

3. C. Spicq argues that the use of Psalm 95 '. . . presupposes an exact correspondence between the successive generations of the people of God, and perfect steadfastness in God's conduct toward them. . . ' citing 1.1-2 as anticipating this idea (*L'épître aux Hebreux* [Paris: Gabalda, 1953], p. 71). I agree with Spicq's observation, but would emphasize that 3.1-6 in particular presents Jesus as the second Moses and the church as the new Israel.

4. There is no demonstrative in the MT. It is added here to smooth out the translation.

forty years. Rather anger is what follows the forty-year period in which they saw God's works.

Why does Hebrews insert διό? Why does he remove the notion of God's anger from the wilderness period, where it certainly seems to belong, and place it after? It seems that he is concerned to portray the wilderness period in a positive light—one that is not characterized by wrath. But why would he want to do this? Because his purpose for quoting Psalm 95 is to warn the *church*, the *new* wilderness community.

To elaborate: the syntax of the LXX and MT equate the period of God's activity with that of God's wrath. After all, the entire forty-year period of wandering is the punishment for Israel's wanting to return to Egypt in Numbers 14. Psalm 95 views the wilderness period negatively. But this negative impression will not do for Hebrews.[5] The church's period of wilderness wandering is not one of wrath but of blessing. The church is not subject to God's punishment as was the first wilderness community. Those that make up the body of Christ are rather 'partakers of a heavenly calling' (Heb. 3.1), or in the language of Heb. 2.4, they have witnessed 'signs, wonders, various miracles, and gifts of the Holy Spirit'. What were the works *they* saw? Not wrath, but the coming of the Messiah and the inauguration of the church age. For the author of Hebrews this is clearly not a show of God's anger, but of his blessing—indeed the climactic realization of his redemptive plan.[6] The new Moses had come and the new Israel was born, and this was attested to by 'signs, wonders, and miracles'. These are the 'works' that the new Israel had seen during her period of wilderness wandering. The

---

5.   The innovation on the part of our author is certainly not in giving a positive evaluation of the wilderness period, since such an evaluation has ample Old Testament precedent. For example, the desert was seen as a place where God showed his benevolence to his people (e.g. Pss. 78.15-20; 105.41; 107.6; 114.8; see also Wis. 11.4-14; *Bib. Ant.* 10.7; 11.15; 20.8; 1 Cor. 10.1-4). The innovation is in the fact that the author interprets *Psalm 95* in this way. Moreover, the fact that the author of Hebrews refers to the *Tabernacle* as the copy of the heavenly sanctuary (8.1-2; 9.1-2, 11) rather than the *Temple* is further evidence of his positive opinion of the wilderness period.

6.   E. Gräßer comments briefly that the purpose of διό is to emphasize the experience of God's salvific activity (*Heilserfahrung*), what he refers to as 'vierzig Jahre Wundererweisungen Gottes' (*An die Hebräer [Hebr 1–6]* [EKKNT; Zürich: Benzinger Verlag; Neukirchen–Vluyn: Neukirchener Verlag, 1990], p. 176). See also H. Attridge's comments (*The Epistle to the Hebrews* [Hermeneia; Philadelphia: Fortress Press, 1989], p. 115).

insertion of διό serves to make the clear distinction between the forty-year period of God's activity, and the subsequent period of his anger. Anger is what follows upon disbelief in God's activity, not what characterizes the period of God's activity. Hence, in applying the psalm to the church, the writer of Hebrews is telling his readers that their wilderness period is one of blessing, not wrath or punishment. If they are unfaithful by following the example of the Israelites, and 'testing with scrutiny God's works', this present age will be *followed* by God's anger in which they forfeit the promise of rest.

That the writer is fully aware of his exegetical technique is made certain in 3.17. There, regarding *Israel's* disbelief (not the church's), he asks, 'And with whom was he angry for forty years?'. Here the writer follows the syntax of the LXX, which reads the forty years as a period of God's wrath. This is the exact opposite of what he did in 3.10. This raises the following question: why would the author of Hebrews give the same verse, which for him was Holy Scripture, two different meanings? Apart from the ubiquity of exegetical techniques such as this in first-century Judaism, I suggest the following theological motivation: in 3.10 he is talking about the church, whereas in 3.17 he is talking about Israel. Simply by quoting this psalm, the author is making a statement regarding the *continuity* between Israel and the church: both have a wilderness period. Yet, the negative overtones in Psalm 95 regarding the wilderness period would not suit the reality of the church age as one of great blessing. This is why he inserts διό in v. 10. The syntax of 3.17, however, is not intended merely to reflect more accurately the syntax of the LXX, as if his exegetical conscience suddenly began to bother him. Rather, he is making explicit in 3.17 what was implied by the insertion of διό in v. 10: there is a distinction between the two periods of wilderness wandering. The Israelite wilderness period was one of wrath: 3.17, 'With whom was he angry for forty years?'. The church's wilderness period is one of divine blessing: 3.10, 'They saw my works for forty years'. Although Israel may have fallen away shortly after her exodus, thus characterizing her wilderness wandering as a time of wrath, the period following the church's exodus is characterized by 'signs, wonders, various miracles and gifts of the Holy Spirit'. For the writer of Hebrews, then, there is continuity and discontinuity between the two wilderness periods. The two are analogous, but not merely so.[7] This is in keeping with what is perhaps the major

---

7.   P.E. Hughes argues that there is an 'ambivalence of association' regarding

theme throughout the book of Hebrews: the new supersedes the old.[8]

Besides the addition of διό in v. 10, a second factor that highlights this emphasis on God's activity is the prepositional phrase ἐν δοκιμασίᾳ in v. 9. Attridge suggests that '... δοκιμασίᾳ has connotations of close and even skeptical scrutiny', which yields the translation, 'Where your fathers tested with scrutiny and saw my works...'[9] We should notice that the object of the testing in Hebrews is not God, as is the case with the MT, but the works. Here Hebrews agrees with the LXX. But our author goes beyond the LXX by changing the verb ἐδοκίμασεν to the prepositional phrase ἐν δοκιμασίᾳ. The effect is to draw further attention to the faithlessness of the exodus community in view of these works. He does not say with the LXX: 'Your fathers tested, *they tried* my works'. Hebrews reads: 'Your fathers tested *with scrutiny* my works'. He is telling his readers that the age in which they live, and the blessings in which they partake, are themselves a certain and true witness to God's ongoing faithfulness in bringing the new exodus community to its rest. Skepticism and disbelief regarding these sure signs are unthinkable.[10]

---

the forty-year period, but the 'overall sense of the passage is not altered' (*A Commentary on the Epistle to the Hebrews* [Grand Rapids: Eerdmans, 1977], p. 143). Hughes, however, may be missing the theological point of the writer's handling of the psalm. Attridge comments, that διό 'is somewhat surprising in view of the association of forty years with the wrath of God in the following exposition (3.17), but it is possible that the author conceived of two periods of forty years, one of disobedience and one of punishment' (*Hebrews*, p. 115). It seems, rather, that these two forty-year periods pertain to two different people in two different eras. Khiok-Khng Yeo suggests that 3.10 and 17 serve to equate the period of testing with the period of God's wrath ('The Meaning and Usage of the Theology of "Rest" [κατάπαυσις and σαββατισμός] in Hebrews 3:7–4:13', *AJT* 5 [1991], p. 5). This solution does not seem to give διό its due force, however, as Attridge also remarks (*Hebrews*, p. 115).

8.   Although for different purposes, Paul's exegesis of Gen. 12.7 in Gal. 3.15-29 is analogous to the author of Hebrews' exegesis of Ps. 95.9-10. Since Gen. 12.7 refers to Abraham's 'seed' (זרע, σπέρμα) in the singular, Paul argues in Gal. 3.16 that its proper referent is Christ. In Gal. 3.29, however, Paul states plainly, almost matter-of-factly, 'you are [plural] Abraham's seed'. That Paul sees Gen. 12.7 as having a dual referent is quite consistent with his understanding of the close identification of Christ and his church elsewhere, e.g., his use of 'in Christ'.

9.   *Hebrews*, p. 115.

10.   Yeo's argument, that the prepositional phrase is '... used to keep the place name כמרימה [sic] of the MT', is unconvincing, since ἐν δοκιμασίᾳ corresponds not to כמריבה in v. 8 but בחנוני in v. 9 ('The Meaning and Usage of the Theology of

A final change that the author of Hebrews uses to actualize the psalm is the insertion of ταύτῃ in v. 10. Reading 'this generation' where the LXX reads 'that' (ἐκείνῃ) further concretizes the psalm—indeed, the whole exodus experience—for the readers. By quoting the psalm the way he does, he is showing his readers that *this* is the generation with which God is ultimately concerned.[11] The commentaries are largely divided over the significance this change has. Spicq, for example, says that this change makes the psalm, 'more urgent for the present community', a position with which I am in agreement.[12] The opposite opinion is represented by Attridge, for one, who sees this as 'a minor variation from the LXX... [which does not] seem to serve any particular purpose in Hebrews' application of the psalm'.[13] But we have already seen with διό that our author's exegesis of the psalm is careful and deliberate. Of course, this does not mean that every change is necessarily theologically significant. There are, for example, two 'minor', or perhaps better 'stylistic' variations, namely the more common verb forms εἶδον and εἶπον in Hebrews rather than the Hellenistic forms in the LXX, as Attridge, too, remarks.[14] ταύτῃ does not seem to be a minor or stylistic variation, but of a completely different order. Perhaps the point should not be pressed too far, but the author's exegesis of Psalm 95 in general supports the understanding of ταύτῃ as a purposeful and deliberate change from the LXX.[15]

"Rest"', p. 4). Another solution is offered by K.J. Thomas who argues that the phrase in Hebrews refers to God's testing of man rather than man's testing of God as the LXX has it. This yields the translation, '. . . where your fathers, during their testing, tried and saw my works for forty years' ('Old Testament Citations in Hebrews', *NTS* 11 [1965], p. 307). The Greek syntax is too ambiguous for such a translation, and hence I do not find this solution as helpful as Attridge's.

11. An insight that cannot be given full consideration here is brought out by Karen H. Jobes ('Rhetorical Achievement in the Hebrews 10 "Misquote" of Psalm 40', *Bib* 72 [1991], pp. 387-96). She argues that the change from ἐκείνῃ to ταύτῃ 'achieves phonetic assonance' with ἔτη in the previous line (p. 391). Jobes gives several strong examples of such 'phonetic manipulation', which '[communicated] the author's intended semantic sense. . . while simultaneously achieving assonance' (p. 392).

12. Spicq, *L'épître*, p. 74.

13. Attridge, *Hebrews*, pp. 115-16.

14. Attridge, *Hebrews*, p. 115.

15. Another argument, this by Yeo, is unconvincing ('The Meaning and Usage of the Theology of "Rest"', p. 5). Yeo argues that the author of Hebrews changes the LXX 'that generation' to 'this generation' because 'that generation' does not occur

For the author of Hebrews, the church is the new Israel. The church has seen the new Moses and God's mighty acts in the new wilderness. *This* (ταύτῃ) is the generation with which God is concerned. What Psalm 95 may have referred to at an earlier time was merely prelude to this new era, 'at the end of the age' and 'in the fullness of time'. The threefold repetition of σήμερον in 3.13, 15 further accents the present fulfillment of what was spoken of in Psalm 95. Both ταύτῃ and σήμερον make specific in Hebrews what is left ambiguous in Psalm 95. The promise of God's rest is for *today*, for *this* generation. In other words, both terms have a decided redemptive–historical dimension. 'Today' or 'this generation' is the present situation of the church, a situation in which those who are partakers of Christ's blessings wander in the wilderness, between slavery and the better, heavenly country awaiting them.[16] The appeal is not merely to the individual in his moment of existential decision (although it is that, too), but to the individual living in the eschatological age when the new Moses is leading his people through the wilderness to their final rest. We see then that both Psalm 95 and Hebrews apply the example of the wilderness rebellion to

anywhere else in the New Testament (See also Kistemaker, *Psalm Citations*, pp. 35-36). He argues further that since the verb προσώχθισα in v. 10 is past tense, 'this generation' must refer to the Israelites, who lived in the past, and not the church. In other words, Yeo cites common New Testament usage to explain why the author of Hebrews changes the LXX 'that generation' to 'this generation', while at the same time arguing that Hebrews' 'this generation' refers to Israel because the verb is in the past tense. The problem with this is that of all the uses of 'this generation' in the New Testament, not once does it refer to a past generation, as Yeo says it does here. Furthermore, one need not assume that Hebrews has in mind either Israel or the church, as if a choice were to be made. To argue, as I do, that the near demonstrative is used to actualize the psalm, is not to argue that in v. 10 Israel is no longer in view. The referent is not either Israel or the church, but both. The author of Hebrews is, after all, citing Psalm 95 and thereby drawing on the past, but his application of the psalm shows that his primary theological concern is the church. The strength of the warning is precisely in bringing the two exodus communities together, to warn the new on the basis of the old without losing sight of either one. The tense of the verb is not the determining issue. Thomas is a bit ambiguous in seeing ταύτῃ as a reminder of Jesus' words (e.g. Mt. 23.36) that strengthens the Old Testament warning, yet 'is not intended to designate some other than the wilderness generation' ('Old Testament Citations', p. 307).

16. But this point is not to ignore the strong element of realized eschatology in the epistle, for example, 12.22, 'But you have come to Mt. Zion, to the heavenly Jerusalem, the city of the living God'.

motivate their communities to obedience. The difference between the two is that the writer of Psalm 95 makes the warning 'timelessly concrete' by leaving the identity of the rebellious generation and the 'today' ambiguous. The author of Hebrews, on the other hand, accomplishes his admonitory purpose in precisely the opposite fashion—by making the psalm as time specific as possible.[17]

The author of Hebrews' understanding of Psalm 95 for the church is reflected first and foremost in how he quotes it. We have seen that διό, ἐν δοκιμασίᾳ, and ταύτῃ are variations from the LXX that reflect his theological motivation to make this psalm more relevant to his readers. This motivation is the same as his motivation throughout the book: to show that the full significance of the Old Testament is realized by the church and only proleptically by Israel.

A second issue discussed here is the author's understanding of creation as a paradigm for deliverance.[18] His participation in this broad theme is suggested by three factors: the argument from Gen. 2.2 in Heb. 4.4, the double meaning of ἔργα, and of κατασκευάζω.

By citing Gen. 2.2, our author is arguing that the rest that is the reward to the faithful new exodus community is to be understood not as physical land, but as an eschatological rest; specifically, the rest that God has enjoyed since the completion of his creative work. Gen. 2.2 reads 'God rested (κατέπαυσεν) from his works'. Our psalm ends, 'They shall never enter into my rest (τὴν κατάπαυσίν μου)'. For the author of Hebrews, creation is the consummation of the exodus. In the

17. It is still a question why Psalm 95 was written in the first place. If the role of the exodus theme in Hebrews is predominantly eschatological, what is the case for Psalm 95? Commentators have remarked on the liturgical use of the psalm in the synagogue, which suggests a more existential function. Still, the issue of the *Sitz-im-Leben* of Psalm 95 is somewhat of a mystery. That it is cultic does not answer the question. One would still need to ask why Psalm 95 was written for the cult. A possible answer is that the psalm has an exilic context. In this sense, the experience of the exodus community had obvious relevance for the 'exodus community' of the exile. This might suggest, although perhaps not a full-blown eschatological perspective, at least an application of Israel's past deliverance from Egypt to the deliverance from Babylon. Hence, both the original audience of Psalm 95 and the audience of Hebrews would be second exodus communities to whom an exodus warning had been applied.

18. Psalm 95 itself is one Old Testament example of the juxtaposition of creation and deliverance. This is discussed more fully in Enns, 'Creation and Re-Creation', pp. 255-69.

Old Testament, for example, creation is typically thought of not as the consummation of the exodus but a paradigm for the exodus. In other words, creation is not the goal of the exodus as it is here in Hebrews, but a broader pattern of which exodus is one example. These two perspectives are quite different, and the distinctiveness of our author's application of this theme should not be lost.

Nevertheless, we still have to deal with the question of why the warning directed to the new exodus community is supported by an appeal to creation imagery. Clearly, an important factor in Hebrews bringing Gen. 2.2 and Ps. 95.11 together is the root καταπαύω, which appears in both.[19] But this merely explains what allowed him to make the exegetical connection, not necessarily what motivated him to make this specific exegetical connection. Why call upon Gen. 2.2 to 'explain' Ps. 95.11 when it appears to introduce a whole new subject into the discussion—creation? After all, the writer could simply have said that the church's rest is not earthly but heavenly and be done with it, without even introducing the subject of God's creation–rest. Or if he really wanted to bring another passage into the discussion, he could easily have found one that contains καταπαύω, but pertains directly to the rest of the faithful, rather than the seventh day of creation. So why introduce this distant verse into the discussion? The motivating factor seems to be in Ps. 95.11. The psalmist says 'They shall never enter *my* rest', not 'they shall never enter *their* rest'. The exegetical problem our author is trying to explain is why Ps. 95.11 refers to the rest in the *land* as '*my* rest', that is, God's rest, when in fact it is *Israel's* rest? It is this exegetical problem in the text that, so to speak, backs him into a theological corner. 'My rest' virtually requires the author to see some sort of relationship between deliverance and creation. The church as the new exodus community, redeemed, or 'created' as it were, has as its goal the original rest of creation. It is the consummate rest—God's rest.[20] Nothing less than God's creation rest can be expected for those

---

19. It is certainly to the advantage of our author's argument that the LXX uses καταπαύω in both Gen. 2.2 and Psalm 95, thereby strengthening the connection between the passages, whereas the MT uses שבת and מנוחתי, respectively.

20. A similar idea is found in *'Abot R. Nat.* 12. Regarding Moses' death we read, 'Moses, thou hast had enough of this world, for lo, the world to come awaits thee: for thy place hath been ready for thee since the six days of Creation' (*The Fathers according to Rabbi Nathan* [trans. J. Goldin; New Haven: Yale University Press, 1955], p. 65).

who are 'partakers of the heavenly calling'. The faithful share God's creation rest because they are co-heirs with Christ (to use Paul's words, Rom. 8.17). The physical rest Joshua (4.8)[21] gave his people as well as the rest of Ps. 95.11 (however this is to be understood) were merely proleptic of this final rest.[22]

The use of ἔργα and κατασκευάζω make this relationship between deliverance and creation more explicit. ἔργα occurs four times in this passage. The first reference to 'my works' is, as we have seen above, in 3.9 (τὰ ἔργα μου), and pertains to the blessings of the church age. The other three references (4.3, 4, and 10) are spawned by the reference to Gen. 2.2 and pertain to the works of God during the six days of creation (τῶν ἔργων αὐτοῦ). The result is a wordplay, which is worthy of consideration in the context of the present argument. The ἔργα in 3.9 refer to the works of deliverance. The ἔργα of ch. 4 refer to the works of creation. Both creation and deliverance are God's 'works'. To take it one step further, in Gen. 2.2, God works (creation) and then rests. In Hebrews 3, God also works (deliverance/second creation), and then, not he, but the *faithful* rest—in *his* rest. This striking parallel suggests an integral relationship between creation and deliverance in the author's thinking.

κατασκευάζω is used in Heb. 3.3 and 4. Attridge comments that in certain contexts this word refers to God's creative activity. He cites Wis. 9.2 and 13.4 as examples,[23] as well as Isa. 40.28; 43.7; 45.7 and 9 (MT = ברא).[24] This verb is used in Hebrews 3 in two ways. First, in v. 3, it refers to Jesus' building of the 'house' (οἶκος). It is also used in v. 4 to refer to God's act of creation. In v. 3, Jesus is the builder

---

21. The fact that both Joshua and Jesus are the same name in Greek ('Ιησοῦς) certainly strengthens the author's typological connection. See also Attridge, *Hebrews*, p. 130; J. Moffatt, *Epistle to the Hebrews* [ICC; Edinburgh: T. & T. Clark, 1924], p. 52.

22. The meaning of rest in antiquity is a diverse and complex matter (both Attridge [*Hebrews*, pp. 126-28] and Spicq [*L'épître*, pp. 95-104] devote an excursus to the subject). Of particular interest are instances where rest is described as a new creation, for example, *4 Ezra* 8.52; *2 Bar.* 78–86; *1 En.* 45.3-6; *T. Levi* 18.9; and 4QFlor 1.7-8 (Attridge, p. 126; Spicq, pp. 95-96). A discussion of this issue would take us far from our topic. In any event, it is clear that the author of Hebrews is making the connection between rest and creation.

23. Wisdom is also a clear example of the juxtaposition of creation and deliverance. See Wis. 16.24–18.4; 19.6-7; and 19.18-21.

24. Attridge, *Hebrews*, p. 110.

(ὁ κατασκευάσας) of a house. In v. 4, God creates all things (κατα-σκευάσας). The question is, what does it mean for Jesus to be the 'builder of a house?' Heb. 3.3 reads, 'Jesus has been found worthy of greater honor than Moses, just as the one who builds the house has greater honor than the house itself'. There seems to be an analogy being made: Jesus : Moses : builder : house. A strict reading of this analogy yields that Jesus 'built' Moses, which does not make much sense. Hence, we should be cautioned against making too much of this analogy. Nevertheless, for the analogy to have any force, we must make something of it. I suggest that Moses is here a metonymy for the people Moses brought out of Egypt—the exodus community. Several commentators mention this possibility.[25] Mary Rose D'Angelo argues on the basis of the Targums, rabbinic literature, and intertestamental literature that understanding 'house' as 'people of God' has ample precedent.[26] If this is so, both Jesus in v. 3 and God in v. 4 are engaged in creation activity: God creates everything; Jesus, the new Moses, 'creates' his people. Creation language is again used to express deliverance.

Conclusion

The author's exegesis of Psalm 95 is driven to a large extent by his concern to bring this portion of Scripture to bear more directly on his readers' eschatological situation. They are witnesses to the climax of God's covenant relationship with his people—first Israel, now the church. Apparently, the author seems to have no difficulty in taking certain liberties with the text in order to make his theological point. His exegetical technique is similar to what we find, for example, in the commentaries of the Qumran community (for example, 1QpHab). They also believed that they were God's faithful remnant living in the consummation of the ages, and therefore assumed that the ultimate meaning of Scripture must be defined in terms of their own privileged place in the unfolding drama of history. The belief of the author of Hebrews

---

25. Attridge cites Moffatt (*Epistle*, p. 42) as well as H. Montefiore (*A Commentary on the Epistle to the Hebrews* [New York: Harper; London: Black, 1964], p. 72) and Teodorico (*L'epistola agli Ebrei* [La Sacra Bibbia; Turin: Marietti, 1952], p. 79) as examples, yet he seems to dismiss this possibility too quickly without offering an alternate solution.

26. *Moses in the Letter to the Hebrews* (SBLDS, 42; Missoula: Scholars Press, 1979), pp. 95-149, esp. pp. 145-49.

that his own age constituted the final eschatological eon (albeit of undetermined length) is further seen in his presentation of God's creation–rest as the church's final destination. Whatever Psalm 95 might have meant at an earlier time, the author of Hebrews tells his readers that its ultimate and therefore proper meaning concerns the church's participation in God's blessing, both now amid certain trouble and temptation, and later in the world to come for those who remain faithful.

THE DIFFERENT FUNCTIONS OF A SIMILAR MELCHIZEDEK TRADITION IN 2 *ENOCH* AND THE EPISTLE TO THE HEBREWS

Charles A. Gieschen

Research on the figure of Melchizedek has developed in three distinct stages over the past century.[1] The first stage of research sought to study the figure of Melchizedek within the confines of canonical literature, with some effort to mine extra-canonical literature for parallels that may shed light upon the canonical depiction of Melchizedek.[2] The second stage sought to study the figure of Melchizedek in various literature, whether within or outside the canon(s), to depict a single growing 'Melchizedek Tradition'.[3] A third stage has emphasized the diverse and

1.   The primary examples of more comprehensive research on Melchizedek during these three stages are: G. Wuttke, *Melchisedech der Priesterkönig von Salem* (Giessen: Töpelmann, 1927); F. Horton, Jr, *The Melchizedek Tradition: A Critical Examination of the Sources to the Fifth Century AD and in the Epistle to the Hebrews* (London: Cambridge University Press, 1976); C. Gianotto, *Melchisedek e la sua tipologia: Tradizioni guidaiche, cristiane e gnostiche* (Brescia: Paideia Editrice, 1984). See Gianotto, *Melchisedek*, pp. 281-98, for more extensive bibliography. I thank Gabriele Boccaccini for helping me to be conversant with Gianotto's work and other recent Italian scholarship.

2.   Melchizedek surfaces in only three texts of the canons of the Hebrew Bible and New Testament: Gen. 14.18-20, Ps. 110.4, and Heb. 5.1–7.28. This first stage of research is visible in numerous commentaries on these 'canonical' texts and in G. Wuttke, *Melchisedech der Priesterkönig von Salem*.

3.   A prime example of this is Horton's *The Melchizedek Tradition*. The discovery of 11QMelch at Qumran gave new impetus to interpret canonical texts in light of extra-canonical texts; for example, M. de Jonge and A. van der Woude, '11Q Melchizedek and the New Testament', *NTS* 12 (1966), pp. 310-26; J.A. Fitzmyer, '"Now this Melchizedek. . . " (Heb. 7.1)' and 'Further Light on Melchizedek from Qumran Cave 11', reprinted in *Essays on the Semitic Background of the New Testament* (Missoula, MT: Scholars Press, 1974), pp. 221-67; and, P. Kobelski, *Melchizedek and Melchiresha* (CBQMS, 10; Washington: Catholic Biblical Association, 1981). As with earlier research, these studies focus on extra-canonical evidence of this so-called tradition which enlightens the exegesis of Hebrews.

pluralistic nature of this so-called 'tradition'; this stage directs scholars to speak in the plural of the existence of different Melchizedek traditions.[4] This study proposes a new stage in the research on Melchizedek by focusing on the importance of identifying not only the various traditions, but also their ideological function within the systems of thought found in the specific documents.

This approach will be illustrated through a systemic analysis of *2 Enoch* and the Epistle to the Hebrews in order to determine the place and function of the Melchizedek tradition in the hierarchy of ideas in these respective documents.[5] The reason for selecting these two documents is because *2 Enoch* has received very little attention in Melchizedek research even though it is an extremely important document for understanding how Hebrews adapted the Melchizedek tradition into its ideology.[6] This analysis will demonstrate that a very similar Melchizedek tradition, which depicts him as a priestly mediator, functions in very different ways in the respective ideological systems of these two documents. This analysis will begin by examining the Melchizedek tradition of *2 Enoch* 69–73 in the context of the ideological system of *2 Enoch* as a whole and within the wider context of Enochian Judaism. Secondly, the Melchizedek tradition of Hebrews will be analyzed within the ideological system of the entire document and also within the broader context of early Christianity. Lastly, the similarity of the

---

4.   See especially Gianotto, *Melchisedek*, which emphasizes the pluralism of these traditions, primarily within Christian and Gnostic literature.

5.   The importance of the ideological system of a document in comparing traditions is discussed by G. Boccaccini, 'Middle Judaism and its Contemporary Interpreters: Methodological Foundations for the Study of Judaisms, 300 BCE to 200 CE', *Henoch* 15 (1993), pp. 207-33.

6.   Even major studies on Melchizedek within the past three decades have not treated *2 Enoch* in their discussions. For example, Horton dismisses *2 Enoch* as beyond the limits of his study which ends with 5th century CE evidence; see, *The Melchizedek Tradition*, p. 81. More recently Gianotto only mentions 2 Enoch in a footnote; see *Melchisedek*, pp. 45-46 n. 1. The reason for the hesitancy to use *2 Enoch* is its problematic textual tradition and disputed date of origin (see n. 9 below). This is especially true of the Melchizedek appendix (chs. 69–73) which was even excluded from R.H. Charles's translation of *2 Enoch* in *The Apocrypha and Pseudepigrapha of the Old Testament* (Oxford: Clarendon Press, 1913) because it was thought to be a later document composed by the Melchizedekians. Thus, this study will also serve to demonstrate the importance of *2 Enoch* in Melchizedek research.

Melchizedek tradition in these documents as well as the distinct ways in which this tradition functions will be compared.

1. *A Systemic Analysis of the Melchizedek Tradition in 2 Enoch*

One of the difficult hurdles in the study of *2 Enoch* is its complicated textual history.[7] It is known only from manuscripts in Old Slavonic. Because of the codicological practices of Slavic scribes, no complete copy of *2 Enoch* exists. The text has been abbreviated, expanded, exerpted, and rearranged. Although a shorter and longer recension are availiable for scholarly study, it is probable that deletions and interpolations exist in both recensions.[8] Even with these liabilities, a growing number of scholars recognize the antiquity of *2 Enoch*, including the Melchizedek appendix, and support the relatively early dating of pre-70 CE for its original composition.[9]

a. *The Ideological System of 2 Enoch*
2 Enoch builds on and continues the Jewish ideas or apocalyptic tradition expressed in *1 Enoch*.[10] It records Enoch's travels through various realms, his ethical exhortations to his family, and the development of an antediluvian priesthood centered in Melchizedek. The section about Melchizedek (chs. 69–73) is distinct from the basic writing and functions as an appendix that was affixed at a very early date in the

7.   See F. Andersen, 'Enoch, Second Book of', *ABD* 2.516-22.

8.   This study quotes from two recensions presented in J.H. Charlesworth (ed.), *The Old Testament Pseudepigrapha* (Garden City, NY: Doubleday, 1983), I, pp. 102-213. The Italian edition edited by P. Sacchi (*Apocrifi dell'Antico Testamento* [Turin: Union Tipografico—Editrice Torinese, 1989], II, pp. 479-594) attempts to assemble more of a critical edition of *2 Enoch*. Sacchi argues that the shorter recension is closer to the original, but it also contains some additions (pp. 493-95).

9.   Andersen dates *2 Enoch* as late first century; see Charlesworth, *The Old Testament Pseudepigrapha*, I, p. 91; see also Andersen, 'Enoch, Second Book of', p. 522. Sacchi asserts that the ideology of *2 Enoch* as well as the content of chs. 69–73 affirms that the document was written before the destruction of the Jerusalem temple in 70 CE and that its Melchizedek tradition predates Hebrews (*Apocrifi*, II, pp. 498-507). See also E. Turdeanu, 'Le livre des secrets d'Hénoch: Son origine, sa diffusion et sa traduction vieux-slave', *Ricerche Slavistiche* 32–35 (1985–88), pp. 5-54.

10.   For a survey of the Enochian traditions in *1 Enoch*, see J. VanderKam, *Enoch and the Growth of an Apocalyptic Tradition* (CBQMS, 16; Washington: Catholic Biblical Association, 1984).

development of *2 Enoch*.[11] There is little continuity in form between chs. 1–68 and 69–73 besides their chronological place in primeval history with a focus on Enoch (1–68) and then his descendents (69–73).

There is, however, ideological continuity in the common concern for deliverance from evil that pervades the entire document. Chapters 1–68 are characterized by a focus on the origin of evil (ch. 18 discusses angelic sin, 29 shows Satan's fall, 30 details Adam's free will and Eve's role in sinning, 31 explains how Satan tempted Eve), the consequences of evil (chs. 7, 10, 32, 34), deliverance from evil (chs. 8, 9, 22–23, 33, 35), the order of creation (chs. 4–6, 11–17, 19, 24–28, 30), and Enoch's teaching to his family which touches on all these themes in ethical tones (chs. 39–68). Because these chapters assume *1 Enoch*, they are not as detailed in recording various ideas.

The concern for deliverance from evil is heightened by a strong emphasis on the degeneration of history in *2 Enoch*. Absolutely nothing is said of the covenant relationship with Israel or events that happened after the flood. There is no reference to the 'God of Abraham, Isaac and Jacob'; God identifies himself as the 'God of your father Enoch' (69.5). The primeval history of antediluvian times and the imminent endtime are all important in *2 Enoch* 1–68. There is no remedy for sin except the destruction and deliverance at the endtime (ch. 41) in which Melchizedek appears to play a role (71.33-34).[12]

Chapters 69–73 are a separate midrashim of Enoch's antediluvian descendents (primarily Methusalah and Melchizedek). In contrast to 1–68, the presentation of 69–73 is principally historical narrative. The generative idea of these chapters is the need for a priestly mediator to provide deliverance from the grip of evil and purity from the stain of sin. Thus, in *2 Enoch* 69–73 we find the creation and continuation of an antediluvian priesthood growing from the priest Melchizedek who was preserved during the flood.

The major elements of continuity between chs. 1–68 and 69–73 are

11. Based upon content, style, and vocabulary, Sacchi argues that chs. 69–73 were written by a different, yet contemporary, Jewish author (or authors) who sought to assimilate the priestly mediator Melchizedek into the Enochian tradition represented by chs. 1–68 and *1 Enoch* (*Apocrifi*, II, pp. 495-507; see also p. 580 note).

12. The only possible exception to this perspective is found in 64.5 where Enoch is called 'the one who carries away the sin of mankind'. However, *2 Enoch* does not assign the role of atonement to Enoch (cf. *2 En.* 53.1-4), but affirms Enoch's role as one who presents prayers of mankind to God.

the continuation of primeval history and the concern for deliverance from sin. The major element of discontinuity is the shift from a focus on Enoch's prophetic warnings about the imminent endtime in 1–68 to a focus on the priestly mediator who will be hidden until the endtime according to 69–73.

b. *The Place of 2 Enoch among Jewish Apocalyptic Documents*[13]

How does *2 Enoch* fit in the chain of Jewish apocalyptic systems of thought? As noted above, *2 Enoch* 1–68 certainly assumes the contents of *1 Enoch* and can best be described as a recasting of the divergent ideas found in this earlier work. Chapters 1–68 primarily follow the pattern of the *Epistle of Enoch* with their ethical tone (*1 En.* 91–107). The Melchizedek appendix (69–73) can be seen as a development growing out of 1–68 that addresses the evil of the postdiluvian situation by raising up a mediator figure. This need for a mediator like Melchizedek is a similar development to the need for a mediator figure present in the *Similitudes* (*1 En.* 37–71). Mediator figures were developed in an effort to inspire hope and assurance in a figure who would carry out God's planned deliverance. It should be noted, however, that the deliverance in *2 Enoch* 69–73 implies a concern for the purity of God's people secured through the priest Melchizedek, whereas the deliverance discussed in the *Similitudes* is gained by the Elect One/Son of Man casting down all the powerful suppressors (*1 En.* 46.4-6).

Why was Melchizedek chosen to play such an important role in literature that is usually dominated by the figure of Enoch? It is possible that *2 Enoch* 69–73 was written in response to competing traditions within Enochian Judaism. For example, *1 Enoch* 106–107 presents a similar post-Enoch tradition involving Methusalah and Noah. There Noah is the one born miraculously and plays the important role in the postdiluvian period. Furthermore, the author(s) of the Melchizedek appendix may have disagreed with the central role in the endtime deliverance given

---

13. For a fuller discussion of the Jewish Apocalyptic tradition as understood in this paper, see G. Boccaccini, 'Jewish Apocalyptic Tradition: The Contribition of Italian Scholarship', in J.J. Collins and J.H. Charlesworth (eds.), *Mysteries and Revelations: Apocalyptic Studies since the Uppsala Colloquium* (JSPSup, 9; Sheffield: Sheffield Academic Press, 1991), pp. 38-58. Boccaccini discusses the periods of development within apocalypic literature, including the Enochian documents; see also G. Boccaccini, *Middle Judaism: Jewish Thought 300 BCE to 200 CE* (Philadelphia: Fortress Press, 1991), pp. 7-25.

to Enoch himself elsewhere (for example, *2 En.* 64.5 or *1 En.* 70–71) or to a mysterious mediator figure like that of the *Similitudes* (Elect One/Son of Man) or the Righteous One who will awake according to the *Epistle of Enoch* (*1 En.* 91.10; 92.3-4). It is very doubtful that this appendix is a response to the Christian use of Melchizedek (for example, Hebrews).

It seems most probable, however, that *2 Enoch* 69–73 was written by a group that sought a solution for the impurity of the Levitical priesthood. Such impurity is acknowledged in the *Dream Visions* of *1 Enoch*:

> Thereafter I saw that, when they abandoned the house of the Lord and his tower, they went astray completely, and their eyes became blindfolded. . .
> I saw how he left that house of theirs and that tower of theirs and cast all of them into the hands of the lion—(even) into the hands of all the wild beasts—so that they may tear them into pieces and eat them.[14]

The vicious attack against the impurity of the wealthy that is leveled in the *Epistle of Enoch* (*1 En.* 91–104) may reflect attitudes towards the priestly class since they also were landowners and had wealth. *1 Enoch* is by no means alone in signaling the need for a new or renewed priesthood.[15] The group originating *2 Enoch* 69–73 clearly desired to depart from that priestly lineage entirely; thus, Melchizedek.

2 Enoch is seeking to answer the same question that the other Jewish apocalyptic documents of this period sought to answer: How will evil be overcome? In its answer, *2 Enoch* reflects the pre-70 CE period in Jewish apocalyptic literature since it neither acknowledges the catastrophic destruction of Jerusalem nor focuses on the role of the Law.[16] *2 Enoch* still reflects a concern for the Temple cult or priesthood as a means for dealing with evil. Such a concern quickly diminished after 70 CE. *2 Enoch* (especially 69–73) is characteristic of the earlier period in Jewish apocalyptic literature when mediator figures—and not the Law—were the focus of deliverance from sin.[17]

---

14. *1 En.* 89.54-56; see also 80.73-75 and 93.8. For the hope of a new heavenly temple, see 90.28-36.

15. Messianic expectations sometimes had a priestly case, partly because of corruption in the Levitical priesthod. For more complete discussion of this phenomenon, see A. Higgins, 'The Priestly Messiah', *NTS* 13 (1967), pp. 211-39, and H. Attridge, *The Epistle to the Hebrews* (Hermeneia; Philadelphia: Fortress Press, 1989), pp. 97-103.

16. See Boccaccini, 'Jewish Apocalyptic Tradition', pp. 38-58.

17. In a similar way to how *2 Enoch* used the priestly mediator figure Melchizedek

c. *Melchizedek in the Ideological System of 2 Enoch*

Although the Melchizedek tradition does not dominate the content of *2 Enoch* as a whole, it is the major focus of chs. 69–73. Here we find a grave concern for a priestly mediator between God and humans, as is visible in the basic plot of this appendix. After Enoch is gone, Methusalam (that is, Methusalah) asks God to raise up a priest (69.5). He is then miraculously shown to be God's choice as priest and he responds by offering animal sacrifices (69.15-17). The priesthood is then passed on to Methusalam's grandson: Nir. He functions as a prince/leader (70.14) and a priest (70.20).[18] However, the evil that would necessitate the worldwide flood once again grows during this period (70.23).

As *2 Enoch* progresses, hope is restored through the birth of a unique priest: Melchizedek. Several details highlight the miraculous nature of this birth. First, Nir's wife is pregnant in her barren old age even though her husband has been celibate for years as a priest and she had no sexual contact with a man (71.2). Secondly, the child delivers himself after his mother dies; his mother contributes minimally to the entire conception and birth experience (71.17). Thirdly, the child appears on the scene as a fully developed and speaking three year old boy (71.18). Lastly, the child has the badge of the priesthood on his chest (71.19). Several of these details are included to emphasize the purity of this child. He was not the product of an impure sexual union or a bloody birth experience; he is a pure priest who could atone for sins. Nir and Noe (that is, Noah) give him the name Melchizedek. It is significant that, in spite of the postdiluvian personage in Genesis 14, Melchizedek is given an antediluvian origin in *2 Enoch*.

In response to Nir's concerns about the possible future destruction of this child with the impurity in the world, the Lord appears to Nir in a night vision and promises to send Michael who will remove and protect Melchizedek during the destruction of the deluge: 'Melkisedek will be the priest to all holy priest, and I will establish him so that he

---

to deal with this question in a earlier period, *2 Baruch* and *4 Ezra* used figures associated with the Law (Baruch and Ezra) as they sought to provide answers to the question of evil in a later period of Jewish apocalyptic literature.

18. This may reflect the union of political and priestly leadership that took place during Hasmonean rule. It is noteworthy that *Jubilees* avoids any discussion of Melchizedek in its rewriting of Genesis, possibly because of its anti-Hasmonean perspective against the joining of the priestly and kingly roles in one person; see Gianotto, *Melchisedek*, pp. 46-61.

will be the head of the priests of the future' (71.29, Rec. J). Nir responds: 'Blessed be the Lord, the God of my fathers, who has told me how he has made a great priest in my day' (71.30, Rec. J). In a manner similar to the tradition in Rev. 12.1-6, Michael descends 40 days after Melchizedek's birth and takes him away to the paradise of Eden for protection during the flood (72.9). The inference is that he will be 'hidden' until the proper moment of his revelation as a priestly Messiah. Such a theme is present in other apocalyptic literature, such as with the Son of Man/Elect One of the *Similitudes* of *1 Enoch* (48.6-7). In addition to these details, there have been interpolations into the text to explain some of the mysteries not revealed.[19]

As can be seen from this content, the generative idea of chs. 69–73 is the need for a priestly mediator to provide deliverance from the grip of evil and offer atonement for sins. These chapters catalogue the development of a priesthood which could truly deal with evil and sin since it has its locus in the antediluvian mediator Melchizedek. This appendix reflects a very degenerative view of the levitical priesthood—and possibly the whole temple cult—which was probably still functioning at the time when this document was written.[20]

2. A Systemic Analysis of the Melchizedek Tradition in Hebrews

Melchizedek, however, was not the only priestly mediator figure proposed by Jewish groups in this period. Using Melchizedek traditions, the author of Hebrews proposes Jesus as the ultimate High Priest who atones for sins of all time. Even though Hebrews also draws on a similar understanding of Melchizedek as an exalted priestly mediator, it will be demonstrated that the author used Melchizedek in a manner very distinct from that of *2 Enoch*.

a. *The Ideological System of Hebrews*
The Melchizedek tradition found in Hebrews is by no means the focal point of this epistle. It is among the several foils used in developing the elevated Christology of this Christian document.[21] Jesus is the mediator

---

19. For example, the relationship between the Melchizedek of *2 Enoch* and the one of Genesis 14 is explained by an interpolation in 72.6.

20. See nn. 9 and 11 above.

21. For a complete introduction to the content and elusive structure of Hebrews, see Attridge, *Hebrews*, pp. 13-31.

figure of Hebrews, not Melchizedek or anyone else. The author compares and contrasts Christ with elements of Judaic belief such as angelic hierarchies, the centrality of Moses, the Levitical priesthood, and the sacrificial system in order to demonstrate to his readers that Jesus is superior to all that various other Judaisms have to offer.[22]

Hebrews is a fine example of epideictic oration that highlights the significance of Christ and seeks to inculcate unswerving faith allegiance in him.[23] It is vital that one sees not only the well-structured argumentation in Hebrews, but also the passionate paranetic exhortations that are carefully interspersed throughout this homily. One must give these sections adequate attention in order to understand the ideology of Hebrews. It is clear that the addressees had undergone some type of persecution (10.32-34) and were still facing it (13.3). Some had withdrawn from the community (10.25; 3.12) and probably had gone back to the former covenant of Judaism which, according to Hebrews, is obsolete (8.13). Others had become sluggish or dull (5.11; 6.12), and had neglected the message of salvation (2.3). The author's emphasis on the coming judgment (2.2-3; 6.8; 10.25, 29-31; 12.18-24, 26-29) and Christ's final role (2.8; 10.13) indicate a weakening of faith, possibly in response to a delayed parousia.

In answer to this situation, the author employs both positive and negative paranetic devices. On the negative side, he issues several severe warnings illustrating the pitfalls of apostasy (6.4-6; 10.26-31; 12.15-17). On the positive side, the community is encouraged to 'hold on to' their confession (3.6, 14; 10.23; 2.1) and also 'to move forward' to a reliable support or deeper apprehension of the faith exhibited in life (4.16; 6.1, 18-20; 10.19-22). The goal of his carefully structured discussion of Christ and his priestly work of atonement is to secure the faith of these people so that they may be saved: 'Consequently he [Christ] is able for all time to save those who approach God through him, since he always lives to make intercession for them' (7.25). Thus, the generative idea is to be faithful to Christ because he is the superior and exclusive means—apart from the rest of Judaism—whereby sins are atoned for and people are saved.

22. 'Judaisms' is used here with the understanding that Christianity was closely related to Judaism until there was distinct separation by the second century CE. See Boccaccini, *Middle Judaism*, pp. 15-21.

23. Attridge discusses such rhetorical method and devices; see *Hebrews*, pp. 13-28 (esp. p. 14; cf. Aristotle, *Rhet.* 1.3, 1358b).

b. *The Place of Hebrews among Christian Documents*[24]

The Epistle to the Hebrews is in continuity with other early Christian documents in its emphasis on the exalted divine nature of Christ as the Son of God and Savior (1.1-4; cf. Jn 1.1-18; Col. 1.15-20). Also like other Christian documents, Hebrews does not hide the human nature of Christ, but sees it as a necessary element for his work (2.14-18).

Like the Pauline corpus, Hebrews draws on the sacrificial under-standing of Jesus' death to explain the scandal of crucifixion. In Hebrews, however, it is not God offering his son as in Paul (Rom. 3.25; 5.6-11), but Christ the High Priest offers himself as the cultic *Yom Kippur* sacrifice that has initiated a new covenant (Heb. 8–10): '. . . he has appeared once for all at the end of the age to remove sin by the sacrifice of himself' (9.26). Furthermore, Hebrews emphasizes the ongoing mediation of Christ before God in heaven on our behalf (7.25; 9.24).

The polemical depiction of Jesus, as faithful to the covenant and also the fulfillment of it through the initiation of a new covenant, is in continuity with other documents of early Christianity. For example, the Fourth Gospel shows how the whole cultic system of Israel finds its end in the person of Jesus. Furthermore, the Gospel of Matthew shows the life of Jesus as the fulfillment of Jewish expectations.

It is clear that there was some loss of Christians from the community that Hebrews is addressing (10.25; 3.12), probably flowing back to various Judaisms centered in the Levitical system. Thus, like several other Christian documents, Hebrews reflects systems of Judaic thought that were in competition (cf. the Fourth Gospel, Matthew, and Gala-tians). Even though Hebrews discusses the cultic system of the taber-nacle period in Israelite religion, it certainly addressed Judaisms where the Temple played a central role in dealing with sin. The group that Hebrews addressed was concerned about purity: Could one sacrifice atone for their sins? While the message of Hebrews does not become obsolete if it was written after 70 CE, it does appear to address the pre-70 situation within a Jewish Christian group.[25] There is no hint of the destruction of the Temple and several pericopes in Hebrews do

24. Like the Judaisms of this period, Christianity also encompassed diversity of thought within various Christian groups as reflected in the extant literature.

25. Attridge summarizes the evidence and indicates that it is very difficult to be more specific than stating that Hebrews was written between 60–90 CE (*Hebrews*, pp. 5-9). J.H. Charlesworth argues for a pre-70 CE date in his *The Old Testament*

imply contemporary sacrificial cult activity (8.4; 9.6-10; 10.1-4; 13.10).

As with many early Christian documents, Hebrews does not discredit the stained covenantal history of Israel, but acknowledges history's salvific nature. Deliverance from sin and evil is found in history and on earth in the great High Priest Jesus of the new and better covenant, even though his work continues in the heavenly sanctuary (note the quotation of Jer. 31.31-34 in Heb. 8.8-13). Thus, the old corrupted covenant is not negated, but is now obsolete (8.13).

Hebrews' focus on Jesus as the High Priest, however, is distinct from many other expressions of early Christianity. Much more prominent is the focus on the prophetic and kingly portraits of Jesus. However, Psalm 110 plays an enormous role in uniting the kingly and priestly messianic expectations. The priestly Christology allowed the author of Hebrews to address the prominent concern for how atonement for sin has been made. Atonement for sin is certainly a central aspect of the generative idea of Hebrews.

Lastly, Hebrews' understanding of the Law differs from other expressions of Christianity. Because this epistle focuses so much on the cultic aspects of the Law, the Law is viewed as weak and ineffectual (7.18-19; 10.1, 28). In contrast, Matthew points to the enduring value of the Law in Christianity according to Jesus (the Sermon on the Mount) and Paul highlights its important role as a schoolmaster to lead us to Christ through knowledge of our sin (Gal. 3.24; Rom. 3.19-20).

c. *Melchizedek in the Ideological System of Hebrews*

As detailed above, the author of Hebrews was writing to people who held allegiance to the priestly sacrificial cult as a crucial institution for the forgiveness of sins. Thus, he is concerned about showing Jesus to be the faithful High Priest who offered the sacrifice for sin and whose priesthood supersedes all that the Levites might offer, especially to those Christians who were becoming disillusioned or discouraged. Therefore, the purpose of Hebrews is not to develop the story of Melchizedek in its own right; rather, the author uses a known competing priesthood tradition (Melchizedek via Psalm 110) to show Christ's priesthood to be more ancient than (Heb. 7.10), and superior to

Pseudepigrapha and the New Testament (Cambridge: Cambridge University Press, 1985), pp. 84-86.

(Heb. 7.7), the Levitical priesthood which appears to have been drawing some Christians back to it.

To demonstrate the legitimacy and superiority of the priesthood of Jesus (who was not a Levite), the author makes frequent use of Psalm 110 where a kingly messianic figure is declared to be '. . . "a priest according to the order of Melchizedek"' (5.6; 5.10; 6.20; 7.11, 15, 17, 21). The importance of this psalm in Hebrews' use of the Melchizedek tradition is difficult to overemphasize.[26] The link between a Davidic messiah and a priestly role in Psalm 110 formed the basis for the unique High-Priest Christology of Hebrews.[27]

It was not enough, however, for this author to simply assert that Jesus was associated with Melchizedek and hope his readers recognized the superiority of Jesus' priesthood. In ch. 7 the status of Melchizedek is carefully evaluated and elevated through a creative exegesis of Genesis 14. The author does the natural things like pointing out the significance of Melchizedek's kingship (7.2), his name (7.2), his city (7.2), his blessing of Abraham (7.6) and the tithe Abraham gave to him (7.4). The author uses the latter two events (the blessing and the tithe) in 7.7-8 to support the superiority of Melchizedek over the Levites (who also bestow blessings and receive tithes) since Levites are descendents of Abraham:

> It is beyond dispute that the inferior [τὸ ἔλαττον] is blessed by the superior [ὑπὸ τοῦ κρείττονος]. In the one case, tithes are received by those who are mortal; in the other, by one of whom it is testified that he lives [ζῇ].

The primary assertion Hebrews seeks to make about Melchizedek in relationship to Jesus, however, concerns the eternal nature of Melchizedek's priesthood: 'Without father [ἀπάτωρ], without mother [ἀμήτωρ], without genealogy [ἀγενεαλόγητος], having neither beginning of days nor end of life, but was made like [ἀφωμοιωμένος] the son of God, he remains a priest forever' (7.3). That this verse implies the eternal nature of Melchizedek and his priesthood is substantiated by 7.8 ('tithes are received. . . by one of whom it is testified that he lives') and 7.15 ('another priest arises, according to the likeness of Melchizedek, one

---

26. For discussion of this, see D. Hay, *Glory at the Right Hand: Psalm 110 in Early Christianity* (Nashville: Abingdon Press, 1973), pp. 143-53.

27. See also Attridge's excursus on 'The Antecedents and Development of the High-Priestly Christology', in *Hebrews*, pp. 83-96.

who has become a priest... through the power of an indestructible life'). This relationship between Melchizedek and Christ can be summarized as follows: Melchizedek *was made like* the (firstborn) Son, thus the (fleshly High Priest) Christ *is according to the likeness* of Melchizedek.

Numerous scholars see an understanding of Melchizedek being without genealogy as developed by an argument from silence, such as is found in Philo and Rabbinism.[28] While this may be part of the puzzle, one cannot ignore that by the first century CE traditions existed that were anything but 'silent' about Melchizedek's genealogy; they understood Melchizedek as an angelomorphic figure without genealogy (e.g. 11QMelch or *2 Enoch*).[29] Furthermore, it is probable that Hebrews drew on the rich Jewish traditions regarding the angelic liturgy in heaven, some of which had priestly angels offering bloodless sacrifices for sinners.[30]

The author's awareness of Melchizedek as an angelomorphic priest is apparent from his interpretation of Psalm 110. He draws on Ps. 110.4, not the 'silence' of Genesis 14, as a primary text for asserting the eternal nature of Melchizedek in 7.3 and 7.8. The author of Hebrews understood the 'eternal nature' of the Messiah's priestly status in Ps. 110.4 ('You are a priest *forever*') as a defining characteristic of Melchizedek: 'He [Melchizedek] remains a priest *forever*' (7.3). Thus, for the author of Hebrews, 'a priest forever' defines 'the order of Melchizedek' set forth in Psalm 110. This interpretation is corroborated by the language of 7.8: 'of whom it is testified that he [Melchizedek] lives'. The 'testimony' the author refers to is not the 'silence' of Genesis as some assert, but the testimony of Ps. 110.4 as it was interpreted by him and others (that is, the Messiah is a priest forever in a manner like Melchizedek who is a priest forever).[31] 'The order [τάξιν] of Melchizedek'

28. See Philo, *Leg. All.* 2.55; 3.79 (Melchizedek) and *Abr.* 31 (Noah). For the rabbinic argument that what is not stated in the Torah is just as important as what is stated, see H. Strack and P. Billerbeck, *Kommentar zum Neuen Testament aus Talmud und Midrash* (Munich: Beck, 1922), III, pp. 694-95.

29. This is especially emphasized by de Jonge and van der Woude, '11Q Melchizedek and the New Testament', pp. 321-22; see also C. Gieschen, Angelomorphic Christology: Antecedents and Early Evidence (PhD dissertation, University of Michigan, 1995), pp. 356-61.

30. *T. Levi* 3.1-4. For further evidence and a treatment of this influence upon Hebrews, see Attridge, *Hebrews*, pp. 99-100.

31. Horton, *The Melchizedek Tradition*, p. 153.

should not be interpreted as having a technical meaning in Hebrews. Note that the author himself interprets what 'according to the *order* of Melchizedek' means with his paraphrase of 7.15: 'according to the likeness [ὁμοιότητα] of Melchizedek'.[32] Jesus is also a priest forever because of his resurrection (7.16, 25).

What must be kept in mind as one sorts out the ideology of these verses is how the author clearly maintains the spotlight on Jesus even as he elevates Melchizedek. *Jesus is the mediator figure of Hebrews, not Melchizedek.* The elevation of Melchizedek serves the purpose of elevating Jesus. Although the precise relationship between these two is not defined beyond Melchizedek being 'made like the Son of God' (7.30) and Jesus being 'according to the likeness of Melchizedek' (7.15), Jesus is certainly not Melchizedek incarnate according to Hebrews; he is the Son of God incarnate.[33] The author maintains a delicate balance in his use of Melchizedek. To delimit Melchizedek in relation to Jesus would downplay the status of the Melchizedek priesthood and discredit the argument that the author constructed against the Levitical priesthood. To put more focus on Melchizedek as an eternal priestly mediator would take Jesus from the center stage of this epistle. The primary likeness between Jesus and Melchizedek is the eternal nature of their non-Levitical priesthoods. The relationship between Melchizedek and Jesus is best described in terms of typology.[34]

As the author seats Jesus in the priestly Messiah throne of Psalm 110, he develops a strong polemic against the Levitical priesthood by contrasting it with that of Jesus throughout ch. 7. Note the following aspects of this polemic:

32. For further discussion of this understanding see Hay, *Glory at the Right Hand*, pp. 146-48, and Kobelski, *Melchizedek and Melchiresha*, pp. 118-19.

33. Since the mediator Melchizedek is already named, it is less probable that he would be equated with Jesus. It is easier to equate an unnamed mediator figure (e.g., Son of Man) with a historical personage.

34. L. Goppelt ably articulates typology as a prominent way that early Christians appropriated the Old Testament, but fails to see a Melchizedek-Christ typology; see *Typos: The Typological Interpretation of the Old Testament in the New* (Grand Rapids: Eerdmans, 1982), pp. 163-70. The typology that the author of Hebrews adopts was already developed in Psalm 110, which testifies to an understanding of Melchizedek as the pattern for the messianic priest-king. Since Melchizedek 'was made like the son' (Heb. 7.3), then he naturally became a pattern for Jesus who, therefore, was 'according to the likeness of Melchizedek' (Heb. 7.15).

1. The inferior Abraham (from whom Levi descended) was blessed by the superior Melchizedek, who is like Jesus, the Son of God (7.7).
2. The eternal Melchizedek priesthood, which resembles that of Jesus, is more ancient, enduring, and superior to the mortal Levitical priesthood; Levi was still in Abraham's loins when the latter gave a tithe to Melchizedek (7.6-10).
3. The indestructible life of the priest Jesus is much more significant than the physical descent of the Levitical priests (7.15-16).
4. Jesus is part of a better covenant involving an oath (7.18-22).
5. The Levites have many individuals in a very temporary office; Jesus is the only priest in a permanent office (7.23-24).
6. The many sacrifices of sinful Levite men are contrasted with the one sacrifice of the perfect son (7.26-28).

Here the ideological place of the Melchizedek tradition in Hebrew comes into clear focus: it is a tool used in developing this polemic against the Levitical sacrificial system in order that Jesus, *the* High Priest, may be exalted and people's allegiance to him may increase (cf. 9.1–10.39).

3. A Comparison of the Melchizedek Tradition in 2 Enoch and Hebrews

Do *2 Enoch* and Hebrews use a similar Melchizedek tradition? Based upon the above analysis of these documents, one can see clear commonalities between their use of Melchizedek traditions on the form/content level. Both documents draw on traditions beyond Genesis 14 to present Melchizedek as an exalted priestly mediator. Both accent the eternal nature of Melchizedek as a priest and not just his so-called priestly line. Both are very deeply concerned with the question of purity from sin and deliverance from evil; this question is central to their ideologies. Both have a deep respect for the role that the office of priest plays in this deliverance from sin. Both have a view of the Levitical priesthood as extremely degenerative. Finally, both use Melchizedek because they want to go outside the Levitical priesthood in offering a solution for evil and sin. Therefore, *2 Enoch* provides us with very important evidence of the type of Melchizedek traditions that influenced Hebrews.[35]

35. Gianotto correctly asserts that there is no direct link between Melchizedek traditions in Philo/Qumran and those in Hebrews (*Melchisedek*, p. 144 n. 62). He

Nevertheless, there are serious differences in the function of this tradition in the ideological system of each document. First and foremost, this tradition is used to develop different central mediator figures. Melchizedek is the mediator in *2 Enoch*, but Jesus is the mediator of Hebrews.[36] Rather than using traditions to develop the person of Melchizedek in his own right as in *2 Enoch*, Hebrews employs this Melchizedek tradition as one component in a larger literary effort to demonstrate the exalted nature of Jesus as an encouragement to backsliding or discouraged Christians and as a polemic against what other Judaisms could offer (primarily angelic hierarchies, Moses, the Levitical priesthood, and temple sacrifices). Therefore, if one wants to make a more proper comparison of systems of thought, one should not compare the two Melchizedeks, but the two mediators: Melchizedek in *2 Enoch* with Jesus in Hebrews.

Secondly, these traditions are used with two different views of history. *2 Enoch* has a degenerative view of postdiluvian history (and, thus, of the Levitical priesthood of the covenant from Moses to 70 CE). Evil's domination immediately before the deluge and during Israel's covenantal history led *2 Enoch* to emphasize the need for priestly mediation through a supernatural Melchizedek who was miraculously born before the flood and would come again at the end of time. In contrast to this, Hebrews maintains the salvific value of history as Jesus fulfills the old covenant and initiates the new in history and long before the end of time.

Lastly, and closely related to these views of history, the Melchizedek traditions are used in these documents to present two different views of atonement for sins or deliverance from evil. Hebrews departs from any Melchizedek or Levitical priestly traditions and practices in emphasizing the self-sacrifice of the priest as the atonement for all sins of all time. In contrast to *2 Enoch*'s use of Melchizedek in a pessimistic context where he holds out hope of a mysterious deliverance and purification from evil in the future, Hebrews presents the deliverance from sin that Jesus has already won in convenantal history through his atoning death as a unique priest 'according to the order of Melchizedek'.

theorizes that Hebrews must have drawn on apocalyptic ideas that are not presently available, but he overlooks *2 Enoch* as evidence of such a contemporary tradition.

36. The ideology of Hebrews was very misunderstood in a later period by Melchizedekians who tried to put Melchizedek ahead of Jesus in their interpretation of this epistle; see Horton, *The Melchizedek Tradition*, pp. 111-12.

HEROES AND HISTORY IN HEBREWS 11

Pamela Eisenbaum

By listing the great biblical heroes and their deeds, ch. 11 of the Epistle to the Hebrews preserves a rare early Christian vision of Jewish religious history. Like all those who recount the past, the author of Hebrews presents history selectively. The *principle(s) of selection*—that is, what criteria the writer uses to include one hero and omit another, as well as what biographical elements of a given hero are included or excluded—is the interpretative key which sets this text in high relief against contemporary Jewish texts to which Hebrews 11 is often compared, texts like Sirach 44–50, 1 Macc. 2.51-60, Wisdom 10, and Covenant of Damascus 2–3.[1]

Like all the other lists and summaries, Hebrews 11 displays peculiarities. Rahab, for example, occurs on no other Jewish list. (In fact, women never appear on Jewish hero lists.) Why is she included here? The traditional answer is that Rahab is an example of faith like all the other members of the list. She risked her own life to protect Joshua's spies. This is partially true, but with so many biblical heroes to choose from, why make the choice of Rahab? Why not Debra? Furthermore, the fact that Rahab appears on the same list as Abraham and Moses makes a statement about her importance in general. Indeed, the analysis of the factors that led the author to choose a particular individual must be kept in a dialectical relationship to the list as a whole. Standard

---

1.   These other hero catalogues are not the only comparable texts, but they have been the most important ones for my study of Hebrews 11. A fuller account of my argument concerning the Hebrews hero catalogue, including discussions of various ancient hagiologies, can be found in 'The Jewish Heroes of Christian History: Hebrews 11 in Literary Context' (PhD dissertation, Columbia University, 1995). There is one other monograph that compares Hebrews 11 to other hero lists, that of M. Cosby, *The Rhetorical Composition and Function of Hebrews 11 in Light of Example Lists in Antiquity* (Macon, GA: Mercer, 1988). Cosby's work, which was very useful to me in my study of Hebrews 11, concentrates on the technical, rhetorical aspects of the text.

biblical images and common intertestamental traditions inform the author in his choice of each hero, but the peculiarity of his list lies in the particular combination of people and events. Only the principle(s) of selection can tell us what Rahab and Abraham have in common.

Usually scholars have taken the principle of selection for granted. The anaphoric use of πίστει has led to the assumption that each hero is an individual who exemplifies faith. Occasionally scholars have noticed that most of those included on the list are not good examples of faith,[2] at least not the best the Bible has to offer. Some scholars attribute the choice of heroes to the author's dependence on a source.[3] The author has then strung together this list with the catchword πίστει. But this is a less-than satisfying analysis. It is highly unlikely that Hebrews 11 is dependent upon a source, although the author was familiar with and may even have been imitating prototypical texts from the LXX.[4]

Although every list exhibits peculiarities, I intend to demonstrate that the Hebrews list differs markedly from any intertestamental proto-types to which one could point (indicated by inclusions like Rahab, and omissions like Joshua and Phinehas). The comment that any Jew could have written this text (with the exception of vv. 26 and 39)[5] —a comment made by more than one commentator—indicates how scholars have failed to perceive the distinctiveness of Hebrews 11. Indeed, the question of the principle behind the selection has remained largely unasked. And, curiously, even those scholars who insightfully point out that the heroes are not the best examples of faith invariably attempt to isolate that element of faith in each example that is alleged to be in the mind of the author.[6]

---

2. H. Windisch, *Der Hebräerbrief* (HNT, 4; Tübingen: Mohr–Siebeck, 1931), p. 99; H. Attridge, *The Epistle to the Hebrews* (Hermeneia; Philadelphia: Fortress Press, 1989), p. 306.

3. Windisch (*Hebräerbrief*, pp. 98-99) and O. Michel, (*Der Brief an die Hebräer* [MeyerK 13; Göttingen: Vandenhoeck & Ruprecht, 1966], pp. 422-23) were influential in disseminating this idea.

4. See Eisenbaum, 'Jewish Heroes', pp. 103-105; and P. Ellingworth, *Commentary on Hebrews* (NIGTC; Grand Rapids: Eerdmans, 1993), pp. 558-59.

5. See, e.g., S. Sowers, *The Hermeneutics of Philo and Hebrews* (Basel Studies of Theology, 1; Zurich: EVZ, 1965), p. 133; and Windisch, *Hebräerbrief*, p. 98.

6. The most striking example of this is Attridge, who explicitly states at the beginning of his commentary on this section that most of the biblical stories referred to do *not* explicitly highlight faith (*Hebrews*, p. 306). And yet in his otherwise thoughtful exegesis of each and every hero, he consistently attempts to find the 'faith element'

As I am about to demonstrate, having faith is not in and of itself a foundational principle of selection.[7] Having faith is only one facet of a multi-faceted profile. I have identified four qualities that the heroes have in common—all of which probably factor into the author's decision to include these heroes. While not every hero possesses every one of the traits that I will identify as the author's principles of selection, the majority of them do.

Furthermore, like the lists of biblical heroes in Sirach 44–50, Wisdom 10, and Covenant of Damascus 2–3, Hebrews 11 also functions as a retelling of Israelite history. Not only is the goal of this study to abstract a profile of the hero, but we must assess the author's diachronic retelling of biblical history. Each hero and event listed plays a role in shaping the author's picture of that history. Thus, whatever criteria the author uses to select heroes apply also to his historiographic understanding of biblical history.

Profile of the Hebrews Hero

Death or Near-Death Experience

All the heroes die or have near-death experiences.[8] Their deaths or near-deaths are then followed by some kind of new beginning.

The first three heroes our author names are Abel, Enoch, and Noah (vv. 4-7). Abel is the world's first murder victim. Even if Enoch did not literally die, he passed from his earthly existence to a divine one. Noah does not die. He in fact is spared while the rest of the world dies. His survival of the flood certainly counts as a near-death experience, which is succeeded by a new beginning. Although the biblical text does not reflect on the post-mortem existence of Abel[9] and Enoch, there exist

---

that must be present in the author's mind. About Moses he says, 'Hebrews is not concerned with extraordinary experiences attributed to Moses in and of themselves, but with his faith' (p. 343). Indeed, the author of Hebrews has not selected arbitrary extraordinary experiences, but neither has he chosen them necessarily because they exemplify a *specific* manifestation of πίστις.

7.   The primary function of the anaphoric use of πίστει is rhetorical, viz., to create the effect of an enormous—even innumerable—number of examples. See Cosby, *Rhetorical Composition*, pp. 41-55.

8.   This characteristic has been observed by J. Swetnam, *Jesus and Isaac: A Study of the Epistle to the Hebrews in Light of the Aqedah* (Rome: Biblical Institute Press, 1981), pp. 95-96.

9.   When the author of Hebrews says of Abel 'although he is dead, he still

intertestamental traditions that do, and it is likely that the author knew of these: Abel was the first figure to ascend to heaven. There he resides as judge of the righteous and the wicked.[10] Enoch was of course known in intertestamental tradition as a visionary as well as an eschatological judge with a God's-eye point of view.[11]

Abraham is said to be 'as good as dead' (ταῦτα νενεκρωμένου)[12] and Sarah 'beyond the appropriate age' (παρὰ καιρὸν ἡλικίας) when a new life, that is, Isaac, is given to them (vv. 11-12). Isaac himself comes as close to death as anyone on the list without actually dying. The fact that he is so close to death but saved at the last minute is, in the words of our author, like the experience of resurrection itself (v. 19).[13] Although the author is very brief in his mention of the patriarchs, Isaac, Jacob, and Joseph, he depicts all of them at the time of their deaths (vv. 20-22): Isaac when he blindly blesses Jacob and Esau, Jacob when he blesses the sons of Joseph, and Joseph when he predicts the exodus.

The connection with death in the description of Moses is more vague, but nevertheless present in two different instances. In the birth story, the child Moses is miraculously saved from death (v. 23). Later, the mature Moses, when he flees Egypt for Midian, believes his life is in danger (v. 27).[14] The mention of the people crossing the Red Sea and

speaks', he alludes to Gen. 4.10, where it says that Abel's blood cried out to the Lord (cf. Heb. 12.24). Thus, the author interprets the Genesis text to mean that Abel did have a post-mortem existence.

10. See 1 *En.* 22.7ff. and *T. Abr.* 13.

11. Most of *1 Enoch* attests to this portrait of Enoch, but see especially chs. 1–36.

12. This description of Abraham is probably traditional; it is found also in Paul, Rom. 4.19.

13. λογισάμενος [Ἀβραὰμ] ὅτι καὶ ἐκ νεκρῶν ἐγείρειν δυνατὸς ὁ θεός, ὅθεν αὐτὸν καὶ ἐν παραβολῇ ἐκομίσατο.

14. An exegetical difficulty exists in v. 27 concerning the statement that Moses was not afraid of the king's anger. Commentators such as H. Braun (*An die Hebräer* [HNT, 14; Tübingen: Mohr–Siebeck, 1984], p. 382); F.F. Bruce (*The Epistle to the Hebrews* [NICNT; Grand Rapids: Eerdmans, 1990], pp. 312-13); and Attridge (*Hebrews*, p. 342) understand v. 27 to refer to Moses' flight to Midian. The problem with this interpretation is precisely the comment that Moses was not afraid, since the biblical text indicates that he was afraid (Exod. 2.14). Thus, other interpreters, such as H. Montefiore (*A Commentary on the Epistle to the Hebrews* [New York: Harper, 1964], p. 204); and J. Héring (*The Epistle to the Hebrews* [London: Epworth, 1970], p. 105) believe that v. 27 refers to the exodus. The problem with this interpretation is chronology. The exodus of the people happens after the Passover sacrifice (v. 28), and up until now the author has not deviated from following biblical

the walls of Jericho falling down (vv. 29-30) are too vague for us to define their characteristics, although clearly the people are in danger when they cross the Red Sea. Rahab, if she had not assisted the spies would surely have perished with the people of Jericho (v. 31). Thus, all the heroes die or almost die, but the event is followed by a new beginning.[15] The author does not always describe this aspect explicitly, but he always pinpoints the end of life/new life moment in the career of the hero.

Ability to See into the Future (The Meaning of the Heroes' Faith)
Most of the heroes on the list have the ability to anticipate the future. Thus, in the midst of adverse circumstances they are confident because they foresee something better. Given the definition of faith ('faith is the realization of what is hoped for, proof of things not seen')[16] by which the author introduced the hero catalogue, this characteristic is the closest we come to seeing the heroes as examples of faith.

Four heroes are explicitly described as having knowledge of the future. Noah receives an oracle, by which he knows what the future will bring and so he builds the ark (v. 7). Abraham follows the instructions of God, even if they do not appear to lead to the fulfillment of the promises. Though he lives in the land of promise as in a 'foreign land', he ultimately knows that a heavenly homeland awaits (vv. 14-16). The author portrays Isaac as 'in the know' when he blesses Jacob and Esau (v. 20), rather than as an old man who was duped by his wife and son, as he is in Genesis 27. Joseph, as I already mentioned, predicts the great event of the exodus from Egypt. Moses has foreknowledge of Christ and the divine rewards that await him in the distant future (v. 26).

For the other heroes, their ability to see into the future is implied by their actions as described by the author of Hebrews. Rahab, for example, helps the spies in advance of the battle (v. 31). As a result, she saves

chronology. This situation has prompted M.R. D'Angelo to argue that the author has conflated the two events (*Moses in the Letter to the Hebrews* (SBLDS, 42; Missoula, MT: Scholars Press, 1979), pp. 59-62).

15. Cf. R. Brawley ('Discoursive Structure and the Unseen in Hebrews 2:8 and 11:1: A Neglected Aspect of the Context', *CBQ* 55 [1993], pp. 95-96) who argues that events like the flood and the splitting of the Red Sea are proto-apocalyptic events in the author's eyes.

16. All translations of Hebrews 11 are mine; other biblical citations are from the NRSV, except when otherwise indicated.

herself and her family. In the case of Abel and Enoch, this quality is more subtle but still present. Both are said to have received divine approval during their earthly life. To be sure, divine approval is something which by definition applies to all the heroes on this list as well as on other Jewish lists. But the approval of Abel and Enoch earns them post-mortem rewards. Indeed, following Enoch's mention on the list, the author makes an exhortative aside: 'For it is necessary that one who approaches God has faith that he exists and that he is one who rewards those who seek him' (v. 6). We may therefore assume that Abel and Enoch's approval stems from their faith in the reality of God and in the knowledge of future rewards.

While the heroes have faith in, or knowledge of, future rewards, their present life is without reward or recognition for their faithfulness. Some scholars have emphasized the suffering which some heroes on the list are said to have endured.[17] In my estimation these scholars have been overly influenced by the concluding verses,[18] which are most likely present for rhetorical effect and not part of the body of the main list.[19] The fact that the heroes are connected somehow with death may also influence scholars to assume suffering plays a key role in the selection of heroes. In my view, as we saw above, while death appears as a theme in the list, it is not necessarily connected with suffering. Of the heroes on the main list, Moses is the only one said to have suffered (v. 25). At the same time, none of the heroes have an easy time of life—Abraham wanders, Isaac is almost sacrificed, and so forth.

Another way of looking at the presence of this so-called theme of suffering is to understand it in relation to the theme of the heroes' ability to see the future. In order for the heroes to focus on future rewards, their present circumstances must be less than ideal. If they

17. Héring, *Epistle*, p. 100; D'Angelo, *Moses in Hebrews*, p. 27.

18. That is, vv. 33-38, which indeed cover a number of trials and tribulations. Vv. 33-34, however, emphasizes not the suffering created by trials, but the overcoming of them. These verses conclude the list for the purpose of drama.

19. V. 32 terminates the anaphoric use of πίστει. In v. 33 and following, the author presents a rhetorical question followed by a rapid-fire list of names, which is in turn followed by a list of deeds without names attached. As Cosby (*Rhetorical Composition*, pp. 58-59) has shown, the point of these verses is to create the impression that examples could be listed *ad infinitum*; the quick listing of names and the use of asyndeton enhance that impression. Thus, for my purposes, the main body of the catalogue ends at v. 32, and only heroes mentioned in vv. 1-32 are dealt with in this paper.

were satisfied with an earthly life filled with material niceties, they would not need to look to future rewards. The heroes' earthly life is filled with adverse circumstances, so as to contrast the poverty of their current existence with their future rewards. This aspect of the heroes' portrayal in Hebrews is closely related to the third characteristic, the alteration of status.

Alteration of Status

One of the most common attributes that biblical heroes are said to possess on Jewish Hellenistic hero lists, particularly Sirach 44–50, Wisdom 10, and 1 Macc. 2.51-60, is honor.[20] Furthermore, this honor is often communicated by demonstrating that the heroes have been blessed with earthly rewards such as wealth, power, and position. In fact, the heroes of Hebrews lack all the glamour and glory of the Jewish heroes as they appear on other lists. In the Hellenistic lists, earthly rewards and honor consistently play a major role. One particularly important characteristic of heroes who appear on the lists in Sirach 44–50, Wisdom 10, and 1 Maccabees 2 is that each hero receives rewards as signs of God's approval, and these rewards are bestowed during each hero's lifetime.

Indeed, in 1 Maccabees 2, the list is structured by the rewards accorded each member of the list.[21] Joseph is rewarded with becoming lord of Egypt, Phinehas receives the covenant of the priesthood, Elijah has great zeal for the law and so is taken up, etc. In Wisdom 10, Sophia rewards the righteous and punishes the wicked in their own lifetime. Sophia guides and protects Jacob for example; 'she prospered him in his labors and increased the fruit of his toil' (v. 10). In the Sirach list

20. See Eisenbaum, 'Jewish Heroes', pp. 42-56.

21. The following chart illustrates how 1 Macc. 2.51-60 is structured by the rewards the heroes receive:

Hero	Deed	Reward
Abraham	tested	righteousness
Joseph	kept commandment	lord of Egypt
Phinehas	zealous	covenant of priesthood
Joshua	fulfilled commandment	became judge
Caleb	testified	inheritance of land
David	merciful	throne
Elijah	zeal for law	taken up to heaven
Hannaniah, Azariah, and Mishael	believed	saved from flame
Daniel	innocent	delivered from lion

rewards also play a crucial role in describing each hero, and these rewards usually involve a position of honor.[22] In fact, the introduction to Sirach 44–50 generically captures the high position in society which the heroes are assumed to enjoy:

> The Lord apportioned to them great glory, his majesty from the beginning. There were those who ruled in their kingdoms, and made a name for themselves by their valor; those who gave counsel because they were intelligent; those who spoke in prophetic oracles; those who led the people by their counsels and by their knowledge of the people's lore; they were wise in their words of instruction; those who composed musical tunes, or put verses to writing; rich men endowed with resources, living peacefully in their homes—*all these were honored in their generations, and were the pride of their times* (44.2-7).

The heroes of Hebrews could not be further removed from this image. They do not receive honor or reward or even recognition in their own lifetime. Furthermore, the heroes are not depicted in the prime of their lives, but rather receive mention in connection with death. In addition, the heroes of Hebrews are not recorded for their impressive accomplishments and talents. None of the Hebrews heroes hold national office and none are said to have made a covenant with God. In short, their status has been altered; the heroes of Hebrews are not considered heroic for the usual reasons.

For example, when the author of Hebrews describes Moses as a hero, Moses' heroic qualities appear circumscribed, situation-specific. He chooses suffering with the people of God *rather than* the fleshpots of Egypt (v. 25). He was not afraid of the anger of the king (v. 27), but no praise is heaped on him as inherently brave,[23] and no mention is made of his many successful confrontations with Pharaoh (avoiding the rivaling magic tricks). The final act Moses performs in Hebrews 11 is keeping 'the Passover' and sprinkling the blood (v. 28). This sprinkling of the blood may be meant to evoke the blood Moses sprinkled on

---

22. B. Mack (*Wisdom and Hebrew Epic: Ben Sira's Hymn in Praise of the Fathers* [Chicago: University of Chicago, 1985]) names the reception of honor/ rewards as one of the seven characteristics of the heroes on Sirach's list. The other six include: 1. designation of office; 2. mention of divine approbation or election; 3. reference to covenant; 4. mention of the person's character or piety; 5. an account of deeds; and 6. reference to the historical situation. Mack's work on Sirach 44–50 was one of the primary inspirations for my approach to Hebrews 11.

23. Statements about the hero's virtue or piety are often an integral part of the description. See Mack's list of characteristics in n. 22.

the people during the covenant ceremony in Exod. 24.8 and referred to in Heb. 9.21.[24] Thus, its mention is more evocative of the blood theme in the document overall than of any special qualities of Moses.

The biographical events that the author chooses to include about Moses portray him as an orphan, a defector, and a fugitive. Moses is not depicted as the leader of the people during the exodus. When the crossing at the Red Sea is mentioned in 11.29, we read 'By faith *the people* crossed the Red Sea. . . ' Indeed, none of Moses' actions as they are recounted in Hebrews 11 portray him as a leader of any kind.[25] Instead of being depicted as a man who leads the people out of bondage, he is a man who makes wise choices for himself.[26] By any Jewish standard of the time, this amounts to a grossly understated picture of Moses as hero.

What are missing in Hebrews' retelling of the Moses story are all of Moses' grand accomplishments, which on other hero lists and in other retellings, are co-extensive with rewards. Because in the author's version the rewards are delayed until some time which lies outside of biblical history, the saga of Moses not only seems incomplete, but Moses himself lacks honor, prestige, and achievement, as do all the heroes in Hebrews. It is not that the author of Hebrews is not paying Moses compliments, but his descriptions of Moses are restrained. While the tendency of hero lists is to be over-the-top, this author holds back.

This holding back is due to the fact that the heroes live in a time prior to the Christ event. Their heroism is not attributable to their achievements in their own time, but to their ability to anticipate a better time, when they will receive their reward (as vv. 25-26 read: 'Moses chose to suffer with the people of God rather than have the fleeting pleasure of sin, since he considered the reproach of Christ greater wealth than the treasures of Egypt; for he looked to his reward'). The heroes of Hebrews function as seers who portend the future, but whose own heroic image is mitigated by their being part of the old world order.

24. For the purposes of typology, the author has an interest in conflating various ceremonies. For a discussion of the matter, see D'Angelo, *Moses in Hebrews*, pp. 244-48.

25. And yet Moses' leadership *is* mentioned earlier in Hebrews in connection with the people's rebelliousness in the wilderness: 'Was it not all those who left Egypt under the leadership of Moses?' (3.16). Thus, Moses is held at least partly responsible for the people's failures, but not given credit for their successes.

26. A. Culpepper, 'A Superior Faith: Hebrews 10:19-12:2', *RevExp* 82 (1985), p. 386.

Hebrews 11 participates in the attitude toward the biblical past which is typical of the document as a whole. The author consistently engages in a hermeneutic of continuity and discontinuity.[27] Like the levitical system of worship, the tabernacle, the Temple, the priests, or other biblical institutions, the author uses the heroes as historical examples for teaching, but at the same time devalues them because they are what make the old covenant *old*. The national realities of Israel, that is, the tabernacle, the Torah, and the priesthood, are only shadows of perfect divine realities (Heb. 8.5). They are both *models for*, as well as *models in contrast to*.[28]

For example, on the one hand, the author makes a strong case for the inferiority of the levitical priesthood, while Christ, on the other hand, is the perfect priest. Christ is shown to be perfect by fulfilling the same needs that the levitical system was trying to fulfill, only he fulfills them perfectly and self-sufficiently. Thus the author allows the ancient Jewish system to set the standard: blood must be shed to expiate sin, the victim must be unblemished, and so forth. But Christ has achieved the perfect version of the standard. Therefore, Christ as priest is both continuous and discontinuous with the tradition. He is a superlative priest who is judged to be superlative by the ancient (and, presumably, inferior) standard of measure. He is unlike the former priests because he is infinitely better, and he is like them because he achieves their priestly goals. Similarly, the heroes of Hebrews represent models for the Christian audience to which Hebrews is directed, but they are also being implicitly contrasted with the ultimate hero: Jesus.[29]

---

27. This idea comes from the work of G. Hughes, *Hebrews and Hermeneutics* (Cambridge: Cambridge University, 1979).

28. There are several discussions of examples in rhetorical handbooks, and they reflect a sophisticated understanding of the different ways an example or model can function. Quintillian lists five types of examples: 1. the similar; 2. the dissimilar; 3. the contrary; 4. the greater-to-the-lesser; and 5. the lesser to the greater (*Inst. Ort.* 5.11.6-7). For an explanation and discussion of these, see B. Brice, 'Paradeigma and Exemplum in Ancient Rhetorical Theory' (PhD dissertation, University of California, Berkeley, 1975), pp. 158-63.

29. One should always remember that a historical example functions propagandistically. The description of an example from the past will always be colored by an interest in the present. See the influential article by S. Perlman, 'The Historical Example, its Use and Importance as Political Propaganda in the Attic Orators', *Scripta Hierosolymitana* (eds. A. Fuks and I. Halpern; Jerusalem: Magnes, 1961), VII, pp. 150-66.

So much of the argument of Hebrews is devoted to distinguishing Jesus from others[30] that the author cannot risk the heroes' status being confused with that of Jesus. If Jesus is the perfect example of faith (12.2), the heroes must be something less. Furthermore, Jesus was not simply the Son of God, but he also had to suffer humiliation and shame (2.9; 4.15–5.8). Since the heroes of the old covenant cannot possess more glory than Jesus, the author's portrayal of them must somehow diminish their grand stature. In addition, because the author describes the heroes as humble in their own time, their image more closely matches the image of the earthly Jesus.

The alteration-of-status characteristic can also help us explain the author's waffling on the position of the heroes' reception of promises. Exegetes have often noted that the author contradicts himself in ch. 11.[31] On the one hand, the author of Hebrews says that the heroes received neither earthly promises (v. 13)—meaning biblical promises like land and nationhood—nor did they receive the ultimate promise given in Christ (v. 39). On the other hand, sometimes the author says they did receive the biblical promises (v. 17, 33).[32] and he certainly implies that they will receive the eschatological promise ultimately (v. 40). I account for this apparent contradiction by distinguishing between receiving a promise and receiving the fulfillment of the promise.[33] Thus, the author's position is as follows: the heroes were promised earthly rewards, but never actually received them. Conversely, God never directly promised them an eschatological reward, but they will presumably receive it.

What scholars have not adequately dealt with is how radical it is for the author to say that the biblical heroes did not receive what was promised them by God.[34] From a traditional point of view, such a statement would have been insulting. But for this author, the heroes' status

30. See esp. Heb. 1–2 and 3.1-6.

31. This observation has been used to argue that the author must be relying on a source. See Michel, *Der Brief*, p. 244. Cf. Ellingworth, *Hebrews*, pp. 558-59.

32. Cf. Heb. 6.15: 'When God made a promise to Abraham, because he had no one greater by whom to swear, he swore by himself, saying, "I will surely bless you and multiply you". And thus Abraham, having patiently endured, obtained the promise.'

33. This is essentially the position of Bruce, *Epistle*, p. 343.

34. Even though the biblical text can legitimately be interpreted this way, e.g., for Abraham, Jewish exegetes contemporary with the author of Hebrews did not read the text in this light. For them, Abraham received all that was promised. See for example, CD 3.1-21; Sir. 44.19-21; and *Pirque Aboth* 5.3.

is not derived from earthly rewards and accomplishments. Their heroic image depends upon other, more humble qualities.

Marginalization

Closely related to the characteristic of alteration-of-status is the characteristic of marginalization. It is the most fundamental quality that the heroes of Hebrews possess. Because the status of biblical heroes is traditionally derived from a position of leadership or connection with a national institution, and since the heroes' station must be altered so as not to outshine Jesus, the author's avoidance of mentioning national accomplishments serves both purposes.

The author of Hebrews depicts his heroes as separate from his/her contemporaries. The language of separation is self-evident in Abraham's case. Abraham lives in the promised land as in a foreign land (παρῴκησεν εἰς γῆν τῆς ἐπαγγελίας ὡς ἀλλοτρίαν; v. 9). Moses, too, voluntarily gives up his status within a nation or society (vv. 24-25). Both men are portrayed as loners.

Even though other characters on the list may not be such obvious outsiders, I think our author views them as outsiders and that this quality is essential. Abel, Enoch, and Noah stand apart from their generations. In other words, none of these men have any real compatriots, but are rather at odds with their contemporaries. Abel was murdered, while the progeny Cain and Seth populate the earth. Because of this event, Abel is taken out of earthly circulation, so to speak. Enoch was taken up and later tradition assumes that this event sets him completely apart from his peers.[35] Noah was saved while everyone else drowned. In the

---

35. Enoch is the first biblical hero to be mentioned in Sirach 44–50 (although Enoch's name was probably not originally in the Hebrew text; see Mack, *Wisdom and Hebrew Epic*, pp. 199-200); where he is said to have been set apart as an example to others: 'Enoch pleased the Lord, and was taken up; he was an example of repentance to all generations' (44.16). A similar sentiment is expressed by Philo in *Abr.* 17–18, where Philo explains that the word 'translation' (μεταθέσεως) found in the LXX implies a turning from a worse life to a better one. For further discussion, see D. Lührmann, 'Henoch und die Metanoia', *ZNW* 66 (1975), pp. 103-16. Finally, the best expression of Enoch as an elect one who was separated from his generation can be found in Wis. 4.10-16: 'There was one who pleased God and was loved by him, and while living among sinners he was taken up. He was caught up lest evil change his understanding or guile deceive his soul. For the fascination of wickedness obscures what is good, and roving desire perverts the innocent mind. . . The righteous man who has died will condemn the ungodly who are living, and youth that is quickly

case of each of these heroes, their contemporaries were in a depraved or at least sinful state, while the heroes somehow transcend that depravity.[36] Finally, Rahab, with whom the list culminates, stands apart from her community of origin as well. Thus, the heroes of Hebrews are not distinguished *by* their comrades, as is the case in the Sirach list, they are distinguished *from* them, and are eventually removed from life with them by God.

Perhaps the best way to measure how far the heroes stand from their traditional place within Israel is to consider what the author avoids saying in his descriptions of the heroes. For example, three of the men named constitute a special class of heroes. Noah, Abraham, and Moses each made a covenant with God. Yet, the author does not acknowledge the covenants made with any of them. Covenants, like the rewards, play a major role in the Hellenistic hero lists, but in Hebrews they are absent.

Surely at least part of the reason the author avoids the mention of covenants is because they are inherently tied up with Israel's national identity. The defining characteristic of Israel's relationship with God is the covenant. Since the author wishes to stay clear of national accomplishments, it makes sense that he would not mention covenants. The covenants are also a traditional sign of status and were usually connected with holding national office. They also imply theophonic contact between the deity and the individual, which the author may have wanted to avoid, because Jesus in Hebrews is the intermediary *par excellence*. Thus, it is not surprising for the author to avoid mention of covenants.

Perhaps the author wished to avoid references to God's covenant with Israel because he thought it would not be well received by a Gentile, or partially Gentile, audience. Josephus downplays the covenant in the *Antiquities*, while stressing that Israel is a virtuous people deserving of God's special attention.[37] But Moses in Hebrews does not possess those characteristics that would typically appeal to a non-Jewish audience

perfected will condemn the prolonged old age of the unrighteous man' (RSV).

36. For an overview of the multifarious traditions about the depraved state of the earth during primeval times, see L. Ginzberg, *Legends of the Jews* (7 vols.; Philadelphia: Jewish Publication Society, 1937), I, pp. 103-41.

37. H. Attridge (*The Interpretation of Biblical History in the Antiquitates Judaicae of Flavius Josephus* [Missoula, MT: Scholars Press, 1976], p. 148), speculates that the theme of covenant is diminished in any setting where Gentiles are included.

either. Among Gentiles Moses was known either as a legislator or as a magician.[38] Neither is referred to in Hebrews 11.

If we use Moses as an example once again, we can further illustrate Hebrews' unique portrayal of the hero. Compared to those in Hebrews, depictions of the great leader in other texts—even New Testament texts—look completely different. For example, while Stephen's speech in Acts is not a hero list, it does rehearse the great events of biblical history while highlighting the works of heroes. In Acts 7 we find everything said of Moses that we expect to find: God speaks to him on Mt Sinai and he leads the people through the Red Sea. Stephen even says '[Moses] received living oracles to give to us' (Acts 7.38). Thus a note is made of the revelation given to Moses and the fact that this revelation is to be handed down. In fact, several direct quotations of God speaking to Moses appear in Acts 7, while in Hebrews 11 Moses is not the recipient of any revelation,[39] and does not act as the lawgiver for the people. The author's omission of these key biographical events indicates that he wishes to avoid the portrayal of Moses as a national hero; Moses is no longer a founding father of Israel.

The heroes of Hebrews are marginalized individuals. Instead of being viewed as leaders, as the center of Israelite society, they stand outside it. It is no surprise then that the list culminates with Rahab, a Gentile woman.

Transvaluation

In the words of the literary critic Gérard Genette, the author has *transvalued* the heroes of Jewish Scripture.[40] Transvaluing occurs when the characters in the hypertext (viz. the derivative text, which in this case is the LXX) acquire roles and attributes derived from a system of values not found in the hypotext (viz. the targeted text, which in this case is Hebrews).[41] In other words, when the author of Hebrews

38. J. Gager, *Moses in Greco–Roman Paganism* (SBLMS, 16; Nashville and New York: Abingdon Press, 1972).

39. Moses does, however, receive a direct revelation in Heb. 8.5.

40. G. Genette, *Palimpsestes: La littérature au second degré* (Paris: Editions du Seuil, 1982). I am grateful to Dennis MacDonald for introducing me to Genette's work. MacDonald's own work (*Christianizing Homer: The Odyssey, Plato, and the Acts of Andrew* [New York and Oxford: Oxford University Press, 1994]) is indebted to Genette.

41. MacDonald, *Christianizing Homer*, p. 6.

composed his miniature re-writing of biblical history in ch. 11, the primary objects of his narrative, that is, the heroes, were transformed by the values of the author. An implicit part of transvaluing is the intentional *devaluing* of the system of values perceived to be originally present in the hypertext. Transvaluing would not be successful if the new values were just added to the text; they must replace the old ones—hence the old ones are devalued so that the audience will reject them. Thus, the author diminishes the heroes' national status in order to highlight aspects of their careers that better reflect his Christian perspective.

The author's understanding of Christology and the new covenant as well as his experience of being a Christian cause him to value the heroes of the Jewish Bible for reasons different from those that had traditionally been employed. National leaders become marginal individuals. A man like Abraham, famous for his power and wealth, is transformed into a wanderer who never received his rightful inheritance. Moses, the hero of the exodus and Israel's lawgiver, is included in Hebrews not for any of those reasons, but because he suffered as an outsider.

The heroes in Hebrews 11 are not primarily examples of virtuous behavior, except in the most general way. The sheer variety of actions ascribed to the heroes makes it difficult to see what behavior is being prescribed or praised. Each hero or event is listed as part of the ancient history of the Hebrews community, existing in an inferior world without the benefit of Christ. Yet, even in this world heroes emerged and heroic events happened through faith. This being established, how much easier is it for the Christian community, which has the benefit of Christ, to have the confidence to abide in faith—that is, to stay the divine course on which they presently travel. Thus, the heroes are an inspiration to the Christian audience because they did so well with so little.

These images of the biblical heroes have both positive and negative functions as examples or models. On the one hand, the author's hermeneutic of discontinuity is evident in the devaluing of the heroes' actual heroism. They lack achievement, high status, and reward. Like examples from Graeco-Roman lists, the heroes of Hebrews are more human than those typically found on Jewish lists.[42] On this level the heroes function as models of contrast with Christ and life in the new covenant. On the other hand, the author's hermeneutic of continuity functions in

42. See Eisenbaum, 'Jewish Heroes', pp. 92-95, 99-102.

that the heroes are models for the new Christian community. Obedience in suffering since the advent of Christ is valued as a sign of high station and not humility, and being an outsider among one's own people need not be a source of shame. The catalogue of heroes in Hebrews reflects a Christian writer who saw the heroes of Jewish Scripture as quintessentially Christian, rather than Jewish.

The Denationalization of Biblical History

Hebrews 11 constitutes what I call a multi-dimensional list. By that I mean that a variety of persons and events appear. (I also include in this category the lists in Covenant of Damascus 2–3, Wisdom 10, and Sirach 44–50.) Identifying this category serves to contrast this kind of list with what I would call a flat or one-dimensional list, in which one particular virtue or type of behavior is illustrated (Graeco-Roman hero lists are almost always of this type). The multi-dimensional nature of a list often indicates that the author was striving for broad coverage of biblical events, so as to better convey the *story* of biblical history—and that is what I think we have in Hebrews. What is most important about the diachronic aspect of the text is that it amounts to a narrative genealogy which functions to legitimate the community addressed by the text.

Because the author concludes the list the way he does ('And all these, although attested to through faith, did not receive the promise, since God foresaw something better for us, so that *they* would not be perfected apart from *us*') the heroes form the ancestral heritage of the community. 'They' meaning the heroes, and 'us' meaning the community, are part of the same story. Hebrews 11 implicitly functions as a genealogy which legitimates the Christian audience by providing them with a biblical ancestry. At the same time, this ancestry is not identified with the nation of Israel, but forms a trajectory independent of it. That is why the list does not include any priests or kings.[43] All the heroes are outsiders. They stand apart from the national history of Israel while at the same time being recorded in Scripture, which is the collection of documents traditionally assumed to contain the story of Israel.[44] In the author's words, the heroes derive their status from

43. David is only mentioned in the summary allusions (11.32), and not as part of the main list.

44. J.A. Sanders (*Torah and Canon* [Philadelphia: Fortress Press, 1972]) makes the point that Scripture was primarily thought of as *story* by the ancients.

πίστις, not from any national role or office. πίστις in this sense is not so much a personal quality, as it is a divine force (perhaps analogous to the Holy Spirit?). πίστις allows the author to establish a non-national, salvation–historical trajectory which includes the Hebrews community.

Effectively, the author's purpose is to *denationalize* the history of Israel. To accomplish this, his task was necessarily two-fold. First, he had to show that the heroes were superior individuals because of non-national accomplishments. Those who are typically thought of as national leaders, like Abraham and Moses, are not depicted in their leadership roles. Furthermore, Abraham and Moses, like the others listed, are treated as distinct from the people or nation. Secondly, he implicitly engages in a polemic against those who would see Scripture as a national history by ending the bulk of his summary just before the establishment of the nation, and by giving the impression that Israel's history dissipates—that is, has no teleological direction—just as she enters what is truly her national phase. Thus, God's promises, which in biblical history are traditionally nationalistic—promises for land, temple, and monarchy—are depicted as not having been fulfilled, in order that a new ending might be grafted onto the story: the heavenly rest now attainable because of Christ (vv. 39-40; cf. Heb. 4.6-11). Indeed, Abraham and Moses are the paradigmatic heroes in Hebrews 11 precisely because they do not receive the fulfillment of those national promises.

It is difficult to imagine an ancient Jewish writer making the remark about the lack of fulfillment of biblical promises, because it represents a perspective so far removed from the traditional laudatory view of the biblical figures.[45] But from the author's transvalued conception, it is a compliment to the heroes, because they will receive a greater promise—the Christian promise. Thus, while most scholars have seen Hebrews 11 as a rather conventional recounting of biblical history, I see it as an innovative Christian reading of that history.

---

45. What I mean by this statement is that while there may have been a variety of Jewish beliefs and practices in the first century, most Jews would acknowledge the biblical heroes as the recipients of fulfilled promises. I simply want to draw attention to the unusual perspective of the writer of Hebrews. Cf. Windisch (*Hebräerbrief*, p. 98) who like many other commentators misses the radical (and rather 'unJewish') reading of Jewish heroes and history in Hebrews 11: 'Bis auf den ὀνειδισμὸς Χριστοῦ und die Schlußbemerkung 39f könnte der ganze Abschnitt von einem Juden entworfen sein. Zum mindesten liegt eine jüdische oder judenchristliche Schultradition zugrunde.'

THE PROVENANCE OF THE CALIPHATE CHURCH:
JAMES 2.17-26 AND GALATIANS 3 RECONSIDERED[*]

Vasiliki Limberis

Most who have studied the letter of James have found the Abraham section puzzling. At best it is a *non sequitur*, with no connection to the letter as a whole.[1] Moreover, the majority of scholars of James hold that the author did not include the section on Abraham as a reaction to Paul's teaching.[2] The chief reason for this position is that James's exegesis of Gen. 15.6 clearly demonstrates that the author had completely misunderstood Paul. This paper reopens the possibility that James is responding to Paul, and proposes that the heart of his argument against him is the Abraham passage.

The evidence for this thesis comes from new social–historical reconstructions of Jewish Christian and Gentile Christian groups of the middle of the first century, and from rhetorical analyses of both the James passage and Galatians 3. In this paper it will be important to establish the context and dating of the letter of James, situating it within the milieu of what Louis Martyn calls the 'law-observant mission to the

*   I thank Alan Segal, Kelley McCarthy Spoerl, David T.M. Frankfurter, and Andrew Dolan for their critical comments on this paper. I first heard the term 'caliphate church' in a lecture which was given by Professor Helmut Koester in 1983. He used it to describe James and the Jerusalem church in the mid first-century. For more details on this idea see E. Stauffer, 'Zum Kalifat des Jacobus', *ZRGG* 3.4 (1952), pp. 193-214.

1.   M. Dibelius, *James: A Commentary on the Epistle of James* (trans. M.A. Williams; Philadelphia: Fortress Press, 1975), p. 149.

2.   P. Davids, *The Epistle of James* (Grand Rapids: Eerdmanns, 1982), pp. 20-21, 127-32, who cites J.H. Ropes, *A Critical and Exegetical Commentary on the Epistle of St James* (ICC; Edinburgh: T. & T. Clark, 1916); R.V.G. Tasker, *The General Epistle of James* (TNTC; London: Tyndale Press, 1965), p. 32; S. Laws, *A Commentary on the Epistle of James* (San Francisco: Harper & Row, 1980), pp. 15-18; C. Burchard, 'Zu Jakobus 2, 14-66', *ZNW* 71 (1980), pp. 44-45.

Gentiles'.[3] From there we shall review what can be pieced together of the message(s) of the law-observant missionaries and the position they gave to Abraham in their preaching. An analysis of Paul's reaction to these missionaries as he elaborates his strong response in Galatians 3 will also be included. This will lead into the analysis of James's own understanding of Paul's worrisome teaching—as he heard it. Finally, the letter of James as representative of the law-observant missions before the Jewish Wars with Rome, 66–70 CE, must be evaluated. Historians of the period have always acknowledged how important these destiny-changing wars were in the history of Judaism, but these wars and the subsequent destruction of the Temple rarely have been thus acknowledged in the history of Christianity. This is due chiefly to the fact that Paul and his mission both have rarely been cast in the defensive, 'underdog' position vis à vis James and the Jerusalem church. The work of E.P. Sanders, James Dunn, Louis Martyn, Raymond Brown, and Alan Segal, among others, has begun to change that; but even Martyn writes that, 'True enough the actual wording of the teachers' sermons is lost to us, since we have no sources written by them'.[4] But I contend that we do, in part, in the letter of James and in Galatians 3.

1. *Dating and Context of the Letter of James*

Establishing a chronological context for the letter of James is essential for this study. For the most part, the importance of chronological context lies in re-envisioning a view of the Christian missions in the 40s and 50s that takes into account three things. First, the spread of Christianity outside Palestine was not in a neat linear progression that grew ever larger and more triumphant. Rather, Paul, Peter, Barnabas and James, as well as a host of other missionaries with a variety of backgrounds in Judaism (for example, Apollos, Prisca, Aquila, Euodia, Syntyche and unnamed disciples of John the Baptist) spread versions of the news about Jesus.

Secondly, for many ideological and confessional reasons, the Acts of the Apostles traditionally has been denigrated by New Testament historians as a *legitimate* historical source for the early decades of Christianity. For the most part, Luke's reliability has been summarily

---

3.   J.L. Martyn, 'A Law-Observant Missions to the Gentiles: The Background of Galatians', *SJT* 38 (1985), pp. 307-24.

4.   Martyn, 'Law-Observant Missions', p. 320.

dismissed because he contradicts Paul in many places, because he writes at least a generation later, and because he presents an idealized view of the spread of Christianity. But this dismissal by historians is a grave mistake. True, when Luke looks back on the early Church from his vantage point of the early second century, he shapes the traditions into a utopian vision of the heroic spread of the Gospel into the *oikoumene*. But Acts' real value lies not in the story *qua* 'truth', but in the treasure trove of traditions that Luke preserves and weaves into his whole version. After the Jewish Wars, Luke was left with a stack of traditions about the early Church that detailed both the law-observant churches and mission and Paul's churches and mission. It is the historian's job not to judge Acts on the merits of its veracity, but to extricate these traditions from Luke's story, and then evaluate each tradition as it stands in isolation from the context of Acts.

And one must never forget that Paul's view of the Christian mission is as much a perspectival and partial (in both senses of the word) version as is Luke's. So a careful historian must untangle the fragile, albeit well-preserved, traditions in Acts that often mirror—or contradict—Paul's letters as well as fill in the gaps. Above all, Paul is not to be taken as the standard for Luke; that is poor history. Finally, paying close attention to these traditions in Acts and Paul's own testimony, we come up with a glimpse of the law-observant mission to the Gentiles that was loosely organized from Jerusalem. Was Paul's the sole mission to the Gentiles? And did Peter really preach Jesus only to the Jews?

Acts 10 recounts the rather convoluted and complicated story of the conversion of the Italian man, Cornelius. Although Peter is not *directly* responsible for this soldier's evangelization, the point of the episode is that God instructs Peter, through a vision, that all animals are fit to eat; and then *after Peter's testimony* the Holy Spirit comes to a group of Gentiles (Acts 10.44-48). Acts 11 continues with Peter back in Jerusalem, explaining that through his vision he knew that God meant for Gentiles to receive the message as well (Acts 11.18).

The clearest indication that Peter converts Gentiles is in Acts 15.7, as he addresses the Apostolic Council: 'Brethren, you know that in the early days God made choice among you, that by *my mouth* the Gentiles should hear the word of the gospel and believe'. Conversely Paul is a missionary to Jews in Acts 13.26, 13.42, 14.1, 17.1-4, 18.8, 19.8, 10, 20.21; 1 Cor. 9.20; Rom. 11.14, even Rom. 11.26-28. He tells us, too, that Peter was in Corinth in 1 Cor. 1.2. Finally we have Paul's angry denunciation of the spies, the men from James, and other teachers whom Paul understood to be encroaching on his mission in Galatia. Paul's mention of James implicates the Lord's brother in this mission, even though James is never mentioned directly as requiring circumcision of male Gentile converts.

Thus the picture we get from both Paul and Acts is that both Peter and Paul were converting *both* Jews and Gentiles. And many other missionaries were doing the same with their own versions of the gospel. There was no 'right doctrine' being promulgated from James and the Jerusalem church, although Jerusalem and the law-observant Christian community there were regarded by all with respect. The simple neat delineation of Paul as the apostle to the Gentiles and Peter as apostle to the Jews simply does not work, and should be abandoned by historians.

Furthermore, what this New Testament evidence points to is that there was a law-observant mission to the Gentiles that was not a reaction to Paul, but simultaneous with his mission. There seem to be varying degrees of adherence to the law of Moses that the law-observant missionaries required. Throughout Galatians and in Acts 11.1-3 and 15.1, circumcision is an issue for the missionaries as well as the dietary laws.[5] But in all the references to Peter in Acts 11, 15, and Galatians the issues are restricted to dietary matters. The 'men from James' in Galatians as well were concerned with dietary matters. In Acts 15.24-29, however, James is remembered only for his promulgation of the Noahide laws that the Gentile converts must observe. Poignantly, he is also remembered for relating the hearsay in Jerusalem—which he apparently did not believe of Paul—that Paul was urging Jesus-believing Jews to desist from observing the law (Acts 21.20-21). But, as we shall see further, for James and all the law-observant missionaries, Abraham and his relationship to the law is the core of their preaching. That Paul reacted so strongly to these missionaries is understandable; there was 'mutual mudslinging' between these preachers.[6]

But if there is such a variety of positions on the law held by the law-observant missionaries, how does the letter of James fit specifically into the movement? And where does it fit with respect to Galatians? I shall attempt to answers these questions in the conclusion.

If we agree that the Apostolic Council in Jerusalem probably took

---

5. J.D.G. Dunn, 'The Incident at Antioch (Gal 2.11-18)', *Jesus, Paul, and the Law* (Louisville, KY: Westminster/John Knox, 1990), pp. 134, 154.

6. Martyn, 'Law-Observant Missions', p. 317.

place in 48, and the Antioch incident no more than a year later,[7] we can postulate the chronology of the events up to James's death in Jerusalem in 63. Not long after the Antioch incident, which so infuriated Paul, he establishes his church in Galatia, traveling from there in 50, returning in 52, then writing his letter to them from Ephesus. Paul has gotten word that teachers from the law-observant mission have begun to corrupt the Galatians and turn them to 'another gospel'.[8]

Although we have no evidence that these teachers were sent from James, the first two chapters of Galatians may indicate that they claimed his authority—and perhaps—his teachings. In these chapters Paul shows that he must 'situate' himself with respect to James and the pillars. They are indeed forces to deal with. If they were not he would not have felt compelled to even mention them. And if these teachers had not referred to James and the pillars as their authority and the reason the congregation ought to believe them, he could just have begun with ch. 3 and lambasted them as upstart innovators. Paul spends a great deal of time in these first two chapters distancing himself from the pillars, alternating in tone from sarcasm to respectful reserve. But he never severs his ties from James, Peter, and John, as his later life attests. 'Jerusalem still served as a source of pride and inspiration and focus of faith.'[9] And because Paul conveniently omits who won the fight in Antioch, it would seem that indeed Paul lost.[10] Dunn points out that in 2.6 Paul is 'relativizing the authority of the Jerusalem apostles in the current situation in Galatia, and aiming at reducing the significance of his earlier

---

7. Dunn, 'Incident', p. 130; and chronology from H. Koester, *Introduction to the New Testament*. II. *History and Literature of Early Christianity* (Philadelphia: Fortress Press, 1982), pp. 103-20.

8. Martyn, 'A Law-Observant Missions', pp. 312-17. Although I agree with a great deal of what Martyn has written in the article, I do not agree with his assessment about the content of the Teachers' message (pp. 314-19). I think his use of the appellation 'Teachers' rather than 'Judaizers' is very helpful here. I think, for the reasons discussed in this paper, that the Teachers are related in some capacity to James. They are either claiming James as their authority or were sent by him. If this were not the case, Paul would not have begun with a history of his relationship to the Lord's brother. Furthermore, as we shall see, I think Jas 2.14-26 answers a great deal of what Paul rebuts in Galatians 3.

9. Dunn, 'Incident', p. 131.

10. R.E. Brown and J.P. Meier, *Antioch and Rome* (New York: Paulist Press, 1976), pp. 39-40.

acceptance of that authority'.[11] It makes sense that the interloping teachers in Galatia were claiming Jerusalem as an authority over and against Paul. And he met their challenge in his arguments in these first two chapters. He shows that all along he had maintained the independence of his mission while having obtained Jerusalem's acknowledgement by his visits to them.[12]

As a result of the letter to the Galatians, in 55 the teachers report back to James in Jerusalem not the entire Galatians letter *verbatim*, but a fairly close summation of ch. 3, emphasizing especially Paul's odd views on Abraham. They also give graphic details about the contentious fighting and bickering that has broken out in Galatia and other communities as well.

James, we imagine, is not only highly distraught by the reports of divisive fighting, but is especially worried about Paul's strange exegesis of Genesis regarding Abraham. Dunn states that the James–Paul polemic is an example of 'intra-Jewish factional polemic of the second Temple' period.[13] Dunn refers to the Antioch incident when he mentions James, but I think it can be applied to the teachers in Galatia as well. James argues with vehemence equal to that of Paul's against the latter's views on Abraham, faith and law, and justification. James probably heard Paul's view on Abraham and faith in person when Paul arrived in Jerusalem in 56. In any case, I posit that James' letter went out after Paul's Jerusalem visit.[14]

Although I completely disagree with most of the conclusions in Gerd Leudemann's book,[15] I do think his insight into the verbal similarities—

---

11. Brown and Meier, *Antioch and Rome*, p. 132.

12. J.D.G. Dunn, 'The Relationship between Paul and Jerusalem according to Galatians 1 and 2', *Jesus, Paul, and the Law*, pp. 118-21.

13. Dunn, 'Echoes of Intra-Jewish Polemic in Paul's Letter to the Galatians', *JBL* 112.3 (1993), p. 477. I include the letter of James here as part of intra-Jewish polemic. Professor Dunn does not do so in his article.

14. P. Stuhlmacher, *Paul's Letter to the Romans* (trans. S.J. Hafemann; Louisville, KY: Westminster/John Knox, 1994), p. 9.

15. G. Leudemann, *Opposition to Paul in Jewish Christianity* (trans. E. Boring; Philadelphia: Fortress Press, 1989), pp. 143-46. He thinks James is an early second-century text, representing a later Jewish–Christian community which has at its disposal the entire Pauline corpus. I, on the other hand, think James cannot be dependent on Romans, and the similarities he sees between them can be explained by the fact that Paul *wrote* both Galatians and Romans. James only responded to Galatians. Paul

and dependence—of James on Galatians are valuable here (Jas 2.24, Gal. 2.16, Rom. 3.28). Furthermore, Paul is responding to the Abraham arguments of the law-observant teachers. *They* were the ones to introduce Abraham as a necessary element in the conversion process, not Paul. And he must respond to this strong argument. Only in Galatians and Romans do we find Paul writing about Abraham and then the law.[16] Abraham had not figured in his gospel message before.

Another indication that James wrote the letter that goes by his name is its emphasis on helping the poor. Paul writes in Galatians one hauntingly simple line about the only request James, Peter, and John made of him: that he remember the poor (Gal. 2.10). It is not an exaggeration to say that it was a prominent feature of James's view of the responsibility of the Christian communities, given the poor economic situation of Palestine since the late 40s, and the volatile, uneasy, political situation there.[17]

Paul was very worried about whether the Jerusalem church would accept his gracious gift of the collection. Dieter Georgi has surmised that James's church accepted the collection only grudgingly, obliging Paul to make himself conspicuous by fulfilling Nazarite ritual requirements in the Temple.[18] The resulting attention from the community subsequently brought about Paul's arrest and imprisonment. There was so much civil unrest during this period in Jerusalem and so many violent factionalists forcing people to conform to their idea of being 'good Jews' that Paul's 'eclectic' Judaism, coupled with the *bruit* caused by his supposed anti-Mosaic views, makes this scenario quite likely (Acts 21.21).[19]

It has even been suggested that James refused to accept the collection.[20] Although this may seem shocking at first, I tend to agree. James

could even have heard James' reactions to his Abraham material when he saw him in Jerusalem, *before* he wrote Romans.

16. Martyn, 'Law-Observant Missions', p. 319.

17. The theme of the poor and doing acts of mercy will figure prominently in the larger book that I am preparing on James. It is out of the scope of this paper to address it here.

18. D. Georgi, *Remembering the Poor* (Nashville: Abingdon Press, 1992), pp. 124-27.

19. E.M. Smallwood, *The Jews Under Roman Rule* (SJLA, 20; Leiden: Brill, 1976), pp. 276-84. Dunn, 'Incident', p. 135.

20. J.D.G. Dunn, *Unity and Diversity in the New Testament* (Philadelphia: Westmister Press, 1977), pp. 256-57.

may have felt the local religio–political pressures from his kinspeople to a greater extent. The late fifties saw an 'increasing nationalism as Israel's position and religious prerogatives were under threat'.[21] Jews of all factions were urged to conform to a 'stricter definition and practice of national religion'.[22] James may have conformed to peer pressure by not accepting the collection in order to distance himself from Paul. Even the account in Acts of their last meeting—harmonious as Luke tries to present it—suggests that James must take precautions not to draw negative attention to the Christian community by entangling it financially with Paul and his diaspora communities, whose reputations are quite suspicious. The fact that Luke 'conveniently' does not mention the collection in this section in Acts perhaps points to his 'embarrassment at the fact that the collection did not succeed in its aim of reconciling Paul with the Jerusalem Church'.[23]

On Paul's less-than-auspicious arrival in Jerusalem (from all perspectives), besides refusing the collection, James would have heard Paul's views once more on Abraham, and this time in person and in an abbreviated form. The tense political situation and Paul's arrest gave James the urgent occasion to write his letter. After all Paul had just been arrested, and the communities would be in need of guidance. Moreover James's letter to the teachers in the diaspora is a serious attempt publically to distance himself from Paul in three ways: he corrected Paul's views on Abraham and the law; he urged the communities to stop the bickering and fighting by showing impartiality and fairness especially between rich and poor; and finally—if they were to do the latter, the poor would be taken care of and there would be no need for collections. In this way he could justify his refusing Paul's financial contribution at a time when it was most sorely needed.

I think Paul was so stunned by the strength of the law-observant teachers and their position on Abraham that he writes Rom. 1.1–15.13 while in prison before he goes to Rome.[24] His letter, especially chs. 10–11, reflects soberness and starkness at his experiences in Jerusalem,

21. Dunn, 'Incident', p. 155.

22. Dunn, 'Incident', p. 155.

23. L.T. Johnson, *The Acts of the Apostles* (Collegeville, MN: Liturgical Press, 1992), p. 208.

24. The debates still rages as to whether Romans 16 is a separate letter. I think it is, as well as ch. 15, which is a fragment of another letter. The majority of ancient manuscripts end at ch. 14. See H. Koester, *History and Literature*, pp. 138-41. I think

both at the hands of James and the Christian community, and at the hands of the non Jesus-believing brothers and sisters. In the letter, Paul's experience of coming face to face in Jerusalem with law-observant Christianity is evident. It is almost as if he was explaining to the Romans what Jerusalem was unable to hear and/or understand. Raymond Brown has pointed out that Paul's tone in Romans is much humbler than in Galatians.[25] Brown suggests that Paul is worried that reports of his strident tone in Galatians had reached Rome, a church tied closely to Jerusalem. Because of this, Paul is apprehensive that he will be spurned in Rome as he was in Jerusalem. Romans reflects Paul's efforts to come to terms both with Jerusalem's powerful message and the difference—even lack—of the eschatological vision he has of the world and the purpose of Christ. For the Jerusalem community Christ had an utterly different purpose.

Paul also must come to terms with the large number of his kinspeople who have not acknowledged Jesus as the Christ. For the law-observant Christians, Jesus Christ's coming became one more 'identity marker' of the Jewish people, along with circumcision, food laws, and sabbath observance.[26] Law-observant Christians saw Christ as a 'confirmation

letters containing what we have of chs. 15 and 16 were written before Paul goes to Jerusalem. Written during Paul's winter stay in Corinth as part of his 'collection letters' (2 Cor. 8, 9), ch. 15 speaks of Paul's hopes to go to Spain and visit a *certain community* on the way there. It could be Rome, but it does not mention the city by name. Ch. 16 was part of a letter to Ephesus. It fits well with this correspondence and his anticipated trip. I am convinced by the evidence Harry Gamble presents for a *fourteen*-chapter letter to Romans, plus 16.25-27, *not* his own conclusion. See H.Y. Gamble, Jr, *The Textual History of the Letter to the Romans* (Grand Rapids: Eerdmans, 1977), pp. 37-47. Nor am I convinced by the arguments of M.A. Seifrid, *Justification by Faith* (NovTSup, 68; Leiden: Brill, 1992), pp. 249-54. The evidence of $\mathfrak{P}$46 only shows that the fragments traveled together in a composite, much as 2 Corinthians was a patchwork of fragmentary letters. That Paul wrote Romans after visiting Jerusalem also explains his need and anxiety to write to a church he neither founded nor knew beforehand, but which he knew had close ties to Jerusalem. Paul was under arrest and had no choice but to go to Rome. He worried about how the law-observant Christians stood on his view of the Gentiles. Also his renewed interest in Abraham and the law—issues he had let go of a bit when he was in Corinth and Ephesus (pp. 54-55)—show that the Jerusalem visit had 'reopened the Galatians wound', as it were. Also, if Paul is arrested and on his way to litigation in Rome, how can he hope to go to Spain?

25. Brown and Meier, *Antioch and Rome*, pp. 113-16.
26. Dunn, 'New Perspective on Paul', *Jesus, Paul, and the Law*, p. 196.

of the covenant and as expiation for the forgiveness of sins'.[27] For them Christ became the ultimate sacrifice, once and for all, in lieu of all the Temple sacrifices, but he did not change 'Sinai as the locus of election'.[28]

Paul could not accept this. For him law-observant Christianity is only a step to a new eschatological vision in which the Gentiles too become God's people, inheritors of the promise.[29] Christ, in his death and resurrection, had bridged the gap between Jew and Gentile: 'Christ's death was effective in Paul's view precisely because it demonstrated that the grace of God was now to be experienced apart from the law'.[30] This summation he gives in Romans, and he hopes the community will understand his position before he arrives. But we have no information about Paul's Roman stay, other than legends from Church tradition. According to them, Paul's death would have occurred around 60.

In the meantime James was facing his own precarious political situation in Jerusalem. With the change in Roman procurators from Festus to Albinus in 62, a new high priest was appointed. Josephus tells us this high priest Ananus was rash and daring, a follower of the Sadducees, 'who are more savage than any other Jews, when they sit in judgement'.[31] It also seems that James had drawn the negative attention of Ananus. Before Albinus arrived in Rome, Ananus took the opportunity to convene the Sanhedrin. He brought charges against James and some others, 'for having transgressed the law'. As punishment James and his friends were stoned to death in 63. Josephus says many in Jerusalem 'who were strict in observance of the law were offended at

---

27. L. Gaston, 'Paul and the Law in Galatians 2–3', in P. Richardson (ed.), *Anti-Judaism in Early Christianity. I. Paul and the Gospels* (Waterloo, ON: Wilfred Laurier University Press, 1986), p. 57.

28. Gaston, 'Paul and the Law', p. 37. I am aware of the myriad of different and new interpretations of Paul's view of the purpose of Christ, especially the commendable new work of S.K. Stowers, *A Rereading of Romans: Justice, Jews, and Gentiles* (New Haven: Yale University Press, 1994). Since this paper is not primarily about Paul, I have chosen to work with the interpretation of Galatians of which I am most convinced.

29. Gaston, 'Paul and the Law', p. 57, and Dunn, 'Works of the Law and the Curse of the Law (Gal. 3.10-14)', *Jesus, Paul and the Law*, p. 230.

30. Dunn, 'Works of the Law', p. 230.

31. Josephus, *Ant.* 9.20.200-204 (LCL; Cambridge, MA: Harvard University Press, 1965).

this'.[32] They told Albinus, still en route, who then threatened to punish Ananus. But King Agrippa took care of the incident by deposing Ananus. With James's death and the subsequent years of war ending in 70, this brief period of the 'caliphate' church draws to a close. Against this hypothetical reconstruction of the interchange and rivalry between James and Paul, we now turn to the law-observant teachers, claiming James's authority, and their message, embedded in Galatians 3.

2. The Teachers' Gospel

It is obvious from a reading of Galatians 3 that for the law-observant mission Abraham and a correct understanding of his relationship to God was central for Gentiles to become inheritors of God's promise. 'Keeping the law' and doing 'works of law' were also paramount in their preaching. Dunn points out that the law-observant Christians' concern about cleanliness and purity laws reflected in Mt. 15.17-20 may be very close to those concerns of the 'men from James', at Antioch.[33] And I think this concern can be applied as well to the teachers invading Paul's Galatian church and to those congregants swayed by them. What 'works of law' meant for the teachers and for Paul must now be deciphered.

From the beginning of the letter to the Galatians Paul's tone is quite angry, calling them 'stupid Galatians'. He sets up antitheses from the very start, placing up his own gospel message against theirs. 'Spirit' (his gospel) is a fruit, or prize, of the 'hearing of faith', is the ἀκοὴ πίστεως.[34] But those teachers have urged the Galatians to 'keep the law', but probably not to receive the Spirit. Paul pits 'works of law' against 'hearing of faith'.[35] For Paul 'hearing of faith' is both an active and passive experience. It is a hearing with obedience, or heeding.[36]

Most of Paul's Jewish contemporaries would understand 'works of

32. Josephus, *Ant.* 9.20.200-204.

33. Dunn, 'Incident', p. 155, and Brown and Meier, *Antioch and Rome*, pp. 53-55.

34. S.K. Williams, 'The Hearing of Faith: ΑΚΟΗ ΠΙΣΤΕΩΣ in Galatians 3', *NTS* 35 (1989), pp. 90-93, as well as J.B. Lightfoot, *Epistle to the Galatians* (London/New York: MacMillan, 1896), p. 135, in which he says ἀκοή is a 'hearing', because it provides a better contrast to ἔργων. The antitheses, nevertheless, are picked up by James in his letter.

35. Gaston, 'Paul and the Law', p. 45.

36. Williams, 'The Hearing of Faith', pp. 90-93.

law' to mean 'remain within all that the Torah lays down', and 'to do what the law requires'.[37] But Paul makes a radical disjunction of the two. Being under the law, in his way of thinking, did not mean one could or did fulfill it. He understood being ἐξ ἔργων νόμου to mean being God's chosen people under the covenant—'Israel *per se*', as that people who are defined by the law and marked out by its distinctive requirements.[38] 'Works of law' were 'convenantal badges'[39] which all Jews and Gentiles who know Jews recognized. Dunn calls this the 'social function of the law'.[40] Hence a diagram illustrating Paul's antitheses:

The prize is the Spirit
Hearing with Faith—opposes—Works of Law
In Faith—opposes—Under the Law

Then Paul must deal with the heart of the teaching that was luring his Galatian church. The teachers had brought up the example of Abraham to convince the Galatians that circumcision was necessary for male Gentile converts. In no letter other than Romans and Galatians does Paul need Abraham for his gospel proclamation. Jeffrey Siker points out that it is not difficult to understand that Paul's Abraham arguments in Galatians are a *response* to the teachers.[41] These are Siker's reasons:

1) The convoluted character of Galatians 3 argument shows Paul has not developed his ideas on Abraham yet. (It takes Romans for that.)

2) The teachers 'bewitched' them with their Abrahamic exegesis, obliging them to become part of the covenantal people through circumcision of the male converts.

3) When Paul introduced Abraham in 3.6, he immediately refers to Gen. 15.6, how Abraham's *faith* made him righteous. This allows him his next move, Gal. 3.7, *these people*, οὗτοι, are the sons of Abraham. What is in everyone's mind after οὗτοι is the contrast, 'not those people', that is, those wretched teachers who are ἐξ ἔργων νόμου, and who have been trying

---

37. Dunn, 'Works of the Law', p. 226.
38. Dunn, 'Works of the Law', p. 227.
39. Dunn, 'New Perspectives', p. 194.
40. Dunn, 'Works of the Law', p. 227.
41. J.S. Siker, *Disinheriting the Jews* (Louisville, KY: Westminster/John Knox, 1991), pp. 33-34.

to convince the Galatians about another gospel. Paul is chal-
lenging them with this demonstrative.

4)   Finally, there is Paul's peculiar exegesis of the 'offspring' of
     Abraham in 3.16. He first tells the Galatians what 'offspring'
     is not: it is not plural. Rather it is singular, and the singular
     offspring is 'Christ'. This counters the teachers' message that
     the Galatian males must become—through circumcision—the
     descendants of Abraham.

Paul assures the Galatians that it is their faith, like Abraham's, that
wins them their receipt of God's promise. Law, on the other hand, puts
people under a curse (3.10-11). He sums his point up with the ingenious use of the Hab. 2.4 quotation, 'The righteous one will live by
faith'.

What Paul has done in his spirited exegesis is to decouple Abraham
from the law. Abraham's faith and the promise are what matter, not
the law, as he later says in Gal. 5.6 and 6.15; neither circumcision nor
uncircumcision makes any difference. This is surprising, for almost all
first-century Jewish literature says that Abraham did the whole law.[42]
Paul's stress on the promise of the Abraham story is unique for his
time. 2 *Bar.* 57.2, 1 Macc. 2.52, Sir. 44.20-21 all associate Abraham's
fulfilling of the law with God's giving of the promise. Paul's strident
tone seems to indicate that he is on the losing side of the battle with
the law-observant missionaries.

A hermeneutical aid to Paul's defensive tone comes from rhetorical
analysis. George Kennedy has classified Galatians as deliberative rhetoric, not judicial, as Betz has posited.[43] So the letter is not an apology
but a wholehearted effort to convince the audience of a certain viewpoint. The reason Kennedy classifies it thus is that Galatians' overall
theme is to persuade the congregation not to observe Jewish law, and
not to practice circumcision of male converts. The 'action is in the self-
interest of the audience'.[44] Although there are elements in Galatians of
Paul's defense (chs. 1 and 2), the theme is persuasive argument.[45] But

---

42. Siker, *Disinheriting the Jews*, p. 210 n. 33.

43. H.D. Betz, *Galatians* (Philadelphia: Fortress Press, 1979), pp. 24-25.

44. G. Kennedy, *New Testament Interpretation through Rhetorical Criticism*
(Chapel Hill: University of North Carolina Press, 1984), pp. 146-47; see also
J. Smith, 'Galatians and Deliberative Speech', *NTS* (1989), pp. 24-25.

45. Kennedy, *New Testament Interpretation*, pp. 146-47, see also D.E. Aune,

this does not obliterate the urgency and defensive tone of the letter. Kennedy sees the mixed quality of the letter to the Galatians, formally defensive in part (chs. 1 and 2) contained within a deliberative whole:

> As Paul's defense, Galatians would be chiefly of historical interest for its picture of the early Church filled with acrimonious dissension and of his personal insecurities and apprehensions; as Paul's exhortation it continues to speak to Christians who are tempted to substitute the forms of religious observance for its essence.[46]

3. James 2.17-26 as a Response to Galatians 3

I must begin by saying that I have found it shocking that the most important commentators on James discount the possibility that James is a response to Paul *on the grounds* that he misunderstands—even misrepresents—Paul![47] It is the nature of disagreements that *opponents do not understand each other*. When they proceed to respond to the person with whom they are emotionally and psychologically at risk, they most often skew the side of their opponent. I cannot imagine any human being not having experienced both sides of these positions in many arguments and discussions. James may be disqualified as a reaction to Paul on other grounds, but certainly not on this count, the flimsiest and least cognizant of the nature of human disputations.

The word 'misrepresentation' itself carries with it a valence that Paul's side is the objective one by which to measure and understand the conflict. I think not. James probably heard of the trouble and dissent in the communities in the diaspora—especially in Galatia—and heard of Paul's response from the teachers.[48] Moreover, James probably heard some of Paul's views when he visited Jerusalem. And we must remember that the visit was strained from the outset, both for theological as well as political reasons. As I have indicated before, James had even more serious problems to contend with when Paul visited Jerusalem. The tenseness of the religio–political situation had become

who also classifies Galatians as deliberative rhetoric, *The New Testament in its Literary Environment* (Philadelphia: Westminster Press, 1987), pp. 198-99.

46. Kennedy, *New Testament Interpretation*, p. 147.

47. Dibelius, *James*, pp. 25, 178-80; Davids, *The Epistle*, pp. 20-21, 30-132.

48. M.L. Soards, 'The Early Christian Interpretation of Abraham and the Place of James within that Context', *IBS* 9 (1987), pp. 24-25. He holds that James could easily be responding to what he heard of Paul's Galatians 3.

so pitched that James truly had to worry about his very life and protect his community's existence. He had to prove to the outside world that he was not too closely associated with Paul. With all these existential worries, it is not surprising that he does not pay close attention to what Paul is saying about faith, works, and Abraham. Paul's arrest was probably like a warning signal. Not only did James have to preserve the Jerusalem church, he had to take responsibility and write a 'brotherly letter' himself to these splintering diaspora communities since: (1) Paul was arrested, imprisoned and on his way to Rome, and (2) Jerusalem needed the churches to help the poor, especially if they refused Paul's collection, and finally (3) Paul had promulgated some very strange ideas about Abraham and the true meaning of 'works' out there that needed attention and correction. Hence he writes the letter to the 'twelve tribes in the diaspora', teachers that depended on Jerusalem in some capacity.

In his article, Soards point out that Jas 2.14-26 is a clumsy, awkward passage, unlike the rest of the letter. 'James', he says, 'falls into an anarthrous style'.[49] He believes that the cause for this is that James has 'entered into a polemic dialogue with Paul', or Paulinists. He cites these reasons: a 'distancing use' of the word 'someone', τις, in 2.18; the antitheses of faith and works that for James is a false dichotomy; the need to reassert and reestablish the traditional exegesis and understanding of Abraham as 'our father'; the peculiarly Pauline use of ἐκ with δικαιοῦσθαι; and finally the clumsy piling up of nouns so characteristic of Paul's style, but foreign to James's.[50] For these reasons, it is not farfetched to begin this section with the hypothesis that James probably did not have a copy of Galatians 3, but he had heard the chapter reported to him verbally in a version fairly close to the original, by the teachers, and then heard Paul's view in person.

James first correction of Paul comes in 1.22-25: He sets up the contrast 'hearing and doing' to counter Paul's ἀκοὴ τῆς πίστεως, a hearing of faith. He exhorts people to be *doers* of the word, not just hearers, ἀκροάται. He repeats this 'hearer' word three times. Paul's phrase in Galatians, however, uses another word for hear, from ἀκούω, the very famous, ἀκοὴ τῆς πίστεως, the hearing of faith. James's phrase resounds in opposition to Paul's phrase which is packed with his evangelical eschatology: his preaching the gospel as a response to the call

49. Soards, 'The Early Christian Interpretation', p. 24.
50. Soards, 'The Early Christian Interpretation', p. 24.

he got from the Christ. James does not acknowledge this. The differences in the word roots of ἀκούω, ἀκρόομαι are slight, the latter
having in some instances the connotation of those who passively listen,
and the former having the range of either being an active hearing or a
more passive proclamation.[51] ἀκούω can also connote 'obedience', a
more active meaning, which would not fit James's polemic intentions.
For rhetorical purposes James plays on the ambiguities inherent in the
word, deliberately giving it a passive and negative connotation, whatever Paul intended it to be. It may be that James wants to avoid Paul's
ambiguity in the passive/active possibilities of ἀκοή, and he chooses
'hearers' in a way that evokes those just listening in an auditorium.

We shall now move to ch. 2. I think that Duane Watson's article has
shown convincingly that the Epistle of James is written as deliberative
rhetoric.[52] James refers to the future and gives moral exhortation.
Like Galatians, James contains the 'two basic forms of deliberative rhetoric, persuasion and dissuasion'. And like Galatians 3, Jas 2.14-26 has
diatribe elements.[53] We must remember that in subjecting these New
Testament letters to rhetorical criticism, 'actual speeches could be more
complex and eclectic than the rhetorical handbooks might suggest'.[54]

David Aune points out quite succinctly that the salient feature of
diatribe is this:

> . . . its dialogical or conversational character. . . which makes frequent
> use of imaginary opponents, hypothetical objections, and false
> conclusions. The questions and objections of the imaginary opponents
> and the teacher's responses oscillate between censure and persuasion.[55]

What the teacher seeks to do is reveal all the possible errors, contradictions, and fallacies the opponent may have.

51. BAGD, ὁ ἀκροατής (οὗ). Thucydides; Isa. 3.3; Sir. 3.29; *Ep. Arist.* 266; as
a hearer, Diognetus 2.1; λόγου, Philo, *Congr.* 70; and Jas 1.23; Diodorus Siculus
4.7.4; (1 BCE) v. 22. Thucydides 3.384a has a similar reproach directed against the
θεαταὶ μὲν τῶν λόγων ἀκροάται δὲ τῶν ἔργων ἀκροάται νόμον in Rom.
2.13, (cf. Josephus, *Ant.* 5.107; 132 νόμου ἀκροάται) ἀκροάται ἐπιλησμονῆς,
the forgetful hearer in Jas 1.25. ἡ ἀκοή is an act of hearing or listening, and can
have the connotation of obeying; it also can be an account, report, or preaching or
fame.

52. D. Watson, 'James 2 in Light of Greco–Roman Schemes of Argumentation',
39 *NTS* (993), pp. 94-121, esp. pp. 100-108.

53. Aune, *New Testament in its Literary Environment*, pp. 199-200.

54. Aune, *New Testament in its Literary Environment*, p. 199.

55. Aune, *New Testament in its Literary Environment*, p. 200.

The most important aspect of diatribe with regard to James's letter and Galatians is that the *genre itself* assumes that the opponent is imaginary with whom he can argue sarcastically and even angrily. This imaginary person synthesizes the entire spectrum of objections and criticism that the audience might voice.[56] The issue and argument become the point, not the person. This is vital for our situation for James. By using the diatribe he does not have to attack Paul *ad hominem*. Paul's Galatian position—quite distilled—is indeed in there, but Paul is not. The genre itself generalizes or neutralizes the potentially bitter debate. Persuasion of the audience is the focus, not decimating the opponent.

This last aspect would be important for James. The focus of his letter, written at such a vulnerable time, is to unite the diaspora church and avoid further factionalism and contention. To make Paul the issue would uselessly create rancor when he had a host of other real problems to control. To heal the diaspora communities is his urgent point. Thus the genre aids him greatly.

Let me begin with v. 14: 'What does it profit, my brethren, if a man says he has faith but has not works?'. James has set up a rhetorical question, separating faith and works, but it must be stressed that they are *not* equal binary opposites. In fact it is here that he begins the 'misrepresentation' or distillation of Paul. He characterizes Paul as having made them binary opposites. James has chosen to prove that faith is inseparable from works; and, in the casuistic event that they are separated, they are utterly unequal. Faith is encompassed by works.

Hence the next section, 2.18-26, famous for causing great difficulty for most interpreters. It begins: 'But someone will say you have faith and I have works'. I do think that this 'but', ἀλλά, is adversative; it is what the missionary teachers have told him Paul will say after they have told him that faith without works is dead (v. 17).

Let us first look at τις 'someone'. Not only is the ἀλλά adversative,

---

56. I find Watson's conclusion to his otherwise outstanding work too cautionary and formulaic. He takes the 'imaginary opponent' thesis much too literally. If 'faith without works' was just a 'perceived problem' (p. 121), who was doing the perceiving? Also he says, 'neglect of the needy and partiality in the community was not actually being exhibited to the degree it was portrayed'. If this were the case, then the author of James must have had a lot of leisure time to practice his diatribe style. Why would he bother? Even a cursory knowledge of the social history of the period warrants the acknowledgement that Paul and James took their missions and their charges *very* seriously, and their precarious situations politically and socially and religiously were all too real.

in this case the 'someone' is a 'distancing term', that is, 'some guy'.[57] It is at this verse that James begins his diatribe. The imaginary dialogue begins with a skillful interlocutor. In good diatribe fashion, James distills the essential characteristics of what he is arguing against, making a generalized synthesis of Paul's identity as the opponent, Paul's argument, and the absurd conclusions such positions lead to. Consistent with the fluidity of the diatribe genre, without naming Paul, he gives a flimsy disguise as to the possible identity of this tricky interlocutor—a guy who talks a great deal about works and faith. Yes, the interlocutor could easily be identified with Paul. James is counting on his readers'/listeners' ability to make the easy identification of τις with Paul.

The τις, someone, becomes the narrator in this section. In other words, James is setting up a scene; note the quotations marks: 'Someone will say, "you have faith and I have works"'. Then James dramatically lets the speaker just take over. In other words, the 'YOU' is the guileless, hapless, gullible believer and Paul is 'I'. Most emphatically the 'I' is not James. He is exposing a position that he is utterly against. The same designations continue in the next sentence.

The next verse, 'Show me your faith apart from your works, and I by my works will show you my faith'. A literalist interpreter will counter my hypothesis and say that is not what Paul favors in the binary opposites in Galatians! And I say, precisely so! James is showing the absurdity of the separation. If they were binary opposites, then this switching of the terms around and representing Paul as saying, 'Show me your faith apart from your works and I by my works will show you my faith', would be completely demonstrable. But it is not at all. In James's view, it is a trap set up by the imaginary interlocutor (Paul) for the poor hapless victim in his congregation. By artificially separating the two, faith and works, the interlocutor (Paul) becomes a trickster, and 'you', the hapless victim, by listening to him fall into his

---

57. Soards, 'The Early Christian Interpretation', p. 24. I have chosen purposely the colloquial translation of 'some guy' because it fits the disparaging tone of the passage. In LSJ (1976b) there are several definitions which support my colloquial translation of 'τις'. 'τις' can refer to a person 'whom one wishes to avoid naming. . . so also is it a euphemism for something bad'. The next fitting definition for support of 'τις' as 'guy' is that 'τις' may be opposed, expressly or by implication' to someone who is boasting that he is great. Finally there is the use of 'τις' before a proper name that conveys 'a sense of contempt'. It turns the proper name into an appellative. I believe, as the reader shall see, that James stops just short of naming Paul on purpose. But the same sense of contempt and disparagement is here.

trap. This is so because the next verse shows that the victim, when taking the bait and answering that he/she believes that God is one is as commendable as a DEMON!! It is at this point that the imaginary dialogue ends, and James takes over as the speaker in the letter. Finally, James names for us his hapless victim, an empty-headed person (parallel to the 'stupid Galatians') and asks him if he wants still more proof of the axiom that faith apart from works is barren.

He assumes that the poor person does want proof and launches into the Abraham section, the central 'doctrine' of the law-observant mission, Jas 2.21: 'Was not our ancestor Abraham justified by works when he offered his son Isaac on the altar?'. He begins with Gen. 22.1-14, the sacrifice of Isaac. According to Soards, James shares a 'marked likeness' to Jewish interpretation of Abraham in two fundamental ways:[58] (1) interpreting Gen. 15.6 in direct relation to Gen. 22.1-14, that is that righteousness was reckoned to Abraham because of his obedience to his command to sacrifice Isaac; (2) referring to Abraham as the 'friend of God'. James expects his audience to be 'fully conversant' with his style of exegesis.[59] James has disregarded the literal meaning of Gen. 15.6 in its original context, treating the verse as a foreshadowing of Abraham's faith in the time of trial, referring specifically to the sacrifice of Isaac in 22.12.[60] In addition, he is in disagreement with the biblical account of sacrifice, where Abraham is a 'God-fearer' (22.12).[61]

James bases this, as the entire tradition does, on Neh. 9.7-8, 'God found Abraham faithful so he made him righteous';[62] 'Thou didst find his heart faithful before thee, and didst make with him the covenant to give to his descendants the land of the Canaanite'. 'Faithful' in this context means that Abraham acted as God had commanded. Isa. 41.8 refers to Abraham as 'friend of God', as does 2 Chron. 20.7, 'friend of God'.

The Apocrypha and Pseudepigrapha writings continue to expand the interpretation of Gen. 15.16 from Gen. 22.14.[63] Note the similarity to 1 Macc. 2.52, 'Was not Abraham found faithful when tested, and it was reckoned to him as righteousness?' and Sir. 44.19-22, 'and when he was tested he was found faithful (v. 21) the Lord assured him by an

---

58. Soards, 'The Early Christian Interpretation', pp. 18-20.
59. I. Jacobs, 'Midrashic Background to James', *NTS* 22 (1975–76), p. 458.
60. Jacobs, 'Midrashic Background', p. 458.
61. Jacobs, 'Midrashic Background', p. 458.
62. Jacobs, 'Midrashic Background', p. 461.
63. Soards, 'The Early Christian Interpretation', p. 19.

oath that the nations would be blessed through his posterity'.[64] Irving Jacobs has shown that *Jub.* 18.15-16; 19.9; 23.10; and 24.11 (c. 161–140 BCE) is the 'earliest source for the motif... portraying Abraham as the faithful lover of the Lord', conforming his own will to the service of God in faithful love.[65]

In support of James's exegesis as well we have the Damascus Document 3.2-3, 'Abraham was God's friend because he kept the commandments'. Heb. 11.17 says, 'By faith Abraham, when put to the test, offered up Isaac'. In later rabbinic literature *m. Ab.* 5.3 gives ten temptations to Abraham and finishes with the sacrifice (*Gen. R.* 55, *Exod. R.* 23).

In other Jewish literature fairly contemporaneous with James, Gen. 15.6 is interpreted in relationship to 22 by Josephus in *Ant.* 18.1.223, and 1.8.4.233, 234;[66] in Philo, *Deus Imm.* 1.4; Ps.-Philo *LAB* 18.5.[67] The 'friend of God' theme is equally strong in Philo, *Sobr.* 11.55-56, Philo, *Abr.*, 15.71; *Apoc. Abr.* 9.6. And in the *T. Abr.*, there is one reference in the long version and four in the short version.[68]

James jumps, as it were, right for the 'friend of God' adage. In v. 2.23 he says, 'Thus scripture was fulfilled that says, "Abraham believed God, and it was reckoned to him as righteousness"; and he was called the friend of God'. Yet this, too, is not unique. Philo, *Abr.* 32.170, put 'friend of God' in the context of the Isaac story. Philo says Abraham both loved and feared God.[69] Jacobs points out that the tradition of not specifically mentioning the Isaac sacrifice, going directly from Genesis 15 to 22 and the promise, was already in Sirach two centuries before James. This shows that James fits squarely within his contemporaneous interpreters of Abraham; James assumes and presumes the sacrifice in his interpretation of Gen. 15.6. Commentators did not have to mention Isaac; the incident was a given. 'Friend of God' is the important phrase, and God's making Abraham the father of all the nations. Jacobs quotes from Ps.-Philo, *Liber Antiquitatum Biblicarum*, that the operative phrase in God's demand of Balaam is the description

---

64. Soards, 'The Early Christian Interpretation', p. 19.
65. Jacobs, 'Midrashic Background', pp. 460-61 n. 4.
66. Soards, 'The Early Christian Interpretation', p. 20.
67. Soards, 'The Early Christian Interpretation', p. 20.
68. Soards, 'The Early Christian Interpretation', p. 20.
69. Jacobs, 'Midrashic Background', pp. 465-66.

of 'Abraham as my friend'.[70] We see that James presents the current, most widespread interpretation of Abraham of his day over and against Paul's more idiosyncratic one. To use 'friend of God' in connection with Gen. 22.12 merged the meanings of 'friend of God' with 'fearer of God'. This was entirely within the exegetical tradition, expanding the meaning of 'fear' to incorporate love.[71]

James ends this Abraham section with an almost sarcastic paraphrasing of Paul's language, the use of ἐκ + δικαιοῦσθαι, δικαιόω:[72] 'You see that out of work is a human being justified, not by faith alone'. The style is clumsy here because James is borrowing language to which he is unaccustomed.

Finally we come to Rahab, who, not coincidentally, is connected to Abraham in much of contemporaneous Jewish literature because of her spontaneous acts of hospitality that brought about good results. In Genesis 18 Abraham is hospitable to three visitors. In the commentaries on Abraham from the period between 200 BCE and 200 CE there is a tradition of collapsing the Genesis Abraham stories. Philo in *Abr.* 167 proceeds directly from Abraham as an example of hospitality to the sacrifice of Isaac as a testing of his faith.[73] Furthermore, Philo in *De Sobrietate* connects 'friend of God' with Gen. 18.17.[74] Heb. 11.31 as well says, 'By faith Rahab the prostitute did not perish with those who were disobedient, because she received the spies in peace'. In *ARN* 1.7 as well as in other Rabbinic sources,[75] Abraham surpassed Job in hospitality to the poor.[76] The same view of Abraham prevails in the *Testament of Abraham*.[77]

In addition, in rabbinic literature the fact that Abraham is not allowed to carry out the sacrifice is understood to be because Abraham had merits, in particular, his *hospitality* (*Gen. R.* 56.5, cf. 55.4). We even have this interpretation in the first century. Josephus had said

---

70. Jacobs, 'Midrashic Background', pp. 462-63.

71. Jacobs, 'Midrashic Background', p. 461.

72. Soards, 'The Early Christian Interpretation', pp. 24-25.

73. R.B. Ward, 'The Works of Abraham, James 2:14-26', *HTR* 61 (1968), p. 286.

74. Ward, 'Works of Abraham', p. 286.

75. Ward, 'Works of Abraham', p. 286.

76. Ward, 'Works of Abraham', p. 286.

77. Ward, 'Works of Abraham', p. 286.

this, too, when he wrote that because God opposed the sacrifice, the deed, ἔργον, was done (*Ant.* 1.233).[78]

Abraham, along with Rahab, is an example of hospitality in *1 Clement* 10, 12.[79] After quoting Gen. 15.6 (10, 6) the author refers to Abraham's πίστις καὶ φιλοξενία (10.7a) and proceeds to speak of the sacrifice of Isaac (10.7b)[80] Just as Abraham is said to have received a son διὰ πίστιν καὶ φιλοξενίαν, so Rahab is saved διὰ πίστιν καὶ φιλοξενίαν.[81] In James, Rahab is an example of πίστις καὶ ἔργα. In the biblical account, Rahab shows her acts of hospitality and mercy and confesses God. Her faith is not referred to expressly in James, but her works are recounted—when 'she received the messenger and sent them out another way' (Jas 2.25). James ends his argument against Paul's Galatians 3 with this grand finale of Rahab's example.

Works in early Judaism are precisely these acts of mercy and hospitality. James did not need to explain the works of Abraham and Rahab to his congregation. It was common knowledge that these were acts of hospitality.[82] Abraham's obedience to God in offering Isaac was a test of his faithfulness—an action—which, in combination with his acts of hospitality, 'justified' him. Rahab's almost reflexive action of mercy showed that she lived faithfully with God. James's exegesis of these two figures assumes that both Abraham and Rahab would have been unable to perform these actions were they not faithful to God. James displays his immersion in the traditional Jewish understanding of Abraham who shows his faithfulness through his deeds and whom therefore God deems 'righteous' and his 'friend'.[83] Ward quotes an apt description of Abraham's 'works' from *Yashar wa Yera*, 42B:[84] 'If one was hungry, and he came to Abraham, he would give him what he needed, if he was naked and came to Abraham, he would clothe him with the garments of the poor man's choice, and give him silver and gold, and make him known to the Lord'. This is not so different from James's instructions in 2.15-16 to take care of the person in need and

78. Ward, 'Works of Abraham', p. 286.
79. Ward, 'Works of Abraham', p. 286.
80. Ward, 'Works of Abraham', p. 286.
81. Ward, 'Works of Abraham', p. 286.
82. Ward, 'Works of Abraham', p. 288.
83. Siker, *Disinheriting the Jews*, p. 101.
84. Ward, 'Works of Abraham', p. 288, as Ward quotes L. Ginzberg, *The Legends of the Jews* (7 vols.; trans. H. Szold; Philadelphia: Jewish Publication Society of America, 1909–68), I, pp. 270-88.

send him on his way. Ward gives a quite useful paraphrase of James: 'Wasn't Abraham justified at his trial? You see his faith cooperated with his acts of mercy, and on the basis of mercy his faith was made perfect.'[85] James's case for his interpretation of Abraham shows how ludicrous and dangerous it is to separate faith and works. Hence the verse that comes right before our section, Jas 2.13: 'For the judgment is merciless for the man who has shown none. Mercy triumphs over judgment.' And because mercy or merciful acts like Abraham's and Rahab's are 'works' for James, he contradicts and explains away Paul's thesis of 2.16b, 'All flesh (human) is not justified by works of law'.

4. *Conclusion*

From this analysis of the Abraham passage, it is evident just how critical for James Abraham was to the correct understanding of a human being's relationship to God. From what James had gleaned of Paul's gospel, he believes the message is utterly wrong since it is based on a faulty exegesis of Abraham in Genesis. James uses Abraham for three purposes: first, to show how fallacious Paul's dichotomy of faith and works is; secondly, to support his own argument against the dichotomy with Biblical proof; and, most importantly, to promulgate the right teachings about Abraham to the new communities in the diaspora. Because of this central place of Abraham exegesis in James's letter alone, it fits squarely within the law-observant mission to the Gentiles.

For James everything unfolds from the Abraham exegesis, ethical behavior explicitly, and law-observance implicitly. Fundamentally James calls into question Paul's Habukkuk quotation (2.4b) in Gal. 3.11b, as we have seen. James through Abraham gets at the very meaning of justification and life. Works for James are acts of mercy, and that is how all human beings shall be judged, just like Abraham and Rahab.

But given such a variety of positions concerning observance of dietary laws, circumcision, and celebration of holidays, where does James's letter fit? Nowhere in the entire letter does he refer to any of these issues. And we have no New Testament evidence that James himself ever demanded that male Gentile converts be circumcised.[86] Yet it seems fairly safe to deduce that the opponents in Galatia who were

85. Ward, 'Works of Abraham', p. 285.
86. Brown and Meier, *Antioch and Rome*, p. 37.

insisting on circumcision of male converts *claimed* James, Peter, and John as their authority. As Brown points out, '. . . in the savagery of Paul's attack he (Paul) seems to lump his opposition to them (the opponents) with his earlier opposition to Peter and James'.[87]

If Paul had been able to filter out any hint of support for his position of not circumcising male Gentiles from James against the teachers in Galatia, I do think he would have done so, instead of implying that the Jerusalem pillars agreed with the infringing Galatian teachers. In other words, by Paul's rhetorical tactic of 'lumping' the teachers with James, he is telling his readers that James would be on their side, not his. Even if James did not require circumcision for male Gentile converts '. . . his party would have supplied the most comfortable haven for those who had opposed any circumcision-free mission'.[88] Ultimately we have no further explicit evidence for James's views on observance of Jewish ritual law.

Nevertheless, it is important to remember from the Abraham analysis that, in James's tradition of exegesis, *Abraham kept the entire law*. This means that it simply went without saying that his teachings on circumcision, holiday observances, and dietary regulations are summed up in James's Abraham exegesis. Whether the letter—through the Abraham exegesis—implies that Gentiles must observe the whole law is not clear. But it certainly is a possibility.

What we do have in James's letter is a view of the law-observant mission from another perspective. James's letter is not general. It is addressed to the diaspora churches right after Paul's arrest, which was a particularly volatile, unstable period. James tries to unite the communities and to correct the mistaken views Paul had inculcated; but this was a very difficult task for him to accomplish without creating further divisions. James must succeed in his corrective task without impugning Paul, the instigator of the problems. I do think his attempts were successful *rhetorically*, given the richness and depth of the Abraham tradition. But politically and theologically I think he failed, but only as as a consequence and casualty of the Jewish Wars.

---

87. Brown and Meier, *Antioch and Rome*, p. 112.
88. Acts gives evidence that James consistently supported the position that Gentile males need not be circumcised.

SOLECISMS IN THE APOCALYPSE AS SIGNALS FOR THE PRESENCE OF OLD TESTAMENT ALLUSIONS: A SELECTIVE ANALYSIS OF REVELATION 1–22[*]

G.K. Beale

1. *Introduction*

Much research has been invested in analyzing John's grammar, especially his unusual grammatical and syntactical constructions, often referred to as solecisms.[1] The purpose of this study is to offer a new perspective by which a programmatic solution to the majority of the significant solecisms can be achieved and which provides a perspective through which better to view John's peculiar Greek usage.

As early as the first half of the third century Dionysius of Alexandria (d. 264/265 CE) observed that John's 'use of the Greek language is not accurate, but that he employs barbarous idioms, in some places committing downright solecisms' (cited by Eusebius, *H.E.* 7.25.26-27). Other modern scholars have accused John of writing poor Greek. The most thorough and important studies of John's grammar are those by Moses Stuart (mid-nineteenth century)[2] and R.H. Charles (early twentieth century),[3] as well as G. Mussies's massive study (latter part of the twentieth century).[4]

---

*   This article is based on a larger paper which was read in the Fall Term of 1994 at the New Testament Colloquium of the Boston Theological Institute and also at the 'Biblical Greek Language and Linguistics Section' of the 1995 SBL Annual Meeting. I am grateful for comments made by members of these seminars, as well as the editorial comments by Greg Goss.

1.   For a brief overview of twentieth-century discussion representing a variety of approaches to the problem of the solecisms see Murphy 1994: 190-91.

2.   Stuart 1845: I, 232-57: 'Peculiar characteristics of the language and style of the Apocalypse'.

3.   Charles 1920: I, cxvii-clix: 'A Short Grammar of the Apocalypse'.

4.   Mussies 1971; cf. also Bousset's introductory section entitled 'Die Sprache der Apokalypse' in his commentary (1906: 159-79).

2. *The Solecisms of the Apocalypse as Signals for the Presence of Old Testament Allusions*

Various explanations have been proposed for the grammatical irregularities in the Apocalypse. Some have concluded that the solecisms are errors, resulting from John's imperfect knowledge of Greek.[5] Others have attributed the unusual constructions to John's writing in Greek but thinking according to the standards of Hebrew grammar and being influenced to significant degrees by Semitic style.[6] There has rightly been a reaction against understanding John's language as 'Jewish Greek', especially conceived of as a distinct dialect and reflecting a unique Hebrew grammatical structure. Instead, the irregularities have been viewed by a number of scholars neither as mistaken slips of the pen, nor as Semitisms, but reflecting categories of unusual, though acceptable, Greek syntax, attested also in contemporary Hellenistic Greek.[7] Some have understood the difficult expressions partly as due to *constructio ad sensum*,[8] which is quite plausible: for example, 1.20a; 2.27; 4.4; 5.6; 6.1; 13.3a; 17.3; 21.12-14. A recent proposal has suggested that the solecisms are the result of John's own attempt to write in the dominant language of the ruling Graeco-Roman powers but to

5.   E.g. E.C. Selwyn 1900: 258.

6.   So Charles 1920: I, cxlii-cxliv, followed similarly by Turner 1976: 146-58, and Thompson 1985, e.g. p. 108 (who both include Aramaic together with Hebrew influence as a factor); generally also Swete 1906: cxiii-cxxv; Ozanne 1965; Torrey 1958 contended that Revelation had been translated into Greek from Aramaic; similarly, Scott 1928 argued that the book had been translated into Greek from Hebrew (for brief but pointed critique of both Torrey and Scott, see Ozanne 1965: 3-4); see Porter 1989a: 583-84, for a listing of other works supporting the general notion that John's style was significantly affected by Semitic influence; cf. also Mussies 1980: 167-77; Sweet 1979: 16.

7.   E.g. so Porter 1989a: 583-84; Turner 1963: 315 (Moulton and Howard's view, but apparently not Turner's); Porter 1989b: 111-61, which is a sweeping evaluative survey of past studies on various degrees of Semitic influence on verbal aspect throughout the New Testament; Horsley 1981-: V, 5-48, which is also a general evaluative survey of the debate about Semitic influence upon Greek throughout the New Testament, especially the notion that there was a 'Jewish Greek' dialect or language.

8.   So Robertson 1914: 135; likewise Stuart 1845: I, 236-38. For explanations of some of these 'constructions from sense', see the commentary by Beale 1997 (forthcoming) on 5.6; 13.3a; 17.3; 21.12-14.

do so in idiosyncratic grammar in order to 'decolonialize' the language and to express an incipient insurgent protest statement against these imperialist powers.[9]

Apparently unrecognized for the most part previously, a significant number of these irregularities occur in the midst of Old Testament allusions. Accordingly, a number of the expressions appear irregular because John is carrying over the exact grammatical form of the Old Testament wording (often from the Greek Old Testament and its various versions, or sometimes from the Hebrew).[10] He does not change the grammatical form of the Old Testament wording to fit the immediate syntactical context of Revelation, so that the Old Testament expression 'sticks out like a sore thumb'. This creates 'syntactical dissonance', whereby, for example, there is lack of concord in case or gender. Just as often, the precise grammar from the Old Testament passage is not retained, but stylistic Semitisms or Septuagintalisms are incorporated in order to create the dissonance. This 'dissonance' is one of the ways that John gets the readers' attention, causing them to focus on the phrase and to cause them more readily to recognize the presence of an Old Testament allusion.

The exegetical analysis in the concluding part of this article indicates that a significant number of Revelation's solecisms function in the above manner to signal Old Testament allusions: see below, especially on 1.4; 1.5; 2.13; 4.1; 11.15; 12.5; 12.7; 14.7; 14.20; 20.2.[11]

The majority of the solecisms examined consist of a violation of concord, whether in case, number, gender or person. Other unusual grammatical features, sometimes included in discussions of the solecisms,

9. Callahan 1995.

10. After finishing a rough draft of this section, I read Bauckham 1993: 286, and Wilcox 1994: 370, who come close to this conclusion. The former says, 'Unusual and difficult phrases in Revelation frequently turn out to be Old Testament allusions', though he appears not be discussing solecisms, since he adduces only two examples, and these are not grammatical solecisms. Wilcox similarly says with respect to the New Testament in general, 'Infelicities in the Greek may also at times mask allusions to Scripture, or in some cases, to midrashic material linked to Scripture, but not immediately identifiable as Scripture', though he adduces only one example, which also does not involve a grammatical irregularity.

11. Because of space, only ten solecisms are analyzed below, but they are representative of others (see further Beale 1997 [forthcoming] on excursuses at Rev. 1.10-12; 2.20; 10.2, 8; 19.6; 19.20; though less certain, see also on 1.13, 15; 3.12; 5.6a, 12; 7.4, 8, 9; 8.9; 9.14; 11.4.

are better categorized as peculiar variations in style but do not approach outright transgressions of more ordinary grammatical rules, examples of which are the following: (1) resumptive pronouns (e.g. 3.8; 7.9); (2) the use of participles as verbs or the resolution of a participle into a finite verb in a following clause (e.g. with respect to the latter cf. 1.5-6; 2.20); (3) the mixing of different verb tenses and moods without any explicit reason for the alteration (e.g. 21.24-27); (4) stylistic expressions which seem to express Hebraisms or Aramaisms (e.g. Rev. 4.9-10).[12] Some of the clear solecisms are difficult to account for according to any theory.[13]

Ruiz argues that the idiosyncratic solecisms are intended to stop the reader and confound a natural understanding of particular portions of the Revelation text.[14] The present discussion indicates that no such hermeneutical intention is present, though a significant number of the solecisms do cause the reader to pause and to reflect on the wording in order to point the reader back to a particular Old Testament reference in order better to understand the meaning of the phrase in Revelation. In the nineteenth century, Stuart argued that the syntactical peculiarities were intended to cause readers to take closer notice of the clause at hand (especially when they were appositional or explanatory clauses), and so were due to rhetorical purposes.[15] The present conclusions refine this assessment. Some, but not most, of the solecisms which can be traced to Old Testament influence could also be explained as due to *constructio ad sensum*. Furthermore, even when both an explanation of *constructio ad sensum* and Old Testament influence are possible, it is preferable to opt for the latter as the reason for the solecism, since the very presence of an Old Testament allusion provides more objective evidence. On the other hand, it is not unthinkable that there could be an Old Testament allusion together with a *constructio ad sensum*, the latter of which might be responsible for the unusual syntax.

12. For further examples of each of these preceding four categories see Bretscher 1945.

13. E.g. 14.12 and 11.18. However, 14.12 is probably due to a rhetorical use by which a discordant nominative (especially the nominative form of the participle) introduces an explanatory clause in order to highlight the explanation before the readers' eyes (cf. Stuart 1845: I, 235). The irregularity in 11.18 merely may be due to stylistic variation.

14. Ruiz 1989: 220.

15. Stuart 1845: I, 235.

Some deny that the solecisms of Revelation reflect any Hebrew or Semitic style, while others contend that such style is the complete explanation for the peculiarities, while still others conclude that the expressions reflect both an irregular but attested Hellenistic (or Koine, vernacular) idiom *and* a Semitic style.[16] Robertson comes closest to the solution when he says that 'it is not so much particular Hebraisms that meet us in the Apocalypse as the flavour of the LXX whose words are interwoven in the text at every turn'.[17]

In the light of the following analysis, and in confirmation of Robertson's general proposal, we will see that stylistic Septuagintalisms have been incorporated into the text of Revelation. They have been incorporated not simply to reflect an Old Testament Greek style, but to indicate the presence of an actual Old Testament allusion. It is true that one could say that such Septuagintalisms 'fall within the range of possible registers' of first-century Greek usage.[18] The question, however, is not about a mere few grammatical irregularities but the great number of the difficulties, and the frequency of the phenomena in comparison with other works.[19] Furthermore, why does John use such peculiar language on occasion and yet keep the rules of standard Hellenistic Greek most of the time? The explanation is that these peculiarities at just these points are not mere reflections of unusual though possible registers of Greek usage, but are stylistic Septuagintalisms; such semi-irregular Hellenistic expressions may occur more frequently in Revelation because they would have felt natural for the author as a result of his Hebrew and especially Old Testament Greek background.[20] Other cases of John's solecisms are even to be more specifically explained as grammatically awkward because they are parts

16. Robertson 1914: 135-37; cf. also Fanning 1990: 271-74.

17. Robertson 1914: 136.

18. As Porter 1989a: 603 says in response to attempts to explain John's Greek as influenced by a grammatical system of Hebrew.

19. So Roberston 1914: 414, 136.

20. Cf. Fanning 1990: 273; Wilcox 1994: 367-68, cites the Babatha Archive papyri, dated at the end of the first century CE, where Aramaic is rendered into Greek. He observes that the evidence there demonstrates that when Aramaic is put into Greek, it resembles closely New Testament Semitisms often attributed to Septuagintal influence. In this light, he cautions against assuming pervasive LXX influence over Hebrew or Aramaic. His caution is perhaps well-taken, though his warning is not relevant in those places of Revelation where a solecism occurs in the midst of or in direct connection with an Old Testament allusion based on the LXX.

of actual Old Testament verbal allusions carried over in their original syntactical form as they stood in the Old Testament passage. The over-all purpose of these Septuagintalisms, stylistic Semitisms, and awkward Old Testament allusions was probably to create a 'biblical' effect in the hearer and, hence, to show the solidarity of his writing with that of the Old Testament.[21]

The excursus in the remainder of this study inductively attempts to demonstrate the above deductive analysis: that a significant number of the Apocalypse's grammatical solecisms indicate the presence of Old Testament allusions. The following solecisms which are analyzed ap-pear to be representative of others which also could have been discussed below (with respect to which see above on note 12).

3. *Exegetical Analysis of Some of the Well-Known Solecisms in the Apocalypse which Points to their Use as Signals for the Presence of Old Testament Allusions*[22]

a. *Solecisms Involving an Irregular Use of Nouns in the Nominative Case*

1. Rev. 1.4: ἀπὸ ὁ ὢν καὶ ὁ ἦν καὶ ὁ ἐρχόμενος. The clause ἀπὸ ὁ ὢν ('from the one who is') is the first and most famous solecism of the Apocalypse, since a genitive construction should follow ἀπό. It is also one of the clearest Old Testament allusions in the book. Does the Old Testament allusion have any significant bearing upon the gram-matical irregularity? Before answering this, the Old Testament allusion must be clarified.

The complete threefold clause in Rev. 1.4, 'the one who is and who was and who is coming', is a reflection of Exod. 3.14 together with Isaiah's twofold and threefold temporal descriptions of God (cf. Isa. 41.4; 43.10; 44.6; 48.12), which themselves may be developed reflec-tions on the divine name in Exod. 3.14. The name of Exod. 3.14 was also expanded in a twofold and threefold manner by later Jewish tradi-tion: (1) 'I am He who is and who will be' (*Targ. Ps.-J. Exod.* 3.14);

---

21. Beale 1988: 332, following Sweet 1979: 16.

22. For discussion of the immediate and broad contexts of each of the following passages in which solecisms occur, as well as further analysis of some of the Old Testament allusions involved, see Beale 1997 (forthcoming); also, see the intro-ductory section therein on 'The Grammar of the Apocalypse' for a text-critical analysis of the most significant solecisms (twenty-five examples are surveyed).

(2) 'I am now what I always was and always will be' (*Midr. Rab. Exod.* III.6; *The Alphabet of Rabbi Akiba*; likewise *Midr. Ps.* 72.1); (3) 'I am he who is and who was and I am he who will be' (*Targ. Ps.-J. Deut.* 32.39; see likewise the gloss to *Targ. Neof. Exod.* 3.14). In *Mek., Tract. Shirata* IV.25–32, as well as *Tract. Baḥodesh* V.25–31, the similar threefold formula describes the God of the exodus in direct linkage with Deut. 32.39.[23]

It is unlikely, however, that John is dependent only on the Deut. 32.39 reference (cf. Trudinger 1966: 87), since the first and last elements of that formula are not the same. Consequently, he is more likely familiar with the general tradition represented by the above texts (especially Old Testament texts) which expands Exod. 3.14.[24] A similar threefold formula is found also in pagan Greek literature as a title of the gods (Stuart II 1985: 16),[25] which may have sparked John's appeal to the Jewish formulae as an apologetic.

Since a genitive construction should follow ἀπό in the phrase ἀπὸ ὁ ὤν, scribes tried to correct the apparent mistake by adding θεοῦ ('of God', 𝔐 (a) t; Vic Prim) after the preposition. But it would be a blunder of modern thinking to judge this as a mistake of one who did not know his Greek very well. In this particular instance, as often elsewhere, commentators generally acknowledge that the 'incorrect' grammar is intentional. The phrase ὁ ὤν is probably taken from Exod. 3.14 and John keeps it in the nominative in order to highlight it as an allusion to Exodus.[26] John's emphasis stems from the fact that ὁ ὤν occurs twice in Exod. 3.14 as an explanation of the divine name Yahweh. Furthermore, it is possible that the full threefold phrase became a general title for God in Judaism (cf. above; cf. Dana and Mantey 1927: 70), and this would have been reason enough for the author to

23. The Shirata reference is also linked to a like threefold formula based on Isa. 41.4; note the threefold formula based on Isa. 44.6 in *Gen. R.* 81.2, *Deut. R.* 1.10, and *Cant. R.* 1.9 §1; for a similar threefold formula for God without reference to a precise Old Testament text see Josephus, *Apion* 2.190; *Ant.* 8.280; *Arist.* 4.5; *Sib. Or.* 3.16; cf. Rom. 11.36.

24. So similarly Delling 1959: 124-26; cf. discussion of the targumic references by McNamara 1966: 105-12.

25. Cf. also Moffat 1970: 21; Lohmeyer 1970: 168, 179, 181; and McNamara 1966: 102; for early patristic references, see Charles 1920: II, 220-21.

26. So also Moulton and Howard 1929: 154; Laughlin 1902: 12; Stuart 1845: II, 15, suggests that the indeclinability of the name YHWH in the same Old Testament passage may have enforced this.

maintain the nominatives. BDF §143, however, note that 'names are usually cited in the case required by the construction; only rarely are they introduced independently in the nominative'.[27] Beckwith (1919: 424), Robertson (1914: 270, 414, 459, 574-75) and others argue unnecessarily that John considered the LXX paraphrase of the divine name as an indeclinable noun, since the unchangeable form would have suited better the majesty, sovereignty, and unchangeableness of God. If such is the case, the same kind of grammatical irregularity has the same significance for the devil's name in 20.2 (cf. Sweet 1979: 65, and the analysis of 20.2 below)!

Possible also is the suggestion that John employs such kinds of constructions here and elsewhere as Hebraisms (in Hebrew the noun in the indirect cases is not inflected; so Charles 1920: I, 13). John's purpose in doing so, as suggested above, would be to create a 'biblical' effect upon the reader and so to show the solidarity of his work with that of God's revelation in the Old Testament. Unconvincing is Mussies (1971: 94), who speculates without any MS evidence that after ἀπό was written the name of God to which ὁ ὤν was put in apposition, and that the name was 'effaced by thumbing or by decay of the scroll', and that scribes misconstrued ὁ ὤν as originally having been written directly following the preposition.

The most probable explanation, however, for the nominative is that it is intended to reflect an allusion to Exod. 3.14.

2. Rev. 1.5: ἀπὸ ' Ἰησοῦ Χριστοῦ, ὁ μάρτυς ὁ πιστός, ὁ πρωτότοκος τῶν νεκρῶν. The phrase ὁ μάρτυς ὁ πιστός ('the faithful witness, the first-born') is nominative but should be genitive (following ἀπὸ Ἰησοῦ Χριστοῦ). The phrase is an allusion to 'the faithful witness' of Ps. 88(89).37 (38) (LXX), which refers specifically to the unending witness of the moon, and which is compared to the unending reign of David's seed on his throne (likewise Ps. 88(89).29). Just as *Midr. Rab. Exod.* 19.7 applies the 'first-born' from Ps. 89.28 to the 'King Messiah', and *Midr. Rab. Gen.* 97 sees Ps. 89.37 as a messianic prophecy, so John applies the phrase directly to the Messiah's own faithful witness which led to establishment of his eternal kingship.

Like the solecism in 1.4 following ἀπὸ, the phrase here is probably

27. BDF cites Rev. 1.4, but it is unclear whether they consider the threefold clause in Rev. 1.4 as an exception to the rule or as maintaining the nominative because it is based on a rabbinical exegesis of Exod. 3.14, or both.

kept in the nominative because it is part of the very wording of the Old Testament allusion, which was also in the nominative in its Old Testament context: Ps. 88(89).37(38) has ὁ μάρτυς. . . πιστός, while v. 27(28) of the Psalm has πρωτότοκον. The author likely wants to keep the nominative to direct attention to the Old Testament allusion, as well as perhaps because, like the phrase in v. 4, it *may* have been a name for the Messiah, as noted above;[28] there is not, however, enough evidence that it was a name at this time.[29] Consequently, 'first-born' has been changed from its Old Testament accusative form either because it had become a name, or, more probably, to conform to the nominative of 'the faithful witness' (ὁ μάρτυς ὁ πιστός) in the Greek Old Testament text.

3. Rev. 2.13: ἐν ταῖς ἡμέραις ᾿Αντιπᾶς ὁ μάρτυς μου ὁ πιστός μου. Moulton (1906: 12) classifies the phrase ᾿Αντιπᾶς ὁ μάρτυς μου ὁ πιστός μου ('Antipas my witness, my faithful one') directly following ἐν ταῖς ἡμέραις ('in the days') as a Semitism which 'contravenes Greek syntax', since the nominative ᾿Αντιπᾶς is a declinable name and should be in the genitive (᾿Αντιπᾶ), as should the following ὁ μάρτυς. . . ὁ πιστός (see also BDF §53-55). Even if the name were indeclinable, it would still stand in a genitival relationship with 'in the days', as should the appositional ὁ μάρτυς. . . ὁ πιστός (cf. Metzger 1971: 734). It is unlikely that the proper name should be considered a nominative of appellation, since indeclinable proper nouns are typically assigned the case demanded by their use in the clause (Brooks and Winberg 1979: 5). Consequently, the modifying phrase 'my faithful witness' cannot be construed as being nominative because it purportedly modifies a nominative of appellation.

Rather, like the solecisms in 1.4 and 1.5, which also should have been in the genitive, this phrase occurs in the nominative because it is part of the same Old Testament allusion as 1.5, where ὁ μάρτυς ὁ πιστός ('faithful witness') also occurs in allusion to the nominative ὁ μάρτυς. . . πιστός of Ps. 88(89).37 (38) (see on 1.5). Again, the awkward nominative is a device directing attention to the Old Testament

28. Whether in Judaism, or formulated newly by John; likewise Turner 1963: 314; Laughlin 1902: 15 is the only one I have subsequently found to come closest to my conclusion: 'The phrase. . . is directly quoted from the LXX of Ps. 89.37'.

29. Cf. further BDF §143 discussed above at 1.4 with respect to the general rule that names are cited in the case required by the syntactical context.

allusion, as well as to the first occurrence of the phrase in 1.5, in order
to make clear the identification of Antipas' faithful witness with that
of Jesus.[30] Therefore, it is unlikely that Ἀντιπᾶς is a careless slip for
Ἀντιπᾶ (as Robertson 1914: 255 and Turner 1976: 146-47 conjecture)
nor that it is a mere feature of the uneducated *koine* style (Turner
1976: 146-47).

It is theoretically possible that the name is a generally indeclinable
Semitic name, since some Hellenized Semitic names were sometimes
declined and sometimes not (Mussies 1971: 94, and Mussies 1964; cf.
Robertson 1914: 255), but apparently no examples of 'Antipas' have
yet been found which are indeclinable. Furthermore, the common practice with Hellenized Semitic personal names ending with nominative
-ας was to decline them according to the first declension (-ας, -α,
etc.; so BDF §53-55; Charles 1920: I, 52, following Lachmann and
others, is so convinced of the declinability of the name that he proposes the conjectural emendation of Ἀντιπᾶ). However, even if the
name were indeclinable, the reason that the following clause ('my witness, my faithful one') has been attracted to the indeclinable nominative
name needs more explanation than that it was a mere 'slip', since the
almost identical clause in 1.5 modifies Ἰησοῦ Χριστοῦ, but its case *is*
different.[31]

4. Rev. 12.7: ὁ Μιχαὴλ καὶ οἱ ἄγγελοι αὐτοῦ τοῦ πολεμῆσαι.
There is a grammatical difficulty in the phrase ὁ Μιχαὴλ καὶ οἱ
ἄγγελοι αὐτοῦ τοῦ πολεμῆσαι, since the nominative (ὁ Μιχαὴλ
καὶ οἱ ἄγγελοι) serves as the subject of the infinitive, instead of the
normal accusative. The articular genitival infinitive (τοῦ πολεμῆσαι),
as is often the case, merely may denote *result* of the initial clause,
'And there came about war in heaven, *so that* Michael and his angels

---

30. Indeed, the other Old Testament text lying behind the idea of 'faithful witness'
is Isa. 43.10-12, which repeats twice that the Israelites were to be 'My witnesses'
(ἐμοὶ μάρτυρες, the latter also in the nominative) together with God and his servant
in the new age of redemption (see further Beale 1996: 144-52).

31. Scribes tried to smooth out the reading by adding 'in which' (αις or ἐν αις)
before Antipas, but the attempt was unsuccessful since the genitive of the name and
of its appositional clause is still required (see Metzger 1971: 734). Stuart 1845: II, 71-
72, tries hesitatingly to solve the syntactical problem by reading in the imperfect ἦν,
'even in the days in which Antipas [was] my faithful martyr', though he acknowledges the problems with this (likewise, but more confidently, Düsterdieck 1980:
143, and Gill 1811: 709).

waged war in heaven'. More generally, Robertson (1914: 1066), on analogy with classical usage, takes the construction as a 'loose infinitive of design' in 'explanatory apposition to πόλεμος', while Moffatt (1970: 426) is content to refer to the construction as 'syntactical laxity'. In line with Robertson, Porter (1989b: 377) refers to the construction as a 'strictly independent' infinitive, which he classifies as part of a larger category of independent infinitives 'long. . . recognized in both earlier and later ancient Greek'. However, the majority of the examples adduced in Goodwin (1890: 310-13, cited in Porter 1989b) form part of idiomatic parenthetical expressions used in speaking or writing to qualify something which has been spoken or written (likewise Smyth 1984: 447); for example, Herodotus uses the infinitive absolute in a very specific manner, often in idiomatic expressions and primarily in the following three kinds of statements about his historical research: (1) when making methodological statements of *'general purport* about his own method', or (2) about problems confronting him in evaluating his sources of information, or (3) when he makes a 'bare *statement of fact* about the problems involved in *obtaining. . . specific* information' (Stork 1982: 107; cf. pp. 89-108 [cited also by Porter); a number of examples cited by Porter are idioms of greeting. No doubt, there are examples of independent infinitives which are not idiomatic, but the question is whether these are typical in any period of Greek. More data must be adduced and evaluated than hitherto could be demonstrated conclusively. The infinitive of Rev. 12.7 does not occur as part of such specialized or idiomatic expressions as noted above.

Therefore, while it is possible that the construction of 12.7 reflects exceptional broader Greek style, or that it is a lax expression, these explanations do not account sufficiently for the unusual construction of the nominative (ὁ Μιχαὴλ καὶ οἱ ἄγγελοι) serving as the subject of the infinitive, instead of the normal accusative. Moule's explanation is that this is a reflection of John's 'barbarous Greek' (1953: 129). But this may be an exceptional formulation, which proves the general rule. In this respect, the strange syntax may be the result of an attempt to transcribe literally an unusually vivid vision (so Farrer 1964: 146). Some MSS ($\mathfrak{P}^{47}$ ℵ 𝔐) omit the genitive article τοῦ before the infinitive πολεμῆσαι, though this likely is an attempt to smooth out the difficulty by simplifying the grammar.

However, the nominative also can be accounted for grammatically by seeing the construction as a complementary or epexegetical infinitive with γίνομαι repeated from the first part of the verse in the more personalized third person plural form of a verb like ἔρχομαι, ἐξέρχομαι or ἀνίστημι (e.g. ἐγένετο πόλεμος ἐν τῷ οὐρανῷ ὁ Μιχαὴλ καὶ οἱ ἄγγελοι αὐτοῦ [ἦλθον] τοῦ πολεμῆσαι; in Rev. 14.15 a number of MSS have the articular genitival infinitive also functioning epexegetically or complementarily to ἔρχομαι. Or, as Swete (1906: 153) proposes, ἐγένετο may be repeated from the first part of the verse directly before ὁ Μιχαὴλ: 'there arose war in heaven; there arose Michael and his angels to make war'. Implied but elided verbs are typical both in Revelation and in Paul, as well as in the New Testament in general (cf. BDF §479-83 on ellipses). In either of the two proposals of supplied verbs, the nominative is not awkward, since it serves as the subject of the implied ἦλθον or ἐγένετο followed by its completing infinitive.[32]

In addition to the above explanations, plausible also is the solution that views the construction as reflective of a Hebrew idiom where the subject preceding the *lamedh* prefix (*le*) + infinitive occurs. Indeed, in these instances the LXX reproduces the wording literally with a nominative subject preceding an articular genitival infinitive, just as in Rev. 12.7 (e.g. Hos. 9.13; Ps. 25.14; 1 Chron. 9.25; Eccles. 3.15). And just as the idiom in the LXX reproductions conveys the idea of necessity, some suggest that the same nuance is included here: 'Michael and his angels *had to make war*' (so Charles 1920: I, 322; Mussies 1971: 96; Thompson 1985: 60-63; BDF §400, 7-8; cf. Moule 1953: 129). In addition to these examples from the LXX, τοῦ + the infinitive elsewhere renders *lamedh* + infinitive, though the same Aramaic construction occurs numerously and the same construction is found in Classical and Hellenistic Greek (cf. Thompson 1985: 61 and Robertson 1914 above).

The attempt by Charles and others to explain the articular genitival infinitive as reflecting an idiomatic Hebrew–LXX Semitism appears to be on the right track. However, the Semitism is not likely due to a general Semitic influence upon John, but is to be accounted for more precisely on the basis of the specific allusion to Dan. 10.20 (from either the Hebrew or Greek Old Testament text), which is present in Rev. 12.7. There also the LXX renders *lamedh* + infinitive by genitive +

32.   *Contra* Charles 1920: I, 322; Thompson 1985: 62 notes that a nominative is the subject of an articular genitival infinitive in listings of Hoskier's variant readings of 4.11, 5.3, 9.6 and 12.2.

infinitive, which serves as epexegetical or complementary to the preceding verb 'return' in the phrase ἐπιστρέψω τοῦ πολεμῆσαι ('I will return to make war'). The first person plural 'I' which is assumed in the verb 'return' in Dan. 10.20 is closely associated with none other than Michael (cf. Dan. 10.21), and this best accounts for 'Michael' being used in the nominative in Rev. 12.7 in allusion to the same Daniel text.

Likewise, οὐκ + the aorist ἴσχυσεν ('they were not strong enough') in Rev. 12.8 may be regarded as reflecting Semitic style (as contends Thompson 1985: 40-41, and similarly Charles 1920: I, 324-25), but it is more precisely the result of an explicit allusion to Dan. 7.21 (beginning in v. 7b; cf. MT, and Theod. [ἴσχυσεν], and also Charles 1920: I, 324-25), which underscores the presence of the Dan. 10.20 allusion. In both instances of Rev. 12.7-8 the same wording of the Old Testament text is preserved, despite reflecting somewhat awkward (in the case of 12.8) or unusual Greek syntax (in the case of 12.7), in order to highlight for the reader the Daniel background.

5. Rev. 20.2: ἐκράτησεν τὸν δράκοντα, ὁ ὄφις ὁ ἀρχαῖος. The nominative phrase ὁ ὄφις ὁ ἀρχαῖος in 20.2 is a solecism (so A 1678 1778 2080), since following the accusative τὸν δράκοντα it should also be accusative. The irregularity could be understood as the nominative of appellation, but probably is not, since there is no early extant evidence of the existence of such a name for the Devil (*Sib. Or.* V, 29 identifies Nero as 'a direful serpent'; *b. Soṭ.* 9.b and *b. Sanh.* 29.a call the Devil respectively 'the primeval serpent' and 'the ancient serpent'). Furthermore, both ὄφις and ἀρχαῖος are declined according to the various cases elsewhere in the New Testament. The reason for writing an original nominative is to conform the name to the same nominative phrase in 12.9 (ὁ δράκων... ὄφις ὁ ἀρχαῖος), thus identifying the passage even further with 12.7-11.[33]

This signposting function of the solecism fits with observations of other solecisms throughout the book which have the same function, usually with respect to Old Testament allusions. Such a grammatical irregularity in this passage is also designed to attract the reader to the earlier occurrence of Satan's title in 12.9; the device apparently had its desired effect on later scribes, as testified to by MSS 051 2030 2377 𝔐 K syh, which add the phrase ὁ πλανῶν τὴν οἰκουμένην ὅλην after

---

33. Cf. the somewhat different reasoning of Metzger 1971: 764, which would still lead to the same conclusion.

ὁ Σατανᾶς in order to conform the passage yet more with the wording of the ch. 12 text, which has the identical phrase. Together with
reference to Rev. 12.9, the phrase in Rev. 20.2 may include allusion
to Genesis 3, where the precise nominative form ὁ ὄφις occurs four
times (and τῷ ὄφει twice), to which Rev. 12.9 alludes. The striking
change to the nominative in 20.2 may highlight the Genesis 3 background more, which may be made explicit by the directly following
addition of 'ancient' (ἀρχαῖος also in the nominative).

b. *Solecisms Involving an Irregular Use of the Nominative Case or of
Gender in an Introductory Participial Form of λέγω*

1. Rev. 4.1: ἡ φωνὴ ἡ πρώτη ἣν ἤκουσα ὡς σάλπιγγος <u>λαλούσης</u>
μετ' ἐμοῦ <u>λέγων</u>. The participle λαλούσης ('speaking') should be
accusative in concord with ἣν, which itself is a relative pronoun referring back to ἡ φωνή, 'the voice'. Later scribes changed λαλούσης to
an accusative in line with ἣν (e.g. ℵ gig Prim Ambr); others changed
it to a nominative, apparently intending to conform it to the nominative
φωνή preceding the accusative relative (e.g. 2329 *pc*; see further
Hoskier 1929: II, 120, for additional MSS. supporting both changes).
Despite these notable attempts to correct the text, the irregularity of
4.1 is intentional. For the rationale, especially with respect to the unusual genitive participle as an indicator of an allusion to Exod. 19.16-
19, see 1.10b-11, where the feminine participle λεγούσης ('saying')
has been assimilated to the genitive case of the feminine σάλπιγγος
('trumpet'), though its antecedent appears to be the feminine, accusative
φωνήν ('voice'). Therefore, in 1.10-11 λεγούσης is out of concord
with φωνήν, since the former is genitive and the latter is accusative.
The irregular assimilation of λεγούσης to σάλπιγγος may be intended
to highlight the trumpet sound of the voice in order to underscore
even more the Exodus 19 background (e.g. LXX), where Moses and
Israel did not precisely hear Yahweh's voice as great but 'the voice of
the trumpet sounded great' (Exod. 19.16) and 'the voices of the trumpet
were going on very much louder' (Exod. 19.19; for further analysis
of the solecism in 1.10-11 see Beale 1997 [forthcoming] excursus on
1.10-11).

In addition, the following participle λέγων in 4.1 should be
feminine nominative in line with φωνή, but is masculine (scribes tried
to conform it accordingly to the feminine λέγουσα: ℵ¹ 𝔐 ᴬ). Many

grammarians see the use of the nominative λέγων probably as a Semitism, representing the indeclinable *lē'mōr*, as it does in the LXX; see likewise 5.11-12; 11.1, 15; 14.6-7 (see on 14.7 below; e.g. Turner 1963: 315). Porter (1989b: 138-39) acknowledges 'at most' only 'LXX enhancement', pointing out that all periods of Greek use λέγων this way; however, his evidence is fragmentary. The use is probably better referred to as an intentional stylistic Septuagintalism[34] (here and throughout the book), since of the 870 times the infinitive construct *lē'mōr* occurs in the MT, 770 are rendered in the LXX by λέγων (Porter 1989b: 138), and because the word is always used in Revelation in conjunction with an Old Testament allusion. Here the Septuagintal idiom further attracts attention to the Exodus 19 allusion, especially since it introduces the phrase 'come up (ἀνάβα)', which likely alludes to God's command to Moses in Exod. 19.24, 'come up' (ἀνάβηθι); an allusion to Dan. 2.28-30 also directly follows.[35]

M. Wilcox (1994: 367-68) has observed that, as in the LXX, the expression 'saying' (λέγων, λέγουσα) introduces direct speech in the Babatha Archive, which is a document dating at the end of the first century AD where Aramaic is rendered into Greek. In the LXX the Greek λέγων is a translation of *lē'mōr* and in the Babatha Archive it is a rendering of Aramaic *lmymr*, and it is likely not a Septuagintalism in the Archive. In this light, Wilcox cautions against assuming that λέγων in the New Testament as an introduction to direct discourse is always a

---

34. There is debate about the distinction between a Semitism and a Septuagentalism. A viable definition of 'Semitism' is an 'un-Greek' construction produced by an overly literal rendering of either a Hebrew or Aramaic source, whether oral or written. A 'Septuagintalism' is discerned by recognizing both a deviation from idiomatic Greek and from Semitic constructions. A 'Septuagintalism is a construction in the LXX of prominence disproportionate to other Hellenistic Greek usage' (Porter 1989b: 118, where also possible examples of Septuagintalisms or Septuagintal enhancements are discussed: e.g. pp. 120-26, 133, 138-39). In particular, the clearest Septuagintalisms are those syntactical peculiarities that are not dependent on or imitative of Semitic syntax but reflect language, 'used to render Semitic constructions into Greek in one of the translation styles in the Septuagint' (Schmidt 1991: 594, upon which discussion in this note is also broadly based). On the distinction between a Semitism and a stylistic Septuagintalism, see further Beale 1997 (forthcoming) Introduction ('The Grammar of the Apocalypse').

35. Cf. Swete 1906: 66, and Beckwith 1919: 495, who see λέγων as masculine because of the author's attempt to align gender with the male person behind the voice (φωνή).

Septuagintalism, but could be from Hebrew or Aramaic influence.

In response to Wilcox, see Beale 1997 (forthcoming) Introduction ('The Grammar of the Apocalypse'). A Septuagintal influence in the present case of Rev. 4.1 is further confirmed from the consideration of the same kind of solecism below in Rev. 11.15 and 14.7 (on which see below).

2. Rev. 11.15: ἐγένοντο φωναὶ μεγάλαι ἐν τῷ οὐρανῷ λέγοντες. Some MSS read the masculine participle λέγοντες (A 2053 2351 𝔐ᴬ), while others have the feminine λέγουσαι (𝔓⁴⁷ ℵ C 051 1006 1611 1841 2329 2344 𝔐ᴷ). It is hard to decide the original reading on external grounds since good witnesses are divided in attestation. However, the masculine reading is certainly the most difficult and best explains how the feminine developed. There would have been more of a scribal tendency to change the masculine to the feminine in order to bring the participle into agreement with the preceding feminine φωναὶ μεγάλαι, which is the subject of the participle. As we have seen, this lack of concord is a characteristic feature of the Apocalypse, and it is always accompanied with scribal tendencies to smooth out the awkwardness. An original masculine may have resulted from John's understanding of the voices as emanating from masculine beings (cf. Robertson 1933: 384, Stuart 1845: II, 240; note mention of the elders in v. 16 and the introduction of their praise in v. 17a with λέγοντες).

Alternatively, this could be an instance of the indeclinable form being equivalent to the Semitic *lē'mōr*. As such, it could be a stylistic Septuagintalism serving to introduce an Old Testament allusion, attracting attention to it through its irregular Greek grammatical form. In this respect, interestingly, λέγοντες also introduces the Song of Moses (Exod. 15.1: 'they spoke, *saying*'), which is significant, since part of that Song is alluded to in Rev. 11.15 (on which see below): cf. Exod. 15.18, κύριος βασιλεύων τὸν αἰῶνα καὶ ἐπ' αἰῶνα. The same participial form is also found earlier in Daniel 2 as part of an introductory question that the entire revelatory dream of Daniel 2 be made known (Dan. 2.7 [LXX]: 'they answered a second time, *saying*'). This is relevant since the prophecy of Dan. 2.44, ἀναστήσει ὁ θεὸς τοῦ οὐρανοῦ βασιλείαν ἥτις εἰς τοὺς αἰῶνας, may also be evoked by the phrase 'εγένετο ἡ βασιλεία... τοῦ κυρίου... βασιλεύσει εἰς τοὺς αἰῶνας τῶν αἰώνων at the conclusion of Rev. 11.15 (cf. also Dan. 7.14, 27). The redundant *lē'mōr* (directly following a verb of speaking) is translated hundreds of times in the LXX by λέγων, λέγοντες and λέγουσα (often indeclinable), and the same phenomenon occurs in Rev. 5.9; 6.10; 7.2-3, 10, 13; 14.18; 15.3; 17.1; 18.2, 15-16, 18; 19.17; 21.9.[36] Especially striking is the observation of Rev. 15.3, where the redundant expression ᾄδουσιν τὴν ᾠδὴν Μωυσέως... λέγοντες (also virtually identical to Rev. 5.9) directly alludes to the Song of Moses in Exod. 15.1, demonstrating that this precise Old Testament passage is clearly in John's mind elsewhere in the book.

3. Rev. 14.(6-)7: (εἶδον ἄλλον ἄγγελον... ἔχοντα εὐαγγέλιον) λέγων ἐν φωνῇ μεγάλῃ. The original introductory λέγων in Rev. 14.7 has been changed to λέγοντα by some scribes in order to harmonize with the accusative ἔχοντα, which also describes the angel in v. 6 (so 𝔓[47] 051. 1611. 2053). Λέγων could well be in the nominative because it may represent the indeclinable *lē'mōr* (Moulton and Howard 1929: 454; Turner 1963: 315; cf. Zerwick 1963: §14), or, more likely, the Septuagintal rendering of the Hebrew typically by a Greek nominative, as in 4.1; 5.11-12; 11.1, 15 (see on 4.1). This may be a stylistic enhancement from the Septuagint in order to signal to the hearer/reader that the background for v. 7 is to be sought in the Greek Old Testament of Daniel 4, which is alluded to in Rev. 14.6-7. It is appropriate that λέγων introduces an allusion to Daniel 4, since λέγων conspicuously introduces an almost identical angelic command to Nebuchadnezzar to 'give glory to the Most High' in Dan. 4.34 (LXX):

Dan. 4.34 (LXX)	Rev. 14.6-7
<u>ἰδοὺ ἄγγελος</u> εἷς ἐκάλεσέ με ἐκ τοῦ <u>οὐρανοῦ λέγων</u>, Ναβουχοδονοσορ, <u>δούλευσον τῷ θεῷ</u>... <u>δὸς δόξαν τῷ ὑψίστῳ</u> ('behold, an angel called me from heaven, saying, "Nebuchadnezzar", serve God... give glory to the Most High'). LXX of Dan. 4.37a expands on v. 34 partly by the following wording: ἀπὸ	<u>εἶδον ἄλλον ἄγγελον</u>... ἐν <u>μεσουρανήματι</u>... <u>λέγων</u> ἐν φωνῇ μεγάλῃ, φοβήθητε τὸν θεὸν καὶ <u>δότε αὐτῷ δόξαν</u> ('I saw another angel... in midheaven... saying in a great voice, "fear God and give to him glory" ').

36. So Thompson 1985: 70; for statistics of LXX occurrence see Porter 1989b: 138-39, who also contends that parallels of the pleonasm occur in 'all periods of Greek', though he has not shown it was a much-used idiom in all periods, as in the LXX; nevertheless, his conclusion that the pleonasm could be a 'well-accepted Greek idiom enhanced by the LXX' is an acceptable qualification of Thompson (see also on 4.1 above).

Dan. 4.34 (LXX)	Rev. 14.6-7
τοῦ <u>φόβου αὐτοῦ</u> τρόμος εἴληφέ με ('from fear of him trembling gripped me'). Theod. of Dan. 4.14 also has ἐφώνησεν ἐν ἰσχύι ('he [an angel] cried loudly')!	

The close parallels point to the likelihood that λέγων is not a general Semitism nor merely a general Septuagintal stylistic enhancement but is actually part of the allusion to Dan. 4.34 (LXX). Therefore, the more precise reason that λέγων is in the nominative instead of accusative is to maintain part of the Old Testament's exact grammatical form in order to create 'syntactical dissonance', so that the hearer/reader would be alerted to recognize more easily the allusion to Daniel 4.

That 14.6-7 alludes to Dan. 4:34 (LXX, not Theod.) receives striking confirmation from the recognition that 14.6-8 is also based on a series of expressions from Daniel 4 about Nebuchadnezzar:[37]

(1)   an angel commands him to 'give glory to the Most High' (δός δόξαν τῷ ὑψίστῳ, Dan. 4.35, LXX; and for the notion of 'fearing' God, see v. 37a);

(2)   the king gives 'praise to the one having made the four-part cosmos (αἰνῶ τῷ κτίσαντι τὸν οὐρανὸν καὶ τὴν γῆν καὶ τὰς θαλάσσας καὶ τοὺς ποταμοὺς, Dan. 4.37, LXX);

(3)   the angelic declaration to humanity through the four-fold formula of universality ('every nation and tribe and tongue and people') is based on the same repeated formula in Daniel, two of which occur in the LXX of Dan. 4.1, 37b (see, e.g., also Rev. 5.9);

(4)   the use of 'hour' (ὥρα) as the time of the latter-day judgment is based on the repeated eschatological use of the same word in Daniel, which is unique to the remainder of Old Testament usage; the approaching time of the Babylonian king's judgment is described as an 'hour' (Dan. 4.17a, LXX).[38] The closest verbal parallel from Daniel for the phrase 'the hour of his judgment came' (ἦλθεν ἡ ὥρα τῆς κρίσεως αὐτοῦ) in

37. See Beale 1986: 541-42; cf. Altink 1984, who attempts to propose 1 Chron. 16.8-36 as background.

38. For fuller discussion of the Old Testament background of ὥρα and its use in Revelation see Beale 1986: 541-42.

Rev. 14.7 is Dan. 11.45, LXX: 'the hour of his end will come', ἥξει ὥρα τῆς συντελείας αὐτοῦ), which refers to the final judgment of God's end-time opponent (cf. also Ezek. 7.7; 22.3);

(5) both passages mention 'Babylon the Great' from Dan. 4.27 (= 4.30, LXX and Theod.; so Rev. 14.8).

c. *Solecisms Involving an Irregular Use of Gender in Adjectival Forms*

1. Rev. 12.5: ἔτεκεν υἱὸν ἄρσεν. The masculine υἱόν followed by the neuter pronominal adjective ἄρσεν ('male son') appears to be irregular, since adjectives should be in the same gender as nouns which they modify. Could John's penchant for alluding to the Old Testament be helpful in explaining this problem?

The language of the woman 'bearing the male child' is again reminiscent of Isa. 7.14, 66.7 and Mic. 5.3-4 (see on 12.2; BAGD: 110, prefer Isa. 66.7). Allusion specifically to Isa. 66.7 is evident from the following observations: (1) the verbal similarity between 12.2, 5 (ὠδίνουσα... τεκεῖν... καὶ ἔτεκεν υἱὸν ἄρσεν) and Isa. 66.7 (ὠδίνουσαν τεκεῖν... καὶ ἔτεκεν ἄρσεν; this clause is repeated in v. 8, with ἄρσεν being replaced by τὰ παιδία); (2) the combination of 'son' and 'male' in Rev. 12.5 is based, at least in part, on the close parallelism of Isa. 66.7 with 66.8 in the MT:

Isa. 66.7	Isa. 66.8
'she travailed, she brought forth. . .she gave birth to a *male* [*zākār*]'.	'Zion *travailed, she also brought forth* her *sons* [pl. of *bēn*]'.

In addition to the verbal parallelism, the singular 'male' of 66.7 is replaced in 66.8 with the plural 'sons', both apparently referring to Israel. (3) The phrase in Isaiah is part of a prophecy figuratively describing that Jerusalem will be like a reborn child when God restores Israel from captivity (see Isa. 66.8-14) and brings about a new creation (cf. Isa. 66.22; 65.17-23). Allusion to an Isaiah restoration and new creation prophecy here anticipates the even clearer allusion to an Isaiah restoration promise later in ch. 12 (see 12.14) and to the new creation allusion to Isa. 65.17 in Rev. 21.1. Isaiah's national promise is applied here to Christ as an individual, presumably because he is ideal Israel and represents the nation as their king, as the Psalm 2 enthronement citation, which also occurs in 12.5, indicates.[39] Indeed, the Psalm 2 reference is applied both to Christ and the believer in 2.26-27 (cf. the identification of the reign of both in 1.5-6, 9; 5.5-12)! (4) The depiction of the woman as having 'fled' (ἐξέφυγε) and consequently successfully bearing offspring (Isa. 66.7) best explains the image in Rev. 12.6 of 'the woman [who] fled [ἔφυγεν]', ensuring the welfare of her offspring (so 12.13-17).

John may intentionally have the neuter pronominal adjective ἄρσεν (instead of the masculine) irregularly modify the masculine υἱόν. As observed above in the textual comparisons of Revelation 12 and Isaiah 66, the unusual grammar reflects the actual wording of the Isaiah text, where *both* the mention of 'male' and the corporate plural of 'son' (or 'child') occur in synonymous phrases expressing Jerusalem bearing in travail. That John has not made a careless grammatical blunder is clear from 12.13, where the masculine τὸν ἄρσενα is correctly used.[40]

On the other hand, some do not see a grammatical incongruity in the use of ἄρσεν, but view it as a noun in apposition to 'son', further describing it (so Fekkes 1994: 183-84, who lists others in agreement). Fekkes thinks this finds possible justification in 12.13 where ἄρσενα is used substantivally. But this still leaves unanswered the question why the neuter occurs in 12.5 and masculine in 12.13; in addition, the substantival use normally would be articular, as in 12.13. Furthermore, in other combinations of υἱός + ἄρσην, which are rare, the latter is masculine and adjectival, and υἱός has the general sense of child, that is, 'male child': Tobit 6.12 (Sinaiticus; see Göttingen *Septuaginta* apparatus); CPR 28.12 (cf. MM, 79); PSI 9.1039.36 (LSJ: 1847).[41]

---

39. See *Midr. Ps.* 2.9, which interprets the Son of Ps. 2.7 and the son of man in Dan. 7.13 as Israel, and equates the figures of the two texts with the nation as God's 'first-born' in Exod. 4.22.

40. Cf. also Torrey 1958: 51, and BDF §136, who have concluded independently that the difficult neuter ἄρσεν is to be accounted for as an allusion to Isa. 66.7 of the LXX.

41. All three of the preceding references are cited in Fekkes 1994: 184. There are apparently only three other extant references in Greek (so TLG): Hippolytus, *De antichristo* 60.8 and 61.10, both of which quote Rev. 12.5 and have υἱὸν ἄρσενα, perhaps following the secondary textual tradition which changes the neuter to masculine, seeing ἄρσενα as adjectival. Also, Theodoret, *Interp. Jer.* 81.616.34, who cites Jer. 20.15 (MT = 'male-son'; LXX = ἄρσην) as υἱὸς ἄρσην ('male-child'), again with ἄρσην functioning as an adjective.

2. Rev. 14.19: ἔβαλεν εἰς τὴν ληνὸν τοῦ θυμοῦ τοῦ θεοῦ <u>τὸν</u> <u>μέγαν</u>. Rev. 14.19 refers to the 'great winepress' as part of imagery expressing divine judgment. The word ληνός ('winepress') is feminine but followed by an irregular masculine modifier: τὴν ληνὸν... <u>τὸν</u> <u>μέγαν</u> ('*the great* winepress').

Mussies 1971: 139, suggests that John's unusual shift to the masculine τὸν μέγαν is due to conforming it to the 'more important component of the word group' (if so, it would be conformed to τοῦ θυμοῦ or τοῦ θεοῦ). Lenski 1963: 450, suggests that the adjective 'the great' is in the masculine (τὸν μέγαν) instead of the feminine to emphasize the appositional phrase, while Beckwith 1919: 664, conjectures that the author put τὸν μέγαν in the accusative as a result of having been so caught up in focusing on the meaning of the symbol as expressed in the apposition. A weakening in the distinction of gender also reflects Hebrew style (GKC §110 *k*, 135 *o*, 144 *a*, 145 *p, t, u*). Some MSS ($\mathfrak{P}^{47}$ 1611 *pc*) change τὸν μέγαν to τοῦ μεγάλου in order to conform it with the immediately preceding τοῦ θυμοῦ τοῦ θεοῦ reading either 'the great wrath of God' or 'the wrath of the great God'. Some MSS (e.g. 181 424 468) omit μέγας altogether, presumably because of the lack of concord with anything which precedes or because of the separation from ληνός, or both.

Rev. 14:19 has several close Old Testament parallels. Cf. Joel 4.13b, πατεῖτε, διότι πλήρης ἡ ληνός, with Rev. 14.20a, ἐπατήθη ἡ ληνὸς... καὶ ἐξῆλθεν αἷμα ἐκ τῆς ληνοῦ. In connection with the 'treading of the wine press' cf. also LXX Lam. 1.15 (ληνὸν ἐπάτησε κύριος) and LXX Isa. 63.2-3: 'Why are your garments red... as though fresh from a *wine press* [πατητοῦ ληνοῦ]? [*I am*] *full of that which is trodden* (πλήρης καταπεπατημένης)... *I trampled* [κατεπάτησα] them in my fury... and brought down their *blood* [αἷμα] to the earth'.

Could this Old Testament background shed light on the problem of the feminine ληνός in Rev. 14.19 being followed by a discordant masculine modifier: τὴν ληνὸν... τὸν μέγαν (though ℵ 1006 1841 1854 2053 *al* gig sy^ph correct with the feminine form τὴν μεγάλην)? The feminine is the typical construction in biblical literature, though the masculine of ληνός occurs rarely, as in Isa. 63.2 (see above, and Robertson 1914: 253), which may have influenced the use of the same gender of τὸν μέγαν in 14.19 (Gen. 30.38, 41, also contain a masc. form of ληνός). In fact, Stuart 1845: II, 303, suggests that to τὸν μέγαν at the end of v. 19 should be added an elliptical masculine ληνόν, so that the final clause becomes epexegetical of the earlier τὴν ληνόν, which could be even closer to the thought of the LXX of Isaiah (see further below). Laughlin 1902: 13, notes that the feminine τὴν ληνόν followed by the masculine τὸν μέγαν [ληνόν] is a construction suggested by the similar pattern of the Hebrew feminine *pôrh* ('winepress') followed by the masculine pronominal suffix *ām* ('them'): 'I have trodden the *winepress*. . . And I will tread *them* in my anger. . . ' John's addition of 'great' to Isaiah's 'winepress' imagery of the Hebrew text could be following early exegetical tradition which also added similar intensifying adjectives: note 'full' (πλήρης) in the LXX of Isa. 63.3a above; the same wording of the LXX Isaiah text could read v. 3a as part of the question begun in v. 2: 'Why. . . is your raiment as from a trodden winepress, [which is] *full* of that which is trodden?' The targumic version reads: 'why will. . . plains *gush forth* like wine in the press? Behold, as grapes trodden in the press, so shall slaughter *increase*. . . '

4. *Conclusion*

Various explanations have been proposed for the syntactical solecisms of the Apocalypse, prominent among which are: (1) that they are the result of carelessness or ignorance; (2) that they are due to various degrees of Semitic or Septuagintal influence generally; (3) that they or mere reflections of somewhat unusual but attested Hellenistic Greek; (4) that many are explainable as being the result of the phenomenon sometimes referred to as *constructio ad sensum*.

This essay has attempted to offer a new approach, though it is to be considered as a subcategory of the second alternative above, which has attempted to solve the solecism problem by turning to a Semitic or Septuagintal background *in general*. Evidently unrecognized for the most part previously, a significant number of the syntactical irregularities occur in the midst of specific Old Testament allusions. A significant number of the solecisms have been analyzed in the preceding segment of this essay which, it has been contended, are representative of many others for which there was not space to study. In this respect, a number of the expressions appear irregular because John is carrying over the exact grammatical form of the Old Testament wording in order to create 'syntactical dissonance', which causes the reader/hearer to pause and increases their chances of recognizing the unusual wording to be an Old Testament allusion. Sometimes the precise grammar from the Old Testament passage is not retained, but stylistic Semitisms or, more usually, Septuagintalisms are incorporated in order to create the dissonance, so that the fuller clause of which the solecism is a part can more quickly be recognized as an Old Testament allusion.

BIBLIOGRAPHY

Altink, W.

1984 '1 Chronicles 16:8-36 as Literary Source for Revelation 14:6-7', *Andrews University Seminary Studies* 22: 187-96.

Bauckham, R.J.

1993 *The Climax of Prophecy: Studies in the Book of Revelation* (Edinburgh: T. & T. Clark).

Beale, G.K.

1986 'A Reconsideration of the Text of Daniel in the Apocalypse', *Bib* 67: 539-43.

1988 'The Use of the Old Testament in Revelation', in D.A. Carson and H.G.M. Williamson (eds.), *It Is Written: Scripture Citing Scripture* (Festschrift B. Lindars; Cambridge: Cambridge University Press): 318-36.

1996 'The Old Testament Background of Rev 3.14', *NTS* 42 (1996): 133-52.

1997 *The Book of Revelation* (NIGTC; Grand Rapids: Eerdmans; Carlisle, England: Paternoster, forthcoming).

Beckwith, I.T.

1919 *The Apocalypse of John* (New York: Macmillan).

Bousset, W.

1906 *Die Offenbarung Johannis* (Göttingen: Vandenhoeck & Ruprecht, 6th edn).

Bretscher, P.M.

1945[1] 'Syntactical Peculiarities in Revelation', *Concordia Theological Monthly* 16: 95-105.

Brooks, J.A., and C.L. Winberg

1979 *Syntax of New Testament Greek* (Washington: University Press of America).

Callahan, A.D.

1995 'The Language of the Apocalypse', *HTR* 88: 453-70.

Charles, R.H.

1920 *A Critical and Exegetical Commentary on the Revelation of St. John* (vol. 1–2; Edinburgh: T. & T. Clark).

Dana, H.E., and J.R. Mantey

1927 *A Manual Grammar of the Greek New Testament* (Toronto: Macmillan).

Delling, G.

1959 'Zum Gottesdienstlichen Stil der Johannes–Apokalypse', *NovT* 3: 107-37.

Düsterdieck, F.

1980 *Critical and Exegetical Handbook to the Revelation of John* (MeyerK, 11; trans. H.E. Jacobs; Ediburgh: T. & T. Clark, 1883; repr. Winona Lake, IN: Alpha Publications).

Fanning, B.
    1990   *Verbal Aspect in New Testament Greek* (Oxford: Clarendon Press).
Farrer, A.
    1964   *The Revelation of St John the Divine* (Oxford: Clarendon Press).
Fekkes, J.
    1994   *Isaiah and Prophetic Traditions in the Book of Revelation: Visionary Antecedents and their Development* (JSNTSup, 93; Sheffield: JSOT Press).
Gill, J.
    1811   *An Exposition of the New Testament. III. The Revelation of St John the Divine* (Philadelphia: William W. Woodward): 691-886.
Goodwin, W.W.
    1890   *Syntax of the Moods and Tenses of the Greek Verb* (Boston: Ginn).
Horsley, G.H.R., and S.R. Llewelyn
    1981–   *New Documents Illustrating Early Christianity*, I–VII (North Ryde, NSW, Australia: The Ancient History Documentary Research Centre).
Hoskier, H.C.
    1929   *Concerning the Text of the Apocalypse*, I–II (London: Bernard Quaritch).
Laughlin, T.C.
    1902   *The Solecisms of the Apocalypse* (Princeton, NJ: Princeton University Press).
Lenski, R.C.H.
    1963   *The Interpretation of St John's Revelation* (Minneapolis: Augsburg).
Lohmeyer, E.
    1970   *Die Offenbarung des Johannes* (HNT, 16; Tübingen: Mohr [Paul Siebeck]).
McNamara, M.
    1966   *The New Testament and the Palestinian Targum to the Pentateuch* (AnBib, 27; Rome: Pontifical Biblical Institute).
Metzger, B. M.
    1971   *A Textual Commentary on the Greek New Testament* (London and New York: United Bible Societies).
Moffatt, J.
    1970   *The Revelation of St John the Divine* (The Expositor's Greek Testament, 5; Grand Rapids: Eerdmans).
Moule, C.F.D.
    1953   *An Idiom Book of New Testament Greek* (Cambridge: Cambridge University Press).
Moulton, J.H.
    1906   Prolegomena A Grammar of New Testament Greek, 1; Edinburgh: T. & T. Clark).
Moulton, J.H., and W.F. Howard
    1929   *Accidence and Word-Formation* (A Grammar of New Testament Greek, 2; Edinburgh: T. & T. Clark).
Moulton, J.H., and G. Milligan
    1972   *The Vocabulary of the Greek New Testament* (Grand Rapids: Eerdmans).
Murphy, F.J.
    1994   'The Book of Revelation', *Currents in Research: Biblical Studies* 2: 181-225.

Mussies, G.
    1964   'Antipas [Rev. 2:13b]', *NovT* 7: 242-44.
    1971   *The Morphology of Koine Greek as Used in the Apocalypse of St John: A Study in Bilingualism* (NovTSup, 27; London: Brill).
    1980   'The Greek of the Book of Revelation', in J. Lambrecht (ed.), *L'apocalypse johannique et l'apocalyptique dans le Nouveau Testament* (BETL, 53; Gembloux: Duculot/Leuven: University Press): 167-77.
Ozanne, C.G.
    1965   'The Language of the Apocalypse', *TynBul* 16: 3-9.
Porter, S.E.
    1989a   'The Language of the Apocalypse in Recent Study', *NTS* 35: 582-603.
    1989b   *Verbal Aspect in the Greek of the New Testament, with Reference to Tense and Mood* (Studies in Biblical Greek, 1; New York: Peter Lang).
Robertson, A.T.
    1914   *A Grammar of the Greek New Testament in the Light of Historical Research* (New York: Hodder & Stoughton).
    1933   *Word Pictures in the New Testament. VI. The General Epistles and the Revelation of John* (Nashville: Broadman Press).
Ruiz, J.-P.
    1989   *Ezekiel in the Apocalypse: The Transformation of Prophetic Language in Revelation 16, 17-19, 10* (European University Studies, 23.376; Frankfurt am Main: Peter Lang).
Schmidt, D.D.
    1991   'Semitisms and Septuagintalisms in the Book of Revelation', *NTS* 37: 592-603.
Scott, R.B.Y.
    1928   *The Original Language of the Apocalypse* (Toronto: Toronto University Press).
Selwyn, E.C.
    1900   *The Christian Prophets and the Prophetic Apocalypse* (London/New York: Macmillan).
Smyth, H.W.
    1984   *Greek Grammar* (Cambridge, MA: Harvard University Press).
Stork, P.
    1982   *The Aspectual Usage of the Dynamic Infinitive in Herodotus* (Gröningen: Bouma's Boekhuis).
Stuart, M.
    1845   *Commentary on the Apocalypse*, II (Andover: Allen, Morrell & Wardwell/ New York; M.H. Newman).
Sweet, J.P.M.
    1979   *Revelation* (London: SCM Press).
Swete, H.B.
    1906   *The Apocalypse of St John* (London: Macmillan).
Thompson, S.
    1985   *The Apocalypse and Semitic Syntax* (SNTSMS, 52; Cambridge: Cambridge University Press).
Torrey, C.C.
    1958   *The Apocalypse of John* (New Haven: Yale University Press).

Trudinger, L.P.
    1966   'Some Observations Concerning the Text of the Old Testament in the Book
                of Revelation', *JTS* 17: 82-88.
Turner, N.
    1963   *Syntax* (J.H. Moulton's A Grammar of New Testament Greek, 3;
                Edinburgh: T. & T. Clark).
    1976   *Style* (J.H. Moulton's A Grammar of New Testament Greek, 4; Edinburgh:
                T. & T. Clark).
Wilcox, M.
    1994   'The Aramaic Background of the New Testament', in D.R.G. Beattie and
                M.J. McNamara (eds.), *The Aramaic Bible* (JSOTSup, 166; Sheffield:
                JSOT Press): 362-78.
Zerwick, M.
    1963   *Biblical Greek* (Scripta Pontificii Istituti Biblici, 114; Rome: Pontifical
                Biblical Institute).

INDEXES

INDEX OF REFERENCES

OLD TESTAMENT

PSEUDEPIGRAPHA

INDEX OF AUTHORS

JOURNAL FOR THE STUDY OF THE NEW TESTAMENT
SUPPLEMENT SERIES